La
GRANDE ARMÉE

La
Grande Armée

Georges Blond

Translated by Marshall May

ARMS AND
ARMOUR

For Ruth – A Sailor's star

Arms and Armour Press
An Imprint of the Cassell Group
Wellington House, 125/130 Strand, London WC2RR 0BB

Distributed in the USA by Sterling Publishing Co. Inc.,
387 Park Avenue South, New York, NY 10016-8810.

First published 1979 by Editions Robert Laffont,
6 place Saint-Sulpice, Paris.
This English-language edition first published 1995.

This paperback edition 1997

Reprinted 1997

Translation © Marshall May, 1995

British Library Cataloguing-in-Publication Data: a catalogue
record for this book is available from the British Library

ISBN 1-85409-411-4

Designed and edited by DAG Publications Ltd.
Designed by David Gibbons; edited by Michael Boxall;
Printed and bound in Great Britain by
MPG Books Ltd, Bodmin, Cornwall

CONTENTS

TRANSLATOR'S NOTE

No attempt has been made to translate the French army designations of its various arms. During the years covered in this work, the equipment and tactics varied considerably. For example, the British army were well ahead in the use of rifle-equipped light infantry; the French had an edge in artillery tactics. To complicate matters further, the Guard, Old, Middle and Young, were specially equipped and trained in their role as shock troops. I have, therefore, chosen to use the author's descriptions. However, for what they may be worth, some common equivalents are listed below.

Chasseurs: light infantry and cavalry; when used as a regimental title, the term was generally used to describe cavalry (*chasseurs à cheval*). Members of the ordinary companies of light infantry regiments were styled chasseurs, the equivalent of fusiliers in the line regiments.

Cuirassiers: heavy cavalry equipped with the cuirass (iron breast- and backplates); although the 8th Cavalry Regiment had been so equipped during the Revolutionary Wars, the other *régiments de cavalerie* were converted in 1801-03, to form twelve (ultimately fourteen) regiments of cuirassiers.

Tirailleurs: infantry skirmishers or sharpshooters, who operated in open order and could fire at will; the word was more a generic term for such skirmishers than used as a regimental title, for which it was used only in the Young Guard and by some auxiliary corps.

Voltigeurs: members of the regimental light companies of both line and light infantry regiments, especially skilled in skirmishing; the Young Guard included some entire regiments of Voltigeurs.

PROLOGUE
The Old Soldiers

The Grande Armée – that was yesterday. In 1935, in the village where I live seven months of the year, I spoke with a farm worker, then seventy-nine years of age, who had seen the survivors of that army with his own eyes. There were some in his county, all octogenarians. One of them had fought at Austerlitz and described in detail the huts which they had built before the battle from branches, the fires blazing in the glacial night to celebrate the anniversary of the Emperor's coronation; then the morning mist and the battle; the imperial Russian guard in white uniform, all mounted on black horses, the clash in the black smoke, the Russians and Austrians in flight and hiding in the marshes. This man spoke half in dialect and half in French which he had only learned after joining the army.

There were five of these survivors in one of these hamlets. In winter, they sat in the cantou – the inglenook by the chimney and its fire. But each morning, regardless of the weather, my informant remembered this detail; the men made their ablutions outdoors. This consisted of plunging their hands into a bucket of cold water and rubbing their faces – army-style, they said proudly. They shaved on Sundays.

In that region in about 1865, there were not thirty-six parties. Either, one was for the government, bonapartist, or republican and in opposition. But even the republicans looked with respect upon the survivors of that epoch. They did not snigger when one of them rose and gave a military salute on pronouncing the Emperor's name, nor did they mock when another, fantasising a trifle, rummaged in his memories, which mingled with tales the old sweats had told him. Thus he claimed and, no doubt, believed that he had been at the Pyramids and had made the retreat in Russia; occasionally, he even claimed to have been in the Indies! These were the lucky men, since none was crippled or one-armed. They would willingly show their scars, which showed violet on their very white skin. They wore flannel which they never doffed. One of them had reddened eyes and wept much: a legacy of Russia, he would say, and refused to go out when it was snowing.

Under the Restoration, all the municipalities destroyed their collections of the Bulletins of the Grande Armée, but in the days of these survivors and even

7

much later, hawkers roamed the countryside, carrying on their backs a variety of small chests whose panels were adorned with what were called Epinal pictures, copies of which they offered for sale. Many started their invitations by reciting tragic tales or by intoning some saga in a monotonous recitative. One big success was 'The Tragedy of the Wandering Jew', of which I myself heard snatches from old people when I was a child. Another big hit was the 'Legend of the Eagle'. The countryfolk did not read Balzac or even Eugène Sue, but they listened to these mountebanks and bought their pictures, thus adding to the prestige of the survivors of the Grande Armée. The cult reached its summit in 1840 when the Emperor's remains were returned to France. In the county which I have described, the survivors did not take part in such splendid ceremonies and Paris was too far away, but the mayors and the municipal counsellors called, they said, to salute them.

Such memories from the mouth of a man for whom I had both affection and respect hold perhaps the genesis of this book. They were little enough when compared with what I was to read later about the campaigns of the Grande Armée, but they gave me valuable guidance which books could not offer. I could never forget these tales heard in my infancy.

As the inhabitants of every country recall, Napoleon's armies swept through Europe. A Hungarian friend asked me: 'What is still left to write concerning Napoleon?' Nothing, of course, after the hundreds of thousands of books that have been published about his reign. One can also say that one can write indefinitely, and this is what has happened; the river has not ceased to flow. Jean Tulard has placed in exergue one of Stendhal's observations: 'From today until fifty years on, it will be necessary to revise Napoleon's story every year.' For myself, it is not in any way the individual that haunts me; indeed, his distrust of men and his ignorance of maritime affairs tended to deter me. What gripped me were the observations of an old countryman who spoke to me of the survivors of the Old Guard, which led to more and more research and to reading books of memoirs – asking myself as I read: 'How had they been able to survive all that; who, in truth, were these men?' The old soldiers who stood to attention when the Emperor's name was spoken had, miraculously, survived nameless butcheries, had marched in serried ranks before the enemy guns, had seen comrades fall beside them, their chests smashed by cannonballs, had seen heads rolling from a sabre-cut, had, in Spain, seen the bodies of friends roasted and crucified head-down over a fire, had themselves fired 'into the brown' on crowds of women and children who had taken refuge in churches. In Russia, leaving their bivouacs of a morning and seeing their friends frozen to death and lying under a tree as rigid as stone, transformed into statues. For months and years they had lived contentedly as an occupying army in towns and villages of all of Europe, dancing with German, Austrian, Polish girls, sleeping with them, and they knew of many comrades who had stayed there, forgetting the army, forgetting France. The French, in an army two-thirds composed of foreigners, had learned a smattering of every European language. They had, also, been pillagers, thieves, rapists, had drunk and guzzled into oblivion and had suffered the worst famines. Heroes, torturers and martyrs, perhaps a unique experience for all time and place. Can we see these men in close-up, beyond the legends to which they themselves have contributed?

Such is the line of approach which I have tried to take, and it was not easy. History according to the official record – including The Bulletin of the Grande Armée which has inflamed the imagination of so many romantics – we know their worth. Thrilling revelations are mixed with coldblooded lies or adroit approximations in all the souvenirs and memoirs of the great, military as well as civilian, when it was necessary at some moment or another to shine or to cover-up a weakness, an error or a crime. Even the testimony of the humble cannot be accepted without scrutiny. All were written after the event, sometimes long after, memory and compassion influence choice and even modest men like to dramatise. Often, too, they like to shine, and why not? That truth one cannot in honesty conceal from the public; the triage of tons of documents, of a million testimonies, cannot guarantee absolute truth. Mathematically exact history does not exist.

That did not discourage me and, besides, sometimes I was virtually under a spell. I wished at all costs to discover the sufferings of the Grande Armée as, at another time, I had wished to record those of the combatants of Verdun. But, as the survivors of Verdun spoke to me, I could see their faces as they spoke and, afterwards, not one Frenchman or one German accused me of inaccuracy. Whereas, not one soldier of the Grande Armée could tell me whether I had showed them in their true colours. However, by dint of care and taking pains, by seeking the human and psychological probabilities – surely they deserve weight? – concerning some event, some remark, I have the inner conviction – accorded to assize juries! – of having preserved the moral essential – no, the differing moral essentials – of this immense venture. If the impartial reader gains the same impression, I may not have failed.

At the beginning of my project, I had thought to recount the story of the Grande Armée while speaking as little as possible of Napoleon – absolutely everything from the point of view of the men in the ranks. That was naïve. Firstly, the man was there, present in the arena, very often in person, risking his life as few of the great commanders have done in modern war, not only surveying the battles through a telescope from the top of a hillock, but galloping under fire. And while present at the summit of Europe and alone deciding the course of his wars, often with genius, the life and death and the sufferings of the soldiers of the Grande Armée. For these reasons, I have mentioned him more often than I had at first expected. And also because he was constantly in the minds of his men, an obsessive father-image, often a father-refuge: '*Le Tondu* knows his business; he'll get us out of this.' Often detested – 'Long live the Emperor!' time and again, but during the retreat from Russia when he abandoned the army to rush to Paris where his presence was politically necessary, an officer of the Guard entered the bivouac and exclaimed: 'So, the brigand has gone?' Sunspots do not prevent a star from shining. We must tell the whole tale.

I

BOULOGNE
The Army Turns Towards the Sea

The Grande Armée should not have marched East. During the weeks when it was falling upon Germany – at a rate of 40 kilometres a day – something no other army had equalled – it should have been sweeping through south-eastern England to reach the London suburbs and the Thames. Its troops should have been terrorising Kentish villagers, not the peasants of Württemberg and Bavaria, without shame but with zest and joy, since for Napoleon's troops, as for nearly all Frenchmen, Britain was the most detested nation in the world. Governed by bastards who would not make peace, who refused the peace so dear to the hearts of the Emperor and to the mass of his subjects because they could not bear the thought of a France serene within her natural frontiers, sheltered from aggression, powerful and respected. For the British government, the very idea of their French neighbour, with twenty-eight millions to the British fifteen, free to disseminate revolutionary doctrines aimed at the overthrow of kings, was intolerable.

The Grande Armée – the third to bear that name – had been formed at the camp of Boulogne in 1803. Some regiments, known as the Army of England, had already assembled there in 1798 when Barras, a member of the Directory, had written to Bonaparte, telling him to: 'Go and chain the huge pirate who reigns over the seas.' The invasion fleet assembled for the purpose consisted of flat-bottomed boats designed by a French Lieutenant Muskeyne. 'They can make the crossing of the strait from the Pas de Calais,' he said, 'provided they are numerous enough and the weather is favourable. The British fleet cannot intercept them all. Those who get through will land and disembark our regiments on the English beaches.'

An engineer of the War Ministry named Pierre Forfait oversaw the construction of the first flotilla. Bonaparte appeared convinced, but shortly afterwards had written to the Directory: 'To attempt such an operation without command of the sea is not only a daring but a *perilous* enterprise.' In fact, he had conceived another idea: to attack the British in Egypt. The invasion fleet rotted in port and the great Saga unfolded at Aboukir, while an Anglo-Russian coalition threatened the frontiers of France, at Paris (18 Brumaire) and in Italy (Marengo).

In 1801, Bonaparte, now First Consul and holding the reins of power, had suddenly ordered: 'Prepare the fleet and assemble the troops.' Was France herself to become Mistress of the Seas? Far from it. I myself formed an opinion concerning the camp of Boulogne when, while writing a biography of Nelson,* I studied the situation from both sides of the Straits of Dover. It was evident to me that Bonaparte had no intention of crossing the Straits; the flotilla was moored at the entrance to the port of Boulogne in a strictly defensive manner, the boats chained one to the next. The First Consul wished to intimidate England, Mistress of the Seas, and after the success of the Peace of Lunéville he could pride himself on being master of the European continent.

Britain was exhausted, bled white by the American war. On 5 August 1801, Nelson had attacked the chained barges of the Boulogne flotilla – clumsily and without vigour, and apparently without conviction. Result – failure. On 15 August he again attacked without success. There was a peace party in England and Bonaparte had his peace, the Peace of Amiens (25 March 1802).

Later, Britain not having implemented all the clauses of the treaty, in particular refusing to evacuate Malta, Bonaparte had upbraided the British ambassador who quit his post at Paris on 12 May 1803. Three days later, the French ambassador in London had been notified of a state of war and two days later the British schooner *Doris* fired on the French lugger *l'Affronteur* in the Bay of Audierne. War once more.

Bonaparte had seen war coming. On 25 March, he had ordered his Chief of Staff, Berthier, to send troops, artillery and supplies to Boulogne. Garrison regiments had moved from the interior by stages towards the Channel and North Sea coasts ('St-Omer must be ready to receive 40,000 men and 6 to 7,000 horses'). This time, he was in earnest.

In 1943, when the overall plan for the Normandy landings had been agreed between the United States and Great Britain, the ministries of war of both countries supplemented their normal programmes with the construction of material for the landings. In Britain, the factories produced prefabricated sections of barges which were later assembled in every riverine town, village and hamlet in Britain, in workshops, garages, barns and even in the streets. Lorries delivered the prefabricated sections and men and women assembled them. The finished barges were manhandled on rollers to nearby rivers and canals and floated down to the sea.

This huge and ingenious enterprise was justly admired. The same could have been seen in France in 1803, except that the boats were wooden. The beat of hammers was to be heard everywhere; construction proceeded not only on the coasts, but in Paris, Saint-Germain, Compiègne and as far away as Colmar and

---

* *The Beauty and the Glory,* Editions Robert Laffont, 1976.

Strasbourg. Once completed, the barges were sent down-steam and, hugging the coast, made their way to Boulogne where they were moored nine or ten deep. More barges were collected at Etaples, Wimereux, Wissant, Montreuil, Ambleteuse and, farther north, Calais, Gravelines, Dunkirk, Nieuport, Ostend and Flushing. (The French coast extended far, to the mouths of the river Escaut, which Britain understandably could not bear to see in French hands.) Gun brigs and river gunboats were built, all to the same plans; small boats of 20 to 25 metres, rigged as brigs or luggers, each carrying 12- or 24-pounder guns and capable of transporting a company of infantry. A considerable number of undecked barges was also built, mostly propelled by oars, all being of light draught and flat-bottomed and capable of beaching on the coasts of England.

The engineer Pierre Forfait was appointed Inspector-General of the flotilla, reporting directly to the Minister of Marine, Rear-Admiral Decrès. 'Take any forest timber you need,' said Bonaparte, 'I want a flotilla of some two thousand units.' In Paris, the esplanade of the Invalides was covered with workshops; an entire section of the left bank was transformed into a vast shipyard which thousands of curious folk came to see. Bonaparte personally supported the propaganda for the flotilla. One afternoon in October 1803 he was seen aboard a barge 'directing manoeuvres' below the Concorde bridge and manning an oar. The loafers on the river banks applauded.

The project to invade England was wildly popular. The towns of Verdun, Foix, Coutances, Moissac and Bernay as well as many communities and corporations offered the price of many barges. Some municipalities voted the motion: 'Ships also are needed!' Paris offered a 120-gun ship, Lyons a 100-gun vessel, Bordeaux one of 80 guns, Marseilles a 74. The population of the Loiret sent 300,000 francs for the construction of a corvette, while that of the Rhine offered an eighth of its taxes; the Nord sent one million francs. Lot and Garonne, less affluent, gave several thousand metres of sail cloth. People were firmly convinced that the invasion would succeed. Most of the French naval officers shrugged their shoulders. Admiral Decrès, Minister of Marine, told anyone who would listen that it was 'monstrous, paradoxical, absurd'. Admiral Bruix, commander of the flotilla, seemed lukewarm. But Bonaparte had spoken. And the bulk of the invasion troops were marching on Boulogne.

On 14 September 1803 (27 Fructidor, Year XI) it was reported that all was ready for immediate embarkation: 114,000 men, 7,100 horses, 32,000 reserve muskets, 14 million cartridges, 1,300,000 flints, 1,500,000 rations of biscuit, 240,000 pints of brandy, 5,000 live sheep, 7,000 rations of bran, and the same of oats, 432 artillery cannon and 90,000 cannonballs and shells. Since May 1803, the engineers had been ordered to provide lodging at Boulogne for five divisions, including 78 infantry battalions. ('The troops must be ready to move by the end of summer.') They were indeed ready by the end of September, but it was not until December that the cavalry regiments stationed at Bayonne, Agen, Lyons, Dole, Belfort and Mainz began to move towards Boulogne. The cavalrymen had to march because the horses 'which would be taken in England' were to serve as remounts.

The passage of all these troops across France excited the curiosity of the populace. Their colourful uniforms were admired by some, regarded with distrust and fear by others. Some of the recruits had no uniform as yet. Some of the troops were content with their lot, delighted at the prospect of marching to ravage England and to bed the English girls, or, simply to gain glory and promotion; their champion was Bonaparte who had led them to so many victories. But many others had long faces.

Conscription was an invention of the Revolution: the decree introducing it was dated 14 February 1793 and it was confirmed under the Directory by the law of 25 August 1799. Napoleon was well aware of the unpopularity of conscription: ('this measure is the most detested by families, but it assures the safety of the State') but he made use of it persistently and in masterly fashion. Service was obligatory for unmarried men of from twenty to twenty-five years of age, but they had a good chance of escaping it through the drawing of lots. Only one in fifteen of the rural conscripts was called and only one in seven of the townsmen. The duration of service varied from one to five years in peacetime to unlimited duration in time of war. Those called could legally escape serving by paying a substitute a price open to negotiation; from 1803 until the end of the Empire, it varied from 1,800 to 4,000 francs. In practice, only the poor were forced into barracks; the system was far from the ideal of universal equality before the law.

Contemporary paintings depict conscripts happily marching, their cockades pinned to their hats, and civilians throwing flowers – but do not be misled. Most Frenchmen regarded the soldier's condition (and the sailor's) as the worst of the worst; they must have murdered both their father and their mother. Most conscripts had only one idea in mind – to desert. Conscription in Year VII (1798) had called-up 200,000 men, but three months later, the depots had received only 50,000. Desertion was rife. In the west and south-west, they formed virtual bands, opposing the gendarmes and even attacking and killing them. On 15 February 1804 the prefect of police at Chartres reported that three gendarmes had been slain. The population lent a helping hand to the deserters, hiding and feeding them.

In Paris replacement by substitutes was not allowed in principle, but there were dispensations and discharges; there were also army doctors who would reject a man in return for a consideration, and forgers of discharge certificates were to be found. Some deserters found it more convenient merely to avoid reporting for duty. On 15 June 1802, 244 conscripts were summoned to the place des Vosges; twenty-five reported. On another occasion, the conscripts reported but began to riot at the moment when lots were to be cast. On 2 December 1802 the Minister of Justice wrote in his 'Review of the Situation' that at the town hall of the Sixth District, the young men had fought with the dragoons who sought to enlist them; these soldiers 'made use of their arms' – result: twenty dead and fifty wounded conscripts, and a boy of twelve among the parents and friends received a sabre cut to the abdomen.

The conscripts were marched willy-nilly to their barracks, but the police reported that a good tenth found an opportunity of deserting before they reached their destination. Many of those who arrived were reduced to tears by the aspect of their new homes. Most barracks resembled prisons: small rooms with low ceilings, small windows admitting little light, comfortless and reeking. Men were piled into them, sleeping two to a mattress. That the barracks were inadequate was due to the fact that there had been no large armies to be housed under the *ancien régime*. Since the Revolution, churches and convents in Paris and the provinces had served as barracks. Furniture had been removed and replaced by piles of hay. Some of the old buildings were serving as stables. There were few troops in barracks in Paris, most having been dispersed to the suburbs, which in those days meant the countryside.

At the barracks the conscripts were greeted by the veterans with mockery, exploitation and bullying. The odious instinct to bully is rooted in the tribal consciousness of many individuals, and in any formed body, military or other-wise, the newcomer must suffer it. The veterans were determined to show the conscripts of 1803 who was boss, and in this they were aided appreciably by the fact that they wore uniform.

To attempt to describe in detail all the uniforms of the epoch of the Con-sulate and the Empire, all the colours of the National Guard: blue uniform, red collar with white facings, white lapels piped with red, brass buttons stamped with the regiment's number, coat and breeches of white wool, gaiters buttoning to above the knee, white for full dress, black or of grey cloth for every day; the uniforms of the light infantry: short-tailed coat of blue cloth with red facings piped in white, waistcoat and breeches of the same blue cloth and short, black gaiters, often adorned with lace and a tassel, a shako with a leather top with the badge of a hunting-horn; the uniforms of the voltigeurs, whose different com-panies each wore a distinctive collar, epaulettes and a flash or pom-pom on their headgear; the fantastic uniforms of the Guard, of the various cavalry corps, would drive me out of my mind without enlightening the reader, who would in any case remember little of my descriptions of uniforms whose cut, colour and a hundred detailed embellishments varied from year to year between 1803 and 1815. Many books, some brilliantly illustrated, have been written regarding these uniforms; open them and turn their pages for hours; beggar yourselves with the purchase of lead soldiers; spend days at the Army Museum at the Hôtel des Invalides where, frozen in their glass cases, are the images of officers and troopers, impressive and slightly menacing in their speechless immobility. You will then have learned, if you did not already know, how these uniforms differed from those of the armies of today, how they were coloured, splendidly embellished – before being drenched with rain, covered with mud or dust, torn, ripped, blood-stained. But they were in good repair when the conscripts saw them on the backs of the veterans for the first time, and if for no other reason the old sweats seemed supermen – mistrusted, often detested, but supermen to whom it was better to submit. The conscripts had no uniforms; some would not have them until many months later although the factories were straining every sinew to clothe and shoe this mass of men. This was a matter of great concern to Bonaparte (the survivors of the Army of Egypt had shivered for awhile in their rags from the Orient; the victors of Marengo had to ransack the Austrian wagons to rig themselves out in more or less military style). Many conscripts received their baptism of fire in Prussia and Poland wearing round hats and the blouses of peasants or artisans, recognisable as soldiers only by their cartridge boxes, haversacks and muskets. In their uniforms, the old sweats were top dog and the naïve conscripts, wrenched from their fields and workshops, had perforce to submit, to spend their last coppers standing drinks, performing all the fatigues and suffering the grossest bullying.

But every tormentor also wishes for admiration. The veterans were nothing loath to recount their glorious exploits, and their stories often contained a fair measure of truth. These men were from a different time, the eldest among them raised under the *ancien régime*. They had fought the Austrians at Jemappes with the old war cry 'Fearless Navarre!'; defended the frontier at Wattignies; won the day at Montenotte, Millesimo, Mondovi, Castiglione, Lodi, Arcola, Rivoli; marched into Milan bedecked with flowers and slept in Venetian palaces. 'You have no idea what they were like, little dirty-arse, these cities like Milan or Venice with their marble houses. You have never seen girls as beautiful as those whom we kissed in Italy. And the Pyramids, do you even know what they are?' The wretched conscripts, fresh from their parishes, certainly did not know. They knew nothing, could neither read nor write – no more could the veterans – but they listened open-mouthed. They had scarcely imagined such things. They had started by sobbing all night on their mattresses, thinking of their homes, parents, sweethearts, but now all that happiness was far away; most of them received no letters because their parents were illiterate. Along with the abuse, the fatigues and the bullying, their reality now embraced this exotic world conjured up by the veterans. Some of the conscripts were too bewildered, too ignorant to comprehend, but others swallowed the bait whole.

The veterans not only boasted of their bravery, their feasts and orgies, but also expressed with pride their mistrust of civilians; they boasted of having been, far from battlefields and barracks, the terror of the populace. This was in fact true. Breaking into shops and cafes, smashing glasses and tables, what a caper! And to embrace the women roughly and beat-up the townsmen if they protested. The police reports were eloquent: 'The son of the proprietor of the Café de Valois had his skull smashed, a young man was slashed by a brigadier of chasseurs in front of the door of the Senate: at the Charonne door, some soldiers killed a civilian; in the plain of Montrouge, three soldiers disembowelled a civilian on the pretext that he 'had looked at them in an insulting fashion'. The incidences of pillage and destruction were numberless, as were attacks on women. A report of the prefect dated 17 September 1804, stated that six soldiers had raped a young girl on the jetty of the grain port and had then thrown her into the Seine. Murders and serious extortion were evidently not daily occurrences and the veterans did not boast of them. Tales of this type at first shocked the naïve conscripts, but to show disapproval could be dangerous; better to feign admiration and this eventually became genuine. In a very short time most conscripts were changed men.

For many years, accommodation at camps had consisted of tents, rented to the military. The first troops to arrive at Boulogne had slept under canvas until the order came, 'Cut down trees and build huts quickly.' The high command correctly assumed that these would be permanent. Engineer officers had supervised the levelling of the ground, laid out access roads and the lines where the huts were to stand, and built metalled streets, some even paved – in all, some four square kilometres of buildings. Neighbouring forests furnished wood, the cliffs stone. Masons built the mud walls of the huts in local style; it took six hours per wall; once dry, the roofers arrived to put on the thatch. Continuous construction, mass production. Each hut was whitewashed inside and out and could accommodate fifteen men who slept on the straw-covered glacis. More comfortable than in barracks. 'The complainers', said the sergeants, 'were not so comfortable in their own homes.' The huts were soon surrounded by grass; the street signs carried the names of past victories: Valmy Street, Jemappes Street, Fleurus Street, etc.; the names of the main avenues recalled past glories of the Revolution: Avenue of the Estates-General, of the Jeu de Paume, of the Constitution – prudently, no names of personages. At the cross-roads were pyramids of stone decorated with seashells. Other camps, more or less similar, were built at Wimereux, Ambleteuse, Ostrohove, Herquelingue, Etaples. Journalists of the *Moniteur Universel* were invited and wrote enthusiastic articles, as required: 'Tree-lined walks, green banks, a carpet of greenery, flower beds carefully maintained contributed to the gracious look of the camps. Springs of clear water provide healthy refreshment for the soldiers and also contribute to the upkeep of the gardens. The senior officers' quarters equal the elegance and the interior decorations of the richest lodgings.' Imagine that! Let us add that for those soldiers for whom limpid water was not entirely adequate, there were grog-shops and barter-shops on the outskirts of the camps.

The bugles sounded 'Soup' at 7 and 11.30 a.m., and at 6 p.m. 'Good and abundant nourishment,' said the articles. The troops found it meagre and unappetising. Four meat days and three meatless days weekly. On meat days, 250 grams of meat per head at the midday meal, fresh meat alternating with salt beef and bacon; on meatless days, 90 grams of cheese replaced the meat. No meat at the evening meal, but peas, pulses, rice or beans, 250 grams of bread and 180 grams of biscuit daily. No wine, but light beer; from time to time there were distributions of alcohol, one litre for every sixteen men. Wine was available at the grog-shops.

Bonaparte inspected the Boulogne camp on 29 June, having left Paris on the 23rd. This was his first journey as Consul for Life and marked his accession to quasi-sovereignty. Josephine accompanied him together with a 'royal' suite comprising Decrès, Minister of Marine; Chaptal, Minister of the Interior; Admiral Bruix; Generals Soult, Lauriston, Marmont, Duroc; innumerable ADCs including the 22-year-old Eugène de Beauharnais, future viceroy of Italy, and a large detachment of the consular Guard. 'Such a glittering procession had not been seen since the progressions of Louis XIV and Louis XV during the Flanders wars,' wrote an eye-witness. Bonaparte wore the uniform of the Guard Chasseurs, green coat, orange trim with, of course, his small black hat with neither edging nor braid, with a small tricolour cockade secured by a black cord. The cortege passed through Compiègne, Amiens, Abbeville, Saint-Valery, Etaples. The populace cheered. Josephine (who was not interested in military camps) left her husband at Amiens; she was to rejoin him at Dunkirk. Bonaparte arrived at 9.30 p.m., greeted by salvoes of artillery, the bells of the church of Saint Nicholas and more cheering, and went immediately to the house that had been prepared for him, the residence of the marquis des Desandrouins, master glass-maker and coal-mine owner.

At dawn next day he was away on horseback, visiting the piers and workshops, the batteries on the cliffs, questioning everyone ceaselessly, as was his habit. At 10 o'clock, he received the authorities at the Town Hall, the bishop, the mayor (keys to the city on a cushion), the prefect, and endured a series of dithyrambic speeches, though he smiled at the cheering crowds when leaving. In case Bonaparte's appearance at this time has escaped your memory, here follows a summary: one metre 68 tall, short limbs, deep and well-developed chest, head size 60 centimetres, rather higher than broad, a little flattened at the temples. The First Consul was no longer the skinny youngster of his first campaign in

Italy; his face had become oval-shaped and his body was growing stouter, forehead very high and hairless, auburn hair cut short. Handsome and most expressive blue eyes, a straight and handsome nose, good and very white teeth 'not wholly regular', small, well-shaped and well-placed ears. By general consent, excellent hands.

He spent the remainder of the day inspecting the troops with his staff and watching naval manoeuvres off the port; he ordered the batteries to fire on ten British cruisers, but these were out of range. At 6 o'clock next morning he left for Dunkirk via Ghent, at that time a French town.

On 15 July, news reached Boulogne that Vice-Admiral Bruix had been appointed commander of the invasion flotilla with the rank of full admiral. The soldiers of his new command had never heard of him. Eustache de Bruix was 44 years old. Senior lieutenant at 27, captain at 34, rear-admiral at 38, Minister of Marine at 39, vice-admiral at 40, he was unquestionably the foremost French admiral so far as intelligence and character were concerned. But he was suffering from tuberculosis ('worn-out by his indulgences' according to Thiers) and was to die two years after taking command of the Boulogne flotilla.

The *Moniteur Universel* wrote discreetly of the dives clustered at the camps' approaches for the repose and the pleasure of the warriors. In fact, one could find there, as in the town, every variety of prostitution. From time immemorial women had followed the armies. Under the *ancien régime* they had comprised in principle the wives of the sutlers and artisans authorised to follow the armies in their little carts; officially they were laundresses and seamstresses. Many of them remained faithful to their men, but some were mere soldiers' molls and these became more numerous during the wars of the Revolution (the Motherland in danger did not prevent the voice of Humanity from making itself heard). A decree of the Convention (8 March 1793) 'authorised soldiers' in vague terms 'to form alliances in marriage without the assent of their superiors' (i.e., any sort of free union was authorised in the army). Moral: a month later, Carnot wrote from Dunkirk to the executive council: 'A terrible scourge is destroying our armies. This is the mass of girls and women who follow them; one must reckon that they are as numerous as the soldiers. The barracks and billets are crammed with them and the dissolution of morals is at its height; these women weaken the troops and destroy them by disease ten times more than those who succumb to the enemy.' Bonaparte, commander of the Army of Italy, was upset by this officially authorised brothel and in August 1796 published an order: 'Women caught at the head of the army in headquarters or in billets will be daubed black, paraded through the camp and expelled from its precincts.' The order proved effective for all of two weeks, the free-and-easies following docilely behind the columns, but let the army halt for merely forty-eight hours and they were all back. Some dozens of the cleverest or the most appreciated even managed to embark for Egypt as 'seamstresses and laundresses by profession' or by disguising themselves as soldiers. In such manner, Pauline Fourès, young and newly married to a lieutenant of mounted chasseurs, won fame as the mistress of the commanding general during the campaign; he almost married her on the day when he learned of the infidelity of Josephine. We shall see more of these transvestites, some charming, others anything but.

There is, naturally, no official record of the numbers of soldiers' wenches present during the various campaigns. One can judge that the high command tried constantly to reduce the damage and to constrain the feminine tide. But it is common knowledge that nothing keeps down prostitution. Raoul Brice has observed: 'Young, vigorous men, ardent soldier-fashion, when resting in garrison or camps, cannot restrain their senses. On the contrary, women are the only target of their desires. They fight among themselves to seduce them; they aspire to heroism, glory and riches in order to please. While officers in love exhibit refined tastes and delay following their hearts, no such superfluous delicacy restrains simple soldiers. The latter have an appetite perhaps more robust and less delicate and seek an immediate attainment of their desire. They appeal to the licentious, to girls whose inclination is to be wedded to the crowd; they are the consorts of the troopers, sought after as the wine runs out at soldiers' debauches when their excited senses seek relief.' We shall refer again to the delicacy of the officers. Brice was closer to the reality when he wrote: 'The Grande Armée encountered venereal diseases everywhere in Europe and had long marched with them, cultivating them on the fertile soil of prostitution and harvesting their fruits itself.'

Not all the women who followed the Grande Armée were prostitutes; we shall see a number of honest women – more or less; after all, the military climate is not that of a private boarding school – among the sutlers more often than among the canteen-keepers. A consular edict of 1799 had fixed the numbers of laundresses and vivandières authorised to follow the armies, ordering the selection of 'citizens with good manners, married to soldiers or NCOs on the active list, chosen as the most active and useful to the troops and whose conduct and morals are superior'. The *vivandières* wore an oval copper plaque with the regimental number. Some were very attractive and there were some cuckolded husbands. One Captain Marcel wrote in his *Mémoires* of a 'very pretty little woman named Reine, canteen-keeper to the 69th Regiment. She lived with a drummer of the 1st battalion who kept a close watch on her so that I could only see her when the battalion was on duty'. Most contemporary illustrations only depict attractive *vivandières* in fetching uniforms, but some, such as those of the Strasbourg artist, Zix, were more realistic. Some of the women had brats; they might be seen giving birth under a tree, catching-up with their regiment one or two stages further on. Most often they were dressed like peasants, but some might sport velvet robes trimmed with fur, pillaged from some château – soon to become filthy from the rough life of the roads and the camps.

Most went on foot at first, shouldering a keg of brandy and a string of sausages; then graduated to a donkey, and a somewhat better array of goods, then to a horse bought from a soldier who had stolen it, and finally to a covered trap – a true mobile shop. In the country the soldiers could not always eat and drink all they stole; to sell to the *vivandières* was a solution; they could hardly have maintained stocks otherwise, re-selling at a profit which was almost always reasonable; lending money to NCOs and other ranks who were temporarily in need, and even to officers. Some persuaded officers to marry them, those thus promoted became '*colonelles*' or '*générales*', but most continued yomping to the end. We can follow them for awhile. One 'Mother Fromageot', seduced at fifteen by a drummer, rose to be the mistress of a captain, then followed a simple gunner who, 'for a bottle of brandy', traded her to a fencing-master, who passed her on to a corporal, a brute who beat her – an unhappy fate for a female. On the evenings after a battle, the *vivandières* could be seen with soldiers searching the dead – sometimes not quite dead – boots were a useful item. Others turned their pony traps into ambulances on the days of battle and could display an exemplary devotion. Catherine Béguin of the 14th Light carried a wounded man five miles on her back to an ambulance; true, he was her husband. The *vivandière* of the 57th Line was mentioned in dispatches for having, at the battle of Guttstadt, 'despite a hail of bullets, twice entered a ravine where our troops were fighting in order to distribute two barrels of brandy'.

We shall meet these courageous women again, and also the wives and mistresses of the senior officers, colonels, generals and even marshals, some admirable, some odious and impossible. Throughout the ages, there has been no mass of females comparable to these followers of the Grande Armée, whose carriages in their thousands jolted through the dust, the mud and the snow.

Bonaparte, First Consul, then Emperor, inspected the camp at Boulogne on seven occasions: 10 February 1798; between 29 June and 1 July 1803; from 4 to 17 November 1804; 19 July 1804; in August 1804. He travelled in a yellow four-horse *berline* with a green boot. Twenty relays on the 270 kilometres of road between Saint-Cloud and Boulogne. Stops of five minutes at the relays by day, fifteen minutes by night. Fresh horses were ready everywhere; the road was patrolled by gendarmes and constantly repaired as the caissons broke it down. Three coaches followed twelve hours behind; one duty coach for the table-waiters, quartermasters responsible for the relays, the great man's *berline* and the carriage for the staff. Couriers constantly rode between these three vehicles. Bonaparte always considered that they were not moving fast enough. He worked in his *berline*, sometimes alone, sometimes with one of the secretaries, even at night, poorly lit by an oil lamp with an adjustable reflector. There were drawers for files and a miniature lavabo. An escort of cavalry of the Guard surrounded the *berline*, an aide-de-camp rode level with the window with the dispatch riders. By night the cavalrymen carried resin torches; dangerous bends were signalled by fires on the roadside. The locals when he passed would say 'It's him' and immediately cry: '*Vive le premier consul*.'

After his stay in November 1803, Bonaparte made his headquarters at Pont-de-Briques, four kilometres from Boulogne on the highway to Paris, in a small eighteenth-century château situated in a quiet park. His full staff consisted of five generals, thirty officers and eleven aides-de-camp, all reporting to General Berthier, chief of staff. 'Work occupied the Consul entirely,' wrote Queen Hortense, during her stay at Pont-de-Briques. 'He neither rested by day nor by night, everything was subordinated to his work.' Never rested – but she immediately added: 'His hours of sleep were no more fixed then those of his meals; he always lunched alone, we only saw him at dinner. On the days when he was preoccupied with some problem, nobody dared interrupt him for fear of encroaching on a serious thought or of receiving a rebuke.' Let us summarise what is common knowledge: that the great man worked constantly, slept little and ate too fast (fifteen minutes). In addition to his quarters at the château (two rooms plus an antechamber where Roustam, the mameluke, slept), Bonaparte had an observation post built on the cliffs near some Roman ruins known as the Odre Tower. This building was 70 metres long by 7 metres wide and included offices for the staff. At the end of the room was a camp bed and a bay window overlooking the port. Bonaparte liked this arrangement. All around were the sockets and the great arms of Chappe's telegraph apparatus. Nearby were the more modest huts for Soult and the servants.

Bruix was commander of the flotilla, but Bonaparte intended to keep him on a short rein. He had in mind a sort of amphibious army and created a battalion of 'seaman of the Guard'. Grenadiers and voltigeurs were made to toil at the oars for hours ('Those who could not row in the roads would row in the port'). Bonaparte left a sketch of his personal activities during this period in four letters written to Cambacérès on 5, 7, 9 and 12 November 1803.

'I was in the middle of the port at 1 p.m. where I had arrived quite unexpectedly. I was most interested in all these works and preparations for the great expedition. At midnight, I was still there. I am housed in the middle of the camp facing the Ocean whence it is easy to measure at a glance the distance which separates us from England. I spent Sunday visiting the ports of Ambleteuse and Wimereux and in exercising the troops there. The work is proceeding. I have just converted a barracks into a naval arsenal. I spent many hours inspecting the troops, man to man, and reassuring myself of the capacity of the various elements. I have more work here for several days. I spent a part of last night in showing the troops night evolutions, which trained elements can sometimes usefully employ against untrained bodies. I spent yesterday entirely in the port, in boats and on horseback, so you will see that I was constantly soaked. At this time of year, nothing can be done without accepting a wetting. Happily for me, all went off perfectly and I have never been in better shape.'

To General Augereau, on 16 November 1803: 'I have been here six days and am inclined to think that I shall attain the end which Europe awaits. We have ten centuries of insults to avenge.'

Bonaparte never wasted time in dictating letters unless they consisted of instructions or contributed to one or other of his projects. Here, he intended by way of the recipients, to spread optimism. An expression in his letter to Augereau is noteworthy: 'In a reasonable time'. In his heart he no longer believed that the flotilla alone could force the Straits and achieve surprise. It would require the support of a high-seas force.

At this time he was preoccupied with the attempts that were being made on his life. Royalist conspirators were active and secretly corresponding with London and Paris by way of Abbeville and Boulogne. In July 1803, the police arrested at Boulogne the very seamen suspected of ferrying the secret agents or their messages to England. They were taken to Paris and lodged in the Temple. Four months later, Baron Bloisel, a member of a prominent Toulonnaise family, visited their dependants, handed over large sums of money and disappeared.

The police recognised him and stated: 'Baron Bloisel arrived from Holland with false papers. About fifty years of age, 1.70 metres, long nose with brown eyes and eyebrows. Try to arrest him and transfer him secretly to Paris.' Orders given too late.

At the same time, Georges Cadoudal had landed from a British cutter with seven companions. Hiding in Paris, he awaited the arrival of other accomplices. On 20 February 1804 the police arrested another individual at Calais in the act of embarking for London. It was discovered that he was an agent in the Cadoudal conspiracy which aimed at assassinating Napoleon, and his arrest implicated General Pichegru. Pichegru, Bonaparte's friend at Brienne, ex-commander of the Army of the Rhine, then the Army of the North, victor at Valenciennes, Condé, Cassel and Courtrai, victor at Fleurus with Jourdan and Moreau, commander of the force that seized the Dutch fleet in the Texel when frozen in the ice, was immensely popular. Having been commander-in-chief of the armies of the Rhine and the Moselle, Pichegru had allowed himself to be persuaded by the Prince of Condé to march on Paris to restore Louis XVIII; the plot had failed and he was arrested and deported. He escaped and fled to England where he made contact with Cadoudal and the princes.

Many of the veterans at the Boulogne camp had served under Pichegru and recalled above all his victories. Sedition was feared and it was decided to act. In an order of the day to the flotilla, the Minister of Justice proclaimed: 'The soldiers and sailors of the flotilla share with every Frenchman the feelings of the most outraged indignation. The enemy Government, instigator of every crime, will cease to exist when the signal to depart is given. The blows which you will inflict will punish the perjurer and the assassin. France will at last be avenged and the First Consul will be assuaged by victory.'

On 28 February Pichegru was arrested in Paris. The officers and some naval detachments in full dress attended a Te Deum at the church of Saint Nicholas at Boulogne. Soult had already addressed a reassuring report to the army: 'Yesterday, the camps presented the signs of a sombre unrest, vague rumours alarmed the soldiers. They learned today of the dangers from which you have just escaped and the camps echoed with cries of joy.' And Soult published an order of the day: 'Soldiers! Banish all your fears, the life of the First Consul is no longer in danger and we, in the front rank facing this enemy nation, will be the shield of the hero.'

Bruix, not to be outdone in eloquence, sent Bonaparte a declaration signed by sixty captains: 'Yes, citizen Consul, the flotilla will cross the short space which separates these shores which are destined to be a new theatre of triumph for the brave armies of this Republic.'

Pichegru would be found dead in his cell on 8 April. Cadoudal, arrested in Paris on 9 March 1804, would be guillotined on 25 June. General Moreau, who had known of the conspiracy and had said nothing, was condemned to two years in prison. That was the end of the Cadoudal conspiracy, but meanwhile the police were convinced that the 32-year-old Duke of Enghien (Louis-Antoine-Henri de Bourbon-Condé) was one of the conspirators. After the Peace of Lunéville, he had moved as a civilian to Ettenheim in the Grand Duchy of Baden. He was abducted on the night of 15/16 March and taken to the château of Vincennes in Paris. Condemned at midnight, he was shot at 3 a.m. on 21 March. This fusillade would have repercussions.

That was not the end of it. In May 1804, Jean-François de Franqueville, a notable of Boulogne, was accused of being an agent of Cadoudal's, convicted of 'criminal correspondence', arraigned before the military commission of the camp at Boulogne, condemned to death on 26 May and shot the following day.

Police surveillance was stepped-up throughout the region. All civilians working at the camp were required to show an identity card; lacking which, prison! But the (British) Intelligence Service was awake and the clandestine correspondence continued to circulate. At the beginning of 1804, fifteen royalists accused of conspiracy and espionage were summoned to appear before the military court at Rouen. Six were condemned to death and three were shot; the others, condemned *in absentia,* managed to escape. 'Among them was a girl of nineteen, Nymphe Roussel de Préville, daughter of a naval captain, extremely pretty, who travelled the roads as far as Dieppe and Amiens disguised as a boy and accompanied by one of her farmers, collecting intelligence, and disseminating mail and money with extraordinary audacity.' A fortnight later two naval officers who were *émigrés* in London landed at Morlaix, destination Boulogne. They were arrested and found to be carrying a thousand pounds Sterling. Arraigned before a military commission at Paris, they refused to speak and were summarily shot.

The echoes of the fusillades directed at spies and conspirators scarcely dampened the atmosphere at Boulogne. The town was a crowded antheap and quite light-hearted; the smallest lodgings were in demand, the smallest business was a gold-mine, the townsmen were amassing riches to last them for the next fifty years. Everywhere were balls, music and embraces. The soldiers sought the girls in the dives in a nearby valley now re-christened the Happy Valley. The officers found their consolations around Pont-de-Briques in the parish of Condette, out-of-bounds to NCOs and other ranks, or in the town. The mayor complained to the sub-prefect that General Loison, billeted on him, had, with her father's consent, installed a girl of eighteen in his house and was living with her. 'You will understand, citizen sub-prefect, how distressed our womenfolk are at such conduct.' The police expelled those girls who created a scandal, but how could one deal with a general's mistress?

Bonaparte decided that there was definitely too much prostitution at Boulogne. An edict forbade non-residents to stay in the town 'without the special authorisation of the Minister of Police' and the soldiers had to undergo medical inspection. The doctors said that 'the totals of venereals and scabials in hospital would drop considerably' but the statistics are suspect, as they lumped both categories together at that time. Scabies was then rife; Bonaparte had suffered from it at the siege of Toulon.

A reduced number of prostitutes was allowed to remain. There were officers' days and troops' days. The 'privileged' girls made fortunes, but killed themselves at it, except for one who has remained famous, a tall, 22-year-old of somewhat masculine appearance. Being lucky, she remained the joy of the camp without compromising her health. The troops called her Madame Forty Thousand Men and believed her to be very rich, but she was to die in poverty in the hospital at Ardres in 1812.

Early in 1804, Napoleon's actions indicate that he was certain that the Channel crossing and the invasion of Britain would go ahead. Several corvettes allocated for his use and that of the general staff had arrived from Havre. Bonaparte was to embark at Wimereux (a closely kept secret). The corvette detailed to transport him had been elegantly furnished and fitted with a Chappe optical telegraph to allow the great chief to remain in contact with France during the crossing.

Precisely thanks to the Chappe telegraph, the news came to Boulogne that the Empire had just been proclaimed at Paris. All units of the flotilla dressed ship overall, the artillery batteries fired salvoes. The troops of the Army of England received double rations and learned that the camp commandant, Soult, had been promoted Marshal, as were thirteen other generals.

Soult immediately addressed the troops in camp: 'Soldiers! Napoleon Bonaparte has accepted the Empire to which the will of the people has called him. A new era begins today and the happiness of France is assured for ever.' That same day, the soldiers were invited to swear an oath of fidelity: 'Soldiers! We will now utter the prescribed oath. This vow, for long graven on our hearts, will be the token of our love for the father of the nation. Soldiers! we swear obedience to the constitution of the Empire and faithfulness to the Emperor!' The troops, 'with one single shout and one common impulse' declared, 'We swear it!' Marseillaise, salvoes of artillery. Some eye-witness accounts reveal that some of the soldiers were not pleased with the title of emperor; who knows whether they had been coached in 'the Republic, liberty and death to tyrants'. But it is true that, for many, Napoleon Bonaparte, even as emperor, continued to be the champion of liberty, the enemy of oppressive kings. Such contradictions have never worried the mob.

The Emperor Napoleon arrived at the camp on 19 July 1804. The town was bedecked with flags, the streets decorated with triumphal arches. At the port, on a wooden column, fifteen metres high, an inscription announced that Albion would be punished and that 'revengeful lightnings' would originate from Boulogne. A crowd assembled on the road to Pont-de-Briques. There were fanfares and young girls threw flowers when the Emperor appeared. He crossed the town rather hurriedly, making a lengthy swing towards the port and the beach. The batteries fired a 900-round salute which lasted for hours. Napoleon embarked in a pinnace flying the new square imperial ensign, sailed towards the massed flotilla and for three hours participated in 'various evolutions for ships' – not too far offshore, because of the British blockade. At 8 p.m. he returned to his Headquarters, crossing the town almost as fast as before, without apparently noticing the public and private illuminations, which momentarily dampened enthusiasm. By 7 a.m. next day he was already back at Boulogne, inspecting everything. The incident occurred at the end of the afternoon of that day.

The weather was so bad – black skies, squalls, a falling barometer, a high sea already running – that, when Napoleon ordered a review of part of the flotilla, Bruix opposed it. What! Dare to say No to the Emperor? For a few minutes, there was such a hot argument that Napoleon brandished his riding whip at Bruix, whose hand went to his sword-hilt: 'Take care, Sire!' For some seconds the two men defied each other, neither yielding; the onlookers were frozen with terror. Then Napoleon threw down his whip: 'The review!' There was nothing to do but to submit. The review was held while a storm exploded and the wind became a tempest. Under a sky slashed with lightning, sloops, barges and gunboats were driven shorewards and many capsized, their seamen and soldiers thrown into the sea.

That is the version which appeared in the memoirs of Constant, the Emperor's valet, and which has been repeated by many historians, one of whom added that, following the quarrel, Bruix had fallen out of favour and been 'exiled'. According to others, Constant was not invariably truthful and the dramatic scene may have occurred on another day or might even have been 'forged' by the famous valet. The Napoleonic faithful can argue as they please. Two facts are known: one month later, Bruix's name headed the list as the first high dignitary of the order of the Legion of Honour, which proves that Napoleon wished to forget the incident; there had been casualties. On 22 July 1804 Soult reported to the Minister of War that eight boats had run aground and that there were 'some fifty victims'. Albert Chatelle repeats this figure; two hundred, says René Maine. In their reports to London, British spies stated: 400. Napoleon himself described it thus to Josephine: 'The wind freshened much during the night, one of the gunboats broke loose and ran on rocks a league from Boulogne. I had thought she was a total loss, but we managed to recover everything. This spectacle was enhanced by the signal guns, the beach fires, the raging and roaring of the sea, the night-long anxiety to save or to see the unfortunates perish. Souls between Eternity, the ocean and the night. At five in the morning, all cleared up, all had been saved and I went to sleep feeling that I had seen a romantic and epic dream.' To each his truth. Napoleon wrote to Latouche-Tréville at Toulon that 'some divisions of the flotilla not having been able to report', the start of the operation had been postponed for a month.

During that same visit to Boulogne, Napoleon dictated a letter to the Minister of the Interior: 'I have just read the proposal of citizen Fulton that you sent to me far too late, seeing that it could change the face of the World. I wish you to refer the examination to a committee composed of the various classes of the Institute. That is where academic Europe should seek the judges of the issue in question. Immediately you have their report, send it to me. Try to complete the business in less than a week.'

Could Fulton's proposal have changed the face of the world by destroying the British fleet or by sowing terror on the seas? It is possible. We must here take some steps back.

In December 1797, Robert Fulton, an American mechanic aged thirty-two who had been living in England for ten years, arrived in France. He wrote to the Minister of Marine, proposing to construct for France a submarine boat capable of carrying and placing explosive charges under enemy ships. He asked in exchange 'a bonus of 4,000 francs per gun for the destruction of a 40-gun ship, 2,000 francs per gun for a smaller vessel'. He also wished to have a regular commission or a letter of marque in order to avoid being hanged as a pirate in the event of his capture. Privateers, as regular combatants, could claim the protection of the rules of war. In the margin of Fulton's letter we can read the reply of Préville le Pelley, Minister of Marine at that time: 'The government cannot recognise openly men who would lend themselves to this type of operation. To do so would in some degree delete from the codes of war the punishments justly inflicted on those who are by nature inclined to wage war in an atrocious manner.'

The following year (1798), Bruix, by now Minister of Marine, in turn examined Fulton's proposal and convened a committee under Admiral Rosily to study it. Verdict negative, project rejected.

In July 1799, Fulton, not discouraged, wrote again: 'It appears that the motives for rejection were pitiable considerations of humanity, as if France was able to protest against the employment of a method destined to avenge her and to deliver her from her most implacable enemy.' His letter might have come from Bonaparte himself. Fulton repeated his proposal to build 'this machine destined to destroy British ships on the high seas and nearly within their ports'. He added that he was not asking for money, but simply permission to try out his machine in Paris. He would pilot it himself to prove that he was no impostor. Permission was granted and construction of the submarine was begun at Chaillot beside the Seine. On 10 April 1800, Fulton informed Minister of Marine Forfait that the machine was complete. Secret trials took place on 13 June in the presence of Forfait and the Minister of War.

The boat was named *Nautulus* (later *Nautilus*). Built entirely of wood, 6.5 metres long, 2 metres beam, with a sail for surface propulsion, submerged propulsion being achieved by a screw propeller turned by hand. To dive, water was admitted to a compartment; to surface, it was expelled by a pump. The boat had two rudders, one vertical, one horizontal, a cupola with a porthole of thick glass, a barometer to measure depth, a compass for direction. What more would the true submarines have, a century later? *Nautilus* could remain submerged for three hours. Three men sufficed to manoeuvre her; submerged, light was provided by candles or an oil lamp. Do not forget her armament: a barbed torpedo loaded with gunpowder; propelled by the submarine, it would be driven into the hull of an enemy ship.

'What do you think of it, citizen minister?' Forfait was impressed; he approached three savants, members of the military council of the Directory, citizens Darçon, Michaud and Alexandre. They shook their heads; here is the substance of their conclusions: the weapon imagined by citizen Fulton is a terrible weapon of destruction, given its silence and absolute efficiency; it is the first concept of a man of genius; it is still imperfect and must be perfected.

Forfait reported to the First Consul: 'All that could be expected of a first experiment has been achieved. It gives grounds for some hopes.' Fulton needed a loan in order to continue his trials. Forfait arranged it. *Nautilus* was dived at Rouen and trials here proved conclusive; at Havre, armed with a torpedo loaded with 30 pounds of gunpowder, she blew up a very large barque. *Nautilus* was transported by road to Brest, where, with only twenty pounds of powder, she sank an old brig – on a day when two British frigates were to be seen anchored in the roads. Fulton visited Admiral Villaret de Joyeuse and Caffarelli, the maritime prefect at Brest. 'I want permission to go myself and to blow-up those two insolent ships.'

The reply was No, and for this reason: 'This manner of making war on our enemy carries in itself such a reprobation that those who undertook it and failed [taken prisoner] would be hanged.' Such a reprobation! The cannon which cut red swathes in the crews massed on deck, the boardings where heads fly, bravo. But no torpedoes. Bayard had already said that the sword was noble and the arquebus ignoble; he died, as we all know, of a shot from an arquebus. In short, on the basis of the report from Brest, the authorities rejected Fulton's proposal. No to *Nautilus*.

How could one discourage Fulton, the American mechanic? Here he is now asking Monge to send the First Consul another project for mines and submarines. 'There are two types: the first with springs similar to that of a clock and which explodes as you choose in between four minutes and four hours; the second are held on the seabed by grapnels and explode on contact with the enemy. They would be kept at a depth of five or six feet. No pilot could avoid these hidden dangers.' What would be used 140 years later but magnetic mines? And, the pioneer added in his best Bonapartist style, 'Citizen First Consul, from the success of this enterprise will spring an order of things worthy of your genius and which merit birth under your consulate ... I am convinced that with patience and the care which so worthy an object deserves, one would attain the goal of annihilating the enormous naval power of England and of establishing the freedom of the seas.'

Forfait and Monge tended to favour the project, but without sufficient conviction. Caffarelli and Admirals Latouche-Tréville and Rosily were entirely hostile, as was the savant Borda. Fulton's proposition was submitted to Bonaparte, but with ten or twenty other fanciful and unfeasible projects: tunnels under the Straits, squadrons of balloons, huge rafts propelled by windmills, kites carrying cannon, etc. And Bonaparte had his head full of a million other things: the employment of this army under arms, the flotilla, the policies being followed by France, European diplomacy – with all its attendant dangers. As for Fulton's project, the reserve or hostility of the savants weighed more with him than that of the admirals. So, with a shake of the head and a gesture, no to Fulton's mines; too bad, other needs are more urgent.

Fulton continued with a frenzy of invention. In the summer of 1803, Parisians were astonished to see a barque of sorts, equipped with paddles, which beat the waters of the Seine in a swirl of smoke. They were looking at the first steamboat in history, and it was this invention which, *Nautilus* and the mines having been rejected, Fulton was proposing to the French government. On the quay where now runs the present 'express road' not far from the Jena bridge, one can read on a plaque:

ON THIS SITE ON THE QUAY CALLED 'THE RUSTICS'
THE AMERICAN ENGINEER ROBERT FULTON
PRESENTED ON 21 THERMIDOR OF THE YEAR XI [11 AUGUST 1803)]
TO CITIZENS
BOSSUT, CARNOT, PRONEY AND VOLNEY
HIS WATER CHARIOT MOVED BY FIRE
WHICH PERFORMED ON THE SEINE
ITS FIRST MANOEUVRES.

It is difficult to understand why there is no mention on this plaque of the fact that, like *Nautilus* and like the mines, the 'water Chariot moved by fire' was refused. There is no limit to blindness.

Fulton persisted. Early in 1804 he again reported to the First Consul, this time through the Minister of the Interior, not about the water Chariot, but about the mines, which he thought might still prove of interest. But the Minister of the Interior was preoccupied with royalist plots, Napoleon's security and police surveillance on a scale hitherto unknown. For six months Fulton's report was shuffled from one bureau to the next. When it finally reached headquarters at Boulogne – in July 1804 – Napoleon while reading it, frowned; and what if this was a marvellous opportunity, an absolute weapon? 'I have just read the proposal of citizen Fulton that you sent to me far too late, seeing that it could change the face of the World ...' And Napoleon wanted a definite opinion in a week. Too late: Fulton crossed to England. In any event, the commission at the Institute also recommended rejection. The chance of changing the face of the world was lost.

Is it a consolation to note that England was as blind as France? Fulton was warmly received, and it seemed as if the British would welcome the redoubtable weapons rejected by Bonaparte. But – no. Once used, their potential would be known to all, with the possibility that sooner or later they would be used against British ships. No to submarines; no to mines. And no to the water chariot moved by fire. What could be achieved by this snail against the world's best warships? Fulton returned to the United States. In 1807, the first steamer, christened *Clermont*, covered the two hundred kilometres of the Hudson separating Albany from New York.. The first naval mines, then called torpedoes, appeared in France in about 1880 for coastal and port defence. The submarine *Gymnote* (electric propulsion) would be built by Gustave Zédé in 1887.

When I was a child, I found in the attic of a country barn an Epinal illustration depicting the distribution of crosses of the Legion of Honour at the camp at Boulogne on 16 August 1804. Napoleon mounted on a white horse, holding a cross and 120,000 soldiers shouting 'Vive l'Empereur!' The ceremony, intended to excite enthusiasm for the new-born Empire, had been the most spectacular of the events aimed at the populace. Such a parade under arms had never been seen before. The troops were drawn-up in an amphitheatre on the plain of Terlinc-thun (today, the old town centre) at the foot of the cliffs north of the town. In the middle, separated from the troops by a vast space, 'a mound in the antique fashion, such as were seen in the Roman camps when emperors wished to harangue their armies'. In the centre of this was a throne for Napoleon, 'an antique chair, used, according to legend, by Dagobert, a canopy, trophies of arms and armour, the whole topped by an enormous crown of laurels. Those troops – such as the Imperial Guard – stationed near enough to see a little of this monument could not believe their eyes. They had toiled for days on the cliffs in a gale of wind in order to stake-out the camps at the pyramids, the triumphal arches loaded with decorations for the glory of the Emperor, a large sundial bearing the inscription 'I shall soon mark the hour of Victory' and allegorical statues. They had for days buffed their arms and equipment, and been woken in the middle of the night to fall-in and march to the foot of the cliffs. Exhausted, even before the ceremony began, but kept awake by the salvoes of artillery, the forty regimental bands, the 2,000 drummers of what was still called the Army of England and, in spite of it all, shouting 'Vive l'Empereur!' when he passed on his grey horse surrounded by his glittering staff. Napoleon wore his immortal working dress of a mounted Chasseur, green coat, trimmed in amaranth, gilt buttons, white waistcoat and breeches, crowned with the no less celebrated small hat.

To salvoes of cannon and drum-rolls. the Emperor had scarcely arrived and taken his seat on the throne when 120,000 soldiers presented arms and

Napoleon read out the 'legionnaires' oath' – yet another oath: 'Commanders, officers, legionnaires, citizens and soldiers, swear on your honour to devote yourselves to the service of the Empire, to the preservation of its territory and integrity, to the defence of the Emperor, the laws of the Republic and the estates which they embody, to fight by every means which justice, reason and law authorise against every enterprise which threatens to re-establish feudal rule. Finally, swear to contribute by every means in your power to the maintenance of liberty and equality, the first basis of our institutions.' Fortunately for his literary reputation, Napoleon produced better texts than this hodge-podge in defence of the Emperor and the laws of the Republic. But it mattered little, because his words could not be heard by the troops. However, when he added 'You swear it!' (which they did not hear, either), all the officers shouted on signal 'We swear it!', and the troops joined in: 'A loud, hoarse noise spread from regiment to regiment'. The 'bad hats' who cried – not too loudly – 'The hell with you!' or 'Shit on you!' were unheard.

The distribution of crosses began to the strains of the 'Song of Departure' and the boom of the salvoes, interspersed with the pealing of the town bells which were carried on the wind. Marshal Berthier escorted to the throne Admiral Bruix, Marshals Ney and Soult, ten civilians including three bishops, officers, NCOs and 2,000 soldiers, including those who had already received 'arms of honour' testifying to their bravery. All received the cross from the Emperor's hands; many were moved to tears. Then in a packed column, headed by the sailors of the flotilla shouldering boarding axes, 120,000 men marched past their sovereign to the music of sixty military bands.

Delegations from the flotilla and the Army of England were invited to two other ceremonies at Paris: the Emperor's consecration and the solemn award of 'the eagles'.

Napoleon's consecration in Notre-Dame de France (2 December 1804) took its place in France's folklore. The invited delegates from the Army of England and the flotilla recalled unaccustomed luxury, interminable spells at attention, and heroic drinking parties. There were also celebrations and rejoicing at Boulogne; the gunfire broke windows. The scene was illuminated. The outnumbered prostitutes, overcome by their labours, were able to fill their chamber-pots with écus.

In Paris, the delegates were invited three days later to the award of the regiments' eagles on the Champ-de-Mars. The eagles were gilded birds which replaced the points and arrowheads of the revolutionary epoch on the staffs of the colours. The tricoloured flags of the Revolution, the Consulate and the Empire did not have the three blue, white and red colours disposed vertically as we know them today; the arrangement varied from regiment to regiment. In 1803, Napoleon, as First Consul, wished to introduce the same flag throughout the army: square, very large (each side 1m 56) with a white diamond in the centre whose points touched the borders of the flag; two triangles in blue and red, placed diagonally, filling the angles and the fixings of the inner cantons being in white. The flag bore the inscriptions 'RÉPUBLIQUE FRANÇAISE' and 'VALOUR AND DISCIPLINE' on a blue globe within the diamond and the legend 'THE FIRST CONSUL TO THE (...) REGIMENT': at the top of the staff, a gilded arrow with a tricoloured collar. As Emperor, Napoleon altered the flag, reducing it to 80cm for each side with the inscription: 'THE EMPEROR OF THE FRENCH TO (...) ' At the top of the colour-staff was a spread-eagle, emblem of the Empire. This bird was feminine, but the troops called it 'the cuckoo'. In 1810, David painted a canvas of the Champ-de-Mars ceremony of 5 December 1804, a fine example of pictorial eloquence with plenty of biceps and braced calves, and highly coloured uniforms, even more glittering than the full dress of the dignitaries. Napoleon and Josephine wore 'imperial ornaments'. The Emperor raised his hand to pronounce yet another oath: 'Soldiers, there are your colours. These eagles will serve you as points for rallying. They will be everywhere your Emperor judges necessary for the defence of his throne and his people. You will swear to give your life to defend him and constantly to uphold them by your courage on your way to victory.' 'We swear it!'

For some days, Paris had been gripped by an arctic cold. Those living on the river banks along the route of the procession (Tuileries, Concorde, rue de Bourgogne, rue de Grenelle, Ecole Militaire, Champ-de-Mars) had been invited to break the ice and scatter cinders. Despite the Siberian weather, there were crowds; towards evening the weather changed and it began to rain. Admiral Bruix caught a severe cold, fatal to his debilitated constitution. He took to his bed and died two months later. There was an 'extraordinary funeral' at Boulogne. Admiral Lacrosse replaced Bruix.

'What the hell are we doing here, what are we waiting for?' The troops in camp at Boulogne grumbled. Winter came, then the spring of 1805; the main troop movements towards Boulogne had started in 1803 – to make an army wait too long is never good, as Napoleon knew better than anyone. Since November 1803, Bonaparte had consulted Ganteaume, then a vice-admiral and naval prefect at Toulon. 'Give me your ideas about this flotilla. Do you believe it will carry us to the shores of Albion? It can carry 100,000 men. Eight hours of a night of favourable weather could decide the fate of the universe.' Bonaparte, already autocratic, reluctant to take advice, nevertheless had confidence in Ganteaume who had brought him back from Egypt four years earlier in the Frigate *Muiron,* running the gauntlet of the British blockade in the Mediterranean. Like most seamen, Ganteaume did not give flat-bottomed boats much chance against a British squadron. 'In the last analysis', he wrote to Bonaparte,

'I consider the expedition of the flotilla , if not impossible, extremely risky and that success would only be attainable thanks to some factor which it is impossible to foresee'.

Bonaparte considered that such a factor could be created ('impossible is not French'); one could wrest command of the sea from the British at a given moment by deploying the French high-seas fleet: indeed, that was the only hope of getting the flotilla through. Briefly, the plan he had in mind was that the Toulon Squadron would weigh and proceed into the Atlantic, being joined on passage by the Rochefort Squadron; the two squadrons would set course for Boulogne. Meanwhile, the Brest Squadron would break the blockade to which it was subjected, or at any rate so engage the attention of the British force that it would be unable to intercept the naval forces coming from Toulon. This adroit plan was repeatedly revised. Every seaman has criticised Bonaparte for his ignorance of the hazards of any naval operation (wind and weather), for giving his admirals orders which were too imperative and too rigid (dates of weighing anchor, courses to steer),for ignoring the possibility that time and distance might work against him. By the time they arrived almost all his orders would prove useless, derisory or dangerous, having been overtaken by events. But, even if the supreme commander had been less imperious, the French navy of the time would have needed a lot of luck to compensate the superiority of the Royal Navy as regards the professional worth of the ships' companies (the French were not lacking in courage), and nothing could reduce the chasm between Vice–Admiral Pierre de Villeneuve, the commander of the Toulon Squadron, and the genius of Horatio Nelson.

According to the (latest) orders from Napoleon, Villeneuve was to sortie from Toulon, dodge the British blockade and, avoiding battle, set course for Martinique in order to entice the British fleet away from Europe. Having ravaged the British West Indian possessions, he was to re-cross the Atlantic and appear 'unexpectedly' in the Channel, attacking the British fleets there, while the Boulogne flotilla, carrying the Army of England, was crossing the Channel. Everybody knows broadly what happened: Villeneuve, pursued by Nelson, sailed to the Antilles (the West Indies), destroyed nothing, and returned to Europe. After an indecisive action against a British squadron 150 miles west of Ferrol (his destination, at the north-west corner of Spain), he took refuge at Vigo (80 nautical miles south of Ferrol) on 27 July 1805.

A few days later Napoleon's coach left Saint-Cloud for Boulogne, passing through towns and villages whose many triumphal arches bore the inscription 'The Road to England'. He arrived at Pont-de-Briques at 4 a.m. and by 10 o'clock was on horseback inspecting the troops in camp; at 9 p.m. we see him again on the quays. Back at his HQ, he dictated a letter to Decrès, Minister of Marine: 'The English do not know what is coming to them. Everything here is in good shape. If we are masters of the crossing for twelve hours, England is doomed.'

A total of 140,000 troops were now assembled in the Channel camps. The plan was right on time: forty thousand men would embark on the same tide, with 16,000 horses aboard the stable-boats. Marshals Lannes, Davout, Murat, Soult and Ney would each command an army corps; the central point of the landings would be Deal, thirteen kilometres north of Dover and less than 100 kilometres from London. Immediately the initial defence had been broken, the army was to march on the capital by way of Canterbury, Chatham and Rochester.

For the past two months Napoleon had known that a coalition in Europe was forming against him. Austria and Russia had signed a treaty, and Britain would be the paymaster. Every contingency must be foreseen. Napoleon had assigned twenty million francs for the repair of bridges and roads from Boulogne–Paris, Brest–Paris, Paris–Lyons–Turin, Paris–Cologne and Paris–Strasbourg. On 31 July Talleyrand had been ordered to send a stiff note to the Austrian court – a form of ultimatum. 'But they must be truly mad to make war on me. There is no better army in Europe than mine.' And Napoleon believed that, in one way or another, Britain would be humbled before his European enemies could achieve anything decisive. So certain was he of this that the Mint had been ordered to strike a medal commemorating the invasion of England, and the first copies of this hostage to fortune were already reposing in a sealed box at his HQ. The face of the medal bore the likeness of the Emperor crowned with laurels, the obverse depicting Hercules supporting the world and 'suffocating in his arms a figure, half man and half fish' which represented Britain. The medal bore two inscriptions: 'INVASION OF ENGLAND' and 'MINTED AT LONDON IN 1804'. Given that this antedated medal would in fact be unusable, it is not known whether Napoleon was responsible for this blunder, but in July 1805 he personally had invited the company of the Vaudeville Theatre to move to Boulogne with its scenery and costumes. They were to cross the Channel and immediately the British army was crushed (no doubt in his mind about this) they were to proceed to London and perform. While waiting to embark, they played at the theatre of Boulogne, a small building lit by whale-oil lamps. The performances included 'Duguay-Trouin, the Portsmouth Prisoner' and 'The Vaudeville of the Boulogne Camp' which were played to enthusiastic audiences who hissed whenever Nelson's name was mentioned.

On 13 August, Napoleon sent a letter to Villeneuve by special courier (these messengers crossed and recrossed France and part of Spain, foundering their horses): 'I am convinced in thinking that victory has eluded our arms after you entered La Corunna (Napoleon did not distinguish it from nearby Ferrol). I hope that this dispatch will not find you still there. Therefore, proceed to the

Channel where we await you anxiously. Proceed boldly against the enemy; the English are not as numerous as you believe and everywhere are kept busy. Provided you can arrive in the next three days, within twenty-four hours your mission will be fulfilled. For the great project of making possible a descent on this power which has opposed France for centuries, we can all die without regretting the sacrifice of our lives.' From now on events moved ever faster and, so to speak, became entangled.

It seems that shortly after Napoleon had dictated this letter to Villeneuve, Gaspard Monge visited him and was asked immediately 'Do you know where Villeneuve is?' How could Monge have known when the Emperor himself did not? But, realising from his tone that the weather was stormy, the savant found a pretext to leave immediately and to call on the Darus who lived nearby and who invited him to share their midday meal. Scarcely had they sat down than a sentry arrived: 'His Majesty requires Count Daru'.

Daru, Quartermaster-General of the Grande Armée, was an important personage in the imperial household. But we must emphasise, once and for all, that in Napoleon's eyes, nobody was important. When Daru arrived he was not reassured. A small, anxious-looking man, his oval-shaped face with its, high, bald forehead, devoid of special features, Daru was then thirty-six, but looked older and had the grey mien of men who are habitually overworked. 'He is a man of rare capacity, my best administrator,' Napoleon would say of him. He had governed Prussia and the conquered countries with an honesty unique to himself. In enemy territory he had lived at his own expense and did not even claim the perquisites to which he was entitled. Daru was born at Montpellier of an old-established Dauphinois family 'which had given numerous servants to the King and the Empire'. His father was senior counsel to the parliament at the regional capital, Toulouse. Educated by the Oratorians, Latin was to his taste more than anything else, but his father distrusted anything poetical or literary: 'You will join the administration, if possible that of the army.' Pierre-Antoine-Noël-Mathieu Bruno, Count Daru, did exactly what his father wished and survived without incident the first years of the Revolution, became Commissioner of War at Brest, then paymaster at Rennes and at Lorient; by 1793 he was Paymaster-in-Chief of the armies of the West and well on his way. But in revolutionary times, weigh your every word and, if possible, never put anything in writing. Early in 1794, mail was being closely examined. The police intercepted a letter in which, jokingly and in pure irony, Daru had called the British 'our friends'. Very wicked. Imprisoned. 'But were you not, moreover, a former nobleman? And did not your mother attend a clandestine mass a year ago?' Worse and worse; Daru's head was in danger. All his friends must intervene and his immediate superior, Chief Paymaster Petiet, approached the minister in order to save him from the scaffold. Transferred to Orleans as suspect, ten months of prison and supervised liberty, finally resuming his functions of Paymaster at Rennes. Some years later he would make a suitable marriage and sire eight children.

In 1800, Daru was Secretary-General to the Minister of War, Berthier. One day Berthier presented a project which displeased Napoleon. 'Who drew this up? I want to see the author.' Daru arrived and defended his proposals. His critic marshalled his arguments. 'Do you agree?' 'No, Monsieur First Consul, I insist.' Bonaparte frowned, repeated his arguments in a somewhat higher pitch. Daru: 'Monsieur First Consul, I insist. But give me your orders and I will obey.' Bonaparte immediately calmed down. Later he would often say to Daru, half jokingly: 'You know that, to calm me down, all you need say is: "I insist".' 'Yes, Sire, but on condition that I add: "Give me your orders and I will obey".'

Daru was appointed Counsellor of State on 17 July 1805 and, a week later, Comptroller of the Imperial Household. This post embraced everything that concerned the Sovereign directly: the palace marshal, the chief almoners, chamberlains, grooms, huntsmen, master of ceremonies, paymaster-general, crown treasurer – with all the assets which these officials controlled and administered. Let us also recall that the Guard formed part of the military household. On 30 August 1805, Daru was appointed Commissary-General of the Grande Armée, and on 1 January 1806 Intendant-General of conquered territories. His task would have been arduous enough had the Grande Armée remained in one place, but this enormous machine, which Napoleon almost always pushed forward at maximum speed, often steam-rollered everything including projects, estimates, and diverse and worthy organisations laboriously set up by Daru. But the duties which troubled him most were those which brought him into personal, often intimate, contact with the Emperor.

'Sire, I have spent my life with books and business. I have not had the time to learn the courtier's trade.' 'Courtiers? They are not lacking around me and I would never miss them, make no mistake. I need an administrator who is intelligent, firm and vigilant; that is why I chose you.' Napoleon said also of Daru: 'He can do anything. He has judgement, imagination, a huge capacity for work and a mind and a constitution of iron.'

But we must return to Pont-de-Briques on 13 August 1805. 'Monsieur Daru, do you know where Villeneuve is?' Napoleon knew perfectly well that neither Monge nor Daru knew the whereabouts of Villeneuve; it is possible that the questions were no more than a sort of external noise, a clicking of the type of computer which was the Emperor's brain, and which had started to process the data recorded during the past days. Napoleon knew, as I have said, that Austria and Russia, pushed by Britain, were preparing to go to war against him. On 31 July he ordered Talleyrand to send the Austrian court a note of warning. But this warning would perhaps be useless and, more and more, he must foresee every-thing. Daru had replied with a grimace indicating that he knew nothing. Napoleon, who till now had seemed to be restraining his anger, relaxed. Then, with a gesture: 'Monsieur Daru, sit down and write.'

Napoleon, in an explosion of rage, had ordered Villeneuve hanged or worse, but afterwards dictated a letter to him that was both imperative and encouraging. He continued to behave as though he still hoped that Villeneuve would appear off Boulogne, but in his heart did he not harbour a presentiment of the grim reality?

That very day, 13 August, Villeneuve sailed from Ferrol. His combined Franco-Spanish fleet was to rendezvous off Cape Finisterre with the Rochefort Squadron and proceed up-Channel. At midday on the following day, lookouts reported a dozen sail to the northward. Villeneuve did not think of sending his frigates to investigate them. Next day he fell in with a merchantman whose cap-tain came aboard the flagship. According to him, the sails sighted were those of a British squadron. Villeneuve gave orders to put about and set course for Cadiz on the south coast of Spain (only 30 miles north of the Straits of Gibraltar). Sub-sequently it would become known that the merchant captain's report of 25 British vessels was false. Worse: the sails sighted on the 14th had been those of the Rochefort Squadron. The two forces had missed each other, neither having dared to close and identify themselves.

Napoleon's manner of dictation has been described hundreds of times: walking up and down, his hands clasped behind him; brief phrases, clipped, ragged sentences, proper names mis-pronounced, the various secretaries catch-ing it on the wing and reconstructing it intuitively. On this occasion, perhaps because he was dealing with higher degrees of secrecy, he chose Daru. What he dictated were movement orders to the army assembled at the Boulogne camp and nearby – not towards England, but towards Austria.

Much has been written about this famous dictation. Napoleon is said to have been dictating 'for several hours'. The exact length of time is not known, but he had Daru set down on paper the entire plan of the campaign of 1805, the campaign of Ulm and Austerlitz.

Seven corps were set in motion. Marshal Bernadotte (I Corps) was to move from Hanover towards Bavaria with 17,000 men. He would be joined at Würtzburg by Marmont (II Corps) marching from Holland with 20,000 men (a good 25 per cent of whom were Dutch). Davout (III Corps) was to move from Ambleteuse (an annex of the Boulogne camp) to Mannheim on the Rhine with 26,000 men (or 28,000, figure uncertain). Soult commanded the largest unit (IV Corps), 40,000 men (32,000 according to some estimates) and was to leave Boulogne for Spire, on the Rhine below Mannheim. Lannes would com-mand V Corps, 27,000 men comprising a division taken from Davout and two others, when they reached Strasbourg. Ney's VI Corps would move from Montreuil to Saverne. Augereau's VII corps (15,000 men) would move from Brittany to Germany.

'Seven torrents' were to crash towards the Rhine. To them must be added the Guard, 5,000 men, plus the cavalry, 22,000 sabres in all, under the command of Murat. 'The cavalry is to leave Boulogne four days before the line and rejoin at Strasbourg. Then, stagger the departure of the infantry units over three different routes on day one, the first divisions of each corps on the next, then the second divisions, and on the third day the third divisions.' All was timed so that, in only twenty-four moves, the army would be recalled from the seacoast to the Rhine between Mannheim and Strasbourg, later crossing and skirting the Black Forest *from above* (whereas the Austrians were anticipating a move through the Basle gap) and crossing the Württemberg above Stuttgart, thus skirting the Danube from the north.

According to a number of historians, Napoleon dictated all this to Daru with 'a staggering mathematical precision' everything down to the smallest moves of regiments, hours of bivouacking and moving on, plus all the orders concerning the replenishment of men, boots and horses. No man had hitherto appeared 'so much in command of events at this stage' according to Madelin. He did everything except detail the hour when the first musket shot would echo and the date on which he would enter Vienna.

Nowhere have I seen the complete text dictated to Daru, but the historic context gives grounds for thinking that some of the orders for the campaign of Ulm and Austerlitz were not dictated on 13 August but on the days following. It is a fact that what was dictated to Daru was more than a mere outline; it was an operational plan more precise and more detailed than most of the plans drawn up a century later by more numerous and self-assured staffs. Plan XVII of the French Army, Joffre's general instructions numbers 1 and 2, the German Moltke and Schlieffen plans, etc., were projects in contrast to which, Napoleon's plan was decisively to succeed.

On 22 August, Napoleon sent an aide-de-camp to Brest with two letters. One was addressed to Admiral Ganteaume in which Napoleon informed him that Villeneuve must have sailed from Ferrol for Brest: 'My intention is that you should not suffer a delay of even a day, so that profiting from the superiority which 50 line-of-battle ships confers upon me, you should immediately put to sea to gain your objective and to enter the Channel with your entire force. I am relying on your talent, your determination and your character in such an important enterprise. Sail and join us. We can avenge two centuries of insults and shame. Never will my soldiers and seamen risk their lives for a greater cause.'

The second letter was addressed to Villeneuve: 'I hope that you have arrived at Brest. Weigh, not losing an instant and, with my combined squadrons, enter the Channel. England is ours! We are ready, all is embarked. Support us for twenty-four hours and it will all be over.' For more than a week, the orders launching the Grande Armée eastwards had been issued, lacking only the word 'Execute'. And still Napoleon wished to invade England. Would he continue to do so?

Scarcely had the courier left Boulogne than Decrès handed Napoleon a letter from Villeneuve dated 10 August, written before he sailed from Ferrol: 'I am sailing, according to circumstances, for Brest or for Cadiz.' Napoleon indulged in a genuine fit of rage, accusing Villeneuve of cowardice and even of treason. Nevertheless lookouts were posted on the cliffs from Dieppe to Boulogne with orders 'to signal immediately the appearance of our squadrons' sails'.

On the night of 20/21 August, bugles and drums awoke the troops. General alarm; everyone to his post! 'This time, this is it! And about time. We've had enough of it here. Let's get at the red-coats. And the English tarts.'

At 4 a.m. 100,000 troops marched off singing towards the port. Each brigade, regiment and battalion knew the exact place where the boat lay in which they should embark. The entire populace took to the streets to see the departure, some calling out, others weeping. In the port could be seen an enormous and organised movement. Part of the artillery, munitions and provisions were already loaded and seamen helped with the rest; horses whinnied on finding themselves hoisted into the air by the ships' tackle.

At Montreuil, Ney, who was in command of the Etaples camp, was giving a ball. They were still dancing when a breathless messenger announced: 'It's starting! The Emperor is embarking with all the troops.' The young officers, frantic at the thought of missing glory, abandoned their partners and galloped down the road to Boulogne. As soon as they arrived, they were told: 'The troops are returning to camp.' What a deception! But the troops were even more disappointed and said so freely.

Had Napoleon wished to force destiny's hand, in one manner or another? He no longer believed in Villeneuve. Not until 1 September was it learned at Boulogne that Villeneuve had returned to Cadiz. But since 23 August, Napoleon had written to Talleyrand that the more he 'considered the situation in Europe the more he saw how urgent it was to take a decisive stand'. If the squadron sailing from Ferrol followed his instructions and, with the Brest force, entered the Channel 'there is still time and I shall be master of England. If, on the contrary, my admirals hesitate, manoeuvre clumsily and fail to gain their objectives ... I must run to help the most threatened. I must break camps and on 1 Vendémiaire [22 September] move with two hundred thousand men into Germany. I will march on Vienna and will not lay down my arms until I have Naples and Venice and until I have nothing to fear from Austria.'

If the admirals hesitate. But now the couriers are galloping the roads, carrying the latest preliminary orders to Bernadotte and to Marmont. The next day, the cavalry started to move. On 26 August, the marshals and generals read to their troops a dramatic order of the day which was to become famous: 'Brave soldiers of the Boulogne camp! You will not go to England. British gold has seduced the Austrian Emperor into declaring war on France. His army has crossed the line which he was to have guarded and Bavaria is invaded. Soldiers, new laurels await you beyond the Rhine. Let us hasten to conquer those enemies whom we have defeated in time past!'

II

VICTORY BY MARCHING
Boulogne to the Rhine

The Army of England was no more. Officially now the Grande Armée, its 200,000 men were marching towards the Rhine along seven routes; all foreseen, all organised. One day's march in front of each force, a commissioner for war and a staff officer alerted local functionaries and arranged for rations and billets. The troops marched with drummers beating at the head and tail of each battalion; bands played during rest halts. Contrary to popular belief, many of the highways of the period were very wide. The troops marched along the borders, leaving the centre free, as did the cavalry. The generals (in carriages) and the colonels (on horseback) led their units. Speed of advance four kilometres per hour (3.9 kilometres precisely: a 'post league'); hourly halts of five minutes; half- or one hour 'smoking halts' at the mid-point of each stage. One hundred paces between battalions. The column stretched back for 35 to 40 kilometres. Each stage was begun early each morning; the second stage was completed by early afternoon when the troops were billeted in threes and fours at farms and domestic dwellings.

Everything that I have here recounted was theoretical. It is generally conceded that from Boulogne to the Rhine everything functioned perfectly smoothly in good weather, and that difficulties only arose when the weather worsened. The troopers' accounts often prove contradictory. According to one: 'Our column stretched out. Those with families near the route were allowed to make their farewells and to rejoin at the double, as no-one wished to miss the first artillery salvo. We were burning to prove ourselves in battle, directed by the Emperor. Only the smoking halts interrupted our march. We sang to encourage ourselves, and when our voices grew hoarse and our footsteps faltered, the musicians redoubled their fanfares.' Another soldier, a Grenadier of the Guard, still the élite units of the army, expressed himself rather differently: 'We had never marched so painfully, we were not given an hour of sleep, marching day and night, platoon by platoon. We kept each other in the ranks to avoid falling. Nothing could reawaken those who fell; they remained in the ditches, despite blows from the flat of a sword. At about midnight, I drifted to the right with the camber of the road. When pushed back to the verge, I staggered and did not stop until I reached a meadow. I held on to my musket but I was living in another world.'

The troops who had left Boulogne on 30 August arrived on 23 September at Spire, south of Mannheim, on the Rhine, having covered seven hundred kilometres on foot. They had made three 24-hour stops at Cambrai, Sedan and Metz. Each man carried his haversack weighing 25 to 30 kilograms; by the time they reached the Rhine their boots were in tatters. A pair of boots was finished 'between Fontainebleau and Poitiers'. Boots were a perennial problem for Napoleon. He dictated hundreds of orders to have them requisitioned and manufactured while the army was sweeping across Europe.

Before leaving Boulogne the Quartermaster services and the staff had issued 'movement orders' and each unit commander could read when he should resume his march; the route he should take to arrive at this or that locality where a stated number of rations would await him; the time when he should leave the next morning and so on. Those responsible for feeding the army on the march were the war commissioners who were detested by the army ('every one of them a thief!'). Napoleon characterised them as thieves or incompetents. They became increasingly dishonest as successive campaigns progressed, but their task was not easy. From the summit of the supply services pyramid Daru laid out the lines of flow from the ration depots, dumps and field bakeries. He even organised 'kneading wagons' to process cereals and stocks of flour taken from the countries through which the army marched. Provisions were brought forward to the troops by land and by water. All this organisation paid dividends, especially to France and her allies because once into enemy territory 'the war must feed the war', in other words, one lived off the enemy. But before that happy state of affairs was reached, the organisation began to disintegrate. The supply service fell behind because the army went too fast ('the Emperor beats the enemy with our limbs'). It is no secret that Napoleon had long gained his victories by using that hitherto neglected weapon – speed. So the troops were obliged to pillage. The same applied to billeting. Orders are all very fine, but how does one fare when the march is ahead of the movement orders and the maps, or when arriving by night in unknown territory? The Grande Armée carried neither tents nor portable shelters. So 'System D' came into operation: forced entry and the theft of anything that would make life less wretched. We shall see plenty of that.

Having listened attentively while Daru read back the campaign orders, Napoleon had said to him: 'Leave immediately for Paris, feigning a journey to Ostend. Arrive alone by night and let nobody know who you are. Stay with Dejean [at that time both Minister of War and Minister of War-Administration]. Shut yourself up with him and prepare with him alone all the executive orders for the marches and the rations. I do not wish even one assistant to be in your confidence. You will sleep in General Dejean's office itself and no one must know who you are. Go.'

On 23, 24, 25, 26, 28 and 30 August and 14 September Napoleon had dictated for the use of Berthier, Bernadotte, Marmont, Murat and Bertrand all the operation orders for a lightning war against Austria. Some historians have tried to 'insert' these orders into the 'Daru dictation', but their detail would fill a volume. Napoleon knew that the Anglo-Russian-Austrian coalition was taking shape. His idea was to appear at Vienna before the Russians could intervene. More exactly: while Bernadotte was coming down from Hanover and Marmont from Holland, to move the other corps of the Grande Armée to the Rhine, then cross Württemberg and the Danube below Ulm in the vicinity of Donauwörth, take the Austrians in rear, surround them, push them into Ulm and defeat them, then march on Vienna to confront the Russians.

This strategy would require him to cross the territories of the German princes. Ney and Lannes' corps would have to cross the Duchies of Baden and Württemberg, and Bernadotte and Marmont's the territory of Anspach which belonged to the King of Prussia. Napoleon's decision to renounce the invasion of Britain and march eastwards had been so sudden that there had been no time to negotiate with the princes. 'Go to Berlin,' he had said to Duroc, 'and persuade King Frederick-Wilhelm to join my alliance. I will take care of the princes.'

Murat had been detailed to leave Boulogne on 26 August and to be at Strasbourg on 11 September having carried out the following programme: to go straight to Mainz without stopping, pass through Frankfurt, reconnoitre Offenbach, finishing at Würzburg for a stay of 36 hours. 'The prince will verify communications with Mainz and the Danube, taking into account the links with the tributaries at Ulm, Ingoldstadt and Ratisbon.' From Würzburg Murat was to proceed to Bamberg: 'He will ensure the communications between Bamberg, Bohemia and the Danube. He will take note of the mountains of Bohemia and will align the advance from Bamberg to Prague, paying particular attention to the gorges of the Eiger.' Murat thereafter was to follow the Regnitz, follow the left bank of the Danube and, having crossed at Passau, would follow the Inn as far as Kufstein and, crossing Munich, would pass through Ulm, Stockach, the battlegrounds of Moskirche with a quick look at the exits from the Black Forest. Well may one find all these details overwhelming, but they do give an idea of the precision of Napoleon's military planning before each and every campaign. Bertrand, the other executor (an engineer officer), was to proceed directly to Munich and to deliver a hand-written letter from the Emperor to the Elector of Bavaria, following which, he too, was to explore a whole region. This would pave the way for an advance of the Grande Armée into Moravia while avoiding the defences of the Inn. 'Austria seems to be set on war,' wrote Napoleon to the Elector of Bavaria. 'I cannot condone such an error. However, she shall have war sooner than she expects. I see that it is in her interest to spend the autumn in fomenting new intrigues, but they will all be frustrated.'

Since 7 September, he had done all he could to collect intelligence regarding the movements of the Austrian and Russian armies: each of their regiments was allocated a card in his unique filing system, and each was constantly up-dated.

On 30 August 1805, the mayor of Strasbourg had received from the Intendant-General, Count Daru, the following letter: 'His Majesty having ordered the preparation of a palace at Strasbourg from now until the end of the month of September, I am sending the architect, M. Blondel, and M. Terrier, the person responsible for the management of the crown furniture, who will be responsible for taking the necessary measures in the selected locality for receiving SS.MM. If this locality is deemed inadequate, it will be necessary to supplement it by renting nearby houses. The suite will comprise: the grand marshal of the court, the master of the horse, three secretaries, two chamberlains, an almoner, eight generals aides-de-camp, a palace prefect, four grooms, sixteen head waiters and valets, twelve major-domos and eight stable hands. On 3 September, he received a memorandum from the Commissioner of War: 'Eight thousand men will arrive in this town, 2,000 forming the garrison and lodging with the inhabitants.' This meant, in effect, find 2,000 rooms in short order, plus 'comfortable lodgings' for the officers of the Guard and for the many notables of the royal suite. It was already known that Napoleon would arrive accompanied by Josephine. The municipality proposed to offer to their majesties the ancient palace of Rohan, the property of an émigré and sold by the city as such. A flock of artisans rushed to prepare it. The bishop lent his bed, many museums sent pictures, linen came from the Tuileries. 'Some Gobelins tapestries, porcelain sets of china together with marble busts and large mirrors provided a suitably worthy and welcoming aspect to this building which had been neglected and run-down over the past fifteen years.' The townsmen set to polishing the rooms and apartments selected for the persons of quality and for the officers of the Guard. As for the troops who were to cross Strasbourg and the Rhine by the Kehl bridge, they were to camp as best they could outside the town in the fields in the worst conditions.

Napoleon and Josephine, accompanied by the imperial suite, left Saint-Cloud on 24 September and reached Strasbourg at 5 p.m. on the 26th. The streets were decorated with flags and garlands of flowers and were 'filled with curious crowds'. As a security measure, explosives and fireworks were forbidden. The mayor, accompanied by the municipal council and a detachment of the guard of honour, welcomed Napoleon at the Saverne gate – keys to the city on a cushion, wines of honour. The guard of honour was superb, white breeches, black boots and hats. Napoleon always replied very briefly to addresses of welcome. A contemporary engraving of slightly later date (from the office of etchings of Strasbourg) shows Oudinot's division of grenadiers marching into Strasbourg on the 26th. Led by bearded sappers (as today in the Foreign Legion) wearing white leather aprons, shouldering axes, marching behind an immensely tall man whose name has come down to us: Drum-Major Sénot, glittering, with embroideries covering every inch of his uniform, including a gold-embellished cross-belt, his staff garlanded with ribbons. Behind, 24 drummers in bearskins with copper drums, 46 musicians in blue uniforms, collars, cuffs and lapels in crimson set off by gold lace, high boots, swords at their sides, cocked hats with embroidery and plumes. Behind them can be seen see a forest of bayonets and bearskins. Urchins ran beside the soldiers while the 'pekins', the civilian men and women, admired them. Alsatians arrived from afar. Strasbourg was as packed as Boulogne had been; not a room vacant, people sleeping on hotel tables, on stable straw with the horses.

On the day after his arrival, Napoleon rode to Kehl 'to supervise the army's crossing of the Rhine' – actually only a part of the Grande Armée; other corps crossed the Rhine elsewhere. The previous day, orders had been issued to the general officers to report at the bridge at 6 a.m. precisely. It began to rain as Napoleon arrived at the bridge and it continued without ceasing. Before even the first divisions had crossed, Napoleon was wet through (the downpour was such that a small lake formed beneath his horse); his cocked hat was so soaked that the back of it fell upon his shoulders in the style of the head-gear of the Paris coal-heavers. He remained impassive.

The Imperial Guard took part in the march-past that day. Thousands of books have been devoted to these troops. The Guard was formed under the Directory, became Consular, then Imperial, and in 1805 mustered about 7,500 men. The legendary image of the Guard, last hope and supreme concept, was the grenadier, the infantryman in the bearskin, although the Guard included all arms, infantrymen, mounted grenadiers, mounted artillery, gun crews, artillery train, sharpshooters (from the NCOs' school), companies of engineers plus, at the Boulogne camp, a battalion of seamen. In practice, the grenadiers were the cream of the cream. To qualify a man had to be at least 1 metre 80 in height, have had ten years service and be graded as an 'excellent possibility': no problem should he be illiterate. The grenadier was not simply a private soldier; his status equalled that of a sergeant and carried the same rate of pay. All grenadiers were required to grow side-whiskers in 'pistol-butt' or 'mutton-chop'; a moustache was also obligatory, as was a pigtail tied with a black ribbon. The bearskin, which came down to the eyebrows, was 35 centimetres high in front, and had a plaque of red copper stamped with an eagle crowned and supported by two grenades, and a tall scarlet plume with tricolour cockade on the left side. The uniform was blue with scarlet trim and lapels of white cloth, lining and facings in white cloth. The straps crossed over the chest supported a large cartridge-box decorated with the imperial eagle and four grenades. On the haversack of untanned leather was rolled the cloak of blue cloth. The infantry short sword and the bayonet-scabbard were also slung from the cross belt. The musket, of a pattern used only by the Guard, was trimmed in brass. Such a uniform cost a lot of money, the officers' even more with their facings embroidered and spangled and trimmed in gold. But the Guard was never to want for anything. It found all the ceremonial companies and, between campaigns, paraded at the Carousel at midday when the Emperor was in Paris. Napoleon, on the balcony with the Empress, the ladies-in-waiting and the guests, stood bareheaded, saluting his favourites grandly.

With the exception of a few details, the full dress of the mounted grenadiers was the same as that of their comrades in the infantry; they too wore the bearskin. Their chargers were all-black with French-type saddles, shabraques of blue cloth, laced in gold, and bearing the imperial crown. The trumpeters were mounted on white-greys and wore a coat of sky-blue with crimson facings and revers, all studded and embroidered with gold-braid.

One picturesque unit which paraded with the Guard was the company of mamelukes, who even headed some parades as advance-guard, trotting or galloping in a wild and brilliant disorder and suddenly stopping dead. The mamelukes had been recruited in Cairo as an escort for Bonaparte in the Turkish manner and in order to impress the population. Most of them were not in fact Turkish, but Syrian. They wore a short embroidered coat, wide scarlet Turkish-style pantaloons with a multicoloured sash, and an enormous turban. Their arms consisted of a scimitar and a short blunderbuss, not to mention a collection of pistols and daggers. A mameluke who became famous was Roustam, 'faithful' according to legend for constantly following Napoleon, even sleeping outside the door of his room, but he was to behave meanly following the abdication at Fontainebleau. The original troop had numbered 25 which had grown in 1805 to 125 by enlisting hussars. Eventually, only a handful were genuine mamelukes, the rest being disguised Frenchmen.

On the march, the grenadiers did not wear the brilliant uniform which I have described, but a felt hat, long blue trousers and a greatcoat. Tradition, however, required that the Guard should always fight in full dress. On the eve of battle, each grenadier removed his carefully-folded blue coat, his white breeches, his gaiters and lifted the heavy bearskin from its cover. At the appointed time, they were fallen-in and, generally, remained where they were. The Guard was an élite body held in reserve at the disposition of the Emperor and was only committed if a battle were going badly. We shall see the artillery of the Guard in action under fire in nearly every battle, and also the chasseurs and the cavalry. But the texts of the battle narratives of the Bulletin of the Grande Armée often ended with the words: 'The Guard was not committed', which meant that they remained with their arms ordered.

'The Guard dies but does not surrender.' Maybe, but the troops of other corps found that this cherished unit did not die often enough and called the grenadiers 'The Immortals'. Overall, within the Grande Armée, the Guard was heartily detested, both in the light of what I have here recounted and because of their privileges: glittering full dress uniform, extra pay and, whenever circumstances allowed, better rations and billets. Even when bivouacking, if there were a better spot, one less miserable, less open to the winds, less muddy, less damp, it went to the Guard and it was a waste of time to protest; the same applied to their officers. Their medical services were superior; they had better doctors and surgeons, more stretcher-bearers, more ambulances, dressings and medicines.

Twenty-two mounted chasseurs of the Guard, commanded by an officer followed by a bugler, escorted Napoleon wherever he went, on horseback or in his coach. If he stopped, four of these troopers dismounted and surrounded him, followed his footsteps, arms at the ready. On the battlefield, the officer posted himself immediately behind the Emperor and only gave way to the marshals. The chasseurs of the Guard were immensely proud of their privilege of guarding the sovereign's person. All the officers of the Guard were besotted with pride and never consorted with the officers of other units. Stendhal wrote that they had 'the stupidity necessary for their job' – and every Guardsman showed the same arrogance. When off duty, the walking-out dress of the grenadiers was, in place of their coats with white lapels, a blue frock-coat, breeches and white cotton stockings, buckled shoes, a cocked hat of black felt. Sergeants even had the right to wear silk stockings. Forty-three sous daily was fine pocket-money; but for these cosseted soldiers it hardly counted, for almost all were maintained by seamstresses, prostitutes or even ladies who had fallen under the spell of their martial bearing. At the last, on the battlefield, if things went badly, these pimps, on command, allowed themselves be cut to pieces.

At 3 p.m. on 14 October 1805, Napoleon left Strasbourg heading for Ettlingen. The Strasburgers' interest in him bordered on indifference. He left Josephine behind with instructions to make herself amiable. This she could do to perfection, and charmed everyone at ceremonies, receptions, feasts and balls which the city offered her almost without interruption from 14 October to 28 November.

Napoleon went to Ettlingen with the intention of persuading the Duke of Baden to let his army march through. This individual having said yes almost immediately, the Emperor summoned General Mouton, one of his ADCs: 'Lose no time! Ride to Stuttgart and announce my arrival to the Elector of Württemberg. Tell him in a few words what it is about.' At Mouton's opening words, his hearer exploded with rage: 'Never will a foreign soldier foul the soil of Würt-temberg. The Emperor will learn of what I am capable, etc.' Mouton remained impassive until the diatribe had ceased and then spoke with common sense: 'Your Highness need not take umbrage at a decision which will, in any event, be implemented. Marshal Ney is not the man to make a detour after being ordered to march straight ahead.' He suggested that to say yes in return for some compensation would be good policy. The Elector, immediately comprehending, not only agreed to the passage, but promised an alliance if the Emperor would elevate his duchy to a kingdom and enlarge it with some territory taken from Austria. Agreed. The future king threw himself before Napoleon and received him with pomp in his palace of Ludwigsburg.

Allow me to recall that Duroc had been sent to Berlin. There he found King Frederick-Wilhelm hesitant and anxious. Closer relations with the powerful Emperor of the French could be advantageous, but to offend both Austria and the Tsar, not to mention Britain, was terribly dangerous. Neither yes nor no. Napoleon informed him that, with or without permission, his troops would cross the territory of Anspach. The objective was Ulm, where the Austrian general Mack had just arrived. The Grande Armée, having crossed the Rhine between Mainz and Strasbourg, would execute a rapid wheel to bring it to the Danube, placing it below Ulm. Mack had concentrated his forces facing west, never suspecting that the Grande Armée was already behind him. A very fine strategic move. But a nightmare for the troops.

The nightmare began on 5 October, a mere month into autumn, but the army found itself marching through a winter landscape. A glacial rain with snow was falling, and within the space of two days the territory became a sea of mud. Successive divisions found the road collapsed, in places become a river-bed, broken vehicles, ruined horses, occasionally, the corpse of a soldier dead from exhaustion. We shall rarely see the speed of the Grande Armée so reduced as during this march towards Ulm. Napoleon was determined to outflank and envelop Mack whatever the cost, so – march or die, but he himself took part in the marathon.

Napoleon had slept in the princes' castles, but now he rejoined the army on its road of frozen mud, well knowing the magnetic effect of his presence. During this race in this dripping hell, he would appear without warning, pass the disordered columns, gasping with fatigue on the brink of despair. As soon as the generals caught sight of the chasseurs of the personal escort, they cleared the road, pushing their men into the fields; fall-in! Watch your dressing! Present arms! The drums beat a tattoo. The Emperor passed, with an all-embracing glance at the troops and a few words for the colonels. The men told one another, 'It's him!' and smartened themselves up, their fatigue forgotten. We shall see that this magnetism, to a greater or lesser degree, was to endure.

At the summit, despite explicit orders from Napoleon, harmony was not too much in evidence. The first battle of the campaign nearly took place between two of the marshals, rather than between the Grande Armée and the Austrians. Murat, Ney, Lannes, Soult and Davout, coming from the north, crossed the Danube and made their first contact with the enemy at Wertingen on the right bank. Ney, on this occasion temporarily subordinate to Murat, criticised his orders which he deemed 'stupid'. These two detested each other. Ney even sought a duel with swords; his aides had to restrain him. Tactically, Ney was right. Murat was wrong and thanks to him, Dupont's division was nearly wiped out by 32,000 Austrian troops. Murat redeemed himself by charging at the head of 8,000 cavalrymen. Let us take a closer look at these implacable enemies.

In 1805, Murat was thirty-eight. In terms of seniority, that meant little. A superb man, almost a giant, he had strong, regular features, fine blue eyes, enormous side whiskers, and black hair falling in ringlets to his shoulders. He was athletic and even a fire-eater. In 1800, when Bonaparte had established his court at Milan, Murat had challenged a young chief of squadron who had claimed to be as strong as he. The brother-in-law of the First Consul could not in principle set aside his rank and consort, even amicably, with all and sundry. But on this occasion a bout of 'iron arms' took place, the adversaries facing each other across a narrow table, right hand gripping right hand, elbows on the table. No score, neither having yielded, but 'after three bouts, blood flowed from the fingers of both champions'.

Bonaparte had had in mind for his youngest sister a husband other than Murat 'who was merely brave'. Caroline was still a student of sixteen when she had met, first in Montebello and then in Rome, this glittering Hercules, gilded and magnificent. She was smitten immediately and made no secret of it. On his part – a fine match and, ye Gods, what a pretty girl! Small and slim, Caroline had been sent back to her convent. On his return from Egypt, Murat had pushed his suit, even to the point where he took an active part in the *coup d'état* of Brumaire. Bonaparte had finally given his consent, albeit without enthusiasm, and was even persuaded to sign the marriage contract on 18 January 1800. Civil marriage was then in style, in the decadal temple, at Plailly. Bonaparte was not present; the religious ceremony took place two years later. Murat and Caroline lived in a private house in the northern quarter of the Tuileries. Sumptuous fare, fine china, choice wines. None the less, General Thiébault saw served on a lace napkin a 'rough earthenware pot containing some grape jam'. 'Please help yourself, it is a treat in my country, my mother made it herself and sent it to me.' A touching faithfulness to his native Quercy.

Murat's parents, innkeepers and farm-owners, had money and useful connections. 'We will make him a priest'. This would be a social promotion. His mother dreamed that Joachim, her twelfth child, would one day become the Curé of La Bastide. He became a student (thanks to Talleyrand's patronage) at the college of Saint-Michel of Cahors, then a boarder at the grand seminary of the Lazarists of Toulouse. But this seminarist, a handsome fellow, had 'adventures' in the city, clandestinely sowing his wild oats.

On 23 February 1787, while watching the advance of a squadron about to join the garrison at Carcassonne, he fell into conversation with a recruiting sergeant: 'I am a seminarist, but I am very unhappy.' 'Did you give a girl a child?' 'Worse. I contracted debts and my creditors are at my heels.' 'And you worry about that? Join up and the devil with creditors! Sign here ...' Scandal and despair in the Murat family. Letters were sent to the Intendant of Languedoc who asked the Minister of War to release Murat – refused. But Trooper Murat would be discharged ignominiously nevertheless – for a disciplinary affair. Another family scandal. His father refused to see the culprit. 'Right. I will go elsewhere.' We now see the future marshal and King of Naples as apprentice-grocer at Saint Céré. But that was in 1790 – liberty, equality, fraternity. He succeeded in being elected as delegate to the fete of the Federation, and Quercy, now the Department of the Lot, rarely failed to support those of its children who showed some gift for politics. Cavaignac, the department's representative, had the army open its doors to the rejected.

Murat, an unabashed climber, used every means – including courage and flattery – to succeed. When Murat was defied by the Convention, the innkeeper's son asked to be allowed to change a letter of his name so that it would match that of the tribune. Not approved, but it had a good effect on the *sans-culottes*. Murat had met Bonaparte in November 1799. November was Vendémiaire and Brumaire followed Vendémiaire. On the 19th Murat led the action at a gallop. At the moment when the dismay and hesitation of the Hero of Italy risked losing everything, he saved the situation by bursting into the Chamber of the Five Hundred with a handful of grenadiers. 'Throw this shower outside,' as he pushed the citizens towards the windows. 'Citizens, you are dismissed!' Bonaparte was far from ungrateful. Murat became commander of the Consular Guard and then, as we have seen, his brother-in-law.

The new victories in Italy enriched him vastly. As a result of economies effected during his government of the Cisalpine Republic, General Murat purchased land and houses for more than a million francs, and this was only the beginning. In 1801, he acquired for 470,000 francs the property of la Motte Sainte-Héraye in the Deux-Sévres; a month later, he paid 500,000 francs for the elegant Thelusson property in Paris, and six weeks later acquired the property of Madame de Bullion at Villiers (Neuilly). In 1803 Napoleon presented Murat with the Elysée palace together with 150,000 francs for repairs, and in the following year the château of the Count of Argenson (more precisely, the so-called château de Neuilly) was added to the household assets. Murat's charges at the head of cavalry became legendary. This gallant always acted 'without a map'; when his flair or mere chance brought him within reach of the enemy, he struck. Napoleon, the strategist–tactician, with his painstaking combinations, was often astonished by the results achieved

Ney, two years younger than Murat, was no less brave but of a different character. Born in Saarlouis, his father, a master-cooper, a substantial man, was ambitious for his children: 'You will be a senior clerk, a Monsieur'. The red-haired urchin became a student at the Augustinian College (high school), and at thirteen was apprenticed to a notary 'to learn the method'; apprentice clerk at the offices of the public prosecutor, apprentice at the office of the company of the mines of Adenweller. A pen-pusher. Not to the liking of a robust young fellow of nineteen. Michel Ney ran away to Metz and signed-on with a regiment of hussars. Sub-lieutenant in 1792, captain in 1794, brigadier-general in 1796, and in 1800 in command of the first division of the corps of the centre of the Army of the Rhine, seeing action at Hochstädt and Hohenlinden.

Under the Consulate, he was still as red-haired as at nineteen, even more robust and even ruddier of complexion, as quick to fly into a rage as to take his pleasure. He had two consuming passions, war and playing the flute – women came a poor third. However, he fell into a fairly gaudy liaison with Ida de Saint-Elme, young and pretty, who had been a mistress of de Marescot and de Moreau among others.

'She is an adventuress. Ney needs a wife.' So said Josephine and Bonaparte agreed – it was more a question of Ney's fidelity than of his happiness. Ney was something of an adversary; he had been republican and the Directory did not upset him, but he did not wholly welcome power in the hands of one man and he let it be known. So he must be brought to heel by means of a good marriage. Josephine and Napoleon looked about for a fiancée and decided that Aglaée Auguié, daughter of a tax commissioner whose solid bourgeois family was of the *ancien régime* rather than republican society, would be a good match. Like Caroline Bonaparte, she had attended Madame de Campan's school, and was an intimate friend of Hortense de Beauharnais. Known as Eglé, she was tall and well-built 'Her face was lit by two magnificent black eyes which later served to kindle a somewhat comic passion in the breast of the ambassador of the Shah of Persia.' Eglé found Ney's 'physique somewhat coarse and Ney found her a bit skinny, but Josephine persisted and the marriage was celebrated on 5 August 1802.

In 1803 Ney, minister plenipotentiary in Switzerland, arranged for the signing by the Helvetic Republic of an act of mediation. In 1804 Napoleon created him Marshal of the Empire, as much to secure his fidelity as to satisfy public opinion. Ney was to pay with his life for that fidelity.

It is 9 October 1805. After Ney and Murat had quarrelled, and Murat's charge at Wertingen had redressed matters, Napoleon declared 'I want to congratulate them and to review them.' A glacial and torrential rain was still falling. Napoleon left Donauwörth at 10 a.m., arrived at Wertingen to hear Murat's account of the battle, and went on to Zusmarschausen where the review was to be held. Fifty-five kilometres on horseback in one morning, The Emperor and his staff were to stop at Augsburg, where the bishop had prepared a sumptuous reception. But first the review. The divisions were drawn up in line before the village. Napoleon passed down the ranks, stopping, questioning, congratulating, while the rain continued to fall in torrents. Did the men consider the business too protracted, unbearable; did they grumble? Not a bit of it. They cheered him. At the big reviews at Boulogne, there had been murmurers. Here there were none; they were at war, and the demi-god had congratulated them. After this interminable inspection, Napoleon ordered the twelve colonels: to select the bravest trooper in each regiment. These he decorated personally with the Legion of Honour; more congratulations, more questions, all under the weeping skies and the failing light. Nightfall. It was now too late to stop at the bishop's palace where comfort, warmth and a special supper awaited him.

'I will sleep here – in the village.' The carriage, the servants, the field canteen, the wardrobe, all the trappings for the Emperor's comfort, were at Augsburg; all that was available in the half-drowned village was the 'portmanteau' always carried by the mameluke, Roustam, which held a cloak and a change of linen. Booted and in his shirt sleeves, Napoleon slept in a chair in front of the fire at an inn, his uniform jacket of a colonel of the chasseurs of the Guard drying beside him.

Mack was at Ulm, but all the army corps must be assembled to surround him completely and prevent his escape. Faster, ever faster. Naturally each corps left behind a trail of stragglers, some of whom would never rejoin. On the night of 12/13 October, Napoleon's coach, escorted by the chasseurs of the Guard, sped down the road from Augsburg to Ulm at a furious pace, but crashed in a pothole. Napoleon was headed for a meeting with Marmont who had marched down from Holland with his corps, and must now cross the Lech, one of the small tributaries of the Danube, now swollen by the rains and flooding the fields. In the light of dawn, however, a bridge was seen to span the river and Marmont prepared to cross it. Napoleon stopped his carriage. He saw passing before him the ghost of an army. Marmont's corps, a mix of French and Dutch regiments, had come down from the north at maximum speed as ordered; the French regiments had lost half their strength, the Dutch many more; the 8th Batavian Division mustered a mere 2,500 men and officers, the remainder having fallen-out along the way, prostrate by fatigue, sickness and despair. Napoleon stopped his carriage, mounted his horse and stationed himself at the approach the bridge, now assailed by rain and snow – would this curse from the heavens never cease?

Napoleon, statuesque as ever, watched the crossing and under his eye the exhausted troops revived. Once across the river, the divisions formed squares into each of which Napoleon entered, questioning, encouraging, explaining patiently that this nightmare would end, that the enemy was already in a desperate plight, already defeated. This leader of men knew that time spent in explanation and encouragement is never wasted, and that strategic psychology is as useful as military strategy. The proclamation which he would read to the assembled army next day would repeat in his theatrical but effective style what he had said to Marmont's exhausted troops: 'Soldiers! It has been only two weeks since we crossed the Rhine, the Württemberg Alps, the Neckar, the Danube and the Lech, famous German barriers which have not slowed our march by a single day, an hour, a moment. Your descendants, five hundred years on, will wish to muster under the eagles round which you now rally and will know in detail all that your corps will have done tomorrow and the manner in which your courage has crowned them for ever. That will be the constant subject of their conversation and you will be enshrined from age to age in the admiration of future generations.'

A great number of the soldiers of the Grande Armée did not understand a word of the Emperor's proclamations, any more than they comprehended his congratulations and encouragement which he uttered while pinching their ears. Of the 200,000 men who crossed the Rhine, some 30,000 were foreigners: Piedmontese, Swiss, Syrians, Belgians, Blacks, Irish, Hanoverians, Ligurians, Badeners, Hungarians, Bohemians, Prussians, Swedes, Russians, Austrians, Poles, Bavarians. These foreigners were not distributed among the French units but were formed into homogeneous bodies. They had been engaged as mercenaries or had been enrolled, *en bloc* or individually, in countries already conquered or ceded to the Emperor by their rulers. in 1805, the Piedmontese (11th French Line Regiment, 26th Regiment of mounted chasseurs, the Legion of the Midi) served France because the King of Sardinia had been one of the first to enter a coalition against the Republic; nearly all his states had been rapidly conquered and annexed. On 10 December 1798, Charles-Emmanuel had to cede all his rights to Piedmont, which became the 27th Military District. Result: conscription.

I have already mentioned the mamelukes. This battalion of oriental chasseurs, another relic of the campaign in Egypt, was formed into a 'Coptic line' and a 'Greek line'. The 112th Line Regiment (Belgian) was one of the units raised from the nine French departments (including Sambre-et-Meuse) which were formed after the annexation of Belgium. The three companies of pioneers were formed of coloured men. Their commander was a coloured officer named Hercules who had distinguished himself in Italy and Egypt. The Irish regiment (originally a battalion) had been formed in 1803 from Irishmen who had taken refuge in France to escape persecution by the English. It would later be enlarged, to the great distress of its chief, the Duke of Feltre, to include English and Scottish deserters posing as Irishmen. The tirailleurs of Po shared the same origins with the Piedmontese. The Hanovarian Legion was formed at the end of the Consulate by General Mortier, then commanding in Hanover.

The Swiss cantonal troops served the French under the terms of the capitulation of 27 December 1803. Initially, recruiting for these regiments had not been pushed, but when the resumption of hostilities with Britain was announced, Bonaparte wanted the terms of the capitulation to be put into effect. 'I note with pleasure', he wrote to the Minister of War 'that you are paying particular attention to the organisation of the Swiss regiments. Be sure that money is not lacking. I am relying particularly on these regiments for coastal defence.' The 32nd Light Infantry Regiment of France consisted of troops from the Roman states, from Naples, Montenotte and Taro. We know how Italy was 'transformed' to the benefit of France. The Bavarian contingent of 38,000 men was the happy result of Bonaparte's benevolence towards Bavaria at the time of the establishment of the Confederation of the Rhine. The regiment of the Tour d'Auvergne, which was formed at Weissenburg on 30 September 1805, bore the name of its first colonel, Godefroy de la Tour d'Auvergne, its original strength of 3,000 men being a mosaic of twelve nations of central and eastern Europe. As for the Baden contingent, we have seen how the Duke of Baden allowed himself to be persuaded into becoming Napoleon's ally. At the time of the Austrian campaign, all the units mentioned above existed, but not all had crossed the Rhine with the Grande Armée. From 1806 to 1814, the Grande Armée absorbed more than sixty foreign units. We shall meet them in the course of the longest military march of all time.

Should one record any major difficulties of language associated with this international horde? We can admire how these simple fellows, speaking different dialects, once thrown together, worked together very well after only a few days. Besides, the reproofs and punishments quickly impressed on their minds – including those of the conscripts from Brittany, Provence and Languedoc who did understand some French – the minimum necessary for understanding the manual of arms, and everyday requirements, As for the rest, Berlitz never invented it. 'French soldiers', noted the pharmacist Cadet de Gadicourt, 'learn German very quickly. Their method is as fast as it is pleasant. They would take a German mistress who did not know a word of French. They would live diligently with her and have her speak of everything of which they had need.'

Marshal Ney had been created Duke of Elchingen in recognition of his brilliant conduct at the bridge of that name on the Danube seven kilometres below Ulm. It was necessary to cross this bridge from the right (south) bank to the left (north) bank to support Dupont's division which was threatened by a sortie of the Austrians who occupied the village and the convent of Elchingen. The bridge had been demolished by the spring floods and little remained save the piles and beams. The first task was to get a platform across. 'We will do that at dawn,' said Ney. Sappers, using doors and shutters wrenched from villages near-by, went to work in the freezing water under the fire of the enemy. Each plank was nailed in place at the cost of three casualties. Sharpshooters and grenadiers then rushed across the partly-restored bridge. Napoleon arrived in person at the bridgehead and to allow him to cross, the officers halted the storming column. The Austrian artillery was firing continuously, the bridge had become a slaugh-terhouse, and the Emperor and his suite dismounted so as not to trample the wounded. The sharpshooters and the grenadiers scaled the scarped banks on the Elchingen side, where every house was a nest of snipers. At the hilltop was the convent.

The storming of this building, transformed into a small strong point, was bloody. Later, Bessières' dragoons were able to deploy on the plateau and charge the Austrian troops, who were also taken in the rear by Dupont's men. The enemy retreated to the heights of Milchelsberg which covered the town of Ulm. Meanwhile, the rain continued.

Napoleon had followed the progress of the attack closely, exposing him-self to he enemy fire. To one gunner whose thigh was shattered by a cannonball, he pinned his own cross of the Legion of Honour. 'Think, you can spend the rest of your life quietly at les Invalides.' 'No, it is bleeding too much. But I don't care. Vive l'Empereur!' For another casualty, Napoleon took off his cloak: 'I want this hero to be buried in it.'

After the fighting stopped, the convent became an ambulance, but in this context, 'ambulance' didn't mean much: the wounded lay on wisps of straw on the ground. The surgeons lacked everything because, like the supply services, the medical service had been unable to keep pace with the army. Larrey, chief surgeon of the Guard, had both the French and Austrian casualties brought to the convent and he did what he could. 'The amputations which we were com-pelled to perform on the gravely wounded did not have their customary success, because most of the wounded had been exposed to the assault of the weather, almost without care for thirty-six hours.' Here, Larrey expresses himself with moderation. Some of the wounded wept when told that they were to be evacu-ated to the hospitals at Augsburg. Hospitals! But conditions at the Augsburg hospitals were ghastly, there were no nurses, even straw was lacking, and there was a semi-famine.

Ober-Falheim was a village on the right bank of the Danube opposite Elchingen. In the evening of 14 October Napoleon, dead-tired from sixteen hours in the saddle, wished to sleep. But there were no doors or shutters anywhere – Ney's sappers had taken them for their bridge. 'Let's try the priest,' said Napoleon. But no there was sign of the priest and his house had been thoroughly ransacked. The Emperor slept there none the less, on a bed of straw and cloaks, having eaten an omelette.

After their reverse at the bridge of Elchingen, the Austrians were also beaten at Haslach by Dupont's troops, and again at Memmingen by those of Marshal Davout. Murat and his cavalry were sent in pursuit of an Austrian corps which had managed to run the blockade of Ulm. Murat himself gave an account of this pursuit: '12,000 soldiers made prisoner together with two lieutenant-generals, 7 major-generals and over 200 officers. 120 artillery pieces were captured as well as 500 wagons of munitions and equipment, including that of Prince Ferdinand; eleven standards were taken; treasure of 400,000 florins was captured and 800 French prisoners were freed.'

Compared with a prize of 400,000 florins, the loot taken from the peasants was small beer, but even so it was not inconsiderable. For example, there was not a horse left on the farms. Many infantrymen were now mounted, as were some bandsmen and civilians. The medics pleaded for these horses to be requisitioned for the transport of the wounded, but – 'We have no orders,' said the colonels. The high command had other things to worry about. Unguarded horses were promptly stolen and sold; there was a thriving traffic in horses, saddles and harness ('people fought and killed for a bridle'). General Thiébault gives some indication in his *Mémoires* of the climate in the Grande Armée at this time: 'The night which followed our move from Memmingen saw a serious blow struck to discipline. The troops of the army corps, who up till now had shown themselves worthy of having been a part of the Boulogne camp, became pillagers and did not hesitate to beat-up the peasants in order to discover their money. One will never know the depths to which they descended in their quest for loot. While searching the house, they would compel the man to accompany them, watching his covert glances carefully and smashing and demolishing the places at which he had looked. They even demolished any newly-built interior walls; they flooded the cellar floors and where the water drained away faster than the rest, they immediately dug. I had left my brigade, I think to have lunch; some other units had passed by and I was trotting to catch mine up. Some frightful cries emanated from an isolated house which I was passing. I immediately dismounted and entered the house, which I found full of soldiers rummaging in the wardrobes. Others had pinioned the woman of the house and her daughter. Laying about with my cane, I cleared them out of the house by the door or the windows. I then noticed that the cellars were packed with soldiers and were awash with wine. I rushed down the stairs, but no sooner did I appear than these ruffians dowsed the lights and cleared out while I broke my cane on I know not whose backs and I then drew my sword. I toured the house to ensure that all the looters had gone and I saw many running through a wooded copse which surrounded the garden. They uttered many threats and curses and one even dared to shout that he would kill me.'

Some officers, to avoid being assaulted, closed their eyes to what was going on, and allowed their troops to burn the contents of houses for fuel. On one occasion, Napoleon made an example: 'You will pay for the house. I will pay six hundred francs and you will give a day's pay. I want the whole sum paid now to the owner.' But how could one stop it? 'Marauding and pillage', as Davout wrote to Berthier, 'are perpetrated without limit. I want authority to shoot some pillagers. Shoot one from time to time.' A useless deterrent; he would have had to shoot half the army. Had Napoleon agreed to have his troops loaded with all the provisions they required, the army would have marched at a third of their normal speed and his genius would have been brought to nought.

On 16 October the rain redoubled and the wind reached gale force. For several hours, the army seemed to disintegrate, duties were abandoned, sentries and outposts disappeared, the guns were left where they stood. In this orgy of the elements, a squadron of French dragoons galloped wildly through the lines of a division of Oudinot's grenadiers, causing panic, disorder and a volley of shots; two dozen men were seriously wounded. Was this the end, a check to the offensive? No.

In Ulm, Mack sat tight, awaiting the arrival of the Russians, not realising that he was surrounded. Lieutenant Marshal Karl Mack von Leiberich, fifty-five years of age, with a square face bearing a scar – 'A present from the Turks,' he liked to say – was an incompetent. In 1798, while commander-in-chief of the Neapolitan forces, he was defeated by the troops of General Championnet and General Macdonald (a Frenchman of Scottish descent), his army corps leaving on the battlefield 1,000 dead, 900 wounded, thirty cannon, nine standards, all his baggage and 10,000 men taken prisoner. The Neapolitan army was certainly not composed of heroes. On that occasion Mack had some good troops but scarcely made use of them. There was one violent clash, it is true, as witness the recollections of Captain Krettly: 'It was raining in torrents, we could hardly move on roads which had become impassable, our horses sank to their hocks in the mud and, despite their strength and their courage, the poor beasts were hard put to move at a slow trot. The regiment of mounted chasseurs of the imperial guard, the mounted grenadiers and the mamelukes found themselves facing the dragoons of de la Tour, whose reputation for bravery was known to every army of Europe. The Austrians always used this corps as advance-guard ... In an instant, there was a cavalry mêlée. Men fought hand to hand on horses thrashing in mud up to the stirrups. The crush was so great that we were unable to use the point of our sabres and we beat at their faces with the heavy guards. The dragoons of de la Tour having stood firm for awhile, finally yielded and retreated.'

The sequel to the battle of Ulm consisted of an artillery duel. From the heights dominating the town, the French guns fired with impunity. At nightfall, General de Ségur told General Mack that he had no alternative but to surrender the town. Mack, still hopeful that the Russians would come to his aid, asked for a week's delay. Napoleon would have been really stupid had he accepted that. At dawn next day, the idiotic Mack stated that he was prepared to surrender on condition that his army could retire to Bavaria. Naturally, the Emperor refused this also. Finally, Mack surrendered unconditionally

On 20 October the garrison of Ulm, 27,000 men, 18 generals, 40 standards and 60 cannon marched past Napoleon who, according to an Austrian colonel, was soaked and covered in mud. The defeated lieutenant-marshal approached the Emperor: 'Here is the unfortunate Mack.' Napoleon refused his sword. The rain had finally ceased, but the weather remained cold. A fire had been lit near the Emperor. The march-past took five hours. Larrey's description of the scene has not been bettered; he was always an exact witness: 'Two distinct parties composed this truly remarkable picture. Our army drawn up in battle formation on the reverse slope of the hill which encircles the town of Ulm, like an amphitheatre with our infantry occupying the tiers. His Majesty was in the centre with his staff on a separated hillock at whose base the enemy army was marching; the various bodies of cavalry and light artillery were posted on the slopes near the high road. The sparkling reflections of the arms, the waving standards, an air of satisfaction and joy illuminated all present, and everything on our side spoke of success and victory. The other party presented a very different aspect. A large corps of infantry, marching in close columns, had just laid down their arms on the glacis. After having marched past the French army, their cavalry dismounted and handed their chargers to our foot dragoons, their new owners.' Larrey added further details in a letter to the painter Girodet: 'Imagine the humiliation on the one side and the jubilation on the other. The glacis and the town were covered with arms and equipment of every type. Many soldiers seemed unmoved by their surrender; others destroyed their equipment and broke their weapons in anger and despair, some shed tears under their helmets and kept profoundly silent. Near our commander-in-chief, the Emperor, with his grey coat and battered hat, stood the generals; his white horse stood behind him; the Austrian generals seemed to belong to another world beside this man ...'

Napoleon summoned the enemy generals and spoke courteously to them. He claimed that their master had launched an unjust war and that, finally, he did not know why they were fighting. 'The Austrian Emperor did not want war,' explained Mack. 'It was forced on him by the Russians.' 'If such is the case', replied Napoleon, 'you are no longer a power.'

Next day, the troops of the Guard heard a proclamation of the Emperor which was posted up as well as read to them. I have already mentioned that most of them were illiterate. Napoleon had drawn up a balance-sheet of the Ulm campaign: 'Of the 100,000 composing this [Austrian] army, 60,000 are now prisoners; they will replace our conscripts as farm labourers. 200 artillery pieces, 90 standards, all their generals are in our power. Fewer than 15,000 men escaped. Soldiers, I had predicted a great battle, but thanks to the miscalculations of the enemy, I have been able to obtain the same success without running any risks, which is an event unparalleled in the history of nations. Such a great result has not cost us more than 1,500 casualties. Soldiers, this success is due to your constancy in accepting the fatigues and privations of every kind, and to your outstanding bravery.' Thanks for the eulogies, but the soldiery thought of little other than that these handsome Austrians were going to replace them on the farms.

III

1805
The Fog of Austerlitz

It was Napoleon himself who named the soldiers of the Grande Armée 'grumblers'. 'They grumbled, but they continued to march.' They grumbled the more because they often did not know why they were marching and, even more often, on a forced and exhausting march, when they had hoped for a rest, a respite, but no – 'forward march, pick them up – quicker!' 'They must reach the Rhine before the allies of England could do so themselves' 'You must march as hard and even quicker in order to outflank the Austrians stationed at Ulm.' Total victory at Ulm was acquired cheaply, as the Emperor himself had said in his proclamation. Now they must continue further, march or die, in even worse conditions; such were the orders from on high; the officers themselves did not understand why, maybe the generals did, but then again, maybe not.

The Russian general who was supposed to come to the aid of the besieged Mack in Ulm, was named Kutusov: aged sixty, one eye lost to wounds, fat, but supposedly intelligent. When the news of Mack's capitulation reached him, he was already on the Inn; he had turned about to wait for the mass of Russian troops and Austrian reinforcements. Napoleon did not wish to grant him the time necessary for this manoeuvre. Never give away time. Always destroy the enemy first. Hence the orders to the marshals and generals – forward, always faster. The nightmare was truly too black. The dark sky, the snow, fifty or sixty kilometres daily, never reaching journey's end before nine or ten in the evening. No billets, just the bivouac. Despite being in allied territory, there was no shelter and nothing to eat, absolutely nothing to hope for from the supply services – pillage the only hope. 'Doors are smashed, the houses cleaned out, the worst excesses unleashed.' A tune we are beginning to know well. Looting for food, then for booty. At Innsbruck, Ney's gunners sacked a church; many soldiers were shot as an example, but the example proved useless. Often the troops arrived in the towns and villages only to find that there was nothing left; the invading Austrians and Russians had already devastated them, once when advancing and again when retreating. Some unlucky Bavarians, hiding in the woods, died from hunger, cold and despair. The Grand Armée, too, in its rush forward, left behind the corpses of those dead from hunger, cold and despair. This was war. Only the Guard was spared something of this hell. The high command tried to preserve this élite unit. The Guard camped around Napoleon each night. Each morning

61

he allowed them to go on ahead of him, then in the afternoon his coach at full speed and escorted by his mounted chasseurs would catch up with them.

This infernal race lasted from about 25 October until 13 November, when the advance guard of the army reached Vienna. It was probably on 12 November that Napoleon received a letter from Decrès, Minister of the Navy, announcing the disaster at Trafalgar. The sea was far away. Vexed, rather than disquieted or moved, victorious at Ulm on the very eve of Trafalgar, the Emperor was to enter Vienna and the sun of Austerlitz was already rising towards its zenith. Waterloo, the consequence of Trafalgar, was as yet, unimaginable.

Vienna, with more than 250,000 inhabitants at the time, was the third city of Europe (London 1 million, Paris 500,000) and by far the gayest. The ladies of the nobility went to mass in robes trimmed with Polish furs, the men wore coats of black velvet, lined with rose satin opening on gilded waistcoats. The theatres were to be found among the maze of alleys in this overcrowded city, often flanked by bourgeois houses or even hovels. Workmen hailed those carriages of which they approved, an aristocrat would stop his coach in order to buy flowers at a stall with a gaudy tablecloth. Flowers, climbing plants and songbirds graced every window; and the Viennese of both sexes sang, in the cafes, the inns, and on the hills – people were music-mad.

'Napoleon's armies are on the march. They are coming!' 'All well and good. They cannot kill us all, and after the war there will be peace.'

A climate of heedless defeatism had reigned for several years following Napoleon's victories in Italy, but an element of disquiet manifested itself during the early days of September. Rumours of the troops' depredations preceded them. Finally, on the 13th, 'They are here!' – curiosity mixed with some fear. What terrible and imposing aspect would this invincible army present?

Would you believe it? What arrived was a horde of beggars or exhausted brigands, shoes in tatters, locks of hair hiding their faces, many in rags. 'One saw some clothed in peasants' blouses, in coats of sheepskin or of other beasts, others clothed in bizarre fashion and carrying long skeins of bacon, ham and morsels of meat hung from their belts – virtual marching larders. Others marched entirely garlanded with bread and bottles of wine.' This description comes from a retired Austrian dragoon officer and has the ring of truth. Every Frenchman who has completed his military service recalls, that even on peacetime manoeuvres, the troops' obsession was: food, snacks at any time, for who knows when or whence the next will come? So, think of these unfortunate pillaging troops, who never knew if, three days ahead, they would enter one of these repeatedly looted towns where there was nothing, absolutely nothing. So, carry the maximum with you.

The impression which these tattered conquerors produced in Vienna was disastrous. Napoleon became aware of it when he entered the Austrian capital on the 14th. And knew how to expunge this image – by employing the Guard, as always, less run down than the army. After some days of rest at Schönbrunn, the Guard refurbished its full dress; the giants shaved, tightened up their pig-tails, combed their side whiskers and pipe-clayed their crossbelts. On a snowy day, behind the impressive grenadiers' band, 9,000 men marched; foot and mounted grenadiers, gunners, generals and glittering officers, not to mention the mameluke circus. All of which was intended to erase – or blur – the sad and disturbing memory of the arrival of the Line some days earlier. In any event, nothing remains in the records of the senior officers of the time. Some even indulged in a little editing of dates to improve matters. For example:

General d'Hautpoul: '13 November was for us a special occasion. We fell-in in battle order opposite the district through which we were to enter Vienna ... Our army made its triumphal entry to the noise of our bands and of our reg-imental buglers. The entire population were at their windows to see us pass.'

General Bigarré: 'We saw the Viennese line the roads to see the passing of this magnificent army of which they had heard so much. The most elegant ladies offered laurels and refreshments to the officers; not one inhabitant was troubled by any French soldier during this triumphal procession.'

Actually, the Viennese were initially curious but reserved, and later quite friendly. In those days the bludgeoning of anti-enemy propaganda did not exist. Discipline was maintained, thanks to the firm hand of general Clarke, appoint-ed governor of the city. Bernadotte had one of his soldiers shot for the robbery in the open street of a working woman's earrings. The officers toured the city and attended the opera where 'The Magic Flute' was played. In the suburban theatres, bawdy pieces were staged, some of which often bordered on the licen-tious but which were well attended. Officers and other ranks 'celebrated brief idylls', or bedded the Viennese prostitutes or women, prostitutes or not, mis-tresses of the moment or longer, or even wives more or less legitimate – I have already mentioned these 'army marriages' – a ragged and straggling troupe which followed the army uphill and down dale in a miscellany of carts and car-riages. They, in the cold and the mud, comprised a fantastic feminine saga which no learned study has ever chronicled and which will never be recorded apart from passing references.

Murat, sent as advance guard, had written to Napoleon: 'As I have had the honour to report to Your Majesty, the city of Vienna has been occupied and, with the help of a degree of ruse, we have secured the bridge.' The ruse had con-sisted of convincing the bridge detail that an armistice had been signed. The Austrians had retired to the left bank of the Danube, pursued by the French. But Napoleon wished to avoid pushing Kutusov too far north because he wanted to destroy him before he could rejoin the bulk of the Russian army, and in a place of his own choosing. The strategic preparation for Austerlitz and the battle itself are masterpieces of the military art. Napoleon started by dissembling, showing himself as timid and fearful, as if dreading a decisive battle – on which he was in fact, set – in order to persuade the Allies to quit their excellent positions near Olmütz, a city situated some 170 kilometres north- north-east of Vienna.

On 20 November 1802, he arrived from Vienna at the village of Pohrlitz, and, bent over a map of Moravia, dictated: 'Marshal Soult is ordered to report to Austerlitz.' Austerlitz is a village 40 kilometres from Olmütz, situated between Pohrlitz and Olmütz. It was here that Napoleon wished to lead the Russians. Less than five kilometres to the west of Austerlitz rose a flat-topped hill, the plateau of Pratzen, crowned by two hillocks. This plateau fell away to the west towards a ravine dotted with frozen lakes fed by a thin stream, the Goldbach. That same day, 21 November, Napoleon moved his HQ to Brünn (20 kilometres west of Austerlitz) and it was from there that he went to visit his chosen battlefield which he had surveyed for several days, observing it from a point of vantage known as the Zuran hillock. He knew the terrain 'as well as the Paris suburbs' and on 28 November he began his hazardous manoeuvre: 'At dawn tomorrow, the troops will evacuate Austerlitz and the entire plateau of Pratzen.'

Napoleon had foreseen that the Russians and Austrians would immediately move to occupy the two positions, which, in fact, they did the following day. The French army, or at any rate that part of the army concentrated in this sector and which was to take part in the battle, was established to the east of the Goldbach ravine. And Napoleon would continue to inspire the Allies' movements. Let us recall that he was no tyro but a highly qualified professional; Austerlitz would be his fiftieth battle.

'My enemies' objective will certainly be to cut my communications with Vienna and its reinforcements. They will try this even more willingly if they see that my right is weak and liable to be turned. I will therefore keep my left strong and I will weaken my right by withdrawing it.'

All turned out exactly as he had foretold. At that time, battles were fought over quite a small space; the Austerlitz battlefield measured about 8 by 8 kilometres and each commander could distinguish enemy movements by telescope. The troops, by contrast, fought without understanding much about the tactical movements in which they took part, often thanks to the thick black smoke which quickly obscured everything. For this reason, I shall now outline the pattern of the Battle of Austerlitz as it unfolded on 2 December. The adversaries' testimony will then be easier to comprehend.

During the night of 1/2 December, the Austro-Russian columns came down from the Pratzen towards the French right, this weak wing which served as a bait. As soon as a part of the Russian force had left the plateau, the bulk of the French forces under the command of Soult crossed the Goldbach ravine and started to climb the hill to the plateau. The enemy counter-attacked but without success. The French cavalry broke the enemy front and advanced as far as the village of Austerlitz. During this time, Soult fell on the rear of the enemy columns which were marching on the French right. By nightfall, the Austro-Russians, caught between the French centre and its two wings, had been annihilated. Some of them tried to flee by crossing the frozen lakes, a very unwise move, as we shall see.

Since 25 November, there had been a form of diplomatic correspondence between Napoleon and Tsar Alexander I, the Emperor first sending one of his ADCs, General Savary, bearing a somewhat vague proposal for an amicable settlement followed by a request for an audience. He still wanted to appear uncertain and rather fearful. The Tsar finally sent Prince Dolgorouki, whom Napoleon received personally on 29 November. The interview lasted only five minutes. Alexander's terms were that he would sign a peace provided France evacuated Italy immediately and if she gave the left bank of the Rhine to Belgium and Holland. Napoleon exploded:

'You dare to speak to me of Brussels when my armies are occupying Vienna? But even if you stood on the heights of Montmartre, you would not obtain Brussels. We shall fight as your master wishes; I wash my hands of it.'

It seems impossible to determine the number of men engaged at Austerlitz. The estimates of the most eminent experts do not agree through no fault of theirs. The Grande Armée crossed the Rhine with about 200,000 men. Ney and Augereau were then in the Alps with 73,000 men. Napoleon left in Vienna under Davout a corps of occupation of 27,000 men who were to join the main body before the battle. The remainder of the Grande Armée was parcelled out in several small bodies in Moravia and elsewhere, moved about by Napoleon like pawns on a chessboard. From this it appears that the Grande Armée at Austerlitz numbered 68,000, 73,000 or 80,000 against 87,000 or 90,000 Allies, Austrian and Russian. The only solid fact is that, on the morning of 1 December, Davout's corps, coming from Vienna, failed to arrive. Napoleon did not appear too disconcerted nor less inclined to put his audacious battle plan into effect, since he sent the 11th regiment of mounted chasseurs, 500 men, to reconnoitre the plateau of Pratzen to see whether the enemy had in fact evacuated it. These chasseurs wore the hussars' green dolman with a black leather shako. Hardly had they climbed up to the plateau when they saw erupting from every direction several thousand Cossacks. It was admittedly the first encounter with these savages. The Cossacks of the imperial guard wore in principle a blue uniform and a cap of red and yellow, but all were distinguished by their filth, their curved moustaches, their lances and very curved sabres, and by their diabolical dexterity on horseback. They charged, whirling their lances in vertiginous circles and howling – a technique which had often shaken seasoned troops. But not this time. Colonel Bessières, youngest brother of the marshal and a competent and unflappable soldier, commanded the 1st Chasseurs. Five hundred against 4 or 5,000 Cossacks – out of the question to see them off, but an orderly retreat would be possible and would also conform with Napoleon's plan to get the Russians off the plateau. The chasseurs detailed as marksmen calmly directed well-aimed carbine fire at the howling horde and dismounted many of them. Others swerved aside, passing behind their comrades, and came on again – always the same pattern, but useless in the face of the orderly retreat of the chasseurs, each squadron deferring its move until their comrades had held the enemy. In the event, not a French soldier or horse was killed or wounded, and this skirmish is significant. These Cossack scarecrows were successful only against retreating, demoralised or harassed troops, or against small, isolated units.

'That morning', wrote General Lejeune, 'I delivered an order from the Major-General to Marshal Bernadotte, whom I found on the heights of Sokolnitz at the foot of a wooden crucifix, full sized and painted red. Here the marshal had had a fire built, before which he was performing gymnastics, stripped to the waist like the Christ. I asked him how he could bear to do this in the cold of the open air. He replied: "My dear friend, I am fortifying myself with a fresh-air bath." And moreover, although he did not then know it, after acclimatising himself to the cold, he would become one of the kings of the North.' Whereas we know that the dynasty of this Swedish monarch with a taste for physical culture would reign in Sweden to this day.

Bernadotte had been one of the best generals of the Republic and a formidable rival to Napoleon. And when he became Crown Prince of the Swedish states, he was to contribute substantially to the ruin of the empire. By the time of Austerlitz, Jean Bernadotte, born at Pau in 1763, had already had a very romantic career, notwithstanding a very pedestrian start: 'You will be an attorney, like me; it is a good life.' 'Yes, father.' A junior clerk in the parliamentary office of the procurator. Jean was bored, but he acquired the good manners which would later please women of the world. 'A man whom one could not meet in a salon without being impressed and asking his name,' would write Madame de Chastenay. And from Madame de Genlis: 'He had the manners of a king.' With a good bearing, hawk-nosed, his admirers claimed that he resembled the great Condé. On the death of his father, he abandoned a legal career and joined the French Navy. On the eve of the Revolution, we see him a sergeant-major at Grenoble in a white uniform with sky-blue revers. The girls giggled at the nickname given him by his comrades: 'Sergeant Fine-leg'. The handsome sergeant gave one of them, a Mademoiselle Lamour (her real name), an infant, who did not survive. In 1780, Bernadotte Fine-leg was a warrant officer at Marseilles and on the point of being promoted sub-lieutenant. Rashly, he saved his colonel's life during a mutiny. 'Oho, so he's an aristocrat!' So no promotion. But it was to come three years later when Bernadotte's career took flight. Another three years and here he is divisional general at the battles of the Army of Sambre-et-Meuse against the Austrians.

At the beginning of 1797, an order from the Directory sent him to Italy with 20,000 men from the Rhine to reinforce Bonaparte, who was demanding help. Leaving Metz with his troops on 17 January, Bernadotte delivered them in 'fine shape' to Bonaparte on 3 March. At this time, Bernadotte sincerely admired the young commander-in-chief, rejoiced at the prospect of service under him and expected congratulations for the promptness of his arrival. Not a word; a cold welcome. Bonaparte scented a rival in Bernadotte and would never like him. After the Peace of Campo Formio, rather than leave him in command of the Army of Italy, he pushed him into diplomacy: ambassador at Vienna on 11 January 1798. On 15 April, Bernadotte left his post following a riot provoked by the tricolore flag displayed on his balcony. And whom did he marry four months later? Désirée Clary, the young sister-in-law of Joseph Bonaparte. You will recognise Napoleon's one-time fiancée; it's a small world. Shortly afterwards Bernadotte left to take command of the Army of Germany, but Napoleon was still worried that he might shine too brilliantly on the field of battle – so he had him appointed Minister of War! This proved to be a blunder, since while Bonaparte was campaigning in Egypt, the seductive and eloquent Bernadotte captured the adulation of the army and the public to the degree that the Directors took fright: 'We are now ciphers; Bernadotte inflames France,' wrote Barras. 'The Minister of War is everything.' And Sieyès manoeuvred to have the too popular minister dismissed. When Bonaparte returned from Egypt, Bernadotte at thirty-six was 'retired'. But Bonaparte was still afraid of him. 'If he becomes ambitious, he will believe that he has the right to dare anything.'

Désirée Clary, Bernadotte's wife, had reserved for her ex-fiancée a curious sentiment; a brand of amorous malice. She had been attracted to Bernadotte as soon as she realised that he was the only one capable of standing up to Bonaparte. Between 18 Brumaire and the proclamation of the Empire, 'Bernadotte had on numerous occasions, given cause for disciplinary action against him, and Bonaparte had several times spoken of having him shot. His hand was seen in every plot which was hatched, not only at Paris, but in the most distant garrison.' But Désirée had maintained amicable ties with the First Consul and, like a good wife, had frequently shielded her impulsive husband, who was thereby not only saved from arrest, but was appointed by Bonaparte to command the Army of the West and to undertake the pacification of Brittany. Consigned to civil life by the Peace of Amiens, ex-Sergeant Fine-leg found himself with the dawning of the Empire an unemployed general. And then, without warning, marshal, commander-in-chief of the Army of Hanover with a choice pew at the coronation, a home in the rue d'Anjou, Grand Eagle of the Legion of Honour. Bernadotte never got over it; so far as he was concerned, whole books could be written about the Corsican's behaviour towards him.

The country around Austerlitz is very hilly and strewn with streams and frozen lakes. The troops had built themselves shelters of branches thatched with straw. They knew that there would be a battle the next day, a big battle, and they all hoped it would be the last. Then, no more bivouacs, no more frantic marches; but rest in comfortable billets with bean feasts while awaiting the march under the triumphal arches. That dream evaporated. The troops would always dream that the next battle would be the last.

Meanwhile, the entire army was hungry. The provisions carried from Vienna had been eaten, and on the line of march the few villages had already been looted. Even the grenadiers of the Guard, the Emperor's pets, had to make do with jam sandwiches. Napoleon passed by one bivouac and chuckled: 'Ah, you old devils, so you have found some jam!' They scrambled to attention. 'Don't move. But you must fit new flints to your muskets. You will need them tomorrow.' Vive l'Empereur! Wherever the great man appeared, the machine came to life. A picket of the mounted grenadiers appeared; black horses, high boots, the same imposing uniform as the foot grenadiers. These majestic centaurs were driving before them a herd of pigs. Without paying attention to the presence of the Emperor, the foot grenadiers threw themselves on the precious flock and proceeded to slit their throats. The mounted men were furious and drew their swords. Blood had already been spilt in the bivouacs over rations, as Napoleon knew. So he decided: six for the cavalry, six for the foot-sloggers. Vive l'Empereur!

The cold day ended. A rumour circulated at nightfall; 'Davout's army corps has arrived.' Half an hour later, it was learned that only a twentieth of the corps had appeared. 'We have covered forty leagues in thirty-six hours.' These men dropped to the ground; the remainder were strung-out behind them for more than forty kilometres. Officers had been left along the route to round-up the stragglers and keep them on the march. The supply service had found some boots in the Austrian barracks, but not enough. Davout's infantry marched on bleeding feet. The whole corps had reported by dawn the next day and would face the Russian assault without flinching.

The night of 1 December was freezing. To alleviate the depression caused by hunger, there was but one remedy: a large distribution of brandy. To transport wine for the army was impracticable – too many casks, too many vehicles. Brandy took up less space. The staff rarely was without wine; here they were drinking Tokay. The junior officers broached the casks and drank through straws. At Austerlitz, the entire army relied on alcohol and enthusiasm. For, at nightfall, the regiments divided into battalions, and were to hear the most effective of all Napoleon's proclamations. First, to inspire confidence, a summary of tactics; true and understandable. 'The positions which we occupy are formidable, and while the enemy is marching to turn my right, I will attack him in the flank.' Then immediately following, the psychological punch: 'Soldiers! I shall direct your battalions; I shall take position far from the firing if, with your customary bravery, you sow disorder and confusion in the enemy ranks, but if victory is in doubt, you will see your Emperor defy the first volleys.' And to finish, the radiant future: 'This victory will finish our campaign and we can return to our winter quarters, where we will be joined by the armies now forming in France. And then the peace which I shall give will be worthy of my people, of you and of me.'

It is well known that Napoleon was neither gastronome nor gourmet and dined and supped (we would say lunched and dined) in fifteen or twenty minutes at most. That night, in his bivouac, supper had lasted longer because the Emperor had talked at length. Not of war or battle, but of the theatre. Junot, who prided himself on his literary bent, had raised the topic and Napoleon had his own ideas about theatre: 'No living author has understood the new principles which must underlie our modern tragedies.' The new principles were politics. 'Look at Corneille, what depth of creativity! There was a statesman! But "The Templars" is a plot devoid of politics; I told the author that it was flawed. Philippe-Auguste ought to have destroyed it, etc.'

So, in brief, politics should be the great driving-force: 'it must replace our classic fatalism in our theatre'. So be it: but the argument became general; Junot talked of the evidence of ardour in the ranks at all levels. The French are happy to fight; they will follow the Emperor to the ends of the earth. No, said one of the company: 'The cheers prove the opposite. The army has had enough; it is exhausted. To drive it further, it will obey, but reluctantly. Today, it only shows a measure of ardour in the hope of seeing the end tomorrow and of returning home.' The speaker was General Mouton, future Count Lobau, then one of Napoleon's ADCs.

'The Emperor, to whom these loyal words will have given little satisfaction, may none the less have agreed with him. He broke off the conversation – "Meanwhile, let us to battle." In fact, he was intending to visit the artillery and the ambulances. A little later he threw himself down on the straw of his hut and slept profoundly.' The grenadiers of the Guard had constructed this shelter for him. (We shall later be able to visit the imperial tent, used in better weather.) In the middle of the night he was woken by one of his ADCs. The Russians had attacked one of the distant villages on the French right, towards the lakes; the attack had been beaten off. Good news, either way; the enemy was nibbling the bait. But the chief wished to reconnoitre the enemy positions once more. He took horse and, with a small escort, rode between the lines – risky, and not for the first time – or the last. On this occasion he ventured too close and stumbled on a Cossack post. According to Ségur who was present:

'The latter advanced quickly towards him and would have seized or killed him but for the devotion of his escorting chasseurs and if he had not galloped towards our lines at full speed. Returning to his own bivouac, Napoleon stumbled over a tree-trunk in the dark. A grenadier nearby seized a handful of straw and lit it, holding it over his head to give the Emperor some light. It was the eve of the anniversary of his coronation, and the light illuminating Napoleon's face prompted the troops nearby to exclaim: "The coronation anniversary! Vive l'Empereur!" "Silence and goodnight. Don't think of anything other than of sharpening your bayonets." But already the same thought and the same cries spread with lightning speed, flew from fire to fire, and all spontaneously seized handfuls of straw and tied them to poles, using these improvised torches to form a line of fire amid cries of "Vive l'Empereur!" repeated a thousand times. Thus was celebrated under enemy eyes the most admirable illuminations and the most touching of accolades. The Russians assumed that we were burning our bivouacs prior to retiring; their illusions grew.'

On 2 December a precious ally joined Napoleon's soldiers – fog. Read again, Tolstoy's *War and Peace*: 'The fog was so thick that even by day, one could see only ten paces in front. The bushes seemed to be enormous trees, the clearings ravines or hills. Everywhere, on all sides, one could fall over an invisible enemy ten paces' distant. The columns marched interminably in the same fog, climbing and descending the hills, crossing the gardens, the vegetable patches in a new world without ever sighting the enemy.'

Napoleon, on horseback, surrounded by his staff and his marshals, kept to the hillock of Zuran, whence he could overlook the battlefield. In fact he could see nothing except banks of fog which concealed the movements of the troops, but he knew the terrain so well and the machine which he had set in movement was so clear in his mind that he could have directed it with his eyes shut – at least at the start. The fog would not last forever. Waiting four paces behind, the marshals upbraided one of their company. Lannes shouted at Soult to his face: 'You are a wretch!'

Lannes, the commander of V Corps, was not a docile man. Thirty-nine at the time of Austerlitz, he would be dead less than four years later. His prickly temperament was perhaps rooted in a feeling of inferiority because he had never attended high school; his father, a farmer at Lectoure in the Gers, had never thought to give him the opportunity. Lannes had received his education from his brother who was a priest; later he was apprenticed to a dyer. As a general, he often suffered feelings of inferiority in the company of his peers. With courage and success, he would complete his education with results that astonished Napoleon. But some self-educated persons can never throw off these feelings of inferiority. The Revolution gave Lannes, as it gave many men, opportunities of promotion; at Lectoure young men able to read and write were not too numerous. Made sub-lieutenant on the day that the 2nd Battalion of Volunteers of the Gers was formed, he climbed the ladder quickly. A hero at Lodi, Arcola, Rivoli, Jaffa, St-Jean d'Acre, brigadier-general in 1797. An active supporter of Bonaparte at 18 Brumaire, he earned Napoleon's gratitude. But why did Lannes persist in addressing Napoleon as 'tu' when Bonaparte did not reciprocate? Still compensating feelings of inferiority perhaps? The First Consul taught him a lesson when informed that Lannes, then commander of the Consular Guard, had rashly misappropriated – with the intention of repaying – some of the corps' funds. Ordered to make immediate restitution, dismissed, 'skirting dishonour' – which was putting it mildly – the general was forced to accept an exile, which might have been worse – minister plenipotentiary to Portugal. At that time such an appointment could pay handsome dividends; when he returned from Portugal, Lannes was rich. And he had at last come to realise that it would be prudent not to *tutoyer* Bonaparte who now however addressed him as 'tu' – 'which he generally did to those generals to whom he wished to show a certain preference', according to Bourrienne. In 1800 Lannes married the beautiful Louise Guéhénuc whose Senator father was a financier and forestry administrator.

If you now wish to know why Lannes had called Soult a wretch on the eve of Austerlitz, here is your answer. The incident occurred some days before the battle at the post office in the village of Welpitz. Murat and Soult had asked Lannes to join them there. They told him that the position of their troops was too exposed and that the enemy whom they were facing was too numerous. Lannes started by saying 'Really?' but they finally convinced him. He agreed to send a note to Napoleon giving their opinion that a withdrawal was needed and he was in the act of writing it when the Emperor entered. 'Good morning, gentlemen, is all well here?' 'We do not think so, your Majesty,' replied Lannes, 'and I was just writing to Your Majesty to say so.' Napoleon took the letter and read it. 'How's this? The brave Lannes is counselling retreat? That is the first time that that has happened. Marshal Soult, what do you think?' Soult saw which way the wind was blowing. No question of diminishing himself before the great chief – on the contrary, one must flatter and profit from the opportunity.' 'No matter in which manner your Majesty may choose to employ my army corps, it will have the better of the enemy, even if he is twice as numerous.' Naturally, Lannes exploded. Turning to the Emperor, he exclaimed 'I have only been here fifteen minutes and I only know of this situation what these gentlemen have told me. Marshal Soult's reply is a shameless reversal which I am astonished to hear. I have been insulted and I must seek satisfaction.'

Then, turning to Soult, he cursed him heartily. As he often did when his subordinates quarrelled – no rare event – Napoleon walked to and fro, pretending to hear and see nothing. Finally: 'I too believe a retreat is necessary'.

We know his plan. Leaving the two marshals to fight it out, Napoleon left to dictate his orders to Berthier. Following their quarrel, Lannes had challenged Soult to a duel; there was no reply to his challenge. On the morning of Austerlitz, the two men found themselves on horseback behind Napoleon with Murat, Bernadotte, Davout, Bessières, Oudinot and Berthier, and Lannes profited from such an audience to address Soult: 'I had thought you a brave soldier and I am waiting for you.' Soult was unmoved: 'We have today more important things to attend to.' Not a word or a gesture more. Lannes had to stifle his fury. It was true that the moment was poorly chosen. Napoleon again pretended to hear nothing.

Shortly after, he was to order Soult to begin the climb up to the Pratzen. A curious type of man, this Soult; a soldier with the temperament of a politician. The son of a notary, he had had a very sketchy classical education, but had acquired a taste for pompous proclamations. He had a haughty manner which went with his severe mien – although he did not look people in the face. As with many senior officers raised under the Revolution, money did not displease him. His contemporaries spoke with admiration, or with snigger of envy, of the magnificent balls followed by suppers which he gave in 1800 at the Duke of Aosta's palace at Turin in honour of a singer about whom he was besotted. Later, his immense fortune, which Napoleon was not alone in regarding with reservations, allowed him to fulfil his obligations opulently. People did not visit him solely to dine or sup, but also to admire – with murmured observations – his superb picture gallery.

On the Zuran hillock, Napoleon issued his last orders to the marshals; one after another they rushed off to their commands. Soult was the last. At 8 a.m., the sun emerged from the fog, red and enormous. Napoleon could see the serried ranks of bayonets as the Russians came down from the Pratzen plateau towards the French right. Then, to Soult: 'How long do you want in which to exploit this moment?' 'Ten minutes, Sire.' 'Away with you, then! But wait fifteen minutes; it will then be time.'

The first effort of imagination which we must make if we are to understand clearly the adversaries' behaviour once battle was joined – how things came out – is to remind ourselves that it all took place more slowly than we would tend to imagine – certainly more slowly than certain films have represented. This was partly a consequence of the slow rate of musket fire.

The standard musket of the Empire, model 1777, modified in 1800 and 1803, was 1.52m long, weighed 4.375 kilograms; calibre 17.5mm. The trim was iron, the balls spherical and of lead, each weighing 29 grams. The cartridge comprised a bag of heavy paper which held the ball and 12.5 grains of powder. Here is what the foot soldier had to do in order to fire: open the priming-pan, tear the cartridge with his teeth, fill the priming-pan with powder and close it, pour the remainder of the powder into the barrel, tamp it down, using the paper bag as a tampon, spit the ball into the barrel and push it down onto the wad, finally, cock the hammer. The instruction manual laid down that the loading operation should consist of twelve movements. An expert soldier could fire once every thirty seconds. If firing were prolonged, the musket required cleaning after forty or fifty rounds, and the touch-hole had to be reamed out with a pin attached to the cartridge-box by a lanyard. A far cry from the automatic weapons of today, or even the 1918 Lebel. Firing was more rapid than the description above might indicate, because the officers controlled the fire 'in two ranks – actually three ranks – of soldiers. It opened with 'fire by file' – a rolling volley from left to right, followed by 'fire at will' with the front rank kneeling and the rear rank merely passing forward the reloaded muskets to the second rank. These muskets had no backsight; the soldiers using the left thumb as a substitute, the accuracy of which can be imagined. Fire was accurate to up to 200 metres and relatively accurate to 500 metres, but beyond that, no. In any case, after a few minutes the battle field was covered with thick, black smoke. The troops fired at will, advancing until in contact with the enemy, and then – the bayonet! This bayonet was 56cm long and its triangular blade was attached to the musket through a socket. It was often the decisive weapon.

The infantrymen's advance towards the enemy was not, however, a blind groping, despite the smoke; nor was it a parade-ground manoeuvre. The tactic developed and perfected by Frederick II set in motion masses of troops, aligned as on parade, moving at fixed intervals and distances; the formations were to be preserved, whatever the weight of enemy fire. The Revolutionary soldiers had spurned this tradition merely because they were untrained. They used open order, taking advantage of whatever the terrain offered, advancing or retiring according to circumstances. The military genius of Napoleon had mastered this mobility and preserved it. A piece on tactics has no place here; let us merely recall that the general principle of the infantry of the Grande Armée was: 'Occupy a front which will permit the use of all arms, multiply the marksmen, changing rapidly from open order to attack column or square as appropriate and vice versa.' The troops formed square mainly in order to repel enemy cavalry.

We shall have many opportunities to see the cavalry of the Grande Armée at the charge. Let us merely say that these heroic charges and counter-charges were not of hurricane force, but slow, 17 km/hr maximum for a charge at a gallop, more often 15 km/hr. Cavalrymen were equipped with either a straight or a curved sword. Thousand of pictures have shown the massed charge, sabres pointed at the throats or the chests of the enemy, heads flying from the curved swords. In addition to the sabre, they had a pair of pistols. Dragoons also had a musket and the light cavalry a carbine, but the carbine fired from the saddle was inaccurate and even a danger to comrades.

Before and during a battle, the mounted and foot artillery fired. Cannon were known as 4-, 8- or 12-pounders according to the weight in pounds of the cannon-ball. Both solid shot and canisters filled with musket-balls were employed. The howitzers fired a hollow, 24-pound shell filled with powder and musket-balls which was ignited by a fuze of reed and wick. The average rate of fire was two rounds per minute for the 4- and 8-pounders and one round per minute for the 12-pounders. In the era of Gribeauval (who reformed the French artillery), the science of gunnery was comparatively rudimentary, and the spread of shot was considerable.

Experts have calculated that the total volume of French artillery fire at Austerlitz was less than that of nine batteries of a field regiment in 1914. Combat losses, however, were very heavy, not only because of the use of cold steel at the end, but because cannon-balls were dangerous beyond the ranges quoted; they would ricochet off hard ground, breaking the limbs of men and horses. And, of course, an enormous number of men died of their wounds.

'The bulk of the French forces, under command of Soult, entered the Goldbach ravine and started to climb the heights leading to the plateau. The Austro-Russians mounted an unsuccessful counter-attack.'

While, as foreseen in Napoleon's plan, the Allies made some passing effort to drive in the French right, the French troops' climb to reach the plateau was proving somewhat difficult. Two divisions of Soult's corps were deployed: Vandamme's on the left and Saint-Hilaire's on the right. At their head, two battalions of light infantry in open order, skirmishing by bounds and zigzags, followed by the first and second line regiments in columns of threes. What I have said of the musketry allows us to picture the soldiers climbing the heights of Pratzen under the fire of the enemy. Saint-Hilaire's division was the first to attain its objective, the Pratzen hillock; a little later, Vandamme's division reached the top of the Stary-Vinohrady hillock. These two divisions then attacked the flank of the Allied centre which was coming down towards the French right. But the enemy had counter-attacked on the Pratzen plateau violently and persistently. Soult had to send six 12-pounders to help Thiébault's brigade which was in difficulty. These guns, firing at a range of twenty metres, slaughtered the Russians. The danger passed, Thiébault thanked Soult in these terms:

'Your cannon arrived in the nick of time, Marshal. I immediately ordered Colonel Fontenay to load them all with canister. "That will wreck them," he replied. "Believe me," I said, "If they last five minutes, that will do the trick." I myself ordered the troops to take careful aim before firing and to fire at the belts of the enemy and the centre of their platoons so that no rounds would be wasted. I allowed formidable masses of the enemy to approach to the planned distance, when our cannon were unmasked along the whole line, and opened the most destructive fire ever known.'

The glorious sun had set and the frost deepened in a glacial east wind; alcohol restored the famished men less and less. The Semenovski and Preobrajenski Regiments and the infantry of the Russian guard, 3,000 gigantic men nearly two metres tall, in white and green, attacked Vandamme's division. The front line was broken, but the second resisted and the two famous Russian regiments fell back in good order. The second attack was delivered by the cavalry of the Russian imperial guard: these handsome, brave men in their white uniforms, riding black horses, were the flower of the Russian aristocracy. They hurtled into the musketry fire, rushed the pointed bayonets, and snatched the copper eagle of the 1st Battalion of the 4th Line. The French had no time to reload – I have already shown what a slow procedure it was. One imagines that 3,000 French infantry would be massacred by a slightly superior number of Russian cavalry, but this was not the case. Napoleon, who was watching the clash through his telescope from a distance of three kilometres, ordered the Guard cavalry to charge, or more exactly, said to Marshal Bessières: 'Send my cavalry forward in support of these brave men.'

Jean-Baptiste Bessières, aged 37 at the time of Austerlitz, promoted Marshal of France with the advent of the Empire, will be seen again in the deadly Spanish sierras and in the bloodstained snow of Russia. Like Murat, he was born in Quercy (at Prayssac, renowned for its foie-gras). Also like Murat, he was educated at the college of Saint-Michel of Cahors, serious study, many priests in the family. There was a Bessières tradition: the eldest son would be a surgeon: 'You shall study at the medical school of Montpellier.' This was one of the most reputable in the kingdom, but Jean-Baptiste was not to go there. A series of agricultural calamities assailed his father's estates and at that time there was no insurance or subsidy. 'Even so, I shall be a surgeon.' He then started a strange apprenticeship under a cousin who was a doctor. As well as a scalpel, he wielded a barber's razor and scissors – one must eat. When the Revolution took place he was 21. Being educated, he co-operated in the editing of the famous statements of grievances which would be sent to Paris. He was also second-in-command of the national guard of Prayssac; he spoke at the local assembly.

In 1792 the departmental Directory named Bessières, his uncle Lemozy and his friend Murat to join Louis XVI's constitutional Guard. But events were accelerating: on 7 June this corps was disbanded and its troops were absorbed into the National Guard of Paris. As a fervent Christian, Jean-Baptiste in no degree welcomed the Revolutionary violence. On 10 August, with some friends, he hurried to defend the royal family, assailed in the Tuileries; too late, the insurgents had already prevailed. But the royalist zeal of these ex-guardsmen had been noted. Branded an anti-revolutionary, he spent the next three months in hiding. He is next seen as adjutant in the cavalry of the National Guard of the Pyrenees. The following year, this unit was to become the 22nd Regiment of Chasseurs. Trooper Bessières became sub-lieutenant, lieutenant, captain. In 1795, in the Army of Italy, with one foot on the ladder; he distinguished himself at Millesimo and at Lodi. Bonaparte appointed him commander of the Guides, a bodyguard made necessary by the daring of the enemy who, on the Mincio, very nearly captured the First Consul. This élite unit would become the Consular Guard and then the Imperial Guard; Jean-Baptiste Bessières' career was set.

Bonaparte liked him; when emperor, he would not change his mind. Bessières would be one of those whom he would always welcome close to him. He would recall that he, like Murat, had participated unhesitatingly in 18 Brumaire, and other aspects of his character were attractive. 'Bessières has many civilian qualities which I welcome in military men.' In other words, he was a wise counsellor. Remember that Lannes had been a suitor for the hand of Caroline Bonaparte and had suspected Bessières of advancing the claims of his rival, Murat. A suspicion perhaps justified, seeing that Bessières had appeared as witness to the marriage of Murat as a so-called cousin. He had also been witness to the marriage of Louis Bonaparte to Hortense de Beauharnais.

Returning to Prayssac after the campaign in Egypt, and now a general, he had married a young girl of his region, a distant relative, for whom in his childhood he had evinced a tender friendship. Marie-Jeanne Lapeyrière was nineteen, with little fortune but of good family, the daughter of a lawyer. The marriage was celebrated in the château of Canussel, owned by the Lapeyrières, after a year-long engagement, then thought to be in good taste. What was more daring was the fact that the priest whom both families had chosen to perform the wedding ceremony was unsworn; it was only a misdemeanour, but there were religious convictions on both sides of the family – Bessières was one of the few army chiefs to have preserved his religious convictions.

Madame Bessières, 'good, gentle and pious', was beautiful and perfectly brought-up. Confronting the 'wide-awake' Parisians was a trial from which she emerged in excellent shape. One can see that the reticence of this country-bred girl was not stupidity and that a madonna-like face can hide a great firmness of character. Marie-Jeanne acquired self-assurance and 'as her beauty grew with her mind' she shone.

Shortly after her marriage, she attended in full mourning, a mass celebrated secretly in memory of Louis XVI. The mass had been observed by policemen in disguise; she was denounced and the report reached Bonaparte ('It was a conspiracy'). The First Consul had a violent interview with Bessières, who advised his wife not to appear in the Tuileries for a spell. But Bonaparte, better informed, asked Bessières to bring to him the 'charming sulker'.

'Madame, I regret to have reproached you by way of your husband. I have since learned that it was by chance that you were moved to attend a mass for Louis XVI.'

Unlike many other women, Marie-Jeanne Bessières knew how to maintain her composure and self-assurance when face-to-face with the intimidating Corsican. 'General,' she said, 'Louis XVI did not deserve his fate. He was victim of a misled people. I had wished to pray for him and had I been in your shoes, I know well what I would have done.' 'And what would you have done, Madame?' 'I would not have allowed the worship of God to be conducted only clandestinely in private houses.' After a silence, Bonaparte replied: 'You are right, Madame. After a while, I will put into force a project which I have had in mind.' Which concerned, of course, the liberty of religion.

Bessières was a methodical soldier. Economical in the expenditure of the lives of his men, he committed merely two squadrons which the Russian cavalry repulsed. The chasseurs of the Guard retired in good order. Bessières understood. He then ordered in two squadrons of mounted grenadiers, and, in succession, two squadrons of chasseurs and all his mounted artillery. At the same time, Bernadotte (on the left wing of the army) detached a division from his corps. Caught between the fire of these three regiment of fresh infantry and Bessières' cavalry, the Russians counter-attacked on both fronts with desperate bravery. Napoleon, always a percipient onlooker, summoned Rapp, an ADC and second-in-command of the chasseurs of the Guard: 'General, there is a mess there; go and put it right.' Rapp charged with two squadrons of chasseurs and the mamelukes. His intervention was decisive: the Russian Guard retreated, leaving on the field 500 dead, 200 prisoners and all its artillery. Rapp, though wounded and covered in blood, escorted to Napoleon a distinguished prisoner, Prince Repnine, colonel of the Russian Guard. Napoleon congratulated them both, returned his sword to the prince and, turning to the glittering officers who surrounded him, said: 'The day is decided, gentlemen, we have fixed them.' Bernadotte was ordered to occupy the plateau of Pratzen, while Soult's corps, the Guard and Oudinot's grenadiers turned about to fall upon the half of the Austro-Russian army which had been trapped. From then on, the battle consisted of no more than a series of fragmentary clashes.

South of the battlefield, the cornered Austro-Russian troops tried to escape across the frozen lakes. The Russians were accustomed to thick ice on which they would walk without hesitation. They advanced with their artillery train and 2,000 men.

'The column covered almost the whole expanse of the lake,' recounted General Thiard. 'The Emperor ordered up an artillery battery, which started to fire, not on the column, but on the ice. After twenty rounds, the ice split with a terrifying noise. In an instant, as if by some stage illusion, the whole column was swallowed up. I well recall the scene of horror before my eyes: hundreds of men seeking to evade death by climbing on horses who were drowning like them. I recall one unfortunate officer, using a pontoon for support while he tried to float on the water above the ice and imploring our help. Needless to say that the artillery train, which must have numbered 65 cannon, had sunk in the lake. The Emperor gave the order to cease fire and we managed to save the men on the banks.'

Here is the account published in the 30th Bulletin of the Grande Armée: 'The enemy corps which had been surrounded and ejected from all the heights was in a hollow and was backed onto a lake. The Emperor brought up twenty-eight pieces of artillery. The corps was driven from one position to another and we witnessed the horrible spectacle similar to Aboukir, where twenty thousand men threw themselves into the water and drowned in the lakes.'

Finally, here is the truth: the 'lake' was in fact a pond whose depth was never more than chest-high. Less than one hundred Russians perished, not from drowning, but from cold. The Bulletin was used all too often as an instrument of propaganda as have other documents across the centuries of history. Many thousand eye-witnesses have recounted their recollections of Austerlitz, more or less honestly, according to their temperament. It is for the historian to nail down the truth as best he can using these materials and assisted by his judgement, his intuition and a modicum of luck.

Lannes was decidedly a sorry character. When Napoleon arrived on the plateau of Pratzen, now conquered and occupied, Soult went to the Emperor to offer his congratulations: 'Besides, Marshal, it was on your corps that I was relying to carry the day.' Lannes knew of the compliment and took umbrage. He had contributed to the victory by paralysing the efforts of the enemy right wing and thought that the Emperor gave too much credit to Soult. 'After a very animated conversation with the Emperor,' states Thiard, 'he left the army. I met him eight or ten days later as he was returning to France.' Lannes went to see Talleyrand to whom he gave his version of the battle. Anger still seethed and coloured all his recollections of the day. 'I cannot stand it,' he exclaimed finally, 'unless you wish to come with me and beat to death these miserable Jews who plunder the dying and the dead.'

We already know, and we will see more in future, that it was not only the Jews who were the scavengers of the battlefields; they were almost certainly in a minority. On the day following the battle, Napoleon slept in the very beautiful château of Austerlitz and it was from there that he issued his famous proclamation which began: 'Soldiers, I am pleased with you...' and ended: 'My people will welcome you with joy and it will suffice to say "I was at the battle of Austerlitz" to elicit the response "Here is a brave man.".' No matter. We have seen something of the circumstances in which the 4th Line had lost its eagle to the Russian Guard. Now, a few days after Austerlitz, Napoleon reviewed Soult's army corps at Vienna 'and surrounding himself with their officers and in a voice which could be heard by the entire regiment, he reproached them in a loud voice in a surprisingly violent tone: "Where is your eagle? Yours is the only regiment of the French army to whom I can put that question! I would rather have lost my left arm than to have lost an eagle! It will be carried to Petersburg and displayed by the Russians with pride...", etc.

This was unjust, because more than twenty men had sacrificed more than their left arms in defending this copper emblem; their lives. But this chastisement had a place in the psychological strategy of the great commander in regard to the troops; flatter the image, but horsewhip them too. And the peroration is significant: 'What will you do to redeem this shame, to silence your old army comrades who will say when they see you "Here is the regiment that lost its eagle."?' The unhappy troops were practically in tears and said nothing. 'At the first opportunity, your regiment must bring me at least four enemy colours and then I will see if I should restore your eagle to you.' History has largely forgotten this horsewhipping; nothing must dim the red sun of Austerlitz.

IV

AN ENORMOUS GROAN
The Army Medical Services

During the battle of Austerlitz, the Allies had lost 40,000 men killed or wounded. On the French side, 7,000 men had been incapacitated. Not for the first time, the sun set on a cemetery. In its sweep across Europe, the Grande Armée would leave behind it a million corpses – not counting those of the enemy. I have heard the comment: 'Over ten years, that is not much.' A thirtieth part of the population of the France of that time; it is true that France did better than that in 1914-18, but the firepower of the armies was much less under the Empire and many fewer men were engaged.

Of the dead of the Grande Armée, some were killed on the spot by cannon-ball, bullet, blast of canister, the cold steel of bayonet or sabre; others died later, next day or the day after, having suffered in truly terrible conditions. One must allow that those killed on the spot were fortune's favourites.

During the evening of Austerlitz, Napoleon quartered the battlefield on horseback, ordering his staff to keep silent 'so that we can hear the groans of the wounded better'. These groans formed an immense and lugubrious lamentation which could still be heard two days later; heard too from the houses to which the lucky ones had been carried – the first comers being casualties among the Guard. Most of the wounded were laid on straw or the bare earth, suffering hunger and thirst, to be operated upon by surgeons, assistant-surgeons and nurses – always far too few of them and more often than not lacking proper instruments and medical equipment. Like the supply service, the medical service could not keep up with the army. The wounded of the Grande Armée, unmentioned in the scholarly tomes, little mentioned in contemporary accounts, formed an army of their own – an army of perhaps two million martyrs. Now read the epilogue to Austerlitz as expressed in the official Bulletin of the Grande Armée (No.31):

'In the evening and for several hours of the night, the Emperor had ranged over the battlefield removing the wounded: a horrible scene if ever there was one! The Emperor passed on horseback with lightning speed, and nothing was more touching than to see these brave men recognised him immediately, some forgetting their sufferings and asking "At least, was victory certain?" Others: "I have been suffering here for eight hours and have been abandoned since the start of the battle, but at least I have done my duty." Again, "You should be grateful to your soldiers today." The Emperor left a guard for each wounded man to take him to the ambulances. Horrible to relate, forty-eight hours after the battle, there were still a great number of Russians whose wounds had not been dressed; all the French wounded were cared for before nightfall.'

This fairy tale, intended to maintain the morale of the home front, was embroidered as events evolved. The day after the battle, Napoleon was apparently shaken by the size of the French losses. He was seen in Austerlitz itself dictating orders for the payment of pensions to widows and orphans, And then? Then Napoleon had to consider armistice terms for the beaten enemy, and make requisite dispositions to ensure the security of the army until peace was well and truly assured. Truly, an emperor commander-in-chief in the midst of remodelling Europe had many other demands on his time than the lot of the sick and wounded.

For centuries even the notion of a military medical service did not exist. The wounded got away from the battlefields as best they could, often assisted by kindly folk, religious or laymen. But most waited for death as they watched the crows circling overhead, waving off the flies while they yet had strength to move a hand. It was at the siege of Amiens that the first French medical service, created by Duke de Sully, had functioned in 1597. It was composed, then as later, of static hospitals whose ambulances followed the armies. The results were immediately excellent; which is to say that a wounded man was not necessarily always a dead man. Louvois, not noted for a tender heart, interested himself in the medical service, saying: 'We gain soldiers if we save them from gangrene and evils like typhoid fever.' As minister, he created the first permanent corps of medical officers and wished that the ring of fortresses conceived by Vauban could be augmented by a second ring of military hospitals. The results achieved by the French organisation so impressed Frederick II that he decided to invite French surgeons to Prussia: 'Gentlemen, organise for me a medical service on the lines of your own.' The principal fault of this concept was that there was practically no help for those wounded left on the battlefield. Louis XVI had laid down by a very detailed edict the pay of the different branches of the medical service. One can read, for example, that the mobile ambulances equipped for first aid or for amputations should keep a league behind the line of battle; the staff were not to collect the wounded until after the fighting had ceased; it must 'collect them in a locality where the ambulance was to arrive as soon as possible'. In reality, these so-called mobile ambulances were wagons so heavy that they needed three or four dozen horses to pull them. Having trailed the army with the baggage train, they rumbled to the places where the wounded had been collected, arriving twenty-four to thirty-six hours or more after the fighting had stopped; by then half the wounded had died.

81

The first reform of the medical service after the Revolution was to prove disastrous; it consisted of appointing officers to the corps who were civilian contractors, and they were paid for their services only in wartime and were then dismissed. They were placed under the orders of the Administration of War. Louvois had taken this step in an endeavour to eliminate the civilian entrepreneurs, most of whom were virtually bandits. The war commissioners – already responsible for the supply of equipment and victuals to the armies (we have seen how that service shone) – had their fief extended to the general management of all military hospitals and ambulances.

Thenceforward, the surgeons and doctors practising in the armies became a burden, almost an enemy, to the commissioners of war, because they protested against the prevalent mismanagement and dishonesty; after each bloody battle they complained of the shortage of instruments, no lint for bandages, no medicines, all the equipment was at the rear of the train. These medical people asked for a minimum of autonomy. Thousands of horses were available, but the administration did not allot a single one to the surgeons and doctors. Only the chief surgeons were permitted a horse, which they had to buy. The young ones did without, willy-nilly, and in any case, such 'extravagance' was unpopular. They foot-slogged, pack on back, in the wake of the infantry, arriving at their work worn-out, covered with mud or dust; hardly in ideal fettle for performing surgical operations! The commissioners complained that the surgeons and doctors would 'become insolent' if they received horses. These men were regarded as virtually supernumeraries because they did not take part in the fighting. This attitude was prevalent at all levels of the hierarchy and elsewhere. Stendhal and Paul-Louis Courier had spoken without admiration of the army medical corps – 'gluttonous Calabrian bandits', drunkards, etc. The targets of this contempt were, admittedly, not the flower of their profession; how could they have been? Recruited from the failures in medicine, very poorly paid, lacking prestige and a future with the army (dismissed, as I have said, at the end of each campaign), their condition was inherently adverse. One must make an exception of the medical service of the Guard, which was privileged, as was everything to do with this cherished corps.

There were no stretcher-bearers on the battlefields. 'We do not have enough men', said the commanders, 'to allow them to relinquish their muskets.' So, the walking wounded hobbled as best they could to the rear; often helped by comrades. 'I have seen some volunteers', wrote Percy, Chief Surgeon of the Grande Armée, 'who carried their comrades on muskets tied together with their kerchiefs, barrel to barrel, passing two muskets so tied under the legs with two more tied likewise under the trunk, using other kerchiefs or a haversack under the armpits in the direction taken by the muskets. Others used a stretcher of branches.' One saw many variants of this 'System D', but it was not looked upon favourably because it was often used as a pretext to leave the field.

The 'front-line' ambulances to which the wounded were carried had available theoretically: caissons of bedding, cut linen, medicines and one or two kits of surgical instruments for amputations or trepanning. Nine times out of ten these items had not arrived by the time of the battle, or could not be located in the disorder of wagons and cannon. It goes without saying that if his army were defeated a wounded man's chance of succour was one in a thousand. I should say here that I have no intention of glossing over the atrocious conditions which were the lot of the sick and wounded in the Grande Armée. Throughout the campaigns, they constituted the reverse of the laurelled medallion.

The army's two best-known surgeons were Larrey and Percy. In May 1780, Dominique Larrey, then aged fourteen, left Beaudéan in Bigorre (later the department of the Hautes Pyrenées) for Toulouse where he was to join his uncle, Alexis Larrey, surgeon-in-chief of the hospital of St-Joseph de la Grave. His father had been a bespoke shoemaker with a smallholding, but as his family had numbered several surgeons – 'You will be a surgeon'. The youth walked more than 500 kilometres to Toulouse, his mother, a widow with three children, being unable to find the money for a seat in a coach. Alexis Larrey took on the task of launching his nephew: 'First of all, you must perfect your Latin. And during your free hours you will study anatomy and will make the rounds of the sick.'

At fifteen, exams, and Dominique became a 'junior assistant', a trainee, something less than a Dresser. He bled patients, washed, applied dressings – all to male patients, as only the surgeons and the Sisters of Charity cared for the women. A junior assistant could only do so in urgent cases, never permanently. Like their seniors, the youngsters had to put their heart into their work; wounds tended to suppurate for a long time, producing 'laudable pus', which was not a cause for concern, or pus known as 'hospital gangrene', for which nothing could be done. These duties seemed pleasant compared to dissection which, like today, was used to teach anatomy. In the absence of any form of antiseptic preservatives, the cadavers were far from attractive, and as religious prohibitions made them difficult to obtain so that the remains were used repeatedly, the slightest scratch could prove fatal to the student. Many of them became disgusted and gave up; the tenacious went so far as to steal bodies from the undertakers, replacing them in the coffins with logs, or disinterred them from cemeteries. Fortunately, the accolade of doctor was awarded more easily than today. At twenty, Dominique Larrey, now senior assistant at the hospital of St-Joseph de Toulouse, submitted a brilliant thesis on bone decay.

'I must now go to Paris. I want to study under Pierre Desault.' He was a famous surgeon. How to get to Paris? But on foot, how else? Six weeks' marching. After a year of hard study (no salary), Dominique, hearing that the commissariat at Brest were recruiting surgeons for Ponant's squadron, left for Brest. Again on foot. The young surgeon was not the only marcher with fine staying-power. Napoleon was to find thousands of pairs of legs equal to every trial.

When Dominique Larrey returned to Paris in October 1792, he was twenty-two and for the first time had had the wherewithal to take the coach; not inside with the rich, but on top in the teeth of a freezing wind. 'Many times, I thought I would die under that blast.' But he was on his way. As senior surgeon in the king's ships, he had sailed to Newfoundland in the frigate *La Vigilante*, had adventured, faced the wide sea. But he was no sailor; seasickness (whose causes he had, typically, analysed) had proved too much for him and Larrey asked for his release. Back in Paris, he obtained a post at the Hôtel-Dieu as assistant surgeon under Desault for whom his admiration increased steadily.

The winter of 1788/9 was terrible. The Seine was frozen from Rouen to Paris, many of the poor perished from the cold. On 27 April 1789 there were riots in the borough of St-Antoine: 500 dead and innumerable wounded were brought to the Hôtel-Dieu. For the first time in his life Larrey found himself treating gunshot wounds.

You shine in your profession, your chiefs praise you, you pass a difficult examination in first place, you think: 'The coveted job will be mine.' No: a minister's recommendation snatches it from under your nose. It was the job of assistant senior doctor at the Invalides which Larrey had failed to secure. Three months later, he was among those who marched on the Bastille. The great ground-swell of revolution was fed also by thousands of individual injustices. Larrey would not obtain his job at the Invalides until 1791. In 1792, as senior surgeon of the Army of the Rhine, his real career would commence.

At that time, Larrey was a man of medium height but well-proportioned, with curly black hair falling to his shoulders, fine eyes, expressive face; in short, a nice-looking southerner. He had pleased a charming and romantic young girl, but the father, a well-endowed functionary, had said No to the marriage. (If only this fellow were a doctor!) A surgeon is little beside a doctor; there was no great distinction between a surgeon and a barber. Dominique and Marie-Elisabeth parted, swearing to marry later, which they did. Meanwhile, the Army of the Rhine. On this first occasion – at the battle of Spire, in Germany, after Valmy – Larrey took his own line which he would follow to the end. The old regulation was still in force; army doctors and surgeons must keep one league distant from the battlefields until the fighting was over. 'I don't want to know about this absurd order,' he declared. With some courageous nurses, he combed the battlefield, giving first-aid to the lightly wounded; the more serious cases were carried on the backs of the nurses – and on Larrey's – to a sheltered spot where he operated on them immediately. That same night, General Custine sent for him. He reported, still muddy and smeared with blood. 'Monsieur Larrey, you have deliberately broken the rules. You are under arrest until further orders.' Then, after a pause: 'Monsieur Larrey, in the name of humanity, I am promoting you to Principal Senior Surgeon.'

Of the forty wounded on whom Larrey operated that day, only four died; an unheard-of success: they had been operated upon in time. This incident gave Larrey the idea of 'flying ambulances' to search for the wounded on the field. At about the same time, his colleague Percy was to suggest the institution of 'mobile ambulances' for the same purpose.

The wheels of the Revolution turned. At the beginning of 1794, Larrey visited Paris to present his project of flying ambulances to the 'Council of Health' which had been established by the Convention. Hardly had he obtained a unanimous vote, than a messenger arrived: 'Citizen Larrey is to present himself before the Committee of Public Safety.' Nobody obeyed such a summons without anxiety.

'Citizen Larrey, we know that you have given first aid to an Austrian prince, and then set him free.' Denunciations are the most abundant fruit of troubled times. Larrey admitted the facts, but claimed that the patient whom he set free had just suffered amputation and never again would be fit to bear arms. 'Hold yourself at the disposition of the Committee.' The Committee of Public Safety only ever pronounced one sentence – death! Larrey hastened to explain matters to his compatriot, Barère, deputy for the Hautes Pyrenées and a ferocious 'Montagnard'. 'I will do what I can,' said his friend, 'but you had better disappear for a while.'

After a quiet, lightning marriage to Marie-Elisabeth, Larrey joined the XIV Army of the Republic at Toulon, under orders for Corsica. It was there that Bonaparte first met him in the autumn of 1794. We know that the expedition to Corsica never left France and Larrey's career took him elsewhere, most importantly, to Egypt.

On 1 November 1800, Larrey was appointed Surgeon-in Chief of the Consular Guard and retained this post when it became the Imperial Guard. On 16 August 1804, he was – like Percy – one of those in the spectacular and primary batch to be decorated with the Legion of Honour. On 2 December 1804, he was invited as an Inspector-General of the Army Medical Services (there were four, including Percy) to the coronation ceremony. He was thankful that the police, then very active, did not find a note which he had written to his wife after that memorable day: 'It was with profound distress that I saw the illustrious warrior grasp the sceptre of kings. Everything leads me to conclude that this instrument of tyranny will be the direct cause of the downfall and ruin of France.'

From a strictly historical view point, 'direct' is the only word to question. His conviction did not prevent Larrey from facing the tyrant respectfully and even as a good courtier – as who would not? He did not seek the personal favours which his position as chief surgeon to a *corps d'élite* offered, but took advantage of his position on behalf of his sick and wounded to ensure that the Guard's ambulance service was exemplary, even lavish, rounded-off by a sedentary ambulance and two mobile field hospitals which, on campaign, were set up when the column halted. It did not matter that, the equipment not having arrived in time, Larrey, his colleagues and their nurses often had to improvise from what was to hand, as in the past. For Percy, who was not of the Guard, the task was much harder.

When he was a child, no one had told Pierre-François Percy 'You will be a surgeon.' In fact what his father, Claude Percy, himself a military surgeon and little satisfied with his lot, had said was: 'I would rather strangle my children than see them military surgeons. You will be an engineer.' But Pierre-François (nine brothers and sisters, five of whom died young) had no gift for mathematics. His father had finally to agree to letting him follow his inclination – 'the call of ancestry'.

Initially the career of Pierre-François Percy, senior surgeon to the cavalry regiment of de Berry at twenty-eight, had been scholarly and academic, marked by prizes and distinctions awarded for of competitions and publications, many of which held sway as standard practice in operating techniques. No battlefields; the Army of the North, then that of the Moselle, then the Army of the Rhine. From the outset of his second career, Percy exposed himself to enemy fire (thrice wounded) and to the hostility of the War Administration. He was the first to claim – forcefully but in vain – a minimum of autonomy for the medical service. I have told how, while Larrey was launching the idea of his 'flying ambulances', Percy was creating 'mobile ambulances', which were much less impressive than those designed by the chief surgeon of the Guard. Comically, the surgeons and ordelies would arrive on the battlefield astride a sausage-shaped vehicle (*Wurst*) adapted from an artillery caisson, drawn by four horses. Each of these vehicles carried eight surgeons and eight aides plus a chest containing first-aid equipment. Alas, these uncomfortable but utilitarian vehicles were even later in arriving than the Guard's medical service and often did not arrive at all, the War Administration having refused to provide any. Another of Percy's ideas was that military hospitals and ambulances should bear a distinctive sign and should be regarded as neutral. 'The enemy wounded', declared this humane man, 'will be taken to hospital along with our own men. After receiving first aid, they would be returned to their respective armies.' General Moreau, in support of this noble project, wrote to the Austrian General de Kary proposing a convention. Reply, No! Neutral hospitals would be detrimental to military operations.

Wounds on the battlefield more readily inspired pity than the colics, eruptions, nose-bleeds, and besides, after Austerlitz, the soldiers of the Grande

Armée, like their Russian and Austrian enemies, had encountered in the hospital at Brunn an enemy as redoubtable as bayonets, muskets and cannonballs: in a few weeks, twelve thousand soldiers died from typhus. This enemy had emanated from the churches to which the Russian wounded had been transported. Already repugnantly dirty on arrival, they became indescribably so after a few days. A good proportion of the sick were sent to France. At each stop, they spread the infection. Percy, then inspector of military hospitals (he would be appointed chief surgeon of the Grande Armée in 1806), had been ordered to organise the hospitals requisitioned in Vienna which, after Austerlitz, also received typhoid patients. According to Larrey, Percy and his assistant, Coste, 'succeeded in curing most of them'. Percy had been a pioneer of hospital hygiene. His paper entitled: 'On the health of the troops of the Grande Armée' had saved as many lives as had the scalpels. One must admire this good-hearted Percy in that he never became discouraged, despite the pessimistic realism with which he viewed the condition of the army's doctors and surgeons: 'To the bureaucrats, we resemble the priests whom custom assigns to the dying. One cares little whether they assure the salvation of souls or help the dying to confront death. They are necessary, that is all. Their absence would provoke scandal.'

At Austerlitz, the entire Grande Armée had fought while doped with alcohol taken on empty stomachs. To restrain it later was impossible. After the armistice on 4 December, the troops had but one idea – food. Ham, bacon, cheese, sweets, no matter what, so long as it was food. This state of affairs lasted for several days, but when hunger had been appeased, thoughts turned again to wine and spirits. After three weeks of orgies, the region was ruined and depleted. At the end of December, a rumour went around: 'Peace has been signed. We are returning to France.' It was true. Austria had signed the Treaty of Pressburg on 26 December 1805. The troops recalled the proclamation of the evening of Austerlitz: 'When everything necessary to ensure the happiness and prosperity of our country has been accepted, I shall lead you back to France.' The Emperor kept his word.

More marching, but without haste. The Emperor had himself written to Berthier: 'I suggest that you only have the troops make very short marches – four-league stages with a rest every three days. They must not be too fatigued by excessively long marches; let there be no stragglers and ensure that their return in no way resembles a rout.'

In Bavaria, in Swabia, in Franconia, the postilions trotting past, announced: 'They are coming!' The inhabitants, ruined by the first passage of these 'allies', ruined again by the advance and retreat of the Austrians, wrung their hands: what to do, where to go? Flight was impossible – the Grande Armée was moving on too broad a front by twenty routes. Everywhere, the same cry: 'Here they are! Here they come!'

Napoleon was wise to suggest that any appearance of a rout be avoided. Since leaving Boulogne and Holland the victors of Austerlitz had covered more than 1,500 kilometres, and they looked more like tramps or *mardi gras* revellers in disguise. The once glittering uniforms were now in tatters, discoloured and stained, and some items had been replaced by Austrian military and civilian clothing. The cavalry's headgear was crumpled, or had been patched-up by village shoemakers. The locals watched this procession of harlequins with astonishment, but there was no laughter or mockery. These 'clowns' had crushed and swept away the best regiments of the Tsar and the Emperor of Austria. They had seen the columns of prisoners marching towards France.

The villagers shed something of their terror on observing that the French soldiers were less savage, less destructive than during their march in the opposite direction. They no longer arrived by night to begin smashing up everything. Detachments preceded them, posting notices in French and German: 'The soldiers must have each morning some bread and brandy; soup, boiled beef and vegetables at dinner; and a good vegetable soup at night.' They had to be provided with a half-pot of wine or a pot of beer at dinner (the midday meal) and supper. In fact, the soldiers always demanded more – bacon, onions (they all wanted onions in their stew). True, they ransacked the cellars, but it was not so bad after all – it could be much worse.

The troops had certainly seen worse. This return by short stages was a picnic. There was time to clean up and make oneself presentable. From time to time they arrived at a town which had not been too stricken, or where the inhabitants were welcoming, amiable even – almost as if they were back in France. The columns were occasionally held up by the slow progress of the contingent of females, always more or less disorganised, 'on their backsides' said the troops. For some of the troops it was the good life. And the essential was that they were moving in the right direction.

It is remarkable that the orders which, at intervals of several days during the second half of February, had halted various corps of the Grande Armée had not provoked a general riot. Official reports mention 'serious discontent' which offers food for speculation. But there was no indiscipline. The men believed they were merely stopping for a few days, to reprovision, to give the towns in France time to prepare a triumphal reception, to receive new uniforms before entering France. Rumours flew through the returning army. The days passed. Anger subsided. No man or beast can resign himself to waiting as can the soldier. The troops said: '*Le Tondu* knows what he is doing.' Finally it transpired that the army would occupy the country until the Austrians had executed all the clauses of the peace treaty. The occupation lasted seven months. It went well because the army was bound for the good times; life was pleasant and there were good relations between the army and the populace. They were allies, after all.

With great ingenuity, and a bit of help from the German women, the soldiers had cleaned up their uniforms. Smart and clean, freshly shaven, they were the valued escorts to the Sunday balls; no rapes, but idylls. Soldiers were seen carrying the baskets of the ladies. Some husbands, of course, were unhappy and the army left behind a good crop of bastards and girl-mothers. But on the whole, was it not preferable to leave children behind rather than cadavers? The officers, compulsorily fed at their hosts' tables, led a peaceful, often rather dull, life. Visits to friends billeted nearby, smoke, play cards, a few receptions at the locals – and, of course, women. The life of the garrison. Let us also note that a good third of the generals, colonels and other field officers were on leave in France. The Emperor was at Saint-Cloud. The Grande Armée was widely spread over Bavaria and Württemberg.

'Napoleon is a monster that has emerged from the mire.' These unwelcoming words emanated from a delicious mouth. Louise von Mecklenburg-Strelitz, Queen of Prussia, was one of the most beautiful women of her time. Every man who came into contact with her was as if transformed, as were even the women. Her perfect carriage, her shoulders and breasts were incomparable, her white hands, scarlet lips, added to her black eyes and streaming blond hair, have been lauded by every historian. Even Napoleon, whom she execrated: 'A beautiful queen wishes to survey the fighting.' Brought up, as in the time of Frederick II, 'in the Parisian manner', she spoke and wrote French better than German. Conscious of her powers and anxious to please, this romantic was the star of the European courts; Frederick-William, Crown Prince of Prussia, was smitten at sight. They were married in 1793, and acceded to the Prussian throne in 1797. Frederick-William III has been treated roughly by the historians, partly because he cut a poor figure beside his dazzling wife. Handsome, a fine horseman, but assessed as 'without much bottom, provincial, irresolute, slow-witted, hypocritical, characterless'. Jealous, and very much in love with his wife, he wanted only a narrow circle of friends and his ADCs around him.

Daily life at the court at Berlin was dismal. The visit of Tsar Alexander I in October 1805 was a welcome distraction. To receive the sovereign of the immense empire was an honour and the Tsar was young and glamorous. He embraced Frederick-William and then his queen 'with a quite remarkable effusion of sentiment'. 'Madam, a thousand obstacles have prevented me from earlier laying my homage at your feet.'

Louise, charmed and enthusiastic, saw herself a national heroine at a stroke. At this time, Napoleon was distributing thrones to members of his family, reshaping Europe, developing a 'Confederation of the Rhine' of which he was the Protector and which was tied to France. This made him the *bête noire* of every sovereign not already enslaved. Louise was resolved, with Alexander's help, to bring about the downfall of this monster emerged from the mire. With difficulty, she persuaded her irresolute husband to sign the Treaty of Potsdam (3 November 1805) which placed Prussia in the camp of France's enemies. To give greater meaning to the ceremony, Louise conceived a ceremony which she endowed with an impressive mysticism. She, her husband and the Tsar crossed the park of Potsdam by night to the little church called the Garrison. They lit torches, which they had brought under their cloaks, and made their way through a narrow doorway to the two plain wooden coffins that held the remains of the Elector of Brandenburg and Frederick the Great, august founders of the Prussian dynasty.

Louise was wrapped in a black cloak 'which set off the paleness of her admirable face'. Hands extended, they swore a triple vow. This secret solemnity in no way hindered the Tsar from ratifying on 23 February 1806 a treaty which his minister, Haugwitz, had signed on the 15th under the unrelenting eye of Napoleon. This he did reluctantly, having no choice except the treaty or war. The treaty provided specifically that Prussia would forbid British Royal Navy ships to enter the rivers feeding into the Baltic and the North Sea. An imbroglio concerning Hanover, which was a British possession, gave Frederick a pretext for denouncing the treaty, which he would have done in any case, under pressure from his wife. Louise regarded any agreement with Napoleon as an intolerable humiliation – 'We will make war', and had him give her the Regiment of Anspach which was thereafter known as the 'Regiment of the Queen's Dragoons'. She could be seen galloping at the head of her regiment, laced into a scarlet tunic (the regimental colours) 'trimmed with sable and lace which embraced discreetly an opening in the front of her corsage. Her blond, silky hair floating behind her seemed to mix with the golden lanyards of her shako with its black visor.' Thus Louise appeared at the head of her regiment parading at Berlin in August 1806. Frederick-William had by then decided on war and even wished to take the initiative in operations. Berlin was full of wild boasting; General Blücher declared that he would get to Paris with his cavalry alone. Prussian officers sharpened their sabres on the steps of the French embassy, while their colonel (or the king himself or the queen: the remark has been generously attributed) exclaimed:

'No need for swords; clubs are sufficient for these French dogs!'
Napoleon, apprised of this sentiment, aware of these warlike preparations, wrote again (12 September) to Frederick-William that he would regret having to declare war, but he wrote that same day to Berthier, who was at Munich, ordering him to put the Grande Armée in movement.

Louis-Alexandre Berthier, Prince of Neuchâtel and Wagram, Vice-Constable, Marshal of the Empire, was both Major-General and Minister of War. He wrote at least twice a day to Napoleon, who was still at Saint-Cloud. A briefcase containing their letters was transmitted from courier to courier who, barring accidents, took 96 hours to get from Munich to Saint-Cloud. In other words, to pose a question and receive a reply took more than a week. True the Chiappe telegraph connected Paris and Strasbourg, but it could hardly be used in view of the need for secrecy. Such a delay made Berthier's task even more onerous because he, like all the chiefs of staff, had to re-edit Napoleon's instructions into detailed orders – and Napoleon did not hesitate to plunge into details.

Here one must give some idea of the huge machine which was Berthier's staff. There was first, the 'major-general's private staff' – the twenty or so aides-de-camp, superb young officers (white dolmans with gold braid; scarlet trousers) riding horses as beautiful as themselves, assisted by liaison officers. Secondly, the 'office' – a self-effacing organisation concerned with practicalities, manned by the officers responsible for liaison with the various services, finance and troop movements, and assisted by civilians or non-combatants. Over and above this private staff was the general staff: three generals ('senior general aides') assisted by ADCs and some twenty staff officers, divided into 'adjutants commandant' of colonel's rank and 'staff assistants' (captains), plus the topographical section, the artillery staff, the engineers, the grand park of the army (the train, horse artillery, munitions), plus the administrative services under Daru. Inevitably, the orders from the authorities of the various services were often duplicated or contradictory, and even the most intelligent officer introduced into this gold-laced antheap, would find it bewildering at first. Berthier directed the machine unerringly and smoothly – though hardly ever without tormenting himself with worry.

Himself unfitted for high command, Berthier was a subordinate of genius. His talent for translating the orders of Napoleon and putting his directives into effect was such that, in the opinion of many military experts, 'it is often difficult to apportion the credit for a given victory between him and Napoleon'. Some have even said: 'Ah, if Berthier had been at Waterloo!' (he died eighteen days earlier).

Berthier was born amid the pomp of Versailles. His father, commander-in-chief of the topographical engineers of the royal army, author of 'the hunting maps of the king' and of the plans of the ministries of war, marine and foreign affairs, had been ennobled by Louis XV. He had encouraged Louis towards the engineer's art, taking care to foster his natural talents for order and method which Napoleon was so much to appreciate.

Berthier became the richest of all the marshals of the Empire (more than a million francs in various gifts), the most congratulated, the most decorated. And the most abused. One day, when Bonaparte, as First Consul, was considering what title he should assume as sovereign, Talleyrand suggested maliciously to Berthier: 'Go and tell him that he had best have himself proclaimed king.' Berthier pushed aside a group of courtiers and made his little speech. Madame de Rémusat recalled the scene. A furious Bonaparte pushed Berthier against a wall and shook his fist under his nose: 'Imbecile, who induced you to come and arouse my bile? Another time, do not take on such errands.'

Berthier was an unattractive person: small, poorly built, head too large, ugly hands with bitten nails which he would hide by thrusting them into his pockets; then, suddenly, he would pick his nose. He was very courteous in his dealings with other officers, and Napoleon appreciated being able to call him, if necessary, six times in a single night – and he would arrive fully dressed, and answer instantly any question concerning the situation and strength of any unit. On his good days, and to compensate for the public insults, Napoleon heaped on him marks of his appreciation. He chose him to go and present his portrait to Marie-Louise, when asked in marriage. Having shown the portrait, Berthier said: 'In fact, the Emperor resembles me.' The young girl was horrified. In 1805, before the great departure of the Grande Armée, Berthier had offered the Emperor a hunt at his château de Grosbois. As there were no rabbits on his property, he purchased one thousand, which were turned loose on the day of the hunt. The guests left the château for the hunt, when a mass of long-eared animals came running towards them, getting underfoot and nearly causing Napoleon to fall. The seller had sent tame rabbits and they thought that they were about to be fed. All Napoleon said, laughingly, was: 'Poor Berthier.'

On the other hand, the Marshal's liaison with the marchioness Visconti irritated Napoleon. As general commanding the Army of Italy, Bonaparte had been wearied by the advances of this no longer young but still very beautiful Milanese. In order to be rid of her, he had thrown her into the arms of his chief of staff, Berthier, still a bachelor at forty. Berthier became immediately and irrevocably besotted by this woman. A little later, and married, he had shown himself still bewitched and was desolate when the war separated him from his idol. He wrote letters to her that were passionate to the point of indecency. Some of these were intercepted by the British, who had copies distributed throughout Europe. Napoleon referred to the affair as 'Berthier's folly', but it was he who had started it.

On 3 October 1806, Napoleon arrived at Würzburg from Saint-Cloud. At Bamberg on the 7th he received a ridiculous ultimatum from Frederick-William, insisting that the French army retreat behind the Rhine. On the 8th the troops heard another proclamation: 'Soldiers! The order for your return to France had already been given and triumphal celebrations awaited you. But war cries came from Berlin. We are challenged by an audacity which demands vengeance. Soldiers! There is not one of you who would return to France other than on the road of honour; we must only return under triumphal arches. What! Have we braved the seasons, the seas and the deserts, beaten a Europe repeatedly united against us, carried our glory from the Orient to the Occident only to return home like deserters, having abandoned our allies and hearing that the French eagle was terrified by the Prussian armies?'

Once more, moving and effective rhetoric. The troops had shown some resentment when the march towards France was halted; rather less when the march east had resumed because the deception had become blurred in their minds, distant. Now Napoleon had found a means to make the resumption of war acceptable. It was the King of Prussia who was preventing the army from returning to France in glory. For each soldier it was now a personal matter between him and the King of Prussia – whose name he did not even know. What did he think he was doing, this fellow? Did he think he could do better than the Austrians and Russians united? They would put him in his place. 'The Prussians insult us,' wrote Lieutenant Putigny. 'We will reduce them to sausages and show the King of Prussia and his wife, this uniformed queen, this dragoon in skirts, that it is the French who wear the trousers!'

Forward! 128,000 infantrymen, 28,000 cavalry, 10,000 artillerymen and other troops, 256 cannon. It was necessary – once more – to snatch the initiative from the enemy by speed, to prevent the Prussians from establishing themselves on the Elbe and bar the road to Berlin.

The Grande Armée advanced in three columns: on the left, Lannes and Augereau: in the centre, Bernadotte, Davout, plus the Guard and the cavalry reserve: on the right, Soult and Ney. The columns were separated from one another by 10, 20, 30 kilometres – the distances varying as the three columns parted, reunited, crossed. The soldier knew nothing of these grand manoeuvres, all he knew was the order – once more – to march or die, as before Ulm, as before Austerlitz. The terrain was hilly, even mountainous, cut by rivers and gorges and laced with forests, yet Soult's corps between 9 and 13 October covered nearly 180 kilometres in 40 hours. The average for the bulk of the army was 36 to 39 kilometres per day; the scouting units, the patrols and the flank-guards covered even more.

There was no question of billets; the troops marched from one bivouac to the next, completing the day's stage in darkness at some village or hamlet where there was never enough shelter even if the dwellings were intact. Within an hour, the place would be totally demolished. There was no physical violence because the inhabitants had fled. 'The army is a torrent flooding the region at a dizzy speed and in indescribable disorder.' Disorder at the level of the rank and file, but the great chief, bent over his maps, once again canalised the torrents. On 9 October Napoleon reached Ebersdorf where he received the reports of Berthier,

Soult, and Murat (who, with Bernadotte, was leading the vanguard) plus the spies' reports – nothing was forgotten, multilingual officers in civilian clothes preceded the army and infiltrated. For several hours he dictated his orders: 'Beyond a doubt, Gera is the junction point of the enemy army, but I doubt they will be able to make the junction before me.'

They must get to Gera with all dispatch, bar the road to Dresden and Berlin and push the enemy westwards. A general order to march towards Schleiz (95 kilometres SSW of Leipzig). Napoleon arrived at this small town, already in the hands of Bernadotte, and issued further orders to the marshals: the second leap will be to Gera (45 kilometres NNE of Schleiz). At Gera, on 11 October at 3 a.m., Napoleon sent for his coach and reached Auma two hours later, where, for reasons of convenience, the HQ and the Guard had been installed. The inhabitants had had no time to flee; some officers entered a barber-shop to be shaved. The owner started work, but suddenly dropped his razor – he had just seen through the window two grenadiers leading away his only cow, certainly not with the intention of milking her. 'My cow!' The general whom he was shaving, his face covered in soap, snapped 'Return the cow!'

Meanwhile the Emperor had received a message from Murat: The enemy was retiring westwards. On the 12th Napoleon reached Gera; Lannes was at Jena (45 kilometres west of Gera). It was between Jena and Weimar (20 kilometres further west) that Napoleon had decided to give battle at the critical point. The army continued its advance unimpeded.

The King of Prussia planned to destroy this army with the following forces: the army of Lieutenant-General von Rüchel, 30,000 men, including General Blücher's 5,000 cavalry; the main army of the Marshal-Duke of Brunswick, commanding von Möllendorf and von Kalkreuth, 70,000 to 75,000 men in all; the army of the Prince of Hohenlohe, 50,000 men whose vanguard (10,000 men) was commanded by Prince Louis, the king's nephew; as a reserve corps, the 15,000 men of the Prince of Württemberg.

On 10 October, during their passage of the River Saale in front of Saalfeld, this force encountered General Suchet's vanguard of Marshal Lannes' V Corps. Saalfeld (40 kilometres SSW of Jena), capital of the Duchy of Coburg, is a small, ancient walled town. The Saale is bordered on both banks by steep hills, forested and wild. The Prussian infantry had retired before the vigorous attack of Suchet's troops. Prince Louis, with the aid of some field police, was trying to rally the beaten troops when a Sergeant-Major Guindey of the 10th Hussars rushed him at sabre point: 'Surrender, General, or you are a dead man.' The prince exclaimed in French: 'Me surrender? Never!' Parrying Guindey's thrust, he slashed at his face with his sabre. He was about to aim a second blow when Guindey ran him through.

A little later, when the French infantry had occupied the courtyard of the ducal château, an officer announced that Marshal Lannes was coming and 'wished to quarter himself at the château and required a supper for thirty persons'. Shortly afterwards, the marshal's baggage arrived, several carriages, some servants, and, finally, followed by a glittering escort, the marshal himself. He had himself announced to the duke. Amélie de Huttenhoven, a lady of the court of Coburg, left a fine description of the aftermath of the battle of Saalfeld: 'During the reception, an officer arrived to announce the death of Prince Louis Ferdinand and delivered his decorations. The following day, 11 October at 11 a.m., a detachment of French troops, most of a company, left the battlefield and marched on the château, headed by a band playing a joyous march. In the cortège was a stretcher on which was apparently a human corpse. The procession entered the courtyard in the middle of which the band ceased to play and the body was placed on the ground. Marshal Lannes and his staff entered the courtyard and approached the bier. The corpse, without uniform, was covered by a torn cloak. The Count of Mensdorf (son of the Duke of Coburg) recognised Prince Louis and could not hide his indignation at the dance music which had accompanied the cortège of a prince of the royal house. He insisted to the marshal that the body be suitably carried to the city church and buried in consecrated ground. The marshal gave his orders: the band played a funeral march and the procession, under the Count of Mensdorf, moved off, followed across the city by a large crowd.'

Napoleon dictated his orders and they were carried out. Piecemeal, and with enormous effort, the troops sorted themselves out from the welter of bivouacs and coalesced into three columns which made their way up to the position where the great captain had decided to strike the enemy an unexpected blow. He knew that when the moment arrived the Grande Armée would prove a solid weapon in his hand. Larrey had real grounds for disquiet regarding his services.

Chief Surgeon to the Guard, Larrey had arranged for his doctors and surgeons not to be dismissed (with a derisory payment) at the end of each campaign. With the resumption of the war, his service was organised and ready to hand. The other troops had no medical staff when they marched off on a new campaign. It fell to the Surgeon-in-Chief of the Grande Armée to recall, by letters and dispatches, those practitioners willing to rejoin the service.

'Just for my ambulances,' Percy had said at the start of the Prussian campaign, 'I must have ten senior surgeons, twenty surgeons and sixty assistant surgeons, all qualified. And I must provide for all the hospitals used by the Grande Armée in the towns to the rear as well as for the temporary evacuation hospitals. According to the estimates, there would be two thousand sick or wounded at Würzburg, six hundred at Bamberg, a thousand at Anspach, six hundred at

Nuremberg and two thousand at Frankfurt.' These figures would be substantially exceeded; at the least, some two hundred surgeons were needed. Replies from those who had returned to France were slow in coming. The situation would have been disastrous, had Percy not been able to call on the native surgeons from the occupied or allied countries. He also knew that he could retain and use all enemy surgeons taken prisoner. When he saw the Bamberg hospital, superb, modern for its day, and well organised, he congratulated his colleague, the Bavarian Doctor Marcus: 'Just so long', as he said in an aside to one of his assistants, 'as the Commissioners for War do not come and interfere with matters here.'

The picture was darker as regards *matériel.* At Bamberg, 'nothing had arrived, no linen, no flannel, no boxes of instruments. Lacking means of transport, all remained at the rear; what a calamity!' The first consignments 'arrived in peasant carts, soaked and damaged. One of the carts carried crutches and wooden legs, which provoked laughter and comment from the troops. They could have been spared this.' In the looted villages, the chief surgeon, a pillager by force of circumstance, had the houses searched in the hope of finding a little linen which, with flannel, the assistants could cut up for dressings. Transportation became increasingly archaic: '13 October, our four-oxen carriage carries two surgeons, baggage and two casks of good wine, the fruits of pillage at Gera.' Percy went to great lengths to find good wine and brandy to fortify the wounded; in those days, such therapy was held to be normal. 'The road is bad, climbing and descending, deep and narrow. On 14th, left for Jena; we had not covered two leagues before we began to hear the cannon.'

The ducal château of Jena was a large building in the French style; we know that at one time everything had to be built in imitation of Versailles. From the windows facing the town one could see a pretty range of brown-tiled roofs, narrow, winding streets and many towers, bulbous and gilded. All such charm has vanished as if the Grande Armée had never existed, thanks to an Allied bombing raid in 1944.

Napoleon arrived at the château on 13 October 1806 at about 4 p.m., but left again immediately by the Weimar gate, escorted by his Chasseurs. Presently, in the recently harvested vineyards, they came to 'a road as narrow as a roof ridge' and were obliged to dismount. The Emperor climbed the Landgrafenberg, a huge butte overlooking the town, dominating the valley of the Saale on the one side, and on the other the plain of Weimar. Napoleon had decided that this height would serve as the point of departure for the offensive battle which he was preparing. Most of the Prussian army was bivouacked farther to the northwest, slightly south of Auerstadt; it was to march next morning.

Having examined his proposed theatre of operations, Napoleon returned to the town (narrowly escaping death from a sentry, having failed to answer his 'Who goes there?'), but then went back to the plateau; on this eve of battle, he wished to 'sleep in the midst of his soldiers', surrounded by the Guard. He had chosen his bivouac; in an hour the grenadiers built him a cabin roofed with straw mats; the servants installed his camp bed, table, campaign armchair, his baggage and two chairs; a dip in the terrain gave access, but only a small fire was lit; this order applied to the entire army; three fires only to a company of 220 men – and it was cold. To temper this austerity, Napoleon had authorised his grenadiers to search for provisions in the town, most of the population of which had fled. 'We found everything that we needed,' wrote Coignet. 'In 45 minutes we were on the return journey, loaded with wine, sugar, cauldrons and provisions of every kind.' The Emperor had invited the marshals to his bivouac, where the food seemed less elaborate than that of the troops: buttered potatoes, cold meats, sweet dishes, hardtack, with, however, the excellent wine of Jena. After a rapid supper, the great man entered his cabin, threw himself on his bed and went to sleep. 'The Emperor slept little,' according to the Operations Journal of V Corps. 'The great event which he was planning might obsess him, but it was difficult to see any sign of it. S.M. had never appeared more calm nor more satisfied.' In fact, Napoleon wished to check every factor up to the last moment. Awakened two hours later, he left to visit the outposts with Lannes, Suchet, Soult and Savary. He returned and was seen bent over his maps, lit only by a few candle-ends. A secretary was seated on a bale of hay. At 2 a.m. there was a report that some of the artillery which was trying to climb the slopes of the Landgrafenberg had got stuck in a rocky defile, the first wagon blocking the road. 'I am going.'

When he arrived the engineers were already at work on the walls with pick-axes to widen the road. The Emperor mounted a hillock at the side of the ravine and gave various orders ('His Majesty deigned to come and encourage the work by his presence.'). Two hours later the artillery was able to advance. The great captain knew that wherever he appeared, efforts were redoubled. He also knew that he must address the troops again: 'Soldiers! The Prussian army is split as was Mack's at Ulm at the same stage; they will only fight to escape. Any unit that gives way will be dishonoured.'

Once again, Napoleon's strategy had already succeeded. Before daybreak on 14 October 1806, the proclamation had been read to the troops and the Emperor had ridden on horseback in front of them by lantern-light. At first light, the mist was as thick as it had been at Austerlitz.

The battle began at 7 a.m. 'The entire army advanced without being able to see one pace in front, but touching the file in front like blinded men, stumbling one against the next', wrote Coignet. 'Hearing noises of movement to our front, we realised that we should halt and prepare to attack. The wretched fog still hampered us but our columns still marched forward and we still had terrain to identify. At about 10 a.m. the sun showed us on a fine plateau and we could see our hands before our faces.'

The most complete accounts of the Battle of Jena are to be found in the two studies by Michel de Lombarès published in *Revue Historique de l'Armée*, nos. 2, 1948 and 2, 1949. It must be borne in mind that Napoleon gave battle with some 50,000 men against an enemy about equal in numbers (Prince Hohenlohe's army) and that by midday some 30,000 men had arrived to reinforce the French forces.

Napoleon had an updated file (Berthier had a copy) on the Prussian army, showing its strengths and dispositions. A great admirer of Frederick II and, to a degree of infatuation, of his genius for military organisation, he tended to over-estimate the Prussian army which, at the time of Jena, was fifty years behind the times.

Their generals were too old. Napoleon was 37, Brunswick, 71; Davout was 36, Soult, Lannes and Ney were 37, Hohenlohe, 60; Blücher, 64; Möllendorf, 81. Gravity and plodding deliberation. To the Prussian troops, a march of four or five leagues was a forced march, an exploit; it moved at a snail's pace with its numberless wagons and carriages of provisions and *matériel*. At each halt, there was no question of billeting on the locals (or of demolishing a village to build shelters); a virtual city of tents was erected to be struck down on the morrow. Before each march, there was an inspection and the troops had to be as well-turned out as before a review at Potsdam. The same hierarchical discipline governed the battlefield. The mandarin marshals and generals were convinced that the secret of victory handed down from Frederick II consisted of rigid and precise evolutions, impeccable and interminable; majesty before everything.

This iron discipline had made automatons of the soldiers who executed commands without thought of death, never moving an arm or a leg unless ordered. Now, at Jena, this machine was to creak to a halt; the soldier-automatons were taken aback. What sort of an enemy was this who disregarded the rules of the game, who did not advance in rigid formations? Despite a heavy and murderous fire, the French advanced from every direction, drums beating. The French, whom the Prussian officers had always represented to their men as being despicable bunglers (the most commonly used expression), were also painted as frightful atheists – atheists maybe, but they were also diabolical. So the Prussian infantry gave way. Rapid victory, some historians have even used the term lightning victory, unfolded between Jena, Naumburg and Weimar on a vast spread of undulating plateaux, some scarped, some crossed by streams, dotted with bulbous-spired villages and surrounded by hedges and gardens.

At 6 a.m. Lannes had been ordered to attack; battle was joined at 9 o'clock when the fog had dissipated. Three Prussian battalions attacked Suchet's troops, two battalions repulsed them. Lannes occupied the whole plateau in front of the Landgrafenberg. Augereau closed; the Prussian defeat began to be apparent; the Grande Armée faced west, as provided in Napoleon's plan. Prussian alarm; Hohenlohe sends 21 battalions and 38 squadrons to the assault of a village (Vierzehn-Heiligen – Fourteen Saints) which is taken amid cries of victory, but Napoleon's reserves continue to flow in, the enemy is thrown off balance and Murat arrives with his dragoons and cuirassiers.

Beyond this abstract technical picture was the reality of war. Rapid victory; the Prussian automatons had not held, but listen to the evidence of Sergeant Lavaux: 'In less than two minutes, by a salvo of cannon, we lost 300 men of our regiment. My hat was lost to the wind of a cannon-ball. I fell backwards and could not rise, as seven or eight men fell on top of me and I was unable to free myself from these unfortunates, some of whom had their arms and legs shot off. I was in no hurry to stand up and played dead until the storm had passed. After a minute, I raised my head a little and saw the regiment, which was still piled up and in confusion. I saw that I could rejoin them without danger; the ground was so covered with dead and wounded that one could not walk without treading upon some of these unfortunates. Some cried: "Comrades, help me!" Others said: "Have pity and lift these men off me." Some, their limbs blown off, cried "Vive l'Empereur!"'

These torn and mutilated men crying 'Vive l'Empereur!' We shall see and hear them thousands of times, often evidenced by their seniors. What is one to think? How many wounded and dying men actually cried this? The legend has embraced many of the most simple accounts, the most convincing, for a start. What is certain is that during the course of this battle Napoleon was seen galloping all over the field and to claim that he was risking his life was no exaggeration.

The Guard 'had not been engaged'. According to some accounts, there was grumbling and the Emperor had reprimanded some skirmishers who, as he crossed ahead of them, cried 'Forward!' 'What the hell? No beardless youngster can tell me what to do. Let him wait until he has directed thirty pitched battles before he presumes to give me advice.'

Tradition has it that two French Hussars, seeing the Queen of Prussia surrounded by young officers, had charged the group, shouting bawdy insults concerning the treatment they intended for her, but her horse outdistanced them and she escaped towards Weimar. 'We saw on the right an elegant carriage and some white horses which we were told was the Queen of Prussia escaping,' wrote Coignet. We can be sure that the beautiful Louise did show herself somewhere along the front.

According to von der Goltz, at 2 p.m. the Prussian army resembled a 'river of fugitives'. Möllendorf had found a glorious end which an octogenarian had no right to expect, but many young lives were also harvested: 15,000 dead or wounded; 15,000 taken prisoner and 200 cannon captured. At 5 o'clock next morning at the château of Jena Napoleon dictated orders to the marshals to pursue the routed enemy. At 8 o'clock he summoned the captured Saxon officers and, with Lefebvre as interpreter, delivered a clever little homily explaining that they ought to regard their erstwhile allies, the Prussians, as their oppressors and their enemy. He, Napoleon, was their liberator and the best thing that Saxony could do would be to join the Confederation of the Rhine. He then dictated a sheaf of letters beginning: 'The battle of Jena will be one of the most celebrated in history.'

The victory on 14 October could equally well have been called the victory of Auerstadt, but Napoleon was not to have news of it until he reached Weimar that evening. At Auerstadt, III Corps, 25,000 men under Davout, suddenly found itself facing the largest of the Prussian armies, that of the Duke of Brunswick, whose 70,000 men had been taken under the personal command of Frederick-William. It was a situation where mere risk-taking would be insufficient.

Davout acted unhesitatingly and showed himself a good tactician, as did his generals, and at Auerstadt even more than at Jena the drive and flexibility of his well-trained troops had triumphed over automatic obedience. The victory was costly to the French – a quarter of their strength – but the enemy was routed. Fewer details have survived about Auerstadt because the Emperor was not there. The editors of the *Bulletin* and others responsible for public relations knew very well on whom they should train their projectors. Napoleon could not divert them from his august person, but when the campaign was over, in 1808 he was to reward Davout by creating him Duke of Auerstadt.

Look at the portraits of the marshals and generals; how many of them are wearing spectacles? It is true, they were young, but good sight or poor, spectacles were worn less frequently than today. On an officer they would have produced a deplorable effect. Davout, however, wore pince-nez, was prematurely bald, and none too well-groomed 'The dirtiest man, the most unkempt that one could meet,' wrote Laure d'Abrantès. A general under the Consulate, he attended the salons with his boots covered in dung, his nails in mourning and wearing 'a greasy old flannel waistcoat'. But it was generally agreed that it was the pince-nez that was the worst of all.

Louis-Nicolas Davout, born at Annoux (Yonne) on 10 May 1770, was a nobleman however, and very well connected. Of a Burgundian family dating from the XIIIth century, he was destined for a military career. Sub-lieutenant at eighteen, he had found one of his cousins, a major in the Champagne Cavalry, who was the first to express concern that his young relative was near-sighted and a bookworm, spending more time in book shops than on the exercise field: 'He reads philosophy and knows nothing of his profession.' We know that the officers of the *ancien régime* were none too receptive of new ideas, even those who had remained in the army. One day, under the Revolution, when at Hesdin the regiment in which Davout was serving offered a banquet to a regiment on the march. An officer proposed a seditious toast: 'I propose a toast that we all carry in our hearts, even though in this time of liberty we are not permitted to do so, and I flatter myself that there is not one idiot among us who would propose another – to the King's health!' Davout bounded to his feet: 'I, gentlemen, am the idiot of which this gentleman has spoken – to the health of the Nation!'

The time spent in book shops had made Davout one of the most cultivated men in the army, but his appearance and his sombre character worked against him. Desaix had introduced him to Bonaparte, who was preparing the expedition to Egypt. The First Consul's opinion after a first conversation: 'He is a stupid blockhead.' But the great man rapidly changed his opinion. Davout distinguished himself at the Pyramids, at Luxor, at Aboukir. By 1800, he was a divisional general, commanding the cavalry of the Army of Italy; in 1801, inspector of cavalry, commanding the foot grenadiers of the Consular Guard.

At twenty-one, Davout, a fine young fellow, had wisely married another Burgundian two years his senior, a woman of good family. Result: blatantly cuckolded shortly afterwards; divorce after twenty-six months of marriage. The woman died some weeks later in 1801. Davout then married Aimée Leclerc, the sister of General Leclerc; he thus found himself brother-in-law to Pauline Bonaparte. This marriage certainly did not hurt his chances when the Marshals of the Empire were nominated in 1804, but Napoleon had sensed that Davout would be one of his most capable marshals.

The Battle of Jena had begun at about 9 a.m. on 14 October. From 10 o'clock the wounded began to arrive in droves at the church where the surgeons had installed themselves. Amputations! Amputations! A solid body of opinion was against the idea: 'It is better to spare limbs.' Unfortunately, to preserve a limb which had been seriously damaged was generally a forlorn hope: haemorrhage or gangrene usually killed the patient. A properly effected amputation allowed the use of a more 'methodical' ligature and dressing. The surgeons labelled as 'primitive amputation' those that must be performed immediately, as opposed to those that could wait, having been dressed, while the progress of the wound was observed.

By 11 a.m. the church was full. Percy had the wounded taken to any acceptable locality; to the college (high school), the Black Bear inn, 'to the vast vestibule at the municipal hall' and even to the mental hospital. The surgeons, sleeves rolled up and arms smeared with blood, operated with a rapidity and dexterity to which modern medicine has paid tribute; using whatever instruments they had brought in their personal baggage, the military caissons having not arrived. Three days earlier, Percy had prudently purchased a saw from an ironmonger in Schleitz. When the patients had stopped screaming under the saw, they groaned. 'These unfortunates had been laid out almost devoid of straw, most without food or water. Some were terribly wounded. Thousands of Saxons and Prussians had been taken prisoner, including nine surgeons, whom I retained.' Some of the houses in Jena were on fire, wounded men where still arriving, but where could they be put?

Collect the walking wounded; they must go the hospital at Gera. Thirty-five kilometres of hobbling. On the day after the battle, Percy visited the wounded in his 'temporary hospitals' in Jena. 'That morning, these unfortunates were still mired in faeces, or surrounded by the excrement of those who could not rise, by amputated legs and arms, bloodstained cadavers, by the stack which produced the small amount of straw on which they had thrown themselves. Some of them had been given a little bouillon and bread. It is hard to imagine how they had managed to survive up to now. My amputees are doing quite well.'

By now, the Grande Armée had split into two columns and was marching northwards. The left-hand column, led by Murat and the reserve cavalry, followed by the corps of Soult and Ney, was pursuing the fleeing Prussians. For the infantry, it was march or die once more, but they saw hardly any fighting because Murat 'by successive fantastic leaps' struck, destroyed or captured the enemy, as far as Stettin (a fortress with 120 guns), as far as Lübeck, where he rounded up Blücher and such men as he had. The right-hand column – Lannes and Davout – had marched on Berlin. On 11 November, the Magdeburg garrison, 22,000 men, 700 cannon, capitulated and paraded past Ney, who wrote to Napoleon: 'Sire. Fighting is finished for lack of enemies.'

The medical service followed from Jena to Berlin. Percy, Surgeon-in-Chief, continued the role of good reporter. His journal will long be esteemed. 'In the approaches to Weimar, the roads and the fields were full of dead, broken muskets, dead horses. Weimar is a pretty town. I have reserved seven Prussian surgeons from the Weimar hospitals, apparently in good health and all speaking a little French. On leaving, I gave senior surgeon Damiens a saw, old but which cuts well, a large knife and some scalpels. We found Auerstadt totally pillaged, having neither food nor hay.' Note that hay was even more precious than food; a man will march further on an empty stomach than will a horse. 'The immense, fertile plain, already sown for crops, was covered with the dead of both nations, broken gun-carriages, abandoned cannon, muskets, cartridge boxes. The two borders of the road were strewn with cadavers; most of the French ones are still there. Two hours from Naumburg, we met convoys of wagons, loaded with some of the 1,800 wounded, both French and Prussian, who had spent the two previous nights in a village. These unfortunates had spent the night of 17/18 in the wagons, crying from thirst and groaning loudly.'

At Merseburg, forty kilometres further north, the wounded were still groaning because it was almost impossible to find them food and drink. Their wagons were jammed among a huge mass of vehicles and troops. Some 9,000 troops halted in the town and on the outskirts, rumour having it that Napoleon was there and would review them. These were the Guard who had stood at Jena with arms ordered, maybe against their wishes, but in any event – they were not employed. The wounded thought that this parade of the 'Immortals' was unjustified and said as much, but those who had the opportunity on that day (20 October) to see le Tondu cried once more 'Vive l'Empereur!' and the parade had gone off well in perfect weather. Percy saw, with a touch of envy, 'the surgeons of the Guard with M. Larrey at their head, all in full dress, and the nurses in uniform and commanded by an officer wearing decorations.'

The army ran into fog when approaching the Elbe. In all directions stretched an immense sandy plain, with crops of barley, tobacco, beetroot – a peaceful region with villages scattered here and there. Standing in front of their clay-brick cottages, some devastated, the inhabitants mutely watched the convoys of wounded and brought water and whatever they had. On through Dessau and Wittenburg; on approaching Potsdam on 24 October they were met with rain and cold. 'Is there a hospital here?' 'Yes the isolation hospital for the king's battalions.'

The well-kept records showed that the lazaret had capacity for 189 persons; Percy had 2,000 sick and wounded to shelter. Finally, they were lodged, as before, in any space that could be found, even in private dwellings. What an enormous volume would be a history of the wounded of the Grande Armée': of those thousands dispersed across Europe, the majority of the survivors finally rejoining the army and eventually getting back to France after many adventures or perhaps none; and the thousands of others who never saw the army or France again – accepted by a family, having found work on a farm, in town or city, and settled down with a wife. But such a history will never be written and we can but imagine.

Potsdam at this time was a clean town with wide streets and well-sited houses, but it was a military town and the atmosphere was severe, not to say sad. By the time that the French arrived, most of the population had fled. The soldiers bivouacked in the gardens, under the trees in the park of Sans-Souci. Hardly had Napoleon arrived than he visited the quarters of Frederick II, intact, nothing disturbed since the death of the great monarch in 1786. He stood in contemplation in front of the simple work table, opened and skimmed several books in French in the library and took several trophies: the great man's sword and sword-belt, his cordon of the Black Eagle, an alarm clock and the colours of the royal guard during the Seven Years War. 'I prefer these trophies to all the treasures of the King of Prussia. I will show them to my old soldiers who campaigned in Hanover. I will send them to the governor of les Invalides who will keep them as witnesses to the victories of the Grande Armée and of the vengeance exacted for the Rossbach defeats.'

We have seen Frederick-William and the beautiful Queen Louise with their guest the Tsar Alexander I visiting the tomb of Frederick the Great by night in a super-romantic setting, On 26 October, Napoleon himself visited the little garrison church and meditated in front of the simple coffin. He remained there for two minutes, 'still and silent as if absorbed in a profound meditation'.

'Soldiers! You have justified and replied worthily to the confidence of the French people. You are the worthy defenders of my crown and of the glory of the Great Nation. So long as you are inspired by this spirit, nothing can resist you. The cavalry has competed with the infantry and the artillery. I do not know to which arm I should in future confide my preference – you are all good soldiers.' (I have to say that I do not tire of citing these proclamations; few documents in History have come down to us that testify as much as they to the psychological manipulation – the husbandry – of masses of men.)

'Now here are the results of our labours: one of the first military powers of Europe, which had earlier dared to offer us a shameful surrender, has been annihilated. We have taken 60,000 prisoners, captured 65 flags, including those of the Guards of the King of Prussia, 600 artillery pieces, three fortresses, more than 20 generals. Notwithstanding, more than half of you regret not having yet been able to fire a musket. All the Prussian provinces as far as the Oder are in our power. Soldiers, the Russians boast that they will soon be at grips with you. We will spare them half of the distance between us. New armies formed in the interior will take your place. My people, indignant, have risen. Soldiers, I cannot better express the feelings which I have towards you than by saying that I carry you in my heart in return for the love which you daily show me.'

Some days later, Lannes was to write to the Emperor that the last sentences of the proclamation had aroused the troops to a delirious state of enthusiasm: 'All cried on hearing it "Vive l'Empereur of the West!" I cannot tell his Majesty how much these brave men adore him; none of them has harboured such feelings towards his mistress as they do towards your person. I ask that your Majesty will tell me whether I should address future dispatches to the Emperor of the West. I pray for this in the name of my army corps.' It is not known whether Napoleon ever replied to this. In any event, in the midst of these extravagant congratulations, sparkles a little phrase which, we may be sure, had contributed much to the delirious enthusiasm: 'New armies, formed in the interior, will take your place'.

Many tributaries of the Spree crossed Berlin, the capital of Prussia. With 160,000 inhabitants in 1806, it was a large city, but only partly built. The centre looked new, with straight and very wide streets, but paved, like many cities of the time, with pointed stones which were often muddy. These were bordered by two-storeyed houses, private dwellings with brilliant façades, but these 'rich decorations hid here and there black alleys'. The most beautiful avenue, 1,300 metres in length and 60 wide, was planted with four ranks of lindens and chestnuts: *Unter den Linden.* It was along this avenue on Monday, 27 October 1806, that Napoleon chose to make his formal entry from the Brandenburg Gate to the royal palace of Charlottenburg. It had rained torrents the night before, but on that day the sun shone in a blue sky. Here, only a small part of the populace had fled. The shops were open, the curious read the notices posted everywhere, signed by the Prince of Hatzfeldt, governor of the city: 'May the memory of the wise behaviour of the Viennese be retained in our hearts. We must hope that this calm resignation will call down on us the clemency of the victor.' Along the length of *Unter den Linden* the crowd pressed behind the hedge of cuirassiers:
'Here they come!' First the mamelukes, galloping, wheeling this way and that, an exotic parade, an unusual circus. Next, perhaps one hundred paces behind them, a bedizened rider preceded by a detachment of the grenadiers of the Guard. The Berliners, many with lumps in their throats, watched these colossal soldiers in their bearskins. Another gap.
'Here he comes!' Down the wide avenue came a group of horsemen, sparkling with gold, silver and feathers, but ten paces in front a single horseman and it was he who drew all eyes: the Ogre, the Usurper, the Monster emerged from the mire, according to Louise of Prussia. Wearing the famous hat 'bearing one sou as a cockade', the green coat of the undress uniform of a colonel of chasseurs of the Guard, sash of the Grand Eagle of the Legion of Honour, Napoleon rode a grey horse with plaited mane and a saddle and shabraque of purple and gold.' I saw at close range the successor of Frederick the Great,' wrote one Berliner. 'He looked to me to have put on some weight since his latest portraits. His complexion is olive-coloured, his features harmonious, striking. One must be endowed with a rare strength not to bow one's head before that look. His serious, almost austere, look is occasionally lit by a strange smile. The effect which it has is like a sunbeam. Some people applauded the conqueror.'
One horse's length behind Napoleon was Roustam, the mameluke, in his oriental costume. Ten paces to the rear, the glittering group of the staffs: the household with General Duroc, Grand Marshal; Caulaincourt, Master of the Horse; Clarke, secretary of the cabinet; Corbineau, groom to the Empress and

her representative; Gardane, governor of the pages; the aides-de-camp: Generals Lemarois, Savary, Rapp, Bertrand, Mouton and ten staff officers; Marshals Berthier, Davout, Augereau, Bessières with their staffs and their aides-de-camp. Twenty thousand grenadiers and cuirassiers, the Guard, mounted and marching, bands playing. Thousands of eyes were wet with emotion – what Prussian had ever been able to resist the pomp of a military parade, especially one so sensational? And how to refrain from applauding when Napoleon galloped around the statue of Frederick the Great while raising his hat in salute? The gilded and multicoloured staff did likewise.

Evening came. The Berliners, reassured and curious, came to watch the grenadiers who were bivouacked in the Lustgarten. Their fires, which were damaging the well-kept turf, threw beams of light on the square leading to the Charlottenburg where Napoleon was installed and where that very evening took place a moving scene which he recounted in a letter to Josephine.

The previous evening the Prince of Hatzfeldt, governor of Berlin, had presented the Emperor with the keys to the city. Today, he had come at the head of a delegation to salute him on his entry to the château. But Napoleon had said to him: 'Do not present yourself, Monsieur, I have no need of your services.' The reason for this rebuff was that Savary's agents had intercepted a letter from Hatzfeldt to the Count of Hohenlohe giving precise details concerning the French troops who had entered Berlin, numbers of caissons, etc. Espionage? After all, the armistice had not yet been signed. But duplicity in any event and Napoleon was furious. Against the advice of Berthier and Rapp, Hatzfeldt had been arrested and it was intended that he be court-martialled by seven colonels of III Corps. Such action would seem to have been justified. His wife, the princess, was young and pretty and eight months' pregnant. Thanks to the assistance of Duroc and other sympathetic ADCs, she got in to see Napoleon, who received her while leaning against the mantelpiece. She threw herself at his feet: 'Sire, my husband is incapable of disloyalty!' 'When I showed her the letter,' he wrote to Josephine, 'she said to me naïvely through her sobs, "Ah, it is truly his handwriting." I replied: "Well, Madame, throw this letter in the fire. Never again will I be so powerful as to punish your husband." She burnt the letter and seemed very content. You see that I like women to be good, naïve, and gentle ... in which only they resemble you.'

On the other hand, there was another woman who would not find pardon. Queen Louise's remark about Napoleon being the monster emerged from the mire had been reported to him as had the fact that she had taught her parrot to utter insulting remarks about the French. She called Napoleon 'Noppel' – pronouncing it 'Moppel' – 'a little mad dog' in Berlin slang. This fanatical francophobe had gone farther. The Emperor's servants had just found in a drawer at Charlottenburg in the midst of a tangle of toilet articles, extended notes on how to avoid the undertakings of Prussia in regard to France; correspondence on the secret negotiations with Russia; Doumouriez' report on how to fight the French and, especially, the file on measures to persuade the King to wage war, even against the advice of his cabinet. 'These pieces', wrote Napoleon, 'show, if proof were needed, how unfortunate are those princes who let women exert influence on political matters.' Louise's provocation and influence weighed heavily when Napoleon dictated the armistice terms, which were more onerous even than those of the peace treaty.

The onset of the French occupation was accompanied by a revival of social activity in Berlin. 'Never', wrote a bitter Berliner, 'was there so much luxury, more elegant feminine toilets, more lasciviousness.' Percy went to the opera: 'They played "Iphigenia in Tauris". I was overcome. I stand by this admiration. The enemy is at Berlin, Prussia is conquered, the king in flight with a terrified army – and, yet, the opera theatre is full, no one seems to give a thought to his country, to pitying the court, nor to have doubts as to the future. Iphigenia's arias were applauded as were, above all, the ballets which were charming. I doubt whether Paris could have done better.'

All prices had taken an upward leap. The nobility were impoverished, the bourgeoisie rich. It was said that the Jews were making their fortunes by speculation – they were deemed to be arrogant. In a bid to spare the poor from the worst of the inflation, Napoleon imposed a tax on bread. It was reported to him that there was a Hôtel des Invalides, the *Invalidenhaus*, situated in the northeastern quarter of the city on the right bank of the Spree. 'Is all well there?'

It was a vast, clean barracks, but the lot of the old soldiers there, who were mostly frail, was miserable. Ill-clothed to the extent that they hardly dared show themselves in the city, sleeping on straw pallets, living on thin soup, very little meat and appalling black bread. Napoleon sent for Daru: 'This scandal must end.' Thanks to the conqueror, the invalids at Berlin now enjoyed an undreamed-of degree of comfort. Later Louise was to interrogate them concerning the conduct of the occupiers: 'Madame, they are endowed with strong arms for fighting and great hearts full of charity.'

On 28 October, Napoleon travelled to Biersdorf where, in full dress, the regiments of Davout's III Corps were drawn up in review order. Davout had been created Duke of Auerstadt, but the troops had yet to be congratulated on their victory. The review lasted for hours because the Emperor stopped numerous times to question, pat shoulders, pinch ears; 'One must be endowed with a rare strength not to bow the head before that look.' But the blue-eyed stare could also be caressing. It is not only women who can obtain a life in exchange for a look. Napoleon could not foresee the butchery of Eylau, but he well knew that he would have to ask a lot of his men: 'I lost some brave men; they were my children. I mourn them, but they died on the field of honour. It was mainly due to the brilliant conduct of III Corps that the great results achieved were due.' Five hundred crosses were awarded and a few days later Napoleon promoted many officers recommended by Davout.

At Berlin, General Hulin, the French governor of the city, whose head-quarters was the palace of Courland, 7 Unter den Linden, received with good-will those citizens who had complaints: cellars had been ransacked; haughty husbands had been roughed-up; but no serious extortions were reported. The regiments of the Guard had been billeted on the inhabitants; the troops having been ordered to 'share the meals that their host was able to provide, according to his status, without demanding more'. That left the matter of wine; as wine prices were exorbitantly high in Berlin, the Guardsmen agreed to accept a jug of beer. But the Emperor, full of solicitude for his troops, sent for Daru: 'I intend that my army should have wine. Take an inventory of the cellars to obtain wine for two months.'

Those inhabitants on whom officers were billeted counted themselves lucky. The young Countess Hönckel de Donnersmarck, whose husband was wandering God knew where with the debris of the Prussian army, played the piano accompanied on the flute by squadron chief Boulard of the artillery of the Guard. The army had just been paid, life was rosy, the billeted troops invited their hosts to the restaurants, more often, to the inns, some of which were famous: the Golden Eagle; the Inn of Russia; the Golden Sun; the City of Paris. The Masonic lodges of Berlin – 'The Royal York lodge', the 'Friendship' – brilliantly received their fellow-masons who were, it seems, numerous. In brief, fraternisation was widespread. It should be noted that those officers who, like their men, boasted of feminine conquests, all made a distinction between the German girls whom they found heavy and lazy, and the Prussian girls who, in contrast, were brisk, svelte, refined, seductive, voluptuous; these were the adjectives that were constantly repeated. To excess, no doubt, thought Surgeon-in-Chief Percy, still hard at it housing his sick and wounded, when he saw with consternation the huge numbers of cases of venereal disease. I shall close this brief account of the occupation of Berlin on a less vulgar note. Louis Lachouque has recounted how his friend, Huard, had found in a Berlin book shop the diary of the pretty Louise Seidler, whose parents had received Senior Surgeon Geoffroy of Bernardotte's corps: 'a handsome man with a serious look, in French uniform. He asked for the keys to the stable, where the wounded were to be hospitalised. This led to conversations and to a request to my parents on his part to be allowed to visit us. We saw each other daily. In a neighbouring room, he read me the works of his favourite poets, Corneille and Racine. We also played music – I played the piano and Geoffroy accompanied me on the violin. Our mutual harmony grew, for I had found in him a sweet disposition and a kind heart. He asked my parents for my hand, to which they agreed.' Her father made inquiries of the authorities of Lisieux, where Geoffroy had been born. 'Our marriage was celebrated in the midst of our family. Those were the happiest days of my life.' A touching idyll amid a war that was brutal but which had not yet engulfed entire populations. But, even at that time, the romance of Louise and Geoffroy was to prove too tender: 'Duty called my dear man and forced us to part. We exchanged letters.' The letters from Geoffroy ceased. One more posted missing in the tempest sweeping across Europe.

V

POLAND: EYLAU
Enter General Winter

Continental blockade may have been an incomprehensible expression for most of the troops of the Grande Armée, but it formed the basis for Napoleon's decision that, with Prussia conquered, they must again be on the march and again suffer and risk their lives. Napoleon could rightly claim that it was Britain that had started it. On 16 May 1806, the British government had decided on 'the blockade of all ports and coasts from the mouth of the Elbe to the coasts of Brest'. In other words, the Royal Navy would forbid ships of any nation to enter or leave any of the northern ports. The continental blockade, decreed at Berlin on 21 November 1806, was a riposte. These were the essentials: all commerce and correspondence with the British Isles was forbidden to all nations; any British subject found in France or territory occupied by France or her allies would be treated as a prisoner of war; all merchandise or property belonging to British subjects would be prizes of war. Finally, and above all, no vessel coming from Britain or from a British colony was to be allowed to enter any port. The object was to asphyxiate England by ruining her commerce. But Napoleon's decision implied that he intended to become the master of the whole of Europe by conquest or alliance.

On 16 November 1806, Prussia, whose armies had been routed, had signed an armistice at the château of Charlottenburg. Napoleon had not wished to appear; Duroc had signed for France; on the Prussian side, two plenipotentiaries. Peace negotiations were to follow, but if they should fail, the two parties pledged themselves not to resume hostilities without giving ten days' notice. It was Frederick-William, who had been decisively beaten and had taken refuge at Osterode (75 kilometres east of the Vistula) who denounced the armistice convention: 'I could not execute the clauses because a part of my States was occupied by Russia.' But in fact he was relying on the Russians to beat Napoleon.

So, once again, it was war, and, once again speed was essential to drive towards the Vistula to prevent Frederick-William from recruiting and replenishing his army on reaching the river, to fortify, build winter quarters and resume the campaign in the spring. Napoleon's spies had reported that the Russian army was marching towards Warsaw in two columns: 60,000 men (General Bennigsen) followed by 40,000 (General Buxhöwden). The Emperor had about 150,000 men who must march east in two armies: one in the north commanded by Lannes, the other in the south, under Murat – as usual, Murat drove into the lead.

'Drove' is misleading given the circumstances. This campaign was to unfold in one of the poorest regions of Europe and, once the Oder had been crossed, an interminable frozen rain fell on the Grande Armée. 'It was an awful sight to see our men soaked, boots in hand, barefoot in the muddy marshes that we could scarcely cross with our horses.' Scattered villages, miserable wooden hovels whose inhabitants lived in indescribable filth; bad roads, or no roads at all, no bridges; it was necessary to cross the streams by the fords or on improvised bridges. The artillery was bogged, carriages overturned; the army crawled.

In 1785 unfortunate Poland had been partitioned for the third time between Russia, Prussia and Austria. In 1806 Warsaw was in Russia. The Russians (like the Prussians) were detested. Having arrived in order to confront the French, their reception was such that, fearing for the safety of his troops, Bennigsen gave the order repeated by so many Russian military commanders and which finally proved the key to success: 'About turn: we are retreating.' This allowed Murat and Davout to make a triumphal entry into the ex-capital of the ex-kingdom of Poland. Here is what appeared in the Bulletin of the Grande Armée: 'It is difficult to describe the enthusiasm of the Poles. Our entry into this grand city has been a triumph and the sentiments which Poles of every class exhibit are reflected not only in the hearts of the people but have been strengthened by misfortune. Their first dream, their first wish, is again to become a nation. The richest leave their châteaux to demand at the top of their voices the restoration of the nation and to offer their children, their fortunes and their influence. Such a spectacle is most touching. They have already donned again their old costumes and reassumed their old customs.' This is dated from Posen (where the Emperor was) 1 December 1806, that is, three days after the entry of Murat's troops into Warsaw, more than 300 kilometres from Posen. Many horses must have collapsed to bring the news so quickly to the Emperor. The editors of the Bulletin must have called on their imaginations for a description of the circumstances. All the same, the inhabitants of Warsaw gave a warm welcome to the first French soldiers who arrived, headed by the gold-belted Murat and his glittering staff.

During this time, the rest of the Army of the South, with its train of wagons, carriages and chariots, was advancing more slowly towards the Polish capital. Percy continued to keep his diary of the march, in which he always described accurately the country and its inhabitants: 'it rains, it snows, it freezes, the roads are terrible. 30 November: arrived at Zirke, a little Polish town on the Warta. Quite good billet with a Pole speaking Latin fairly well. The country resembles that around Ambleteuse, all is sandy and sand so fresh as if the sea had covered this sad country, which is surely never did. All one sees here are men with moustaches or tufted beards with a sort of robe or long dress with a belt: all wear boots and a fur cap. In a few villages can be seen some pretty cottages with thatched roofs. All the roofs are thatched, some very untidily.' Let us salute these thatched roofs as we pass; they will long be the only food available for the horses. On 2 December the train arrived at Posen (today Poznan) which was decorated with triumphal arches, Napoleon having arrived there from Berlin three days earlier. This day was the anniversary of Austerlitz, and the arches were decorated with allegorical figures and inscriptions: 'To the Victor of Marengo', 'To the Victor of Austerlitz'. 'To the Restorer of the Polish nation.' Like the soldiers, these had been assailed by the climate and already were discoloured, their inscriptions barely legible. But nothing deterred the organisers of the ceremonies; everywhere lamps were hung, though wind and rain extinguished many, but the illuminations were maintained 'as well as possible'.

Napoleon wrote that night to Josephine: 'I have been to a ball in town. It is raining. I am well. I love and desire you.' All the imperial letters sent from Posen are interesting, for different reasons. To Murat: 'I shall not proclaim the independence of Poland until I am satisfied that they will maintain it, when I see 30 to 40,000 men under arms, organised, and the nobility on horseback ready to sacrifice their lives.' To Cambacérès, Minister of War: 'I need 90,000 men in order to assure the peace.' To Daru: 'Write to the commissioner to Marshal Ney who is at Bromberg that Bromberg and Thorn have resources and that one can find shoes there. And if no shoes are available, let him take the leather so that the industrious soldiers can repair their old shoes.' This sentence alone gives an idea of the troops' situation in a campaign that was merely starting. While waiting for the leather and to encourage them to wait, a proclamation: 'Soldiers, a year ago today at this same hour, you were on the famous battlefield of Austerlitz. The terrified Russians were fleeing. Soldiers, we shall not lay down our arms until a general peace has confirmed and assured the power of our allies, and has restored to our commerce liberty and our colonies. We have conquered on the Spree and the Oder, Pondicherry, our establishments in India, the Cape of Good Hope, and the Spanish colonies. What gives Russia the right to hope to change their destinies?'

But now the glacial silence of General Winter gave effective reply to proclamations. Many soldiers made no secret of the fact that they did not give a hoot for Pondicherry or the Cape of Good Hope; they did not even know where they were. More or less surreptitiously, when leaving for the next stage, many hid, made-off, disappeared into the countryside, holed up in the villages, the peasants' cottages, having threatened them at gun point. Later, the Emperor would have parties sent out to round them up, but not all of them would be found. From Posen, the Emperor wrote to Murat: 'Announce at Warsaw that I shall soon arrive. I long to hear that the bridges over the Vistula and the Bug have been restored.' These bridges had been destroyed by the retreating Russians.

The many carriages of the imperial cortège left Posen on the night of 15/16 December. Icy rain fell in continuous torrents, the roads became rivers or bogs, no landmarks could be seen and the procession lost its way repeatedly. Eventually a dismal hamlet of wooden huts was sighted. Riders from the escort sought directions, but found only serfs in tatters, sleeping with their beasts, crawling with vermin and terrified at the sight of uniforms. The convoy left again somewhat uncertainly and by chance reached Kutno and Lowicz. An unexpected thaw prevented the Emperor from using his coach and he had to make do with a local barouche. It took a week to cover 300 kilometres.

Five leagues from Warsaw, Duroc's carriage, preceding the Emperor's, fell into a bog and was damaged. It was 4 p.m. and already dark. The chasseurs of the escort, already muddied to their thighs, rescued the Grand Marshal from the wreck with some difficulty. He had a broken collarbone – what to do? He was carried to the nearest village and lodged in the least sordid cottage. They would come for him the next day. Napoleon arrived at Warsaw at midnight on 18 December. Murat had outshone himself as master of ceremonies; all the Poles were present; the welcome was delirious.

On the following day the Emperor sent for the Surgeon-in-Chief. He had had a talk with him at Posen and was well aware of the sad state of the medical service. He regarded it as more than a mere detail and certainly would have wished to be able to devote more time to it. And on this particular morning the Emperor was furious at the administrative service: 'The French nation has become the most barbarous in Europe as regards its hospital services. Our army is at the bottom of the list in comparison with our neighbours; the Cossacks treat their wounded better than we do! But I don't see M. Coste; where is he?' Coste was the Chief Doctor. 'Sire, he has returned to Kustrin.' 'It is to the Invalides that that good man should be returning. It is not men like him that I need for the army. I want them young, active, a bit lusty – with balls.'

Suddenly the Emperor called Daru to take dictation: 'A senior doctor in an army corps is absurd and useless. All doctors are to leave the corps and divisions to which they are attached and are to remain, either at the hospitals or at General Headquarters. A senior army surgeon must also act as doctor. There will only be surgeons in the army.' He went on to dictate a detailed plan of the ambulance organisation. Percy took notes feverishly at the same time as Daru and he thought that he was hearing a fairy tale when he heard Napoleon add: 'It is to be hoped that the surgeons will be responsible for the safety, upkeep and equipment of the wagons attached to their division of ambulances.' The Emperor pointed his finger at Daru: 'I am shocked at what happens to the material for the hospitals, to the crowds of employees paid but absent, at the means of trans-

port, and so on. They have ruined my corps of surgeons as a result of tormenting them and of using them for their stupid projects.'

Daru said not a word, but he was goggle-eyed: 'They have ruined my corps
of surgeons' – 'They' were the commissioners for war. Daru knew this. These
men reported in principle to him, but in fact constituted a powerful and obstinate Mafia in face of whom the Emperor, who could do anything, but had so
much to do – was impotent.

'It is to be hoped that the surgeons will be responsible for the safety,
upkeep and equipment of the wagons attached to their division of ambulances.'
Alas, this qualified hope was to remain a hope; other cares, other projects,
engrossed the Emperor's attention, above all the war – forward, forward, always
forward.

We must now focus our attention on Bennigsen who aimed to swamp the
Grande Armée from the left, thus cutting the road to Berlin. On 22 December
the bridge over the Narew was completed, the cavalry reserve crossed the Vistula at Praga and, with Davout's corps, marched on the enemy. Next day, the 23rd,
Napoleon left Warsaw. Percy went too because the Emperor now wished the
ambulances to accompany the main body of this Army of the South which was
now marching upstream. 'We shall give battle tomorrow or the day after. I foresee at least six thousand wounded.'

What a beautiful river is the Vistula! A simple line on the map, but actually eight times wider than the Seine. Some 100,000 men got across on 'a rick-
ety pontoon, half boats, half wagons', and then, what roads! One passed
peasants' carts which had fallen into bogs, mired in mud, their occupants sig-
nalling for help, but, time was pressing. Cannon could be heard far ahead. '24
December. From 10 p.m. until 3 a.m. we heard cannon and musketry,' noted
Percy. 'We reached a wretched village where a bridge had been built. Already
300 wounded: amputations. Helped with several dressings and showed the
young fellows how to pinch and elevate the skin in order to cut a fold quickly
over a bullet which they wished to extract from a Russian hussar. During another operation, a purse was stolen from M. Bousquet, senior surgeon of an infantry
regiment, containing 40 louis which was all his savings, since a fire had ruined
his regiment at Posen.' On 25 December they arrived at Nasielsk where Davout's
corps had fought victoriously. 'A very Jewish town, wooden houses, full of mud,
ruined by the Russians who had stabled horses in every room. Debris and rubbish, traces of barbarism everywhere. Some men wished to do likewise. I saw a
dragoon running, a loaf of bread in his hand, while some Jews were crying out.'
Percy arrested the thief and found hidden under the bread 'a golden Decalogue
and a large silver cross'. Yesterday's battlefield was thick with the corpses of men
and horses. Who would dream of celebrating Christmas?

On that day Napoleon who, like his troops, had bivouacked in rough conditions, rested for some hours in the château of Lopaczyn. A courier brought disturbing news: a hundred suicides in the army, including the Guard.

The problem was both moral and physical. First, the Russians seemed unassailable. Each time one thought they were cornered they melted away into the dark forests and when one followed – nobody. The countryside was becoming increasingly dismal: ochre clouds sailing at ground level, torrential frozen rains, mixed with snowstorms, three hours of true daylight daily, one might have been in the Arctic. The ground did not absorb the water; one could not even see the soil under this huge covering, if one tried to walk one stuck in mud up to the knees. Try to extract a foot, the strap of the gaiter under the shoe would break, the shoe would remain stuck. The horses were in water up to their bellies, losing shoes in the mire; many fell down from sheer hunger. If the infantry covered more than fifteen kilometres in twenty-four hours it was held to be a miracle. When the army arrived by chance at a village, it piled into the hovels: 'where the inhabitants had left nothing but vermin'. Bivouacking was a martyrdom. One sought a pine forest where the mud might be less thick than elsewhere, but everything was so soaking wet that it was out of the question to light a fire. A malignant fever emanated from the swamps and attacked the soldiers, particularly the young ones. Like the horses, many died on the road; their bodies would remain where they had fallen.

The surgeons, too, were exhausted. Percy, who had been coughing since their departure, was now on the brink of pneumonia and had to return to Warsaw. He met Marshal Lefebvre: 'The Marshal was followed by the Guard, very dirty, very tired, having covered twenty leagues in unbelievable mud, muttering under their breath and without a crust of bread; that is what the army had come to; it lived on meat when there was time to cook it, on potatoes – here, turnips when any could be found, for the peasants buried them in the fields.' For the French soldier, a peasant to his marrow, no bread was worse than no meat. Not only had the soldier no crumb of bread, but 'not a drop of brandy, no time to dry clothes and he was dying from fatigue and starvation. They were dying in the ditches for want of a glass of brandy which would have revived them.' Hence the suicides.

Napoleon himself bore witness to this in a letter to Joseph Bonaparte: 'We are in the midst of snow and mud, lacking bread, brandy, wine, eating meat and potatoes, making long marches and counter-marches without any kind of comfort and generally fighting with the bayonet against canister; the wounded compelled to escape in sleds for fifty leagues in the open air. Having destroyed the Prussian monarchy, we are now fighting against the rest of Prussia, against the Russians, the Kalmuks, the Cossacks and the tribes of the north which have invaded since the days of the Romans. We are making war in all its power and its horror.' A neat conclusion, and it is true that this army, bordering on despair, could, when at grips with the enemy, summon up surprising reserves of energy and would fight victoriously at Putulsk, Golymin and Soldau.

At Golymin, the vigour of General Rapp's cavalry forced the Russians to retire. Rapp was wounded. In the stylised battle manoeuvres one could readily pick out the Emperor's aides-de camp – among them Rapp – from the brassard which they wore on their left arm. Many were the sons of the old nobility, such as Ségur, Castellane, Fezensac, Flahaut; but not Jean Rapp, thirty-four years of age, born at Colmar of an obscure family. Not all the generals and marshals had been as worthy as this old NCO, intelligent, humane, brave on every battlefield. A lieutenant-colonel at Marengo, he had been ADC to Desaix who died in his arms. Bonaparte had lauded Rapp's valour – 'You shall be one of my aides-de-camp.'

The First Consul had also sensed that Rapp might be a good diplomatist. In 1802 he was instructed to indicate to the Swiss that France was planning to intervene in their quarrels and Rapp accomplished this delicate task brilliantly. General of brigade, divisional general after Austerlitz, in Prussia and Poland Rapp earned the nickname from the troops of 'the intrepid one'. But at Putulsk his left arm was shattered, his sixth or seventh wound. Napoleon wrote him a very cordial letter and a few days later visited him in hospital. 'Well, Rapp, wounded again!' 'Not surprising, Sire; battles all the time.' 'They will finish when we are eighty-four.'

Napoleon stayed two days at Golymin, having ordered Murat to follow the Russians and try to deduce their intentions. 'I am in a bad situation,' he wrote to Josephine. 'I have beaten the Russians and taken 30 guns and 6,000 prisoners. But the weather is frightful and we are in mud up to our knees.' Forty-eight hours later, again to the Empress: 'I believe that all is over for this year; the army will enter winter quarters.' And he himself was to meet Marie Walewska.

On 29 December, Napoleon arrived at Putulsk from Golymin. On 1 January 1807 he left for Warsaw, stopping *en route* to change horses at Bronie where his barouche was immediately surrounded by a crowd, through which two elegantly dressed ladies tried to approach him. One of them, young and very pretty, with large blue eyes, spoke to Duroc: 'Please, Monsieur officer, help me.' He took her hand and escorted her to the carriage. 'Here is one, Sire, who has braved the dangers of the crowd for you.' 'Napoleon took off his hat and leaned towards me and I do not know what he said as I was too intent on expressing my message.' The young woman had, apparently, memorised a small compliment which she recited in a sing-song voice in French with charming conviction: 'Welcome, a thousand times welcome to our country. Nothing that we can do will prove more decisively the sentiments we bear towards you nor the pleasure we feel at seeing you grace the soil of this nation which waits for you to restore it.' 'Napoleon looked at me attentively. He took a bouquet which was in his carriage and gave it to me, saying: "Keep this as proof of my good intentions. We will meet again at Warsaw, I hope, and I will claim a kiss from your beautiful mouth."

Such was the start of one of the most touching romances in history: on the one hand this all-powerful man who quite simply desired a beautiful woman and who would possess her through blackmail under circumstances none too honourable; and she, impelled to the sacrifice of her conjugal virtue by the great Polish patriots.

Even though this tale has been recounted a thousand times, I would have liked to have forgotten for a moment the horrors of war to follow this pretty blonde, but the drums and bugles call us away. One last look at Marie Walewska, clutching to her bosom Napoleon's bouquet. She was nineteen, and would bear the Emperor a son; in ten years she would be dead, as he would in fourteen.

How many months of winter quarters were spent at Warsaw? For Napoleon, exactly one month, but it was the sort of rest that he enjoyed. He had ('let us profit from the goodwill of the Poles!') invited Berthier to raise a Polish corps of light horse. To be eligible to join it was necessary to be 'a landowner or son of a landowner, aged from eighteen to forty, to possess a horse, a uniform and a set of equipment and accoutrements conforming to pattern'. This light horse was only a beginning; the Grande Armée would receive two 'Legions of the North', a Legion of the Vistula and some other Polish units. From 1808, the 1st Regiment of Light Horse would sing without embarrassment on the roads of Spain its war song, words by Lasalle, their instructor and regimental chief:

The French were in Poland,
Spain sees the Poles,
Europe will see without shame
That French and Poles shall reign.
What nation is so strong
As to oppose their endeavours?
Poles, Frenchmen, act in such a way
That the whole world is facing death.

In January 1807 the first detachments of the reinforcements demanded of Cambacérès arrived: conscripts who had received only the most rudimentary tuition. Batch after batch, they would continue their training in Poland during a very hard winter. The weather had suddenly grown colder, but it was easier to get about because the ponds and swamps were frozen. Three-quarters of the young soldiers had arrived very poorly clothed; the corps chiefs purchased whatever cloth they could find, and civilian clothing which could be converted one way or another. Napoleon reviewed regiments in different uniforms, feigning to notice nothing, speaking to the men, ceaselessly questioning, where are you from? what does your father do? ears were pinched, his riveting blue eyes fixed on the flustered youths.

Flour was ordered, ovens and storehouses were built; Napoleon knew that without bread the troopers felt lost, but there would never be enough. The billets of the Grande Armée were scattered over an area of more than 150 square kilometres 'the corps could thus find some of the necessary food on the spot, the rest being brought in by foragers from the hinterland and from the interior of Prussia'.

True, convoys of provisions from the occupied territories were continually on their way to the army, but the system often failed, as for instance, in the province of Hesse. At Kassel, where General Lagrange was in command, rebels made off with twenty cannon and hundreds of muskets. Napoleon wrote to Lagrange to burn the village which was the principal source of the rebellion and to execute thirty of the ringleaders: 'The region must realise that any armed revolt will be severely punished.'

The couriers from Paris did not only bring good news. The last conscriptions, 420,000 young Frenchmen in two years, had aroused anger; defaulters were everywhere. From the officers sent back to France, from the repatriated sick and wounded, through letters sent to families – luckily, many were illiterate! – the Grande Armée's sufferings and losses became known. The victory bulletins did not suffice to calm mothers' fears. There was growing opposition, particularly among the bourgeoisie, which had to be faced. From the depths of Poland, while bridgeheads had to be organised to ward off a Russian counter-attack, Napoleon was governing France, Prussia, Italy and the Confederation of the Rhine. He digested, chapter by chapter, the budget proposed for 1807, was alarmed by the decline in the receipts of customs dues resultant on the exclusion of cotton fabric spun in England (the continental blockade), which he redressed by a new tax. He ordered Champigny, Minister of the Interior, to find a site in Paris where the Bourse could stand, to transform the unfinished Madeleine into a temple of the Grande Armée, to change the name of the Military School bridge to the bridge of Jena. It fell to him to convoke the Jewish elders on whom pressure must be exerted to persuade it to modify the temperament of the Jews: 'They must strike from the law of Moses all that is intolerant.' He interested himself in the creation of a new ballet 'The Return of Ulysses' – to Fouché: 'There is no reason why it cannot be given. Tell M. de Luçay to put it on.'

None of these concerns upset the vital phenomenon which was Napoleon. The civil departments functioned at Warsaw with the same precision as they had at Paris. Twice a week at the Blacha palace the Emperor heard a concert, after which there would be a court reception. So many beautiful Polish women! And not just beautiful: compelled to spend half the year on the estates which their husbands managed, they read, improved their French, played music, studied all manner of subjects, and prepared to spend the winter in town 'where they showed themselves superior to their rivals from other countries'.

We know that Napoleon found the time to play the happy lover of Marie Walewska. Josephine, having quickly learned of the affair, had spoken of rejoining her imperial husband. He sent the letter which every husband sends in this situation: 'I am touched by everything you tell me. But the season is cold, the roads very bad and insecure. I therefore cannot expose you to so many fatigues and dangers. You really must abandon the idea of covering three hundred leagues at this season across enemy territory and in the rear of the army. It costs me even more than it does you to put off for a few weeks the joy of seeing you, but events require it as do our affairs. Farewell, my love, be happy and show character.'

On 28 January, Napoleon, still at Warsaw, received disturbing news from Bernadotte concerning the Army of the North. Ney, who was not happy in his quarters at Neidenburg (130 kilometres north of Warsaw) had marched north without orders, pushing his cavalry as far as Guttstadt and Heilsberg (90 kilometres further north and only 60 from Königsberg). Result: Bennigsen, breaking the winter truce, advanced with 70,000 men and Bernadotte had had to make a general retreat.

Shouting that Ney was a disobedient imbecile, the Emperor bent over his maps and the strategy-making machine started up. Here is the plan for a simple manoeuvre to surround and destroy Bennigsen's army. Let Bernadotte, instead of resisting while waiting for reinforcements, continue to retreat in order to draw Bennigsen after him. In three days, the Grande Armée would be concentrated and would advance northwards by forced marches – again forced marches! The Russians' lines of communication would be cut. Orders were sent to the marshals laying out the overall plan down to the last details. But – and is this a sign of Destiny on the road to so much success? – an unforeseen accident: the officer carrying the order to Bernadotte was captured by a troop of Cossacks. He was searched before he had time to swallow his despatches, which went through channels to Bennigsen. And that generalissimo, determined to avoid the trap, resorted to the old Russian strategy, so useful in open country – retreat. His army would confine itself to rearguard actions at Allenstein and Hoff.

At Allenstein, the 2nd Chasseurs attacked and threw back a large body of Cossacks which was covering the Russian rearguard. As the Russians were endeavouring to regroup, Napoleon (who had rejoined the army, having left

Warsaw on 27 January) ordered a new attack and a dogged pursuit of the Russian rearguard. Accordingly, the regiment formed column of squadrons and advanced but, while passing in front of the great leader, instead of their usual 'Vive l'Empereur!', they loosed another cry: 'Kleba! Kleba!' (In Polish, 'Bread!' Napoleon frowned for a moment, then quickly conceived a reply. Standing in his stirrups, sword uplifted, laughing loudly, he shouted: 'Daley! Daley! Kleba!' ('Forward! There is bread!') This went down well; the French cavalry advanced, dispersed the Cossacks, attacked the rearguard right and left and handled them roughly over six leagues. The pursuit continued, but the army was still suffering. Arriving at their bivouacs on the hard snow, the unit chiefs sent foraging parties to ransack neighbouring villages. If inhabitants were found, their wagons were requisitioned and loaded with anything that was eatable. Such good fortune was rare; more often the parties returned empty-handed to face the fury of their comrades: 'You don't know where to look!'

Individually, or in small groups, foragers wandered aimlessly over the darkening plain; the Cossacks, lurking in the woods, ambushed and cut them down. The more disciplined soldiers were furious that the cold did not destroy the bugs, from whose bites they were constantly suffering; the frost also burnt their eyelids. But from the moment that the army advanced, Napoleon was content: 'The enemy is flying in the greatest disorder,' he wrote to Daru. 'He has lost thirty guns, many standards, and baggage and wagons in immense quantities. The depots at Guttstadt and Leibstadt have been taken. The Emperor is very well.'

The Polish town of Hoff lies 30 kilometres south-west of Eylau. The Russian rear-guard – twelve battalions with cavalry – had ceased to retreat and faced the pursuing French. Soult's infantry had not yet arrived, but Napoleon, full of ardour, had ordered Murat to 'charge immediately'. To the right was a coppice and in front, a small bridge, which was swept by Russian canister. The bodies of men and horses were scattered in a ravine.

'Advance the dragoons!' The dragoons, in dark green uniforms with white waistcoats and breeches, wore a crested helmet garnished at the edges with sealskin and topped by a black mane. Now these helmets were dented, the mane reduced to a few shreds. The dragoons thundered away without hesitation, charging the small bridge which was still being swept by canister. The ravine in front of Hoff looked increasingly unhealthy, but Napoleon remained optimistic: 'Engage d'Hautpoul's cuirassiers!'

These cavalrymen wore a helmet and breastplate that were supposed to be bullet-proof. The breastplate was of wrought iron and doubled, that is, it covered both chest and back, the two halves joined by brass shoulder-straps and a belt at the waist. The iron helmet, of the same pattern as that of the dragoons, was topped by a brass comb and a mane of black horsehair.

D'Hautpoul, fifty-three years old, was a very tall, robust individual. Descended from an ancient family of lords in Languedoc and an ex-officer of the *ancien régime*, he was somewhat foul-mouthed. A divisional general in 1797, he had narrowly escaped court-martial in 1799 for a failed manoeuvre at the battle of Stockach. Later, however, he had shone with the Army of the Rhine, then at Raussnitz (1805) and at Austerlitz and Jena. His troops were known as 'the terrible cuirassiers of d'Hautpoul', and in front of Hoff he led them forward in the slow, thundering gallop of the heavy cavalry, shaking the bridge over the ravine so that it seemed in danger of collapse. Bullets clanged against the cuirasses, men and horses fell, but the survivors pressed forward, slashing furiously; the Russian battalions broke. An hour later, Napoleon embraced d'Hautpoul in front of the entire division: 'To show myself worthy of such an honour,' cried the giant, 'I must give my life for Your Majesty!' Then, turning to his men: 'Soldiers, the Emperor is pleased with you. He has embraced me on behalf of all of you. And I am so pleased with you that I kiss all your arses!' Cheers. D'Hautpoul was to keep his promise to Napoleon; he was killed the next day at Eylau.

The battle at Hoff had lasted all day. The houses in the town were crowded with wounded and more were arriving all the time. Many had spent most of the day lying on the frozen soil of the battlefield and some would remain there overnight. One survivor wrote: 'What a frightful night I spent. Many times I regretted that I was not one of those dead bodies which surrounded us.'

Eylau today is Bagratronovsk, an industrial town in Russia of 7,500 inhabitants. At the time of which I am writing it had 1,500, was called Preussich-Eylau and was in East Prussia. Most of the books give the Battle of Eylau as taking place on 8 February 1807; in fact part of the battle was fought on the 7th, but that day is less documented because Napoleon had not yet arrived – without him, less to record. It seems likely that the first action had been joined during the night of the 6th/7th when the Emperor's quartermasters, coming from Landsberg (near Hoff), stumbled on the Russian outposts, who had not imagined that they were so near. It was snowing. Come day, Soult's advance guard arrived, and then the Guard. Furious fighting took place in the town itself; the cemetery changed hands several times, both sides' artillery boomed. In the streets, guns and caissons rolled over the dead and dying. A Russian detachment had barricaded itself in a wooden mill in the town. The French set fire to it. The screaming unfortunates died to the last man. Before nightfall on the 7th, the bulk of the Russian troops had retired to the hillocks which formed a semicircle around the town.

During the night, or later – accounts differ – Napoleon arrived and established himself at the post house at the entrance to Eylau. 'Established' is rather grand, given that the building was largely empty, the Russians having sacked the place. The Russian artillery was still firing and Napoleon wanted to go and see what was happening, but his staff dissuaded him: 'Why does not Your Majesty take a short rest?' Finally he went to sleep in a chair, but was woken before 6 a.m. 'Sire, the Russians are attacking!' The battle had been resumed, a confused assault in the black night. The Russians again seized the cemetery; the 26th Line Regiment ejected them. At dawn, the whole of Eylau was in French hands. But this time Bennigsen decided not to retreat.

On the Russian side, 80,000 men including 8,000 Prussians. Napoleon had only some 54,000 effectives, dog-tired and starving. Ney's corps was then on the Königsberg road north of Eylau. Since daybreak the Guard had taken position in the cemetery destined for fame. 'What was so painful', wrote Captain Parquin: 'was the heavy snow, whirling in our faces with rare violence, so that we were blinded. The pine forests which were common in this country and which bordered the battlefield rendered it even more dismal. Add to that, a foggy sky whose clouds seemed to remain at tree-top level and which gave to the whole scene a funereal cast which reminded us that we were three hundred leagues from the beautiful skies of France.' French guns replied to Russian guns, firing at point-blank range which meant that after every round men fell on one side or the other – an apparently futile manner of waging war, but Napoleon must have felt that, for the moment, there was no alternative: 'I am hoping that Davout can attack the Russian left flank.'

In the cemetery were the Guard. It so happened that, when a bullet whistled by, two or three grenadiers instinctively ducked their heads, earning a reprimand from their officers. The Guard was rarely engaged, but was required to know how to die impassively, a convention which earned them all their privileges.

The Russians were drawn up in two long lines and were also taking casualties. Doubtless they were growing impatient, because Napoleon saw their first line form column and march on a mill situated to the left of Eylau. Some French infantry intervened and drove off the attack. Napoleon ordered Augereau's corps to advance in column on the centre: 'We must stop the enemy from attacking Davout's corps. If my manoeuvre succeeds, the Russian left will have to fall back on the centre.'

At that moment the blizzard of snow became so thick that visibility 'was reduced to two paces' and the French columns wavered. The Russians, their backs to the storm, were less blinded than the French. Their cavalry began to advance on the cemetery, supported by 4,000 grenadiers. Level with the cemetery, Napoleon saw that the position of the French was none too good; he slashed with his crop at the snow covering the ground: 'What cheek!, what cheek!'

Augereau was carried in, wounded by a large-calibre musket-ball. He complained that his force had not been supported, but what could one do, what could one see in this tempest? A moment later, the visibility improved a little. 'Send in the mounted chasseurs and the dragoons of the Guard,' ordered Napoleon, 'and send me Murat'. Murat arrived, covered in snow. 'Are you going to let those fellows there devour us?' Murat made off; he would lead eighty squadrons of chasseurs, dragoons and cuirassiers.

Usually cavalry would advance on an enemy formation in 'battle formation'. This was a tactical, rectangular formation: close order, with the longest side towards the enemy, that is, at right angles to the line of advance. The cavalry did not gallop madly; when, as they most often did, they charged at the gallop, their maximum speed was three hundred metres a minute, about 18 kilometres per hour. At Eylau, Murat's cavalry, 'animated by heroic fury', advanced much more slowly, thanks to the snow which covered the ground and was still falling, stirred by the wind. In some battles, the cavalry of the Grande Armée was seen to charge at the trot or even at a walk if the terrain were difficult. Normally, at the gallop, the squadrons were slightly obliqued, but it was wholly according to circumstances. If the ground were at all constricted, or if the cavalry had to pass through gaps in the infantry columns, they charged in close column by platoons or by divisions.

When the French infantry was threatened by a cavalry charge, it 'formed square'. In practice, this was most often a rectangle, though in principle each 'square' measured 150 by 25 metres and was composed of an entire division, with six ranks of infantry on each side. The soldiers were closed-up shoulder to shoulder, the front rank kneeling. In three-rank formation, only the first two fired, the third rank behind keeping the muskets loaded. Fire was withheld until the cavalry was nearly upon them. At Auerstadt, Davout's infantrymen held fire until Blücher's cavalry was ten metres away, and they drove off every charge. The square formation fostered in the men a great sense of security. They had the impression of constituting a living fortress. At the battle of the Pyramids, 16,000 infantrymen held more than 50,000 cavalry in check. The fortress was not always invulnerable however. First, because while it was being attacked by cavalry it was also being bombarded by artillery. If a breach were made in one of its sides, the cavalry charged into it. Even without artillery support, the assaulting cavalry could breach the living walls of the square by wave after wave of charges, as Murat had done at Eylau.

The death rate among the horses killed during the campaigns of the Grande Armée was horrendous; no meaningful figures can be given because as the horses from France were killed in battle, or died from hunger, neglect or disease, along the interminable roads, they were replaced by horses requisitioned, bought or stolen. When Bonaparte sailed from Toulon, he took only 300 horses for the 3,042 cavalrymen who accompanied him; the rest were acquired in Egypt. And it was because Napoleon reckoned that he could always or often find enough horses in enemy or allied territory that he had formed foot dragoons who could fight both as infantry and as cavalry.

In France, the Grande Armée purchased their horses from breeders and farmers, mostly from the *départements* of the Orne, Calvados, Manche, Aisne and Ardennes. The horses had to be younger than eight years old, and the army paid 400 francs for each beast, cash down. At one time colonels were responsible for mounting their regiments, but then Napoleon transferred the task to large depots commanded by retired cavalry generals unfit for active service as a result of war wounds. The colonels were furious and put it about that these generals would buy bad horses and fill their own pockets. The method of buying remounts changed frequently between 1800 and 1813.

Those army horses destined for combat had to be trained for manoeuvres and familiarised with the sounds of war. In this respect, 'Instructions for the manoeuvres of mounted troops, Year X' is a monument of precise detail: 'Horses will be habituated to fire by firing pistols at the stable doors when they are being fed their oats. Take care to dwell for a pause between the shots at first, but as the young horses become more accustomed to the fire, repeat the pistol shots more frequently. If among the young horses, there are some who are sufficiently upset to affect the troupe, you must lead them to the stable before beginning the lesson, which should be continued, morning and evening, while they are eating their oats, and to habituate them, separately and little by little, to the noise of firearms. In this way the horses will also become accustomed to the movement and the flapping of the standards and, when in company with the infantry, to the noise of their drums.'

Admirable theory. Touching and abiding solicitude for the poor nag requisitioned from his farm in Bavaria, Austria, Poland, pushed day in, day out along dusty roads or in mud or snow, often their only food the straw from thatched roofs, and then thrown into the turmoil of cannon-fire. None the less, the enormous machine which was the cavalry of the Grande Armée functioned, manoeuvred under fire, in battle formation or in column. Its cuirassiers, dragoons and chasseurs certainly knew how to ride and fight on horseback, and the famous Instruction of Year X is as precise and detailed regarding the training of the cavalryman as of his mount. The drill for loading pistols when mounted comprised twelve steps; the drill for the presentation of arms for inspection differed as regards the heavies, the dragoons and the lights.

I will confine myself, for the benefit of today's cavalrymen, to quoting the paragraph headed 'To draw the sabre'. 'Pass the right hand over the reins, through the strap, seize the sabre at the hilt in order to draw the blade from the scabbard for about four fingers' breadth. Draw the blade quickly and hold, placing the back of the blade against your right shoulder, the wrist resting on the top of the right thigh, the little finger behind the hilt. The cavalryman will present his sabre in three movements to the inspecting officer when the latter stops in front of him: 1. Present the sabre forward, the arm half-extended, the thumb at the height of and six inches from the chin, the blade perpendicular, the flat of the blade to the front, the cutting edge to the left, the thumb across the right side of the hilt, moving the little finger forward. 2. Turn the wrist inwards in order to present the other side of the blade. 3. Shoulder the sabre once inspection is finished.' When Murat's cavalry charged at Eylau, the men in the front rank leaned forward, aiming the points of their sabres with their arms extended to the front. Those in the second rank remained upright, their short swords pointing upwards.

'The Russian attack had been literally nailed to the ground' according to some reports, but this is a little too condensed. It is true that the French cavalry had driven off the Russian cavalry and had driven a breach in the infantry following them, but the clash was frightful. Men were gutted by sabres and bayonets under a hail of cannon-balls and canister; the bodies of men and horses were scattered on the white ground. Some Russian reserve artillery, firing from a clearing in the forest into the confused mass, mowed down the combatants indiscriminately. It was at this time that General d'Hautpoul fell, whom Napoleon had embraced a day earlier.

As the Russian infantry continued to march towards the centre, Napoleon decided to engage the foot Guards. But we must withdraw our gaze for a moment from the observatory used by the high command. The surgeon Percy had left Hoff for Eylau. 'Scarcely more than a quarter hour from the battlefield, was a large house full of wounded with more to come. The surgeons were operating energetically, Around this haven from despair, were numberless vehicles, regiments awaiting the signal to move, and a crowd of poor wounded who could neither enter nor have their wounds dressed.' In the area immediately surrounding Eylau were wounded grenadiers of the Guard making their way back covered in blood. 'This shook me, as the Guard was a reserve unit only engaged as a last hope. A bad omen.' Larrey and the other surgeons of the Guard were hard at work, not in the mobile hospital provided for this privileged corps, but 'in miserable huts' in the same conditions suffered by Percy and his subordinates who were working on the wounded from the line units. Among the wounded were many generals: Augereau, as already mentioned; Laval, bullet under his Achilles tendon; Heudeley, bullet in his lower abdomen; Dahlmann, ten lance thrusts. General Corbineau, ADC to Napoleon, died from a thigh lost to a cannon-ball. D'Hautpoul had merely a fracture above the knee, but would die since it was not amputated in time. 'Many of the houses in town were on fire. The roar of the guns, the smoke from the fires, the cries of the wounded under the knife, will remain for ever in my memory. The battle was raging, but even so individuals and small groups were pillaging the town.'

At this time, Davout was deploying behind the enemy, but at about 3 p.m. 8,000 Prussian troops attacked, and Napoleon had only thirteen battalions of the foot Guard in reserve. On horseback, Davout harangued his troops: 'The cowards will die in Siberia; the brave will die on the field of honour.' The outlook was grave, but as evening was approaching Ney arrived on the enemy right. As soon as he learned of it, Bennigsen began thinking about retreat. Meanwhile, Percy and three colleagues climbed to the highest point in the cemetery 'to see the outcome of this battle between the two redoubtable armies. The plain was immense and one could readily see the two opponents on the snow-covered terrain, the infantry aligned, the cavalry standing by to intervene. The movements of the troops, the noise of their firing, the artillery, the marching men, the innumerable corpses, what a curious and harrowing spectacle! Rivers of blood had flowed on the reverse side of the cemetery towards the plain. Around the church, in the streets of the town, everywhere dead men and horses. The traffic rolled over them, artillery caissons crushed skull and limbs. And still the starving soldiers were pillaging under the cannon-mouth, risking death for a handful of potatoes. It was impossible to reach the wounded lying on the battlefield, so I returned to our huts which were humming with activity. Amputated arms and legs were tossed outside with the bodies of the dead.'

Napoleon, too, had re-entered Eylau. General Billon recalled: 'I was seated on a stone slab, back to the wall, when he passed in front of me. The Emperor would go to great lengths to avoid his horse treading on so many human remains.' according to Billon, the Emperor wept. He then rode over to the village of Ziegelhof, a half-league from Eylau, where he stopped at a small farm. He seemed exhausted and upset. He slept there 'fully dressed and booted, on a mattress beside the fire'. He was awakened in the small hours of the 9th to be told that Saint-Chamans, Soult's ADC, was asking to see him on an 'urgent matter'. The officer was admitted: 'What is it?' asked the Emperor in a tired tone of voice. 'Sire, the enemy is retreating. The Marshal is asking for orders.' According to Saint-Chamans: 'It was easy to judge from the lightening of his expression, the pleasure which this news had brought him.' Until now Napoleon had been very anxious. Would the Russians, who had shown themselves so tough, not return? No, they would not. Eylau would be a victory.

At dawn the next day Napoleon rode across the battlefield. No abattoir could have been so revolting. The corpses of men and horses were intermingled and spread over the ground covered with thick snow. This snow was no longer white, but yellow, stained with red, or sometimes a mass of reddish matter mixed with red or grey entrails or torn limbs. Some of the wounded were uttering harrowing cries and one could hear the cries and the death-rattles of horses with broken limbs who were dying of thirst.

The various reports and documents concerning the numbers of casualties at the massacre of Eylau do not agree, any more than do those of Verdun, 110 years later. The 58th Bulletin of the Grande Armée dated 9 February admitted to 1,900 dead and 5,700 wounded on the French side, figures corrected in the years following to at least 3,000 dead and 7,000 wounded: twenty generals killed or wounded; in those days senior officers also risked their lives. The Russians paid even more dearly: at least 7,000 dead and 10,000 wounded. 'Darling,' Napoleon wrote to Josephine, 'there was a great battle yesterday. We were victorious but I have lost many; the enemy lost even more which does not console me.'

While he surveyed the field of battle, pensive and grave-faced, Napoleon said little and that under his breath. Here is what he said. Facing a hillock where the 14th Line Regiment had been roughly handled, Bessières remarked of the dead: 'They are laid out like sheep.' 'Rather, say, like lions,' corrected the Emperor. Viewing the dead of the 14th, Napoleon said: 'What a massacre! And without a decision! A scene well calculated to inspire in princes a love of peace and a horror of war.' Facing the survivors of the 43rd Line, who had garlanded their colours with crepe because their colonel had been killed: 'I never want to see my colours in mourning. We have lost a good many friends and brave companions but they died on the field of honour and their lot is enviable. Let us work to avenge, not mourn, them, for tears belong only to women.' Then, a little later, turning over a corpse: 'It is but a short step.' This last remark has been repeatedly questioned and none of the other versions has been reliably confirmed. A group of aides-de-camp and senior officers followed Napoleon on these visits, but never closer than a horse's length away, and, seeing that he never turned when addressing a remark to one of them, what could these soldiers have heard? Later, they recollected as best they could.

After this visit, the Emperor passed through the midst of his troops. 'Vive l'Empereur!' was heard, still the ritual acclamation, but there were also new cries: 'Peace!' 'Peace and France!' 'Bread and peace!' Napoleon gave orders for the distribution of brandy, then – another departure – assembled his marshals and aides-de-camp for consultation: should they pursue the enemy without delay? Soult suggested a retreat behind the River Passarge (50 kilometres to the west) and, after fortifying, to rest the troops and await reinforcements. 'I agree with that,' said Napoleon. The Bulletin announced: 'The army will return to billets and enter winter quarters.'

VI

TILSIT, 1807
The Empire Extends to the Niemen

At the beginning of the century Eylau was a compact town of about 1,500 inhabitants. After the battle it was crammed with troops and officers of all ranks, plus about 4,000 French and an unknown number of Russian wounded, and thousands of dead from both sides lying in the streets. Snow everywhere. No food to be had, and the civilian population had fled.

On 9 February, stretcher-bearers and ambulances and even the doctors, doctors' assistants and surgeons spent the day transporting to the town centre the wounded rescued from the frozen huts, open to the four winds, where they had spent the night, and searching the battlefield for French and Russian wounded who, to avoid being buried in snow, had burrowed among the corpses of their comrades.

There was neither a hospital nor a large building available. That left the church, crammed since the previous evening with 400 Russians, both healthy and wounded. The only possibility: houses abandoned by their inhabitants – except, of course, those occupied by officers and troops.

The most grievously wounded were laid on the ground floor. There would be up to 70 in a small living-room, on the bare earth or, perhaps on dirty straw brought from the huts. Parties were sent out to find fresh straw, but if they found any they fed it to their horses.

When the ground floors were full, the so-called lightly wounded were hauled upstairs; some of them would be dead by morning. These men had been brought from the huts or from the snow-covered battlefield on carts or stretchers through streets which were choked and blocked, carts rolling unsteadily across the corpses of humans and horses. With a minimum of decorum, these had mostly been pushed to the borders of the roads to rot. 'It is lucky', said the surgeons, 'that the cold staunches the haemorrhages and limits infections.'

On the morning of 9 February, Percy was summoned by the Emperor. Except during actual combat, one did not wait on him without ceremony. The Surgeon-in-chief rapidly doffed his jacket of wolf skin and his sheepskin hat 'which made him look like a hussar', and, pulling on an embroidered frock-coat *en route*, ran to the 'palace', 'a hut as humble as mine and not one hundred paces distant'. Napoleon was stretched out fully dressed on a mattress, his face showing 'serenity and security'. One M. Lombard, a commissioner (quartermaster-general responsible for the materials for hospitals and ambulances, an important person) accompanied Percy. Here is a summary of the conversation: 'How many wounded?' 'Sire, about four thousand.' 'How many dead?' A third, certainly.' 'Were many wounded by cold steel?' 'Many, Sire, the lances and the bayonets do much damage.' 'How many generals wounded?' 'Many, Sire.' He named them, those doomed, those who could be saved.

Napoleon turned to Lombard: 'Have you people to help you?' 'Sire we lack neither linen, flannel nor instruments, but we need managers, staff and nurses.' 'What organisation, what barbarity!' In fact, the situation was worse than Lombard had admitted, since only the Guard had enough linen and instruments. 'Sire, when one is sure to find himself without a job when there is peace, regardless of how well he had behaved in war, it is difficult to be zealous and to decide to stay in the army as an employee or nurse. This very title would be a negative recommendation on return to France.' 'It is true that almost no one but confidence men and vagabonds throw themselves into the hospital service, which they quickly abandon once their affairs have ceased to prosper.' Percy intervened: 'Surely your Majesty will never confuse such men with the surgeons, whose future, however, is no more assured.' 'I am pleased with their efforts and devotion, and I wish that all that should be better organised in future, each being sure to retain his post.' 'Sire, in your Guard, the ambulance service offers a fairly good career, despite the time and place, because you have given them employees who are officers and soldiers. We also need that, and it is above all essential that the surgeons should be formed into a corps. 'Good. What is happening to your wounded?'

Percy gave more details. It is clear that Napoleon, once more, evaded the issue. No privilege of the Guard could be extended to the entire army. We shall see this refusal confirmed. One might conclude from this conversation that Napoleon's principal interest was to know how many active soldiers remained to carry on the war. Percy received a bonus: on 11 February the Emperor awarded him two hundred supplementary 'nurses', who were in fact common soldiers selected by chance. Percy wrote: 'I have assigned them to the different hovels where the wounded are cared for. There are doubtless some good ones in the bunch, but many devour the little food allotted to the wounded.'

On the day after the battle and on the next day the wounded received a cup of thin bouillon and a crust of very coarse black bread. Nothing else could be provided, the town and its surroundings having been thoroughly ransacked. On the evening of 10 February, however, the wounded in the makeshift ambulance where Percy and his assistants operated though that things were improving: less thin soup, a little more bread and, wonders – fresh straw! But, a sudden noise, and a flood of grenadiers invaded the ambulance. 'We are his Majesty's foot guards. All this is requisitioned for us.' In a matter of minutes the stew and the bread had disappeared, the fresh straw was wrenched from the wounded and the surgeons were thrown out. 'I arrived', wrote Percy, 'at an empty room in a pastor's house; he had seen the Guard smashing in the front doors of houses, breaking everything and making an unholy noise, and had fled with his four sisters. I took possession with my four companions, determined to defend ourselves. The ground floor of the house was occupied by sixty wounded men. The gangrenous leg of one of them gave off a charnel-house smell which was unbearable. I proceeded to cut it off. I had just had two Prussian prisoners remove twenty-five French and Russian corpses which lay around the house, plus four wagons of rubbish which were proving noisome.'

In the church were crammed 400 Russians, some well, some wounded, some dying. The unwounded men lit a fire which they replenished with benches, partitions, organ, altar – producing thick smoke. From time to time, they threw out a dozen corpses, then shut the doors again. A Frenchman who managed to get in to distribute bread was horrified to see that the Russians were keeping still-warm corpses to sleep upon. Percy had tried to persuade some Russian surgeons to come to the aid of their compatriots, offering them bread and brandy, but they refused; besides, what could they do?

On the night of 10/11 February a strong wind had backed to the southwest and next morning the temperature had risen by twenty degrees centigrade. A warm sun shone all day, turning the snow into a blackish swamp in which, up to the knees, the soldiers lost boots and stockings. After the hunt for food came the hunt for boots. With the heat, suppuration and gangrene increased; dirty dressings were tossed out together with the day's crop of corpses. 'Some Russian prisoners were harnessed to sleds which were piled with the dead. Enfeebled, they resembled corpses themselves. Everywhere was excrement, rubbish, the crushed remains of horses, rotting and putrid debris.'

On 12 February, Napoleon dictated an order: 'All the wounded are to be evacuated in the next twenty-four hours. The wounded from the line are to be sent to Thorn by stages and, from there, to Warsaw. Those from the Guard will go to the château of Inowraclaw.' This stood beyond the Vistula and had been requisitioned by Marshal Bessières. The evacuation of the Guard's wounded passed off fairly well; that of the Line was rather different.

Early on the 13th, Percy had assembled his entire force in the church square, where the Russian prisoners deposited the night's crop of 25 corpses – a routine affair. The surgeons and doctors were pale and thin. One of them read out the names of the seriously wounded who were to be moved first: 300 amputees, 500 fractures, 200 serious head wounds. There were also fever and diarrhoetic cases, particularly among those who had drunk too much melted snow, plus victims of frozen feet and gangrene. Add to these an unknown number of wounded who had already been sent to châteaux around Eylau; some three hundred at Plirchten, at least as many at Merwitz and as many again in a third château.

'His Majesty', said Percy, 'wished that the evacuation should be ended by this evening, but that will be impossible. We will do our best. Each convoy will comprise fifteen vehicles for which two of you will be responsible. Do not over-load the wagons. The walking wounded must follow the convoy on foot. They can help you at the stages.' The vehicles were wagons or sleighs; the latter could slide over frozen soil and mud. The convoys laboriously assembled, while the artillery caissons rumbled past, throwing up sprays of mud; officers' carriages, some carrying wives or mistresses, many of whom had had time to catch-up, added to the chaos. On the broken-down roads of Eylau carriages, carts, wag-ons, collided; insults and scuffles ensued. The sleighs and requisitioned carts became embroiled in the disorder, the peasants trying to control their little rus-tic horses which were frightened by the commotion. Some had loaded their vehicles with straw which served as cover and mattress for the wounded and, ultimately, as food for the horses – straw was treasure.

In the houses assigned to them, the surgeons were still changing soiled dressings and operating on last night's crop of gangrenous patients. Percy: 'We dressed, amputated, the wounded screamed; we set fractures and we loaded.' Loading the wounded on to low vehicles was relatively easy, but to hoist up and into the high army wagons those unfortunates to whom the smallest movement caused acute suffering, was another matter. 'Would they survive after twenty-four hours?' Another agonising question: could one distribute before departure to each wounded man a cup of hot bouillon and a small glass of brandy? The pillaging Guardsmen had taken everything except two steers which Percy had acquired at the last moment.

Move off! The convoy elbowed into the mass of artillery and troops. By evening 600 wounded had been evacuated. The Emperor expressed his pleasure to Percy: 'Your surgeons have shown courage, zeal and devotion.' This convoy of suffering was to cover more than 200 kilometres. On 18 February, Napoleon, hearing that many of the wounded assembled at Landsberg (25 kilo-metres from Eylau) were unable to move for lack of vehicles, sent Percy his own carriage; he would go on horseback. He also gave orders to requisition 'all car-riages using the road, including those of general officers and of the canteen women'. Senior officers and *vivandières* protested in vain. Most of the surgeons would ride horses, some went in sleds, including Percy who was suffering from persistent bronchitis.

The convoys moved slowly by short stages, over bad roads which were either frozen or rivers of icy mud. Some sleighs were unable to keep going, some carriages got stuck. The ambulance caissons carrying linen, lint, etc., had to sup-ply several convoys, which slowed up changing the dressings. At the stages, food was a problem. The surgeons tackled every task, including the most menial. How were those with leg or stomach wounds to relieve themselves? One could not be continually stopping to lift a patient and remove his breeches; some of the patients were diarrhoetic in addition to having multiple wounds. Percy: 'The wagons are infected by pus and excrement. Our surgeons can scarcely stand the reek.' Another problem: the peasants conscripted as drivers took every opportunity – overturned wagons, bottlenecks, disorders – to make off. 'Some surgeons were obliged to use violence against the peasants.'

The walking wounded following the convoys looked like ghosts. 'A mass of men passed by who were suffering fevers and diarrhoea. So thin and debilitated that one could not conceive how they could walk. Pale, wrinkled, yellow, covered with spots.' The Liebstadt–Osterode stage, 60 kilometres in three days, was one of the worst. It was often at such moments that devotion was manifested. Percy pays tribute to one junior assistant surgeon, named Lecat, slight, bright-eyed, pleasant featured. This lad had learned some words of Polish 'those needed for survival in this rough land' and he showed a remarkable talent for exciting the sympathy of the peasants for the plight of the wounded. In this way he obtained bread (only black, but what a joy to bite into it!) and often poultry or ham and then – what a marvellous bouillon!

Before reaching Osterode, the route led through a magnificent pine forest. The road was wide, but the passage of so many vehicles, the snow and the frost had made it dangerous. Horses fell and broke their legs, a wagon overloaded with wounded fell into a concealed ditch. It was necessary – and once again young Lecat showed his devotion – to transfer the wounded, stinking, groaning, crying, into other wagons which set off, running over the fallen horses – and all in the teeth of an icy blizzard.

A rumour had run through the convoys – 'There are hospitals at Osterode'. In the imagination of these unfortunates, Osterode was a haven, a paradise. They arrived at a large market-town covered in snow, pillaged successively by French and Russians. Percy: 'I visited three houses, so-called hospitals. What hospitals – my God!' The only care consisted of parsimonious distributions of bouillon and hard-tack. The wounded fumbled in their filthy rags for a cup or a bowl. The distribution suddenly stopped: no more bouillon until tomorrow. The streets were choked with rubbish, detritus, animal entrails. Everywhere were soldiers, in rags, muddy, shuffling on feet swollen with chilblains and swaddled in dirty rags. They looked at the sleighs and the wagons full of wounded: 'How they stink!' Not a drop of pity for their brothers in arms, faces blue with cold, soaked, filthy, pitiful. Human feeling no longer existed. Even some surgeons and their assistants seemed to be overcome by so much misery. Percy even found some who claimed to have lost their convoy. 'I threatened them with dismissal and forced them to retrace their steps back to their vehicles. I am sorry to confess that I upbraided them, for they were themselves suffering much.'

On 24 February, at Osterode, Napoleon once again sent for Percy, who first remitted his statement of personnel (numbers and ranks of the surgeons in each of the various ambulances). The Emperor liked nothing better than such statements and read them attentively. Then, to Percy: 'That is accurate.' Did he really know? It was, in any case, more an expression of satisfaction, a compliment. Then followed questions: 'Are you losing many wounded?' Always this concern for effectives. 'Sire, we would lose more in bad hospitals. In spite of the difficulties and miseries of this evacuation, we are losing fewer than if we had left them at Eylau or Landsberg. The open air, the cold and even the snow are less dangerous than the infected air in the hospitals.' 'Is tetanus taking a toll?' 'Only one case, Sire. It is great heat alternating with great cold which brings on tetanus. Our wounded have not been exposed to this contrast. It is in the hospitals that these noxious fevers develop and spread. Diarrhoea empties them and the diet precedes the first stage of feverish delirium.' 'And chilblains?' 'More than two thousand men cannot march due to chilblains on the foot or the heel, many have feet torn by ice. And there are two or three regiments where all are coughing from the colonel to the drummer boy.' 'I see. Thank you.'

The harder the winter, the more one searches attentively for the tiniest precursor of spring. As early as 23 February, Percy recorded an event: 'I heard a lark today. Here comes gentle spring.' In fact, spring was still far away; the milder temperatures brought first a thaw, and mud and stenches increased; but in the reeking carts the word ran from one sufferer to the next – the lark is singing. How many times had they heard, instead of the lark, the mournful croaking of the crows? The lark brought a message from the gentle France which they longed to see again.

Whether it would be better to desert or wait for a normal return was much debated by the soldiers of the Grande Armée in Poland. At least thirty thousand desertions – where did these men get to? How on earth could they get back to France from here?

The convoys of wounded continued to crawl along. At Strasbourg there was a minor miracle; all the prostrate wounded were able for the first time to leave their rotting beds on the wagons. A convent of poor Capucins welcomed the worst cases, the most chilled. There was little straw, but it was clean. The remainder were billeted on the inhabitants who received the wherewithal to feed them – from God knows whence in this disorder. But the real miracle was at Gottlob. How Gottlob had escaped pillage was a mystery. When they arrived, the wounded wept tears of joy to see in the shops little rolls like brioches, cakes and bottles of brandy. 'We could have anything if we paid.' Even those who could not afford all these luxuries were happy to be billeted on the inhabitants who proved helpful in welcoming such stinking guests. There was even linen and lint for the three surgeons sent on ahead by Percy to 'hurry from house to house to change dressings'.

One is never permitted to remain long in an earthly paradise. Next day the unfortunates found themselves once more groaning under a driving rain. The roads were terrible, many streams had to be forded, more wagons overturned. Between two downpours, a lark was heard singing and some claimed that they had seen it 'perform the Holy Spirit', an expression from old France describing the bird hovering at a low altitude, its wings beating.

Thorn, 27 February. Here, after a rest, the convoys were reorganised for the remainder of the journey towards Warsaw. Thorn, on the right bank of the lower Vistula, is an old and historic city (birthplace of Copernicus), but the wounded found it crammed with people and rubbish (why didn't we stop at Gottlob?). Sod it! I'm going back! In the confusion, either alone or in small groups, the healthy and walking wounded vanished. The other wounded from Eylau were dispersed among the already overcrowded hospitals. When they would leave again, nobody knew.

This convoy of pain, which I have wished to follow at the risk of disturbing the reader, could find its counterpart a hundred times over, with little difference save climate, on all the roads followed by the Grande Armée in its drive across Europe. But, with regard to this particular journey, we must now state a fact *a priori* that is incredible – from Eylau to Thorn, only one in ten died. The cold had been a blessing in disguise, and perhaps the hunger too. In warm weather, suppuration and gangrene would have been much worse and one should not forget that diet can remedy the worst intestinal infections. We should remember too that these men, exposed to a lack of hygiene which we would find horrendous, had, like all Europeans of that epoch, been screened by an infant death rate which spared only the most robust.

After Eylau the Emperor had said that the army would go into winter quarters. It certainly needed to do so. As a priority it had to recover 60,000 missing, wounded, deserters. Reinforcements were summoned from every region in the Empire, and these were marching towards Osterode, the 'bad village' whose inhabitants had fled. Napoleon decided to build a vast camp there. He took up quarters temporarily in the old château of Ordenschloss and summoned the engineers. They constructed a palisade around a vast square inside which were streets bordered by fairly comfortable wooden huts. Each street bore the name of one the latest victories. The Guard had its own camp, built with a degree of luxury; in the centre a brick building where the Emperor installed himself. He worked, ate and interviewed personnel in the single room. When he went out, the grenadiers presenting arms were shaved and powdered as if in their barracks at Courbevoie. Arriving at one block at mealtime, the Emperor did not wish the men to stand as he entered: 'Do not disturb yourselves. I am pleased with my grumblers. They have lodged me well, and my officers have paved rooms. When we leave, the Poles can make it a fine city.' The Poles did in fact come long distances to see this wooden city constructed by the French; it was a curiosity. Berthier pleaded with the Emperor to retire behind the Vistula where he would be more comfortable. Napoleon refused, knowing that any such move would be interpreted as a retreat. The news from France was not good. The slaughter at Eylau had had the worst effect, the stock market fell. According to Savary: 'This decline was due to the terror which struck everyone each time they saw the destinies of France and of every family subjected to a salvo of cannon.' Disturbed by these tales, Napoleon wrote to Fouché: 'France's position has never been so great or so favourable. As for Eylau, I said and said repeatedly that the Bulletin had exaggerated the losses and what are twenty thousand dead in a major battle? When I bring home my army to France and to the Rhine, it will be seen that not many are absent from roll-call.' In truth, the numbers would be there, thanks to conscription, but many names would be missing.

Napoleon would have been glad to parley and make peace, seeing that the bloodshed had not been decisive. While still at Eylau, he sent General Bertrand to the King of Prussia with proposals: the states belonging to this sovereign would be restored to him as far as the Elbe and a peace would be signed. 'I must consult my ally, the Tsar.' Napoleon, in an order of the day dated 16 February, endeavoured to allay the discontent of the army: 'Having thus frustrated all the enemy's projects, we will return to the Vistula and take up our quarters. Anyone troubling us will regret it for, beyond the Vistula as beyond the Danube, amid the frosts of winter as in early autumn, we will still be French soldiers and French soldiers of the Grande Armée.' This eloquence was now more defensive than victorious.

At the beginning of March 1807 Napoleon had his HQ at Osterode, in the centre of his army which had moved towards the Baltic to cover Danzig, the siege of which had begun. All enemy attacks were contained and repulsed without difficulty. The field police combed the rear areas to round-up deserters, who were often labelled stragglers. The officers of the gendarmerie before whom they appeared were ordered to instil a feeling of shame for their cowardice: 'How could you run away when the Emperor brought you victory?' The search produced meagre results. The imperial orders concerning provisioning and *matériel* were more successful. Three lines of 'major warehouses' were established. At Osterode, 200,000 rations of hard-baked bread were stored, together with 140,000 rations of biscuits, 30,000 quintals of flour, 1,600 quintals of wheat, 300,000 rations of brandy. Bread and brandy were the main props to morale.

On 1 April Napoleon, who had had enough of his one-room quarters, left Osterode for Finkenstein, 30 kilometres farther west, where he found a very nice country house belonging to the King of Prussia's court chamberlain. The Guard and Oudinot's corps were billeted nearby. 'I have just transferred my headquarters to a very beautiful château,' he wrote to Josephine. 'It has many chimneys which is very nice. Often having to get up at night, I like to see a fire. My health is perfect. The weather is fine but still cold.'

Napoleon was to remain at Finkenstein until 6 June. Twice a week he received from a functionary of the Council of State the dispatches of ministers. He immediately studied the files, even rising if they arrived at night, when secretaries were immediately summoned. More than 2,000 kilometres from Paris, he continued to oversee the administration of the Opera. To Fouché: 'If things do not work better, I will send them a good soldier who will make them march to the drums.' To Daru, he expressed his anger at being asked for 16,000 francs for the 'upkeep' of the hut he had used at the Boulogne camp. The Emperor was virtually free from money cares, given that his private budget was in practice intermixed with the State budget, but he knew that all who circulated in the corridors of power or nearby filled their pockets, and he became irritated at being fleeced. On the other hand, he congratulated General Denniée, Secretary of State for War Administration, who had sent him a report: 'I have received and read with great interest your Statement A, giving the estimated number of effectives after the induction of the 1808 conscripts. It was so well drawn that it read like a beautiful piece of poetry.' A revealing compliment. Conscription was beginning to disgust French opinion, but the Master was re-assured to learn that the gaps in the Grande Armée would be filled.

At Finkenstein from the outset, Duroc, Grand Marshal of the palace, had strictly insisted on etiquette. The Guard paraded daily in the grounds of the château; the marshals and the high dignitaries attended in full dress, grouped around the Emperor according to rank. One oriental costume stood out – that of the envoy of the Shah of Persia – which says much for the conqueror's prestige. The receptions were naturally less brilliant than were those in Warsaw, but then Finkenstein was rather remote. The most discreet of the guests was undoubtedly Marie Walewska, uneasy at first as we know, then amorous. Josephine was aware of the situation and complained. Her husband replied: 'I do not like to see my little Josephine, who is good, sulky and capricious and who knows how to quarrel with the grace she brings to everything, for she is always amiable, except when she is jealous and then she becomes wholly devilish.' Then came warnings against strangers, even of ambassadorial rank; never to receive at Malmaison anyone who would not be admitted to the presence of the Empress if the Emperor were there.

Towards the end of April Percy came from Osterode to submit a plan for the reorganisation of the surgical service of the Grande Armée. He trusted that the Emperor was in a good mood; all the rewards which Percy had asked for his subordinates and colleagues after Eylau had been granted: the Legion of Honour for eight senior surgeons, five senior aides promoted to senior surgeon, forty surgeons of every grade received 300, 200 or 100 francs gratuity. 'It is a triumph for the surgeons of the army,' said Percy, whose project had been entitled 'The creation of surgery for battle.' This organisation would need to be self-sufficient, independently administered, with sufficient nurses to escort the convoys, guard the parks and the wagons, collect the wounded from the battlefield, bury the dead, care for the sick in the field hospitals, see to the cleanliness of the camps, the hospitals and the headquarters. 'In this way,' explained Percy, 'all the soldiers will be kept in the line. Not one will be diverted to help the wounded, the hospitals or the convoys.' The confusion, disorder and the struggles for influence which engendered a multiplicity of administrations would all be eliminated. The surgery for battle would be an independent corps like the engineers and the artillery.

Napoleon paced up and down in the main room, listening with goodwill to the Chief Surgeon, interrupting to speak on other subjects, for example of Coste, Chief Doctor of the Grande Armée, an old man of whom Napoleon deplored yet again 'his conservatism, his lack of spirit, his fear of death'. Coste had asked to be relieved. Profiting from a silence, Percy resumed, describing his project. 'Sire, we could have a senior surgeon of the army, plus three senior surgeons as inspectors-general, plus sixteen senior surgeons with the rank of lieutenant-colonel.' Napoleon reached for the Percy's notebook which had been carefully written, flicked through it and stuffed it into his pocket. 'We will see about that.' The interview was ended. 'With the rank of lieutenant-colonel' had been one sentence too much. Merge the surgeons and doctors into the officer corps: No! Only the Guard had received this privilege. Napoleon knew that the mere mention would produce howls of protest from 80 per cent of the corps of officers. It was asking too much to risk that for what he regarded as a secondary cause. And, at bottom, Napoleon, ex-officer himself, agreed with the feelings of these officers. Improve the conditions of service of surgeons and doctors, yes, if possible; not to intermingle too much the various arms of the service is the aim of every war leader. But the Emperor already had so much to occupy his attention. He had wished to end this campaign with a major victory. Attention at Finkenstein now turned towards Danzig.

From the 10th century to our own day, Danzig has seen it all: independence, vast riches, many sieges, devastation, domination by many powers. Her situation at the mouth of the Vistula on the Baltic coast made her a strategic key point.

Napoleon wished to take this fortified city so as to lay hands on her immense stocks of munitions. He also felt that, with Danzig taken, the left wing of his army would be safe from any military threat. Marshal Lefebvre's troops were already investing the fortress. David's portrait of François-Joseph Lefebvre, Marshal of France (promoted in 1804), Duke of Danzig, depicts above his gaudy panoply the brown, robust and regular face of a man of the people. He must have been 53 years old at that time. Born at Rouffach, Haut-Rhin, his father was a miller who left the child with his brother, a village priest. 'Teach him Latin; he can be a priest like you.' This miller had been a hussar and was now a widower. He told the lad that to be a soldier was the worst of trades, but at the same time had regaled him with tales of the soldier's life – at 18 the boy had rushed off to join the French guards. He was not ignorant, as some have said. He wrote a good hand and had a smattering of Latin, thanks to his studies at the presbytery. Speaking German better than French, he would give lessons in that language to his comrades after he joined the army. As sergeant, he married; on the register he gave as his profession 'master of languages'. A decade later, he was a captain and in another two years divisional general of the Army of Sambre-et-Meuse. There seems to be little of special note concerning his military talent, where courage dominated. Commander of the military division of Paris in 1800, his tastes and friendships should have inclined him more towards Bonaparte's adversaries, but the latter had won him to his cause on the very eve of 18 Brumaire. Sword in hand, Lefebvre had saved the First Consul from the fury of the Five Hundred, an action which later did no harm to his chances.

For the most part, Lefebvre is less well-known than his wife: Madame Sans-Gêne (Free-and-Easy), the heroine of the celebrated play by Sardou and Moreau. In fact, the name had not been invented for her. The dramatist Moreau had written a play featuring a female soldier named Thérèse Figuier, whose career as a dragoon had lasted from 1793 to 1815. Sardou believed that the play would enjoy greater success if someone better known and with the same traits of character as this Figuier were written in, Maréchale Lefebvre, for example. Ultimately, Madame Sans-Gêne is a caricature of the Maréchale.

In Paris on 1 March 1793, Lefebvre, then a sergeant in the French guards, had married his mistress, a laundress named Catherine Hubscher from the rue Poissonnière, an Alsatian as was he, thirty years old, illiterate, as were most working people. He taught her to write and the marriage was very successful. The laundry flourished – and an NCO of the guards was not just anyone.

Catherine watched the rise of her husband's fortunes with distrust. When she heard that there was talk of offering General Lefebvre a place on the Directory, she wrote to him: 'You must tell them NO. What would become of you in the middle of all that? They must be poorly off if they want to make a king of an idiot like you.' At any rate these words are attributed to her, but they are no more verifiable than nine-tenths of others she is said to have uttered. The only certainty is that the ex-laundress was out of her element in the salons which became open to her under the Consulate. She was completely aware of this and realised that she was too old to acquire manners and a veneer, so she sensibly decided to do without and continue to use the language of a plain housewife. She would say 'It is I who does my hair' as opposed to 'I do my own hair' and would refer to 'the wife of so-and-so'. She talked with more spirit than did her gossiping listeners. Some of her linguistic errors were deliberate and not due to vulgarity of character, for she was full of common sense, but she was determined to show these frequenters of salons that they were not going to impose on her. All the same, when her husband was created Duke of Danzig, she used his title proudly. She went to the Tuileries to thank the Empress Josephine and the major-domo introducing her omitted her title. Josephine had noticed this and said 'And how is Madame the Duchess of Danzig?' Catherine turned to the flunkey and said 'Hey, sonny, that's telling you!' A little later, still at the Tuileries, as Napoleon was holding her hand and presenting her to a glittering circle, the Duchess of Lusignan said in a stage-whisper: 'Your majesty has seen fit to lower the title of duchess down to Madame Lefebvre.' 'I have seen fit', corrected Napoleon tartly, 'to raise the title of duchess up to Madame Lefebvre.' Later, tiring of the guerrilla warfare of the salons, she chose to speak little. Having seen her, Madame de Chastenay, who had expected to meet something of a 'card', wrote that she had met only 'an old fat foreigner. I had thought to find her otherwise grotesque. However, spirited Frenchwomen are everywhere and this woman is among them.' The Lefebvre family had fourteen children, twelve of whom were boys. Twelve died in infancy, which was not unusual at that time.

Napoleon placed great confidence in Lefebvre, but had seen fit to send him an engineer, Chasseloup, and the artillery General Lariboisière ('siege warfare is a specialised affair'). Danzig was being defended by 13,000 Prussian and 4,000 Russian troops. The fortifications were of wood, but could withstand musketry. Redoubts and earthworks had been erected around the city. The defenders could let loose the waters of the Mottlau and the Vistula to flood the area to the south, west and north. A vast swampy plain, the Nehrung, extended from the city to the sea; it bordered a canal, a reach of the Vistula and the island of Holm, which was garrisoned by the Russians. In short, a defence to discourage all but the most determined enemy.

The French troops under General Schramm had succeeded in establishing themselves in the Nehrung. Consultations between Lefebvre, Lariboisière and Chasseloup concluded that Danzig could only be attacked from the west, defended on that side by two works: the Hagelsberg and the Bischofsberg. Chasseloup suggested a diversionary attack against the Bischofsberg ,while putting the main weight against the Hagelsberg. Agreed. Initially Lefebvre had only

18,000 men at his disposal, but at the end of March two army corps (44th and 19th of the Line) plus a train of artillery arrived. From time immemorial, siege warfare had begun with the digging of parallel trenches which were edged closer to the fortifications yard by yard.

On 2 April the sappers had begun a first trench, 1,200 metres long, on the Ziganberg, a height opposite the Hagelsberg; the sandy soil made the work very arduous. A Russian redoubt was taken the following night, but the defenders retook it and let loose flood waters around it – a serious check because the enemy could fire at will on the French trenches. The sappers continued to dig in the most adverse conditions until 7 April. The sand was collapsing all the time, and the diggers were under sniper fire during the daytime. Chasseloup ordered the attack on the Bischofsberg to begin on the night of the 7th/8th: 'This secondary operation will allow us to establish batteries there which can take the Hagelsberg in reverse and even to fire on the city. Four days of short-range butchery ensued. The Prussians counter-attacked; the French attacked again – and so it went on. On the 12th Marshal Lefebvre personally headed an attack which secured the Hagelsberg.

At Finkenstein, Napoleon, bent over his maps, was daily informed of progress by his couriers, and followed the attack as if there in person – or so he thought. He wrote to Lefebvre that he hoped that Danzig would be taken within two weeks; that he had sent him a large siege train; that General Schramm should be reinforced in order to cut the canal. He dictated a communiqué for the Bulletin of the Grande Armée (71st Bulletin of 19 April): 'Marshal Lefebvre displays the energy of a young man. The Saxons, the Poles, the Badeners, with the hereditary prince at their head, compete in ardour and courage.' To Lefebvre on 15 April: 'You are really starting to hit your stride. I continue to hope that fire can be opened seriously on the city itself on the 20th. I am therefore hoping that for my 1st May bouquet you will send me the keys to Danzig. I have noted with pleasure the energy which you have displayed in developing the siege works; it is the utter determination to conquer which transmits this energy to the minds of others.'

On 15 April French troops under General Gardanne advanced the length of the Laake Canal in order to interdict navigation on this channel and on the Vistula. Marshal Kalkreuth, commander of the Danzig defenders, threatened with being cut-off from the sea, intervened with 3,000 Russians from the Weichselmünde fort (on the Baltic, north of Danzig) and with 2,000 Prussians from the city. These counter-attacks were repulsed. Elsewhere, Lefebvre's troops reached the left bank of the Vistula, which meant that the river was now secured on both sides.

On the 20th there was a strong spring gale in the Baltic, and snow filled the trenches – little activity. On the 23rd the city was bombarded by 58 heavy guns. Lefebvre's troops cheered as flames engulfed the houses, but – disappointment; the flames subsided and only smoke could be seen, and that dissipating. The besieged had succeeded in dowsing the fires. On the 25th, a further bombardment, more fires, again extinguished by the garrison. But the sappers had been working hard. During the night of 25th/26th, a third trench was completed; the noose was tightening, enemy sorties were repulsed. But Lefebvre, remembering Napoleon's wish for his '1st May bouquet', became uneasy and impatient: 'Order a general assault immediately!' Neither Chasseloup nor Lariboisière agreed, nor did any of the engineer officers. 'We have not yet sufficient artillery. Our men must invest the town more closely. The enemy still has too many redoubtable bastions. To attack now would be suicidal. Ask the Emperor's opinion.'

In substance, Napoleon replied: 'You must not be impatient. You must not ignore the engineer officers and the foreign auxiliaries. I am sending you reinforcements, but the grenadiers' chests will not overturn the walls of Danzig. Listen to the opinion of General Chasseloup.' I must make a comment here. Since the beginning of the siege Napoleon had continually pressed Lefebvre; now he was restraining him. Economy in human lives had never been, and would never be, the major concern of the conqueror. So, why restrain Lefebvre? I suspect that Napoleon had an ingrained conviction that he and he alone understood the totality of the military art, and this, coupled with a drive for total domination, might produce contradictions, but if so – too bad.

Lefebvre had abandoned his general attack, but he wished to secure two dangerous strong points: the island of Holm and the redoubt of Kalke-Schanze opposite, on the bank of the Vistula. A successful attack was launched on 6/7 May. Accounts mention the brave conduct of the sharpshooter Fortuna, an incident mentioned repeatedly in military history. Landed on the sandy soil of the island, Fortuna, scouting forward in the dark, was ambushed by the Russians, disarmed and captured. Shortly afterwards the column which he was preceding approached. The officer in command heard noises, glimpsed silhouettes and, suspicious, cried: 'Who goes there?' A Russian officer replied in French, 'France! Forward!' But Fortuna shouted: 'They are Russians, captain. Open fire!' The French charged, the Russians were routed, killed or taken prisoner. In the mêlée, Fortuna survived by throwing himself into a ditch. He was decorated and promoted sergeant. That same night, the foreign auxiliaries (the Legion of the North and the Saxons) had taken the redoubt of Kalke-Schanze. On the island of Holm 400 Russians were surprised in their wooden huts and put to the bayonet.

The noose around the city tightened. On the night of 7/8 May, troops of the 19th Line and 12th Light reached the covered road in the fortifications; the sappers demolished the palisades with their axes. Next day the sappers dug around the bastions. From 11 May, both besiegers and besieged had the impression that the final assault was imminent. We have here a brief note from Percy which is less impersonal than the military accounts of this siege war. The Chief Surgeon had been present since 1 May; he must have been feeling happy, having recently learned that he had been made a Commander of the Legion of Honour and a member of the Institute. 'I went into the trenches with M. Ramoret, senior surgeon of the 19th Line. The place was ploughed up with cannon-balls. One saw women with their infants searching for these and for musket-balls; they get five sous and one sou for them. Our soldiers exposed themselves even more to win the wretched five sous. Women and children are constantly digging with spades in those places where a ball had fallen. I saw eight or ten soldiers cutting up a horse for its flesh; they had surely killed it for that purpose.'

'Between the artillery salvoes there was a mournful silence. The trenches were smeared with blood. We kept close to the breastworks without exposing our heads, as otherwise the enemy aimed a musket at you and killed you. The soldiers rarely stood upright but stood in niches cut into the earth of the communication trenches which sheltered them from the rain, the cannon-balls and the bullets. But the balls and the bullets sought them out everywhere. A company would think itself lucky if they did not lose two or three of their number after twenty-four hours in the trenches. The regiments are being bled white at an alarming rate.'

On 12 May the Russians (General Kamensky) landed some 4–5,000 troops at the mouth of the Vistula near the fort of Weichselmünde. It became known later that during a council of war, Tsar Alexander, the King of Prussia and Grand-Duke Constantin agreed that they no longer had the means to fight a major battle against the French which in any case would force them to expose the city, but that they could try to relieve Danzig by sea. The idea seemed ridiculous to Napoleon when he learned of it. 'This hope of succouring Danzig by a seaborne expedition', he wrote in the 74th Bulletin, 'must seem quite extraordinary to every intelligent soldier who knows the terrain and the position of the French army.' He was correct. The attempt failed dismally, and cost the Russians more than 2,500 dead and wounded. The Danzig garrison had not even attempted a sortie. On the evening of 22 May, the ships that had brought the landing force left for Königsberg, carrying as many wounded as they had been able to collect. Marshal Kalkreuth managed to send a message to the Grand-Duke: 'I am running out of ammunition.' His hopes rose next day when he learned that the British corvette *Dauntless* was bringing him replenishments. The French watched this spanking little vessel, helped by a brisk wind from the north, sail into the estuary with a determination bordering on suicidal courage.

Scarcely past the Weichselmünde fort, artillery and musketry fire smashed into her. Dismasted, she struck her colours and sank.

There was no further hope for the besieged though they continued to resist. Their guns hammered the French trenches which approached ever near-er; casualties were heavy. Lefebvre wrote to the Emperor that Chasseloup's tac-tics were too costly and that it would have been better to attack Bischofsberg directly, rather than take the Hagelsberg first. Napoleon, bent over his maps, still followed the siege step by step, still anxious to convince Lefebvre that he alone knew what must be done. Lefebvre received two letters from Finkenstein, one dated 17 May, 8 p.m, the other 18 May, 11 a.m. Here are the main points: 'Your letter caused me the greatest surprise. I had thought that you had more charac-ter and conviction. Is it at the end of a siege that one must change the system of attack, thus discouraging the army and calling into question your own judge-ment? You have no right to state that my opinion was that we should attack the Bischofsberg: my opinion was that we should first attack the fortified camp, invest the place closely, and then attack the point which the engineers and the artillery judged the most vulnerable. After the council which you convened, you decided not to attack the fortified camp, but the Hagelsberg.'

As we can see, Napoleon had edited the record quite freely; he had merely counselled Lefebvre to listen to Chasseloup. Here is what followed: 'You are about to take the Hagelsberg. Administer a swift kick to these petty critics. Attack the Hagelsberg; master of the Hagelsberg, the city is yours, firstly, because you will have the Bischofsberg and, finally, master or not of the Bischofsberg is quite unimportant: you can advance across the low ground of the city under cover of the Hagelsberg. Danzig has always been taken via the Hagelsberg. Furthermore, the engineer and artillery officers had decided that this was the point to attack. They know more of it than the subalterns and the gossips, who, rather than advance the trenches, amuse themselves by criticising. I am aware of the frivolity of the French character. Have them throw bags and casks of earth in the trenches, and under the protection of this earthwork, breach the palisades and loose the assault. Consult only Chasseloup and Lari-boisière and ignore the rest.' The subalterns and gossips were those officers of Lefebvre's who thought that this slow approach was proving too costly in lives. The Marshal had to resign himself to this attrition. Happily, two days later, when the assault was scheduled to begin at last, Marshal Kalkreuth announced that he wished to negotiate his surrender.

Some merchants installed at the city gates were selling wine at 32 sous the bottle – both to the French and to the besieged, who were fraternising already, toasting and guzzling together. Everybody had had enough of the siege; the capitulation was signed on 26 May. The garrison was to march out with the honours of war, but surrendering its arms and ammunition, artillery and magazines, etc. All royal and regimental property was to pass to the French army. Marshal Lefebvre entered the town at the head of all the besieging troops, led by the engineers. From Finkenstein on 28 May, Napoleon dictated a letter instructing the French bishops to address special thanks to the God of armies so that he would deign to continue to favour the arms of France and to watch over the country's prosperity. They were also to pray that the British cabinet, 'persecutor of our holy religion and also the eternal enemy of our nation' should cease to influence the continental ministries.

In conquered Danzig, the troops and officers made a discovery: 'Here they drink porter and the wine of Oporto; two liqueurs of considerable strength. The English find the Portuguese wine too weak and cut it with arrack.' Napoleon left Finkenstein in his six-horse coach, preceded by an escort of chasseurs and followed by the entire train of senior officers. 'We rushed away thus, like a storm, at a brisk trot day and night, covering many leagues and those who had to follow this whirlwind were none too comfortable.'

Lefebvre went to meet the Emperor at the abbey of Oliva, near Danzig. Etiquette was expected, and Lefebvre had to wait in an ante-chamber. After a quarter of an hour, he was admitted to an office where Napoleon was breakfasting with Berthier. 'Good morning, monsieur le duc, sit down. Do you like chocolate?' 'Yes, Sire.' 'Well, you will not have any for breakfast, but I am going to give you a pound of the same city of Danzig for, since you have conquered it, it is just that she should bring you something. Duke of Danzig, accept this chocolate; small presents foster friendship.'

Lefebvre thanked him and breakfast proceeded; the Marshal understood nothing regarding this present. As for the title of duke, he thought it must be a joke. Only after regaining his quarters did he understand that he now really was Duke of Danzig. A note in the package informed him that the chocolates consisted of a wad of 300 bank notes of 1,000 francs denomination. The valet Constant says that from then on and for many years, officers and men said 'Danzig chocolate' when speaking of money.

Napoleon was to spend two days at Danzig 'studying ways and means to exploit all the city's resources, which were immense. The local city taxes amounted to 20 millions.'

Lefebvre was finally to receive a gratuity of two and a half millions, 'for the purchase of a fine dwelling, producing 100,000 francs net, and situated in old France on the Loire, the Seine or the Saône'. Each man wounded at Danzig was to receive ten francs; unwounded soldiers ten francs and a bottle of wine. On a much later day, Lefebvre was to receive an individual who spoke with envy of the riches he enjoyed. 'You can have the lot at cost,' said the old Marshal-Duke. 'Come down into the garden. I will fire sixty musket rounds at you and if you are still alive after that you can have the lot.'

At Danzig, Percy was occupied in trying to evict fifty bad-hats from a house known as the Bourse which he wished to turn into a hospital. 'It was also decided to open a hospital there for 500 venereals. But this establishment did not fit in with the plans of certain people who intend to exploit the city.' Percy noted that the army pharmacists responsible for requisitioning dressings and medicines were filling their own pockets. He attempted to limit the trafficking and peculation.

After a spell of frost and bad weather, things improved. The apple and plum trees had only small buds, but one could see violets on the banks. These signs of a late spring were touching. 'On every face was a yearning to return to France,' wrote Percy on 4 June. 'I doubt if His Majesty will spend the winter here, but the army will doubtless remain for a long time yet. 5 June – The weather is fine; there is hardly any dark. All come to see Danzig, spend a day or two drinking good wine and leave again. 6 June – It is said that the Russians have launched a general offensive.'

During the siege of Danzig, the Russians had established a fortified camp at Heilsburg, on the Allee, between Guttstadt and Bartenstein, where about 170,000 men were concentrated. At the same time, the Grande Armée was resting and training. After the city was taken the troops did not lack for bread, boots or munitions.

On 5 June Napoleon learned that the Russians had launched an attack on Ney's VI Corps which was in barracks at Guttstadt. 'I am very happy', he wrote to Davout, 'to see that the enemy wished to avoid our coming to him. My intention had been to move on him on the 10th and I had made all the necessary dispositions of supplies for that purpose.' An endless pursuit of the Russians, masters of the retreat, was not to the taste of the master tactician, or kind to the limbs of his soldiers. Ney had been ordered to retreat as far as Deppen if he found himself too outnumbered.

It was for the Russians to seek contact. German and Russian historians have acknowledged the masterly way in which Ney had manoeuvred. Plotho: 'The calm and order, coupled at the same time with the rapidity with which Ney's corps concentrated at the signal of three rounds of artillery, the coolness and caution with which his retreat was executed, during which he offered continuous resistance, and at the same time, profited from each situation – all attest to the skill of the captain commanding the French and to the arts of war which they had brought to perfection, as well as the achievement of perfect dispositions and the most skilful mounting of an offensive operation.' Ney had held 50,000 Russian troops with fewer than 15,000 men. From Finkenstein on 6 June, Napoleon expressed his 'satisfaction at the coolness and courage with which he had effected all his dispositions'.

The Russians had also attacked Bernadotte's VI Corps and Soult's IV Corps. Everywhere they met stout resistance. Napoleon left Finkenstein on the evening of 6 June, riding in an open carriage and surrounded by his Guard. He wrote to Bernardotte, who had been wounded at the battle of Spanden: 'I have yet to deduce what the enemy was trying to do. The whole thing had a smell of a rash move. I am concentrating my infantry and cavalry reserves at Mohrungen and I shall try to fix the enemy and engage him in a general action which will finish him off.'

During the following days, the movement of the different corps of the Grande Armée are as gratifying to watch as a General Staff *Kriegsspiel*. The Russians called off their offensive and Napoleon no longer knew the whereabouts of the bulk of their army. Quick now, a small attack to compel them to reveal themselves, and from prisoners it was learned that the main body was now (8 June) at Guttstadt. Good; but when he arrived there – no Russians. They had returned to their fortified camp at Heilsberg. Their chief, General Bennigsen, was suffering from the stone, which occasionally subjected him to the tortures of the damned. He slept in his bivouac fully dressed, wrapped in his cloak. He showed no talent other than for retreat, but the near defeat of the French at Eylau had somewhat gone to his head and he saw himself now as the master of the offensive and he was obsessed by turning movements – taking the Grande Armée in reverse by its left – a lack of imagination which was to be his downfall.

On 9 June the French entered Guttstadt and next day began to march towards Heilsberg where the Russians had dug in. The foot-slogger and even commissioned officers knew nothing about *Kriegsspiel*. Forward! They marched; they halted, they marched again – there were the Russians (they always said the Russians, though there were Prussians there too). One killed or was killed, one was wounded and felt life ebb in a ditch, groaning and awaiting the arrival of the ambulance.

The Poles in the Grande Armée had wantonly wrecked the small town of Dirschau because it had been defended by Prussians – only 500 of them, but General Dombrowski had first battered it with artillery. Then the Polish troops had opened fire indiscriminately on both the enemy and the population. Some houses remained miraculously intact amid the carnage. Percy: 'I dined well at the table of the host of our senior surgeon, where I saw some beautiful women, including a brunette with concupiscent eyes and a brazen manner.' But for the army, there was scarcely a halt.

It was now high summer; the country between Dirschau and Marienberg was superb. The rye was ripening, the wheat was high and the oats were burgeoning. The roadsides were planted with willows, the villages were huge and well constructed. At Marienburg, an army of peasants was pressed into service

and worked like convicts, digging ditches and erecting embankments and palisades. By order of the great captain, the town must form a strong point in case
the Russians counter-attacked. In the burning sun, the unpaved roads were thick
with dust from the passing traffic. As the ambulances neared General Headquarters, they loaded wounded covered with blood and dust and panting with
thirst. On the approaches to the town of Mohrungen, the air was foetid with the
stench of putrefying corpses left on the ground or partly buried. The countryside was changing. Percy: 'The land here is poor and arid as if at summer's end.
No cultivated land and the few fields and meadows had been stripped by our
army. There were many lakes and forests. Deppen, when we arrived, had been
burned by the Russians, the houses still smoking in the extreme heat. Everywhere putrefying corpses of men and of horses.'

'The misery and distress of the population was extreme. We had stopped
that morning for a snack; a young and beautiful girl cast famished looks at my
crust of black bread. One of our surgeons threw her a handful of small coins
which she picked up more from gratitude than from need: it was bread which
she craved. I offered her a crust; she blushed and immediately put it into her
mouth. While eating with difficulty she turned aside and wept. I had given her
a good glass of brandy which she had only swallowed from politeness.'

Forward! With Guttstadt taken, the Grande Armée marched at dawn on 10 June
for Heilsberg. What we call a road network was miserable in this region. Fortunately, there was a road between Guttstadt and Heilsberg which wound along
the left bank of the 50-metre wide Allee, through a landscape half valley, half
plain. At one point it ran through a lengthy gorge. Now, one does not hazard a
large body of troops in such a spot without taking precautions, as no one knew
better than Napoleon. 'The advance guard must be strong. Murat will command it, having with him part of the cavalry and Soult's and Lannes' corps This
large detachment will enter the gorge; should the Russians attack, it will be able
to hold them, to prolong the fight until the bulk of the army has had time to
enter the gorge and to outmanoeuvre the enemy, fixed by the advance guard.' At
about midday, Napoleon left Guttstadt with the main body of the army. *En
route* he left the columns in order to climb a hillock. Naturally, he was surrounded by his staff and by the chasseurs of the Guard. 'Berthier – my maps!'
So the ceremonial began. Caulaincourt, Master of the Horse, signalled the staff
officers in charge of the maps. The latter, bowing, passed the map case to Berthier who, likewise bowing, spread out a large map which Napoleon examined, first
leaning on his hands, then kneeling, concentrating, drawing lines with a small
pencil. This study in the open air, under the sun, was conducted for more than
thirty minutes while those present kept a respectful silence. Then Napoleon
rose, laughing and showing his fine teeth. He had just worked out his entire tac-

tical scheme – not just for Heilsberg, which in his mind was no more than a transient element in the plan, but as far as another town along the Allee which he had chosen for the general and decisive battle to 'finish it' – Friedland.

Heilsberg, a transient element perhaps, but much blood was to flow there on that same 10 June. At Heilsberg (on the Allee towards Friedland) the Russian army was encamped on both sides of the river and on the heights whose frowning redoubts bristled with cannon. Once there Murat's mission was to sound the enemy and hold him until the main body came up, commanded by the Emperor in person. Instead Murat hurled himself on the redoubts with his cavalry and a part of Soult's corps, without even waiting for Lannes, who was following close behind: 30,000 against 90,000 Russians. 'The consequence would have been serious had Bennigsen known how to exploit his earlier success and the present situation.' The arrival of the main body saved the day, but the word 'butchery' occurs in many accounts of Heilsberg. Amputated arms and legs were scattered around the ambulances. There were many corpses: 9,000 French killed or wounded; 12,000 Russians. During the fight, the great captain came and went where he would despite the cannonade. 'Sire,' said Oudinot, 'if you remain exposed under the musketry, I shall have you carried by my grenadiers and shut in a caisson.'

This was not mere court flattery; all the marshals believed sincerely that if the Emperor were killed it would be disastrous. And they were not alone in this: even those soldiers who were ready to curse their hero-tyrant believed it. Napoleon, fuming, at last consented to remain sheltered in the midst of his Guard.

The Russians retreated once more; Bennigsen marched his entire force up the right bank of the Allee. At 4 a.m. on 11 June the French entered Heilsberg where they found many thousand quintals of flour 'and all kinds of provisions'.

Henri Lachouque, perhaps the most meticulous commentator of Napoleon's campaigns, has written of Friedland: 'We note that, of the imperial battles, it was, perhaps, the only one which, by the simplicity of its plan, the speed of its development, the decisiveness of the result, compares with Austerlitz. The latter is the model of defensive battles, fought on ground studied at leisure. The former is the model of the offensive battle, fought according to improvised dispositions on a battlefield chosen at a glance. Both bear the stamp of a willingness to combine, to conduct, to consummate by an artistic manoeuvre a single, decisive battle.' Let us consider the 'artistic' manoeuvre. Then let us try to inspect the rough and painful reality, which is the material, the clay of the 'artist'.

Bennigsen, always as doleful as a sick dog, led his troops in retreat along the right bank of the Allee in the direction of Königsberg. To prevent him reaching that fortress town Napoleon advanced Murat (150 squadrons, 21,000 horses), Davout (III Corps, about 24,000 men), Ney (VI Corps, about 16,000) plus a section of the Guard. Soult's IV Corps of about 25,000 men) marched towards Landsberg to throw back the Prussians, together with I Corps (about 20,000 men) under the command of General Victor who had replaced Bernardotte, wounded at Spanden, as we have seen, on 5 June. Only the dragoons of Latour-Maubourg and Lasalle's division were directly pursuing the Russians. By the evening of the 12th, the army was more or less concentrated at and in the vicinity of Eylau. Napoleon kept the main body ready to manoeuvre and threw Lannes as vanguard towards Donnau opposite Friedland.

Friedland (today Pravdinsk, USSR, 18,000 inhabitants) in 1807 was a large, quite pretty market town, whose houses had pointed roofs and were surrounded by gardens. It is situated on the left bank of a loop of the Allee, about 25 kilometres ENE of Eylau. During the afternoon of 13 June Bennigsen learned that the French vanguard had entered the town, and his reasoning was as follows: 'The mass of the French army is driving on Königsberg. The forces which have penetrated Friedland cannot be more than a fraction intended to protect his right flank. I will roll them up and then attack that right flank.' With this intention, he moved the mass of his army across the river. An error which he would regret for the rest of his life.

The Russian artillery remained on the right bank and bombarded the town while the infantry and cavalry attacked and initially drove the French back. Bennigsen had some 70,000 men and could see before him no more than about 10,000 French. Supported by his artillery, he felt that his position was good and was not worried when he heard that Oudinot's corps of 16,000 men had arrived; 70,000 men against 26,000 were good odds. He little suspected that the mass of the French army was no longer marching on Königsberg, but on Friedland, and that he, with his back to the river, was trapped.

Now ensued what has been called the first battle of Friedland, which in fact was no more than a prologue. Lachouque: 'Lannes was an advance guard commander of the first order. Reinforced by Mortier, and then by Oudinot's infantry and the cavalry divisions which were the first on the scene, he held out for four hours, first with 10,000, then with 20,000 against 70,000 Russians troops, and assured the advance of the bulk of the French army through the narrow valley of Posthenen.'

Napoleon, 'beaming' at the thought of fixing the Russians at last, had left Eylau at about 8.30 a.m. on the 14th. He was to cover in two and a half hours the seven leagues separating him from Lannes, 'galloping his Arab charger' according to many accounts. It would be inaccurate to portray the Emperor riding alone like a scout. He was always surrounded by an escort whose composition and strength varied according to the theatre and the operation.

'On horseback, we rode in the following sequence,' wrote Caulaincourt: '4 chasseurs as advance guard, 3 staff officers, 2 or 4 general ADCs, this group being 80 paces in front. The Emperor, with behind him the Master of the Horse, the colonel-general, the major-general, behind them, several general ADCs according to the Emperor's orders: 6 officers of the Emperor's general staff, 2 ADCs and two officers of the major-general's staff: the duty cavalry officer and his picket were 500 paces behind as were the duty squadrons.' There were four such squadrons chosen from the Imperial Guard regiments, namely, a squadron of mounted chasseurs, one of Polish light cavalry, one of dragoons and one of mounted grenadiers, all commanded by the duty general ADC. Assigned a position in the cortège, these cavalrymen would thrust aside any one who might get in their way. ' When one of them, carrying a note or returning from some mission, rejoined the escort at the gallop, he had to overtake everyone and take station on the Emperor's right, when the latter would question him. One day, a Captain Thiard, returning from a reconnaissance, overtook the Emperor slightly and had to rein back. "Stay where you are," said Napoleon dryly, "the first place is always where I am." Should we come to a narrow bridge, a narrow passage or some place which might hide some danger, the Master of the Horse would ride ahead, preceding the Emperor.'

'The number of saddle horses of the imperial escort consisted of ten brigades, each of 13 horses: two battle horses and a fast horse for the Emperor, a horse for the Master of Horse, a horse for the duty groom "or another", a horse for the duty Page, a horse for His Majesty's Mameluke, a horse for any guide – for example, a local peasant – three grooms' horses, a horse for the duty scout. When there was a lengthy stage, the brigades were echeloned in advance along the route, so that Napoleon would always find fresh horses every ten or fifteen kilometres.

'A pair of pistols formed a part of the equipment of any horse the Emperor might ride. The duty Page carried a telescope slung on a bandoleer, and on his saddle bow carried saddlebags containing a kerchief and a pair of gloves for the Emperor and a small assortment of writing gear, pens, paper, ink, pencils, compass, sealing wax; he also carried on the crupper a small valise for the Emperor. The duty surgeon also carried a valise with a set of instruments and everything necessary for first aid.

'I seem to recall that five other horses were often needed, one for the house valet with flannel, salts, ether, water, a half-bottle of Madeira and some surgical instruments, and three for three butlers, each equipped with a small canteen.'

Napoleon preferred Arab horses though he often had to make do with other mounts. Constant says, 'They were schooled with the greatest care by the scout Jardin, who accustomed them to every kind of object. He even went so far as to drive pigs and dogs between their legs.' Was Napoleon a good or a passable horseman? The *Mémoires* and other accounts are vague and contradictory. Chlapowski: 'We schooled Arab horses, which he preferred as they would stop immediately and when [the Emperor] started suddenly without holding the reins, he would have fallen had not the necessary precautions been taken. He liked to ride downhill at a rapid gallop, regardless of the risk of a broken neck to those following him. He never used spurs nor did he use leg pressure to put the horse into a gallop – he started it with a blow of his whip.'

Many witnesses describe Napoleon as an 'indefatigable rider' Caulaincourt: 'When the Emperor was on horseback at Warsaw, he started normally at a gallop, even though it was only for two or three hundred paces. Despite all the zeal and precautions taken, it was difficult for an escort to be always at his side at the moment he started.' Odeleben: 'Napoleon was a tireless but mediocre horseman, jolting in the saddle, bunching the reins in his left hand and letting his right hang down.' I leave it to the horsemen among my readers to form an opinion if they can.

What horseman has never fallen? Parquin, an old soldier under the Empire, says in his *Souvenirs et Campagnes* that one day a chasseur of the imperial escort fell and Napoleon had called him clumsy. He then fell himself and the chasseur, galloping to regain his station, observed aloud: 'It looks as if I am not the only clumsy one, today.'

From the time of leaving Eylau, Napoleon had with him a Captain Marbot, who having come from Friedland explained what had been happening up to the time of his leaving the battlefield. 'Have you a good memory?' asked the Emperor, smiling. 'Passable, Sire.' 'Well what anniversary is it today, 14 June?' 'Marengo.' 'Yes, yes, and I am going to beat the Russians in the same manner as I beat the Austrians.'

At the end of his ride, the Emperor reached Posthenen, 2,500 metres from Friedland, where he was surrounded by a crowd of senior officers, including Oudinot, whose coat was torn and his horse wounded and bleeding slightly. Oudinot bowed and addressed the Emperor: 'Sire, see the river there, just behind the enemy. I could dip his arse in it if I had the troops,' or the bowdlerised version: 'Be quick, Sire, my grenadiers are exhausted. But give me reinforcements and I will throw these Russians into the river.' One should remember that we often come across differing versions of conversations between Napoleon and his officers and men; the popular version is almost always the more probable.

After listening to Oudinot, Napoleon sent all available officers to determine whether the enemy was continuing to cross from the left to the right bank of the Allee. Yes, they were. At midday, the Emperor arrived at the plateau beyond which lies Friedland. A chair was found and he dined off a crust of humble black bread. The battle had subsided. The Russians seemed to be hesitating in the face of the determination of such French troops as they had faced up to now. Bennigsen was told of clouds of dust on the road from Eylau, indicating that French reinforcements were *en route*. He hesitated.

Napoleon sent for his telescope and spent some time examining the position of the two armies. The Russians were in front, facing west with Friedland right behind their centre. Friedland and the river.

The gilded staff kept quiet. Most were thinking 'The day is too far gone for the grand, decisive battle today.' Someone, I have not discovered who, must have told the Emperor of this near-unanimous opinion. He replied firmly: 'No, no – we won't catch the enemy making a mistake like this twice.'

The orders followed. His tactical plan called for the centre to be broken first and then the two wings to be defeated in detail. While the enemy was held on the left (north), the French right (Ney) would attack vigorously. The left would not attack until after the right had secured the bridges. In his *History of the Consulate and the Empire*, Thiers, to whom Marshal Mortier recounted the episode, has recorded, in suitable words, Napoleon's orders to Ney: 'This is the objective: advance, looking neither right nor left, bore into this thick mass, cost what it may. Enter Friedland, seize the bridges and pay no heed to what may be happening to your rear, right or left. I and the army will take care of that.' Napoleon to Mortier: 'That man is a lion!'

At 5.30 p.m. twenty guns from a French battery fired simultaneously – it was the signal. Ney had ordered the French right to advance without firing, muskets shouldered. Both sides' artillery rumbled; the battlefield was swathed in smoke. The contradictory nature of the various versions indicate that none of the witnesses could have had more than an approximate idea of the movements of the units involved.

At best one can say this: General Bisson's division, blinded by the smoke, veered too far to the right, leaving a gap between themselves and the next division – a gap which was soon filled with Cossacks. The result was disorder. Ney's troops, who had advanced shouting 'To Friedland!' but by now were doubtless, beginning to have had enough of advancing in the teeth of the Russians' heavy fire, began to retreat. Their officers spurred them on with the flat of the sabre and cries of 'Forward! Fortunately, Dupont's division was able to stabilise the situation and drive off the Cossacks. The centre and the left started to move. General Boulart: 'There was a horrible butchery, especially in the Russian centre covering the town. A 30-gun battery of General Sénarmont was disposed in tactical groups in front of the infantry, thus opening the line of advance. In front of the infantry! One may well suppose that this novel concept must be credited to ex-captain of artillery Bonaparte. Artillery was henceforward no longer to be a static arm, but would be the point of advance, opening the road. This role in offensive warfare would accrue to the artillery more and more — until the advent of tanks and tactical aviation.

Sénarmont's artillery smothered the Russian batteries, and the French had gained the victory of Friedland in less than two hours. Next day Napoleon wrote to Josephine: 'My love, this will be but a short word as I am very tired. I have been bivouacking for several days. My lads well and truly celebrated the anniversary of the battle of Marengo. The battle of Friedland will also be as celebrated and glorious for my people. The whole Russian army put to flight: 80 cannon, 30,000 men killed or prisoners, 25 Russian generals killed, wounded or prisoners; the Russian Guard annihilated; a worthy sister of Marengo, Austerlitz, Jena. The bulletin will tell you the rest. My losses have not been large, I manoeuvred the enemy successfully. Do not worry and be happy. Good-bye my love. I am off on horseback. Napoleon.'

The 'not large' losses amounted to 7,000 killed or wounded. The dark side of these battles was always the same. In front of an ambulance set up: 'In a large red house a cannon shot from the battle, were thrown the corpses of those wounded who had died on the way.' Percy: 'In a ground floor room and behind the door, a mound of amputated limbs, blood flowing from each; one could hear the cries, groans and howls of the wounded carried on ladders, muskets, poles, a harrowing picture, always the same and to which I shall never become accustomed.' Even the Bulletin of the Grande Armée gave a glimpse of the price of victory: 'The next day the sun rose on one of the most horrible battlefields ever seen.' It was so hot and the corpses of men and horses stank so badly that the usual order for gravediggers was cancelled; instead, 'Take them to the river and throw them in.' Before beginning this repellent task, a generous issue of brandy. The soldiers laughed as the corpses tumbled down the slopes of the ravine.

In his report to the Tsar, Bennigsen had toned down the extent of the Russian defeat, but concluded that it was time 'after this unhappy day' to treat with Napoleon. And, not daring to tell the whole story, he wrote to the Tsar's brother, Grand-Duke Constantine: 'Ask him whether he does not wish to stop the flow of blood; this is not a combat but a downright butchery.'

'Good-bye my love. I am off on horseback!' Escorted by his cavalry, Napoleon set off in pursuit of the Russians along the Allee, but these masters of retreat had outdistanced him. At Wehlau, where the Allee flows into the Pregel, they burned the bridge behind them; another must be built. For more than an hour, Napoleon joined the sappers, hatchet in hand. 'Then he sat in the shade nearby for an hour and drank a glass of red wine with a snack. He then swam his horse across the river with the water up to the beast's back.' The crossing of the hastily erected bridge was picturesque. Percy: 'It is a pleasant thing to see 100,000 men on foot, in carriages, hastening to be the first, swearing, threatening, brandishing sabres, occasionally using them. From the viewpoint of my little shelter, I saw the cuirassiers stopping the artillery by using the flat of their sabres on the horses' noses, and the artillery officers and the train shouting to the troopers riding the horses to ride over the cavalry. Then a general arrived who struck one, sabred another.' This is known as *esprit de corps*! At 6 p.m. on 16 June, the bridge collapsed. A ford was found nearby, but it was deep and many horses were drowned.

While Napoleon was beating the Russians at Friedland, Murat's cavalry, followed by Soult and Davout's corps, drove on Königsberg, the fortress city which held the last of Prussia's resources. Murat arrived under the walls of Königsberg (today Kaliningrad, USSR) on 14 June, and heard the news of the victory of Friedland. The Russian Generals Lestocq and Kamensky also heard the news and evacuated the town; Soult's troops immediately took possession.

It was 19 June and raining. The army was marching on Tilsit. The countryside was pretty, though marshy. Nearly every soldier was a peasant; they cast knowing looks on the crops. Rye five feet high, excellent hemp, superb fields of flax. In France, flax was much cultivated. 'It's nicer than my place! And the spuds! Look at the spuds!' The villages were wooded, each house with its meadow, its orchard; here and there, pigs, geese, poultry. A procession of carriages and carts loaded with families, their clothes and cooking utensils was encountered; refugees, who, fearing a battle as the Russians retreated, had fled. Now they were returning, wet through, fearful. The soldiers of the Grande Armée stopped them, searched the bundles and took the best articles of clothing and any valuables. This was war.

Tilsit (today Sovietsk, USSR, 32,000 inhabitants) was a 'quite pretty' town with long, wide streets, but nearly all paved with enormous stones placed haphazardly, the largest in the centre to serve as stepping-stones if the streets were flooded. The Russian army had retired to the far side of the Niemen; the bridge was still burning. The Niemen is a fine river, two-thirds the size of the Rhine; its waters were blue and fast-flowing. At Tilsit some French prisoners were found who had been there for three months. Most of them were tubercular, and they said that a good two hundred of their comrades had died. 'As the Prussians had treated us so badly, the Russians had not seemed too bad.'

The army was bivouacking behind the town. It was raining glacially and hard, the ambulances were filled with sick. There was meat, but no bread. Morale would have been low had it not been for rumours of peace; in the bivouacs there was talk of little else. The Emperor was going to make peace with the Russians – the Prussians no longer counted. One day, it was settled, peace would be signed tomorrow, and tomorrow, nothing. Ah, when would it be finished? Chasseur Barrès wrote to his family: 'We have had enough of this war. It seems to us in one sense that we are at the end of the civilised world, five hundred leagues from Paris, And everyone is tired to death.'

The desire for peace was universal. Talleyrand wrote to Napoleon, congratulating him on the victory of Friedland: 'But it is not only in the light of the reports of glory that I dream. I like to look on it as the herald, the guarantor of a peace which will provide Your Majesty with the repose which so many privations, fatigues and dangers have been earned by his peoples.' The French people were tired of war, as were the Russians. Grand-Duke Constantin wrote to his brother, the Tsar: 'Sire, if you do not wish to make peace, give each soldier a loaded pistol and order him to blow out his brains. This will produce the same result as a new and final battle which would infallibly open the gates of your empire to French troops, battle-hardened and invariably victorious.' The Tsar finally decided to negotiate; messages were exchanged, diplomacy, bargaining. Finally, Prince Labanof, the Tsar's representative, asked for an audience of Napoleon, who received him graciously and invited him to dinner. He told him that he held the Tsar in high esteem, then, indicating the Niemen, said: 'Here is the boundary between the two empires. On one side let your sovereign reign, and I on the other.' The Niemen, limit of the French empire!'

It was still raining on the bivouacs, but hardly a thought was given to the weather. All were listening for the gun which would signal the armistice – for a change. The great news broke over the army on the morning of 22 June – the soldiers embraced. And the two Emperors are to meet – to sign the peace!' The troops listened to the imperial proclamation which was read to them by their officers and those of their comrades who knew how to read:

'Soldiers: on 5 June we were attacked in our quarters by the Russian army. The enemy had misjudged the cause of our inactivity. Too late did he discover that our repose was that of the lion. He now repents of having disturbed us. During the days at Guttstadt, at Heilsberg, on that ever memorable day at Friedland, in short, in ten days campaigning, we have taken 120 guns, 7 standards, have killed, wounded or made prisoner 80,000 Russians, deprived the enemy of all his magazines, hospitals, ambulances, the city of Königsberg, the 300 ships in this port, loaded with every kind of ammunition, 160,000 muskets which England had sent to arm our enemies.'

The troops heard all this with a touch of impatience. They knew the song, the paean to glory; now they expected something different. Expert manipulator of the psychology of crowds, Napoleon had husbanded his assets. The readers, drawing breath, continued:

'From the banks of the Vistula we have arrived at those of the Niemen with the rapidity of eagles. You celebrated the anniversary of the coronation by Austerlitz; this year you have worthily celebrated that of the battle of Marengo which put an end to the war with the second coalition.'

'Frenchmen, you have proved worthy of yourselves and of myself. You will return to France covered with all your laurels and after having secured a glorious peace which carries with it the guarantee of its permanence. It is time to finish and to let our nation live and rest sheltered from the influence of malign England. My favour is the proof of my gratitude and the wide extent of my love for you.'

At last! At last the words which all had been awaiting were the present and no longer the future: 'a glorious peace which carries with it the guarantee of its permanence'. Not 'will carry', but 'carries'. The least intelligent soldier felt instinctively that this time 'this was it' – Peace – and Return to France.

In his proclamation, Napoleon had only anticipated a little. Peace was not yet signed: the armistice conventions included provisions should one of the signatories wish to resume hostilities, but no one paid heed to that; the text said in plain language that an armistice existed between the French and Russian armies in order that, meanwhile, they could 'negotiate, conclude and sign a peace which would end the effusion of blood so contrary to humanity'. Berthier had signed for France, Labanof for Russia.

That left Prussia. Marshal Kalkreuth was received by Napoleon on 24 June. He signed the conditions for a suspension of hostilities dictated by the Emperor but without learning anything of future arrangements. There was every reason to fear that they would be harsh. The Prussian court trembled from fear and anxiety. Queen Louise wrote to Tsar Alexander: 'I would despair were you not the arbiter of our destiny.'

The troops knew nothing of this bargaining in high quarters, but the thought that the two Emperors were to meet aroused more and more enthusiasm. The Bulletin of 24 June gave the news officially: 'Tomorrow, the two Emperors of France and Russia are to meet. For this purpose, a pavilion has been built in the middle of the Niemen which the two monarchs can reach from each bank. Few occasions will be as important. The two river banks will be manned by the two armies while their chiefs consult on the means of re-establishing order and bringing tranquillity to their peoples.' Tranquillity – it was hardly credible; 'we went round in circles, asking if it could be true'. On 25 June the banks of the Niemen were crowded with troops. One could clearly see in mid-river a house built on a raft and covered in canvas. 'The engineers built it in eight hours. And it is furnished inside like a palace.'

Midday. The Emperors took their seats in their boats; Napoleon's, garlanded with greenery, was the first to reach the raft, accompanied by many Marshals of the Empire. They waited for five minutes until Alexander set foot on the raft. Napoleon stepped briskly forward and embraced the Emperor.

The Tsar was wearing the uniform of the Preobrajensky Guards: dark green with red facings, gold laced, white breeches, sash, bicorn hat with black and white feathers. At thirty, he was a blue-eyed blond, extremely handsome. The French called him 'the Greek lover'. A born seducer, courteous, gallant, perpetually smiling, with all the symptoms of a sensitive heart easily moved. Six years earlier, he had coldly allowed his father, Paul I, to be murdered. Bursting into tears at the news of the murder, he had loaded the assassins with honours.

The two sovereigns exchanged a few words that could not be overheard with certainty, but which did not prevent generations of historians and memorialists from reporting them:

The Tsar: 'Sire, I hate the English as much as you do.' Napoleon: 'If that is the case, peace is secure.' The two then entered the small house unaccompanied. Their discussion lasted for 90 minutes, but no one will ever know what was actually said, because each later reported whatever best suited him. Napoleon wrote to Josephine: 'My love, I have just met the Emperor Alexander; I was very pleased with him. He is a very handsome, good and young emperor. He has more spirit than people might think. He will be lodging in the town of Tilsit tomorrow.'

On that day, the 26th, there was a second interview in mid-river. The sovereigns' boats were be-flagged in white – a sign of peace. The troops massed on the banks admired them. The previous day the Tsar had asked Napoleon's agreement to inviting the King of Prussia, Frederick-William, and Napoleon had said yes. The Prussian, in hussar's uniform and with a shako and waxed moustaches, was skinny, seedy, ill-assured. The meeting lasted about the same time as the first, and the two emperors then retired, each to his side.

At 5 p.m. Alexander entered Tilsit which, by agreement, had been neutralised and barred to all but the two emperors, their staffs and their guards. He was greeted by a gun salute and then, mounted on one of Napoleon's best horses, inspected the French Guard. The Marshals trailing behind the two emperors 'were glittering with gold and braiding'. Napoleon escorted Alexander to the house which had been prepared for him and invited him to dine with him that evening.

The Tsar was to stay several days at Tilsit, attending the manoeuvres of the Guard, dining with Napoleon, inviting him to take tea with him. The soldiers saw with surprise and admiration, the two monarchs walking together arm-in-arm, naturally, surrounded by the resplendent marshals. The two men also rode together, often in the company of Frederick-William, who had been billeted in a miller's house. A much less accomplished rider than the other two, he was consistently outdone. Napoleon judged him severely: 'He is an extremely limited man, lacking character or talent, truly a simpleton, a dunce and a bore.' He had bullied him since their first meeting, speaking of the defects which he had noticed in the Prussian army and offering him humiliating advice. In anguish,

Frederick-William asked himself what sort of peace Napoleon would impose on his country.

On the 28th the weather changed and the sun came out, though there were several showers of rain and hail during the day. The engineers had built a large wooden hut in which the officers of the Guard were to feast their erstwhile opponents. On the 30th the sun shone brilliantly in a cloudless sky. In a well-chosen meadow, a cannon-shot from the town, planks nailed to trestles formed picnic tables for the 'brotherly feast', arranged around a square in which the band would play. The meal consisted of soup, beef, mutton, pork, goose and chicken. To drink: beer, schnapps (brandy) in barrels at the ends of the tables. The Guards ate standing. The Russians, initially suspicious and awkward, were reassured by the French. Coignet has left a detailed account of this feast, and although he may have exaggerated some details, he did so inadvertently, having written his *Mémoires* more than thirty years after leaving the service and one can understand that this was in no way a formal banquet.

'These hungry men [the Russians] could not restrain themselves: they knew nothing of the reserve which one should exhibit at table. They were given brandy to drink, which was the drink of the meal and, before offering them a glass, it was proper to drink and then to pass them a goblet in white metal containing a quarter of a litre. The contents immediately disappeared; they swallowed a morsel of meat as large as an egg with each swig. They were quickly uncomfortable and by signs, invited us to unbutton, as they were doing. We saw that, in order to exaggerate their manly chests, they were swathed in cloth, which we were disgusted to see them discard. Two aides-de-camp then arrived to warn us to stay put as the Emperors were about to pay us a visit. Here is what happened: with a gesture, our Emperor indicated that none should move and made a circuit of the table. The Russian Emperor declared: "Grenadiers, you have deserved this." On their departure, the Russians fell-to again with renewed gusto.'

The two emperors were well advised not to have lingered. To 'make room in the stomach', the Russians put their fingers in their mouths. The end of the feast was nauseating. Many were snoring under the tables, sleeping in their vomit.

No dramatist could have written a better part for Louise of Prussia than that which she played during those days. She arrived in a carriage wearing a white crepe dress (court mourning) and a pearl diadem of pearls – distressed, it was said, but still beautiful. The grenadiers, who presented arms – including Coignet, apparently – were dazzled. She came reluctantly, her heart in her mouth, at the insistence of the royal counsellors, who hoped that her charm would induce Napoleon to offer terms more lenient than those that they feared.

At the miller's house, when she appeared, she was overwhelmed with suggestions. 'Oh, have pity,' she said, 'give me a little time to collect my thoughts.' Napoleon arrived shortly. 'Is the queen there?' He was shown the narrow stairway. 'What would one not do to gain such a prize?' Gallant, but he was to show himself inflexible and even a touch sadistic. The Queen immediately embarked on a pathetic catalogue of the Prussian misfortunes; 'One would have thought her a new Duchenois in Chimène,' the Emperor wrote in his *Mémorial.* He cut her short: 'How could you have dared to declare war on me?' 'Sire, the glory of Frederick the Great misled us; it was so dazzling that it allowed us to make this mistake.' Louise went so far as to ask the Emperor to restore a part of Westphalia to Prussia, especially Magdeburg. He again interrupted to compliment her on her dress. 'Is it crepe, Italian gauze?' 'Sire, must we talk fashions at a moment like this?' This beauty's eyes filled with tears. That night, at dinner, she was placed between Napoleon and the Tsar. A moment before they sat down at the table, Napoleon went to a table and took from it a perfect rose which he presented to the Queen 'whose hand first expressed a sort of unstudied refusal'. Then she corrected herself: 'Yes, but with Magdeburg at the least.' 'But', replied Napoleon, 'let me recall to Your Majesty that it is I who gives and you who will receive.' 'The dinner and the remainder of the time was passed in that way,' Louise displaying her charms. Napoleon invited her to dine the next day. On returning to Pictupoehnen, she believed that she had achieved her ends. For this second dinner, she wore a red and gold dress with a muslin turban. Just as she was leaving for Tilsit, she received a note from her husband: 'The terms have been changed and the conditions are frightful.' She burst into tears and no longer wished to go to dinner. The Tsar, informed of this, came in person to persuade her. She finally left, sick at heart.

'How's this?', asked Napoleon with heavy humour. 'The Queen of Prussia wearing a turban? Surely not to impress the Emperor of Russia who makes war on the Turks?' 'It is rather to impress Roustam.' The notoriously boastful Mameluke was standing behind the Emperor during most of this banter, much of which was repeated in his *Mémoires.* He should be treated with extreme caution. What does seem certain is that at this dinner, excruciating for her, Louise behaved stoically, truly regally. After the meal, Murat approached her, unaware apparently that only those of equal rank should question a sovereign. 'How does Your Majesty divert herself at Memel?' 'By reading.' 'What does Your Majesty read?' 'The history of the past.' 'But the present epoch also offers deeds worthy of being remembered' 'It is already too much for me to live in it.'

According to the *Mémorial,* when Napoleon was escorting her and, halted on the stairway, she squeezed his hand and said to him with an appearance of sentiment: 'Is it possible, having had the privilege of seeing at close quarters the man of the century and of history, that he will not allow me the liberty and satisfaction of assuring him of my attachment for life?' Napoleon's reply: 'Madame, I am to be pitied; it is the result of my unhappy destiny.' Louise of Prussia said to Duroc on leaving: 'Ah, I have been cruelly deceived in this house.' The next day, Napoleon wrote to Josephine: 'My love, the Queen of Prussia dined with me last night. I had to defend myself against her wish that I should make some more concessions to her husband; but I was gallant and held to my policy. She is most amiable. I cannot here give you details without making this letter very long. By the time that you read this letter, peace will have been concluded with Russia and Prussia and Jérôme proclaimed King of Westphalia with three million population. This for you only.'

The peace treaty was signed on 7 July. The beautiful Louise had obtained very little. Napoleon, 'in token of his regard for HM the King of all the Russias', restored to the King of Prussia, vanquished and at his mercy, the Kingdom of Prussia as it had been on 1 January 1772, with many small duchies and earl-doms, including part of the Duchy of Magdeburg, though not Magdeburg itself. In brief, Prussia kept only four provinces and five million inhabitants.

Louise of Prussia was not the only woman to shed tears on learning the fate of her country. Where was the kingdom of Poland, for which Marie Walewska had sacrificed herself? All that appeared on the new map of Europe was the 'Duchy of Warsaw' placed under the sovereignty of Frederick Augustus, King of Saxony.

The peace treaty was matched by a far-reaching treaty of alliance. France and Russia agreed to make common cause by land or sea in any war that either of them engaged in or supported, committing all their forces and neither of them making a separate peace. The Tsar accepted Napoleon's proposed media-tion to make peace with the Turks. Napoleon accepted the Tsar's, with a view towards peace between France and Britain; a complete procedure was delineat-ed in an endeavour to make that nation accept peace. A summons would be addressed to her and, lacking a 'categorical and satisfactory' reply by 1 Decem-ber, the Russian Ambassador would be ordered to ask for his passports and quit London immediately. Napoleon could feel himself master of Europe – conti-nental Europe. At St. Helena, later, he would be asked during what period in his life he had felt happiest. 'Perhaps it was at Tilsit. I found myself victorious, dic-tating laws and with emperors paying me court.' The troops billeted in and around Tilsit had heard little of these carefully chosen words which claimed to control the destinies of millions of human beings. They were content to see the two sovereigns appearing constantly together, and continued to fraternise with the Russians. There were other fraternal feasts which lasted well into the night. The French grenadiers learned to shout in Russian 'Long live our father, the Tsar!' and their new comrades to shout in French 'Long live the Emperor!' The Russians showed little talent for languages. The French that Napoleon's grenadiers tried to teach them was vivid and included a number of slang phrases used at the time only in the Grande Armée; some have passed into general and popular use. Let us profit from this pacific lull at Tilsit to compile a random glossary:

Le patron; le petit Tondu (the Boss, little Shorn one): Napoleon

Le lampion (Chinese lantern): his cocked-hat

La bamboche (the cross): the Legion of Honour

Le brutal: the artillery

La noce; la fête; la musique (wedding, party, music): war

Donner un fameux coup de peigne (really comb one's hair): take part in an unusually hard fight

Tourner l'oeil; descendre la garde; défiler en parade (roll one's eyes; drop one's guard; march off): die in action

Les pékins (muftis): civilians

On déchire de la mousseline (they are ripping muslin): sound of a fusillade

Crucifix à ressort: pistol

Le coucou; l'oiseau (the cuckoo; the bird): the eagle atop the colours

Friser (to graze): a near-miss

Avoir sa pente (slope): to like one's drop of liquor

Mettre les dents au crochet (set one's teeth on edge): starving

La débine: poverty

Faire une bosse: to celebrate; to eat well

Le jus de l'arbre (*tortu*) (sap of the (crooked) tree): wine – many variants: *le rogomme* (booze); *le casse-poitrine* (rot-gut); *le riquiqui* (little runt); *le sacré chien* (damn dog); *le sauve-la-vie* (life-saver) (Brandy was more drunk than wine, which was too bulky)

La bouffarde (puffer): short-stemmed pipe

Trouver (to find; to 'liberate'): to steal

Les musikos: brothels

Piler du poivre (to grind peppercorns): sentry duty

Etre mis aux mites (lodged with the maggots): put in the cells

Dur à cuir; vrai bougre; vieille moustache; briscard; brave à trois poils; crâne (hard as leather; true fellow, etc.; old moustache; old sweat; three-haired slugger; baldy): long-term soldier; a three-stripe man

Marche à terre: foot-slogger, yomper

Les Immortels (the Immortals): sardonic name for the Guard

Gros talons; gilets de fer (high heels; steel vests): cuirassiers

Les carabins (sawbones): surgeons

Céléris; riz-pain-sel (celery eaters; rice-bread-salt): commissariat staff

Marche à regret (forced march): conscript

Les Goddams (pronounced godans): the British

Les kaiserlicks: the Austrians

Etre abîmé, hypothéqué (ruined, mortgaged, to have 'stopped one'): to be wounded

Le rasiné (grape-juice): blood

La charmante, la gale (delight; the itch): no pain and a hospital berth

La mie de pain (breadcrumbs): fleas

La côte de boeuf (side of beef): the sabre

Du cormant (hardwood): beef

Un rafalé, un frileux (a squall/short burst of fire, someone sensitive to cold): a scared soldier

Les cousins de l'Empereur (the Emperor's cousins): Corsicans.

And so forth, including many expressions for girls, the sexual act, venereal diseases, etc. The memorialists have not seen fit to quote all these in their works and, the mass of the soldiers in the Grande Armée being illiterate, this chapter in the history of language has been lost. One may well conclude that some present-day slang words and phrases in the 'venereal' vocabulary are the heritage of the 'grumblers'.

The latter did not merely try to teach the Russians to speak a few words of French, but also introduced them to their games and amusements. One popular open-air game was 'cat and rat'. Two 10–15-foot cords were tied to a stake driven into the ground, each cord tied around the waist of a blindfolded man. The 'cat' had a club with which he tried to strike the 'rat'. Both men tried to move around the stake as quietly as possible, listening for the other, the cat to locate the rat, the rat to avoid being clobbered. This was popular with the Russians, but another was even more so. Into the Niemen was thrown a cat attached by a cord to a goose. The cat would try to climb on the back of the goose which in turn would dive to get rid of the cat. Generally, both drowned to the delight of the spectators. Barbaric times.

On 8 July, during a farewell ceremony, Napoleon took the Legion of Honour from his own coat to decorate the 'First Grenadier of Russia', one Lazaref of the Preobrajensky Battalion. The man kissed first his hand and then the hem of his coat. Next day Alexander re-crossed the Niemen, to signs of friendship from Napoleon on the bank; on that day, Prussia signed the capitulation.

On 10 July, the Emperor of the French reached Königsberg where he dictated orders for the army to evacuate the vast area of conquered Europe across which it was scattered. Some marshals returned to Paris, others remained to direct the units that were retiring by stages. The Guard was to move 'by very short days and without tiring itself' to Berlin. Old Prussia was to be evacuated in two stages, although Napoleon knew that the Prussians would not agree to pay war indemnities without a struggle. 'It must be paid down to the last sou,' he wrote to General Clarke, 'and this is not conditional on our evacuation. Therefore, let the Berliners know that unless they pay the ten millions, they will have a French garrison perpetually.'

The general dispositions of the army did not provide for the evacuation of Poland.

Before leaving Königsberg, Napoleon decided to send one of his ADCs, General Savary, as a temporary representative, pending an exchange of ambassadors between France and Russia. He wanted to keep an eye on the situation there, and prolong the goodwill of Tilsit as long as possible.

'In your conversations, avoid anything that might prove shocking. For example, never speak of the war. Never criticise any custom, however ridiculous. You have seen how I was deceived by the Austrians and the Prussians. I trust the Russian Emperor and there is nothing between the two nations to prevent a complete rapprochement. Go to work.'

Accompanied by a staff, and bearing a letter of warm recommendation, Savary crossed the Niemen and set out for St Petersburg from where he reported that the Russians still detested the French; he had even had difficulty in finding lodgings. Napoleon might have been better advised to chose another emissary rather than the officer who had orchestrated the execution of the Duke of Enghien. There was a sizeable colony of French *émigrés* resident at St Petersburg and elsewhere in Russia.

After Königsberg the Emperor moved to Dresden, where he drew up the statutes for the Duchy of Warsaw. Here he learned of Portugal's refusal to close her ports to British vessels and immediately instructed Talleyrand to inform the Portuguese ambassador that if Portugal persisted in this defiance, war would be declared.

In Poland, the troopers of the Grande Armée were telling one another how wonderful it would be to return to France without having to fire another shot.

VII

SPAIN, 1808
The Disasters of War

The return to France had been postponed, but the disappointment was accepted. The high command had acted wisely for once in its management of the occupation. No large camps, no barracks; more than 150,000 men dispersed in small towns, communities and villages throughout Poland, East Prussia, Mecklenburg, Brandenburg and Silesia. The population had to accommodate them, but they were used to it; they had seen everything – except, as yet, pillage, extortion, rape.

And the troops seemed to be easy-going, as who would not be, having survived the battlefield? Those who had done the fighting were going to return to France, that was certain since they now had a victorious peace and an alliance with Russia; if further proof were needed, witness the gradual arrival of occupation troops to replace them. So, patience, especially since the weather was scorching. March on the roads and eat dust – no thanks. Wait until it's a bit cooler.

With total inaction, soldiers become bored. Those of the Grande Armée, mostly farm workers in civil life, were by no means unwilling, after a few months, to help the locals with the field work. As were the artisans – France has been a nation of handymen since time immemorial. One saw infantrymen, cavalrymen, gunners repairing houses, furniture, carriages – in short, taking a part in the daily life of the community. And in the amusements too. Dancing was more popular than it is today. The French soldier, welcomed at the balls, smartened himself up, played the gallant. So here we return to the eternal topic – women.

The army's camp-followers must have been a pretty battered lot by now; the troops chatted-up the local girls, and their correspondence is instructive. The worthy young man determined to remain faithful to his promise: 'Even though I am a soldier, my heart has not changed. I seem to see you always before my eyes.' If the girl were illiterate, the letter went to a neighbour who could read: 'Please offer many compliments to my little friend, for I embrace her with all my heart. I am hers for life. Each night I go to bed, I wish she was at my side, my sweetheart.' Others, seduced by the charms of the girl at their billet, wrote that as soon as they could get out of the army they would return to marry her. Some admitted that there was no need to marry to find an ideal in this country.

As before, the Prussian girls 'pleasant and accommodating' were the most popular. Jean-Claude Quennevat in *The True Soldiers of Napoleon* has accurately described the reasons for this popularity: 'In fact, few of these Gretchens succumbed from vice or licentiousness; they were generally hyper-sentimental romantics, inclined to accord a holy gloss to the sexual act, even outside marriage', and were therefore ready to sacrifice anything for their lovers.' And their French lovers were often just as smitten, as witness the many duels occasioned by a pair of beautiful eyes that crop up in the annals of the occupation.

Few duels were fought with pistols. The cavalrymen used sabres, the infantry short-swords or bayonets. Fencing, taught by the regimental masters-at-arms, was a part of military education. But duelling was forbidden, so it often took place at night by torch light.

For one category of soldier in the Grande Armée the Peace of Tilsit did not herald rest and feminine consolations. Convoys of wounded crawled from Königsberg to Berlin, accompanied by clouds of flies and spreading a nauseous stench. Dysentery killed many. The overworked surgeons and doctors received as reinforcements from Paris 'assistant surgeons' of eighteen who could not even be employed as nurses. They had joined the medical corps to escape conscription. Can you guess the nature of the first-aid administered to a convoy of wounded on stopping at a hospital? Each patient was given a sprig of greenery to keep the flies off.

The French director of the hospital at Marienburg was a drunkard who resold the rations, as was the case at Kutash described by Percy. Do not shrink from dwelling on the details; they are part and parcel of the era. 'The courtyard is poisoned by the substances emptied into an open ditch, which overflows. Corpses are piled at the foot of the stairs leading to the main rooms, where they empty themselves, spreading a frightful odour. The stench is general in the wards, each mattress having harboured ten or twelve patients without ever having been being washed. The meat ration has been cut by half in order to enrich the director and the bursar. The chief provisioner, one Rosé de Hagueneau, a fraudulent bankrupt, joined in order to re-establish his affairs. The Emperor knows that such a situation is nearly universal: he swears, raves and the evil continues.' The evil was not to end. Napoleon showered words on Percy, but declined to launch a basic reform of the medical service, and I have already explained why: except in the Guard, no surgeon or doctor could ever aspire to officer's rank.

A year has passed. At the beginning of 1808, the Grande Armée is still spread throughout Poland and the German states, covering an area of 15,000 square leagues. The troops have almost become assimilated into the population, letters are rare and France is distant; they are becoming used to this peace in exile. To those who are impatient, comrades say as they did a year earlier that it was better to wait for the end of the hot weather and avoid the dust. And, suddenly, it's all changed: 'We're leaving!' The rumour spreads like fire before the wind, and then comes the official order. We are leaving for France. Vehicles are requisitioned for weapons and baggage. The first departures will be spread over three weeks from 3 August. But, note, not everyone will leave; about one-third of the occupation force will stay behind. But these men persuade themselves that they will form the second batch. The joy of the men mingles with the sobs of the women: 'Ah, you promised to take me with you.' 'I'll come back.'

And what of the baby already born and the infant to come? Some soldiers, already married or engaged in France, had made false promises, though others had been sincere, believing that the general peace in Europe would last for ever and that they could return!

By carriage to France – but after the first days, there were murmurs that to return by marching easy stages would be more comfortable than being packed in and unable to move. The requisitioned carts were a job-lot, no springs, no hoods, the men roasted in the sun and half-drowned by the rain and sleet of summer storms. The endless columns of packed carts rolled towards the Rhine by day and night, two stops every twenty-four hours. At these halts, finally able to stretch one's legs and relieve oneself, the troops found a meal prepared: bread, meat, beer, brandy. The officers found their meals ready at tables seating thirty or forty. Excellent organisation, in contrast to the chaos of so many of the marches towards the guns. But this very perfection dismayed, and even more this urgency: 'What does it mean? Where are we going?' Was there some other war in some other place? 'We know nothing apart from the fact that the Emperor gave this order. We are moving without let-up or rest. By night, the convoys collided, carts overturned, there were killed and wounded, arms and equipment lost. Too bad! Keep going.'

France, at last, and no more carts; on foot, shouldering packs. Southwards. In the towns were triumphal arches, municipal receptions, banquets, speeches. But from the population – nothing. Before their houses, the people regarded the marching grumblers without uttering a word, expressionless. Often, even the shutters were closed. Questioned, little by little, the civilians talked: 'We thought we were going to have peace, but no, it is war.' A French army had been beaten in Spain. 'In Spain?'

One could write of the Spanish war from the viewpoint of the soldier in the ranks, who knew nothing of cause and effect; or deal with it on a different level – that of the chancelleries, the palaces, the thrones. I feel that both are required if one is to come to an understanding of this huge and complex affair, of its fury and ferocity, the equal sufferings of the troops and the populace, the calculations, ambitions, intrigues and plotting of the great powers.

The immediate causes of the war in Spain are set out in the scholarly works. Let me summarise them. The primary cause was the obduracy of Britain who, mistress of the seas, wanted Napoleon's skin and refused every offer of peace – including that of the Tsar after Tilsit. We know that in order to bring her to her knees, the Emperor had conceived the continental blockade, but for the system to be effective all the ports in Europe must be closed to British goods.

Now, by the end of 1807, only one country's ports remained open – Portugal, which for centuries had lived almost entirely on its commerce with Britain. Napoleon had no choice other than to seize Lisbon and eject the Braganza dynasty which had virtually transformed Portugal into a British colony.

Portugal is separated from France by a wide expanse of Spanish territory; since 1795 Spain had been an ally of France, often reluctant but always finally compliant. Napoleon would encounter less difficulty in rallying Spain to his views now that the Spanish monarchy was in the throes of disintegration.

But let us get to the bottom of the business. The Emperor sought not only the help of Spain in the conquest of Portugal. He also dreamed of reviving the Carolingian concept of establishing a French border territory stretching from the Pyrenees to the Ebro, giving the Spanish king a conquered Portugal in exchange. But which king of Spain? Although Charles IV (the reigning sovereign) had always been an accommodating ally, it was a continual source of irritation to Napoleon to have a throne bordering his own occupied by a member of that Bourbon dynasty whose memory he wished to expunge from France. In the federal system of which he dreamed, the crowns would be awarded to members of his own family – a disastrous idea, as we know. So much for his intentions. To clarify the sequel, there follows a chronology of events:

  28 July 1807 – France by ultimatum, backed by Spain, invites Portugal
     to break her alliance with Britain. Ultimatum refused.
  3 August – Junot takes command of an expeditionary force of 22,000
     men assembled near Bayonne.
  18 October – The first French battalions cross the Bidassoa and are courteously welcomed by the Spanish authorities.
  22 October – War is officially declared on Portugal.
  27 October – Secret agreement between France and Spain for the partition of Portugal. This is the moment to see who reigns and who governs in Spain.

One of Goya's masterpieces is his portrait of King Charles IV in the bosom of his family. At first glance, it is a majestic group, glittering, florid, but close study reveals faces of ferocious cruelty. One wonders how Goya evaded immediate execution after delivering his picture, but the great are so imbued with a sense of their own importance that it blinds them.

Charles is in the foreground; quite huge, Bourbon nose and mouth, the features coarsened, though wearing an almost benevolent expression. This sovereign (52 years of age when Goya painted him) was in truth a brute. He liked to fight with seamen, porters, grooms. However, his life was strictly controlled. He had dozens of clocks which all had to keep exact time – an obsession of his. Wakened at 5 a.m., he attended two masses and then went to his 'workshops' where he became woodworker, cabinet-maker, joiner, shoemaker. Thence to the stables – his horses were his best friends. Dinner at midday. He ate alone, gluttonously, quickly, until 1 p.m. when it was time for the hunt, in all weathers and all seasons. On his return, he was surrounded by diplomatists and courtiers. Though he hardly listened to what was said, he addressed everyone familiarly except priests. At night, he visited the queen and the ministers attended him according to custom: 'Well, what's going on in the country?' This took all of half an hour, after which they were dismissed: 'It is time for my music.'

He played the violin, not solo, but in an orchestra assembled for him, and would curse the leader if he ventured to observe that he was coming in three bars too soon. After music, supper, then cards (*el Hombre*) during which he slept until awakened to go to his room. He slept alone and never honoured the queen with his presence, having been told by the priests that 'to exercise marriage rights would hurt his health'. Absolute continence, no mistresses.

Let us take another look at this portrait of Goya's. On the king's right between two of her children is the queen, Marie-Louise of Parma, granddaughter of Philip V on her father's side and of Louis XV on her mother's; cousin of her husband. Fifty years old at the time of the portrait, she has an authoritative air. She looked frightful, deeply décolletée, she displayed a ravaged bosom with greenish skin. No teeth; she often ate alone because she could take nothing but pap. She spent vast sums on her toilette, ordering everything from Paris and choosing the most gaudy and shimmering confections. A pharmacist and several specialists in beauty products formed part of her entourage. She loaded herself with diamonds; when it thundered, she augmented them with relics and rosaries although she had no religious faith. Fearful and superstitious, she was said to be amiable in casual relationships. Leading an outwardly austere life (never a ball or a play at court), one interest regulated her conduct: the volcano which seethed beneath her skirts. She took lovers from every walk of life, from ministers to soldiers of the guard.

Ferdinand, the crown prince, appears in the portrait in a light-blue costume. 'Though young, he already had the looks of an old roué' according to Michelet. It is true that the prince, on becoming Ferdinand VII, would be frightful, but that was still to come. 'Tiger's heart and mule's head,' said the queen. Victim of an asphyxiating education, he was introspective, solitary, sly. Married young, to a daughter of Queen Marie Caroline of Naples, it was said that he had never approached her. He knew of his mother's excesses and he hated her – the hatred was mutual.

One need not bother about the others in the portrait who have no part in the tragi-comedy that was to unfold. But let us add a character whom Goya obviously couldn't include. Godoy, the queen's lover at 21, when she was thirty-seven. The Spanish called him *el choricero* (sausage-seller) because he came from Estremadura, where pork is the principal industry, but his nobility, although minor, was beyond question. Manuel Godoy y Alvarez de Faria: lifeguard at 14, grandee of Spain, prime minister and Duke of Alcudia at 25; the volcano was grateful and Godoy had tamed the royal household.

The queen was so successful in concealing the irregularity of her life that the blinkered Charles IV was unaware that she was deceiving him. As was Godoy and she herself, because they went their own ways. After a long affair with one Josefa Tudo, the prime minister, at the sovereigns' instigation, made a dynastic marriage with the Countess of Chinchon, a featherbrained blonde who, speaking of her husband, was to say: 'I hate him so much that I do not love my child because she is his daughter.' Let us here lower the curtain on this sketch of the climate at the court of Madrid. Napoleon's spies had reported to him that Charles, Marie-Louise and Godoy were known to the Madrileños as *el cabron, la pute y el alcahurte* – the goat, the whore and the ruffian.

According to Corporal Martial Joseph Delroeux: 'We crossed the Bidassoa, a sad trickle of a river which forms the boundary between France and Spain. Then we marched to Irun, a small town situated in the province of Biscaya. The inhabitants are filthy, eaten by vermin. Marching down a street, we were showered with fleas from those at the windows above who were watching us pass. Our captain already had several on his cloak and said jokingly to the officers "I have already been attacked by the Spaniards".'

The French army which entered Spain on 18 October 1807 comprised 20,000 men, including 2,000 cavalry, and 36 cannon. There was no comparison with the soldiers of the Grande Armée. According to witnesses: 'Most of them are skinny youths, sickly and in rags. Some have no breeches and hide their nakedness under their cloaks; others scarcely know how to hold their weapons.' Napoleon, making haste to deny Portugal to the British, had had to make do with whatever was to hand, the fruit of a hasty levy. At the head of this destitution was 36-year-old General Andoche Junot, tall, broad-shouldered and narrow-hipped. His long, curly and delicate hair framed his face to the mid-point of his cheeks. A noble nose with narrow nostrils, a long chin and a mouth with tender lips. Happily, one might say, a long scar crossed his face from the right temple to the left side of the mouth. This souvenir of Lonato, in Italy, corrected any tendency to the feminine in his features.

'Valour carried as far as temerity,' wrote General Maillot, whence the nickname of 'the Tempest' attached to Junot when he was still a grenadier under the Revolution; at the same time, he was elected sergeant. Before entering the army, he had studied law, wrote a very elegant hand, as they said in those days. One anecdote is well known: during the siege of Toulon, Junot was writing to Bonaparte's dictation. A cannon-ball fell between them, covering the paper with earth. 'Good, said Junot, I won't need any sand [as blotting-paper].' Bonaparte esteemed Junot, who worshipped him, and shared his purse with him. His bravery was displayed in Italy and Egypt. In 1804 he was disappointed not to be included in the mass promotion of marshals. The personality of his wife, Laure Permon, damaged his career. She had called Bonaparte, then with slender limbs in boots too large for him, 'Puss-in-Boots'; he called her 'The little Pest'. To rid himself of this somewhat irritating couple, Napoleon had had Junot appointed ambassador to Lisbon in 1805. The ambassador had quit his post without permission to rejoin the Grande Armée, an action for which he was forgiven, since we see him at Austerlitz as ADC to the Emperor.

Appointed Governor of Paris in 1806, Junot attracted attention by his dissipated life style and extravagant expenditure. It was his liaison with Caroline Bonaparte that partly prompted Napoleon to send him to Portugal at the head of this new army.

This is not the last we shall see of Junot, but in case we become overwhelmed by the great events unfurling, let me here record his sad end. In 1813, governor of Venice, temporary governor of the Illyrian Provinces, he could not reconcile himself to the irrevocable disapproval of the Emperor. He suffered acutely from facial pains, the result of his wounds. Syphilitic to an advanced degree, he became mad. Consigned to the care of his father at Montbard, he jumped from a window and broke his thigh. The leg was amputated, but he tore off the dressings and died some days later. But that is in the future.

At the head of his miserable army, Junot marched on Lisbon via Bidassoa, Valladolid, Salamanca, Ciudad Rodrigo, la Sierra de Gata, Alcantara, Abrantès, Santarem.

The Spain which unfolded to the first French soldiers who entered at the end of October 1807 was as exotic as China or Patagonia to most inhabitants of western Europe. First, the country: rocks, brush, no cultivated land, wild sheep and cattle, predatory birds sailing over the heights, streams at the bottom of deep gorges. The only sound, the ear-splitting squeaking of the wooden wheels of the rustic wagons.

The inns were hovels where the only habitable room was the stable; no furniture, the fireplace stood in the centre of the communal room. Through the smoke one could discern the guests seated on the ground, wrapped in sheepskins or brown or black cloaks. Only part of the face visible, as were two fingers holding a cigar. Their silence broken by a few words every quarter of an hour or so. 'The army was warmly welcomed by the population,' according to some reports; this means that people simply looked mutely at the soldiers.

What most astonished Junot's recruits was the universal plethora of churches, convents and priests, and particularly the immense hats with upturned brim worn by the priests. Beneath this, a face of brown wax barely emerging from a long robe of green-black. 'Scarecrows,' said the soldiers. But they had not yet become aware of the predominant and incredibly repressive role of the clergy in Spanish society.

The better to consolidate their dominance, the Spanish priests insisted that learning was fatal to the people and must be confined to the servants of God. A teacher was worse paid than a workman; small communities had none and stagnated in total ignorance. Religious observance was often little more than the grossest superstition. The peasants, not content with loading themselves with scapulars and pious images, placed around their children's necks silver-set ribbons plaited with the tail of a black mare. An amulet said to be very efficacious was the tooth of a hanged man. Such superstitions existed also in France in the more remote regions, but the custom of burying the dead in the churches had been abandoned many years earlier. A widely held Spanish belief was that burial under the high altar assured salvation. The churches' foundations were crammed with coffins. When they became full, specialised diggers arrived and disinterred the skeletons, attaching them in skeins to the vaults of the holy ground. This in 1808 – the French soldiers who, during the halts, went to look at the churches were astonished by this macabre proceeding and disgusted by the odour.

Here still reigned, more powerfully than the throne, the Inquisition. Still mouldering in prison cells were those rash souls who had let it be known that they did not believe in miracles or that all who died unshriven went to Hell, or who had simply defended wife or daughter against the lust of some monk or priest. The result of this theocracy was apparent on quitting the homes of the rich, or the convents or the workplaces of the artisans who lived poorly; everywhere was poverty and mendacity. Beggars were legion and arrogant; it was not politic to tell them to go and seek work: 'I am asking for alms, not advice.'

Brigandage arose naturally from the army of beggars; no road was secure, no one ventured to travel singly. This social condition, as senseless as it was backward, did nothing to reduce the boundless pride of the Spanish people. Should a traveller ask a peasant to serve as a guide: 'I cannot. I am hildago.'

Hildago meant noble, a man whose ancestors had recovered their lands from the infidel, the Moors.

Napoleon had ordered Junot to record all the provinces he crossed, with details of the roads and the nature of the terrain, and have the engineer officers make maps and sketches showing distances, topography and resources of each place. 'And stay with your army, firstly, because a general should never leave it; secondly, because he is only great when with his army, but is small at court. Regardless of invitations, march with one of your divisions.'

The entry into Spain began well enough, but the march began to deteriorate thanks to the discomfort and lack of hygiene at the halts. It rained incessantly and the soldiers had no linen or spare clothes; they lost their shoes in the mud. The horses, fed on barley and straw, wasted away or died, often being replaced by requisitioned mules or oxen.

During this period, the curtain rose at the Escorial on a tragi-comedy from another age. On 29 October 1808, Charles IV dictated a letter to Napoleon: 'My eldest son has organised a horrible plot to dethrone me; he was moved so far as to make an attempt on his mother's life! An attempt so frightful as to merit the most condign punishment which the law allows. The law which named him as successor must be revoked. One of his brothers will be more worthy to replace him in my heart and at the court. I am now seeking his accomplices in order to plumb the depths of this blackest criminality and I wished to lose not a moment before informing Your Imperial and Royal Majesty and praying for the help of his counsels and insights.' The Spanish monarchy was taming itself through the king's person.

In fact, the infante Ferdinand had never attempted to kill his mother. But, on the advice of François de Beauharnais (brother-in-law of the Empress), the French Ambassador at Madrid, he had hatched a fairly clumsy plot and committed to paper a draft decree against the possibility that, his venerated father having been called to God, he would become king, and of course would dismiss Godoy, the Prince of Peace, denouncing him as seducer and procurer to the queen. Through treason, the paper came into the king's hands. Godoy neatly assumed the role of mediator and advised him to exercise clemency. On 5 November, the son signed a letter of unconditional apology: 'My father, I have failed you, I have been wanting in regard to Your Majesty in your station as king and father, but I repent. I pray your Majesty will allow your grateful son to kiss your feet.' Marie-Louise also received an equally abject letter. The lawyers proceeded to unmask the plot.

Junot's troops continued to march towards Portugal. They crossed snow-covered plains between Salamanca and Ciudad Rodrigo. There were no reliable maps and they had to rely on guides. They often lost their way. 'What is the name of this mountain range towards which we are marching?' 'La sierra de

Gata' 'And is Alcantara beyond it?' 'Yes, a long way beyond.' That was true, but the sierra was snow-covered and vehicles could not cross. Provisions had to be carried on the backs of the men; half were lost. The starving troops spread out through the woods in search of food. They found neither village nor food, but bandits whose first French victims these juvenile soldiers became. To cross the mountains it was necessary to widen a passage through the rock for the artillery; the guns were hauled by cables, which often broke. Peasants recruited as auxiliaries would tip their loads into the ravines by night, cutting the traces and making-off with the oxen.

At Ciudad Rodrigo, Junot had received a letter from Napoleon which could well have enraged him, as it showed how little Napoleon understood of the hardships facing these young recruits. He must take Lisbon as quickly as possible, occupy the Portuguese ports, seize the fleet, hoist the French flag on all vessels, each to be garrisoned by two hundred infantrymen. The Portuguese army must be disarmed; political suspects were to be sent to Paris. But at the same time, he must be diplomatic: 'I know I need not counsel you not to give grounds for any complaint. It is up to you to set an example of the greatest impartiality. Above all, make sure that the army receives its pay. The receipts from seizures of jewels and from the shops stocking English merchandise should be half to the private sector and half to the army.'

In the meantime Junot's army was dying of hunger, and pillaged the few houses. They groaned when facing torrents swollen by the rains. Before Aravil, General Delaborde, who commanded the advance guard, dismounted and, though crippled with rheumatism, entered the stream: 'Learn, boys, how to cross a river without a bridge.' The division followed and gained the opposite bank. Junot, 'the Tempest', inspired all to follow his example of boundless energy, but the advance guard arrived at Abrantès in Portugal, 'in an indescribable state'. Fortunately they were entering a cultivated region. Junot requisitioned cattle, bread, wine, clothing, and then summoned his officers: 'Choose four thousand of the strongest men. They must form an élite column for the march on Lisbon.'

The Portuguese Regent had told Napoleon that he was breaking with England, but Portugal was in fact playing a double game, and Napoleon knew it. 'Continue your march,' he had told Junot. The latter had written from Abrantès to the Portuguese Minister of Foreign Affairs and War, complaining that he had been poorly welcomed in Portugal whereas he came as a friend. Bluffing, he gave the impression that his tyro soldiers were seasoned troops: 'My soldiers are disappointed not to have fired a shot. Do not force them to do so, or you may regret it.' He had no idea as yet of the situation in Lisbon.

Portugal was at that time inhabited by a poverty-stricken people, over whom had reigned since 1786 Maria of Braganza, who was insane, which was why her son Joao was regent. At his side to counsel him was the British Minister Plenipotentiary, Lord Strangford. Despite the official declaration of 20 October (rupture with Britain), he was still *en poste* and trying to convince Joao to resist the French army. It is true that a single Portuguese regiment, well deployed in the mountains, would have sufficed to stop Junot's army in its tracks. But the Braganza dynasty was also 'stopped in its tracks' and, such was the reputation in Europe of the Grande Armée, that even its most miserable recruits were a source of terror. 'We cannot resist,' said Joao. Within an hour Strangford (better known as an author of light fiction than as grand diplomatist), had removed the British coat of arms from over the door of his house, demanded his passports and transferred himself to the *Hibernia*, flagship of the British squadron cruising off Lisbon. The following day, the royal family embarked in numerous vessels of the Portuguese fleet, destination: Brazil, their only colony. The entire court, ministers, most of the nobles and the rich who lived in Lisbon followed their example.

In pouring rain, the populace silently surrounded the carriages making for the Tagus. Heading this lugubrious procession was the old queen's carriage; it was the first time in sixteen years that she had been seen by her subjects. A ray of lucidity pierced her mental decay, alerting her to the shameful character of this flight. 'How's this, we are leaving the kingdom without a fight?' And to the driver: 'Not so fast, they will think we are fleeing.' Howling, she refused to embark and was carried forcibly aboard the *Prince Royal* (80 guns).

This abdicating fleet comprised eight ships of the line, three frigates, three brigs and twenty merchantmen. 'Never was an embarkation made in such disorder. The highest in the land found themselves mixed with soldiers, valets, with people of all ages and both sexes whom fear, need or interests unconnected with those of the prince had carried in the crowd to the ships.' The 132nd Regiment had been detailed to protect the royal family, but, arriving at the port, it was found that every ship was full. 'But surely there is a place just for me?' groaned their colonel. He was taken aboard, but his regiment was left behind. Once the passengers had embarked, their baggage was loaded. 'The furniture of the royal palace and of the richest houses in Lisbon, the funds from the public treasury, the money which the Regent had been amassing for some while, funds which the fugitive families had managed to assemble, all this was piled on the banks of the Tagus, half covered in mud.' Did the crowd throw itself on these riches, storm the ships and haul back the high and mighty passengers and ill-treat them? No. In the face of this shameful spectacle, the spectators merely displayed the terrible resignation of the poor.

On the 27th the flotilla anchored in the middle of the Tagus, which at Lisbon is as wide as an arm of the sea and is called the Straw Sea, awaiting a favourable wind. The British fleet cruised off the river mouth to protect the fugitives with its guns. At this point, anger surged through the abandoned watchers, anger mixed with fear: how would the French, whose arrival was said to be imminent, conduct themselves? There were some disorders in the old quarter of Alfama which had been untouched by the earthquake of 1755. The floating exodus finally weighed anchor on the 29th – twenty-four hours before the arrival of the first French detachments.

Junot had left Abrantès on the 26th at the head of his advance guard. He had galvanised his wretched troops to the extent that next day they were at Santarem, having covered sixty kilometres in the rain, often in water up to their knees. Junot handed a proclamation to a deputation of notables which had come to meet him: 'And the members of the council of regency will answer with their heads for the preservation of order.'

They were only two leagues from the capital, but the soldiers were dropping with fatigue. Junot allowed them one night's rest and in the morning – forward! It was still raining. The French general made his entry at the head of his staff and followed by just one regiment of grenadiers. 'The state in which we entered', wrote General Thiébault, 'was beyond belief. Our uniforms no longer had colour or form. My feet were peeping out of my boots.' Given his state, that of the troops can be imagined. Marching to attention at command, they traversed this city of 300,000 as far as the port. Junot was received by the members of the new government presided over by the marquis d'Abantos 'and by what remained in the city of the most distinguished elements'.

He had narrowly missed capturing the royal family and its treasure, but, wrote Adolphe Thiers: 'Some precious stones, some coins, and finally a family whose capture would have been highly embarrassing, did not equal the advantage of becoming master, without firing a shot, of the most important positions on the European littoral and of having prevented a rising which could not be contained had it displayed the least spark of opposition. General Junot and his soldiers have thus harvested the reward of constancy.'

On 20 February 1808, Murat, Grand-Duke of Berg and Cleves, was in Paris; he intended to leave next day to visit his estates. Late that afternoon, he went to the Tuileries where he had a few words of little import with the Emperor and then returned to his palace, the Elysée. As he was finishing supper, a secretary delivered an urgent and confidential letter from General Clarke, Minister of War:

'My lord, I have the honour to announce to Your Imperial Highness that His Majesty the Emperor has nominated you as lieutenant-general in command of all the troops in Spain. His Majesty intends that Your Royal Highness should leave tonight to transfer your headquarters to Bayonne. His Majesty wishes that Your Highness should arrive in that city by the 26th or at the latest the 27th

February. His Majesty has appointed General Belliard as chief of staff to Your Highness. I am ordering him to Bayonne accordingly and, pending his arrival, I have ordered the senior adjutant Bailly de Monthyon to proceed there immediately in order to carry out his duties temporarily. General Lariboisière has been appointed in command of the artillery. I have also the honour to inform Your Imperial Highness that His Majesty is considering the command of the engineers, the auditor-general and the commissioner who will be appointed to discharge the functions of quartermaster-general.'

Murat was to have under his command the II Corps of the Gironde (General Dupont), the coastal observation corps (Marshal Moncey), the division of the Pyrenées-Occidentales (General Merle), the division of the Pyrenées-Orientales (General Duhesme), a detachment of the foot and mounted Guard (General Lépic), the troops forming the 16th, 17th and 18th Provisional Regiments and the five battalions of the Reserve Legion (foreigners). Total, about 80,000 men. We have already seen that, except for the detachment from the Guard, temporarily separated from the Grande Armée, all were drawn from the recruits of the latest call-up; very young soldiers but, according to reports, 'well officered and of good morale'. Most of the Grande Armée was still resting in eastern Europe, totally ignorant, as we have seen, of the events in the Iberian peninsula.

Murat finished both his supper and the reading of the message: 'Your Imperial Highness is authorised in all unforeseen cases to issue instructions and orders to assure the tranquillity and security of his forces. I have the honour to be, &c.' Napoleon had made his decision: to liquidate the Spanish Bourbons and replace them with members of his family. The preparation of this fateful coup d'état was a masterful mix of dissimulation and brutality.

On 5 February, Charles IV had written a letter to the Emperor expressing his alarm at the arrival of more and more troops marching into Spain. He recalled that Spain was allied to France and ended, in effect, 'What are the intentions of Your Imperial and Royal Majesty?'

No reply! And Napoleon ordered Mollien, Minister of the State Treasury: 'Have sent to Bayonne in the most secret manner possible, in a well guarded eight-horse wagon, two millions in gold: the sinews of war. As for physical resources: concentrate at Bayonne a large park of artillery, sixty artillery caissons of ammunition for the artillery and forty for the infantry. An order to Marshal Bessières, commanding the cavalry of the Guard, to send to Bayonne four battalions of fusiliers, detachments of chasseurs and dragoons. An order to General Lépic to leave Bordeaux with the whole Guard in order to be at Bayonne on 3 March at the latest.' All these orders were dated 18 February. We have already seen the later orders to Murat.

François de Beauharnais, still ambassador at Madrid, was instructed to say that the movements of French troops in Spain were designed to protect the country against the British 'who are threatening Gibraltar and Cadiz'.

That same week, an agent of Godoy's, one Izquierdo, was in Paris, anxiously interrogating Talleyrand on the Emperor's intentions. 'And why not marry a French princess to the Prince of Asturias? That would cement Franco-Spanish friendship. I am authorised to assure His Imperial Majesty that King Charles IV agrees to cede to France our Ebro provinces in exchange for a part of Portugal.'

Talleyrand pricked up his ears. Here was a concrete proposition which, it seemed, agreed with the Emperor's plans. But Izquierdo suddenly received from Duroc on behalf of the Emperor the urgent suggestion to return to Madrid 'to dissipate the thick clouds which have arisen between the two courts'.

This deliberate use of bad faith was to continue. On 25 February a very dry letter from the Emperor to Charles IV, which recalled to the King of Spain that on 18 November 1807 he had asked for a French princess for his heir, Ferdinand, Prince of Asturias: 'Your Majesty in his letter of 5 February no longer mentions this marriage,' wrote Napoleon. 'This leaves obscure many important goals of interest to my peoples.' How can one refrain from crying 'What an idiot!' But any pretext is good for a monarch who must think only of the interests of his peoples. This letter to Charles IV was entrusted to M. de Tournon, chancellor and staff officer to the Emperor, with instructions to stay five or six days at Madrid while giving the king 'vague information and nothing which might arouse suspicion that he had information of the Emperor's projects'. Threaten, arouse fear, keep up the anxiety.

There was a French squadron at Cadiz under the command of Admiral Rosily – their mission, to prevent any attempt by the royal family to flee to America. Spies had reported that this possibility had been discussed at the Escorial and the Braganzas' example must not be followed.

Murat would enter Spain on 7 March. A few days later he would receive a letter from Napoleon: 'If there is no further development and the Prince of the Peace (Godoy) has written to you, you may reply in a banal manner stating that your orders have brought you to Spain to inspect my troops.'

Three days earlier, a ciphered message had been sent to Beauharnais informing him that a French army of 50,000 men would enter Madrid on 22 or 23 March. The ambassador should put it about that the intention of the Emperor was to proceed to Cadiz to besiege Gibraltar and then pass over into Africa. Napoleon was confident that he had concocted a seamless cover plan.

Murat left for Spain in a state of extreme excitement. What the Emperor wished to accomplish in that country, what he wanted of him, Murat did not know exactly, but nothing stirs the mind so much as ambition, and the ambition of the Grand-Duke of Berg – constantly stoked to white-heat by his wife Caroline Bonaparte – was boundless. 'The Emperor keeps mum on his plans and has chosen me to command this army which will enter Spain and which will march to Madrid. Why Madrid, and why me? Joseph and Louis Bonaparte, neither with any military reputations, are they not seated on the thrones of Naples and of Holland?' The throne of Spain as a step up the military ladder – why not? Forward!

At the frontier, on 7 March a delegation from the province of Guipuzcoa saluted the Marshal; the village mayors offered homage. Murat sent Napoleon an elated note: 'Your lieutenant who has been sent to Spain to take possession in your name and with the consent of all the Spaniards could not have been more warmly received.'

Two days later at Vitoria, Murat heard that the priests were protesting from the pulpit the entry into Rome of the troops of General Miollis. 'Send for all the clergy!' The priests came and listened without saying a word to a somewhat menacing harangue. 'The Guard has none the less been welcomed by the population,' according to Moncey's report to Murat. On 15 March he reached Miranda, on the 19th Castillejo and it was there that the Grand-Duke of Berg received the first knock-out blow to his ambition.

Fifty kilometres from Madrid, the estate of Aranjuez on the banks of the Tagus contrasted with the surrounding sterility. In 1808 it was a town of fountains and gardens, the summer residence of the kings of Spain. In March 1808, the court was already there. On the 5th, Izquierdo, Godoy's diplomatic agent, arrived breathless from Paris: 'Napoleon wants the Spanish throne for one of his brothers.' Nobody had told him this at Paris, no one spoke openly of it, but the secret intentions of the powerful often leak out and Napoleon had already given to his military chiefs and to Beauharnais so many convergent orders that the secret was out. 'Ah,' cried the queen. 'There is nothing for it but to flee to America.' Charles hesitated. To leave his horses, his hunting, his little concerts, and even the card parties at which he would fall asleep – what a wrench! 'We might lose much more,' said Godoy. 'Our lives, for example. We must go!'

It was not Napoleon's soldiers marching on Madrid whom the Prince of Peace feared, but his compatriots; he could feel their hatred swirling around him. They held him responsible for the invasion and for the humiliation of Spain and he sensed that a faction was forming around Ferdinand to encompass his downfall. Godoy hatched a plan of escape: we will summon troops from Madrid; establish a camp at Talavera which will protect our departure. Eventually the king said 'So be it, but Izquierdo must return to Paris and do everything he can to deflect this blow which is being aimed at us. Give him full powers.'

Ferdinand showed himself hostile to the plan for flight (fearing to become the prisoner of the queen and Godoy), and opposition developed within the Council of Castile; an agreement with Napoleon must first be attempted: 'And if no solution is found, we will raise the people against the French. In any event, we must remain.'

Godoy did not even pretend to listen; he left for Madrid, issued orders, Spanish troops must be sent to Andalusia and be stationed along the route which the royal family would take to the port of embarkation. The Council of Castile had divulged the news of Godoy's preparations. People are generally unhappy to see themselves abandoned by their sovereign. On 14 March were to be seen around the palace at Aranjuez rough, poorly dressed strangers of sombre mien, types rarely seen in this garden city. Their numbers swelled steadily and they were dominated by a strange person, the Count of Montijo. Once the queen's favourite, he was now very unwelcome at court and Godoy had exiled his mother in 1805. 'I must avenge her,' he had said, 'and liberate the nation from the monster which is devouring it.'

Disguising himself as a peasant and taking the name of Tio Pedro (Uncle Peter), he got together a band of monks, priests and vagabonds, all expert in fomenting disorder and uprisings. Initially these ruffians distributed money to the peasants and put it about that Godoy (who had returned to Aranjuez) planned to abduct the royal family to Seville and thence to Mexico

The Prince of Asturias was the beneficiary of this propaganda. In the evening the royal family promenaded before the public gaze. Ferdinand was acclaimed; silence for the king and queen. Godoy himself found it prudent not to appear. In front of his small house near the park and the suspension bridge over the Tagus, strollers passed sniggering. In the shadows of the gardens, there was coming and going; consultations. When the royal family withdrew into the palace, a clamour grew under the windows. 'I don't like that,' said the king to the queen, and next day had the lifeguards read a proclamation: there was no reason for alarm at the imminent arrival of the French allies, who had come to repel a possible invasion of the coasts of Spain by the British. 'As for myself, I will not leave Spain, but will remain in the midst of my people.' 'Long live the king!' But that was not the only cry; even louder was 'Death to Godoy!' and a frenzy of obscenities and curses.

There was an interval of calm as evening drew on, but during the night the crowd surged once more around the palace. There was a rumour that the royal family and Godoy would flee on the following night. Godoy returned home at about 10.30 and 'sat down to supper with his brother, Diego, and the commander of the hussars'. At about midnight, a shot was heard. Who it was that fired it will never be known; many accounts, as contradictory as they are romantic, have been recorded. In fact the affair appears to have taken place in accordance with a well-thought-out plan.

A light had appeared in a window of Ferdinand's apartments, and this had been followed immediately by the shot – a signal. The soldiers came running from their barracks, Montijo (Uncle Peter) led his priests and monks towards Godoy's house, accompanied by a crowd holding torches and brandishing weapons. The house was surrounded, the doors smashed in, the crowd climbed the stairs, burst into the salons, smashing everything, burning the carpets, the curtains, savagely wrecking the treasures of the royal pimp. But Godoy, sought everywhere, had vanished.

He had been preparing for bed when he heard the shot. Quickly donning a military cape, he rushed to the top floor of his home and took refuge in the room of a faithful domestic, a groom, where he remained for the rest of the night and throughout the next day (18 March), hungry and thirsty, terrified at the noise in his house of shouts, cries, and laughter. At nightfall he ventured down another stairway opening on to a hut full of trunks and carpets where he collapsed from exhaustion to pass another night of agonising thirst. At the end of his tether, he quit this second refuge. A soldier was sitting on the stairs, smoking a small cigar. 'For God's sake, a glass of water. I'll pay.' The soldier hesitated for a second and then, 'No, I cannot,' and he ran downstairs: 'Here is the prince!' The kill. The royal guards arrived first and would escort Godoy nowhere except to the king. But to do so entailed crossing Aranjuez and the populace was running riot with clubs and stones. 'Clutching the saddles of two horses, almost suspended in the air, half blinded from a wound over his eye which was bleeding, the Prince of Peace, pursued by threats of vengeance and death, by the curses of a furious mob, was taken, not to the palace as the king had ordered, but to the stables of the guards' barracks as had been decided by 'a certain authority unknown to one and to all'. Which meant that Ferdinand's partisans would stop at nothing in order to propel him to power.

The king and queen were dumbfounded; the ministers and the great ones wished only for the return of calm. 'There is only one thing for Your Majesty to do which, at the same time, may save the life of the Prince of Peace: strip him of all his functions and honours.' The king assented – the queen groaned. Immediately the news became known there was an explosion of joy from the populace; there was dancing around celebratory fires, not only in Aranjuez but also in Madrid. Under the balconies of the royal palace came shouts of 'Long live King Ferdinand!'

Charles IV still wished to spare his ex-favourite the worst: 'Let him be tried, since the people wish it, but not here. Transfer him to the Alhambra at Grenada. That will give passions time to cool.' It was necessary to send a six-mule team and a carriage to the stable where Godoy was crouching in the straw.

The crowd assembled there was not deceived. The mules were unharnessed and in a few minutes the carriage was wrecked: 'Death to Godoy! Death to the ruffian!' And still under the windows of the royal palace others cried: 'Long live King Ferdinand!'

At about 7 p.m. on 19 March, Charles sent for his principal ministers. He asked to see the document which Philip V had used to renounce the throne, and with the help of Marie-Louise he drafted an act of abdication in favour of his son Ferdinand and signed it: 'He shook his shoulders like a man shedding a burden, and, addressing the Russian Ambassador – the reason for whose presence I have been unable to discover – 'I have never done anything in my life with more pleasure.'

The letter which Murat addressed to Napoleon after learning of the events at Aranjuez was one long lamentation: 'Sire, I cannot hide from you all my distress. I foresee that blood may flow and Europe will not refrain from saying that it was France who had ordered it ... Sire, I command your armies and represent Your Majesty and certainly no one would believe that I am there without knowing your plans and if Madrid should become agitated and if heads fall, regardless of whose, what will be said? My loyalty is wounded and for the first time in my life I regret my inability to know how to serve Your Majesty in such a critical situation.'

A free translation: 'The abdication of Charles IV has ruined my hopes. Must I give it all up?'

According to the official account, Murat entered Madrid at the head of two of Marshal Moncey's divisions, with numerous detachments of cavalry and regiments of the Imperial Guard. Here is what actually occurred:

Leading was the Grand-Duke of Berg's staff, composed of rich young men, dressed in luxurious uniforms and riding parade horses, then the circus of mamelukes with their scimitars; the cuirassiers, at whom the Spaniards marvelled, never having seen such admirable cuirasses. But, following them, were the raw conscripts, in rags, skinny, under skakos too large for them, looking harassed. This spectacle provoked first astonishment, then laughter, then distrust. What, are these the conquerors of Europe? The Guard regiments bringing up the rear did not succeed in effacing this unfortunate impression. The Captain General of Madrid and the officers of the garrison were there to welcome the French Marshal: 'But where are the civic and ecclesiastical authorities?' No one knew. 'And where am I to lodge?' The home of 'the Tudo ladies', sacked by Godoy's enemies, was suggested. 'Are you mocking me?' Finally, the admiralty palace would be assigned to Murat.

Ferdinand – now King Ferdinand VII – entered his capital the next day on a white horse; no troops, only lifeguards. The crowd threw itself under the hooves of his horse, kissed his hands, his knees, his spurs; the horse walked on a carpet of capes, hats and fans, kerchiefs were thrown in the air. All the church bells were rung, maroons were fired, the nobles, knights and ladies applauded from the balconies.

Murat, who twenty-four hours earlier had been struck down by the abdication of Charles IV, now reacted, not wishing to despair of his star: 'Ride to Aranjuez,' he ordered General Monthyon. 'See the old man, talk to him, make him speak. Have him write to the Emperor that his abdication was made under duress and that his ministers are traitors who wished to assassinate him.'

Tired, hesitant, Charles IV let himself be convinced and wrote the letter dictated to him. In order to increase the impression on Napoleon, the letter was ante-dated to 21 March, that is, before Murat's arrival; and Murat also wrote to the Emperor: 'The King (Charles IV) has formally declared that he abdicated only to save his life and that of the queen, that he was convinced that he would have been murdered that night. He has asked me to solicit Your Majesty's generosity which he has so often enjoyed in the past in order to allow him to purchase a farm in France where he might live out his days quietly with the queen.' A fairly blatant lie, but well edited; the abdication was invalid; Ferdinand was not an impostor, but as Charles IV did not wish to resume his throne, it was accordingly vacant. Another letter from Murat to the Emperor was even more explicit: 'I had thought of protesting to the king about the events at Aranjuez and then having him abdicate the throne in favour of Your Majesty, who would then be free to dispose of it as you might see fit.' In favour of whom, if not Murat himself?

We know that Murat did not become king of Spain and that his schemes did not come to fruition. There is a curious letter from Napoleon to him dated 29 March 1808, which was included in the *Memorial from St. Helena*, though Jean Thiry states that he has been unable to find either the original or any copy. Adolphe Thiers (*History of the Consulate and Empire*) thought that it might have been written but not sent. It is of interest as it shows that the Emperor, having totally misconstrued the truth about Spain, had perhaps given some thought to the events at Aranjuez. Here follow some extracts from this odd missive:

'You have to make over the people anew with all the courage and enthusiasm which are displayed by men without political convictions. The aristocracy and the clergy are the masters of Spain. If they fear for their privileged lives, they will ferment mass risings in order to prolong the war indefinitely. I have supporters, but if I present myself as conqueror, I shall have none. The Prince of Peace is detested because he is accused of having delivered Spain to France: this is the grievance which has supported the usurpation of Ferdinand; the popular party is the weaker. The Prince of Asturias has none of the qualities necessary for the head of a nation, which will not prevent him from aspiring to be a hero in order to oppose us. I do not wish to use violence against this family; it is never effective to court odium and to inflame hatred. Spain has more than 100,000 men under arms, which is more than is necessary to sustain effectively a civil war; divided on several issues; it might serve as a means for a general uprising.

'Should I come to Madrid? Should I establish a wide protectorate by choosing between the father and the son? It seems difficult to me to allow Charles IV to reign; his government and his favourite are so unpopular that it would not last three months. Ferdinand is the enemy of France, which is why he has been made king. To place him on the throne is to serve the cause of those factions which for twenty-five years have worked for the destruction of France, etc.' In short, Napoleon insists that a rigorous discipline be maintained for the protection of the population, the convents and the churches. 'Should war break out, all will be lost. The destiny of Spain must be decided by policy and negotiation.'

So far as Spain was concerned, Napoleon's support of policy and negotiation was that of all dictators faced with a weaker antagonist. It involved, quite simply, the employment of force, while taking a minimum of Jesuitical precautions. Murat, still hoping to obtain the Spanish crown, would manipulate as best he could the unavowed goals of his master. Persuaded or pushed by him, Ferdinand, then Godoy (in order to save himself from popular retribution), the royal couple, would turn up at Bayonne, the snare where *Raminagrobis* (the monster Napoleon) would devour them.

At Madrid, Murat showed himself, went riding in sumptuously extravagant uniforms. When he attended mass (as advised by Napoleon to please the Spaniards) a hired chorus would cry as he passed 'Long live the Grand-Duke!' He held grand reviews, flourishing his Marshal's baton. Whether it was his own idea or had been suggested to him is not known, but he went so far as to reclaim from the Spaniards the sword of Francis I, defeated at Pavia! He had it formally presented to him – and spouted a ridiculous speech, saying that it would be carried to Paris: 'where it will remind those generations to come of the centuries of the great Napoleon and that of Charles V'.

Spanish pride was incensed and Murat, as Napoleon's lieutenant-general in Spain, started to run wild. Napoleon in his strange letter had written, 'If war flares up, all will be lost.' War did flare up.

Throughout the country, the young soldiers found little to eat but plenty to drink. At first they had been bemused by the army of priests and religious orders, and the almost hysterical displays of piety on the part of the populace, but now they began to deride them. The scuffles and disorders had started in Catalonia at the beginning of March; some drunken soldiers had broken crossroads crucifixes, had spat on pious relics and pulled Capuchin beards; others had stolen sacred vessels, raped some girls.

It was not only the extortions; the taxes levied on the towns, the obligatory billeting of troops, the requisition of provisions and forage which outraged the people. The French were attacked by night. At Zamora, the Spanish mistress of an officer warned him charitably that his comrades would never see France again. And, when he laughed: 'You will see. I implore you to stay close to me or you will die like the others.'

At Barcelona, the early morning patrols stumbled over the corpses of French soldiers stabbed in the back. In many regions peasants were arrested for wearing bonnets inscribed 'Death to the French!' Murders and reprisals began to escalate.

In Madrid Murat cultivated the high society ladies – or those who would accept his invitations. He wrote to the Emperor: 'Your Majesty can decide on whatever course he sees fit; his wishes will be executed without opposition.' Without opposition! His spies were reporting that more and more peasants were entering the capital, buying daggers, powder and ball. Murat laughed: 'How can they say that feeling in the capital is against the French when we see soldiers strolling the streets with the Spaniards?'

Yes, but while so doing, they could read on the walls placards such as: 'By general consent, it is ordered that the chamber-pot should be named Napoleon and the lavatory Buona-Parte.' In the poor quarter, the Plaza de la Cebada and the calle San Anton, with their crowds of filthy beggars, mules, flaunting prostitutes, half-naked children, wounded or dying soldiers were found every morning. By night on the banks of the Manzanares, snipers fired on soldiers returning late to barracks. In the Carabanchel district, a priest knocked on the door of a French officer: 'Señor, here is your chocolate.' The officer got up, opened the door and received a pistol-ball in the chest. In the centre of the city, a fanatic stabbed an officer and two soldiers. Arrested, he gave as his excuse: 'Ah, I was suddenly inspired to kill three Frenchmen.' Popular uprisings were reported from Burgos and Toledo. In April, forty-four men of Moncey's corps were killed by axe or daggers. French soldiers retaliated by deliberately killing civilians. A Spanish police officer explained to a French officer: 'The Emperor does not know the Spaniards. They are vindictive and their hate of Godoy is justified. They will never forgive you for having deprived them of their prey.'

Ferdinand left Madrid for Bayonne on 10 April. Murat had persuaded him to ask Napoleon for his mediation, rule on who should reign, he or his father (who had retracted his abdication). Throughout his journey he was acclaimed as the man held to be king by the Spaniards, but behind in a separate carriage rode General Savary, Napoleon's envoy, whose task it was to monitor Ferdinand's progress. At Valladolid, Ferdinand wished to halt. 'No, Sire, we must go on.' 'How dare you speak to me thus? Will not people say that I am your prisoner?' 'No, Sire, but those are my master's orders and they must be obeyed.' At Vitoria, the Spaniards urged Ferdinand not to go on to Bayonne and during a halt of several days, a guard of armed supporters was formed. Savary had to push his intimidation to extremes. Ferdinand's carriage moved off to shouts of fury and the groans of the women: 'God go with him! So young and we shall never see him again.' The beggars sang an improvised dirge in the streets: 'Unhappy Spain! Fernando, where are you going?'

He arrived at Bayonne on 19 April. Napoleon, who had arrived two days earlier, received him with favour (at the château of Marrac some two kilometres from the town), but without greeting him as Majesty or Highness, an ominous omission. Napoleon's gave his opinion of Ferdinand in letters to Talleyrand and Caulaincourt: 'I have here the Prince of Asturias, whom I have received kindly, but whom I do not recognise [as king]... The Prince of Asturias is very stupid, very cunning, and very much the enemy of France. You will understand me when I say that with my experience of appraising men, his inexperience at twenty-four years of age did not impress me.'

Six days later, Godoy, an Ishmael, arrived after a menacing journey crouched on the floor of General Exelmans' carriage, passing through towns by night and changing horses only in open country under the protection of troops. He was accommodated in a country house near Bayonne whence Savary fetched him to present him to Napoleon. 'He looks like a bull,' said the Emperor, but in public he displayed kindness ('The Spanish nation has treated him with unparalleled inhumanity').

The royal couple arrived on 30 April and were received with pomp and every sign of friendship. Napoleon called at the house prepared for their use, then escorted them to the château Marrac. As they were sitting down at table – Napoleon had wished Josephine to be present – Godoy was absent and Charles became uneasy: 'And Manuel? Where is Manuel?' Napoleon sent for him. The Queen talked fashions with Josephine. Napoleon's opinion of the couple: 'He is a booby and she is a fright. With her yellow skin she looks like a mummy. She has a false and malicious manner and it is impossible to imagine a more ridiculous person. At sixty years of age, she wears a décolleté dress with short sleeves and without gloves.' After the meal, Napoleon sent for Ferdinand for the decisive explanation which was to be made in the main hall of the château. The scene was grotesque.

Charles, standing, grasping his long walking-stick, demanded that his son return his crown. Ferdinand was evasive: 'Such a renunciation, made outside Spain, would never be accepted by the Spanish people. It would need to be made in Spain and approved by the Cortes.' This infuriated them. Charles brandished his stick, Marie-Louise spouted curses, but Ferdinand said nothing more. The impasse would be broken a few days later thanks to Godoy's agency, invoked by Napoleon. But in the mean time Madrid had had its *Dos de Mayo*.

'Madrid is a large, sad city,' wrote Larrey, 'whose streets, although paved with black, pointed stones, are dirty.' Early in the morning of 2 May 1808, the capital wore its normal look.. Peasants urged donkeys loaded with panniers, merchants rigged their stalls in the open, half-naked urchins were running about shouting, one could see mules bearing individuals wearing broad-brimmed hats like the priests', but their clothing was coloured – doctors en route to visit their patients.

Groups of peasants from the suburbs gathered in front of the churches; many had slept in the church porches. The rumour had reached them that the French planned to carry off to Bayonne the infante Don Francisco, the youngest of the king's sons, and his sister, Marie-Louise, ex-Queen of Etruria. On the previous day Murat and his escort had been whistled at on the Puerta del Sol. Those Madrileños who had French soldiers billeted on them advised them to stay home: 'There's trouble brewing; the people are furious.'

French troops had fallen-in in front of the palace where, at about 7 a.m., two carriages had pulled in. The ex-Queen of Etruria appeared and got into one of the carriages with two companions. There was no reaction; Marie-Louise was of interest to nobody. But when the infante appeared, there were shouts: 'Treason! Don't let them take the Prince! Death to the French!' Some of the demonstrators cut the traces and unharnessed the carriage. A gentleman appeared at a window of the palace; he shouted 'To arms! They are taking the Prince!' The crowd rushed forward. A moment later, Francisco appeared on a balcony, bowing and waving kisses. At that moment there arrived one of Murat's ADCs, white pelisse, red breeches. 'Kill him! Kill him!' A picket of the guard just managed to rescue him. From that moment there was riot and insurrection.

The ringleader, a locksmith named José Blas Molina, sent men to the armoury whose guards allowed them to take weapons, and the hunt was on for individual French soldiers who could be seen running, desperately seeking shelter. But all doors were closed to them. They were pelted with roof-tiles and stones. Unfortunate victims were cornered and slaughtered. Within an hour dead bodies were everywhere. In the hospitals dozens of sick and wounded had their throats cut by the Spanish nurses.

Murat had 10,000 troops in the city, 20,000 camped outside. First reaction: the Guard grenadiers appeared on the palace esplanade and sited two cannon in battery. The first salvo was fired in the air, the second, of canister, horizontally. The servants of the royal palace were mown down, the mob retreated, dispersed and then re-formed in the neighbourhood of the calle Mayor and the streets nearby. In the crowd were men, women and even children armed with pikes, axes, iron bars, knives, clubs and a few muskets. Death to the French!

From his post at the San Vincente gate, an extension of the royal palace, Murat deployed four columns of troops through the city gates and they converged on the Puerta del Sol. Some lancers and mamelukes made their way down the calle de Alcala under a hail of tiles, paving-stones and even furniture. The insurgents fired from windows and from embrasures at street level. '*Muerte a los gavachos!*' (cowards).

The most detested unit was that of the mamelukes, descendants of the Moors, the ancient masters of Spain. They wore wide red pantaloons, a white turban and a shimmering belt. Clusters of Spaniards attached themselves to their spurs, to the horses' tails, disembowelling the animals, throwing the riders to the ground and stabbing them. Those of them that who free charged again and again, plying their curved scimitars with amazing skill; heads flew.

The French troops, enraged by the sight of the bodies of their comrades, gave no quarter. Any house from which they were fired upon was invaded, sacked and the inhabitants bayoneted. The monks of a monastery in front of which a mameluke lay dying were all decapitated and their heads thrown from the windows.

The detachment guarding the artillery park at Monteleone were disarmed and massacred. The insurgents took two cannon and set them up. A French column retreated; a cuirassier fell from his horse; a woman transfixed him with his own sabre. A soldier had managed to warn Murat of what was happening on this side of the city. 'Let's finish off this wild mob!'

A Spanish workman appeared with a white handkerchief on his sword. He wanted to parley, but the mob left him no time. Battle was resumed, but this time the French prevailed. By 1 p.m. the fighting had died down and delegates of the *junta* ran through the streets with white flags: 'Peace! Peace! Everyone go home!'

But retribution was already under way. 'A military court, sitting at the post building in the Puerta del Sol, will pass summary judgement on those found with weapons in their hands,' proclaimed Murat. Any Spaniard found in possession of a knife, scissors, a razor – a barber had them on him – was arrested, pinked with bayonet thrusts and dragged in front of the court where he was summarily condemned.

There was no lack of execution sites: at the Prado, at the top of the Retiro, in the courtyard of the church of Buen Suceso, against the walls of the Convent of Jesus, on the hill of the Principe Pio. All windows in town had to be shut; fire was opened on anyone who showed himself. As usual, the ringleaders had already made off and it was the innocents who were arrested. Those with money attempted to bribe the soldiers. But without success; the thirst for vengeance was too great. An old Madrileño did not deny that he had killed three soldiers and even boasted of it: 'I die happy. If every Spaniard will do as I did the country will be saved.'

Night fell. A clear night under the stars. The streets were strewn with corpses: soldiers and civilian men, women and children, and horses. The walls of the houses were pock-marked by bullets; troops were posted at the junction of the main streets with cannon loaded and aligned. But all was now silent, except for a distant cannon and the final fusillades from the firing-squads on the heights of Principe Pio.

From his home at 9, Puerta del Sol, Goya, old Goya, deaf but in no way blind, had watched the revolt and later had interrogated witnesses. The most inspired televised reporting would lack the impact that Goya brought to his engravings and paintings of the Dos de Mayo in his 'Disasters of War'. His painting of the executions at Principe Pio, with the shirtsleeved Spaniard facing the muskets, arms outstretched in a gesture of imprecation, the waiting batch of victims, the soldiers taking aim, the whole illuminated by a single lantern – is a tragic masterpiece.

How many killed in total? As usual, the figures were initially fantastic, then reduced. Finally, serious historians stated between 400 and 500 on the Spanish side, 150 French, but those killed in uprisings have the greatest impact on history.

Shortly afterwards Murat wrote to the Emperor: 'The results of the events of 2 May confirm a decisive victory for You. The Prince of Asturias lost his crown on that day; his party was completely defeated and stands at the side of the victor. Your Majesty can dispose of the crown of Spain and there will be no further disturbance. All are submissive and only await the new king which Your Majesty will give to Spain.'

The new king, thought Murat, could be none other than himself. He had no idea that on 2 May 1808 at 11 p.m. Napoleon was engaged in dictating a letter to him which began: 'I intend the King of Naples should reign at Madrid and I wish to give you the throne of either Naples or Portugal. Reply to me giving your thoughts for it must be done within a day.'

On 5 May, Napoleon was out riding near Bayonne when a messenger from Murat delivered his report of the events of the Dos de Mayo. The Emperor did not appear astonished. 'Every conquered people needs an uprising. The incident at Madrid was nothing; it is a pity that Barcelona did not revolt. One could have swept away the dissident subjects there as well.'

After which he informed Charles IV, who sent for Godoy and Ferdinand. The king threatened his son once again with his stick. 'What news do you have from Madrid? Well, I have some news and I will tell it to you. Do you think you can persuade me that you had no part in this destruction? Who advised you to commit such a monstrous act?' Marie-Louise was present and threatened to strike her son, going so far as to call him a bastard! And she mentioned execution, the guillotine. 'What a woman; what a mother!' Napoleon was to say. 'She horrifies me.' And he told Ferdinand: 'I am only obligated to your father, the king. He it is whom I recognise and I will accompany him to Madrid.'

This was deceit, since in his mind his brother Joseph was already king of Spain. But, faced with this offer of the throne, Charles IV took fright. 'But I do not want to be king! And what would I do in a country where my son has inflamed passions against me?'

Then Napoleon passed judgement: if, before midnight, Ferdinand had not recognised his father as the legitimate king, he would be treated as a rebel. The following day, Ferdinand renounced his claim to the crown and Charles exchanged his realm for a royal residence in France, first at Chambord, then at Compiègne, plus an income of six or seven millions. A 'proportional salary' would be paid to all the princes of the royal family. They were to go to the château of Valençay, Talleyrand's home.

'Your Majesty can dispose of the crown of Spain and there will be no further disturbance.' Napoleon wished to believe what Murat had told him. He spoke to Talleyrand of 'the salutary lesson which had been given at Madrid and which would promptly settle things'. And he pushed ahead.

On 10 May Napoleon informed Joseph that he was to have the Spanish throne: and what a present! 'Spain is not the kingdom of Naples: it is eleven million inhabitants and more than 150 millions in revenue without counting the immense income and the possessions in the Americas. I wish that immediately on receiving this letter you confer the regency on whomever you choose, the command of the troops to Marshal Jourdan and that you leave for Bayonne, etc.'

On 12 May Napoleon ordered Murat to convene the Council of Castile who were to 'ask' him for Joseph as king of Spain.

On 25 May he himself addressed a proclamation to the Spaniards: 'Spaniards, after a long agony, your nation was perishing. I have seen your hurts and I am bringing you a remedy. I will place your glorious crown on the head of another like myself. Spaniards, remember what your fathers had been and look at what you have become. It has not been due to any fault of yours but to the poor government which has ruled you. Be full of hope and confidence in the present circumstances, for I wish that your furthest descendants should remember me and say: "He was the saviour of our country."' Foolish presumption: whom God would destroy He first makes mad! Even before Napoleon had dictated this proclamation, Spain had burst into flames.

The rebellion began at Oviedo (Asturias) where Canon Llano Ponte had summoned the entire populace of the region. At midnight on the 24th, the tocsin sounded. Guided by the monks, the insurgents marched on the magazine where, unhindered by the officers, they removed 100,000 muskets. One hundred thousand! The local *junta* solemnly declared war on Napoleon. Murat, when told, declared that it was 'a stray spark'.

On the same day at Valencia, Canon Calvo began the hunt for *afrancesa-dos* (collaborators). The Count of Cervalloni, reputedly one of them , was assassinated – by a monk, Fra Rico – and his head was paraded on a pike. Frenchmen were massacred on the plaza de Grao, others at the plaza de Toros, more than 300 victims.

From their pulpits, the priests apostrophised Napoleon: 'You are the king of the shadows who is surrounded by clouds of locusts; you are the one named in the Apocalypse, named Apollyon, that is, destruction. This French army will be scattered like straw.' Almost everywhere the clergy headed the resistance. The Valencian army had 1,400 ecclesiastics in the artillery alone. Recruiting took place in the churches, the convents; no uniform, merely a red scarf with the words: 'Long Live Ferdinand VII! Religion and Country!' Murat, warned this time, sent Moncey's army corps which clashed with a horde of 'Kamikazes'. Moncey did not try too hard to take Valencia, as we shall see.

After Valencia, Murcia, after Murcia, Seville. There it was a layman, a Catalan named Nicolas Tap, who, learning of the abdication at Bayonne, led the populace to the arsenal (the officers offering no resistance) and armed 20,000 men. Colonel Pedro de Echavarry addressed them: 'Soldiers, the lewd Murat has had 40,000 iron collars made in order to lead you north like the most filthy animals. Is it not better to spill your blood in defence of the Church, the kingdom and yourselves? Twelve million countrymen are watching and envying you your glory!'

At Badajoz (Estremadura, near the Portuguese frontier) the governor, Count de la Torre, had forbidden all ceremonies on the saint's day of St. Ferdinand in order to avoid trouble. A crowd burst into his house and beat him to death, and his quartered corpse was exposed on the bridge. Many French officers coming from Portugal had the misfortune to arrive there at that moment. Thrown off their horses kicked, spat upon, they would have perished under the knives, when a more refined torturer suggested that it would be better to keep them as hostages in case the French came. One of these unfortunates would survive.

Murat sent Dupont to punish the Andalusian insurgents. 'The first salvo of cannon that you aim at these wretches should ensure the tranquillity of Andalusia for ever, and I dare to say, of Spain, too.' It was from his bed that Murat dictated this blindly optimistic note. He was suffering from the 'Madrid colic' mentioned in many of the memoirs of the soldiers of the Grande Armée. Larrey, chief surgeon of the Guard, entering Spain with a column of the imperial Guard, has left us a clinical description. 'The illness starts with very violent pains, the patient howling and rolling on the ground, he vomits copiously and often; after a period of abatement, there is a new crisis.'

As to the origin of Madrid colic, Larrey cites the wide differences in the day and night temperatures during the Spanish spring, bathing in the Manzanares still too cold, night sentry duty and especially the abuse of Spanish wine. Larrey had had some wine analysed and had discovered 'narcotic substances which the merchants and tavern-keepers add to the wines, harmless to the Spaniards, but troublesome for foreigners'.

Murat suffered acutely from gastritis and a delirious fever; by night, he uttered such resounding roars that his ADC came running, sword in hand, fearing an assassination attempt. Leaving Madrid, the Grand-Duke had himself moved to Chamartin, a property of the Duke of l'Infantado. Here he was seen prostrated, head in hand, refusing all food and all business. He recovered and on 5 June returned to the royal palace at Madrid, but had to take to his bed again next day. On 12 June he asked the Emperor to replace him.

The blaze of fury continued to spread. At Zamora, officers, monks and notables agreed to serve under a shoemaker in order to rouse the people. At Santander, the bishop, crucifix around his neck and pistols at his belt, ran through the streets shouting: 'Hail Jesus! Children of Jerusalem, let us march to victory!' There were 5,000 children of Jerusalem, armed with old muskets, forks, clubs. One of Bessières' columns arrived, drove them off and occupied the town. The bishop escaped in civilian garb, but continued to organise resistance in the mountains.

The governors of Cuenca, of Cartagena, of Tortosa, who were Spaniards but 'governors for Charles IV', the king who had knuckled down to Napoleon, ceding the crown to him – all were assassinated. The governor of Malaga's body was cut into pieces which were burned in the square at Grenada. At Grenada too, the mob killed General Trujillo, who had had the misfortune to marry the sister of Josefa Tudo, Godoy's mistress.

At Madrid, Savary had replaced the ailing Murat. The French held the city securely. A state of siege was proclaimed, all meetings were forbidden, all those arriving must sign in at the town major's office. But the Madrileños whispered to one another with wild joy news of the smallest success of the insurgents in the provinces. They would stroll past the barracks each morning in order to ascertain how many Spanish officers and men had deserted during the night in order to join the insurgents. The garrison melted away. It was announced that the *junta* at Aranjuez had ordered a mass rising; all unmarried men, all men married or widowed without children, were to enrol without delay.

A leaflet entitled Catechism was clandestinely circulated throughout Spain; it was an initiation to resistance and it began: 'Tell me, my son, who are you? Spanish, by the grace of God. Who is the enemy of your happiness? Napoleon, Emperor of the French. What is Napoleon's origin? From evil. And Murat? From

Napoleon. Godoy? From the fornication of both of them. Who are the French? One-time Christians become heretics. Is it a crime to be born French? No, a Frenchman is only damned when over the age of seven years. Is it a sin to kill a Frenchman? No, it is a meritorious act and will deliver the country from its aggressors.'

A French officer billeted on some Spaniards had protected them from the reprisals after the Dos de Mayo. This was the compliment addressed to him by his host at the moment of his departure for another garrison: 'I am greatly obligated to you. My wife owes her life to you and I owe you that of my children. Well! I must tell you what a true Spaniard feels at the bottom of his heart. If you were the last Frenchman remaining in Spain, I would kill you with my own hand in order to free my country completely.'

His spies continually reported to the Emperor the details of the risings in the provinces and the state of mind of the population, but he refused to accept that there was any danger: 'If it still persists it is because Murat used too light a hand after the 2nd of May.' And around him was the same blindness. 'For centuries', wrote Roederer, 'the Spaniards have been governed by monks and eaten by fleas; they are wretched, ignorant, bigoted, lazy and not over-brave.'

At this moment, however, Spain was becoming the cockpit of torture. The soldiers of one French column arriving at Manzanares (in the province of la Mancha where the peasants were reputed to be the most fanatical) saw, in a field bordering the road, some pigs eating what appeared to be human remains. Two hundred French soldiers had been massacred there: their hands had no nails and their faces no eyes. At Lerma were other corpses whose genitals had been cut off. General René left Madrid on 24 May with his ADC – his young nephew – and was captured by the insurgents in the Sierra Morena. His two companions were sawn in half between two planks. René was wounded, but escaped. A compassionate Spanish officer had him moved to a hospital, but peasants broke in and stabbed him.

Reprisals and vengeance took their course. Lerma was burned and pillaged. Soldiers, 'dressed in monks' cassocks, marched in procession around the flames imitating the sacred chants with unholy garrison parodies'.

On 7 June, the army of General Dupont – Pierre Antoine comte Dupont de l'Etang – left Valdepeñas and marched on Cordoba. At La Carolina, between Almuradiel and Linarès, they saw that their road was bordered on both sides by the corpses of French soldiers spitted and roasted; others had been buried alive up to their necks; frightful remains of cut-up bodies, a little further on, three corpses, an officer, his wife and his daughter, on which had been perpetrated 'indescribable indecencies'. That day this army smashed the Spaniards at the bridge of Alcolea on the Guadalquivir. Now, Cordoba is ours!

Not so fast. Cordoba, the city with the mosque of a thousand columns, consists in part of crooked streets, relic of the Moorish occupation. The defenders fired from the houses and the churches, but the defence could not hold out against an army. The doors were stove-in and the massacre began. The soldiers only stopped to visit the cellars. Those who did not drop dead drunk returned even more enraged. They raped and killed. Monks and nuns were among the first victims, for fire had also been opened from the convents and monasteries. The city became a nightmare desert where pigs could be seen gnawing at the breasts of women killed in the streets.

The sack of Cordoba lasted several days. The army camp became a bazaar where anything could be found: sheep and goats, furniture, gold and silver objects, family portraits, gilt mirrors. And one also saw – astonishingly – peasants from the region who purchased everything, very cheaply, from the soldiers. According to one witness: 'The generals' wagons groaned under the weight of gold and silver, of sacred vessels from churches. We did not know which weighed the heavier, the execration heaped on us or these riches.'

Dupont de l'Etang, veteran soldier of the Revolution, small, skinny, bronzed, dressed in the old way and with powdered hair, was not a bad soldier; he had a good service record, having distinguished himself at Marengo and Pozzolo, where his 15,000 men had routed 45,000 Austrians. He had been brilliant at Friedland to the degree that he was deemed destined for a Marshal's baton. But his destiny lay elsewhere.

Dupont is one of the few captains of war not to have a street named after him in Paris. Not because he authorised the sack of Cordoba – other famous generals and marshals had loosed similar horrors in Spain – but because he was later defeated at Baylen.

At Cadiz, the French Admiral Rosily had good reason for awaiting General Dupont's arrival with impatience; his squadron – five ships of the line and a frigate – had been bottled up by a British squadron cruising some miles offshore. Exceptionally, the Spanish General Solano, commanding the city, was a francophile; like many other foreign officers, he had served in the Grande Armée in Germany and had happy recollections of the campaign. The monks denounced him to the population – he is an *afrancesado*! – and one day Solano was ordered to burn Rosily's ships. He refused and was cut to pieces by sabre and dagger and then decapitated. General Thomas de Morla replaced him and immediately opened fire on the French with twelve batteries. The British squadron closed the trap. The French seamen resisted the bombardment for some days, and then Rosily struck his colours. He and his staff were allowed to return to France and his ships' companies were sent to the prison hulks.

In order to make some sense of the bloody disorder which ensued, let us here recall the composition of the French army in Spain at the beginning of July 1808. General Headquarters were at Madrid; Marshal Bessières commanded the corps of the Pyrenées Occidentales with 23,000 men covering Saint Sebastian, Viscaya and the mountains of Santander and Burgos. General Verdier had under his command the troops in Aragon, 10,600 men; Catalonia was occupied by some 11,000 men under General Duhesme with the divisional Generals Chabran and Lechi, supported by the 9,000 men of Reille's division. To these should be added General Dupont's observation corps of the Gironde, which we have seen at Cordoba, and Moncey's coastal observation corps, each having three divisions totalling 40,000 infantry and 8,000 cavalry. To these must be added Junot's 23,000 men in Portugal. These figures are approximate and changed according to losses and replacements sent from France.

In France, Napoleon studied his maps, bent on controlling the entire strategy in the peninsula. On 10 June he wrote to Berthier, then a major-general at Bayonne: 'It is much to be desired that the reduction of Saragossa should be quick. It seems that such an event can have a great influence upon events in all Spain.' At that very moment General Verdier's troops were already besieging Saragossa. As soon as their presence had become known, crowds of peasants, workmen and beggars had taken to the streets and the *junta* had armed them – poorly, the muskets were old, and some of the defenders were given blunderbusses and other relics of the past century. They had thrown themselves in the path of the French advance guard, but the cavalry of Lefebvre-Desnouettes had swept them aside.

Saragossa, lying between the Ebro and one of its tributaries, is composed of houses and convents within massive walls dominated by the enormous bulk of the château of the Inquisition. Inside the city is a labyrinth of narrow streets feeding into the principal street, the Coso. Most houses are built from solid stone, many of them vaulted at street level. On 1 July, Verdier's gunners began their bombardment; on the 2nd, the infantry were sent forward to assault the breach.

This was the day on which a 22-year-old girl, Maria Agustina, 'a goddess, incomparably beautiful, dressed half in man's and half in woman's clothes', according to a young infantryman named Billon, who saw her for a moment, would pass into legend in Spanish history. As the defenders were retreating from the French assault, Maria Agustina seized a linstock from a dying gunner: 'By Our Lady of Pilar, I will die rather than abandon this post!'

The defenders rallied and their volleys slowed the French whose losses mounted to 500 men including many officers. Verdier recalled his troops. The siege of Saragossa was to be lifted on 13 August without a decision. Agustina was given a promotion in the Spanish army, the *junta* awarded her a medal and even her name was changed – to Agustina Zaragossa. Byron lauded this heroine. Told of this unsuccessful assault, Napoleon decided that the fate of Saragossa was no longer of prime importance: 'The corps of Marshal Bessières is the most important; everything must be done to ensure that it encounters no reverse. Then comes that of Marshal Dupont. In third place is the action at Saragossa and Valencia in fourth place.'

The situation had reached a stage where the French troops were no longer facing a mere rabble of insurgents and fanatics; now professional army corps were being formed in the provinces. Don Gregorio de la Cuesta and Don Joaquin Blake had assembled a force of 28,000 men at Medina de Rio Seco (40 kilometres north-west of Valladolid; 200 kilometres from Madrid) on a rocky plateau. Bessières attacked with Merle's division, Reynaud's brigade from Mouton's corps and Lasalle's division, in all 10,000 infantry and 1,000 cavalry. The charges of Lasalle's cavalry and those of Mouton at Medina de Rio Seco have become famous. At the heels of the cavalry, the infantrymen of the 4th Light were engaged, firing was brisk and men fell; Mouton exhorted his men: 'Remember, you are the 4th Light! Forward – with the bayonet!'

As depicted in the Epinal pictures, a drummer boy of fifteen beat the charge; the Spaniards broke. Some tried to hide in bales of hay but were winkled out by the bayonets and killed: 'No quarter – they are brigands!' Lasalle's cavalry, unleashed on the 25,000 routed Spaniards, completed the massacre. The sack of Medina followed with the killing by cold steel of the Franciscan monks who had fired on the French. The French casualty list at Medina de Rio Seco proved that the *fureur française* had paid off: a mere 70 dead, 300 wounded. Napoleon wrote to Bessières: 'This victory will be one more laurel in your military reputation. Never was a battle won in more vital times; the fate of Spain depended on it.'

At the very hour when he was writing this, Dupont was preparing to sign the capitulation of Baylen.

At the end of July 1808, Andujar on the River Guadalquivir, 60 kilometres east-northeast of Cordoba, was a large market town where were produced the *alcarazas* or earthenware pots. Far to the north lay the peaks of the Sierra Morena. The plain of the Guadalquivir is fertile, but this is the summer solstice, which here is known as *la sarten,* the frying-pan, forty degrees at midday. About 6,000 French troops were bivouacked along the river on the burning sand. The banks were packed with a thousand or more wagons, carriages and vehicles of every sort, loaded with baggage, sick and wounded including many cases of venereal disease and scurvy, and the women – officers' wives, *vivandières*, laundresses, prostitutes, the usual gaggle – plus a number of officers and civilians who preferred to ride in carriages rather than on horseback. A soldier wrote: 'Every captain has his carriage and six mules.' The mules and the horses jostled one another in an endeavour to drink from the rivulets of the nearly dry river. We are looking at one of Dupont's three divisions. The carriages and wagons (116 of them according to the Spanish) had served to carry off the booty from the sack of Cordoba. Napoleon himself was to speak of the 'impure gold' crammed into the generals' wagons. Dupont's troops had gold chalices and crucifixes in their haversacks, but at Andujar they were issued with 120 grams of bread per day and some tepid water; no wine. What were these troops, shattered by fatigue and heat, doing here? They were awaiting an enemy attack!

On reaching the Guadalquivir Dupont had deployed his three divisions as follows: himself at Andujar, General Vedel at Baylen, General Gobert at La Carolina. Baylen is an old town surrounded by olive trees in a basin at the junction of two roads. The French numbered about 18,000 men plus 2,000 Swiss mercenaries. The enemy totalled about 40,000 men in four divisions, commanded respectively by General Reding, of Swiss origin; the Marquis of Coupigny, a French émigré; one Jones, an Irishman; and Don Manuel de la Pena, all under the command of the Biscayan General Castanos, known as 'the Gypsy'.

The action which was to follow was slow, ill-coordinated and confused; the French planning was very shaky. The only way one can make sense of this famous defeat is to present events in their chronological order. On 14 July, the enemy troops, coming from the south, appeared opposite Andujar and 'exerted pressure' on Dupont's outposts; that is to say that they fired continuously for some time, then retired, returned for a repeat performance and retired again, but without giving any indication that they might attack in earnest.

Dupont ordered Vedel, at Baylen, to send him reinforcements. The order was either ill-written or incorrectly transmitted because Vedel arrived with his entire division, having evacuated Baylen – which Reding immediately occupied to threaten the French left.

Gobert, realising his colleague's mistake, hastened from La Carolina and charged at the head of his cuirassiers to eject Reding. The Spaniards, at least three times more numerous, routed the French and Gobert was mortally wounded. General Dufour replaced him but, fearing another attack by the Spanish, retired on La Carolina. It was now the evening of 16 June. Dupont, learning of Gobert's death, ordered Vedel's division to return to Baylen: 'Attack the enemy wherever he is found.' He himself did not move. Vedel, having returned to Baylen, found neither Dufour nor Reding: 'Reding must surely have moved north to cut Dufour's advance. Forward to the sierra!'

The result of these poorly co-ordinated and irrelevant deployments was to split Dupont's army in two. In the south, Dupont himself was now imminently threatened by the bulk of the enemy forces: in the north, Vedel had rashly? (we shall see) marched towards the sierra.

'We must concentrate my army,' said Dupont to his staff. 'We must return to Baylen and attack Reding and rejoin Vedel. Forward!'

Forward, but the heterogeneous caravanserai which was Dupont's division looked as frisky as an old saddle horse, and Dupont had scruples, albeit honourable ones: 'We must not abandon our sick and wounded to the enemy.' 'Nor the women, general.' 'Nor the women, naturally. They must be evacuated to the north with the sick and wounded.' But not all would be.

The division took an interminable time to get organised and it was not until the night of 18/19 July that they set off for Baylen. At 3 a.m. the advance guard under General Chabert reached a tumbling stream called the Rumblar: 'General, the Spaniards are here!'

Fighting began at daybreak. Dupont had split his battalions into penny packets which were mown down as they reached the field. The Spanish – blue uniforms with red revers – charged vigorously supported by lancers called *garrochistas*; these were men who herded the wild bulls from Andalusia to the bullrings.

By midday the heat had become torrid. After fifteen hours on the march, plus seven more in combat, the French were exhausted; more than 2,000 had been killed. It was at this stage that Dupont's Swiss confronted Reding's Swiss. A sacred convention of these mercenaries was that they should not kill one another. They hoisted their shakos on their bayonets and embraced. Fighting ceased at this point; Dupont had only 3,000 effectives left. One more try. We must break through to rejoin Vedel! No! The wounded died untended, soldiers refused to replenish with cartridges and went to drink in the Rumblar stream, others lay on the ground awaiting death.

Vadel was still hastening northwards when on the morning of 19 July he heard the cannonade – but to his rear. He gave the order to turn about, but the division marched in a leisurely manner. His soldiers had also marched a long way and they demanded a halt: Vedel agreed. They started off again, but stopped once more to chase a herd of stray pigs. Forward again; the column arrived in the vicinity of Baylen at about 4 p.m. 'Close up! We are going to attack!'

But then two Spanish officers appeared with a handkerchief on the point of a sabre. 'Flag of truce! An armistice has just been agreed between our general and General Dupont.' 'I don't believe it, and anyway it is of no importance. My troops will advance.' They advanced, the troops, suddenly embued with the courage of saviours, brushed aside the Spaniards and encircled one of Reding's battalions. 'Surrender!' 'No – wait!' This time it was a glittering French ADC, his horse lathered: 'General Dupont has ordered a cease-fire!'

Vedel had arrived too late. Dupont had sent General Marescot to negotiate with the enemy commander. 'Negotiate? Out of the question. The three

French divisions must capitulate.' This was Castanos speaking. His own troops had not taken part in the battle, but he was senior commander – Castanos, 'the Gypsy' was an unusual man. Camp commandant at San Roque, opposite Gibraltar, after the rising of 2 May he had dared to congratulate Murat on his 'magnanimity': 'You can count on me as on a French general.'

Completely taken in, Murat had given him money for his men with which Castanos immediately reinforced, re-armed and trained his force. Against the French. Against the French, any deceit is legitimate and commendable. Now the Gypsy had the pillagers of Cordoba in the hollow of his hand, trapped in the basin of Baylen. To let them die amid their booty would be just, so prolong the negotiations! Finally Castanos received Dupont, who surrendered his sword. The loser still wished to shine: 'You can be proud of this day, General, for it is a fact that I have never lost a pitched battle until today. I have won more than twenty.' 'It is even more remarkable', replied the Gypsy dryly, 'that this is the first battle I have fought.' He had, in fact, served longer at court than in the camps.

Vedel did not wish to surrender: 'My troops have not been beaten. I demand that General Dupont authorise me to resume hostilities.' To the officer who brought this message Dupont said No, but he was quite willing that Vedel should escape with Dufour (Gobert's replacement) and to try to reach Madrid. Vedel set out, but Castanos, having been informed of this, summoned Dupont: 'If you do not recall your general, I shall have all the men of your division shot.'

Vedel's division had already reached St. Helena in the defiles of the Sierra Morena, when on 21 July at midday Captain Baste caught up with him, bringing an order from General Legendre, chief of staff to Dupont: 'Halt your march; return to Baylen in order to lay down your arms.' Vedel hesitated, but General Pryvé arrived shortly with a signed order from Dupont: in substance – 'Return. The capitulation agreed provides that your division, without being prisoners of war, will be disarmed and repatriated to France under the Spanish flag.'

This was untrue, or at least had not yet been agreed. The conditions of the capitulation of Baylen had been negotiated in a atmosphere of great confusion and not, in fact, signed until the 22nd, whereas Dupont had quoted the clauses to Vedel on the 21st.

Vedel's troops were on the point of mutiny when they learned that they were to return to Baylen to surrender. They wanted to compel Vedel to march them to Madrid. 'In order to make us abandon our wise and honourable intention,' wrote Corporal Martial-Joseph Delroeux in his *Souvenirs*, 'they explained to us the advantages of this capitulation, which stipulated that we were to be taken directly to Cadiz and from thence transported to France. That, moreover, in view of the sufferings and privations which we had undergone during the past three months, some three-quarters of us were so exhausted that it would be almost impossible to regain Madrid, seeing that the mountains of the Sierra Morena were in the hands of the Spanish; and, finally, that the capitulation was in no way humiliating and that, if we refused to submit to it, the 1st Division would be pitilessly put to the sword. This blackmail was successful and Vedel returned. Could he have done otherwise? Colonel Bugeaud, the future marshal, managed to escape with his regiment and return to Castile.

Many soldiers in Dupont's three divisions have testified concerning the battle and the capitulation of Baylen. None of their accounts is really convincing. Corporal Delroeux, already quoted, has stated that when Vedel heard cannon-fire behind him, he hesitated for a long time before ordering a turnabout and that it was the soldiers who compelled him to do so: 'It was in spite of him that we flew to the aid of the 1st Division.' One is baffled at this sudden urge to get a move on, given the dilatory nature of the division's return to Baylen. On the other hand, one can readily accept the assertion that it was by holding out the prospect of a happy repatriation that the division was persuaded to return after the capitulation.

Furthermore, Delroeux makes a serious accusation: 'General Dupont, commander-in-chief of the army corps, had amassed a considerable amount of treasure. He wished to remain the sole owner, whereas other generals, and particularly Vedel, wished (sic) to claim a share; whence the disunion: Vedel, being denied his share of the loot, had perhaps wished to trick Dupont by not marching promptly to his aid. All of which tends to convince me that Vedel wanted to trap Dupont ...' Another survivor of Baylen, Captain François, wrote in his Mémoires: 'Vedel seemed to relish the predicament of General Dupont.' Finally, a certain moral laxity at the top did nothing for the morale of the troops.

On 23 July, 'while the corpses rotted in the sun', Dupont's soldiers, more than 8,000 men, laid down their arms and paraded before the Spaniards who were mad with pride at having humbled the conquerors of Europe. The next day, it was the turn of the 9,000 men who had returned with Vedel. Certain articles of the capitulation were dishonourable to both sides. Castanos had stipulated that the troops' haversacks should be searched to ensure that they contained no sacred objects from the sack of Cordoba. On the other hand, Dupont had succeeded in arranging that the generals and officers should retain their arms and their possessions.

We can resign ourselves without too much regret to saying farewell to Generals Dupont and Vedel, with a few notes regarding their fates.

Dupont: embarked at Cadiz on 5 September 1808, arriving at Toulon on the 21st. Arrested on Napoleon's order, dismissed on 1 March 1812, placed under house arrest at Dreux. Liberated on the restoration of the Bourbons, appointed Minister for War and later given a military command. Dismissed again on Napoleon's return from Elba. Appointed counsellor of state under the second restoration, later elected deputy. Enjoyed a peaceable retirement from 1832. Died in his bed in 1840 aged seventy-five.

Vedel: disembarked at Marseilles on 12 November 1808. Arrested and imprisoned, dismissed on 14 March 1812. Held to be less culpable than Dupont, he next appears with the Army of Italy in 1813, restored to his rank. Commandant of the 1st army division at Lyons during the first restoration, then commandant of the 1st military division at Cherbourg during the Hundred Days. Removed from the active list on 25 July 1815. Died in bed, as did Dupont.

The capitulation convention provided that all the French, having laid down their arms, would be repatriated. The generals who had served under Dupont and Vedel were in fact sent home as were some of their officers. The rest were not. The *Junta* of Seville had refused to recognise the capitulation.

Columns of prisoners were marched across Andalusia, in a temperature of 37° in the shade, of which there was little; destination: Cadiz. These unfortunates believed that they were to be repatriated at the same time as the generals. No. 'Only the generals embarked and we were dispersed to various places. In this way, those who committed the faults whose consequences we were now suffering returned to France while we were held hostage.'

Castanos had ordered that the columns of prisoners should avoid the large towns 'so as not to be exposed to popular vengeance'. Did he know that the peasants would be worse than the townees? Throughout their journey, men, women and children formed ranks on either side, always with the same cry 'Cordoba! Cordoba!' The sack of Cordoba was a reproach deserving worse than death. The children dodged in and out of the ranks to bite the French 'and not letting go until they had secured the morsel'.

The soldier who made the error of breaking ranks for an instant (to find a drink or relieve himself) was captured and killed by the peasants with atrocious refinements, eyes gouged out with scissors, genitals wrenched off. Muleteers mixed French blood with the wine in their goatskins. The 'intox' of the populace by the priests reached new heights. 'We know that you kill children,' said one Spaniard to an unfortunate captive. 'Do you eat them also?' The officers who shared the fate of their men – many did so voluntarily – were accorded the same treatment. At Aralar, townees brandishing knives, laid siege to the inn where they were incarcerated. 'Cordoba! Cordoba! We will cut off your heads at midnight!' Many officers committed suicide and a Spanish doctor, summoned by the mayor, cried: 'Ah, what a beautiful sight!' At Jerez, the authorities narrowly prevented a massacre of a column surrounded and being spat upon by the crowd. At Lebrija, 75 dragoons, officers and men, were massacred in a convent and a barracks. One of the killers cried: 'There are still some rolling their eyes,' and the dying were finished off.

In a little town called Los Gabescas, 200 dragoons were massacred on 8 September, the feast of the Nativity of the Holy Virgin – 'Cordoba! Cordoba!' Some of the scenes were unbelievable – for instance, peasants trawling through the soldiers' excrement in the hope of finding gold coins. Gille, in his *Memoirs of a Conscript of 1808*, recounts how one of his comrades had saved 22 gold pieces in this way: 'He retained them for a week in his body and it was only at the end of this time and following some acute pain that he finally recovered them.'

Recovery from the French pillagers was an obsession. The seams of their clothes were ripped apart, epaulettes opened, dressings torn from wounds. At Port Sainte-Marie, a wounded officer was attacked by a young woman, well built and pretty, who wrested from him his watch and his cross, and who undressed him and 'inspected his most intimate parts'. Furious at not finding the treasures she had hoped for, she 'butchered his genitals'. One must remember that wives and mistresses, and of course the *vivandières*, had accompanied their men on this nightmare journey.

On 3 August 1808 Napoleon was at Bordeaux where he had arrived from Bayonne. He was making his toilette in an apartment reserved for him in the municipal building when a courier arrived from Spain with news of the disaster at Baylen. 'Thunderstruck, his face distorted', he seized the porcelain washbasin and hurled it to the floor. 'A French army capitulates in open country! What a crime! A defeat, a massacre can be repaired, soldiers can be replaced. But honour lost in capitulation is irrecoverable. Dupont should be shot in front of his troops.'

Having paced up and down in a fury, the Emperor recovered himself and it was then that he uttered the famous phrase, justified to a high degree, 'Everywhere where I am absent, they commit nothing but follies.' Therefore, he will go to Spain. He dictated orders an hour later: 80,000 grumblers must leave Germany and march on Spain; two divisions will come from Italy.

The situation was worse than he suspected. His brother Joseph – now King Joseph I of Spain – had left Bayonne on 8 July, arrived at Madrid on the 20th and left again on the 30th. Alarming rumours concerning Dupont's situation had reached him on the 27th. He had immediately written to Napoleon: 'I do not believe them all, but it is feared that they will prove to be true in part. In that case, an army of 100,000 men will march on Madrid. I can muster 20,000 to confront them. I will reinforce them with the remains of Dupont's corps and we can beat the enemy. If not, Madrid must be abandoned and we must join with Marshal Bessières and await the help which in any event will be needed.'

On the 29th, about to leave the capital, he wrote again: 'I do not have to tell Your Majesty that it will take 100,000 men to conquer Spain today. I must repeat that the whole nation is outraged and is determined to follow with arms in their hands the course that they have chosen.'

The situation was bad, not only in Spain but throughout the entire peninsula. On 1 August, Sir Arthur Wellesley landed in Portugal at the mouth of the Mondego (40 kilometres from Coimbra). For those for whom the name Wellesley strikes no chord, I hasten to substitute that under which he was to become famous – Wellington: thirty-nine in 1808, large nose, haughty air, a taciturn disciplinarian, already famous in his own country as 'the Sepoy General' having shone in India; a member of Parliament since 1806, recently promoted lieutenant-general and in command of the army 'destined to intervene in the affairs of the peninsula'.

The affairs of the peninsula were to move quickly in Portugal simply because Junot did not have sufficient troops, while Britain, mistress of the seas, could land all the regiments she wished.

Wellington landed with 15,000 men and started to march south towards Lisbon. Junot ordered General Laborde, the commander of his advance guard: 'You are to leave today to meet the English. You are to harass them while awaiting my arrival with the main army.'

For the first time in their war against Napoleon, the British themselves were to confront the French on land, rather than by some interposed force. It must be remembered that, as often happened during operations where Napoleon was not commanding in person or was not present, there are fewer details concerning the war in Portugal than those of the war in Spain. What is certain is that the 'redcoats' were sound troops and initially had the advantage in numbers.

Wellington was advancing with 15,000 men, whereas Laborde had 3,000. Laborde manoeuvred well, killing 1,500 redcoats, then, in danger of being overwhelmed, retreated on Torres Vedras to join up with Junot who was coming from Lisbon, and with General Loison who was marching from Abrantès. Junot, who could not strip all his garrisons in Portugal, could muster only 9,000 men. Meanwhile the British had landed two more brigades, so that it was with 18,000 troops seasoned in India that the British would confront Junot's 9,000 conscripts.

Junot could perhaps have awaited the British in the mountains surrounding Lisbon north of the Tagus, but such a move would have been foreign to his temperament, and in any case all Napoleon's generals not under his direct command feared to be taxed with cowardice. Junot therefore marched on Wellington who had occupied the heights of Vimeiro. The conscripts, led by Generals Kellermann and Foy, were to show themselves courageous, but two to one are long odds and the British had a mass of artillery. Having lost 1,800 soldiers, Junot retired on Torres Vedras where he learned that two more contingents had disembarked and that the British now had 28,000 men. The idea of holding Portugal to enforce the continental blockade had become an almost comic illusion; Junot, sick at heart, decided to send General Kellermann to the British with orders to propose an armistice and the evacuation of Portugal.

'The French army will retire with the honours of war and all its equipment. It will be returned to France in British vessels which will land them at the ports of Lorient or la Rochelle or in ports nearby. The sick and wounded will be repatriated as soon as they are fit to travel. The French may take no property of the Portuguese and those Portuguese who have helped the French army will be neither pursued nor disturbed in their persons or their goods.' The Convention of Cintra, signed on 30 August, would be scrupulously honoured by the British. In the first days of September, the 22,000 French troops remaining in Portugal had been ferried to the coasts of Brittany or the Saintonge. And the (few) Portuguese more or less guilty of having helped the French army were not harassed in any way.

However, the British public were outraged when the Cintra conditions became known. A press campaign was followed by a 'court of inquiry' charged with determining whether Wellington had betrayed his country's interests. The future conqueror of Napoleon was declared not guilty.

Napoleon was at Erfurt when he learned of the Convention of Cintra, and he had Clarke, Minister of War, write to Junot. He agreed that there was nothing in the convention contrary to honour, since the troops had not laid down their arms and had returned with their eagles. He only wished to know why Junot had not built a fortified camp where he could await rescue.

Napoleon had invited to Erfurt (near Weimar) Tsar Alexander and all the kings of Europe because he wished to secure his lines of communication before proceeding to Spain. Austria was arming and the loyalty of his ally of Tilsit was beginning to have a hollow ring. The grumblers whom we have seen in Germany and the troops in Spain, alternately martyrs and butchers, would have been quite incapable of imagining the pompous diplomatic fantasia so brilliantly described by André Castelot, during which the megalomania of the Emperor erupted and which gave Talleyrand the opportunity to stab Napoleon in the back. Finally, Napoleon authorised the Tsar to seize Finland and the Danubian provinces, in exchange for which the Russian sovereign would say Amen to the conquest of Spain; he even undertook to fight Austria if the latter dared to attack the French empire. The two emperors parted on 14 October.

Queen Hortense recounted in her *Mémoires* that Josephine had sighed long when her husband left for Spain: 'Will you never cease to wage war?' 'But do you think that it amuses me? Don't you think that I would prefer a good bed after a good dinner, rather than to suffer all the privations which await me? Do you really think that I am made differently from other men? I agree that I know how to do other things than to make war, but I must bow to necessity, to my duty towards France and I am not the one who controls events, I obey them.'

Events got under way in Spain, where he would often be obliged to share the worst discomforts with his soldiers. On 29 October 1808, he left Paris for Spain, still with one major illusion: that the Spanish army was a gang of brigands without military chiefs worthy of the name; he was soon to be disabused.

He had to move quickly, for he was none too reassured by the Tsar's promises at Erfurt. His carriage and its escort flew over the old highroads to the Pyrenees: Rambouillet, Vendôme, Tours, Angoulême, St-André-de-Cubzac (Gironde). The Emperor thought that he was not moving fast enough by coach – so to horse. 'I met the Emperor riding a pony on the sands of the Landes,' wrote Percy. The Landes at that time was a poor and miserable region, all the peasants were dressed in sheepskins or in a sort of monk's hooded cassock of rough brown cloth.

Bayonne at 2 a.m. on 3 November. Napoleon got everyone up, inspected the magazines and depots recently established. All in disorder, only provisions, not one item of clothing! 'What's going on here – who is in charge?' After its journey from eastern Europe, by cart and on foot, the Army of Germany's uniforms were in tatters, its boots worn-out. Muddlers in office had ensured that there would be yet another exhibition of an army in rags. The Emperor dictated or, more accurately, shouted a letter to General Dejean, Minister for War Administration: 'I have received your report of 2 November with the statement attached to it. From that, I should have at Bayonne 83,000 pairs of shoes, 140,000 shirts, 83,000 haversacks, 39,000 shakos and a large number of cloaks. All that is a child's fairy-tale. I have nothing, I am naked. My army is in want and your clerks laugh at me. The providers are thieves who will be paid while I have nothing. The whole of your clothing service works badly, directed by idiots and rascals. Never has anyone been so poorly served and betrayed.'

Still on 3 November, at 3 p.m. Napoleon summons the managers to the château de Marnac, shakes them, shouts at them, and finally: 'Since there is nothing more to be done, load everything left in the depots on to wagons and let them follow the army. Now I want to see the light cavalry squadron.'

But the imperial army which flooded into Spain bore little resemblance to that which had accompanied Murat. One saw a few youngsters, but mainly old sweats, 'tempered on the field of battle', plus most of the foreign regiments from every region of Europe. We have seen something of the recruitment of Poles in Warsaw; volunteers, sons of Polish high society who had asked to be allowed to serve as close to the Emperor as possible. 'Send them here and have them manoeuvre a bit.'

According to some theorists, Napoleon had an idea at the back of his mind when sending for these young fellows. At Châtellerault during a fete they had 'forced' ladies and girls after roughing-up their husbands and brothers; this deserved retribution. So the story runs. In any event, the light cavalry manoeuvred under that blue stare which could be supremely demanding. After some minutes, they had been assessed: sensational horsemen but totally ignorant of the manual of arms. 'Let them march with the Guard, but have Durosnel teach them on the road the basic elements of the cavalryman's trade.' General Durosnel was one of his equerries.

Napoleon left Marnac at midday on 4 November and at 8 p.m. he was at Tolosa (25 kilometres south of San Sebastian). Joseph had arrived there with his court after quitting Madrid:

'I will have re-established the situation in Spain even before the Emperor arrives.' He drew up a plan for an offensive, had it approved by Jourdan, his major-general and sent out such ridiculous orders that the marshals refused to carry them out. Moncey to Jourdan: 'The Emperor has not confided to me one of the best army corps in order to have its glory and safety compromised in this way.' Likewise Ney: 'There can be no doubt that this letter was written by a man who knows nothing of our calling. Tell the king that I am not here to play the part of Dupont.' Napoleon upheld these refusals. At Tolosa he told his brother: 'The general who undertook such an operation would be a criminal.' After some plain speaking Joseph was forbidden to meddle in any way so long as the Spanish nation had not been brought to heel.

Joseph was embittered. He had had no enthusiasm for this exchange of kingdoms. Now he had to recover Spain, but that would be the task of Murat. To abdicate would be to admit his incapacity. Joseph was ordered to follow the General Headquarters, but at a distance and to show himself as little as possible.

Napoleon had already taken over command in the field and issued his first order – to Bessières at Pancorbo: 'Scour the whole plain of Burgos, beat up the Spanish infantry, send strong raids of cavalry and infantry towards Villarcayo. I would like to know what is moving in the rear of General Blake.' (Blake was an Irishman in command of a Spanish army.) Before leaving Tolosa Napoleon ordered the superiors of the convents in the town to send him a delegation: 'Gentlemen, if you take it into your heads to meddle in military affairs, I shall have your ears cut off.'

The true Grande Armée, with some conscripts in the ranks, entered Spain. As they crossed the frontier, they met the sick and maimed who were being evacuated to France. 'You will find out that this is not a war like the others.' 'We have seen the others!'

Yes, but. At Mondragon between Bilbao and Vitoria, they saw a French officer nailed to a door and 'one could see between his teeth the proofs of the mutilation he had undergone'. Then, in the middle of the road, a *cantinière* and child with their throats cut. At Zamora, in a butcher's shop was a corporal of the Guard hanging from a hook, split from top to toe and drained like butcher's meat. At the first of these spectacles, the conscripts turned green, vomited, tried not to look. The veterans laughed at them, but in their hearts they wished they were back in Germany or even Poland.

And now, at the start of this march on Madrid, men who had held their heads high when facing cannon-balls and canister bowed to the blows of sickness. This was the result of fatigue, poor food, vermin; sleeping on the bare stones of churches and sacked convents had never been good for anyone. The sick left in the hospitals along the route were not coddled. Nearly always, the hospital was an old convent where palliasses were piled. 'Much diarrhoea and chronic dysentery with intestinal ulceration. The sick were living corpses dying slowly and painfully. Wounds turned septic. The air was so polluted that meat started to stink in a few hours if not quickly dropped into the cooking-pot.'

Therapy depended heavily on the 'kina' or quinine, a decoction of the febrifugal bark of tropical trees. Percy and Larrey had arranged that the supply service would bring quantities of kina, but the war commissioners (including one Tornan) diverted most of it to France where it commanded very high prices.

The hospitals were ante-chambers to death; the sick were tended by Spanish nurses who were waiting for an opportunity to kill them, and by French auxiliaries, soldiers who had often inflicted their own wounds and, at the first opportunity, would vanish into the human scum of both sexes which followed the columns.

Napoleon knew all this, but he had less time than ever for the sick. He had lost none of his magnetism for the soldiers. As soon as he appeared, the most exhausted, the most ragged among them, bawled 'Long live the Emperor!' The welcome he received at Miranda was so frenetic that he himself was astonished: 'Oh, oh! Here's a lot of heart.' Then, he added perceptively, that in all this there was more of Bacchus than of anything else. Absolutely correct. Miranda was a wine-growing region: in the cellars, soldiers floundered up to their knees in the wine leaking from the broached hogsheads. In the churches the altars had been burned, the tombs opened, ornaments and sacred vessels stolen. The bivouac fires were stoked with gilded containers and altar ornaments.

On 10 November, this is what Napoleon could read in the official reports: Lannes had defeated the Spanish left, Victor and Lefebvre had cut the right 'into pieces'. Mouton, supported by Bessières and followed by Soult, was in the course of mopping-up the enemy forces of the centre north of Burgos.

'To horse!' After a day on horseback, the Emperor arrived at nightfall at the market town of Cubo on the Burgos road. He was almost alone, having left his staff and escort behind him. A messenger appeared at midnight: 'Sire, the road to Burgos is open. Marshal Soult's troops have occupied the city.' 'Ségur, leave immediately. Prepare me a billet at the archbishopric.'

An hour's rest and again to horse. The Emperor had with him only his ADC, Savary, the mameluke Roustam and a few chasseurs of the Guard. By night they trotted or galloped, the escort carrying torches. The pace only slowed when crossing the battlefield of the previous day, covered with Spanish dead. Among the casualties, monks in hooded robes, crucifix tucked into belt, still clutching musket, sword or long knife.

Napoleon, Roustan and Savary entered Burgos at 7 a.m. It was not yet daylight, but an enormous fire which had ravaged a whole district on the far bank of the River Arlanzon, lit up the scene. The streets were full of drunken soldiers, staggering and brawling. Every church door was stove-in and one could see inside strewn on the flagstones broken statues, pictures, candelabra, confessionals.

The whole city was a sewer, crammed with the bodies of men, horses and filth. At the archbishopric they found Ségur who apologised for not having had time to clean things up. He had also had difficulty in finding enough soldiers in a fit state to form a guard of honour for the Emperor.

The troops were there, bivouacked in the main square. Huge fires were roaring away, fed by musical instruments, missals, precious furniture. In huge vats looted from the convents were whole forequarters of meat. Officers sat smoking in gilded chairs. Napoleon passed by without comment. What could he say?

'This way, Sire.' The stairway was cluttered with every sort of debris. To gain it one had to step over a river of urine in the courtyard, avoiding heaps of manure mixed with bones, meat and excrement. By the light of a candle, Ségur showed him to the archbishop's quarters. The rooms were smeared with wine stains, here and there were broken bottles, the whole giving off a foul smell. 'Too bad, I'll sleep here.' The Emperor was covered in mud, worn out with fatigue, hunger and cold. He helped Ségur to get a fire going while Savary and Roustan went in search of food.

'Ségur, that smell is really too much. Open a window.' The ADC opened the curtains to reveal three armed Spaniards, motionless, backs to the wall. Had they known that the Emperor was coming? Had they come to rob? Either way, three pistol shots might have changed the course of History. They did not move, frozen with fear. The Emperor had not even thought to draw a weapon; he smiled and made a gesture of pity: 'Disarm them, Ségur and turn them over to the guard.' Savary and Roustam returned bearing food obtained from the soldiers who were cooking in the square. Napoleon ate quickly and stretched out fully dressed. Physically, this man could adapt to anything. He never needed pomp to demonstrate his power.

At this moment, less than five hundred metres from this filthy room where he was sleeping, a frightening episode was unfolding. At the foot of a large tower of the cathedral, an urchin signalled to some passing grenadiers – they could climb the tower. Some women who had taken refuge up there, ready for picking – why not? In many countries, urchins work as scouts. This one signalled that they should go up one at a time and one grenadier followed him. A moment later the boy signalled to the next one. But the third soldier became suspicious; was this a trap? Several grenadiers went up together until they reached a closed door. They broke in and found eight monks installed with weapons and provisions. In the middle of the room were two decapitated grenadiers. Their comrades threw the monks and the urchin from the window and watched them crash to the ground.

Percy arrived at Burgos on 16 November. The place was still filthy, only the archbishop's palace having been cleaned – by a detail from HQ. In the town, Percy saw Spanish prisoners who were burying the bodies of their compatriots, having removed their clothes. Here every piece of clothing was precious. Percy saw the wrecked abbey of San Juan, filled with soldiers, horses, carriages, debris of every kind. The abbey's pharmacy, one of the finest in the world, had been wrecked. The monastery of Las Huelgas was serving as a stable, the tombs broken open by treasure-seekers, skeletons scattered about the floor.

Napoleon was to stay at Burgos until 21 November. While there, he learned that Victor with 10,000 men had routed the 32,000 men of Blake's army in the Cantabrian mountains at Espinosa. Soult, meanwhile, was marching on Santander. Marbot, on a mission to join him, had seen, among other things, 'A young officer of the 10th Mounted Chasseurs nailed by hands and feet to a barn door, head downwards over a small fire.'

The wounded from the battle of Espinosa – 80 wagon-loads – reached Burgos on the 21st. Percy received them. 'None had left the wagons for five days, their straw was fouled, some lay on mattresses covered with pus and excrement. They were covered with rags and pieces of carpet. We got them out as best we could and as many wished to relieve themselves, we had to hold them suspended for the purpose. These manoeuvres took a good two hours in a frightful stench.'

The wounded were taken to the Convent of the Conception, where there was nothing to sleep on, not even straw; no linen, no food and, when night fell, not a single candle – the soldiers had taken every one. No one came; there was no help. Well, at about 9 p.m. a representative of the supply service arrived, but only to count the wounded! Next day, Napoleon had gold distributed to the wounded who had arrived in the convoy: eight or nine napoleons to each officer, three to each soldier. Napoleon left Burgos on 22 November for Aranda – eleven leagues distant. The road was awful, virtually destroyed. 'The Emperor cared little about the road, the mud or the rocks. The officers risked foundering their horses to keep up with him.' At Aranda, Napoleon learned that Lannes had advanced on 23 November towards Tudela, defended by Castanos the Gypsy (officially the victor of Baylen) who had 40,000 men. This army had been routed, as had Blake's. The victorious French had pillaged for two days. Napoleon had forbidden pillage, but I Corps had arrived before he did and had raked over practically everything. The infantry of the Guard had got wildly drunk, grenadiers were lying everywhere, dead drunk, many had to be hospitalised for several days. Napoleon himself was tireless: 'On horseback by 9 a.m., ordering everything, reviewing a corps, deploying another.'

During a review, a soldier of the 95th broke ranks and told the Emperor that for seventeen years he had served bravely and honourably, taken part in the most demanding campaigns and had always saved a few sols from his pay to send to his aged mother. His colonel confirmed this. Napoleon awarded him the Cross: 'And I will send four hundred livres to your mother's address.' 'Vive l'Empereur!' At another review a lieutenant of dragoons told him: 'Sire, I have been four years in this rank without the prospect of promotion.' 'Well, I was a lieutenant for seven years and that did not hurt my chances of promotion.' 'Vive l'Empereur!'

Now for a disturbing tale. The town commandant of Aranda, having drunk unwisely, had mortally wounded twelve soldiers with sabre cuts to the head. 'We do not know what will be the outcome of this business, wrote Percy. 'Napoleon will stay in this town until we have beaten the 30,000 Spaniards said to be between us and Madrid.'

Separating Old Castile from New Castile were several mountain ranges, rugged and steep – the sierras – nearly parallel, some 8,000 feet high and rising like a barrier between the north and south of the peninsula. At their feet, stretched high plateaux, bare and windswept, cut by narrow valleys. To travel from Aranda to Madrid it would be necessary to cross the Sierra de Guadarrama. There was only one pass in this range: Somosierra at 4,750 feet; not so much a pass as a defile, 2 kilometres long, only 3 metres wide at some points, winding, hemmed in by debris.

Since Napoleon had entered Spain, the intelligence service had been functioning better and he knew that after the disaster to the Spanish army north of Burgos, the *junta* had assembled at Madrid a corps of 28,000 men with 28 cannon: 'Benito de San Juan had been appointed in command. A fanatical Castilian. All the Madrileños were convinced that he would deny us the crossing of the Guadarrama.'

On 29 November Victor's corps took the village of Bocaguillas at the foot of the sierra. Napoleon bivouacked there and issued his orders. Ruffin's division will lead, marching in three columns. The centre column will follow the road to the pass, the flanking columns will climb the rocks and will beat down any resistance. They set off at dawn next day, Napoleon accompanying them. Fog favoured the advance, but pessimistic messages soon arrived from the flanking columns; progress over the rocks would be extremely slow and painful: 'As soon as the infantry gets within cannon and musket shot, there will be a massacre; the centre column will then have to advance without protection.'

Something else must be tried. Napoleon took but a few minutes to reach a decision. Only a lightning attack could succeed – in other words, the cavalry must charge. Piré, colonel of the Guard's chasseurs, reconnoitred the defile – 2.5 kilometres to the summit and three right-angled bends, each defended by several hundred Spaniards and four cannon, enfilading the road. At the pass itself was a 16-gun battery. Piré concluded that it would be impossible to get through. Napoleon's reply: 'Sir, I do not know that word!' The affair, immortalised in the Images of Epinal to the tune of hundreds of thousands of copies, was about to start. The Polish light horse was there, close to the Emperor. Dark blue uniforms with tall Polish chapska, they had furbished their uniforms under the worst possible conditions and carried themselves proudly. There were 250 of them, and they had never been under fire.

A tall, well-built cavalryman left the group of staff officers. This was General Montbrun, temporarily without a command, 'attached' in military parlance, a state of affairs that pleased him not at all. He bowed: 'Sire, let me lead these youths.' Napoleon nodded his head. Another officer sought permission to charge; this was Philippe de Ségur of the staff, a future general. Forward! First at the trot, then a gallop. 'We charged flat out,' Ségur wrote. The slope was quite steep, yet the Poles did manage a gallop.

In two minutes, the first bend with the four Spanish cannon. Their salvo mowed down the leading platoon; the commander, Kozietluski, was killed. Forward! The squadron approached the second bend. Another salvo; the same result, fifty troopers shot down: 'a defiant shout of "Vive l'Empereur!" – the spirit is irresistible'.

I was not present. I don't know whether these Poles in full charge cried 'Vive l'Empereur!' or whether they 'shouted their war-cry' as some versions have it. I don't know whether, as has also been said, they held a sabre in one hand, a pistol in the other and the reins between their teeth – not very convenient for crying 'Vive l'Empereur!' I don't know how many were cut down by each salvo.

Many details differ in the accounts of witnesses and participants of the action of the Somosierra, but I think we can accept that the drive was truly 'irresistible', since a hundred troopers reached the top led by Montbrun and Lieutenant Niegolowski. A cloud of black smoke; the battery at the pass fired. Ségur and Niegolowski fell and with them some sixty Poles. That left forty survivors, some wounded. The Spaniards must not be given time to reload. Montbrun, still alive and in the saddle, waved his sword. Forward!

Now occurred the phenomenon of collective panic – rare, but not totally unknown. The Spanish defenders couldn't understand why their salvoes hadn't stopped these cavalrymen. They must be invulnerable devils. Every man for himself! Benito San Juan breasted the torrent of fugitives, cursing, beating with the flat of his sword, but nothing stopped this panicky rout – and it was Spanish muskets that shot down San Juan the fanatic. Around his corpse, the Polish sabres cut down the Spaniards.

'Vive l'Empereur!' It was indeed Napoleon who appeared at the gallop with his staff. Ruffin's division followed at the double. Napoleon dismounted, approached Lieutenant Niegolowski who was on the ground, alive but covered in blood. Napoleon removed his own cross and pinned it to the chest of the wounded man in a gesture which is today legendary. Ségur, also, was in a bad way with five wounds: 'You are a hero. You shall carry to Paris the standards taken here.'

That night the Emperor slept at Buitrago on the far side of the sierra. Next day, he ordered a parade of the survivors, some forty of whom (a good third) were wounded; bloodstained bandages around the head, arms in slings, some on foot supported by a cavalrymen of the Guard. Napoleon rode up to them and doffed his hat: 'You are all worthy of my Guard. I honour you as my bravest cavalry.' 'The Poles wept for joy. The road to Madrid was open.'

Since the French defeat at Baylen, Madrid had been in a state of victorious exaltation. The British would eject the French, not just from Portugal, but from the entire peninsula. The 'king of dreams' Joseph, would never return to the capital. The news of the crossing of the pass of Somosierra tempered this enthusiasm, but not the sprit of resistance. The *junta* left Aranjuez for Badajoz to organise resistance in mid-country and, at the same time, a temporary *junta* was set up at the post office in Madrid. 'We will defend Madrid. We will expel Napoleon in the same way that we have expelled his brother.'

There were 6,000 infantry and 100 guns in the city, plus a large number of armed peasants who regarded the soldiers with suspicion because the regular army had fled at Somosierra. 'There were traitors in their ranks.' In defeat or imminent danger, traitors are seen everywhere. Who it was that accused the marquis de Peralès is not known. Until now he had been thought a loyal Spaniard, but, he had had sand added to the cartridges!

In such circumstances, the more unlikely the accusation, the more weight it carries. Peralès was garrotted and his corpse was exhibited in the city, especially in the Retiro. Hundreds of monks spilled out the (good) powder from the cartridges and refilled them with equally good powder. Another cry was heard: 'There are two mamelukes in Madrid; they have remained hidden since Joseph fled.' Two Jews were singled out – 'Here they are, that's them!' – murdered and then flayed, their bodies dragged through the streets. At the same time, barricades were erected everywhere, windows were protected by mattresses, and the streets and courtyards were denuded of paving stones. Before retiring south, the regular *junta* had appointed two men to command the defence of Madrid: General de Morla and the marquis of Castellar.

It was 2 December 1808, the anniversary of the Emperor's coronation and of Austerlitz. At midday Napoleon reached the heights overlooking Madrid; the weather was splendid and not at all cold, 'like the best days in France of the month of May'. Three divisions of dragoons welcomed him; the infantry was some three leagues behind. While his tent was being erected, Napoleon contemplated Madrid.

The tents of the great captains have always been an interesting study. Let us profit from the lull to look more closely at this one. It bore no resemblance to a camping tent. Here the mules are arriving, prodded by their drivers. They are carrying the canvas, the stakes, the furniture, the beds, all packed in rolls of leather. Napoleon could hear behind him the officers barking at the valets who were unpacking the heavy rolls. Not more than thirty minutes may elapse before the blue/white canvas, bordered in red wool, snapped in the breeze – that was an order.

The tents (there were three), Napoleon's, that of the officers of the imperial household, and Major-General Berthier's, were all double-walled, the outer skin tensioned by stakes. Between the two skins was a corridor where the baggage was kept; the Emperor's valet and his mameluke slept there. The imperial tent had two rooms, office and bedroom. The office was divided into two by a curtain: the space adjoining the bedroom was private to Napoleon, the other served as an ante-chamber for those he had summoned and for the ADCs and the duty officers. It was there, too, that Napoleon ate, the food being brought in from outside. The bedroom was carpeted and was also divided into two by a curtain. In the smaller area was the bed; in the larger, communicating with the office, could be seen the furniture: a large table covered with the maps of the current operations; an armchair in red leather, two settees, two tables at the corners for the secretaries. Every item of furniture was collapsible.

We can now see on this day of 2 December 1808, in the larger room, a man studying the map of Madrid. Rarely mentioned in the accounts of the wars of the Empire, he was none the less an important person. This was Bacler d'Albe, aged forty-seven, the Emperor's topographer and an eminent geographer, painter of battles; a fine portrait of the Emperor by him is now at Malmaison. Along the line of march of the Grande Armée, Bacler d'Albe highlighted in colour on his maps everything that the Emperor needed to survey the situation rapidly: rivers, mountains, breaks in the terrain, etc. Now, knowing that Napoleon would shortly arrive, he had worked over the map and inserted pins with different coloured heads to mark the positions of the French and of the enemy.

By night, some twenty candles lit the operations map which the Emperor might consult at any moment; there were also dividers to measure distances. When the map was very large, Napoleon would stretch out full-length on it, as did Bacler d'Albe also on occasion, and often the two men would knock heads. Bacler d'Albe was also responsible for the 'portfolio' which, apart from papers, contained two or three mahogany boxes with compartments, and the travelling library.

As I have said, the Emperor's bed was at the end of the room, separated from the rest by a curtain. Collapsible, like everything else, it was a marvel of construction by Desouches. The steel frame was surprisingly light. The bed, 1.80m long by 0.90m wide, was curtained 'in rich green with green silk trim'. There were many copies which were used during other campaigns. Napoleon only slept a few hours at a time. He would get up and work in his dressing-gown of white piqué, his head wrapped in a scarf and with green slippers on his feet. He would call his valet Constant and order coffee. He wore out those around him as much by his work as by his rides. On awaking, he would wash in eau de Cologne, using a gold-trimmed travelling case. The household officers kept as strict an eye as possible on everything brought to the headquarters. His clothing was all over the place. Everything that he wore soon became very dirty. As for meals, when campaigning the maximum time allowed was ten minutes.

The conquest of Madrid had not been a major military operation. There had been an ultimatum, followed by an attack, a second ultimatum and refusal, followed by a second attack, a third ultimatum followed by a surrender. On Napoleon's orders, the first ultimatum had been carried to the Spanish outposts by an ADC to Bessières; this officer had been attacked by armed peasants and barely escaped. The first attack was launched at 7 p.m. by moonlight. French troops captured the Retiro palace, the main barracks and several other positions. The second ultimatum, signed by Bessières, was carried by a Spanish officer made prisoner at Somosierra. Reply: 'we must consult with the people and the authorities'. At dawn on 3 December, Napoleon personally directed the second attack from the heights where he was positioned, and the French achieved more gains. At 11 a.m. the Emperor suspended operations and a third ultimatum was dispatched, this time to the *junta*: 'A general attack will be launched. But I would prefer that the surrender of Madrid would be due to reason and humanity rather than to force.'

The defenders' morale, particularly that of the army, had declined substantially. At 5 p.m. three delegates, including General Morla, arrived at Napoleon's tent. 'The *junta* is disposed to surrender, but the armed peasants and the last class of the population are still opposed. We will try to convince them and ask for tomorrow to do this'

Berthier introduced the delegates to Napoleon, who received them coldly. The Bulletin of the Army of Spain published his rebuke, edited into high-flown language: 'You invoke in vain the name of the people. If you do not succeed in calming them, it is because you yourselves have aroused them and misled them by lies. Assemble the clergy, the heads of the convents, the mayors, the principal landowners and let the city surrender not later than 6 a.m. tomorrow or it will cease to exist.' There followed violent reproaches concerning Spanish atrocities and the violation of the terms of the Baylen capitulation, ending with: 'Return to Madrid, I give you until 6 a.m. tomorrow. Return, only if you can tell me that the populace has submitted. If you fail, you and your troops will all be put to the sword.' At the given hour on 4 December, Morla and General Don Fernando, governor of Madrid, presented themselves at Berthier's tent to announce their surrender. At 10 a.m. General Belliard took command of the city and all posts were turned over to the French.

The French troops made their entry. The column did not consist, as earlier, of a majority of green conscripts, sickly and poorly uniformed. The ADCs in winter dress wore the Hungarian pelisse, a white dolman with gold braid, a shako in scarlet cloth topped by a plume, a black and gold silk belt. Their horses displayed panther skins, trimmed with gold and scarlet. The grumblers in their full dress were superb, a human river in shimmering colours flowing down the calle d'Alcala. Many Madrileños were unable to conceal their admiration. But Lucas-Dubreton recorded a conversation between two monks overheard by a staff officer: 'Oh', said the younger one, 'what admirable troops; they are irresistible. If Murat had arrived with such troops, we would have had to be on guard against a revolt which would have lost us everything.' 'How many do you think there are?' asked the elder of the two. 'At least twenty thousand.' 'Well, at fifty dead daily, as much from fighting as from sickness, fevers, the knife, the women. That totals eighteen thousand dead a year. How many would be left?'

Meanwhile, Napoleon tightened the screw. Here are the provisions of four decrees all issued from the imperial camp at Madrid on 4 December 1808: abolition of all feudal rights in Spain; suppression of the tribunal of the Inquisition and sequestration of their goods; suspension of the religious orders and novitiates; reduction of convents by one-third, the goods of confiscated convents to accrue to the Spanish crown; abolition of customs barriers between the provinces.

On 7 December Napoleon addressed a proclamation to the Spaniards, explaining the grounds for these measures, telling them that they had been led astray by perjured men and deceived by the English. 'I have destroyed all that was opposed to your prosperity and grandeur.' And he, Napoleon, was giving to Spain, not only his brother Joseph as king, but a liberal and beneficial constitution. 'But if my efforts are useless and you do not respond to my confidence, then I shall have no choice but to treat you as a conquered province and to place my brother on another throne. I would then place the crown of Spain on my own head and I will see that the wayward respect it, for God has given me the strength and the will necessary to overcome every obstacle.' This declaration was received in silence. The Madrileños stayed indoors, going out only when necessary. Many shops closed.

Some days after the surrender, Napoleon moved with a party of his staff officers from the tents to the nearby château of Chamartin, a country house belonging to the Duke of Infantado; not one chimney, rooms could be heated only by braziers placed in the centre. Joseph, humiliated at having been excluded from all the business touching his kingdom, had retired to the hunting lodge of Pardo, one league from the capital. Napoleon went rarely into Madrid. On one day, however, he did enter early in the morning accompanied by Joseph. Visiting the palace, he placed his hand on one of the stone lions guarding the stairway: 'I shall hold it in the end, this delectable Spain!' Madrid still personified the defiance of Spain. On Belliard's orders, the theatres, dance-halls and cafés had been reopened, but remained empty. Napoleon tried to overcome this enmity by measures of clemency and protection. Having learned that General Morla had been one of the signatories of the capitulation of Baylen, an agreement which was later violated, he took no further action. He pardoned the marquis of Saint-Simon, a French *émigré* condemned to death for having fired on the French during the assault on Madrid.

He had given strict orders forbidding all pillage in Madrid. Two skirmishers, caught red-handed breaking into a house, were condemned to death. Their colonel pleaded for a pardon in view of their habitual good conduct. Clemency was refused. The two men were shot on the glacis of the city. Not a single Spaniard attended the execution.

On 18 December 1808, Napoleon was reviewing Lefebvre's corps when numerous officers arrived, surrounding two British prisoners – at least, they wore red coats, though these were in a bad way, dirty and torn. 'Sire, here are two Frenchmen.' They were very young soldiers, taken prisoner at Baylen. At the end of the terrible march which we have described in part, they were put in a prison-hulk, then transferred to an island prison. In order to escape from their situation, the two young fellows had agreed to join one of the corps being raised by the British. They were assigned to General Moore's army, but had deserted a week ago as soon as they learned that the French were in Madrid; marching by night and hiding by day, they reached the French outposts. 'Sire, their information is interesting.' 'Send them, here.' The escapers did not appear stupid. They had deserted from Moore's army as it crossed the Portuguese frontier, heading for Salamanca. They insisted that they knew all about the plans of the British, which were common knowledge; seize Burgos and cut off the French from the Pyrenees.

Moore, forty-seven, a lieutenant-general of three years' seniority, had been chosen by the cabinet to replace Wellesley (the future Wellington), discredited in British public opinion for having signed and observed the Convention of Cintra. Moore, according to a number of British military experts, was 'the best trainer of men which this army has ever had'. We shall see in which direction he will this time lead his troops. Having listened to the fugitives, Napoleon interrupted the review, hastened to his office and studied his maps. Moore was a week beyond Salamanca and marching on Burgos; he must now be somewhere near Tordesillas. 'I will march northwards. Soult is to come down from Santander. Moore will be caught in a vice. Either he will accept battle or will seek to escape to Portugal, perhaps by one of the Spanish ports in Galicia. But I will arrive early enough to cut off his retreat.'

Napoleon would march with Ney's 32,000 troops; Soult had 30,000. But when one looks at the map, one sees that the Sierra de Guadarrama is still there, solidly planted north of Madrid and, again, it would have to be crossed. Not, admittedly, by the restricted defile of the Somosierra as was necessary when coming from Burgos, but further south-west and at a lower altitude. The map shows that from that side the slopes are 'wide and gentle'.

On 21 December, the Guard and Ney's corps marched towards the foot of the sierra; they had been ordered to scale it during the following day and night, a distance of six kilometres.

Next day Napoleon, in turn, approached the mountains. It was very cold with a violent wind almost from the moment of departure at Chamartin; the sky darkened, became orange, then nearly black. Then, suddenly, a blizzard. Castile has its furies.

Having gained the foot of the sierra, Napoleon and his accompanying officers, half-blinded by the white torment, glimpsed in the fields bordering the road an immense crowd, or rather, a chaos of thousands of men, horses, guns, caissons, convoys – all motionless as if lost, frozen by disaster. These were Ney's troops sent ahead the day before. Here is a summary of the reports made to Napoleon: The troops had not been able to climb the mountain. The slopes were icy, the horses skidded, breaking their legs and falling, the snow formed drifts where the men floundered up to their waists. The artillery, even with tripled teams, could not get even half-way up the slope. The teams had turned round and descended again, sowing panic among the infantrymen following them. Units were intermixed and men got lost. A colonel recalled that his men were repeating what the villagers had told them: they had seen a Spanish regiment try to climb the mountain in weather like this. Not a man had come down again. And night falls quickly at that season. 'Sire, we must postpone the operation, at least until tomorrow morning. Perhaps the weather will improve.'

No-one knew where the chasseurs of the Guard had got to; Savary went to find them. Napoleon had never seen such a disorder caused by the violence of the elements. Occasionally the swirling snow became so thick that it was impossible to see ahead ten paces. Eventually Savary returned with the duty squadron of chasseurs of the Guard. With the Emperor leading, it moved towards the base of the mountain. The road was choked by infantrymen trying to advance in the same direction.

'Make way! Make way for the Emperor! Move to the right!' The men obeyed, pushed by the NCOs, but an infantryman of the Empire on the march with his pack, his musket, his ammunition, had little in common with a ballet dancer. The overloaded footsloggers slipped on the ice, bruised or wounded themselves. The Emperor was welcome to go first; not one cheer. All that could be heard were curses, insults and a rising fury which was just beginning.

Even at the foot of the mountain, the Emperor's horse had nearly fallen several times on a level road. Dismounting, the officers and chasseurs imitated their leader, advancing in Indian file, leading the horses as the wind whipped up the snow ever more fiercely. They were advancing at two kilometres an hour, often less; from time to time being forced to retire. Napoleon was sometimes supported by Savary, sometimes by Duroc; the staff officers linked arms for mutual support with the Emperor in their midst. At thirty-eight, the man was indefatigable on horseback, enduring, indifferent to discomfort, but, unaccustomed to marching, he staggered, muttering imprecations about this 'damned business'. Now astride a cannon man-hauled, a less painful means of transport, but as the Emperor passed two regiments which were lagging, what he heard was hardly encouraging. 'Dirty bastard, blackguard. Someone put one up the spout for him! Enough of this!' Men who so often had shouted 'Long live the Emperor!' swore at one another, one inciting the next: 'If you're too yellow, let me pass and I'll blow his brains out!' Such quick transition from adulation to vilification. We know that this is nothing new historically.

The generals and marshals with their huge cavalry boots could go no further, so here they are astride the guns. Marbot: 'We continued to march in this curious way and finally managed to attain the summit of the mountain.' Or rather the summit of this slope. Going down was a little less frightful for everyone. Orders provided that Headquarters and General Lapisse's VI Corps were to be billeted at Villa Castin, five leagues beyond the foot of the sierra. Napoleon realised that this was out of the question. He sent for Lapisse: 'General, your men have taken a beating. Spread them out between the local villages and try to find them food and fire.' Napoleon himself stopped just at the base of the descent at Espinar, where a small post office offered shelter. A fire was lit for him; some servants of the imperial household had managed to push a mule laden with provisions over the divide. Napoleon wished that all those who had made the crossing should share his meal equally.

Outside, the chasseurs of the Guard bivouacked under the freezing rain. 'Divide the men among the local villages' was a good idea, but there was nothing there except some mud hovels sheltering a few humans in the last degree of misery, a condition that the soldiers were to share for a long while to come. On 24 December Napoleon received a message from Soult: 'II Corps has clashed north of Valderas with detachments of the British army.' Napoleon's immediate order: 'If Soult is attacked have him retire for a day to the east in order to draw Moore in that direction.' And Napoleon would lead Ney's troops to attack the British in the rear or the flank .

A perfect manoeuvre in theory, but this is Spain. The officer carrying these orders was captured and killed by the guerrillas, and the dispatches were immediately sent to Moore. And from that moment Moore had but one thought, to drive north at maximum speed and embark at Coruña. Napoleon also had but one idea: to catch Moore before he could embark. Consequence for the soldiers: once more, march or die. For many, that would mean march and die.

Fifteen leagues daily, that was the Emperor's target. Such a performance was possible in good weather with rested troops. But now, with the Guadarrama behind them, rain had replaced snow, a glacially cold rain. The fields were flooded, the roads became rivers of mud, worse than in Poland. Each successive regiment passed the wrecks of the one preceding it; vehicles engulfed in mud, often with their mules and asses still in harness; cavalry horses and even men bogged down and dead. This is the kind of thing that was happening: a soldier – not a conscript, not soft – a chasseur of the Guard, stops suddenly and addresses his comrades: 'I am a good soldier. You have seen me under fire. I would never desert, but this is too much for me.' He puts the muzzle of his musket to his forehead and pushes the trigger with his toe – finish. He will not the only one. On 28 December, a dozen soldiers of the Guard committed suicide: 'I would never desert,' said the first. To desert was to risk worse than a quick death; the guerrillas were still there in the countryside, more or less on the flank of the columns. Deserters would hardly travel a half league before they fell into their hands, which meant torture followed by death. However, there were others who, though desperate, hesitated to end it all with a musket shot and simply lay down in the mud. Their comrades said they were mad. 'No it's not me who's mad. It's *le Tondu!*'

The suicides during this race to the sea – this race to death – have never been counted, nor the numbers who disappeared along the way. The army resembled a funeral cortège strung-out over dozens of leagues. Units were mixed-up, brigades, divisions. The Guard itself was at the end of its tether and broke up. Percy followed with his ambulances: 'No need to ask the way: dead horses, mules, asses showed the way. No warrior or nomadic people can have equalled us for destruction and vandalism.' The perpetrators were nearly always rank and file who terrified miserable inhabitants in their hovels. If they saw an officer, they besought him to stay and protect them, offering all that they had,

Poverty, filth, vermin. Percy: '*La padrone de la casa*, though aged about 43 years, had a healthy baby which she was suckling. The women are ugly and as dirty as Hottentots. A woman even older and uglier was also suckling. I have a filthy room and a blanket to appall.' 'Who cares, said these stalwart peasants, whether it is a Bourbon or a Napoleon who governs us, provided that he governs us well. Hypocrisy? Galicia is not Castile and below a certain level, the wish for survival kills even fanaticism.

The chase continued, Ney leading with his advance guard. No British at Aquilar del Campo, no British at Valderas where Napoleon, having cut across country with only a small escort – dangerous because of the guerrillas – arrived shortly before Ney. The inhabitants stated that the British had left not more than two hours earlier towards Benavente. 'We will keep going,' said the Emperor. 'Sire, the army is in a terrible state. Give them a little rest.' 'Approved. A halt of twenty-four hours. We will regroup the units.'

On 30 December, the divisions sorted out as far as possible, the pursuit was resumed. Before dawn, Lefebvre-Desnouettes, colonel-general of the chasseurs of the Guard, was sent with his regiment and a squadron of mamelukes to see if the British were in Benavente, on the right bank of the River Esla. Lefebvre-Desnouettes, brilliant cavalryman, a thruster, reached the left bank and found that the town appeared to be abandoned. He crossed at a ford with 1,500 horsemen and rode beyond the town, making contact a little farther on with 5,000 British cavalry. His troops came well enough out of the encounter, but he himself was taken prisoner.

Despite this sudden turn of fortune's wheel, the pursuit continued – Napoleon growing increasingly furious, more and more determined to finish it. On 31 December, the army, now reinforced by Soult, also crossed the Esla. At nightfall the exhausted men dropped where they were, even into the mud, while vehicles of every sort splashed their way through the ford half-submerged. That night the army was no more than one vast and exhausted disorder, but officers with lanterns passed among the units: 'Departure at dawn tomorrow.' Catch the British at any cost! The Emperor ordered that Astorga be reached next day. Sixty kilometres to go in the mud and rain, mostly by night, for this was 1 January 1809. The less dazed soldiers sniggered while wishing one another a happy New Year. Many agreed that the best thing would be for *le Tondu* to stop one as soon as maybe – yes, it had indeed come to that.

It would be wrong to suppose that the lot of the pursued was any better than that of the pursuers. The British corps commanded by John Moore had crossed the Hispano-Portuguese frontier on 11 November. On the 13th it was at Salamanca, some 20,000 troops plus some bands of armed peasants.

'Here are the English. We are saved!' This welcome assured Moore that his movements, his objectives would not be compromised. We know that his first intention had been to march towards Valladolid and cut French communications with the Pyrenees. We also know that, having learned that Napoleon himself was marching on him, Moore had only one idea: to get to Coruña and embark. His troops marched through the same mud and the same rain as the French and their orders were the same – march or die. The roads they had covered were littered with bogged vehicles, with corpses – and dead horses, but with a difference. These horses had been killed by a shot to the head in order to deny them to the French and each horse lacked a hoof. Every soldier forced to abandon his horse had to bring a hoof as confirmation. The British troops behaved in exactly the same manner as the French: pillaging and getting blind drunk whenever possible. Very soon those Spaniards who had hailed the British as their saviours came to detest them; their dearest wish being 'to see the French hanged by the guts of the British'.

Soult and Ney's troops collected from the roadside and the cellars red-coated infantrymen, helmeted dragoons, blue-uniformed gunners. And women, too, young English women often pretty, well-dressed and blooming. British regulations allowed six women to each company on continental expeditions, and all legitimate women for veteran units. These unfortunate captives wept copiously as the French soldiers auctioned them off.

The chase continued. Marbot: 'A glacial rain soaked uniforms, and the horses floundered through marshy terrain. It took enormous effort to advance and, as all bridges had been destroyed by the British, our infantrymen were obliged to strip five or six times daily and to brave the freezing streams with their weapons and clothes on their heads in order to cross.' Not all the bridges had been cut because we do not read that Napoleon was forced to cross in this fashion, but no doubt Marbot speaks truth when describing the hardships of the soldiers – and the suicides continued. According to Percy, Ney's army had lost half its effectives since leaving Madrid.

The workings of Napoleon's intellect are almost incomprehensible. In the midst of this deadly pursuit he was able to distance himself completely. On 21 December, he wrote to Crétet, Minister of the Interior, and to Gaudin, Minister of Finance, concerning the beautification of Paris. The Bastille and all the great squares should be embellished by 'vast and splendid fountains', using the waters of the Ourcq which had recently been linked to the city, and large expanses of water were to beautify the Champs Elysées and the Tuileries; the mass of buildings in the space between the Louvre and the Tuileries was to be demolished.

On 2 January at Benavente, perhaps the worst time during the chase, the Emperor spent the morning dictating orders intended to keep the Ministers in Paris busy, and in organizing and maintaining his sprawling empire. This lasted until midday, when he mounted his horse, galloping across the snow to the head of the columns of men staggering with fatigue.

Not one cheer as he passed; no more 'Vive l'Empereur!' and the looks directed towards him were impassive; men at the end of their tether have no room for hate; only how long have we been marching – and are still marching! The Emperor, stern-faced, feigned to see nothing; this is war in Spain – which must be taken as it comes. Once the British were caught and beaten, as beaten they surely would be, the enthusiasms and acclamations would be heard once more. But the fatal course of destiny born here in Spain is now irreversible.

Half-way to Astorga; the night was black and freezing, no longer any prospect of galloping. Two leagues before the next halt a staff officer coming from Benavente found him: 'Sire, a courier from Paris is searching for Your Majesty and will shortly be here.' 'I'll wait for him here.' Dismounting, the escorts built a huge fire by the roadside, the Emperor being just as soaked and shivering as his troops. The dispatch-rider arrived. Berthier opened the pouch and handed a wad of confidential dispatches to Napoleon, who read them by the light of a lantern. Without a word he crumpled the sheets and stuffed them into his pockets, mounted his horse and walked it in the direction of Astorga.

Here is a summary of the messages: Austria had formed two armies which were threatening the frontiers of Bavaria and Lombardy. Tsar Alexander, contrary to the Treaty of Erfurt, had not only failed to intervene, but had shown his approval of the action of the Austrian Emperor. From France, disquieting news. The Catholics were indignant about the use of force against the Pope; the Jacobins were up in arms over the costly war in Spain. Conscripts deserting everywhere, more than a third in some departments. The stock market was falling; in recent months stocks had lost twelve points (from 93 to 81).

According to reliable police reports, Talleyrand and Fouché were openly committing treason. According to them, the Spanish affair would be fatal to Napoleon, either by a military disaster or by enemy fire in battle, or by an assassin's dagger. With his death, what would transpire? The subject was being discussed with their accomplices, including Caroline née Bonaparte. None of the conspirators envisaged any of the Emperor's brothers as a successor, and Talleyrand and Fouché, as two ex-Revolutionaries, would find the return of the Bourbons dangerous. Their choice was finally Murat, glittering, fairly popular, and a cipher whom they could manipulate. Things had progressed to the stage where the police had intercepted a message sent to the King of Naples: 'Prepare relays on the road to Paris so that we can present you in the capital on the first signal.'

What to do? Napoleon wasted no time. Clearly he must return to France. Soult must take command of the troops, continue the pursuit and destroy Moore's army before it could embark. He must abandon to Joseph, at least for now, the task of 'pacifying Spain'. Joseph would accordingly have under his orders the 250,000 men of the Grande Armeé, commanded by Soult, Ney, Victor, Moncey, Mortier and Gouvion St-Cyr.

Napoleon knew that his brother could certainly reign acceptably over a Spain that was friendly or resigned and submissive, but was quite incapable of dealing with the present situation. The Emperor thought that he could oversee and redress matters at long range, and that once Austria and the conspirators had been brought to their senses, he would return.

For the moment, he would go to Valladolid where news from Paris could reach him with only five days' delay. But he was reluctant to leave Astorga, still hoping to hear that Moore had accepted battle in which case he would hasten to deal him the mortal blow. But No. Nothing. He reached Valladolid on 8 January and stayed there for nine days.

Napoleon 's departure for France was prepared in secret; no announcement to the troops, no communiqué. But the news leaked as far as the grenadiers of the Guard and their reaction was anything but cordial: '*Le Tondu* is abandoning us after all that we have endured for him! If he is not comfortable in Spain, then neither are we.' Napoleon overheard the widespread comment: 'We would like to return too.' 'I will review the Guard in one hour's time.'

As soon as the commander-in-chief appeared, the Guard sensed that this time there would be no kind words or pinched ears, but even so the violence of his manner surprised them. Napoleon approached one grenadier, grasped his collar, shook him, disarmed him and, pushing him back into the ranks, addressed the men: 'I am very willing to pardon you this time, but what are these grumblings that I have heard? You want to rejoin your girls in Paris? Ah, they are far away; you'll see plenty of others! When I am eighty I'll still see that you keep your dressing!'

On another occasion Napoleon reviewed the 17th Line Regiment, known as General Legendre's, still at Valladolid. Legendre had been chief of staff to Dupont, vanquished at Baylen. The imperious voice crackled: 'How can you show your face when your shame is everywhere blazoned, when your dishonour can be read on the faces of your brave men?' Astonishment – dead silence! 'We blushed for you from farthest Russia to the lands of France when, following the proceedings of the high court, we learned of your capitulation. When has a unit ever capitulated on the battlefield? On the battlefield, Sir, one fights and if one chooses to capitulate rather than fight, one deserves to be shot.' Timidly, Legendre suggested that at Baylen the commander had wished to save the artillery.

'It was not the artillery you wished to preserve, it was the convoy of wagons loaded with your loot. You behaved neither as Frenchmen nor as generals, but as thieves and traitors!' 'We only tried to save Frenchmen.' 'France needs her honour, not her men.' Napoleon seized the wrist of Legendre's right hand and shook it: 'How could this hand not have withered having ordered Vedel to lay down his arms? By what right did you wrench from these brave men the arms that they had honourably borne up to then?'

Here, as so often, witnesses' accounts differ in detail, but agree on the essential, that is, the tone and the violence of the words and the wish to humiliate. A general can be dismissed, but to humiliate him publicly is neither politic nor profitable for a supreme commander. Clearly, here and before the Guard, Napoleon lost control of himself. 'This unfortunate war was my downfall,' he was to say at St Helena. 'All the elements of my destiny were to stem from that fatal knot. It divided my forces, compounded my problems, destroyed my integrity in Europe.' A fair judgement in retrospect, but at Valladolid in January 1809 Napoleon had not yet accepted this setback. Basically furious at himself, he turned his anger against others.

At the same time, and which is perhaps more serious – he was still looking to conceal the truth from others. Wishing to reassure his brother, who was upset over his departure, he wrote that his kingdom was being pacified; calm had been restored in the provinces of Leon, Asturias and New Castile, Saragossa would shortly fall and General Saint-Cyr would soon finish his work in Catalonia; the British, chased out of Spain, would not be keen to return. In short, things were going well in Spain.

Or nearly so; while the Emperor was at Valladolid the body of a French officer was discovered down a well in a monastery. Two servants were hanged, the monastery closed and Napoleon harangued the monks in such a terrifying fashion that they approached him on their knees to kiss the hem of his garment.

And now there were new suggestions to his brother on means of 'pacification'. 'Some twenty dissidents must be hanged. I will hang seven here tomorrow, all known to have committed excesses. You must do likewise in Madrid. If we do not free ourselves of a hundred brigands and firebrands all will be wasted. As to the hundred, shoot or hang twelve or fifteen and send the rest to the galleys in France. I only restored quiet to France by arresting two hundred firebrand assassins and bandits whom I exiled to the colonies. Since then, the climate in the capital has changed as if in response to a blast on a whistle.' In his view, 'the mob only loves and esteems those whom it fears' and, finally, the mob consisted of all who resisted him. Every despot has harboured this illusion.

On 15 January 1809, Napoleon had received some even more alarming reports concerning Austria's intentions. He left Valladolid secretly on the 17th, accompanied only by Duroc, his ADC General Savary, and the mameluke Roustam, plus a picket of chasseurs from the escort. The rest of the household was to follow by easy stages. Berthier was to stay a further six days in Spain in order to handle the details of the transfer of command.

Thirty leagues from Valladolid is Burgos, the first planned halt. Tradition has it that the Emperor covered the 120 kilometres in six hours. Savary took the lead, followed by Napoleon who constantly beat his ADC's horse, which Savary also was spurring harshly. Behind came Duroc and Roustan who could barely keep up. Then, strung out over more than a kilometre, came the 25 chasseurs of the escort, who were relieved at each halt which lasted only long enough for the horses to be changed. Then off again at the gallop.

The speed of their progress and the secrecy of its preparation plus an element of luck meant that at no time did the guerrillas put in an appearance. At midday Napoleon was at Burgos which he left an hour later in a light carriage. The stage-horses were distributed along the length of the route, and the party moved by night and day. Napoleon reached Bayonne at 4 a.m. on 19 January, but left almost immediately. At 8 a.m. on the 23rd he was at his office in the Tuileries: 'One might have thought that the place had been struck by lightning.'

VIII

WAGRAM, 1809
The Last Great Victory

'You are a thief, a coward, a man without faith, you do not believe in God. All your life you have failed in your duty, you have deceived, betrayed everyone. Nothing is sacred to you, you would sell your father. I have heaped you with gold and there is nothing which you would hesitate to do against me. In the past ten months you have in this fashion had the impudence, because you assumed without cause that matters were going badly in Spain, to say to anyone who would listen that you had always disapproved of my enterprise in that kingdom, whereas it was you who first gave me the idea. And this unfortunate man [the Duke of Enghien]: who was it who first told me where he was living? Who encouraged me to pursue him? Where are you aiming? What do you want? What are you hoping for? Dare to tell me! You deserve breaking like a glass, which is within my power, except that I despise you too much to take the trouble!' And, finally, the famous phrase: 'You are shit in silk stockings.' Thus Napoleon confronted Talleyrand on his return from Spain. Neither Hitler nor Stalin would have bothered with such a theatrical denunciation; they would simply have had him 'liquidated'. Napoleon let him live and even allowed him his liberty. Fouché, his accomplice, trembled, but the Emperor did not wish to alienate his chief of police. The other conspirators had gone to ground.

Napoleon said, and wrote at that time, that on his return to France, the Austrians retreated to their own territory, but in fact he was certain of nothing and needed to provide against any contingency. He must now create a new army – but with what? After Baylen, he had raised 80,000 conscripts from the classes of 1808 and 1809. On his return from Spain, he called up 300,000 men of the class of 1810, indifferent to the cries of outrage which arose from the entire nation. But, kept well in hand (the police were ever vigilant), the people protested but were silenced. As for the conscripts, Napoleon thought that he knew how they would react. Initially despondent, they would, like their predecessors, be brain-washed by the veterans into believing that *le Tondu* was a god who would lead them from victory to victory.

Of the army, known as the Army of Germany, at whose head Napoleon advanced upon Austria, only a third consisted of seasoned French troops; one-third were foreigners and one-third of youngsters who did not even know how to shoulder a musket. They totalled about 110,000 men. Of these, 70,000 were the remnant of the Grande Armeé, occupying Germany. The Guard had been recalled from Spain and reinforced, and before leaving Valladolid Napoleon had created the 'Young Guard', an élite troop developed from the elements of the Old Guard. Little by little, the difference between the Young and Old Guards would disappear. In 1809, they numbered about 30,000 men.

The contingents of foreigners had been provided mainly by the princes forming part of the Confederation of the Rhine and were commanded by French officers. In detail: 12,000 Württembergers (Vandamme), 7,000 Germans (Rouyer), 4,000 Westphalians (Jérôme Bonaparte), 12,000 Poles (Poniatowski), 5,000 Badeners. With VII Corps commanded by Legendre, 30,000 Bavarians plus some Italians and Spaniards, a total of 100,000 foreign troops.

There were 100,000 conscripts, evenly spread through the regiments which meant that they were often in a majority: thirty days in service, knowing nothing, it was expected that they would receive their tuition on the march. The first result – the first difficulty – was a tactical one: not enough seasoned troops that could be reliably deployed under fire, which could mean disorder and panic. To preserve some cohesion, the battalions would march in formation in depth, thus providing an ideal target for artillery.

Another problem was command – new officers would not drop from heaven. Napoleon decided that all the young men studying at the military schools should be promoted to sub-lieutenant, and that all retired or unemployed officers fit for service should be recalled. Use every means to attain this end.

Napoleon would wield this imperfect weapon with masterly skill. Military experts agree that the Austrian campaign represented Napoleon at his best in terms of strategical and tactical brio. In Spain we have seen him cat-called, insulted, detested. Let us cross the Rhine and glide like eagles over the German campaigns: what do we hear? 'Vive l'Empereur!' This renaissance is for me the most striking feature of the lightning campaign which culminated at Wagram.

At his office in the Tuileries on 10 April 1809, Napoleon was listening to a report from Archchancellor Cambacérès (56 years old, jurist, a contributor to the Civil Code) when General Lauriston, the duty ADC, entered with a dispatch from Berthier, just received from Donauwörth (in Bavaria, on the Danube, 40 kilometres north of Augsburg): 'They [the Austrians] have crossed the Inn.' Napoleon said to Lauriston: 'This is war!' Lauriston wrote that the Emperor's eyes were moist and lifeless as though some great sorrow weighed on him. Sorrow at having to campaign once more? At having the enemy seize the initiative? Either way, Napoleon reacted quickly: 'I shall leave tomorrow at 4 a.m. Cambacérès will preside over the council of ministers.' Secretaries were called and took down orders on the wing. To Clarke, Minister of War, to Eugène de Beauharnais, Viceroy of Italy, to Jérôme, to Berthier. To Fouché, who came to assure the Emperor of his complete devotion. Reply: 'Send spies immediately into Germany.'

During supper, Josephine had insisted on accompanying her husband part way and Napoleon had finally agreed. Many ADCs would follow in the second carriage and a picket of dragoons would protect the whole. They travelled night and day. On 14 April at 3 a.m., passing through Bar-le-Duc, the Emperor cried 'Stop!': it had occurred to him to visit the Oudinot family. Napoleon esteemed Oudinot, whom he called Bayard. His family were solid businessmen and his parents had initially done all they could to divert him from the profession of arms. Now, here he was Duke of Reggio, commanding the corps of grenadiers, and in a fair way to becoming marshal. An ADC knocked at the door: 'The Emperor wishes to see you. He is coming.' The family, startled, were running about in their night clothes and, suddenly, there was the Emperor, smiling: 'I would like to kiss the little girls.' The two children, woken, startled by the noise, the lights, the kiss of the strange man, cried, but Napoleon laughed heartily: 'I will tell the Duke of Reggio that all is well here.'

All aboard! Travelling day and night. On 15 April, an exhausted Josephine was left at Strasbourg. Duroc took her place next to the Emperor in the jolting carriage. Rastadt, Durlach, Stuttgart, Ludwigsburg, with brief halts, for example, to visit the grand-ducal family at Baden and the King of Württemberg (one must reassure one's allies): 'What is Your Majesty's plan of war?' 'We are going to Vienna.' 'We await with confidence the first thunderbolt from today's Jupiter.' 'We are going to Vienna', but at Ludwigsburg Napoleon received a dispatch from Berthier, describing the dispositions he had made against a sudden thrust by the enemy: 'But this is madness!' The essential task of a chief of staff is to have his chief's orders executed. Many officers could do this to perfection, but left to their own devices were totally inadequate. Such was the case with Berthier. Persuaded that the Austrians would attack from every direction simultaneously, he had so dispersed his troops that in no direction were they superior: precisely the contrary of Napoleon's doctrine. Having skimmed through the message, Napoleon dictated a letter changing it all: 'You must do just the opposite of what you have done.' No recrimination, no wounding comment. Napoleon realised that he had asked of Berthier more than he could fulfil.

At 10.30 a.m. on 16 April, on the road again. The countryside of Baden is varied: wooded, hilly, and the weather is usually superb in spring, but today is windy and stormy. The Emperor, dictating to Duroc, scarcely glances out of the window. The carriage is being escorted for a while by Württemberger dragoons, a signal honour for the Confederation of the Rhine. As they were crossing a large forest a storm burst violently, lightning, thunder, squalls, torrential rain. Barns at the roadside sheltered the riders, and the Emperor took shelter in a fairly large

house, the home of a forest ranger. He and his wife, impressed but not embar-
rassed, bustled about and provided an excellent meal for the master of Europe.
In this simple but sparkling clean room with its polished furniture and neat curtains, Napoleon was pleased to be waited on by the young daughter of the
house, a tall, pretty and gracious girl. 'But how comes it that such an attractive
girl as you is not married?' 'Alas, sire, we are poor and she has no dowry.' 'Can
the young Württembergers really be so stupid? Send me Ferbois.' Ferbois was
the headquarters paymaster and kept the imperial cash box. 'This is for this pretty girl's dowry.' A solid amount, too, so here is a happy family; for once, the war
was not a great misfortune.

The imperial carriage rolled away into the squally dusk. During the night,
at Dillingen, Napoleon had Maximilian, King of Bavaria, awoken; he had taken
refuge there from the invading Austrians: 'Sire, all is lost unless you act quickly!' 'No, in a few days you will be back in Munich.'

All aboard! At 6 a.m. on 17 April, General Headquarters was established
in a convent. Berthier and his aide-de-camp Monthion, who had not expected
the Emperor so early, were absent on some inspection. A staff officer led
Napoleon to a large map covered with pins. 'Where is the enemy?' 'Sire, see
these red pins. The Austrians having crossed the Inn, turned right and marched
on Ratisbon.' 'What are you saying? That is impossible.' 'It's true, Sire.' 'Then
I've got them! That's a lost army. In a month we shall be in Vienna.'

The bulk of the Austrian forces, commanded by their best general, the
Archduke Charles, was in Bavaria. In four days, from 19 to 23 April, Napoleon
was to turn them from the south, forcing them on to the Danube in a series of
victorious battles which costthem 50,000 men. Charles, having narrowly
escaped encirclement at Eckmühl on 22 April, retreated eastwards pursued as far
as Vienna by Napoleon.

The famous 'Four-day Campaign' was not devoid of risk. At the start, the
morale of the troops and the officers was not of the highest. No one understood
the deployments ordered by Berthier and the Emperor's whereabouts were
unknown; had he only just left Paris? Napoleon, on being told of this, immediately ordered each division to fire a salvo of twenty-one guns: 'That's it! Here he
is. Now you'll see!' And once again the recruits had to listen to the veterans
recounting their exploits, their past glories.

The Emperor issued a welcome proclamation, starting with 'I am coming
like a lightning flash,' and ending with 'Our past victories are a certain guarantee of the victory which awaits us. Let us therefore march and on our appearance let the enemy recognise his conquerors.' The youngsters had never heard
the like of this before, and even if they understood only some parts of it, the
words 'victory' and 'conquerors' and these veterans who cried constantly 'Vive
l'Empereur!' worked like magic.

Another worry for Napoleon at the start of the campaign was this: to what degree could he rely on these foreigners of the Confederation of the Rhine? On these officers and soldiers who spoke the same language as the enemy? How would they resist a propaganda invoking Germanic solidarity? One Colonel Meda of the lst Chasseurs had found in a presbytery at Hirschau, near Stuttgart, the text of a prayer, printed in Austria, which a number of clergy in Baden and Württemberg had read from the pulpit.: 'We pray to you O God, in love and gratitude for our saviour the Archduke Charles. It is You who have sent him to our aid. Order the cherubim to carry him in their arms ...' Unctuous stuff, but it might be effective. Napoleon's parry would be two-fold. First, a proclamation: 'Bavarians! Until today you have been fighting alone against the Austrians. Not one Frenchman is in the first rank; they form a reserve corps of which the enemy knows nothing. I have complete confidence in your bravery. I have already extended the boundaries of your country, but I now see that this was not enough. I shall make you so great that if in the future you need to make war against the Austrians, you will have no need of my help. For two hundred years the Bavarian standards, protected by France, have resisted Austria. We shall march on Vienna where we shall soon punish the evil that she has long inflicted on your country.'

Secondly, Napoleon took a personal risk. Since the beginning of the battle of Abensberg (20 April) he had marched with the Bavarian divisions in the front rank; behind him were only a few of his staff officers, and he took his stand wherever the fire was hottest. 'Troops are like macaroni,' Patton, the most aggressive general of the Second World War, would write, 135 years later. 'If you want to move macaroni forward, you must pull it. With troops, you must be in front.' How many of the great captains of war did this. 'Yes, but the supreme commander should not risk his life like a section leader. If he is killed, that might provoke a catastrophe ...' Here practicality parts company from logic. Which great captain had ever been more essential to his army than Napoleon? And, by exposing himself at Abensberg he took an additional risk; if he had been hit, who would know whether the ball had come from an Austrian or a Bavarian? But these foreigners were won over by his confidence in them and by his ignoring the risks. They faced the enemy; they charged with the bayonet. Abensberg was the first victory of the Four-day Campaign.

Numerically, the sides were unequal: facing Napoleon's 300,000 men were 500,000 Austrians, but in terms of strategy and tactics Archduke Charles was a lightweight and moreover, none of the enemy commanders exposed himself as Napoleon did at Abensberg, and would continue to do.

The procedure placed an additional heavy burden on him. Between battles, he was occupied much more intensely than his troops; while they were marching, pack on back, his nights were spent studying his maps, organising, ordering. At Ziegelstadel, watching the march past of Davout's corps, he looked so exhausted that a baker in front of whose shop he had paused brought him a chair and he sat down to watch them pass. This did not shock them; on the contrary they pitied him: '*Le Tondu* is exhausted. He drives himself as hard as he drives us.' And 'Vive l'Empereur!'

Napoleon wanted to defeat Austria rapidly; his magnetic hold over the troops must be exploited to the maximum – he sought constantly to maintain it. Rewards were one means and he had a new idea: do not await the reports of the unit commanders before distributing the Cross. Immediately after a battle, with the men fallen in, he would send for the officers: 'Give me the name of your bravest soldier.' The choice must be very quick, following which the Emperor would call the soldier from the ranks: 'You are the bravest man in the regiment. I award you the Cross.' This simplification, this return to basics, was so popular that the choice was never challenged. Often with the Cross, there was another phrase: 'I promote you officer.' The Emperor had probably had to check that the man was not completely illiterate. Such promotions aroused enthusiasm, especially when it concerned an NCO. The Emperor would announce in a loud voice: 'I promote you lieutenant, baron of the Empire, with a gift of four thousand francs income.' Yes, for the first time, titles of nobility and gratuities transmissible to descendants were awarded impromptu to junior officers, NCOs and even to common soldiers. General Pelleport, promoted from the ranks: 'It was for us poor soldiers of fortune, having only our swords, a great moment in which we received a reward which would perpetuate in our families the record of our services.'

The capture of the hearts and minds of his soldiers, NCOs and junior officers accomplished, it was only a question of maintaining their devotion. To keep the devotion and support of the high- ranking officers was not so easy. These marshals, these generals in line for promotion to marshal, were already glittering with decorations, distinctions, titles, loaded with cash which some hardly had time to spend. Scarcely did they decide to enjoy a little pleasant relaxation when along came another war. Some of them, not yet fifty years of age, said that they felt old. 'I would very much like to hang up my boots,' was a sentiment often heard among the staffs. And, since the start of the Spanish affair, anxiety was expressed: 'The Emperor is on the wrong track. We are caught in a whirlwind of wars which will never end.'

Napoleon, always alert, was aware of these opinions, but did not attach much importance to them until Lannes returned, recalled from Spain. Of all he marshals, Lannes was his favourite. He reported on 19 April shortly after General Headquarters had been established at Vohburg. The Emperor, cheered by the victory of Tengen, greeted him in an improvised office, lit by candles removed from the local church. To the sovereign's surprise, Lannes was unrecognisable, in the depths of gloom, notwithstanding that he too had a victory to claim. But what a victory!

We have already taken a long look at Saragossa, whose convents and buildings resembled a citadel. When Lannes' troops approached for the second time, on 20 December 1808 (the first siege had lasted from 15 June to 13 August without result) the garrison numbered 30,000 soldiers plus about the same number again of armed peasants and townsfolk. The French numbered 30,000. At the start, the bombardments and harassing attacks made little impression on the besieged. The heart of resistance was José Rebelledo de Palafox y Melsi, known simply as Palafox, a general of thirty-three, ex-bodyguard of Ferdinand VII, not over-brave, totally without military experience, but well-spoken, popular with the ladies. In truth he was a false hero whom Spain would later place upon a pedestal as Duke of Saragossa because he had been made an idol of every form of resistance.

Napoleon, irritated by the slowness of the siege operations, had ordered Lannes to take charge of them personally. On 26 January all the French artillery fired simultaneously and the large monastery of San Engracia fell to the Poles of the Vistula Legion. In the refectories, chapels, corridors and even in the cells, the monks, covered in blood, fought like demons; one Pole was brought down by a crucifix. An equally savage battle raged within the gilded walls of the baroque church of the Capuchins, Spaniards firing from the upper galleries, the organ loft. They fired from the house windows; to cross an open space was suicidal. It was necessary to advance very slowly, using low walls and buttresses; lacking the time to seek and use stones, the French soldiers used sacks of grain, bales of wool, and especially the books taken from the library and the churches; priceless folios were piled up like bricks,

Progress underground was equally slow, the sappers digging by the light of lamps and torches whose smoke was suffocating. Often their picks broke antique vases filled with gold, silver, Carthaginian and Roman medallions. The sappers broke into one cellar where the defenders were hiding among jars of wine and oil, and a hellish battle ensued in lakes of oil, wine and later blood. The cost in dead remains unknown. On the French side, there is a report of 600 dead daily, but nothing can be confirmed. There was a battle to take an asylum, bitterly defended though on fire, the inmates throwing themselves from the windows; some of the bedridden were burned alive. Directly opposite was the huge monastery of Saint Francis, still resisting though mined. On 10 February an enormous explosion blew up an entire company of the grenadiers of Valencia. A moment later, the last defenders were hurled from the tower to the ground. Next day heaps of corpses were found in the cellars where families had taken refuge.

Every religious building was the scene of furious resistance. In the Church of the Recollection there was a battle amid the coffins: 'from one of them the livid and fleshless head of a bishop protruded, swathed in his episcopal robes'. At the convent of Saint Lazarus, the defenders retreated to the foot of the altar, crowded with women and children, Who could be spared in this welter of blood and thick smoke? The French soldiers fired into the brown.

The French army was camped under canvas outside the town. Supplies of every kind were lacking, as the whole province of Aragon was in revolt and the convoys could not get through. The camp presented a wild aspect: pictures from convents and churches, Velasquezs, Murillos and Goyas, served as improvised roofs; underfoot old parchments served as straw, fires were stoked with altar ornaments and the statues of saints.

The French sick and wounded were piled into the convents outside the walls by conscripted Spaniards who made no secret of the fact that their dearest wish was to dump more corpses into the communal graves. Underground in Saragossa, the air was unbreathable. Typhus was killing 200 to 300 persons daily – and where could they be buried? Large graves were dug in the streets and courtyards, bullets ripped through the piled-up corpses awaiting degrading burial. The horrors became indescribable.

On 16 February Lannes could be seen in the front rank of the French troops attacking the university; anxious to make an end, he 'exposed himself like a cadet'. A cannon-ball cut in two his ADC, who was standing behind him.

On 19 February Palafox sent a request for a suspension of fighting for three days. 'A poor joke,' said the Marshal. Next day Palafox transferred his powers to a *junta* of 40 persons who were to decide whether or not to surrender. These worthies asked for an armistice and firing ceased. When the Spanish delegates arrived, Lannes showed them a map of the city with six emplacements marked on it: 'There are six mine chambers, each containing 3,000 pounds of powder. I demand immediate and unconditional surrender. Otherwise all will be blown up tomorrow.'

Having yielded on all points, the negotiators did not dare to re-enter Saragossa. But that very day resistance ceased. Next day, some 8,000 defenders marched out of the town past Lannes after laying down their weapons. Many still swaggered, cigarillos in their mouths. Palafox, discovered shortly afterwards in a cellar, received no consideration. Sent to Vincennes, as Napoleon had ruled: 'My intention is that he should live sequestrated without means of writing or of making himself known.' Imprisoned under the name of Pedro Mendoza, he was released in 1813 and returned to Spain where he resumed his career.

The second siege of Saragossa had cost the French nearly 4,000 dead, including many of the engineers' sappers. The victorious and occupying French found a putrefying necropolis. More than 6,000 corpses filled the streets, the squares, the church porches. Lannes methodically attempted to restore order and a semblance of hygiene. Corpses were thrown into deep graves and sprinkled with lime; huge fires were lit as in times of plague. The level of the reparations set by the Marshal amounted to 800,000 piastres. 'The city cannot pay such a sum,' said the president of the *junta*. 'We will offer you the treasury of Notre-Dame-del-Pilar.' The bargain was struck, not without advantage to Lannes personally – a million francs, according to gossip. The Duchess of Abrantès has suggested an incredibly exact figure of 4,687,949 francs, but no serious historian has placed much weight on the memoirs of Junot's widow. The General died on 23 July 1813, leaving more debts than assets, and Laure d'Abrantès never reconciled herself to a modest way of life. Writing was her last means of raising a little money, of appeasing her creditors. Encouraged by Balzac, she wrote her *Mémoires* under the Restoration with less exactness than the wish to please those in power and the wider reaches of the public. Théophile Gautier called her the Duchess of Abracadabrantès. Her writings saved her from oblivion, though not from poverty; she died sick and an opium addict in a garret, owing her creditors 1,400,000 francs.

'Sire, this is a horrifying war,' Lannes wrote from Spain to Napoleon. When he arrived at imperial headquarters on 19 April 1809, he had in one sense lost his faith. The succession of wars over seventeen years had been too much. Sire, they compare you with Gengis Khan and the French with the Mongols.' 'What! Was it I who started this war?' Heir to the wars and conquests of the Revolution, with Britain as the irreducible enemy, it was essential to continue. Napoleon argued with Lannes, as he would argue until his dying day; 'an extended conversation' according to memoirs of the time. Finally, Lannes murmured: 'Sire, I will do all that you command me to.'

In one month and three days he would be dead. Napoleon himself had another twelve years to live; despite the number of times when he exposed himself to danger, death would have none of him. At Ratisbon (23 April) he advanced until he was under the walls, from which the defenders were constantly firing. He was on foot with Lannes by his side when a ball hit his left big toe. 'I am hit,' he said coldly. 'That must have been a Tyrolean, they are the best snipers.' Not a dangerous wound, but a painful one. First aid was needed. The surgeon Yvan dressed it on the spot, Napoleon sitting on a drum, surrounded by his staff. 'The Emperor is wounded!.' If their god, their fetish, the great soldier is dead, all is lost. One must absolutely confirm this news. No orders, no pleas, no threats could restrain the soldiers, gunners, cavalrymen who broke ranks and came running. 'Sound the Assembly', ordered Napoleon, 'and help me mount my horse.' He realised that this was the only remedy – to be seen. '*Le Tondu* is still alive.'

His charisma was at its zenith. The next day in the conquered city, still burning, half destroyed, Napoleon reviewed the regiments that had taken part in the assault. In front of the 7th of the Line, he ordered the bravest NCOs to step forward. One of them was a superb fellow, martial expression, two scars on his face, a recommendation in itself. 'How many wounds?' 'Thirty.' 'I did not ask your age, but the number of times you have been wounded.' 'Thirty.' Seeing the Emperor's perplexity, the colonel intervened: 'Sire, he understood. He truly has been wounded thirty times.' 'How's this? Wounded so often and still without the Cross.' But this sergeant did have it and he displayed it under his cross-belt which had hidden it. 'I do have one, but I damned well deserve a dozen, Emperor!' 'Well, I promote you officer.' Cheers rang out through the ranks. Often a ranker would have nothing except his bravery. An old grenadier, created Knight of the Empire, protested: 'Sire, I'd prefer the Cross.' 'You have it, since I have made you a Knight.' 'But I would prefer the Cross, sire.' 'All right.' Napoleon took the Cross from his own chest and pinned it on the soldier's, who then cried like a child.

The Napoleonic magnetism aimed at the higher ranks, initially without exciting much enthusiasm, could be counter-productive. The fixed idea of pleasing the Emperor often ended in useless butcheries, such as at Ebersberg. Masséna was ordered to pursue the Austrian General Hiller, whose army corps of 35,000 men was completely cut-off from the other Austrian forces and had retired along the right bank of the Danube. Napoleon's order had ended with these words: 'Activity! activity! Speed! These I recommend to you.' Masséna passed the advice on to his subordinates.

Hiller, having crossed the River Traun, established himself at Ebersberg and turned to face his pursuers. His position was the most advantageous imaginable: a town, fortified during the Middle Ages, overlooking the river from a scarped cliff. The river was wide, divided into several arms; the bridge which crossed it was very long and narrow and exposed to the fire of the defenders. The best course was to wait; Lannes' corps had just crossed the Traun, seven leagues farther south. Threatened with being bottled up, Hiller would clearly have to abandon Ebersberg. Masséna knew this and, having given orders to demolish the first section of the bridge, established himself on the first island to wait. But General Claparède, who commanded the leading division, had taken to heart the Emperor's counsel: activity, speed, the more so as a day earlier, he had been taxed with having let Hiller escape. The commander of the Corsican and Italian Brigade which preceded the column was the Dutch-born General Cohorn, who enjoyed the reputation of an indomitable hero. Forward! With the first island taken, the drive continued under the fire of the Austrian batteries. Bodies started to tumble into the river. Forward! The cliff was climbed, Ebersberg entered; the houses were packed with riflemen and the killing continued. Masséna, who was watching, banged his fist: 'Ah, why does he thrust his head into such a hornet's nest?!'

Activity, speed ... Cohorn's brigade advanced 'at the cost of heavy losses' but, in front of the castle, came to a halt. Claparède tried to deploy eastwards outside the town which was by then in flames, Masséna brought up his artillery and opened fire. But the Austrians counter-attacked with forces five times greater and drove the French into the blazing town.

In brief: Masséna sent Legrand's division to the aid of Claparède's and also launched an attack with his mounted chasseurs and hussars. At about 7 p.m., Hiller ordered a retreat, but his troops blocked inside the town did not receive the order and in any case could not disengage from the French who were giving no quarter. Not only were the Austrian troops attacked, but also the inhabitants found with them: 'In a burned house, 68 Tyroleans were suffocated; an Austrian officer received seventeen bayonet thrusts and a child of eight who had seized a sabre had her head crushed by a musket butt.'

Savary described the fight at Ebersberg as 'one of the greatest extravaganzas of courage which military history offers'; 2,400 French killed or wounded according to the archives of the war; other sources cite 4,000 dead. Between the burned houses of Ebersberg, the streets were piled with dead, among them the bodies of women with children clasped in their arms. The army transport crossed the town, crushing these frightful remains. 'One marched in a slough of human flesh which gave off a frightful stench.' Napoleon, it is said, was sickened: 'All those who agitate for war should see a monstrosity such as this. They would then know what their activity costs in terms of harm to humanity.'

He spoke sincerely. For him, the nation responsible for the butchery of Ebersberg was Britain, bent on his destruction. He declined to establish his headquarters in a house in the upper part of town which had escaped damage, and chose to pitch his tent in a garden farther away, and refused to see anyone for two hours. When finally Masséna entered, Napoleon received him with a frozen expression. But that bluff soldier argued without letting himself be intimidated; Cohorn had been seized by an heroic folly; Claparède had followed him. 'Could I let this division be annihilated or made prisoner? I would not have been pardoned for such a breach of my duties. Sire, you will receive an exact report of this incident.'

As for Cohorn, the Emperor had spoken to him 'sympathetically', observing however that he would have lost fewer men if he had waited for the troops behind him to come up before attacking. What the Emperor would have said if Cohorn had done just that, nobody knows. Of course, there was a distribution of the Cross, of pensions and honours. To have omitted it would have been unfair and there could be no question of applying the brakes to the war machine which powered the campaign.

Vienna in 1809 was still the most charming city in Europe, the gayest, most care-free. People knew that Napoleon was approaching with his army, but continued to attend concerts, the theatre, balls, to exchange on the least pretext presents and bouquets, repeating what had been said three and a half years earlier: 'Napoleon, bah! he cannot kill us all.' The French had then entered Vienna, and what happened? Nothing. Had the city suffered? No. And this time indifference was spiced with a certain optimism. 'The French are not what they were. Napoleon believes he is Master of Europe, but his dominion is everywhere challenged. Prussia, thirsting for vengeance, is simmering and awaiting a favourable opportunity. France's annexation of the Papal States will outrage Italy and others too. The Tyrol is in revolt, guerrillas have reduced French occupation to impotence. As for the guerrillas in Spain – well! Napoleon's grave is being dug in Spain. Such was the supper and theatre gossip.

Napoleon's victories while on the march towards Vienna scarcely made any impression. The Archduke Charles had retreated, but he knows what he is about. His army has retired in good order behind the left bank of the Danube and it may well be that Napoleon will be trapped there.

And, since Austerlitz, our troops have been seasoned. Vienna itself was defended by Archduke Maximilian, brother to the Empress, at the head of 16,000 men. On 10 May, Napoleon and Lannes reached the suburb of Mariahilf. 'Send an ultimatum to Maximilian!'

Since the bearer of the message had been mistreated, Napoleon sent for howitzers which began to bombard the city. When fire ceased, a delegation of Austrians appeared, but nothing was settled; the bombardment was resumed and fires could be seen. Maximilian retired beyond the Danube and a second delegation materialised. As the members temporised, Andréossy (the French Ambassador to Austria, who had joined Napoleon) sent a last ultimatum to General O'Reilly, to whom Maximilian had delegated his authority before retiring: The Emperor is about to renew the bombardment and Vienna will be completely destroyed. On the other hand, if they surrendered, their persons and property would be respected and no-one would be pursued for his opinions. 'The Emperor shuts his eyes to the past. I desire your reply within an hour.'

The capitulation was signed that evening. The French troops occupied the city on the morning of 13 May, disarming the Austrian garrison. Napoleon had a proclamation read, celebrating his victory, and stigmatising the fleeing Austrian princes. In short, lines intended to avoid exaction and pillage: 'Soldiers! The people of Vienna, forsaken, abandoned, bereft, should be the object of your respect. I have taken the inhabitants under my special protection. As for the turbulent and wicked spirits, we shall in justice make examples of them. Be good to the poor peasants and to the good people who have such a claim to our esteem. We do not vaunt our success; we see in it evidence of that divine justice which punishes the ingrate and the perjurer.'

The author of this noble text did not deceive himself unduly as to its efficacy because at the same time he formed mobile columns to sweep up the pillagers who at a pinch would commit murder. Known euphemistically as 'stragglers', these malefactors, more or less uniformed, continued to operate in the wake of the army. When captured they were court-martialled and, in serious cases, immediately executed.

'I will live here amid the souvenirs of the great Maria Theresa,' said the Emperor, on occupying the Schönbrunn. Next evening, his voice could be heard echoing around the courtyard: 'You shower of idiots!' This blast was directed at officers of the foot guards who were trying to form up a party of old sweats for guard duties. The twenty-five men were in such a parlous state that some were using their muskets as crutches. This is what had happened. The 1st regiment of foot chasseurs of the Guard had been transported in wagons across Europe as far as Ulm where there was a depot of arms and clothing. Then, footslogging and it was time to show the Emperor what they could do. Eighty kilometres the first day, sixty on the next six days, halting only for food and three hours' sleep nightly. On the last day, within four leagues of Schönbrunn, the regiment was prostrate. 'All right,' said the colonel, 'you can rest here, but I need 25 volunteers for a night guard for the Emperor.' The honour of the Guard was at stake. Some at least of these men must have forgotten how much they had cursed *le Tondu* in Spain, for the colonel had only to choose from among those who stepped forward. They fell-in immediately under the command of a major and two captains.

The Emperor had not yet retired when the volunteers arrived, in the state which I have described, at the château after midnight. Frightened by the anger of the great captain, the officers discreetly vanished. Napoleon addressed the commander of the mounted grenadiers: 'Build a big fire. Spread some straw here that these poor fellows can sleep on. Warm up a cauldron of sweetened wine.' The volunteers were unfit for duty for several days. But now Napoleon's attention was diverted elsewhere.

At Vienna there is only a small arm of the Danube (today a canal); the water is not blue, but dark-brown. The main channel runs some three kilometres from the city centre with numerous arms; in some places it is very wide – one kilometre or more. In May 1809, swollen by melting snow, the waters were virtually torrential. It was essential to cross; the Austrians, now on the left bank, had destroyed the bridges behind them. Archduke Charles and his army had taken up positions on the plateau of Wagram, north-east of Vienna. After marching the length of the right bank and consulting his senior engineers, Napoleon said: 'We will cross here.'

The river was more than four kilometres wide at this point, a little downstream from Vienna, but in mid-stream was the isle of Lobau, four kilometres by six, and between it and the left bank were some smaller islets. Finally, it would be necessary to cross two branches, one 480 metres wide, the other 240 metres, and beyond the isle of Lobau a small branch 120 metres wide.

The isle was wooded, so while working the engineers would be under cover. The few Austrian troops on the isle were chased off without any great difficulty and the experienced bridge crews started work on 19 May. Drays brought to the river banks the flat-bottomed boats which would support the bridge. Built in sections, they were 2.15m wide and their length varied from six to ten metres; they had to be anchored upstream and as Vienna lacked anchors sufficiently large and heavy, Napoleon had the bright idea of using barrels filled with cannon-balls. The sections were joined together with beams, and transverse planks formed the road-bed. At 3 p.m. on 20 May Napoleon came to watch the completion of the bridges. With Lannes he spent the night at a small house on the isle; the weather was fine and the staff officers lay on the grass and sang arias.

The main bridge was finished that night and the troops started to cross from the right bank to the isle of Lobau. The smaller bridge for the branch beyond the isle was finished at 3 a.m. next morning and Lasalle's light cavalry passed over to the left bank, where there was a vast expanse of crops and meadows – the 'plateau' of Wagram, which forms the north-eastern boundary and, in fact, is no more than a levee a few metres in height. Between this and the Danube, about a kilometre away, lie the villages of Aspern and Essling. During the morning of the 21st, Berthier climbed the bell-tower of Essling and observed the Austrian army which was descending from the plateau like a stream of thick cream seeping over a pie. He reported to Napoleon that he estimated their strength at 90,000 men. At the same moment, a message was received that only some 20,000 men had crossed to the left bank and that the main bridge over the Danube had broken. 'Evacuate Aspern and Essling immediately!' False alarm! The bridge had already been repaired and General Molitor reported that he would easily hold the two villages with the troops that he now had. Counter-order – Stand firm!

The enemy was still moving; the thick cream continued to flow in a convex arc. The guns fired and the scene was obscured by black smoke. It was between 1 and 2 p.m. and the weather remained good. Chroniclers have written of the butchery of Aspern, the butchery of Essling. The second was just beginning; the French were fighting against odds of four to one – the Austrians advancing with 103 battalions, 148 cavalry squadrons and 300 cannon. Even the recruits of the last call-up had by and large behaved well during the battles along the Danube from Abersberg to Vienna. But now there were 300 guns firing salvos at them, and all that their officers could do was to order them to close ranks as the cannon-balls cut swathes in their formations. Coignet: 'The cannon-balls ploughed into our ranks, mowing down three files at a time.'

Reinforcements were arriving from the right bank, but in penny packets like water dribbling from a tap; men, horses, cannon, munitions were getting across at a snail's pace – the little bridge to the left bank was a bottleneck. Then the bridge cables broke and all movement ceased until the sappers, up to their necks in water, were able to make repairs. Meanwhile, Aspern was taken and lost six times: cavalry charges relieved the hard-pressed infantry to turn back the Austrian tide. By nightfall, General Molitor's troops had managed to secure Aspern and those of Lannes were protecting Essling. General Espagne had been killed – the two villages burned.

The opposing armies were at a standstill – the Austrians had the greater number of troops – and were so close to each other that at some points the sentinels could make out uniform details and faces. At 9 p.m. Napoleon wrote to Davout: 'The enemy attacked with his whole force and we had only 20,000 men to hand. The battle was a hot one but the field is ours. You must send us all your artillery and all the munitions possible. Send all the troops you can spare, retaining those necessary to guard Vienna. Also, send us some provisions.' The bottleneck at the bridges was still serious, and the files of wounded heading back were making matters worse.

By dawn next day (22 May) 34,000 French troops had crossed to the left bank, still facing the better part of 90,000 Austrians. A thick mist had covered the river banks, but it suddenly dissipated. The artillery opened up and again all was covered by black smoke. The Austrians launched four bloody attacks on Aspern, only to be repulsed yet again.

Napoleon's object again was to drive in the enemy centre particularly since he was now hard pressed. Lannes led the attack with Oudinot on his left, Saint-Hilaire's division in the centre and Boudet's on the right, in a superb manoeuvre over this plain where the barley was ripening. But the Austrians were not blind and Archduke Charles advanced his artillery.

When Napoleon's horse was hit, troops nearby shouted that they would lay down their arms unless the Emperor retired. With him dead, they would be lost: *le Tondu* was their mascot. He returned to the isle of Lobau where he had a platform built around a pine tree whence he could survey the battlefield. At a distance it was an impressive sight – a slow ballet. The battalions advanced, one after the other, the charges of the cavalry flowed around them and forced them to move diagonally. The freshening breeze thinned the smoke; lighter columns of smoke arose from the burning buildings in Aspern and Essling.

Close in, it was the same story as the previous day, the cannon-balls ploughing through the close-packed masses of men and the terrible cry, repeated constantly, 'Close up!' and the lifeless bodies strewn behind them. Now the Austrians, though by far the more numerous, retreated; no one knows why. Possibly Charles had wished to fight the decisive battle on the plateau and nowhere else. It is also possible, and I am convinced that this is the case, that the French troops had been pushed forward more firmly and with less regard for losses.

Thus the grand design became apparent: the French advancing in virtually symmetrical formations, preceded by and seemingly escorted on the wings by continuous cavalry charges. Then, in mid-morning, the entire army, advancing northwards – in this costly advance to victory – without apparent reason, as if a huge hand were holding it back, slowed down and then began to retire. This was a staggering development, but it was not from the heights of his tree that Napoleon was now observing it.

The Emperor had left his pine tree and had ridden to a small hillock north of Essling which gave a good view of the battle. It was there that General Bertrand of the engineers approached and in a low voice gave him the disastrous news that the main bridge (from the right bank to the isle of Lobau) had broken. Upstream, the Austrians had thrown tree trunks into the river as well as boats loaded with stones, some fireboats, some destructive rams. Their repeated attacks had forced a breach of three hundred metres. Nothing more could cross and repairs would take at least forty-eight hours, maybe more. According to the testimony of all present, Napoleon – who often exploded at a poorly executed or misunderstood order – took this blow of fate calmly. As to the consequences, the most wooden-headed NCO could assess them. The section of the army on the left bank – about 50,000 men – was isolated; no more reinforcements and, after an hour or so, no more ammunition. Then massacre and defeat. Napoleon took the only rational decision – retreat.

To keep control when retreating is the most difficult task confronting a commander, one which puts his capacity and imagination to the test. To hold the enemy, repeated counter-attacks were required, but here and now the Austrian artillery was firing constantly, whereas the French were almost out of ammunition.

At one moment it was feared that the Austrians, who had retaken Essling, might cut off the French retreat by getting to the bridgehead from the small bridge linking the left bank and the isle of Lobau, but No: the rifle brigade of the Guard retook Essling, by now no more than a brazier, and held it until the army had retreated, when Napoleon gave the order to evacuate the village.

It was largely thanks to the authority and competence of Marshal Lannes that the retreat did not degenerate into a rout. But on the evacuated left bank were lying 18,000 dead or dying Frenchmen. The Austrians had lost 27,000 men.

Newly arrived from Spain, Lannes had said to the Emperor: 'Sire this war is frightful.' Then at the end of the same conversation: 'Sire, I will do all that Your Majesty commands.' At dawn on 21 May he said to his ADCs while mounting his horse: 'I don't like the look of this business. Besides, whatever the outcome, this will be my last battle.' A presentiment or did he wish to retire? For two days he had commanded the French right wing brilliantly in the Essling sector. At the end of the second day the retreat was going well. Lannes, tired from long hours on horseback, had dismounted and was talking to a brigadadier general named Pouzet. The Austrian artillery fire and musketry was continuing, and suddenly a stray ball struck Pouzet full in the face and killed him outright. Lannes, upset and feeling that he had had enough corpses for one day, wished to distance himself and walked some hundred paces towards Enzerdorf, a village not far from the small branch of the Danube. Here he sat, pensive and sombre, watching the retreating troops. Some officers surrounded him, including General Marbot.

A ricocheting ball hit Lannes legs at the precise point where they were crossed. 'I am wounded,' he said, 'but it is not serious. Give me a hand up.' No question of standing upright. An officer: 'There is an ambulance down there.' He and several others tried to carry the casualty, but this pained him beyond endurance. 'We need a stretcher, or at least a cloak. Hey, grenadiers, what have you got in there?' It was, in fact, the corpse of general Pouzet and Lannes saw it. 'I don't want that cloak, it is covered with my friend's blood.' Finally, the grenadiers brought a stretcher covered in branches. At least half an hour had passed. He was carried to a first-aid post established in the bridgehead of the small branch of the river. Larrey, surgeon in chief, was there; they had been friends since Egypt and Larrey had treated Lannes for other wounds. Nurses pulled off his boots and the surgeon slit his breeches: 'The wound in the right thigh does not look dangerous. But ...' The but was the sight of the left knee, which was dreadful, broken bones, torn ligaments, rupture of the tendons and the popliteal artery. 'We must amputate,' said Larrey. Other surgeons protested, including Yvan: 'It is too warm. Besides, look at the state of the patient.' Larrey felt his pulse; he was unconscious, his face pale, his eyes dull, respiration irregular. 'This was to be one of the most difficult decisions of my life,' Larrey was to write. However, he decided to operate. This was the epoch when, lacking anaesthetics or antiseptics, the surgeons had but one weapon, except for their scalpels: speed. Larrey was a great surgeon; the operation lasted exactly one hundred seconds.

The Emperor arrived as the last sutures were being made. He knelt to embrace his friend, tears in his eyes. The story goes that Lannes' blood smeared the white kersey waistcoat of the Emperor. 'Montebello: do you recognise me?' 'Yes, Sire, you are losing your best friend.' 'No, Lannes, you'll live. Is not that so, Larrey, that you will answer for his recovery?' Naturally, Larrey said Yes and, according to Marbot, Lannes said: 'I shall be happy to serve long both France and Your Majesty.'

Carried to the only house on the isle of Lobau, he spent a quiet night. Next day, he was taken to Ebersdorf in a boat or on a raft (accounts differ). He spent four days there, so calmly that he was thought to be out of danger. Napoleon came to see him every day, accompanied by Berthier. According to Cadet de Gassicourt, then pharmacist in ordinary to the Emperor, ex-lawyer and prolific writer of plays and songs; also according to the valet, Constant, and in a letter from Metternich to his mistress, Countess Wilhelmina de Saxen, Lannes is said to have addressed violent reproaches to the Emperor, saying that he sacrificed uselessly the men who served him best, that his insatiable ambition would be his ruin, etc. The story even went that Lannes had died cursing the Emperor.

Such assertions have, in my view, been demolished by Dr Guy Godlewsky, a meticulous historian, especially in matters touching the health of the Emperor. Having recalled that Cadet de Gassicourt had not been present when the historic conversation was supposed to have taken place, and that none of those present recorded these diatribes and curses, Dr Godlewsky reproduced three photographs in *Souvenir Napoleonien*, no. 297, January 1978, which show that the paragraph stated to report the words described did not appear in the manuscript of *Journey to Austria, Moravia and Bavaria, in the train of the French army during the campaign of 1809*, which manuscript was stated by Cadet de Gassicourt in his *Preliminary Reflections* to have been written in 1812. The paragraph was inserted in the proofs of the book which appeared in 1818. Dr Godlewsky offers three hypotheses for this addition: (1) it was not easy to pass the royal censor in the first years of the Restoration with anything less than an anti-Bonapartist broadside. It therefore is very possible that Cadet de Gassicourt did it in order to obtain approval. Or maybe this gesture had been suggested to him by the police, which amounts to the same thing; (2) that the author had traded it for the Legion of Honour, which he had just received; a far from honourable deal; (3) (which is not incompatible with the first two) that he 'simply inserted the rumours which were current even under the Empire regarding Lannes' diatribe'. As to the origins of the rumour – and of all the rumours in History – one could speculate endlessly.

On the fifth day after being wounded Lannes contracted a septic infection with fever and delirium, which was followed by a general collapse. He died at dawn on 30 May 1809. Napoleon arrived shortly afterwards. Marbot had wished to prevent him from entering the room 'poisoned with putrid miasmas', but the Emperor pushed him aside and embraced his dead friend, and remained with him for more than an hour. Would he have done so if they had quarrelled as reported?

On Napoleon's orders, Larrey, assisted by Cadet de Gassicourt and one Valériaud, embalmed the body for its return to France. The word 'embalm' suggests subtle odours. To embalm a corpse is another matter. Cadet de Gassicourt has recounted the embalming of Lannes' corpse – which took three days – with a plethora of detail over which it were better to draw a veil.

Up and down the Danube, preparations were afoot for the next clash. The Austrian army had been reinforced by troops levied in Moravia, Bohemia and Hungary and all the peasants' horses had been requisitioned. On the left bank, the engineers of the Austrian army constructed redoubts protected by palisades, the gunners installed fixed batteries.

The French had but one obsession – the bridges. On the main section (600 metres), three bridges were to replace the shattered boats: a 60-arch bridge on piles across which three vehicles could pass abreast. Upstream, a second bridge on piles 2.60 metres wide, exclusively for the infantry. Farther still, a pontoon bridge – this, as far as one can make out, was the original bridge, repaired. The army could thus cross the bridges in three columns. At the small branch from the isle of Lobau to the left bank, where there had been but one bridge, there would now be four, the original one and three others, even wider.

To build the bridges, piles had to be sunk on which to place the transverse beams that would support the roadway. The bridges across the small branch were built on large trestles driven into the river bed, four metres apart. The construction of these bridges in the midst of a campaign, more ambitious than any before, took twenty-two days in all. Napoleon spent his days supervising the work. He also spent hours studying from a leafy tree on the isle of Lobau the work that the Austrians were developing on the other bank of the river. This rustic island, wooded, half isolated, was transformed into an industrial and military city 'with workshops bordering the streams, forges, magazines, hospitals'. Notably, ambulances replaced the primitive first-aid posts set up during the two days of the battle of Essling. Other works included entrenchments and batteries – 112 guns on the small branch to protect the crossing. The Guard grenadiers controlled the traffic. The high command anticipated that this time, thanks to the bridges, the army would make an easy crossing. Meanwhile communications between the isle and the right bank were difficult and the men crowded there suffered from hunger and thirst. 'No other water', wrote Grenadier Pils, 'than that of the river on which floated the corpses of men and horses from the two-day battle.' The Austrian sentries posted on the left bank often hailed their

French counterparts, sometimes in French: 'You will soon starve to death on this island; we are collecting picks and shovels to bury you.'

During all these preparations, Napoleon was living in the Schönbrunn, which is to say that he slept there and could be seen there except when he was inspecting the work in progress. As soon as he was away from the dangers and discomforts of his soldiers, the sovereign exacted a protocol and ceremonial as rigid as that at the Tuileries.

Let us watch a person of rank, summoned to the Schönbrunn. Before being ushered into the offices, the visitor must cross the 'waiting-room' , always crowded with officers, chamberlains and functionaries and then pass into the 'duty room' in which the general ADCs kept a twenty-four hour watch and who, in turn, had their own aides-de-camp there also, as well as the staff officers, the Master of the Horse and the pages on duty: all ready to jump to fulfil the least wish of their master.

Let us assume that our visitor had been invited to lunch. He would enter the dining-room immediately behind Napoleon, himself preceded by the 'Palace Prefect', who stood throughout the meal, hat under his arm, behind the Emperor's chair. A none too onerous duty, seeing that no meal lasted more than ten minutes.

Daily at 11 a.m., Napoleon would witness the changing of the Guard battalion in front of the palace. He would be surrounded by some sixty bedizened senior officers. Also watching this spectacle would be numerous Viennese; a slender cordon of gendarmes kept them in place.

In the crowd would be seen French officers who had brought their Viennese women to watch the spectacle; the officers had time on their hands while the bridges were being reconstructed. Vienna has never had the reputation of being a puritanical city. 'Since the French took over the city, and were notable for their liberality, one saw mothers insinuating themselves into the homes of strangers on various pretexts, proposing their daughters, collecting the price and remaining witnesses to their dishonour. Likewise, the working girls took the soldiers to their fathers' homes who, without stopping work, opened the door to the bedroom and politely saluted the lover of the moment. The Jews and the monks managed the intrigues of those more socially elevated.' Testimony which we must accept, taking into account the desire of these Don Juans on campaign to portray themselves as forced into debauch.

In truth, many of their partners were pushed into prostitution by the poverty induced by the war. 'I have seen countesses, baronesses, young and pretty, whose husbands were absent, seeking to exchange their jewels, their diamonds for food and, finally, offering themselves.'

Cadet de Gassicourt mentions a *vivandière* of the Army of Germany washing her linen in the Danube, a pleasant picture to record in the too often brutal annals of the Grande Armée: 'She had an infant at her breast, two other small ones nearby in her unharnessed wagon.' Thirty years of age, with an expressive face, a skirt of coloured cloth, a grey coat, an old felt hat tied with a scarf. 'How you must suffer', said the pharmacist, 'with the burden that you bear and with the fears which it must cause you.' But no, she was not unhappy: 'Why should you think so? I have made my bed and I could not live away from the army. I have made eight campaigns and this one has been the best. I followed the regiment because I loved a sergeant. He was wounded and I took care of him. He gave me a child, I bore it in the ambulance.' Likewise two other brats which the regiment had adopted. During the halts, the grenadiers played with them.

'When the regiment deploys against the enemy, I stay with the rearguard and put my little family in shelter. Once the business is finished, I come out and help the poor weary ones. And she explained how she ran her little business: 'None of my stock has cost me a sou. It all came from the regiment. The old ones set aside a share of the last pillage for me. And it is to these same soldiers that I sell the provisions that they willingly pay for and which they did not trouble to keep or to transport. With the money I earn, I could set up in a town, but I decided to wait until the regiment is disbanded because I would be unhappy if we were separated.'

Farewell, *vivandière*, the guns will soon be sounding again.

Since 2 July his troops on the isle of Lobau had been packed like sardines. Napoleon had decided that the army – 150,000 men with 600 cannon – would debouch on to the left bank on the 4th, and throughout the previous night the munitions wagons had rolled across the bridges ceaselessly.

The two armies –160,000 on the Austrian side – would face each other on the plain from which the Wagram plateau rises for some metres. Archduke Charles would try to flood the French left and cut off the bulk of the French army from the river – we might better say the Napoleonic army, for let us recall that one-third of it was composed of foreigners. A symmetrical manoeuvre would be sketched by the French against the enemy left. As soon as Napoleon was satisfied that his positions on his left were holding, he would deliver the hammer blow to the enemy centre with an enormous battery of one hundred cannon, followed by a mass of infantry and cavalry. At 3 p.m. on 6 July, Charles ordered a retreat.

The 150,000 soldiers of the Army of Germany had certainly never envisaged the above schema of this famous battle which has been studied, analysed, dissected, ten thousand times and more in the military schools of the Western world. For the soldiers, the battle was, like those preceding it, nothing but noise, fury, confusion and suffering, and I am inclined to have reservations concerning any too precise reconstructions, made long after the event. But certain major and confirmed events characterise Wagram, the last great victorious battle of Napoleon's reign.

On 4 July at midday, Napoleon told Masséna that his army corps, posted on the left, must at all costs contain the enemy pressure, since it would be the pivot for an anti-clockwise turning movement by the French centre and right wing. Madelin compares this judiciously to a gigantic scything swing anchored on Masséna's army corps. The Marshal said confidently: 'I will stop the Austrians.' Bravo!, but the day before, his horse having tripped on a root, this ardent warrior had well and truly hurt his thigh. 'I'll have myself carried in a chair,' 'No,' said the Emperor, 'you must use a carriage to go from one division to the next.'

So we see the Duke of Rivoli – so many dukes *in partibus* among these marshals – moving around in a carriage on the battlefield. On the evening of 4 July, after a blood-red sunset, there was a violent and prolonged storm. The troops, crossing the river on the pontoon bridge which had no freeboard, were as soaked as if they had swum across. The thunder drowned out even the noise of the French and Austrian artillery, which was firing continuously. The cuirassiers' horses, frightened by the noise, reared, throwing their riders into the river; goodbye, everything is going to pieces. Berthier ventured to suggest to the Emperor that the attack should be postponed. 'No, another twenty-four hours and we shall have the Archduke Jean on our hands.' The latter was toiling up from Italy with 30,000 men to join Archduke Charles. The French artillery was pounding Enzerdorf where the Austrians were dug-in, one kilometre beyond the small river branch. The garrison of Enzerdorf capitulated shortly afterwards; a good start. The sun rose at 4 o'clock on 5 July 1809. The French troops started to advance on to the plain in good order. The infantry were happy to see that the artillery, rather than themselves, were leading the way; lots of artillery. By 9 o'clock 70,000 men (perhaps more, accounts differ) had been deployed; the artillery was still leading, then two columns of infantry with the cavalry on the wings.

Napoleon rode constantly from one corps to the next, his progress marked by the multi-coloured staff who accompanied him. Austrian cannon-balls were falling all around. The Guard and the cuirassiers were in the rear as reserves. Napoleon stopped his horse for a moment and, through his telescope, saw that the bulk of the enemy was retiring to the plateau of Wagram where no doubt they intended to give battle.

The infantry were reassured to see that Napoleon was staying with them; 'Vive l'Empereur!' each time he passed in front of a battalion. They continued to march under artillery fire, still without making contact with the enemy. The army was still deployed in two lines: front line, Masséna's corps on the left, Oudinot's in the centre, and Davout's on the right; rear line, Bernardotte on the left, Marmont in the centre, the Army of Italy (Eugène and Macdonald) on the right.

Now, here's something new: a mass of white uniforms, many columns of infantry, numerous cannon, still more cavalry advancing eastwards in a move to swamp the French right. In that direction lay the village of Rutzendorf which had been lost. Napoleon, who had seen it, sent an ADC to Oudinot: 'Re-take Rutzendorf.' Order executed.

At the troops' level, it was running through high crops, stopping to fire, running again; much black smoke, white-uniformed cavalry which charged – the terrible flash of sabres! But the French cavalry was also there; and still the cannon-balls from all directions, comrades falling but we must advance. The French artillery were firing and the Austrians were not playing games, either. And suddenly, they were in the village and no more Austrians. From midday to 9 p.m. all the villages on the plain were occupied in succession. All was going well.

Napoleon's turning movement was under way. He intended to cut the enemy force in two by seizing the village of Wagram, thus obtaining a decision by nightfall. 'The attack will be carried out by Bernardotte's Saxons and by the divisions of the Army of Italy under Macdonald, who will lead. Oudinot's corps will act in support. There are two more hours of daylight – that should do it.'

That did not do it! Napoleon was to learn that to march with an army composed of one third of foreigners was plenty.

The attack on Wagram started well. The troops, covered by a mass of artillery, crossed the stream called the Rüssbach under enemy fire and, pushing back the Austrians, gained the plateau. Bernadotte's Saxons on the left were the first to deploy; Macdonald's Italians followed. Seeing on the crest some unfamiliar uniforms, the Italians believed that they were confronted by the Austrians – fire on the enemy! But these were Bernadotte's Saxons. Suddenly under fire from two directions (the Austrians were continuing to fire) the Saxons turned tail and fled. The Italians, still believing them to be Austrians and that they were charging furiously, recoiled and fled in their turn.

The true Austrians, bewildered by this sudden rout, fired into the brown at will. Faced with this shambles, Oudinot was obliged to retire also in order to re-establish a line of resistance. Napoleon gave orders to round up the fleeing troops and to re-establish the front. He was furious. No victory that day.

'I will stay here. Have them put up my tent opposite Aderklaa just behind Oudinot's bivouacs.'

Aderklaa is a village on the edge of the plateau, two kilometres from Wagram. That night, when the Emperor entered the square formed by his Guard, his ADCs could hear him murmuring imprecations against 'the stupidity of Bernadotte'. Bernadotte was in no way responsible for the muddle that had occurred; it was not his fault that he had Saxons to command. It was not

Macdonald's fault that he had Italians to command. But we have already met Bernadotte at Austerlitz and we know that Napoleon did not like him – an old and deep-seated grudge. However, the Emperor did not pass the evening grumbling about the future king of Sweden. He had the next day's operations to think about. To Berthier: 'Send for the corps commanders. And have them build me a fire.'

Although it was June, the nights were cold on this plain of corn and there was not a tree to be seen. The foot servants ran as far as the village of Raschdorf and managed to find some straw and the remains of some doors. Thin smoke rose next to the tent. A famous engraving, 'The Eve of Wagram', shows the Emperor asleep on an old chair, fully dressed and booted, one foot on a plank on which are draped some maps, but, in fact, at 1 a.m., after his meeting with the corps commanders, he entered his tent and slept on his camp bed.

At 4 a.m., gunfire. At first light, the Austrian left wing attacked Davout's corps: 'This clash was the start of the battle of Wagram.' It was a major clash, everywhere black smoke, cannon-balls, swathes of casualties. Through the smoke riders could be seen galloping in all directions. In their midst the Emperor, often arresting all movement and using his telescope, galloping off again, ordering, directing. An ADC said to him: 'Sire, be careful, they are firing on your staff.' 'Sir, in war any accidents can happen.' It is almost impossible to recount any happening to the Grande Armée without mentioning this man. To say that he was the soul of every action is no more than the truth. Say what you will of him, that he was pitiless, cruel, but what cannot be denied is that he was never afraid and he never spared himself.

So far, the results were not too bad: the attack on the left wing had been stopped, the Austrians were retiring on Neusvedel at the foot of the Wagram plateau. Napoleon was reassured to see that even the latest batch of conscripts, these green troops who had received such training as was possible during the long march to the Danube, were fighting well – that is, that despite the enemy fire, they continued to obey their officers who cried unceasingly 'Close Up! Forward damn you!' On the other hand, he considered that the command was stodgy. Lannes was dead and Ney and Soult were in Spain.

At 9 o'clock a messenger announced that on the left wing Masséna's corps was in difficulty – Masséna, the pivot of the grand movement, the handle of the scythe which was to mow down the enemy. The 18,000 men of his corps were up against 60,000 Austrians and he was giving way; if the enemy could turn him, it would be all over. Already, some Austrian regiments, having pushed him back, were marching towards the bridges. Masséna's troops heard the cannon almost behind them, a frightful feeling. General Boulart: 'One did not dare to dwell on the anxiety one felt, but one could read it on the faces of those nearby.'

Napoleon galloped towards the menaced corps. As the Marshal was still unable to mount a horse, his carriage had to remain behind the lines from where he would direct the troops. Or at least that is what the Emperor thought was the case. But no, the carriage was in front, under a hail of fire, repeatedly attacked by the Austrians, as repeatedly saved by the sabres of his staff officers, a third of them killed or wounded. The carriage had a postillion and a coachman in Masséna's livery to drive the four superb horses. Napoleon dismounted and climbed in beside the Marshal. Here is a cameo quite rare in the midst of battle. We have scarcely done more than glance at this man, Masséna.

The Napoleonic era is not so distant from us. Twenty years ago, an octogenarian living in the place Masséna at Nice told me that in the same part of town, his great-grandfather had seen Masséna as a child in a shop in the rue Saint-Jacques, working a wooden machine for making vermicelli.

The future Marshal, Duke of Rivoli, had been orphaned when quite young and had been brought up by uncles and aunts. He was born on 6 May 1758, a Sardinian subject. At thirteen, he had left Nice to seek his fortune in France. At seventeen, illiterate, having drudged as a cabin boy in a merchant ship commanded by another uncle, he enlisted in 1775 in the Royal Italian Regiment in which a cousin was a junior officer, learned to read and write and found his vocation. Corporal, sergeant, warrant officer and adjutant (1792) of the 3rd Battalion of Volunteers of the Var. The Revolution offered promotion to gifted soldiers. On 22 August 1793 André Masséna was general of brigade; on 20 December 1793, a divisional general.

We know that not all his generals and marshals had been life-long admirers of Bonaparte. Under the Consulate, Masséna, previously a divisional commander in the Army of Italy, headed the protests against the Concordat. 'I've done enough for that bastard,' he said of the First Consul. Furious at being obliged to attend a Te Deum at Notre Dame, he had behaved scandalously in creating a disturbance because there were insufficient chairs for the generals. Created Marshal, he said to Thiébault, who was congratulating him, 'We are fourteen!'

With the establishment of the Empire, he dropped his opposition. Only two things obsessed him: glory and money, especially money – he was madly avaricious. Napoleon had to discipline him repeatedly (financially, for it would not do to deprive France of such great military talent) for shameless extortion on the part of this needy orphan who had risen to become Duke of Rivoli.

Now we see Napoleon sitting beside him in a carriage in the midst of a battle. The situation was serious, the artillery was booming, yet the Emperor could not but admire the superb horses, the liveried attendants. These two were civilian servants of Masséna's: 'There are three hundred thousand men on this battlefield,' exclaimed Napoleon, 'but those two men are the bravest of all. We are here to do our duty, but they are risking death without any such compulsion. Splendid!' And, to the coachman and postillion, 'You two are brave men!'

Marbot recalls that, after the battle, the Emperor suggested to Masséna that he give his two servants some monetary reward. Masséna dragged his feet for two months. Finally: 'I will give four hundred francs to each one.' 'Four hundred francs annuity?' questioned one of the household. The Marshal choked: 'Annuity? I would rather see all my ADCs shot and stop a bullet through the arm which had signed the gift of a life annuity of four hundred francs to anyone.' Napoleon, on learning of this, told Masséna that he ought to make the sacrifice nevertheless. The miserly Marshal obeyed reluctantly. But we are getting ahead of our tale and it was on quite different topics that the Emperor was speaking to his Marshal. 'I will defeat these Austrians by piercing their line between Aderklaa and Wagram. But in order to do that, my Guard must retreat no further and must retake the lost terrain. Your objective must be Essling.' 'But, Sire, that would mean marching two leagues with my flank exposed to the enemy.' 'Masséna, Masséna, you will do it notwithstanding. I am leaving for the centre.'

Napoleon was then seen riding a very white horse which distinguished him to the troops before whom he passed ('Vive l'Empereur!') and made him conspicuous to the enemy – he drew fire from all quarters. Bessières received the order to charge with all the cavalry and outflank the Austrians who were exerting pressure on the French left wing. As Bessières moved off a ball hit him in the thigh and he fell, and was thought to be dead. Napoleon asked, 'Who is that who fell?' 'Sire, it was Bessières.' 'Carry on, I haven't time to weep.' Was Napoleon thinking of Lannes and his death? A little later, he sent for news of Bessières. The Marshal was alive, but his leg was paralysed. General Nansouty replaced him. Six regiments of cavalry charged; that is, they advanced at the trot under fire. During this manoeuvre, the enemy artillery killed 1,200 horses and doubtless many of their riders.

At what point did Napoleon conceive of using the artillery as a battering-ram? Well before the battle, no doubt, since the guns had deployed on the left bank before the bulk of the infantry and cavalry and had been ordered to concentrate. But it was necessary to choose the right moment to unleash the thunderbolt. That moment arrived at 11 o'clock – while Masséna was still threatened and the Austrians appeared to be doing none too badly.

There were 102 horse-drawn guns, commanded by General Lauriston, the largest concentration of artillery ever seen on the battlefield at that time. Napoleon ordered General Drouot to guide them, indicating with his sword the position which each battery should take up. They took post at half cannon-shot range.

Let us remember that. The range of field artillery varied greatly according to calibre, but fire was more generally opened at 600 metres. Given Napoleon's intention to strike a devastating blow, the French gunners had to advance to within 300–400 metres from the Austrians, and naturally came under their fire which left a trail of dead and dying men and horses amid the black smoke. Finally, at 11 o'clock the order was received, 'Open Fire!'

The French guns fired 36,000 rounds, using 250 million pounds of powder. The cannonade rolled continuously from one end of the line to the other, and the military chiefs of the time were impressed. Marshal Marmont: 'One can imagine the beauty and majesty of this scene.' Napoleon could see the results through his telescope: Austrian guns knocked out, caissons blown up, brown-clad artillery men cut down as were nearby infantrymen. The scene was becoming more and more visible, the smoke thinning on the Austrian side as their artillery was destroyed.

Napoleon had already ordered that the cavalry be unleashed as soon as the enemy artillery ceased firing. Now they had done so and their infantry were retreating, and a large pocket could be seen developing on their front. The French cavalry threw themselves into it under Nansouty (Bessières being wounded): six mounted regiments, followed by the four regiments of General Saint-Sulpice. The guns, then the cavalry, then the infantry supported by the cavalry. It would be Macdonald who would deliver the decisive blow.

Macdonald, whose Italians had fired on their allies and then decamped? Yes! Napoleon placed confidence in this man and, in addition to the Army of Italy, he would march at the head of Broussier's and Lamarque's divisions to deliver the knock-out blow. Grenadiers and skirmishers would be massed and his infantry would be flanked by Nansouty's cavalry on the left and by that of the Guard on the right. This mass would advance, passing to the left of the artillery.

Jacques Alexandre Macdonald, a descendant of Scottish immigrants, born at Sedan, forty-four years old at the time of Wagram, stood out from other Marshals. By his Nordic face, his absolute abstention from boasting, exuberance and even loquacity. As to his honesty and devotion, they seem fabulous in the light of the standards observed by his glittering colleagues.

After Wagram, Macdonald would be appointed Governor of Styria. The inhabitants, astonished not to be burdened with taxes, and seeing that the Marshal observed a modest way of life, wished to express their thanks. The city of Graz alone offered 200,000 gold francs. 'No thank you. If you feel indebted to me, there is another way to discharge it. Take good care of the sick and wounded that I must leave here temporarily.'

Macdonald had become popular as a result of his campaigns in Germany and Italy under the Republic; he also distinguished himself on the River Trebbia (1799) and in Switzerland (1800). When he led the forces intended to break the Austrian centre at Wagram, he had just emerged from a sentence of five years' disgrace: he had been a friend of Moreau's, who was condemned to two years imprisonment (June 1804) for apparent complicity with the royalists; pardoned, but struck off the strength, Macdonald defended him courageously. Spied upon by the police, harassed, he too, narrowly escaped indictment and found it prudent to retire to his estate at Courcelles and to keep quiet. At the start of the Austrian campaign, Napoleon, rather short of first-class generals, sent him a message: 'Return. I will give you a division responsible for operations in Northern Italy.' A division in a secondary theatre? To the astonishment of the high command, Macdonald in the correct manner, but with equal firmness, replied No. 'All right. Then join me with the Army of Italy.' So that was how we see Macdonald at the head of the assault troops on this famous battlefield. From a self-esteem of sorts, he wore his old uniform as a Republican general.

The hundred-gun battery had driven in the Austrian centre, but the enemy had not been defeated. He still had artillery and it was still inflicting damage. Savary: 'Macdonald closed the ranks as entire files were mowed down and adjusted their dressing as if on the parade ground.' When the Austrian artillery finally ceased firing, squadrons of white-uniformed cavalry arrived at a brisk trot; these were seasoned troops.

We have seen at Friedland the method used by the infantry to resist cavalry charges: a square was formed in the manner which I described. This particular square was enormous and the Austrian cavalry crashed against four walls of fire. Horses fell, the white uniforms crushed the crops. When the charge had been defeated, the squares were opened and columns formed – Forward! Shortly afterwards Macdonald was able to see through a clearing in the smoke that the enemy were retreating in great disorder. Napoleon, eye to his telescope, exclaimed several times, 'What a brave man!' The Emperor saw the Austrians retreating and, according to some accounts, it was at this moment that he said in his 'clear and penetrating voice', 'The battle is won!'

And he dismounted and signed to a page to spread a bearskin on the ground. The Emperor threw himself on it face down. He had slept only two hours the previous night and had carried in his head that day the entire battle plan. The Austrians retreated, but their artillery was still firing. On his bearskin, screened by a pyramid of drums, Napoleon slept the sleep of the dead. But an hour later he was on his feet and as fresh as a daisy.

Masséna on the left wing had stopped the Austrian advance and on the right wing Davout was advancing. Macdonald was also making progress at a walk with bayonets fixed under a hail of musketry and cannon fire which, however, was decreasing. It was now 3 o'clock and the Austrians were retreating on all fronts. The Archduke Charles, fearing to have his communications with Moravia cut, had ordered the retirement An unforeseen incident marked the end of this day. Napoleon had had his tent pitched in the middle of his army. At nightfall, there was suddenly a cry: 'To arms! The enemy is here!" and a huge trampling on the plain, thousands of shadows running towards the Danube. Napoleon was already mounted, buttoning his breeches and looking for his hat and sword. The Guard formed square around the tent and messengers were dispatched for news. Could this be the Archduke Jean with his relieving army? No, false alarm. Some twenty Austrian hussars had strayed behind the French outposts and had been seen by some storekeepers who raised the alarm. The story runs that their cry sowed panic among the 'marauding soldiers' who were going through the pockets of the dead as was then customary. Half an hour later calm had been restored and Napoleon was asleep in his tent. He was to sleep for two hours and was up again at dawn.

Macdonald was also asleep, in a house at Sussenbrismar, when shouts of 'Vive l'Empereur!' awoke him. He got up and, in his own words, 'I saw the Emperor surrounded by my troops whom he was congratulating. He came to me and embraced me cordially saying: "Let's be friends from now on." I replied, "Yes, in life, in death," and I kept my word, though not as far as that, but up to the abdication. The Emperor added, "You have conducted yourself valiantly and have rendered me the greatest service during this campaign. It was to you on the battlefield of your glory that I owe a large part of the achievements of yesterday and so I create you Marshal of France [he used that word instead of Empire] which you have long merited."' Oudinot and Marmont were also promoted Marshals: Berthier, to general surprise, was made Prince of Wagram. Some called him 'the office chief'. Napoleon found him useful and efficient in that role.

According to Lachouque, French losses were 34,000 men, five generals killed and 37 wounded. The Austrians lost 25,000 men plus 12,000 prisoners, seventeen generals disabled. André Castelot: on both sides, more than 50,000 killed or seriously wounded. According to Jean Mistler: French losses, 10,000 killed, 14,000 wounded, of whom 8,000 did not recover. According to Amédée Augustin-Thierry (brother of the famous author of *Tales from Merovingian Times*), French losses, 26,772 killed, wounded or prisoner: Thiry: 'French losses amounted to 66,772 men.' Comparing that with Augustin-Thierry, I assume that one or other figure was misprinted.

To try to number accurately losses in battle has always been very difficult and the figures are only approximate. It is hardly necessary to recall that the dead of Verdun have never been fixed other than to within some 100,000: approximately 300,000–400,000, both French and German. Compared to that, I am told, Wagram was small beer. Yes, but Wagram lasted two days, whereas Verdun (the true battle) lasted some five months. And the relative fire power bears no comparison. Wagram was a superb tactical victory – the last great Napoleonic victory – but was also by the standards of the time a notable butchery.

Among the names of the fallen generals is that of Lasalle, who had shown himself in Spain to be competent, courageous and rigorously honest – 'Amiable

Lasalle' according to Stendhal who could hardly be called a militarist. Antoine Charles Louis de la Salle, the 'de' particle dropped during the Revolution, was born at Metz. The bullet which struck him full in the forehead expunged a mix of qualities rarely found in the same person: youth (general at 31 years) good looks, refinement, athleticism, intelligence, easy going, infinitely brave, while by adroit tactics sparing of his soldiers' blood. Roederer advised him to take care of himself. 'I have lived long enough,' was Lasalle's reply. 'Why do we want to live? To gain honour, to make one's way, to gain a fortune, That is of itself as great a satisfaction as making war. One is in the smoke, the movement, the noise, and when one has made a name for oneself, one can savour the pleasure of having done so. When fortune is gained, one is sure that one's wife and children will want for nothing. All that is enough. I may die tomorrow.' A friend asked him, 'Do you then wish to be killed?' 'My friend, any trooper who is not dead by thirty is a coward and I don't anticipate exceeding that length of time.' He did in fact do so, but only by four years. His wife received his last letter: 'My heart is yours, my blood the Emperor's and my life belongs to honour.'

On Friday 7 July, Napoleon toured the battlefield. The cries of the wounded were a chorus of continuous and agonising misery – as at Austerlitz; but at Wagram the weather was warm. 'In the high corn, one could not see the wounded on the ground, some put their handkerchiefs on their musket barrels and hoisted them up to attract attention.' The medical service was completely swamped; the stretcher-bearers came and went constantly, but they were, as always, pitifully inadequate. Some of the wounded would spend five days there and be found still alive in an insupportable stench, attacked by flies and surrounded by comrades on whom the worms were already at work.

The dead are dead and life goes on. The army pursued the routed Austrians – indolently, because of the extreme heat and the fact that they considered the battle already won. On 10 July, when Napoleon rejoined his troops at Znaim, he saw infantrymen climbing the laden fruit trees, which covered the plain – 'It quenches one's thirst,' they said. At about midday the Archduke Charles asked for an armistice.

'Armistice, while we have them by the throat and can finish them – down with Austria!

These were the Marshals who were protesting: Masséna, Oudinot, Macdonald, Davout. Napoleon had summoned them to his tent to ask their advice. He listened sympathetically. He was aware that he had no reserve, that his soldiers were tired and what would the Tsar do if he pursued the Austrians too far? Perhaps he also gave a thought to the immense cry of agony of the wounded on the battlefield? He closed the debate firmly. 'Enough blood has been shed. Let us make peace.'

IX

SPAIN, 1811
The Guerrillas Will Win

It is 1810 and we have Peace. On the map of Europe, France is huge. Not France, but the Napoleonic empire for, as in the Grande Armée, there is some of everything in it. Incorporated are Belgium, Holland, large tracts of Germany and Italy. The Confederation of the Rhine is a far-flung protectorate stretching from Prussia and Poland to the frontiers of Russia.

Over this enormous empire reigns a despot. Before him all tremble, including his family, gorged with honours. André Castelot has recounted how one day Napoleon insulted all his relations: 'Lucien is an ingrate, Joseph a Sardanapalus, Louis a basket-case, Jérôme a rascal. Then, describing a circle with his hand: 'As for you, ladies, you know what you are.' Nobody flinched; nobody flinched in France, where the lustre of the era tended to blind people to the fact that they were living in a police state.

Decrees of 1810 authorised only one newspaper in each department and four in Paris, of which one, the *Journal de l'Empire*, had been wrenched from its owners and was now managed by the minister of police. A part of each branch of the administration was subordinated to the police. Fouché, hostile to the Austrian marriage, had been replaced by Savary and, for extra security (Fouché had too much power) Napoleon had created, outside the police ministry, special police sections in each of the ministries of foreign affairs, interior, finance, war, the city of Paris, plus a private force whose agents served him directly. Opponents and malcontents spoke in whispers, for in the state prisons at Vincennes, Mont St-Michel, Joux, Lourdes, the Château d'If were men who had been put there without trial.

Nevertheless, on 20 March 1811, when the cannon began to fire a salute, 'the capital held its breath'. If Marie-Louise bore a daughter, twenty-one guns, if a son, one hundred and one. At the twenty-second round, people embraced in the streets and throughout France as the news spread men shouted hurrahs. The French – like some other peoples – had always preferred sovereigns who kept them on a short rein, leaving them souvenirs of glory and their eyes with which to weep. In the ranks of the Grande Armée, the repudiation of Josephine had been very unpopular. But the grumblers had wet eyes at the birth of the King of Rome.

Where were they, these hundreds of thousands of soldiers? Scattered around Europe; many in barracks in France. Peace was not a reality and reigned only on the continent, aside from Spain, since Britain still said 'No!' So, limited leave for the troops. Did this provoke protests? Nothing serious. Captain Tascher: 'For the first time in many years, the soldiers heard talk of leave and retirement but, difficult to believe, the desire no longer existed in most of them. Time, absence, changes in folk-ways, had broken or loosened the ties which had bound them to their families and the surroundings of their childhood. And as men must find some anchor, habit had formed for them a new family, their comrades replacing the originals. Few men had admitted to wishing to take off their uniform.' Many others have confirmed this. 'I am a soldier for life,' the soldier Duchesne wrote to his parents. 'If I was offered release I would not take it.' The poverty and insecurity of so many country-dwellers explains this preference for guaranteed meals. The mass of occupying troops in Germany and Europe no longer yearned for their barracks in France, even though the officers disliked the idea of not being allowed to pillage and had to rely on their salary, insufficient and always paid late. Commandant Coudroux, serving in the army of occupation in Germany: 'With ready money, all would be well. The officers are in general fairly economical in this regiment; but I do not know one who has well-lined pockets. 150 francs does not go far with a captain.'

But there was one country to which no soldier wished to be sent, and that was Spain. Because Napoleon was not there; even the marshals and generals who were filling their pockets were not really happy, because only close to the Sun-Emperor could one aspire to the highest distinctions. The rancour of those exiles sharpened their disputes with others even more. The rank and file found the Emperor's absence demoralising; they fretted at not being able to see him, even though they had often detested him in the past.

During this period of more than three years of peace, Napoleon could have returned to Spain ('when I am not there, they commit all sorts of follies'), but his divorce and remarriage had engrossed him, as had the joys of parenthood. And the business in Spain displeased him. To tarnish his glory in a country where nothing transpired logically, according to his idea of logic – definitely not. It is pointless to imagine what might have happened if he had returned to Spain; one can only record the result of his absence – mistrust among the senior officers, each one intent on extorting the greatest profit. We must here cast a glance backwards.

After Junot had capitulated (honourably) in Portugal and his troops had been repatriated, the British invaders had marched into Spain. Other French troops – just over one-third of the 190,000 Napoleon had left in Spain – had then marched into Portugal under the orders of Soult and Victor. On 29 March 1809 Soult had taken Oporto without much difficulty. And there, without warning, he had been seized with the same giddy megalomania as had possessed Murat: why not a king's crown on his head? 'In the relaxed climate which we enjoyed after taking Oporto,' wrote General Thirion, 'the Duke of Dalmatia was engaged in two pursuits: to carve out a kingdom – already in his acts and decrees, he was calling himself Nicholas I; secondly to increase his treasury by acquiring diamonds and items such as pictures, statues of the Virgin, saints, angels and archangels – any saints, provided they were cast in precious metal, would find a place in his wagons.' Many officers, including Generals Loison, Merle, Thomières and Marmet, state that they had heard Soult addressed by the Portuguese as 'Sire' and 'Majesty' at receptions given by him.

Napoleon's personal police were active in his armies and reported everything to him. He was resigned to the depredations of the marshals and generals, but he was displeased by those who coveted thrones without his permission. To Daru: 'Have you seen that that prize idiot, Soult, wants to make himself king of Portugal?' Soult received an admonitory letter which ended: 'The esteem which I have for you and the recollection of the services which you have rendered me at Austerlitz and elsewhere have persuaded me. I will forget the past. I hope you will serve as is customary and I appoint you major-general of my Army of Spain.' In other words, Soult was to oversee everything for Napoleon; military capacity counted more than anything else.

The Marshal's subordinate officers found him increasingly eccentric, so much so that they formed a conspiracy against him. They chose a Captain Argenson of the 18th Dragoons: 'You will go in secret to the English general and invite him to march on Oporto to rid us of this madman.' Wellesley was that English general, London having restored his command, and he marched on Oporto. He knew that Victor was coming down the valley of the Tagus, but he regarded Soult – mad or not – as the more dangerous adversary. On 11 May 1809, 20,000 redcoats reached the approaches to Oporto on the left bank of the Douro. Soult had the means to resist, but through lack of vigilance, or the treason of the conspirators, he remained unaware of the presence of the British until they had already seized part of the town. The enemy found his dinner untouched on the table. Sword in hand, with an escort of chasseurs, he cut a way to safety, northwards, followed by his entire army, 'abandoning the sick and wounded to the generosity of the British, who were at our heels, while the peasants harassed our flanks and picked off the stragglers. We replied by shooting all who fell into our hands and by burning the villages. The march of our columns was marked by clouds of smoke.'

In the French armies, only a tiny fraction of the troops, 45 per cent of whom were foreigners, had ever seen a map of Iberia or even knew which country they were in; the names of the towns were no more than sounds to them. Ney arrived at Lugo in Galicia (80 kilometres east of Compostella) with reinforcements. 'The orders from Paris', he told Soult, were 'to chase the British from Galicia. I will march on Vigo.' Soult said, 'I shall march on Zamora.' That was in the direction of Madrid, but, he added, 'I will join you with reinforcements.' Ney waited for him in vain, then retreated to Astorga, also in the direction of Madrid. On the way he wrote to King Joseph letters full of complaints about Soult.

Wellesley was also having difficulties. As liberator of Portugal, he had asked the *junta* at Seville for the command of all the armies in the peninsula. The reply was negative: the Spanish generals did not wish to serve under foreign command and the populace only accepted help from the British reluctantly – the French were the sons of Satan, but the British were heretics, also destined for hell. Wellesley would find it difficult to co-ordinate his operations with those of the Spanish generals. However, on 23 July 1809, 25,000 British and 35,000 Spanish troops arrived together in front of Talavera de la Reina, 70 kilometres to the west of Toledo. Talavera lies in the middle of a plain, bordered by hills to the west and planted with olive trees and vines. King Joseph Bonaparte, alerted to the threat to his capital, had recalled all troops that could arrive in time – 22,000 men under Marshal Victor, 17,000 under General Sébastiani. Joseph himself arrived with his guard and two regiments of Desolle's division. It was understood that Soult would come down from the north with the army that had fought (*sic*) in Portugal, regrouping at Plasencia (110 kilometres west of Talavera) and then joining in the action. He advanced slowly, his regiments trailing wagon-loads of provisions, booty and women.

Victor on his own initiative launched an attack late on 27 July. The cannon rumbled under a cloudless sky; as the black smoke spread, the infantry of the 16th Regiment charged with the bayonet – that is to say, these soldiers, bent under the weight of their 30kg packs, advanced slowly along the rows of vines, bayonets fixed and without firing, facing the British volleys. These poor devils, who had seen it all, obeyed orders with a sort of fatalistic automatism. Die here or elsewhere, what did it matter? And better to die on the battlefield than be crucified by the guerrillas. The enemy retreated and it looked as though a decision might follow, but night was falling and fighting ceased.

Next day, the 28th, the same scorching heat. Victor had in mind the enforced check to his offensive of the night before. 'We must launch a general attack,' he told Joseph. 'If IV Corps attacks the centre and right of the enemy, I will roll up the left and turn it.' 'No,' said Joseph, 'wait for Soult before making a general attack.' Just at that moment a message arrived from Soult: 'I cannot regroup my army at Plasencia before 3–5 August.' 'But they may get reinforcements from Toledo,' said the king. 'We should attack before they arrive.'

Orders were issued and the troops deployed. At 2 p.m. all was ready. Once more, flanked by the troops of artillery bumping over the furrows, the soldier-porters advanced slowly under the scorching sun. Nothing went right. The leading battalions were trapped between the British left and the Spanish right. Few troops will stand firm against assaults from two sides simultaneously; that is an axiom of tactics; retreat was necessary and some artillery was abandoned. Shortly afterwards, General Lapisse was mortally wounded and the troops retreated. King Joseph sent a message to Sébastiani: 'Suspend your attack and remain on the ground you occupy.'

The British had ceased to advance. The two armies were face to face at a half cannon-shot, but neither opened fire. The dry grass and brush had caught fire and the cries and groans of the wounded surrounded by the fires could be heard. Night fell. The brush fires spread more than two leagues, their light punctuated by yellow geysers as artillery caissons exploded.

King Joseph had retired within his guard (following the example of his illustrious brother) with the intention, he said, of renewing the fight next day. At 10 p.m. some officers of I Corps (Victor) came to report that the corps was turned on its right. This was rectified at dawn next day and the corps was withdrawn to Cazalegas along the line of the mountains; Sébastiani announced that, in consequence, he too must retire. Joseph had to order a general retreat.

The movement went off in good order without interference from the British who had lost 5,000 men including two generals. The Spanish had lost 3,000 killed and the French 6,000. We can read in Marshal Jourdan's *Mémoires* that Victor and General Sébastiani exchanged insults, each accusing the other of having forced them to retreat by abandoning their position.

The British government hailed Talavera as a great victory and, shortly afterwards, Wellesley was created lord Wellington, Duke of Talavera. Such honours did not go to his head. Fearing (as always the British do) to see his communications with the sea cut off, he decided to retire to the south-west and re-enter Portugal with his army.

To the Spaniards, Talavera was a Spanish victory: 'Even without the English, we would have won.' Hundreds of thousands of Spaniards repeated this boast. Pushed from behind, the Seville *junta* (when speaking of it, the Spaniards referred to it as 'his Majesty') raised before the autumn another army of 50,000 men – On to Madrid!

On 18 November, General Don Juan Carlos de Areizaga had stationed himself and his staff in the belfry of the little church of Ocaña (12 kilometres south-west of Aranjuez, only 60 kilometres from Madrid). 'From here, we will have a good view of the battle.'

The battle was to be joined on a flat expanse of country between the *junta's* army and 30,000 men commanded by King Joseph, 'assisted' by Marshals Soult and Mortier and General Sébastiani. Areizaga lit a cigar: 'Gentlemen, after Talavera, we have no grounds for anxiety.' His staff made no comment; what they could see was in no way reassuring as the first cannon smoke dissipated. Facing a charge of the French cavalry, the first Spanish battalions, instead of forming square, broke and began to flee as if a wind had blown them away. Once again, one saw the smoke of the French artillery, the infantry advancing – not too quickly – other Spanish battalions in flight and yet others allowing themselves to be surrounded and taken prisoner. In short, for the Spaniards the battle of Ocaña was a ghastly defeat: 5,000 casualties, more than 13,000 men taken prisoner, 50 cannon, 30 standards, munitions and baggage lost.

The French soldiers who were victorious at Ocaña had much to avenge. They couldn't forget the great number of comrades massacred, martyred, and looked at their prisoners with no friendly eye. King Joseph harangued them: 'My good friends, spare these poor Spaniards. They will one day be your brothers in arms!'

This was a bit much, but they obeyed – grumbling. To assuage themselves, they pillaged Aranjuez en route for Madrid, wrecking the palace, burning in one night 500,000 quintals of quinquina, and throwing furniture and pianos into the streets: 'The twanging of the breaking strings amused them.'

Each time that a French victory was proclaimed in Madrid, the Spaniards said: 'It's a lie!' To convince them of the victory of Ocaña, Joseph had the 13,000 prisoners marched through the capital – the Madrileños closed their shutters. To show that he was king of all Spaniards, Joseph released almost all the prisoners, thus gaining some applause. 'I've got them, they recognise me! I will now go into Andalusia. The Seville *junta* will recognise me as has Madrid. The arms will fall from the insurgents' hands and we shall have peace.' The announcement of the liberation of the prisoners had made Napoleon roar: 'When I see this sort of conduct I ask: Is this treason or foolishness?' When Joseph confided his noble dream – to win over the *junta* – he first said No, then agreed but imposed conditions: 'Joseph can march into Andalusia, but with Soult as mentor. Meanwhile, Masséna is to attack Wellington in Portugal. The two Marshals are to co-ordinate their movements and the peninsula will be swept clean.'

January 1810. Joseph left Madrid in great style at the head of a fine army. With him were ministers, chamberlains, courtiers and women in a cortège of gleaming coaches. 'My object is not to obtain submission by force, but to dispel illusions. I will arrive at a union of hearts.'

The astonishing thing is that this succeeded. The march into Andalusia was a military parade in the course of which one could almost count the number of shots – less than two hundred dead. Most astonishing was this: at Cordova – Cordova, where we saw the worst and which still bore the scars – Joseph was welcomed by young girls bearing flowers. It was winter, but the sun shone marvellously and the orange trees were fragrant. A cathedral (an ancient mosque) celebration with chants and incense and the chapter saluting 'José

Primero'. On leaving, vivats, bells, cannon – but these were salutes and the soldiers wondered if they were dreaming.

Amid the plaudits of the crowd, the bishop handed Joseph two eagles taken at Baylen and deposited *ex voto* in the cathedral. This was on 27 January 1810, eighteen months after the atrocious and unforgettable sack of the city. Joseph addressed the crowd: 'Use your intelligence; it will show you that French soldiers are your friends ready to defend you. There is yet time. Rally around me. Let this day unfold for Spain a new life of glory and happiness.'

Cheers, and the historic walkabout continued. Grenada, then Malaga were occupied without difficulty by Sébastiani's corps, while the bulk of the army moved towards Seville. Thirty-five kilometres short of the city, at Carmona, Joseph called a council of war.

'Instead of attacking Seville, which seems disposed to resist, I think that it would be better to march straight to Cadiz, which, it happens, is undefended. We had best take the port before the British get the idea of doing so from the sea. The Seville *junta* will find itself isolated and that much more disposed to conciliation. Most of the council agreed, but Soult's voice was heard: 'Seville must first be taken. Once we have it, I will answer for Cadiz.' To say No to the mentor must not be thought of, so Joseph gave way. The army, rather than swerving towards Cadiz, kept straight on to Seville.

There is rarely complete agreement in temporary governments. In January 1810, Seville was in ferment. There was even a form of terrorism following a popular declaration against the *junta*, accused by some of feebleness, by others of rigour. A Capuchin revolutionary had just had the prisons opened, the mob had sacked the arsenal and a new *junta*, 'The supreme national *Junta*', had been elected by acclamation, the members of the old *junta* fleeing towards Cadiz. 'The French are coming!' This cry provoked a new and farcical upheaval, the masters of yesterday fleeing in their turn to Cadiz – no more *junta*. On 31 January 1810 Joseph's troops, arriving at the city walls, discovered a strange scene. The rooftops were black with men and women and even some children brandishing weapons and shouting. Greetings? No, insults. Resistance – a fight for honour? No. Not a shot fired! This manifestation of Andalusian humour remains incomprehensible, for next day at the first ultimatum, the city opened its gates. Joseph made a triumphal entry and, as at Cordova, was censed by canons and, again as at Cordova, was presented with trophies of Baylen. And a few days later each of his appearances was applauded. The Sevillaños had had enough of the insurgents and the fanatics.

Meanwhile, Cadiz was fortifying itself, reinforced by fresh troops; a British squadron blocked the harbour entrance. Soult was to send Victor to invest the town, but without stressing any urgency.

Joseph had decided to make a tour of Andalusia, his peaceful conquest. And Soult preferred Andalusia to anywhere; he lived in a magnificent palace, giving banquets and balls. On Sundays his bodyguard in full dress lined the streets between the palace and the cathedral, where he heard Mass surrounded by the civil authorities. No royal title, since Napoleon had forbidden it, but 'the Marshal appeared to be more the monarch of the kingdom of Andalusia, rather than a simple lieutenant of the Emperor, according to Apolinaire Fée (the army pharmacist) in his *Souvenirs of the War in Spain*. No monarch had ever surrounded himself with more majesty, no court was ever more deferential than his. His entire staff courted a smile, or just a look, which he distributed with studied dignity. Aping the Emperor's style, he cultivated sober gestures and words.'

This pseudo-monarch had not lost his taste for the arts. His choice now ran to the works of Murillo which he 'collected', that is to say, he stole them from the churches of Seville. After the Empire, he was to sell to the Restoration government the famous 'Virgin in the Blue Mantle', which hung in the Louvre until 1941, when Marshal Pétain returned it to Spain.

'This was to be a strange tale,' wrote Lucas-Dubreton, 'this business of the works of the old masters of Spain, Flanders, Italy, falling victim to the rapacity of the warriors of the Empire. Murat had a taste for Correggio and confiscated almost all his works, in particular the "School for Love" which had belonged to the Duke of Alba. Soult collected Murillos and the Rubens which hung in the Dominican monastery in the village of Alcarrica; in Toledo, el Greco only escaped because his works appeared strange and Gothic. Raphaels were looted from the Escorial.'

Other senior soldiers preferred treasures more easily converted to cash – pyxes, chalices, statues which, melted down into ingots, purchased elegant houses in Paris. Still others made money more directly by taxing for a while the provinces over which they reigned. Ney milked Avila so thoroughly that Madrid could no longer exact the smallest sum from there. Yet others requisitioned the crops and sold them to the supply service.

Underlying this rapacity from on high, minor racketeering flourished. A Spanish prisoner who could pay plenty could be sent home rather than taken to France; one notable, taken hostage against exaction from his village, paid for his release. Everything had its price. The petty thieves and extortioners at the bottom of the scale said: 'We have no choice, our salary is late,' and this was often the case. But the biggest depredations were at the top. 'Sire,' wrote Joseph to Napoleon, 'for the sake of the ties between France and Spain, recall Loison, Kellermann, Thouvenot. These men are costing us a fortune.' Kellermann, according to Napoleon himself, was the champion of dishonesty. Joseph regarded as honest Suchet, who certainly was (we will meet him later); Mortier,

Reynier and even Soult! He doubtless wished to deal gently with his mentor. He gave the concession for army equipment to a bankrupt friend of Soult's.

At Grenada, Sébastiani showed himself a to be a great lover of sacred art. Rumour had it that he had in his train two wet-nurses whose milk he found to be a comforting drink. Some witnesses and writers doubtless blackened the picture here and there, envy often nourishing their indignation, but Napoleon's final and laconic judgement was grave: 'Of all the generals who were in Spain, a certain number should be arrested and hanged.' To be fair, one should recall the fact most of these senior officers displayed on the battlefield personal courage quite rare at that level. No war fosters the development of virtues other than courage, and in Spain the moral climate was of the lowest. Long after the French had departed, the resentment of the troops could be detected from the semi-effaced inscription on the walls of Burgos, Toledo, Valladolid, Badajoz and Salamanca:

'SPAIN
GENERALS' FORTUNE
OFFICERS' RUIN
SOLDIERS' DEATH'.

We last saw Joseph visiting Andalusia. Napoleon, dissatisfied at seeing (among other things) a resistant *junta* in Cadiz, suddenly decreed a new organisation of the occupying forces which transferred the northern provinces of Spain to direct French control. Joseph, furious at not having been consulted, returned to Madrid.

The commanders of the army corps charged with ejecting the British from Portugal were Ney, Junot and Reynier, whose 50,000 men were all under the supreme command of Masséna. Napoleon used to call Masséna 'the child of victory'. 'He has talent and luck.' Once again, the interminable procession of infantry, artillery and supply wagons wound its way along the road from Salamanca to Ciudad Rodrigo, which was broken up and gouged by dry ruts. At the beginning of June 1810 it was hot. I have a fond recollection of arriving at Ciudad Rodrigo at dusk under an immense sky gently illuminated, of gilded houses within its ramparts, the coolness and the quiet of the *parador* (inn). In 1810, officers considered this fortified city austere. 'Officers out of favour at court were sent there,' was frequently heard at Madrid. The governor, Don Andres de Herrasti, was an old gentleman with perfect manners. When Ney, personally tasked with clearing Ciudad Rodrigo, sent him a first ultimatum, he replied: 'I have sworn to defend this city to the last drop of my blood and I intend to keep my word.' A siege was unavoidable. The inhabitants, counting on the British to rescue them promptly, withstood the bombardments with great courage and unity.

On the besiegers' side, however, there were daily quarrels. Ney was furious at being subordinated to Masséna. 'He's an old dolt, worn out by his mistress.' At merely fifty-five, it was difficult to recognise the child of victory. On his arrival at army HQ, at Valladolid, the generals who welcomed him found him aged and slowed. They were surprised to see sitting beside him in his carriage a young officer of dragoons, decorated with the Legion of Honour, with delicate features and a figure anything but masculine. 'My aide-de-camp.' This was his mistress, Madame Leberton, who had left her husband, a captain of dragoons, to follow the Marshal. She always rode at his side, he saw everything through her eyes. The soldiers said without envy, 'Masséna's bird!' She had suborned Masséna to the point where, if she felt tired, he halted the entire army. It destroyed his authority and under the walls of Ciudad Rodrigo his staff fought with one another like Kilkenny cats.

The sappers and the gunners did their duty, the city was invested more and more closely, bombarded more and more heavily, and still the British did not appear. On 9 July the governor had the white flag hoisted. In civilian clothes, he climbed the shattered ramparts: 'Please forgive my being dressed thus and unable to surrender my sword to you.' 'Governor, you have made too good a use of it to have it taken from you.'

All the officers were permitted to keep their swords, their horses and baggage; the soldiers, their packs and equipment. The city, which had stubbornly resisted, was not subjected to tribute, pillage or disorder, an unparalleled exception in the chronicle of the Spanish war.

The French army marched in the direction of Coimbra. On learning that Wellington was retiring before their advance, the campaign seemed to be off to a good start. Masséna: 'We are sixty thousand and Wellington has no more than 25,000 redcoats.' This omitted the 40,000 men of the Portuguese army, courageous, indefatigable, and the *ordenenzas* – a ferocious militia of guerrillas. Both knew the country, whereas the French were groping their way forward with only one map for the entire army, and that dating from 1778 and full of errors. 'We requisitioned a peasant each morning as a guide. We were obliged to execute him in the evening, for we were sure that he would inform the enemy if we set him free.'

On 25 September 1810, the army arrived at the foot of a steep chain of granitic mountains, some 100 metres in height. 'That is the Sierra d'Alcoba,' said the guide. He added that the Anglo-Portuguese had fortified the monastery of Busaco which could be seen at the summit of the cliff. 'We'll attack at dawn the day after tomorrow,' said Masséna. 'Frontally?' asked several officers. 'Naturally, why not?' It was necessary to use steep goat tracks. Hardly had the first assault troops gained the summit than they received a withering blast of canister full in the face. The survivors climbed over the dead and also fell, and so it went. The epitome of a mindless assault. At 9 o'clock they had to call off the assault and come down again.

Masséna went through the camp trying to maintain morale. 'Bravo, that's the way to attack the enemy!' That provoked sotto voce murmurs and a Piedmontese soldier shouted that it was an attack of *coglioni*. Many officers thought said that the army should bypass the position, and next day another guide led them by a route which did just that. The frontal attack had cost 4,000 dead.

Coimbra was occupied without difficulty. Masséna decided to leave the wounded at the convent of Sainte-Claire – the army must continue towards the Tagus and Lisbon – 'A detachment will suffice for their protection.' Eighty wounded were left behind. The British were not far off and retook the city a few days later. The Portuguese militia immediately massacred all the wounded.

Wellington retreated slowly towards Lisbon. He was sure that reinforcements were on the way by sea. He left behind him an empty countryside, deliberately ruined. The inhabitants were ordered to destroy their crops and to leave with their cattle, destroying bridges and mills as they went. The Portuguese militia enforced these orders. The French army, once its provisions had been consumed, faced famine. The troops said that this re-conquest was worse than a retreat. In barracks, shots were exchanged between one corps and another over a few sacks of bread or potatoes. Masséna still tried to encourage his troops: 'Forward! We'll have them!'

One day, the scouts reported that the British had ceased to retreat. But at the same time there came an unpleasant surprise: in the space of ten months Wellington had had constructed on the heights of Torres Vedras, covering Lisbon, a fortified line – 45 kilometres of defences, including 32 redoubts. Masséna and his subordinates had been totally unaware of them. This was in October 1810. 'We go into winter quarters,' ordered Masséna. 'Time works for us. The British and Portuguese will be rent by quarrels.'

The two armies were to remain face-to-face until March 1811. The British, well-fed from Lisbon, were comfortable enough; their officers rode on horseback in front of the French lines. Soon came the rain and the cold and both sides stayed close to home. But the French were suffering increasingly from hunger.

Groups of soldiers rummaged through abandoned villages, often finding hidden provisions. One of these parties took up residence in a neighbouring convent, owing allegiance only to their chief, a sergeant with a capacity for organisation, nicknamed Marshal Chaudron, because of the provisions which he produced for his followers. The latter also rounded up those girls and women who had imprudently remained in the region; the convent became a liberty hall. Deserters from the British, Portuguese and French armies found their way to 'Marshal' Chaudron's band. Masséna decided that this was setting a deplorable example and sent word to Chaudron that he must dissolve his troop. Fire was opened on the messengers. A veritable expedition had to be mounted to attack the convent. Chaudron was shot, as were several of his lieutenants.

Throughout Spain the war dragged on. Between campaigns, officers and men led a mostly dull garrison life. Each general governing a province assembled a little court, somnolent and riddled with intrigues. If the weather were not too hot, they would drive out with the ladies for a country picnic. Occasionally, in the midst of dinner under the trees, shots would suddenly ring out and the air would be full of bullets – the guerrillas – everyone would lie down flat.

The officers played a great deal and not just at cards. As well as the prostitutes, the roulette kings followed the troops, setting up shop in cafes where the gamblers congregated. Spaniards mingled with the officers and even priests could be seen, poorly disguised as civilians; the demon of chance dominated all of them.

Meetings in the Masonic lodges provided another distraction. There were lodges for officers, others for NCOs and, for the women, 'lodges of adoption'. Many were installed in the palaces of the Inquisition, the ritual tests and initiations being held in abandoned dungeons, where the friends of enlightenment could inspect with horror the instruments of torture. At Madrid, there was a lodge of the Scottish rite, the Estrella, placed under the high protection of King Joseph who, unable to preside in person, delegated to one of his aides-de-camp the duties of Grand Master.

I have already mentioned those women who made available to all that most widespread and universally appreciated of pastimes. What I have not so far mentioned was that during the attacks and the pillaging of the towns, innumerable nuns were raped before being killed; others, when things were quiet, fulfilled for the occupying officers and soldiers the role of ardent and gifted mistresses. One should recall that many of these girls – like many in France and elsewhere – had been forced into a religious order, pushed into convents by their families; for example, the youngest daughters of poor families who had failed to find a husband of their rank or who had affronted the authorities by some indiscretion. To assure calm in their establishments, many superiors had closed their eyes to illicit love affairs. Long before the war, they had likewise had to ignore the activities of certain priests and monks who were directors of the consciences of their young nuns.

In every province in Spain, even when the war was static, there was one unceasing activity – the guerrillas. Napoleon had developed a great dislike of these people whose activities he compared to those of smugglers. 'It is from laziness and not from bravado that the Spanish peasant prefers the dangers of smuggling and the ambushes on the highways to the fatigues of farming. The Spanish peasants have taken advantage of the situation to adopt this nomadic life which is much to their taste and which mitigates their poverty. It has no connection with patriotism.' None of the soldiers who fought in Spain has endorsed this judgement. The guerrilla movement against the armies of Napoleon drew its force from the most profound and powerful feelings, both patriotic and religious, of a people convinced that their vocation and historic mission was to rid their native land of the infidel. Napoleon had replaced Mahomet. 'The inhabitants of the occupied provinces', one can read in an order from the Seville *junta* dated 17 April 1809, 'may arm themselves, even with forbidden arms, to attack on every occasion that presents itself, French soldiers, both individually and in groups.' The popular resistance bands were auxiliary to the regular armies, but had the approval of the high authorities. It was a national service; the widows and orphans of guerrillas killed during operations or dying from wounds received a pension. The authorities of towns and villages were required to furnish the guerrillas with food and help, 'always with the utmost precautions'. The effectiveness of the guerrillas quickly became apparent in their control of the lines of communication of the army of occupation. Couriers were seized less than a kilometre from their points of departure and their dispatches delivered to the Spanish or British authorities (the latter paid better). After a month, Joseph never knew whether a letter sent by him to his illustrious brother had reached Bayonne or not. But he read in the Cadiz *Gazette* (sent to Madrid by a French spy) the gist of one of his conversations with one of his ministers! When a French column entered a town, its commander would send for the mayor: 'I need one thousand rations of food and one hundred of forage.' 'Mr Officer, I know how many rations you need. I will have delivered to you one hundred and eighty rations of food and fifty of forage.' This would be the exact strength of the column in men and horses.

The French command soon learned that the guerrillas were not content just to control their communications; the courier from Valladolid to Salamanca was found murdered and nailed to the door of the church at Tordesillas. The situation got worse. General Foy, who had travelled to France with an escort of 60 men, narrowly escaped capture by guerrillas in the defile of Pancorbo. Agile and determined, he had jumped from his carriage, crossed a stream and, assisted by some of his men, managed to climb the bank opposite while the guerrillas were ransacking his coach. The escort lost 25 men.

The staffs became convinced that any journey carried a 50 per cent risk of death or capture, and the custom began whereby an officer leaving on a journey first settled his gambling debts. The guerrillas came from all walks of life, from the ex-bandit sought by the police in his own country and for whom resistance provided a moral alibi (he was killing and pillaging from patriotism), to the desperado whose wife had been violated by the invader. Religious orders were well represented. Fray Luca Raphael, a Franciscan whose father had been shot, boasted of having killed 600 Frenchmen with his own hands. Near Valladolid three monks captured a sutler and his wife. They killed the man and took the woman to their little monastery – situated inside Valladolid, even though it was under French occupation. For weeks, the monks' prisoner could hear soldiers passing in the street speaking French, but she was closely guarded. Finally, she escaped and took refuge in a French outpost. Her ravishers were arrested and condemned to death; the hangman, having refused to execute the monks, was replaced by French soldiers.

Occasionally, during a fight with the guerrillas, an unmistakably French voice would be heard in the Spanish band: 'Is General So-and-So still as much of a robber as before? And are you still dying of hunger?' This would be one of Napoleon's soldiers who, disillusioned by poverty and insecurity, had deserted and joined the bandits. And not only Frenchmen, but Poles, Italians, Dutch deserted. In one of these bands, which the Spaniards called a *cuadrilla*, Urquijo counted 10 Spaniards and 90 foreigners – Poles, Italians, Dutch, French. The procedure for deserting was simple: merely report to an outpost with your shako on the point of the bayonet. Another hardly credible fact, British deserters were seen in the *cuadrilla*s. There is no limit to the taste for adventure.

The guerrillas often mixed with the civilian population. They wore no uniform and looked like poor peasants: a tall, pointed felt hat, rough wool shirt, belted black breeches of leather or velvet, open at the knee, espadrilles – see Goya's paintings and drawings. On operations, the guerrillas also wore a cartridge belt and often, from bravado, some part of the Napoleonic uniform – scarlet woollen breeches, hussar's pelisse, busby with plume – all esteemed as trophies.

Some guerrillas shunned these disparate garbs and wore brown uniforms with red revers for infantry, green and blue for cavalry. These formed a part of the cuadrilla of Juan Martin Diez, the Empecinado, the 'Grabber', as a kind of parallel army and would number some 6,000. Diez, who had joined a cavalry regiment in 1792 during the war against France, had raised after the invasion of Spain a band which operated as guerrillas in the districts of Aranda and Segovia. Several times captured, he escaped, and became a folk-hero, but his reputation rested upon a hundred cruel exploits. He recruited the peasants, using reassuring language: 'My friends, I have never lost a battle. When the French press too hard, I retire with your children to keep them safe. The French wear themselves out pursuing me.'

The most implacable enemy of Juan Martin Diez was General Hugo, father of Victor. This 'hero with the so gentle smile' went so far as to disguise himself as a Spanish officer and spied on Diez in his own camp – without much success, it must be admitted. But he finally defeated the celebrated guerrillas in uniform at Cifuentes in September 1810 and near Alcocer in July 1811.

This notorious *cuadrilla* committed several memorable atrocities. In August 1810 at Villafranca in Navarre they captured twenty French grenadiers and a *cantinière*. Diez' men stripped the woman, smoked her until blackened, paraded her on a donkey facing backwards with a placard 'The Whore of the French', then having put out one eye and cut off one ear, they exposed her in a wicker cage. As for the grenadiers, five of them chosen by lot were buried up to their necks in a bowling alley. When one of their heads was hit, the crowd applauded; the game lasted until the martyrs died. The rest were reserved for the 15 August, when the French celebrated the Emperor's birthday; the executioner struck them down, while the canteen worker, by now dying, was nailed to the church door. The priest and the mayor, sickened by the spectacle, tipped off the nearest French troops. Villafranca was surrounded and burned and its inhabitants massacred.

Francisca Espoz y Mina, known simply as Mina or Uncle Francisco, was a guerrilla chief no less renowned. Originally a Navarrese peasant, a lithograph portrays him with a haughty expression and wearing a general's uniform. He was said to be a man of austere tastes; no women in camp; iron discipline and organisation of all services: hospitals in isolated villages, powder factories in caves. His intelligence service reached as high as General Reille who was responsible for tracking down the guerrilla chief. Reille's mistress, a Navarrese, would give Mina two or three days' warning of French movements in the region. Traitors were rigorously punished: any Spaniard who had helped the French had his right ear cut off and was branded with a hot iron with the words: 'Viva Mina' on the forehead. Thanks to this Mina, Navarre saw a huge increase in reprisals. In 1811, having learned that the parents, women and children of guerrillas were being held hostage in the cells of Pamplona, Mina declared 'war to the death and without quarter on the chiefs and soldiers of France, including the Emperor'. Three Spaniards surprised while making powder were hanged at Pamplona. The following night, three French grenadiers were captured and hanged. The accompanying placard in French was worthy of Goya: 'You hang ours; we hang yours.'

The soldiers' comrades swore vengeance; fifteen monks were arrested and hanged and the regiment marched past the gibbets. A few days later, before the gates of Pamplona, two officers and four French soldiers were hanged. General Abbé had six Spaniards shot and a placard warned Mina: 'For each Frenchman, ten Spaniards will be executed in future.' Reaction: the guerrillas hung four French soldiers up by their feet, having cut off their noses and ears and put out their eyes. Nearby, a new placard by Mina: 'For each Spanish soldier twenty French soldiers will be executed: for each Spanish officer, four French officers. General Abbé's reply: 40 Spanish prisoners will be shot. His notice: 'General Abbé will, if necessary, round up Spanish prisoners in France and execute them.'

This butchery on the spot was succeeded by atrocities in the country. When twenty Frenchmen had their throats cut at Tordesa, general Abbé pursued Mina, who was on the move and now had a price on his head. The guerrilla had prisoners with him. Tightly bound, they were pushed over a precipice; those who still stirred were stoned.

Two resounding victories would carry Mina to the summit of his glory. On 25 May 1811, a French column commanded by a colonel – 400 soldiers, 100 vehicles, plus 1,000 Spanish prisoners – entered the gorge of Arlaban on the road to Salinas. Mina's men attacked at 6 a.m. The Spanish prisoners lay down at the first shot, then rushed to join their compatriots. The 400 Frenchmen fought bravely until 3 o'clock when fighting ceased. Cost: every vehicle ransacked, 65 killed, including three women frightfully mutilated. Hearing of the arrival of French reinforcements, Mina and his men fled with their prisoners. As the latter held back, he had them pushed at bayonet point into a ravine.

One year later, in April 1812, at the identical place, same scenario. This time, the convoy that was ambushed stretched back over four kilometres. Included were prisoners and sick, but the escort of grenadiers and Poles (number unknown) must have been fairly strong since Deslandes, one of King Joseph's secretaries, had not hesitated to join the convoy with his wife and children. On this occasion Mina attacked by night – with 3,000 men it was later learned. Again the escort fought bravely in the darkness and disorder. The French lost seven officers and 279 NCOs and soldiers killed. Deslandes had his throat cut and his wife was made prisoner. The French relief force arrived much too late and found nothing but the horrible remains of the battle – corpses gnawed by dogs, etc.

Among the papers Mina's men found in the ransacked vehicles was a letter from Joseph in which he expressed to the Emperor his wish to abdicate. This appeared in the Cadiz *Gazette*. Mina, guilty of numerous atrocities, showed himself merciful to the extent of sending Deslandes' children to Vitoria and exchanging their mother for his own sister, who had been interned at Pamplona.

This was the last triumph of this austere guerrilla. He will be seen later, still pursued by the French and still evading them. Then following the British into France with a reduced troop. Finally, Ferdinand VII did not want him in Spain (too well-known, too popular) and it was in France that this assassin of so many Frenchmen ended his days in exile with a pension granted by Louis XVIII.

The name of Juan Palarea – generally called El Medico, as he was something of a healer and a bone-setter – is best known for the capture of Colonel Lejeune on 6 April 1811. Lejeune was returning from Andalusia on completion of a mission for the Emperor. Not far from Madrid the 25 dragoons and 60 Badeners of the escort were attacked by 800 mounted guerrillas. 'Surrender!' The escort fought well; only four survived – naked, their uniforms taken from them. Lejeune was one of them. Up rode a horsemen with officer's insignia – El Medico himself. He interrogated Lejeune. 'Who are you?' 'Colonel,' replied Lejeune. 'If he is colonel, do not kill him. We can exchange him.' He was given shoes and a bloodstained shirt then, a little later, an old coat. Lejeune, so dressed, would be handed from one *cuadrilla* to another across a Spain theoretically under French occupation, his life in danger whenever a French force was expected, for then the cry arose: 'Hang him!' At Plasencia, the ladies, fanning themselves, cried: 'Hang him, slit his throat!' On the Portuguese frontier, he narrowly escaped stabbing by a young hunchback and his brothers. Finally he was turned over to some fine red-coated cavalry; still a prisoner but at least alive.

Everywhere the Spanish women helped the guerrillas, rarely fighting but as auxiliaries, nurses, providers, lookouts. Seated motionless for hours on a rocky crag, as some French detachment passed, they would sing a hymn to the Virgin; at this signal, the concealed guerrillas would open fire and charge.

A women would be seen hiding a wounded man with her body. The French would pull her out of the way and bayonet the prostrate man: 'One must not have pity on these brigands. They make as if to ask for quarter and then they slit your throat if you are not the stronger.' Still unending hatred; even the children are raised on it. At Salamanca, Laure Junot embraced a tiny child and noticed a knife around her neck on a small silver chain. She wanted to take it off as being too dangerous for an infant. The child pushed her away: 'Don't touch that. That's to kill a Frenchman.'

And here perhaps is the depth of hatred. One night, seven French soldiers stopped in front of a merchant's house in Los Cabezas de San Juan on the road between Seville and Cadiz. One of them knocked at the door. A very beautiful woman opened it. 'Could we come in and rest for a short while?' 'Of course, come in. I can even make you some supper.' No husband visible, but four charming children with whom the soldiers played while the woman was preparing the meal. As they were about to sit down, one of the hussars became suspicious: 'We would like you and your children to share our repast.' The beautiful hostess raised her eyes to Heaven: 'Ah, always this mistrust. If only you knew how I love the French!' Everybody ate and drank and the cavalrymen, a little guiltily offered apologies. 'But I understand you, gentlemen. There are so many bad men.' 'You have a pretty voice. Is it you who plays this mandolin? Will you sing us a bolero?' The notes of the delicate song filled the room, one, two, three staves, then the rhythm and the voice changed and there was no more singing, but a cry: 'Death to the French!' The mandolin was on the floor, the singer pale: 'I have been poisoned, but God, the Virgin and the saints be praised, so have you.' One solitary hussar survived in hospital for a few days. It was he who told the tale: 'a really beautiful woman ...'

At the end of 1809, Napoleon had formed a corps of gendarmes intended specially to counter the 'brigands'. These men were prepared to put up with anything in pursuit of their duties – climate, hardships, hunger, thirst. Local history has retained the name of only one of them: Foulon, speaking excellent Spanish, a tireless detective, operating mostly alone, nemesis of the guerrillas since his capture and execution – before a crowd of 200 – of the bandit Amoroso. Following another bandit, le Roco, in the mountains, he made life so hard for him that the man surrendered unconditionally. Promoted sub-lieutenant and decorated, Foulon continued his vendetta, especially against those Frenchmen who had defected to the guerrillas and had them formally executed. He was killed in 1813 near Bilbao.

Spain was peppered with resistance strongholds whose position and operations were known, but which even the army of occupation did not attack; why lose men for such small gain? The French also had blockhouses; miniature fortresses comprising usually a large, isolated house to which a moat, earth rampart and palisade were added. They might have a garrison of some forty men, sometimes fewer, at times no more than four or five. They would have orders to keep an eye on the movements of regular Spanish troops and guerrillas, but in practice they were usually bypassed and impotent.

By day, the local villagers might stop to gossip, drink a glass of wine, sell a few provisions, and then suddenly, one night or at dawn, the guerrillas would attack and there would be casualties. Or at dawn after a quiet night, the soldiers would find twenty paces from the palisade a post bearing a notice: 'Go no farther under pain of death.'

Some men of these small garrisons could not stand the eerie isolation and deserted or joined the guerrillas. Or an entire garrison would quit to join a band of 'demoralised' men whose feelings were neutral towards French and Spanish, and simply wished to live off the country as best they could. Men without a country, they would take over a village for as long as they could find food to eat, and then move on. Some might attach themselves to a convoy of sick and wounded headed for France. If recognised and identified, their fate was sealed, but some were fortunate and finally regained their homes in France to spend the rest of their lives recounting imaginary adventures.

The soldiers of Soult's army corps complained of being told nothing, of understanding nothing. Why had they quit Andalusia where the climate was so agreeable, where the occupation went off well on the whole, to come here in the cold and the fog in the brush at the foot of an escarpment on top of which glowered powerful fortifications? Was it going to be necessary to assault these nests? Some officers claimed to know the answer: It is Badajoz, we are not far from Portugal. The idea of returning to Portugal was greeted with no enthusiasm – especially among those who had already fought there. But Soult had new orders from the Emperor: 'March from Seville on Santarem and on the left bank of the Tagus combine your operations with those of Masséna manoeuvring on the right bank. Combined, your two armies will swamp the fortified lines of Torres Vedras and throw the English back, first to Lisbon and then to the sea.'

On 1 January 1811, the units stationed at Seville and its environs moved off. Progress was slow as they slogged north-westwards through the rain and mud. At the halts it was necessary to post a guard against guerrillas, and compel the peasants to drink the well water first; despite all precautions, many men were lost along the way.

Badajoz stood on the left bank of the river Guadiana. The town was encircled by Vauban-style fortifications at the foot of which was a muddy ditch. Spies reported that the garrison amounted to 10,000 men, and there was a fortified camp beyond the right bank of the river. The populace was armed and inspired by the cult of a glorious past. Liberated from the Moors, the town had suffered four sieges from the Portuguese: 'The French do not make us afraid.'

In the rain, the engineers laboriously dug trenches for the next three weeks. The artillery, moving with difficulty along the muddied roads, had not yet arrived. The morale of the besiegers was not good, nor was it improved when, in February, a rumour circulated that two Spanish divisions had arrived at the camp beyond the river. They would surely try to lift the siege of Badajoz.

The satrap Soult had not lost all his military acumen. On a hastily drawn map of the region, he demonstrated a tactic to his staff: 'The Spaniards believe they are safe within their camp. We must surprise them. Like this ...'

During the night of 18 February and the following morning, assisted by a thick mist, and thanks to the swift improvisation of the engineers, 6,000 infantry and 2,000 cavalry crossed the river by boats, rafts and pontoon bridges. Despite heavy fire from the defenders, the camp was surrounded and captured. The Spaniards lost 2,000 killed or wounded, 5,000 were taken prisoner and the rest fled.

But Badajoz still held out. Soult had but one thought; to find a pretext for not joining Masséna, and return to his beloved Andalusia. A timely message reached him: 'An Anglo-Spanish corps has just landed at Tarifa point. They will certainly try to raise the siege of Cadiz.' 'We will return down there.'

To raise the siege without having attempted an assault was out of the question. The sappers were digging galleries beneath the ramparts in order to place mines, but Soult was impatient: 'Attack the fortifications with pickaxes!' 'With pickaxes, Monsieur le Maréchal?' 'Yes, by day and night.' Almost anything is possible if the human cost is disregarded. The number of wielders of pickaxes melted according to the intensity of the fire of the defenders. The artillery arrived and took post; this reduced the casualties. Badajoz capitulated on 10 March.

Rumour had it that money played a part in this capitulation – Soult was very rich. Be that as it may, hardly had Badajoz been occupied than his army turned about and headed for the sun.

Masséna's army was still shivering in front of the British lines of Torres Vedras, waiting for reinforcements – Soult's army! – before attacking. The British launched several half-hearted attacks, as if to let the enemy know that they were still there. They were repulsed, and prisoners were taken; these men said that Wellington admired 'the extraordinary tenacity of the French'.

At the end of February, there was a rumour that Masséna had called a meeting of his commanders and that they had all but come to blows over their disagreements. Among these commanders quarrelling was by now a way of life. Two days later the company commanders ordered their men, discreetly, almost under their breath: 'We are leaving. Get ready.' 'Where?' 'To the north, in Spain.' Yes, a retreat. But careful! Not a sound. If the British realise what is happening they will attack.' An assault on an army which is packing its bags can be murderous. Few details exist concerning this movement, but it was so quietly executed that the British did not become aware of the departure until two days later – 6 March 1811.

It is difficult adequately to describe this army streaming northwards. Some men were still wearing remnants of uniform, others were swathed in cloaks made from bed curtains in striped wool, of red, yellow or brown, the colours scarcely discernible beneath grime and grease, old blankets, shepherds' coats, monks' habits, picadors' sombreros, mantillas – a carnival.

The start of the retreat was fairly orderly, as the men wished to put some distance between themselves and Wellington's troops, who by now would surely have been ordered in pursuit. But Masséna's soldiers had long been deprived of everything; the first time they got their hands on some wine they threw discretion to the winds. While the commanders were squabbling, the regiments received confused orders with shrugged shoulders. The retreat slowed down.

First on the heels of this army were the Portuguese militiamen, mopping up isolated groups. Their ferocity rivalled that of the guerrillas in Spain. One of their habits was to fix a man between two planks and saw him in half. In an isolated house near Thomar a flat and bloodstained object was found nailed to a wall beneath a notice which read: 'Skin of a dragoon, burned alive.' In the course of their pursuit the British would see in a field a circle of burning straw, in the middle of which was a wounded Frenchman. Each time that he tried to emerge from this brazier he was driven back by jabs of a pitchfork. Rescuing this unfortunate from his tormentors was not easy.

'It would all be even worse if the Bravest of the Brave were not in command of the rearguard.' Since Friedland the troops never called Marshal Ney anything else. Not only brave, but competent, it was thanks to his watchful authority that there were very few stragglers on this retreat. 'We would have even fewer if we moved faster,' said Ney. Many of the soldiers said, 'It's Masséna's chick who is holding us up.' Ney could no longer stand to see the ex-Child of Victory: 'He's senile!' Only fifty-three, but aged, worn-out, still besotted by his mistress disguised as an officer. She was certainly not the only one to follow a man – husband or lover – on this campaign, but the whole army detested 'Leberton, Masséna's chick', both because Masséna insisted that she should enjoy the honours due to the wife of a marshal and because she was all too often an insupportable hindrance. Between Fuentas de Cuberta and Miranda do Corvo she announced that she could not ride horseback, or walk on the steep and rocky mountain trails. Masséna had the soldiers carry her. While admonishing his men not to abandon his mistress, he lamented: 'How stupid I was to bring a woman to the war. I should have listened to the Emperor.' Napoleon had spoken harshly to him: 'Good God! One should leave women at home. Look at me. There are times when I have a dog's life.'

At the Spanish frontier, Masséna told Ney, who was still with the rearguard, that he should face about and march to meet the British. Ney flatly refused, and left for France. When Wellington heard of it, he said it was the equivalent of a battle won.

Despite disputes at headquarters and the disorder of his movements, from October 1810 to March 1811 Masséna had lost but a single cannon. Only 3,000 men had died in battle, but 20,000 had died from sickness. Wellington exploited this attrition. Patience, temporising, the slow preparation of impregnable lines, such were his methods. On his arrival at the Spanish frontier, he learned that the French had faced about.

With Ney's departure, Masséna decided to abandon his mistress, leaving her in her carriage with other women in the wake of the army. This regained liberty allowed him to seize the initiative.

The two armies met on 3 May 1811 near Fuentes de Oñoro, 30 kilometres west of Ciudad Rodrigo. The British cavalry, brilliant horsemen who had challenged the French in front of the lines of Torres Vedras, were routed, but, surprisingly, when facing this counter-attack, the red-coated infantry formed square in a manner the Guard could not have bettered and held firm. As at Talavera, fighting ceased at sunset and resumed next day; for about an hour the French had hopes of victory, but again – as at Talavera – the mutual distrust of the commanders spoiled everything. Masséna retired. Wellington said: 'If Boney had been there, we would have been beaten.'

He was anxious to take Badajoz, where the French flag had floated for two months at the summit of the old town. Beresford, one of Wellington's subordinates, had invested it. Soldiers and civilians suffered hunger. The energetic General Philippon exhorted his soldiers: 'Help will soon be here. Meanwhile the English can do nothing to us. Look at their ridiculous cannon!' Indeed, the Seville *junta* had sent to Badajoz cannon that were two centuries old; even from the citadel, one could see their excessive length.

On 15 May, the defenders noticed movement among the British besiegers. Soult was en route with 17,000 men from Andalusia. But Beresford was marching to intercept him with 42,000 men: British, Spanish and Portuguese. On 16 May, battle was joined in front of the Albuera, a tributary of the Guadiana. Soult had said that he would win 'even if the entire British army on the continent were concentrated'. He attacked first and the affair was murderous. The precise fire of the redcoats devastated the French regiments: an entire British brigade was wiped out by the cavalry of Latour-Maubourg. The Polish lancers refused to take prisoners. 'O Albuera, name of glory and grief,' wrote Byron. At nightfall, the two mauled armies (3–4,000 dead on both sides) remained facing each other – and what now? With 13,000 men facing 32,000, and with no hope of surprise, Soult had no prospect of victory. He retreated. The cannon-fire ceased; the French did not appear and the besieged in Badajoz realised that they had been abandoned once more.

Napoleon, so long a protagonist of Masséna, had not forgiven him his defeat in Portugal. He relieved him of command on 10 May, several days before the battle of Albuera, replacing him with Marmont. In 1811, Auguste-Frédéric-Louis Viesse de Marmont (of the lesser nobility) was 37 years old. When a youth, a lively affinity for the exact sciences had attracted him to Bonaparte. A close friend, he unreservedly admired the young general with the sparkling military genius. How disappointed he must have been not to see his name listed among those promoted marshal in the coronation honours! 'He's only thirty,' said Napoleon. He liked Marmont ('he's my pupil, my son'), but he was not yet entirely convinced of his capacity for high command. Evidently he became convinced because Marmont was made commander-in-chief of the Army of Dalmatia, then Duke of Ragusa in 1808, and marshal in 1809.

Marmont scarcely shone in the peninsula, but who did? Here we see him on 12 June 1811 replacing Masséna, who had just reached Merida (60 kilometres east of Badajoz) where he joined Soult who, according to every witness, welcomed him with joy. Soult had, in fact, written to both Joseph and Napoleon asking for reinforcements for the army in Portugal – and here was the answer. And, as an added bonus, Wellington, having learned of the Soult-Marmont concentration and not wishing to take any risk, recalled his troops to Portugal.

Would Soult and Marmont pursue him and settle the account left open at Talavera? No.

'I am very disquieted at the situation in Andalusia,' said Soult. 'And I have decided to return there with my troops.' I have not been able to trace the details of the 'lively argument' between the two commanders. It matters little, the consequence can be seen: Soult returned towards his cherished kingdom, his cosseted extortioners, his adulterous court. Marmont, who said he experienced towards Soult 'an iron opposition', would take up winter quarters in the valley of the Tagus. Would the Spanish war ever end?

Thanks to the internecine war between the generals, the campaign faltered in the north, in the south, in the west and in the centre of Spain, fuelled by their shameless greed, their immorality in every sphere, while their troops behaved more and more like bandits. Elsewhere in the country, the Napoleonic troops were uniformed, disciplined, tactically trained; not pillagers and, overall, not unwelcome to the local population. The local authorities accepted their administrative functions and fulfilled them faithfully, even to the extent of aiding the fight against the guerrillas

The soldiers and the functionaries were regularly paid and even the widows of the Spanish troops received their pensions. Major public works projects were undertaken. The pacified region included Aragon and Catalonia. Its commander-in-chief was General Suchet. 'Only Suchet is on top of his job,' said Napoleon in 1812. 'Had I had two top generals like him to lead my troops in Spain, this war would already have been finished; but each one chooses to do his own business, rather than mine.'

When reading biographies of the generals and marshals of the Empire, one constantly comes across the expression 'distinguished himself': he distinguished himself at Austerlitz, at Jena, at Eylau, at such and such siege or campaign. This refers mainly to bravery or to military talent. Louis-Gabriel Suchet, forty-one years old in 1811, distinguished himself by his bravery and military talent, by his competence as an organiser, by a superior aptitude for reflection, by his humanity. And, above all in the Spanish cauldron, he was a phenomenon of integrity and scrupulous honesty.

Born at Lyons, the family were silk manufacturers in very comfortable circumstances, young Suchet was excited by the Revolution. In 1791, he was a sub-lieutenant in the national guard of Lyons, but he encountered there some police aspects which he found displeasing and so enlisted as a simple soldier in a free company of the Ardèche and shortly afterwards was elected lieutenant-colonel; men who could read advanced fast in the free companies. Suchet was to take part in the siege of Toulon and obtained a transfer to the Army of Italy (only as battalion chief, but this was more serious). He fought at Lodi, Castiglione, Arcola, Rivoli. By 1798 he was general of brigade, by 1799 general of division. Suchet 'distinguished himself' at Austerlitz and Jena. On 15 November 1808 he made a marriage of both reason and love with a Marseillaise niece of Julie, née Clary, the wife of Joseph Bonaparte, who became king of Spain. Count of the Empire in 1808, Suchet took part in numerous battles, mostly victorious, but he also conducted a retreat (notably in Italy under Joubert) without loss, in good order, displaying the necessary capacity. He fought on the plains and in the mountains. He listened attentively to the accounts of the survivors of the insurrectionary war in the Vendée and of those comrades who had fought the guerrillas in the Appenines, the Abruzzi, in Calabria. He had been a chief of staff (to Brune in Switzerland and to Joubert in Italy). A true professional, but he had, and voiced certain ideas that were quite unorthodox in his day.

'The art of conquest is nothing,' he said, 'unless the troops are fed.' To meet this alimentary need, Napoleon had quite simply adopted the great Revolutionary principle: 'the war must feed the war'. In other words, the armies must live off the conquered countries. 'This principle', said Suchet, 'has always recoiled on us, even in those countries where we were welcomed as the bringers of liberty. The people become quickly overwhelmed with taxation, requisitions, and matters degenerate into pillage, exaction and the guerrilla. France cannot supply everything herself, but everything should not be exacted by force from the foreigner.'

At the end of 1808, shortly after his marriage, Suchet had crossed the Pyrenees. Marshal Lannes, who at that time was commanding III and V Corps in the laborious siege of Saragossa, sent Suchet to Calatayud (75 kilometres south-west of Saragossa). 'You are to protect the siege and keep open our communications with Madrid.'

We have seen in other regions of Spain some military chiefs who left matters to fate alone, the only ally of the couriers and of the convoys crawling along the roads. The guerrillas were no less fierce in Aragon than elsewhere, but Suchet seems to have achieved good results against them by the meticulous organisation of his defence . Small mobile groups with one or two cannon shuttled continuously between the small outposts.

Until the capitulation of Saragossa, Suchet had commanded a division in Junot's III Corps. When Lannes returned to France he lauded this divisional general to the Emperor: 'Sire, he should command an army corps.' Although he admired him greatly, Napoleon had up to then questioned his capacity for higher command. Lannes' advocacy impressed him. 'Agreed. I will have him given III Corps; and he will at the same time be governor of Aragon. He must hold this province because I am sending V corps elsewhere.'

On 5 April 1809, from the Tuileries, Napoleon moved his units about the map of Spain like chessmen, with mixed results. The old kingdom of Aragon had absorbed Catalonia, the kingdom of Valencia and even the Balearic Islands. In 1809, reduced to the three provinces of Saragossa, Huesca and Teruel, it stretched from the Pyrenees in the north to the Sierra Iberica in the south. In the west it was bordered by Navarre, by Castile to the south-west, the country of Valencia to the south and Catalonia to the east and by France to the north, some 600,000 inhabitants, including 50,000 'notables', monks and domestics, divided from north to west by the River Ebro; fine harvests from the valleys.

Suchet's III Corps comprised three infantry divisions, eight squadrons of cavalry, good artillery, a paper strength of 20,000 men but actually not more than 10,000 effectives, thanks to desertion, sick, and ceaseless provision of escorts for parties of sickness and prisoners heading for France; on the return journeys, they escorted recruits. The 10,000 resembled those widely scattered elsewhere in Europe: sloppy workers, poorly disciplined, given to pillage. 'All that must change.' Suchet was the opposite of the tough chief; from natural humanity and because he obtained his best results from well-treated troops. This last tenet was given lip-service by all the military chiefs, but the vicissitudes of war often ensured its neglect. 'The general's life-style', said Suchet, 'should never be so comfortable as to outrage the rank and file, who are suffering hardships. The leader should observe an absolute integrity and live appropriately but without extravagance.'

That the officers and men of III Corps were paid regularly seemed miraculous to the army in Spain, but it happened because neither the money sent from France, nor that raised from war taxes, was misappropriated. The officers and the staff clerks of the supply corps no longer stole – or perhaps they stole much less.

The rank and file responded to this fair treatment and to a type of paternal protection by changing their ways. Discipline was improved, as were training and exercises. They accepted as normal that deserters, pillagers and malingerers should be tried, condemned and executed. *Esprit de corps* revived, that primitive, tribal sentiment whose manifestations can be adverse or helpful, according to the chief's style of command.

While he was taking his army corps in hand, Suchet learned that Blake's army of 20,000 men had reached the frontier of Aragon, and he marched to meet this enemy force. And on 23 May 1809 his troops were beaten at Alcañiz (100 kilometres south-east of Saragossa). Or, more accurately, they fled without fighting. Most fortunately, Blake, 'who could not believe his eyes' did not immediately exploit his advantage. 'I wish to know exactly what happened,' said Suchet. A drummer had started the rout. Seized by panic, he had suddenly shouted 'Every man for himself,' and his company had fled, then the regiment, followed by the others – one stitch undone, the rest unravel.

'A court martial must judge the drummer.' Condemned to death and shot in front of the troops, who were shocked, but the execution solved nothing. Suchet thought of a horse who has run-out at a jump; he must be put to the obstacle again. But in favourable conditions. Reducing the garrisons to a strict minimum, he called in reinforcements and again confronted Blake. The Spanish army was beaten and shattered on 18 June at Belchite (59 kilometres south of Saragossa).

Aragon had traditionally been a prosperous agricultural region and most of the inhabitants chafed at the economic semi-paralysis which resulted from the activities of the guerrillas. But how to persuade them to back the activities of the occupying power? 'We must obtain the active support of the population,' said Suchet.

Pacify – first conquer and then win hearts and minds – is the dream of most conquerors. Suchet dreamed of it following his campaigns in Italy and Germany. Now, he was Master of Aragon. 'The Aragonese must be administered according to the usage and customs of their country by responsible Aragonese, disposing of real power and adequate means. Under our protection to begin with.'

A proclamation in Spanish was posted in all the towns, villages and hamlets: 'My troops will not damage the crops or disrupt your cities. They will live in their camps, ready to protect you. The maintenance of the army will be divided between the occupation authorities and by those of your province. Religion and its ministers will be respected.'

A central *junta* for Aragon was created at Saragossa. Known and esteemed notables agreed to participate, partly because they had been assured that the president of the *audiencia* would remain responsible for the Department of Justice as well as the *Contadoreria* – the general treasury and tax collection centre. Furthermore, all public posts were reserved for Aragonese, except that of secretary-general of the government of Aragon, responsible for relations between the *junta* and the French authorities, to which Suchet appointed a Frenchman of Spanish descent, one Larreguy. 'Don't expect to receive orders from Madrid,' wrote Napoleon. 'This will be between you and me, Monsieur Suchet.' The Emperor intended to give his brother a minimum of causes for complaint.

One of the first messages from Madrid to the government of Aragon was to demand the transfer to the capital of the treasure of Notre-Dame-de-Pilar. Suchet, warned, said no, and the refusal touched the hearts of the entire province.

Detachments of French troops protected the Aragonese workmen who were attempting to restore the lateral canal of the Ebro, built under Charles Quint for irrigation and navigation between Navarre and Aragon. In many cities, water supply works were in course of construction. At Saragossa, squares and promenades were built in the spaces left vacant by buildings destroyed during the siege.

The Aragonese are less ferocious than the Castilians, living as they do in a richer agricultural region. Furthermore, the landowners and peasants were happy to be protected against the guerrillas' rackets. There was a grain of hope that the pacification might succeed. In 1810 and 1811, Madame Suchet came and spent some months in Aragon with the husband who had had to leave her so soon after their marriage. On horseback, she often accompanied him on his tours of inspection far from Saragossa. The inhabitants were touched by this mark of confidence and no untoward incident occurred.

But a pacified Aragon was not a closed kingdom sheltered from any invasion. Its security, the maintenance of the order established by Suchet, required that the French be established at many strategic points in Catalonia. Suchet drew up a plan which the Emperor approved. The first objective was Lerida (130 kilometres east of Saragossa), dominated by a castle which overlooked the plain of Urgel, the 'granary of Catalonia'.

The town was besieged, but the governor refused the usual ultimatum, and the artillery bombarded the town. The lower town was taken and the inhabitants were trapped between the French fire and that of the defenders of the castle. In bombardments the artillery made no distinction between civilians and the military. On 14 May Lerida capitulated. According to Bugeaud, harmony succeeded the killing: the victors and vanquished strolled arm-in-arm. Carmelites, Grey Sisters, old folk, young nuns, all enthused over the grenadiers and many exclaimed: 'If only we had known that it would be like this we would not have been so afraid.' So runs the story, without confirmation. What is certain is that Suchet immediately organised the city administration, using Catalan personnel.

He continued to guarantee security by holding the strong points in Catalonia. His finger pointed to Tortosa near the mouth of the Ebro: 'The Spaniards who are there launch attacks on both sides of the river, with reinforcements which they receive by sea from the British.'

To invest Tortosa, situated in a fertile plain near the sea, it would be necessary to clear the countryside and establish a form of blockade. The engineers made a start by cutting down thousands of olive and carob trees which provided the city's livelihood, and blowing up some of the houses in the suburbs.

The inhabitants believed that a precious relic preserved in their cathedral would protect them, but suffered a blow to their morale when the cannon opened fire. On 2 January Suchet sent an ultimatum; the governor replied with a note saying that he had so little command of his troops that it would be necessary to send him help if serious trouble were to be avoided. Suchet and his staff entered the breach with a company of grenadiers and the capitulation was signed on a gun-carriage. Some grenadiers told the besieged that they had been wrong to yield. 'Your chiefs betrayed you. If you had resisted a bit more, we would have been obliged to raise the siege.' In fact, these men much regretted not having been able to take the town by storm, which would have allowed them to plunder it. Well clothed, well fed, paid regularly, yes, but it was often impossible to prevent nostalgic thoughts of the 'good old times' of towns sacked and packs crammed with gold pyxes.

Thus Suchet took one town after another, penetrating into areas beyond the control of the occupiers. 'To assure the security of my communications, I am raising six companies of Aragonese sharpshooters.' Aragonese! One must admire this commander, celebrated for his prudence, who took the risk of arming men who, after all, were Spaniards. And it succeeded. One may ask oneself: Had Suchet at this point won his campaign of pacification in Aragon? Would such a success have been possible elsewhere in Spain? Were the Aragonese who served the French pursued later as traitors? The disturbances in the French armies occupying Spain do not allow us to seek the answers. One must also bear in mind that ten languages or dialects were spoken in the army which Suchet led from town to town in Catalonia. With the French were Prussians, Saxons, Bavarians, Bohemians, Moravians, Swiss, Poles, North Italians, Neapolitans. Why not Aragonese? The Napoleonic torrent was jumbling up Europe.

Napoleon had dismissed the colonel who reported the fall of Tortosa with the words: 'Tell Suchet that a marshal's baton awaits him at Tarragona.' Napoleon had never been to Tarragona, but the maps, files and plans etched in his mind a picture of its military significance: the amphitheatre built facing the sea, pivot of the defence of Catalonia, solid refuge in case of defeat. The British fleet defended the port through which supplies and reinforcements arrived. Beyond the lower town a smooth road climbed to a plateau beyond which was a rocky valley and thence to the fort of Olivo, a solid position with a large garrison.

Suchet would conduct the siege of Tarragona with 20,000 men and a strong artillery train. On 21 May 1811, at nightfall, four cannon-shots gave the signal to attack. Shortly afterwards the amphitheatre resembled a brazier wreathed in black smoke. The lower town was taken under fire by both the French troops and the British ships, which fired into the brown without too much care for who received the broadsides.

At the same time, Suchet's troops attacked the Olivo fort. Despite the artillery and the defenders' volleys and the six-metre ditch which encircled the fort, it was carried. The bombardment of the town and the port had ceased. Black smoke smudged the pink colours of the sunrise. Suchet sent an emissary to the governor: 'I ask a suspension of fighting in order to bury the dead.' Refused. Soldiers started to dig large graves while still under fire from the town.

This work had to be stopped, not because of enemy fire but because rock was encountered so near the surface that the graves were too shallow.

The dead bodies were piled in heaps and set on fire; the vast pyre burned for three days, giving off a frightful stench. A great silence spread over the entire town and the besiegers' camp. In the roads could be seen the sails of ships coming and going. The British removed the Spanish wounded, ferried in reinforcements, munitions and food. The fall of the fort had altered nothing. The siege could last months or years.

No! On 21 June, Suchet launched a new night attack, taking the port and the lower town. This meant the loss to the defenders of everything that the mistress of the seas brought in: sugar, sardines, tobacco, cotton, coffee, quinine, and even leather and porcelain. The pillage was on a royal scale. Neither the soldiers nor the *cantinières* nor the traffickers who habitually followed the armies could carry it all away, but the morning was but half gone before hundreds of Jews appeared, who bought the booty from the victors. Quinine at ten sols the pound, sugar at five sols, the Jews piled their carts high, loaded their mules and disappeared.

The Spaniards still held the upper town and the governor, Contreras, still declined Suchet's invitation to surrender. When, on 28 June, the French attacked the upper town, the inhabitants fired on them from the windows of their barricaded houses. Driven into the street which leads to the cathedral, they took refuge, still intermixed with the soldiers, in this church, already jammed with 900 wounded, women and children. Suchet's troops entered and there was a massacre.

Other Spaniards had been driven towards the sea and on to the beaches where many were mown down by the broadsides of the British warships which were once again firing into the brown. The night of 28/29 June was to be horrible for the soldiers, continually urged on to further efforts: 'Come on! One more time!' and exasperated by the opposition which they were encountering. Four thousand corpses, at least a half of them civilians, were scattered throughout the city. Many witnesses stated that the Poles and Italians were 'even more ferocious' than the French and that blood 'ran in the gutters from the upper town to the lower quarter of the port', which was perhaps an exaggeration but which gives food for thought. Not until next day were the officers able to restore a semblance of order.

Suchet must have thought that the pacification and security gained in the region entrusted to him justified the price paid, since he attended a Te Deum, not in the bloodstained cathedral, but in the church at Reus, three leagues distant. There the inhabitants thought it politic (as a sign of submission, fearing to share the fate of Tarragona) to organise a celebration with a 'dance of the giants' which can still be seen in Belgium (*les Gilles*) as a relic of the Spanish occupation.

At Tarragona there were also celebrations for the return of the victorious general. Catalonia appeared overall as pacified as Aragon. On 8 July Napoleon had made Suchet a Marshal of the Empire; he was the only French general between 1808 and 1814 to be rewarded in this manner for military operations in Spain.

One region subdued, pacified; there was always another farther off that threatened security. At the end of August 1811, Napoleon ordered Suchet to take Valencia, the third city in Spain, with a large population which had always displayed a particular hatred of the French. On 15 September 1811 he set off with 20,000 men. It was necessary first to invest Sagunto, 25 kilometres north of Valencia and not far from the sea. The inhabitants compelled the commander of the fortress to capitulate when Blake's army, coming to their rescue, was repulsed with losses by Suchet's army. Blake had then dug-in at Valencia with 30,000 men.

Suchet sent for reinforcements. Siege works were started, trenches dug, artillery brought up as close as possible. The monks furiously exhorted the populace. Standing on the ramparts, they held up small children and defied the French to fire on them: 'Kill, Frenchmen, kill!' The governor, the marquis del Palacio, had the statue of Notre-Dame de los Desemparados paraded in procession and declared that she would always protect the city.

Starvation prevailed to the extent that people were eating grass. Many families tried to escape across the marshy plain – the Albufera – which separated the city from the sea. The soldiers surrounded them, seized the women. 'When will we cease to torment the world?' wrote Bugeaud. 'Ah! Without patriotism, I would be weary of the first of all the callings.'

Blake capitulated on 9 January 1812. The French took 18,000 prisoners, including Blake, 23 generals, 900 officers, 21 standards, 2,000 horses, 392 cannon, 42,000 muskets. A Spanish disaster. 'I wish there to be no pillage,' said Suchet.

Feverish from a wound received at Saragossa and poorly healed, he camped in the middle of his army in the gardens outside the city and detailed General Robert, appointed governor and assisted by Bugeaud, to take possession of the city. The latter had 1,200 grenadiers and voltigeurs as police.

All went well and he made his entry on 14 June 1812. It had been necessary to clear a passage for him for the debris in the streets reached in some cases as high as the first storey. The surprising sight which now greeted them was attested to by many witnesses. Those houses that had escaped damage were bedecked and decorated 'as on the feast of Corpus Christi', orchestras played in the plazas and women applauded the conquering Marshal from their balconies.

Those monks who wished to organise hostile demonstrations were reduced to silence by the populace itself – and by the execution of a few die-hards a few days later. Suchet wanted order; order restored, he organised his conquest in his usual 'Valencia must be run by Valencianos'. Even the running of the police force was left to a Spaniard.

Napoleon, having learned that the conqueror of Valencia was still suffering from his wound, sent him his chief surgeon, Baron Boyer. He did not recover until after two months' intensive treatment, but when he next could mount a horse he was Duke of Albufera. He noticed some time later that the old Moorish castle where his wife had stayed during the siege had been within range of the defenders' heavy artillery: 'Why was not fire opened in that direction?' 'As a courtesy, Monsieur le Maréchal.' The city's commandant, learning that Madame Suchet was living in that tower, had ordered that no gun be aimed in that direction. Suchet's personality inspired respect. In the regions he held – conquered by fire and iron and administered thereafter by local people – the occupation wound on without incident.

Elsewhere, at the same time, the war god remained the stronger. At the beginning of January 1812 Wellington appeared without warning before Ciudad Rodrigo and after less than two weeks' siege, the French hoisted the white flag. Despite this formal capitulation, despite the joy of the inhabitants, the British chief could not restrain the savage rush of his soldiers, led by an Irish regiment – blind drunk. The town burned for six days.

The 'Iron Duke' then chose to finish off Badajoz, whose loss had so irritated him. The town was again invested – for the third time – and bombarded as never before. Once again, the gallant Philippon inspired his soldiers: 'As prisoners – you know what that means – the Cadiz hulks.' The reputation of these ante-chambers of death, which had been the lot of the prisoners of Baylen, was such that many of the defenders of Badajoz felt it better to die fighting. As for the British, they were elated by the remembrance of the sack of Ciudad Rodrigo. They launched a night attack – no moon – into the breaches opened by their artillery. Mines exploded beneath them, mangling redcoats. Scarcely checked by this horror, the survivors threw themselves against the carefully prepared defences, beams with blades and sharpened points of hardened steel gutted them, but others passed over their corpses; one assault followed another; the French were swamped. Philippon, who had retreated to the citadel of Guadiana, capitulated, while Soult, marching to his aid, turned about.

The sack of Ciudad Rodrigo had been a picnic compared to the fate of Badajoz. To welcome their liberators, the inhabitants illuminated the town as best they could, and their reward was pillage, rape and massacre. Spanish and Portuguese vagabonds, brigands, assassins mixed with the British troops. It was useless to try to hide, to bar the door; musket shots shattered the locks, doors were stove-in, woe to the women, woe to him who tried to defend his own! Hogsheads were rolled into the streets and broached; a shocked officer over-turned some casks and the brutes crouched down to drink the wine in the gutters. The drunks opened fire on anyone, on their own officers, who tried to restrain them, on their comrades. The professional robbers concentrated on pillage; profaners, having robbed the churches, paraded the priests nude through the streets – 'Papists!' From outside the city, Wellington sent parties to stop the Bacchanal, but they too joined in. In the cathedral cellars soldiers dropped dead-drunk amid the cadavers. Two days and two nights of hell, 5,000 dead and the streets red with wine and blood. An Englishmen wrote that the victory of Bada-joz was 'sullied by an exhibition of barbarity without equal in any other army'. According to Toreno, Wellington was powerless to stop it and was himself threatened by his troops. Poor Spain!

After the surrender of Baylen, Dupont and Vedel's forces had been marched away at 4 a.m. on 23 July 1808, not knowing that they were destined for the hulks; the Andjudar agreements had specifically provided for their repatriation to France. I have given some account already of their terrible martyrdom on the march south. They had been divided into two columns. The first followed the left bank of the Guadalquivir. As the agreements provided, the officers had retained their arms, horses, carriages and wagons, and the soldiers had kept their haversacks. They were escorted by a battalion of Murcian infantry and 100 cavalry.

On the first night, arriving at the city of Bujalancia, the chief of the escort told General Dupont that the soldiers in this column would be billeted on the inhabitants. Fortunately, a woman revealed that the town was surrounded by 1,200 militiamen and guerrillas who intended to slit the throats of the French during the night. They bivouacked outside the town and kept going. I have already mentioned running the gauntlet, being spat-upon, insulted, threatened in each town they came to.

'Any prisoner who left the ranks to relieve himself, or who through weak-ness could no longer remain in the ranks,' recounted Henri Ducor, a marine of the imperial Guard, 'became an immediate target for the inhabitants who has-tened to assassinate him. We had only to turn back to be witness of these mur-ders and, had we not done so, the cries for mercy and the savage chants of the throat-cutters would indicate the murders all too clearly. Women, children, the aged – all joined in.'

The other column (Vedel and Lefranc's division) followed a different route, encountering everywhere the same hatred and perils. Amid their worst tri-als, the soldiers repeated the names 'Rota' and 'Sanlucar de Barrameda', said to be the two ports from which they would embark for France. For France – this hope made any torment bearable.

On 2 August the escort's chiefs addressed the French officers: 'Please tell your men that you will all have to stay for a week or so in the region because the *junta* of Cadiz has encountered difficulty in assembling enough ships to transport you. But that has now been done and the ships are being converted.'

One week, two weeks, three weeks. On 20 August the French officers were given 'plans of billeting' which were posted up widely. The troops swore. 'We shall never see France again!' Look at what it says, said the optimists: 'While awaiting embarkation'.

Those words were inscribed in their hearts. About 7,000 men were spread through some twenty towns and villages in southern Spain which already harboured the seamen from Admiral Rosily's squadron and prisoners from other regions. Two or three weeks later, the rumour circulated in the billets that Generals Dupont and Vedel had left for France. 'The bastards! They're ratting! They're abandoning us!' A broadsheet announced to the soldiers that 'in spite of his protests' Dupont had been compelled to embark in the *Saint George* with 80 officers, including Generals Legendre, Barbou, Fresia, Rouyer, Pannetier and Colonel Schramm. Vedel himself had been 'compelled' to board a Genoese brig, the *Minerva*, which was to transport to France Generals Poinsot, Cassagne, Le Grange and some others. None of this calmed the indignation.

To stay with their men, the naval officers had voluntarily declined to take passage in the 'generals' ships' – as had General Lefranc. He was ordered to march his men towards Malaga – another dispersion, this time into three sections. 'The officers will be billeted at Malaga hospital, the soldiers at Velez-Malaga and at the fortress of Puente del Rey.' Hopes of repatriation faded as the days and months went by. In less than two months, one third of the French soldiers penned at Puente del Rey died of sickness. On 20 November, General Lefranc 'succumbed to a slow fever'. His officers asked that he be buried with military honours; the governor of Malaga said No! And forbade them to follow his coffin.

On 7 December at 2 a.m. about a hundred armed Spaniards guided by monks climbed up to the monastery of Lebrisa where 200 French soldiers were held. Seventy-five of these disarmed men, including many officers, were murdered. On 10 December the survivors were told that they were to leave for Guadix, near Granada. At Santa Fe, they learned that this was a mistake and that they should go to Cadiz: 'That is where you will embark.' On 13 December – No, the embarkation will be from Sanlucar, one of the ports previously chosen for the purpose.

At Sanlucar, the officers were separated from the men. Four days later: 'Prepare to leave for Cadiz.' General exasperation and anxiety. Finally, no question of repatriation – all prisoners in the extreme south of Spain were taken aboard the hulks at Cadiz between 25 December 1808 and 1 January 1809.

A prison hulk was an old sailing-ship stripped of cannon and rigging. That is easy to visualise. One went down from the top deck to the next deck which, still above the waterline, had some light. Beneath this was the half-deck, below the waterline and rather dark, the only light coming through hatches giving on the deck above. In the floor of the half-deck were one or more hatchways leading to the hold, the ship's dark stomach. On arrival the prisoners were put in the half-deck. 'The first night', wrote Turquet, 'it was literally impossible to stretch out. The floor served as bed, and space was so limited that we agreed to range ourselves in two lines turned one against the other with our feet touching. In the space between, it was necessary to place a third line of men whose feet touched the chests of some or the heads of others. After trying many alternatives, it was necessary that we all retired at the same time and facing the same way. When wishing to change so painful a position, it had to be executed with the precision of a military manoeuvre.'

In any prison, individual, or collective, the first days are the worst; later on the prisoners exhibit an amazing gift for improving their condition, even in the worst circumstances. The men in the hulks were helped at first – by death. Some one hundred deaths in January and February 1809 made more room for the survivors, and the prisoners were allowed to take the air on deck in turn. Initially, the corpses remained on deck, the prisoners not daring to throw them overboard, Then the Spaniards organised an undertakers' service; boats came alongside and collected the previous day and night's harvest of corpses, which were towed ashore for burial in common graves in the cemeteries or even in graves dug in the sand, where the tide uncovered them – Cadiz faces the Atlantic.

Most of the prisoners died from scurvy, dysentery or typhus. Mortality was horrendous during the first weeks because there was no medical assistance. The sick considered beyond help were pushed, despite their protestations, into a corner of the deck known simply as 'the abandoned'. The horror of these noxious corners was Dantesque. Hulk prisoners were vulnerable to any disease because they were cruelly under-nourished. Every four days a pinnace which they called 'the Mule' brought them water and food. According to Ducor, this consisted of hard-tack, black and adulterated, wormy biscuit, salt meat decomposing with age, spoiled cod, rice, peas and beans, all equally spoiled, 'all in very small quantities'. No wine, no vinegar, nothing in which to prepare our food.'

Quartermaster Gilles wrote: 'On many days, we saw neither bread nor vegetables. We used rainwater to cook straps, braces and haversacks, after heating them to remove the fur, as we did the gaiters. The dogs which had been on board had long been eaten.' Thirst was another torment on those hot days when

The Emperor: Napoleon wearing the uniform of the Grenadiers of the Imperial Guard.
(Print after Delaroche).

Left: A fusilier of line infantry, c. 1809; with grenadiers in the background. (Watercolour).

Below: Officer of the 5th Hussars in campaign dress. (Print after Edouard Detaille)

Right: Officer (right) and gunners, Foot Artillery. (Print from 'Job')

Right: On the march: a voltigeur (left) and carabinier of light infantry, 1809. (Engraving after Hippolyte Bellangé)

Opposite page, top:
'Passage of the Ford': a regiment of chasseurs à cheval prepares to cross a river in the vanguard of the army, the regiment's élite company leading the way. (Print after H. Chartier).

Opposite page, bottom: On the march: the wearisome nature of marches on campaign is exemplified in this illustration of Pino's division of IV Corps in the Russian campaign of 1812. (Print after Albrecht Adam).

Upper right: 'Coquin de temps!': grenadiers of the Imperial Guard on the march in bad weather. (Print after Horace Vernet).

Right: Reconnoitering: a staff officer with telescope and sketch-book observes the terrain in advance of the army. His horse is held by his orderly, a chasseur of the Imperial Guard. (Print after Jean-Louis Ernest Meissonier).)

Left: Foraging: on campaign, private property was not respected if it could be utilized by the army, as in this scene showing Italian Guards of Honour of the Grande Armée's IV Corps in the Russian campaign of 1812, using fencing for firewood. (Print after Albrecht Adam).

Left: Foraging: chasseurs à cheval round up cattle for use as 'rations on the hoof'. (Print after F. de Myrbach)

Left: 'Baked potatoes': grenadiers of the Imperial Guard offer to share their frugal rations with their emperor. (Lithograph after Raffet).

Above: Soldiers of the Grande Armée take a few moments' rest after an exhausting day's march in the Russian campaign of 1812, as observed by Albrecht Adam. Note the use of shakos as pillows.

Below: Dinner on campaign: officers of the Italian Guards of Honour in bivouac during the advance into Russia in 1812; note the use of an upturned cooking-pot as a table.
(Print after Albrecht Adam)

Above: On the night of the battle of Bautzen, 20-21 May 1813, Napoleon works upon his maps by the light of a camp-fire, watched over by his faithful grenadiers of the Old Guard. (Lithograph after Raffet).

Below: 'The Emperor is watching!': infantry advance into heavy fire with determination, in the knowledge that Napoleon's eyes are upon them. (Lithograph after Raffet).

Above: The 14th Line at Eylau: surrounded and without hope of relief, the 14th entrusts its 'Eagle' to Baron Antoine de Marbot in an attempt to save it from capture. (Print after Lionel Royet).

Below: French infantry engaged in a desperate fight in the streets of Essling. (Print after F. de Myrbach).

Above: The advance of a cavalry brigade: a scene near Ostrowno, July 1812, showing one regiment advancing in column, with another deployed in line reserve. (Print after Albrecht Adam).

Below: 'Bravest of the Brave': Marshal Ney (centre), musket in hand, commands the rear-guard during the most desperate stages of the retreat from Moscow. (Print after A. Yvon).

Right: Regimental standards represented an almost spiritual connection between Emperor and army, epitomised by the 'Eagle' carried by each regiment. This print after Charlet shows the Eagle-bearer of a regiment of Grenadiers of the Imperial Guard.

Right: The plight of women and children who accompanied the army was sometimes desperate, most notably during the retreat from Moscow. (Lithograph after Raffet).

Left: 'The misery of war': a column of French troops on the retreat from Moscow. (Print after Charlet).

Left: Napoleon aims a cannon in person: battle of Montereau, 18 February 1814. (Print after Eugene Lamy).

Left: War spreads to the homeland: the defence of the Clichy gate at Paris, 1814. (Engraving by P. Aiken after Horace Vernet).

Above: Fall of empire: Napoleon surveys the wreck of his army while the Imperial Guard still stands firm: Waterloo. (Lithograph after Raffet).

Right: Field surgery: Napoleon with Marshal Lannes, mortally wounded at Essling. At the left stands Dominique-Jean Larrey, chief surgeon of the Imperial Guard, who performed the amputation of Lannes' leg. (Print after E. Boutigny).

Above: 'Wounded': most of those injured in battle had to lie where they fell, if unable to make their own way to the rear. This grenadier has fabricated a tourniquet out of his musket-sling. (Lithograph after Horace Vernet).

Left: Casualty-evacuation: this scene, observed by Albrecht Adam at Smolensk in 1812, shows a common method of carrying a wounded man, using a musket as an improvised stretcher.

Above: Arresting réfractaires, those who attempted to avoid conscription, and deserters. (Print after T. de Thulstrup).

Below: French prisoners of war in custody; the sentry (extreme right) can be identified by his long breeches as a fusilier of Hungarian infantry. (Print after J. A. Klein).

Above: A regimental vivandière finds a loved one dead upon the field of battle. (Lithograph after G. Böttcher).

Right: 2nd (Dutch) or 'Red' Lancers of the Imperial Guard. (Print after F. de Lalauze).

no rain fell. Caltil-Blaze: 'Some straws in the mouth helped to withstand the pangs of thirst.'

At least half the prisoners were suffering from the diseases already mentioned. As the French armies approached Cadiz, The Spaniards transferred these sick prisoners from the hulks to the permanent naval hospital at Cadiz, the Hospital de l'Aguada, in order to be able to show, if the French conquered, that the prisoners had been well treated. According to a Spanish report, of a total of 859 sick, eight died on the first day (25 January 1809), eight on the second, five on the third. 'This total includes nine women, and one officer who died on 26 January 1809.' On 4 February, 'of 242 patients, 6 died within 24 hours'. This was much fewer than on board the hulks. 'Each day', wrote Gilles, '30 to 40 of our unfortunate comrades died.'

The hulks had been ships of Rosily's fleet, to which had been added some old tubs of the Spanish fleet, in ruins since Trafalgar. At first there had been seven, but their number varied. I have found no confirmed list of these ships. Likewise, it is impossible to establish the number of prisoners put in the hulks: 8–10,000 according to the Swiss surgeon Chapuis, or even 12,000 according to the Commissioner of War, Demanche.

The Spanish authorities, alarmed at the numbers of sick transferred to the Hospital de l'Aguada and fearing that contagion might spread to the town, converted the *Terrible* to a floating hospital. She was cleaned up and modified somewhat for the purpose, but ten such hospitals were needed and the epidemics were still raging in the hulks. 'It was only the soldiers' wives and the *cantinières* who stayed healthy,' wrote Gilles. 'There were several hundred with us and not one fell ill.' We have seen a number of women die at the Hospital de l'Aguana, but perhaps they were the wives of officers? What I remember here is a very approximate estimate of several hundreds, but as yet no military historian has given any indication as to how many women had followed the convoys of prisoners across southern Spain, survived this calvary and reached the hulks. These women, whose condition must have been even worse than that of the men, were but one detail in this immense saga. The few mentions we find in eye-witnesses' accounts lead us to conclude that they displayed moral and physical courage superior to that of many of the men. But in all the hulks were some good-hearted men who put their minds to the production of 'distractions' for their comrades. They arranged for concerts and even dances, for gymnastics on deck. The unfortunates could see boats full of sightseers for whom a 'visit to the hulks' was a distraction; these ghouls were likely to hear some pretty vulgar insults directed at themselves.

As I have said, the officers had been separated from their men before the latter were embarked; they were accommodated in the *Vieille Castile*. Men from the hulks who succeeded in getting assigned to the latter ship as servants, have

289

recorded their surprise on coming aboard. Castil-Blaze: 'One did not see here any thin, pale faces. Senior officers with three chins, fresh and healthy complexions, ample stomachs, such were the inhabitants.' Let us assume that this witness exaggerated the contrast a little. Here is the soldier Froger: 'Our officers were better off, but they were treated very differently from us! They had everything which they needed. Often there was luxury in poor taste. But I said nothing.' Gilles: 'Many officers had private means, so they could buy anything which was not issued to them. They never lacked fresh water, for example, and could have as much wine as they wished.' I have read in many memoirs that officers and soldiers, on the road, or before or after embarking in the hulks, were closely searched and robbed of everything, and that they were paid a miserable wage as prisoners. In fact, the zeal of the searchers must have varied considerably depending on time and place, and some of the victims obviously managed to retain valuables; witness the number of officers who were able to buy extra 'comforts' right up to the end of their detention, though this did not prevent them from falling sick and dying.

The survivors led an acceptable life for prisoners. They read books lent them by the naval officers, smoked cigars, fished over the side, For a while, they had permission to go swimming, but with the approach of the French army, this was withdrawn as too likely to lead to escape. The married officers had brought mattresses with and couples would surrounded the bed with a partition made from old skirts or brown paper; a degree of privacy from their neighbours' gaze though not their hearing.

On 28 March 1809 all prisoners, officers and men, seamen and soldiers, were suddenly ordered to prepare for embarkation in the transports in the roads; for some days there had been a concentration of shipping, but this had happened before – Cadiz was a port of transit for Spanish troops and supplies.

Now, they were off, leaving, no one knew where. Only a few still believed in repatriation, especially since the Spanish soldiers had said that the hulks would not long be empty. Other French prisoners would be coming 'from the Sierra de Tolox or from the region of Granada'. But perhaps, after all, they were going to be sent home in batches. The suppositions, calculations, kept up their spirits for the two or three days occupied in the move to the transports aboard small craft crammed to bursting. The transports now numbered twenty-three and – which made repatriation seem less likely – many of the ships and frigates were wearing British colours.

No sooner aboard than it was get between decks: 'Hurry up! Move! Yes, down here, just duck your head'. The Spanish commissioners, in order to get more in, had installed floors of planks to split each deck into two levels so that the prisoners had to crawl without much headroom to find a place. Their rations of biscuits and beans and the canteens of brackish water were passed hand to hand in the darkness: 'They want to make us die!'

Some of these unfortunates would never quit their lairs alive; each day, corpses were thrown overboard. The voyage – whither no one knew – was to last twelve days and more. The worst time was when a storm hit them off Cape Palamos. The inexperienced and seasick Spanish seamen thought of nothing but their prayers. The captains had to beg the help of French naval officers among the prisoners. But where do you want to go? To the Balearic Islands. Not all the prisoners embarked at Cadiz were destined for the Balearics; the seamen of Rosily's squadron were to be sent to the Canaries. And of the transports sent to the Balearics, those that suffered the worst storm damage had to put into Algeciras or Gibraltar.

Finally, on the morning of 17 April, the coast of Majorca came into sight. The convoy stood off and headed for Minorca. But there was no disembarkation at Minorca; the authorities had no wish to welcome some thousands of prisoners rumoured to be pest-stricken. For two weeks the unhappy convoy sailed from one island to the next while the Majorca *junta* deliberated – rejected everywhere. But these wretches have got to be landed somewhere. On 1 May, the commandant of the port of Palma was finally told to send an order to the captain of the *Cornelia*: the senior officers, having passed quarantine, would be authorised to stay at Palma. The junior officers, NCOs and soldiers (including the marines of the Guard) would be landed at the island of Cabrera. All the ships moved with deadly slowness; the disembarkation which started on 5 May would not be finished until 11 May.

Cabrera is a rocky isle, sixteen kilometres south of the southern-most point of Majorca, Cape Salinas; an area of seventeen square kilometres, five kilometres at its greatest width. On the north side, two large bays with narrow entrances; one, the *Puerto* (port), has an excellent anchorage.

Close in, Cabrera is a rock. Here and there are stunted trees, dingy green brush, in fact, brambles, which when cut emit a foul odour and cause swelling to anyone handling them. In a few sheltered corners one can find myrtle, rosemary, gorse, arbutus and spiny cactus. No fauna other than insects and green lizards.

The first NCOs and soldiers who landed on Cabrera at 7 p.m. on 5 May 1809 found the place welcoming. Not a human being in sight, the few families living there having been evacuated, but overhead an immense sky, a feeling of peace and almost of liberty after the confines of the hulks and the hell of the crossing.

Such is the power of military discipline that the units mustered obediently around their chiefs. Patrols were sent out to find firewood, others sought temporary shelter, yet others fresh water. The skippers of the small craft pointed towards a source of fresh water, called they said, 'La Fuenta'. Buena, buena!

Night was falling, the watering parties did not return. Those who went to see for themselves pressed around the spring. 'A trickle of water for 6,000 men,' one seaman would write . It was necessary to bivouac in order not to lose one's place in the queue; scuffles broke out.

Pure water, that was all. The sloops had departed. On the second day and the two following, other drafts arrived, but not an ounce of food. Cabrera is only 200 kilometres from the coast of Africa and the May sun strikes hard. The men took refuge in the caves. In the first days, 83 dead.

On the sloops' third visit, three officers were landed; their accommodation consisted of tents brought in by a Spanish gunboat, and the Castillo, an old fort dating from the XIVth century, some 72 metres above sea level. All faced famine; not a sail to be seen. The soldiers said: 'We were brought here to die of hunger.'

On 12 May two ships, the *Berta Catalina Tomas* and the *Santo-Cristo de Santa Eulalia* were sighted and soon entered the port. They brought the first provisions. The Palma *junta* had awarded the victualling contract to one Nicolas Palmer; his sole aim was to extract the maximum profit from the sum allotted him (less, of course, the kick-back to the Spanish commissioner). In so doing he had avoid cutting the rations to such an extent that many prisoners died of starvation – which would reduce his revenue. A periodic head count was instituted.

The daily ration consisted on a pound of hard-tack, 60 grams of rice or vermicelli, 120 grams of chick-peas, with 30 or 45 grams of oil 'replacing both butter and soup meat' and a little salt. During the first months, this food was shared in common by 'messes, but then, too many men feeling cheated, it was divided into individual rations. Any theft of food was severely punished, even by death. Palmer's rations only arrived in good weather. When he failed to appear, the prisoners boiled thistles, which injured their mouths; others fried green lizards on skewers in the sun – these went into the soup.

As in the hulks, the officers fared better. Occasionally they received from Palma some sheep, goats and a cow. But these were alive and on what could they be fed at Cabrera? Killed, they hardly kept; much of the meat went bad.

The prisoners feared above all to miss the distribution of rations. The NCOs soldiers and seamen were grouped on the heights nearest the port, in the numerous caves, in fissures in the rock, in shelters of branches. When winter comes, said the veterans, we must find something else, or we shall all die.

The imagination of prisoners has no limit. The structures that rose on the island of Cabrera to shelter 6,000 men was one of the most astonishing sights seen in the Grande Armée. Some 700 shacks, each sheltering about a dozen men, were built of wood and stone and contained chairs, tables, and beds made from leafy branches.

An instinctive self-preservation, a vague hope of repatriation some day (for the NCOs, soldiers and sailors, the accursed exile at Cabrera would last five years, but a certain number of officers would be released much earlier) had encouraged the prisoners to group themselves by battalions and companies around three hills. A thousand troglodytes not wishing to construct huts, preferred their caves.

The first eight buildings were reserved for women and were known as 'The Royal Palace'. We know that several hundred women were present in the hulks, but it seems that there were only twenty-four or so on Cabrera – some survivors said that there were only fifteen. How many perished during the transfer (one of them gave birth to twins, who survived as she did) or on the island during the early days, we have no means of knowing.

There must have been some women with the officers in the Castillo; the accounts give only slight details concerning the life-style of those who shared the fate of the 'Cabrerian' officers. Ducor mentions the *cantinière* who gave birth to twins: 'She was their only support, but none the less she was seen constantly working to help the sick prisoners and to be useful at every opportunity.' And he mentions the case of Madame Daniel, known as 'Mother-of-the-Winds' because she had so little clothing. Widowed in Spain, and having her 15-year-old son with her, she had built a hut which sheltered the two of them until they were repatriated. 'We were touched by the devotion of this mother who did not hesitate to save her ration to give to her son.'

As for the inhabitants of the 'Palais Royale', having established ties with the sailors who ferried-in the provisions, they managed to procure a little wine for their men. 'This was because they had the advantage over the men in being able to arouse sympathy more readily.' Let us allow a witness to speak; his brief account is more eloquent than anything else. Gilles: 'Most of the women lived with the men with whom they had come to the island. But also the bait of gain gave birth to the idea of speculation. Such women passed often into the arms of the island's capitalists, that is, those who had succeeded in saving some money, some voluntarily, others by arrangement with their so-called husbands, who in exchange for a sum of money, renounced all their rights. Those who had made such a deal quickly tired of their new companions and re-sold them at a profit. This sort of trafficking had the effect of lowering prices. I have seen a woman for sale who was by no means bereft of charm and youth for the paltry sum of ten francs dressed or five francs completely naked.'

After the Second World War, a number of ex-prisoners of war in Germany told how the fever of cultural activity had simmered in the camps at the beginning of their captivity – debates, theatricals, readings, music. Precisely the same thing happened in Cabrera, this island of the deprived. Half the prisoners gave lessons to the other half. 'What were most plentiful', wrote Lardier, 'were educators of every hue; there were masters of mathematics, of music, of languages, of drawing, and especially of fencing, dancing and quarterstaff.'

On 8 September 1809, the 'Theatre of Nature' opened with great ceremony and offered '*Le Désespoir de Jocrisse*' and '*Monsieur Vautour*'. Some of the officers of a British brig were present. Other plays were later presented. The only way that the actors could learn their lines was by listening to a gunner captain named Foucault who was endowed with a fabulous memory and who knew most of Molière's plays by heart. Occasionally one of the actors might forget his lines, not having eaten for twenty-four hours.

The weather and the storms decided everything. In autumn one saw at Cabrera a horrifying return of sickness: typhus, scurvy, dysentery, ophthalmia, scabies, as in the hulks. This fever extinguished the cultural variety. In November 1809 on the night of All Saints, a storm flattened the tents where the sick were tended. It was then necessary to bury many corpses, but to dig in the rocky soil was painful, sometimes impossible. The bodies were burned in what is today called Figtree Valley – surprising evidence of fertility in the midst of the Cabrerian desert.

In winter, no more theatre, no more lessons or debates – dismal apathy. In the rifts in the rocks the prisoners vegetated and rotted, 'weather-beaten' hermits drained of energy, savage, blackened, frightening to see. They sold their miserable rags for a crust of bread, went about nearly naked, increasingly skeletal.

The following spring and summer saw a marked diminution of the spirit that had been evident during the first year, The theatre was not reopened; the only collective activity was on 15 August, the Emperor's birthday, when around the shack of the marines of the Guard the men had a banquet – some beans in a mess-tin. They talked about 'the Emperor, Paris, France, the Carousel parade, the hundred-gun salute for the birth of the King of Rome, the illuminations and fireworks, the dances and the free spectacles'. Then one of them stood up: 'The Emperor's health!' All standing, hand to the salute in sign of respect, drinking water from battered goblets or broken glasses, they repeated the toast. 'Never had a toast been proclaimed with more true sentiment,' wrote a quartermaster of the *Pluton*. 'When we sat down, our eyes were wet with tears.' Most of these men had been plucked from their homes and families by pitiless conscription. Survivors of a calvary, at the very nadir of misery, one might think that they would be cursing their sovereign – Not a bit of it: 'Vive l'Empereur!'

Cabrera was 28 kilometres from Palma, 200 from Africa, 240 from Spain. At the beginning some of the marines of the Guard had escaped by taking over the 'bread barge'. In February 1810, a further attempt at escape was frustrated by the prisoners themselves, furious at the thought of the barge making off with several days' bread ration. Later, a sergeant named Bernard Masson succeeded in stealing a felucca towed behind a Spanish frigate. He was never recaptured, but details of this exploit are lacking.

At this time prisoners from the hulks, who had succeeded those deported to Cabrera, tried to put an end to their martyrdom. On 15 May 1810, those aboard the *Vieille Castille* cut the cables during a gale, hoping that she would drive ashore on a part of the coast held by the French. She was fired on by a British corvette. During the night, she sank some 700 metres off the coast. Under fire from the British and burning, a raft was hastily built and the women and children were piled on to it – there were children too in this floating prison. Help finally arrived from ashore and the escape succeeded at the cost of about 100 dead out of 800 prisoners.

Eleven days later, on 28 May, encouraged by their example, the sick aboard the hospital ship *Argonaute* mustered their last strength in an effort to do likewise. The British opened fire and boarded, and a frenzied hand-to-hand struggle between the British marines and the typhoid patients ensued, while the hulk, surrounded by a circle of fire, drifted towards the shore. Of the 600 prisoners, some 250 reached safety.

The last celebration of the Emperor's birthday at Cabrera took place on 15 August 1811. After that nothing – hopes of survival, diminishing daily. The numbers of hermits and deranged increased. There were scenes of cannibalism in the caves. Gilles recounted how two men wearing the uniform of the Swiss army dissected the bodies of two of their comrades, 'dead of scabies'. Another man alleged that he had seen a Pole kill a comrade and eat his liver.

Napoleon had never made a secret of the fact that prisoners were of little interest to him: 'One should die!' and Cabrera recalled the nagging defeat of Baylen. In 1810, and in 1811, he did order that the captives be rescued, but nothing came of it and later he had plenty of other worries – in Russia and elsewhere.

On 16 May 1814, after the fall of the Empire, two French schooners wearing white flags appeared off the island. The naval officers who landed were horrified by the appearance of the spectres who came to meet them: 'Nothing written by the writers of fiction equalled the frightful reality which I found before my eyes.' A flotilla was expected to repatriate the prisoners.

Since May 1809, many contingents of French prisoners had been brought to Cabrera from various provinces of Spain: the maximum number was 16,000 according to some writers; others said 9,000. When the survivors were landed at Marseilles, they were carefully counted: 3,639. The royalist city commandant delivered a speech about the usurper Bonaparte who had drowned Europe in blood, which provoked murmurs: 'What's this? You still love him after all the evil that he has done to you?' 'Yes, we still love him!'

X

THE SCORCHED EARTH
OF RUSSIA

The heat was unbearable. The dust raised by the army marching rapidly was so thick that men could barely see the file in front of them. The dust was neither white nor grey, but rust-coloured. It penetrated the nostrils, the mouth and the eyes. Some soldiers swathed their heads in cloth, leaving spaces for nostrils and eyes, which gave them the appearance of phantoms. Others claimed that they suffocated in the cloths and preferred to tie branches to their shakos against the sun. Entire battalions could be seen thus adorned, looking like moving woods. The men, bent under the weight of the haversacks, 30 kilograms or more, marched as fast as they could, urged on by the NCOs. They looked apprehensively at the verges of the wide road...

Where was this? Still in Spain? No, in Russia between Vilna and Vitebsk. This mass of men marching towards Moscow was the Grande Armée, new version: 400,000 men, one-third of them French.

The recall of men to the depots on 1 June 1812 gave the Grande Armée a total of 678,080 men, of whom 322,167 were foreigners, but there were so many foreigners in the so-called French armies that overall not more than a third were French nationals. The strength return included the occupying troops in Germany, who took no part in the campaign. About 400,000 troops had crossed the Niemen at many points, heading east between 24 and 30 June 1812. Two-thirds of this mass included Belgians, Carinthians, Croats, Dalmatians, Saxons, Bavarians, Rhinelanders, Poles, Italians, Swiss, Danes, Westphalians, Württembergers, Mecklenburgers, Prussians, Austrians, even Spaniards and Portuguese. All these uniforms, all these military orders, twenty languages or dialects competed or mixed; how could this Babel be mastered, as it must be? At bottom, insults and blows are an international language.

Most of the French contingents were composed of recruits of the conscriptions of 1811 and 1812 and had never campaigned. The 1812 recruits were untrained. These levees had caused disaster in France. More than ever, any way to avoid conscription was legitimate. As married men were exempt, the number of marriages increased fantastically – youths of eighteen married women in their sixties. Deserters, hiding in the forests and mountains, formed bands to resist the mobile columns searching for them, and some hard fighting resulted in hundreds of dead. Everywhere, these dramas were recounted in whispers; nothing appeared in the papers.

The foreigners, except the Poles who comprised V corps, served without enthusiasm, often reluctantly. Their slackness or slowness affected the morale of the French. Until the Niemen was crossed and even for some time after, the morale of the young officers had been fairly good. They had felt that the Grande Armée was invincible, that the Emperor would make himself Master of Europe and that their careers would follow those of the top commanders, today loaded with honours and riches.

The spectacle of the concentration at Kovno, facing the river which marked the Russian frontier, would have moved anyone. 'The sky was unclouded, the Emperor's tent was pitched on a bluff 300 metres above the Niemen; all around were masses of immobile men and horses. The Emperor had ridden away at 5 a.m., crossing the river to reconnoitre the Russian side, then returning to his tent to watch his troops march past, standing near a rustic throne of branches and turf made by the gunners of the Guard. He fidgeted with his riding-whip and hummed: "*Malbrouk s'en va-t-en guerre*".' The Polish cavalry, in their elegant national costume and riding superb horses, carrying long lances with pennons snapping in the breeze, resembled a moving stream of colour. The sun sparkled on the wall of steel of the cuirasses, the cannon gleamed, the Guard was 'as smart as in the Tuileries'. While marching past, the troops shouted 'Vive l'Empereur!'

The marshals and generals grouped near the Emperor forced themselves to appear happy and full of spirit, but some found this difficult. For the first time since the Empire had been proclaimed, they were staking all their honours and riches – most of them had come from such modest backgrounds that their rise had seemed a fairy tale. Three years had passed very quickly, and now they detested the thought of their past warrior existence; not the dangers, for they were brave, but the nights in bivouac, the cavalcades under the hot sun, the rain, the snow, the discomfort. They resented this campaign and had to restrain themselves from voicing their opposition, their desire to see an end to these conquests. Conquests? Some spoke of the war in Spain with sniggers, sometimes in front of the troops, the rank and file hearing them say, 'Bloody war!'

Napoleon, too, would have liked well enough to enjoy his power and glory and domestic happiness in peace; father of an adored child, Emperor and son-in-law of an emperor, what more could he want? He was seen to have discarded habits that had become second nature: meals at fixed times and now, a miracle, he even lingered at table. He had become fat and stooped slightly, his hair was thinning, and if his look still remained piercing, his normally pasty complexion occasionally took on a greyish tint. And the hardships of warfare were beginning to make him feel that his body would not always respond to the spur of his will.

Napoleon's motive for invading Russia was precisely the same as that for Spain, namely to enforce the continental blockade. Since Tilsit, his ally the Tsar was unshakeably convinced that the system would ruin his empire. The Russian economy complemented that of Britain; commerce between them was vital to both. Russian ports were piled high with timber, tallow, tar, potassium, hides, iron which Britain, before the blockade was clamped on Europe, imported with relish and in return sent to Russia manufactured goods vital to a country with virtually no manufacturing capacity. The deficit of the Russian trade balance was enormous, the rate of exchange of the rouble was plunging. Alexander had finally said No to the blockade. The port authorities had been told to turn a blind eye to the arrival of British ships disguised as neutrals, and Russian ships sailed by night for Britain.

Moreover, Alexander knew that Europe had had enough of Napoleonic domination. He was prepared for war and Napoleon had decided to strike first. Since 1811, the topographic office overseen by Bacler d'Albe (whom we have seen at work in the Emperor's tent) had received secret orders to prepare maps for the future campaign. When the news of this project leaked out, none of the great captains had dared say a word. 'He'll' ruin us': only one voice was raised – his name overlooked in the major histories – that of the modest and intelligent colonel of engineers, Ponthon. After Tilsit, Ponthon and one or two other officers had served a spell in the Russian army on an exchange basis, as often happened between allied nations. Ponthon had kept a sharp eye out and had rendered such accurate reports that Napoleon had assigned him to his staff.

Questioned frequently by the Emperor, he had been one of the first to understand his intentions towards Russia and had dared to speak his mind:. 'Sire, such a war carries with it terrible dangers. Conquered peoples will never be your true allies. The immensity of the Russian theatre changes the facts of war. You would advance into wildernesses where you would find neither food nor forage. With the first rains, the terrain becomes impassable and if the campaign drags on into winter, how will your troops withstand temperatures of minus twenty or thirty degrees?'

Napoleon had listened without a word, 'fixing the colonel with a severe eye'. Finally, Ponthon had dropped to his knees: 'Sire, in the name of the prosperity of France and of your glory, I implore you, abandon this war.'

Napoleon dismissed him with a gesture. For several days the Emperor was seen coming and going with a thoughtful look as if hesitant. Then, resolution returned: 'This war will be short.' France and Russia had hastened their preparations, and then let drop the mask. On 8 April 1811, the Russian government had sent the Emperor of the French an ultimatum demanding the evacuation of Prussia, Swedish Pomerania and all places occupied by France beyond the Elbe. The *Moniteur* announced that the Emperor had left to inspect the Grande

Armée concentrated on the Elbe: 'Her Majesty the Empress will accompany His Majesty to Dresden where she hopes to have the pleasure of meeting her illustrious family.'

The 'encumbrance of kings' which assembled at Dresden to welcome Napoleon was a strange demonstration of sparkling gaudiness worthy of Panurge, of sovereigns great and small hypnotised by the Corsican Ogre, now Emperor of the West, their master and ally, whom they detested and whom many of them had already betrayed. The Chancellor of Austria, Metternich, and the King of Prussia had both written to the Tsar telling him that they would make war to the minimum. Metternich: 'We would only be auxiliaries and towards an end as much in Your Majesty's interest as in ours.' The Prussian: 'If war breaks out, we would not do more than strict necessity dictates: we would constantly bear in mind that we are united, that we must one day again become allies.'

With the Niemen crossed, Napoleon had divided the Grande Armée into three major corps of different sizes (Macdonald in the north, himself in the centre, Jérôme Bonaparte, King of Westphalia, in the south) with the intention of fixing and manoeuvring the Russian forces in front of him to a decisive battle.

Now, during his advance into Russian territory, those armies were no longer there: 'The Russians were retreating, leaving behind them a void and destroying everything, the tactic of scorched earth.' This is what children in the primary schools read in their books. What they will not read are the details, the figures showing how the adventure quickly went wrong.

After less than one hundred kilometres into Russian territory, between Kovno and Vilna, the Grande Armée had already lost 5,000 horses, 50 per kilometre (other accounts put it at twice that figure). The horses died because the only forage that could be found for them was green rye, and also because of the climate. In the evenings the torrid heat frequently gave place to extremely cold, torrential rain. Only the horses suffered from this climate. For years, the old sweats had said: '*Le Tondu* wins his battles on our legs.' The Russians were retreating at top speed, and had to be pursued. The veterans could manage fifteen leagues daily without undue trouble, but not the young recruits. At eighteen, they could not cover 60 kilometres daily with a pack, plus musket and ammunition. They were left by the roadside. After 48 hours of marching, the Grande Armée had 50,000 stragglers – fifty thousand!

Behind the army came an enormous train, wagon-loads of provisions, ammunition, supplies, all drawn by mediocre horses and driven by requisitioned drivers. These rigs were mixed up with innumerable carriages of officers and women, and individual wagons, which collided and overturned in wild disorder. Some wagons were even drawn by oxen, This train never reached the front which was advancing in a region denuded of population, cattle and food. Enraged at finding nothing in the villages, the soldiers set fire to the hovels.

Some young recruits who could not keep up with the rapid march killed themselves by a bullet in the mouth; even before Vilna had been reached there were several hundred suicides. Other stragglers formed themselves into units, electing leaders, spreading out on both flanks of the line of march; if they found an inhabited village they would stay there and stuff themselves with food – the Cossacks or the partisans came by night to cut their throats.

'My love,' wrote Napoleon to Marie-Louise on 30 June. 'I am at Vilna and very busy. Things are going well, the enemy has been completely foiled. I am in fine health. I think of you. Vilna is a very fine town of 40,000 souls. I am in a very fine house where, until recently, the Emperor Alexander was lodged, never suspecting that I was so close behind him.'

We have just seen how well the Emperor's affairs were going. Vilna (today Vilnius, capital of Lithuania, 264,000 inhabitants) was a city of 20–25,000 souls, rather Jewish, where could be seen comfortable houses and miserable hovels. On 1 July, Napoleon received M. de Balachof, the Tsar's minister of police, sent by his master to express the Tsar's surprise at seeing Russia invaded without a declaration of war. Balachof was instructed to state on behalf of Alexander that, if the French retired to the Niemen, negotiations could immediately be opened to arrive at a good understanding. Napoleon received him courteously, expounded at length the usual arguments that invaders employ to justify their action (non-observance of earlier treaties, feelings of being threatened, and so forth), finishing by expounding on the frightful fate of a vanquished Russia.

'Sire,' said Balachof, 'we acknowledge the bravery of the French and the genius of their leader, but the Russians will fight with resolution and even with despair and God will doubtless favour their cause, for they have not sought this war.' Napoleon invited him to dine and was patronising: 'What is Moscow? A large village. How many churches?' 'More than two hundred and fourteen, Sire.' 'Why so many?' 'Our people are devout.' 'Bah! No one is devout today.' 'Pardon me, Sire, maybe they are no longer devout in Germany and Italy, but they still are in Spain and Russia.' The word Spain cast a chill; Napoleon saw fit to react grandly: 'Which is the road to Moscow?' 'Sire, the Russians say, as do the French, that all roads lead to Rome. You can take whichever road you like. Charles XII went via Poltava.' And the Swede had suffered a sharp defeat. Napoleon left it at that. He gave Balachof a letter for the Tsar in which he once again threw the blame on Russia for the war.

Napoleon allowed his troops ten days' rest at Vilna, but on 7 July he ordered them forward again. He had learned that the Russian army which he was pursuing (that of the Russian General Barclay de Tolly) had just gained the fortified camp of Drissa which the Russians had been building for more than a year to cover the road to St Petersburg. He would attack them there.

A few days later, he learned that another Russian army (that of General Bagration) was also retreating – whereas he had hoped that it would be encircled by the forces commanded by Jérôme.

Why Napoleon had appointed his younger brother, 28 years of age in 1812, a general of brigade with no experience of land warfare whatever to head what amounted to an army – three infantry and one cavalry corps – and commanded by such seasoned commanders as Vandamme, Reynier, Poniatowski, Latour-Maubourg is impossible to say. This promotion is the more surprising if one remembers that Jérôme had done little during the last twelve years apart from infuriating his illustrious brother. His play-boy life-style, blatant and enormously pretentious, would be suitable material for a television drama.

Youngest child of Madame Letizia, Jérôme Bonaparte, fifteen years younger than Napoleon, had lived in court circles since the age of thirteen, at the château of Montebello in Italy, a magnificent residence whither the victorious general had summoned his entire family. Before departing for Egypt, his elder brother had placed him in the college at Juilly – but in 1800, here is the 16-year-old with a personal suite of rooms in the Tuileries and with a large staff of servants. Even though he still wore the uniform of an ordinary hussar, the sentries presented arms to him: brother of the First Consul.

In every administration, money circulates freely in the corridors of power, and the young brother, who had never experienced the family's lean years, spent heedlessly. He ordered from Biennais, a fashionable jeweller, a gold-mounted dressing case that cost ten thousand francs. He amassed debts, sowing his wild oats with relish. A slim, handsome youngster, with fine features and a cupid's bow mouth, he believed everything was allowed him. He went too far when he appeared for dinner in riding boots, whip in hand. 'You are off to sea!' said his big brother. So, off to Brest where he was promptly enrolled as second class cadet in Admiral Ganteaume's flagship, the *Indivisible*. Off Candia, *Indivisible* engaged the *Swiftsure* of Admiral Keith's force and captured her. Jérôme had shown courage – which he never lacked – and, as reward, was detailed to carry to Paris the vanquished captain's sword. Another reward: the stripe of first class cadet.

He was then appointed to the *Foudroyant* which, under command of Villaret-Joyeuse, sailed for Santo Domingo where she took part in the recapture of Port-au-Prince. A further promotion, to second lieutenant. But the uniform lacking in glamour, Jérôme appeared on board one day in the guise of a lieutenant of the Bercheny hussars: sky-blue breeches, dolman and pelisse, scarlet waistcoat. The astonished Admiral sent him back to Paris in April 1802.

In Paris, the second lieutenant/hussar's behaviour was such that Napoleon again intervened. 'You are going back to the West Indies! 'and a rather dry letter: 'As a second lieutenant I wish to see you aboard your corvette at sea, studying a career which is your road to glory. Should you die young, I would be consoled, but not if you lived sixty years without glory, not having served your country and without having left a record of your existence.' Jérôme must have had something about him since in 1803 we see him in command of the brig l'*Epervier*. But still – *la dolce vita* – as little on board as possible. Naval life bored him. After a further dispute with Villaret-Joyeuse at Pointe-à-Pitre on 20 July 1803, he abandoned his command and headed for America – a serious offence.

At Baltimore, Elisabeth Patterson, very pretty, daughter of a rich merchant of that town, shone at every ball. But when the handsome Jérôme appeared, she blushed, paled and shortly thereafter she had, in the contemporary phrase: 'nothing more to offer him'. She was pregnant. 'Come what may, I love you and will marry you.' On 21 December 1803, the marriage took place in secret at her father's house; Jérôme's family received no notification.

Jérôme was not of age and consequently the marriage was legally invalid, but Mr Patterson, in order to assure his daughter's future, stipulated in article 4 of the marriage contract that if for any reason a separation were demanded, Elisabeth Patterson would have the right to 'the ownership and unhindered use of one-third of all real property, personally and jointly owned, of the said Jérôme Bonaparte, now and in future, for herself, her heirs and assigns, etc.'

Napoleon, now Consul for life, head of the family, spluttered and in the Corsican dialect pronounced these fateful words: 'I strike him out of our family. I will never see him again.' Later, when Emperor, and long besought by Madame Letizia and Lucien, he consented to say: 'I will never see him again unless he submits. In any event, Elisabeth Patterson will never be allowed to land on the territory of the Empire.' Jérôme disregarded these terms two years later when he visited Italy with the intention of asking clemency from his brother and to present his wife to him. Before meeting him, Napoleon wrote to tell him what he had decided: 'There is no fault which cannot be atoned for by one truly repentant. Your union with Miss Patterson is nul in the eyes of religion and of the law. Write to Miss Patterson to return to America. I will grant her a pension for life of sixty thousand francs on condition that under no circumstances will she bear my name. You will tell her yourself that you have been unable to change the way things are. Once you have voluntarily annulled this marriage you will regain my friendship, and I will resume the feelings which I have had for you since your childhood, hoping that you will prove worthy of them by the efforts which you make to acquire my gratitude and to distinguish yourself in my armies.' Not a word about the little son (named Jérôme) – as though he didn't exist. The brothers corresponded for a fortnight without meeting. Finally,

Jérôme gave in. Sick at heart, he sacrificed his wife and son for the somewhat vague prospect of titles, honours and fortune: 'I will have you appointed captain of a frigate.'

In the West Indies Jérôme, in command of the frigate *Le Vetéran,* captured eleven British merchantmen, and on return succeeded in running the British blockade to reach Concarneau. He was now vice-admiral.

Napoleon had evidently done more than just pardon him; on 24 September 1806, a senate decree created him a prince with the grand cordon of the Legion of Honour. More. Napoleon, knowing that so long as he reigned, there would be less opportunity to shine at sea than on land, awarded the Vice-Admiral an army title, general of brigade. Better still: by a clause in the Treaty of Tilsit, Napoleon obtained European recognition of Jérôme as sovereign of the new kingdom of Westphalia, which Napoleon had created from a clutch of Prussian provinces. Jérôme I, King of Westphalia at twenty-two, and more of a playboy than ever.

'He must be married off without delay,' said Napoleon.

Pell-mell, a fiancée was found: Catherine of Württemberg, daughter of the duke, now also a king by grace of Napoleon for whom king-making had become a game. Catherine was a trifle heavy, not pretty, but her kindness and spirituality lighted her face enough to capture Jérôme the seducer for a while: she would give him three children: Jérôme Napoleon Charles; Mathilde; and a Napoleon who would marry Clothilde of Savoy, daughter of Victor-Emmanuel II, King of Italy.

Napoleon realised that Jérôme's salad days had marked him for ever when he saw the list of dignitaries appointed to the tiny court of Westphalia: a grand chamberlain, fifteen ordinary chamberlains, a grand master of ceremonies, eight masters or assistant masters of ceremonies, plus twenty ADCs, a grand master of horse, six honorary masters, a secretary of the treasury, not to mention the domestics and the inevitable French theatre, indispensable for amusing the court at Cassel – 400,000 francs annually. In brief, for a kingdom of 7,000 square kilometres, a staff about equal to that of the imperial court. Napoleon was soon assailed by demands for money; furious, he refused. He knew that the mothers of Cassel refused to allow their daughters to attend court balls or celebrations; the moral climate, it was said, was not what one would desire.

In giving Jérôme command of an army, Napoleon had perhaps thought that he would be a docile subordinate – in 1806, after all, he had written to Berthier: 'Carry out my orders to the letter. I am the only one who knows what should be done.' This tendency of his had increased since then. 'In this profession and in a large theatre,' he had written to Jérôme in 1812, 'One only succeeds with an established plan. You should therefore study your orders closely and do neither more nor less than I tell you to.'

Napoleon's plan had envisaged separating the two Russian armies, initially standing on the Dvina and the Dnieper, and defeating them in detail, but the Russians' immediate retreats rendered it impossible to implement. That said, Jérôme's army might perhaps have been able to trap Bagration's if he had pursued him as energetically as had the main corps sent by Napoleon on the heels of Barclay de Tolly. On learning that Jérôme was deaf to the advice of his chief of staff, General Marchand, and was not pressing forward, Napoleon transferred the King of Westphalia to the command of Davout, until then, his subordinate. This provoked the reaction of a spoiled child: with his entire Guard, 25,000 men, Jérôme quit the Grande Armée and returned to his kingdom.

'There are no records to show just how extended the main army corps became in its pursuit of the Russians. As before reaching Vilna, the great heat of July sometimes turned to storms and cloudbursts. The horses continued to die, the number of stragglers grew ever greater and the entire army was suffering the pangs of hunger. Many staff officers were unable to conceal their disquiet at the insufficient number of effectives deployed when, at last, they trapped the enemy. 'Here and there on the roads were dead and dying, victims of forced marches, of malnutrition and the rigours of the climate,' wrote staff captain F. de Kauster. 'The châteaux and the highways were littered with stragglers, some trying to rejoin their units, others deliberately keeping to the rear of the army in order to live as they wished. Herds of cattle driven by soldiers, long lines of Russian wagons loaded with provisions followed the columns and conjured up the spectacle of a nomadic people on the march, rather than the finest army of Europe commanded by the greatest captain of the century.'

The casualties of the march on Moscow were not only the victims of forced marches, lack of food and the rigours of the climate. In his *Mémoires*, Larrey writes of another cause of death, hardly mentioned in the military reports: 'The unrestrained use of Schnapps was also fatal to many conscripts. Obtained from wheat, the addition of narcotic plants gives it a stupefying capacity.' We have seen the surgeons and physicians of the Grande Armée using brandy as a restorative and complaining when they were unable to obtain replenishment. One must also remember that other types of alcohol were available. The old sweats could cope with rot-gut liquor, but it was too much for the youngsters. 'All those who died from the effects of this liquor exhibited the following symptoms,' wrote Larrey: 'loss of muscular control, vertigo, collapse, eyes half-open, watering, they crouched in the ditches and on the roadway itself and died almost immediately.' According to later calculations, between the Niemen and Smolensk and without having fought a single battle, the Grande Armée lost a third of its effectives.

All this time, there had been practically nothing in the way of fighting beyond skirmishes and minor encounters between cavalry. On 15 July, after crossing the Dvina, the Russian cavalry (which a few days earlier we had seen retiring in perfect order) turned about and faced the pursuing forces; a regiment of Polish hussars was surprised while sleeping and the greater part of a squadron was taken prisoner.

The army debouched into a region of vast prairies, covered with waving fields of rye. The villages consisted of groups of semi-buried huts, the inhabitants, wearing long robes, were bearded, greasy, wild-looking. 'We marched, destroying everything,' wrote René Bourgeois, senior surgeon of the Dauphiné regiment. 'We bivouacked in the midst of the crops which were trampled and which we pulled up to make shelters. The soldiers scattered in search of provisions, they beat the peasants, chased them, pillaged their houses, led away their cattle.'

Cannon-fire was heard for the first time at Ostrowno on the Smolensk road, six leagues from Vitebsk. Murat's cavalry charged the enemy rearguard. For the first time the French could see the Russians' uniforms, mostly dark-green. The grenadiers and infantry wore white breeches, the hussars were bedizened as in all armies, the cuirassiers wore white.

The first clash was between cavalry. The Russians showed great talent for sudden withdrawals into the woods. In the second fight that day, the infantry were more in evidence. The Russians lost 4,000 men killed or taken prisoner, the French 1,300; nothing like the losses hitherto from fatigue, the climate, sickness, alcohol and despair among the young recruits. Next day, 27 July, a detachment of scouts from the left wing suddenly found themselves surrounded by hordes of Russian cavalry which had emerged from the woods. The scouts were seasoned troops and fired steadily on the horsemen, many of whom were brought down. Charged, they had no time to form square, so adopted a back-to-back stance and fired calmly at point-blank range. The main body watched from a distance. When the Russians retired the scouts returned and the Emperor questioned them: 'What unit are you lads from?' 'Skirmishers from the 9th of the Line, all from Paris.' 'Well, you're a fine lot and you shall all have the Cross.' 'Vive l'Empereur!' On the 28th, Napoleon learned with disappointment that the entire Russian army had decamped during the night. Not a soul in view, not a single peasant to be interrogated. Patrols examined in vain the tracks that led in several directions. Later in the day he heard that the advance guard had already entered Vitebsk, abandoned by nearly all the inhabitants, and that the Russian army had already passed beyond it.

Vitebsk was quite a large city in a forested region cut by many clearings. Once again, the Russian rearguard turned and fought, then retired, burning the bridge over the Dvina. H. von Roos: 'The town with its houses, convents and churches appeared to be swathed in clouds of smoke – a striking spectacle. On the morning of 28 July, while our camp was astir, all was quiet on the other bank of the river. The smoke enveloped the town and spiralled up in the rays of the rising sun.' The fire had not only burned the bridge but nearly all the shops. The town was ruined and four-fifths of the population had fled: scarcely anyone was to be seen, except for a few Jews. They were selling flour which they had hidden and it was possible to buy bread. The sick and wounded were billeted in the churches and houses; as usual their lot was most pitiable.

With the pursuit halted for the moment, officers and men of a reflective turn of mind wondered whether the Emperor might not suddenly declare that the aims of the campaign had been attained. The whole of Lithuania had been conquered, the right wing had entered Mohilev and the left extended to Riga; the Russians had been thrown back over the Dvina on one side and over the Dnieper on the other.

The Emperor had only threatened to burn Moscow in order to compel the Tsar to make peace – at worst we shall not go beyond Smolensk. Napoleon was lodged in the palace of the Prince of Württemberg, governor of White Russia. It was said that many repairs were in hand; perhaps they were not going farther? He had a modest apartment which contained all that he needed when campaigning: maps, book box, the large portfolio, dressing-case, little iron bed. Rising at 5 o'clock, he came down to the parade at 6 when a brigade of the Guard marched past him, a ceremony which has been called his Mass. As the esplanade was too small for these ceremonies, the engineers demolished some of the houses.

He summoned the army chiefs to hear details of his projects. His first words made it clear that there was no question of stopping at Vitebsk or Smolensk. 'The Tsar will make the peace which I want once we have taken Moscow, not before. To remain behind the rivers would be to invoke a false security. When winter comes, you will see them full of ice and covered in snow. Why should we stop here for eight months when we can be in Moscow in twenty days? We must strike quickly or risk losing all. We must enter Moscow within a month or risk never reaching it.'

Napoleon added that neither Moscow nor even Smolensk would be taken without a battle, and the earlier they engaged the bulk of the Russian army the better.

He thought for a moment that this hope was to be realised on 9 August when he learned that on the previous night 12,000 Russian cavalry, including some squadrons of Platov's Cossacks had surprised General Sébastiani's advance guard near the village of Inkowo on the Smolensk road. The arrival of the French cavalry had saved three regiments from disaster. Inkowo was no more than a bare defensive success, but Napoleon had received the news with joy. The commitment of 12,000 sabres at a time told him that the bulk of the Russian army was ready to give battle at last. Some hours later, came disappointment; the Russians were continuing to retreat towards Smolensk. Well, so be it; the pursuit continued.

The Cossacks! We see them at Inkowo; Platov was one of their most famous leaders, few others are known, but the name Cossack occurs in history like a whip-crack. 'The Cossacks', said Napoleon, 'are an affront to humanity.' Ye Gods! they had harassed his army to death! Let us take a closer look at these strange horsemen.

'At Inkowo, the Cossacks fired arrows at us,' wrote von Roos. 'We kept two of them for a good while.' Yes, some of the Cossacks, not all, bent their bows and launched their obsolete projectiles at the gallop with incredible skill, recalling the North American Indians. But they had other weapons: in 1812 the personal weapons of the Don Cossacks might include lance, sabre without a guard, pistol and carbine, often bow and arrows as well; their was no hard and fast rule, each man arming himself as he thought fit. Spurs were not used, but each Cossack had the *nagaika* – a long leathern whip; remember how in the great Russian stories, the Cossacks descend on the villages and whip the recalcitrant moujiks.

Cossack officers wore a fairly long blue tunic, those of the Cossack Guard wore a red one. Uniform of the rank and file could differ widely depending on the unit. However, one can describe fairly accurately the uniform of the Don Cossacks: a very long dark-blue tunic, dark-blue trousers, broad bottomed and tucked into their boots, fur bonnet and hood.

Albert de Muralt, a Swiss-born lieutenant in a regiment of Bavarian light cavalry, has left us a good account of the Cossacks in the Russian campaign. He had seen bearded men in rough wool clothing, often red or blue, wearing fur toques with long hairs, or flat cloth bonnets. They rode wiry little ponies that appeared to be buried under the high wooden saddles covered with sheepskin blankets. 'We had many scuffles and skirmishes with the Cossacks who were covering the retreat of the Russian armies, but we rarely had the opportunity of engaging them in a serious fight. They would only face us when they were very much superior in numbers. On the other hand, they continually harassed us and often charged when we least expected it, on our flanks or even in our rear.' They made use of the forests to gain surprise. Their scrawny ponies were fast and durable. 'Cossack cavalry used the lance with skill, both to deliver blows and to parry. If they missed with the point, they whirled the haft so that they could not be reached by a sabre. Our cold steel did not have much of a chance.'

307

The Cossacks were exceptional horsemen, their martial skill having been developed by successive generations. They could ride by day and by night, sleeping in the saddle if necessary. They moved fast and in silence, having nothing that might make a noise, not so much as a click; no chain on the bridle, no metal buttons; it was a point of honour never to entangle their weapons. Many could use a lasso.

The Cossacks were mainly used as scouts and light cavalry, but some Russian generals used them indiscriminately, lacking other troops, and indifferent to their losses.

The Cossack civilisation had an interesting history. These were the pioneers who first thrust into the endless wastes of unknown Siberia until they reached the Pacific coast. They had contributed to the defence of Christendom against Islam. From 1600 to 1800, they had headed numerous revolts against Russian rule. Celebrated horsemen, but also pirates on the Caspian and Black Seas, pillagers, rapists, genocidal, but also peaceable fishermen and trappers, competent farmers.

They were not a tribe or a separate ethnic group, and they had never been a nation. They were first seen in the XVth century on the southern steppes of Russia as the tide of Asiatic nomads ebbed. Seeking new lands, they ejected groups not well anchored to the land, often mixing with them, living at first from hunting, fishing and harvesting and often by pillage. Although their origins were substantially Russian, their way of life always differed from that of the Muscovites, who originated in the forests. The Cossacks were children of the steppes. The Muscovites erected an authoritarian state as a protection against invasions and to assure interior order. The Cossacks, raised in the dangerous frontier region between the northern Russian foresters and the Tartars of the southern steppes, mistrusted any form of settled life. They elected a chief, but continually opposed him, hence their frequent rebellions until they were won over and furnished the Russian state with their indispensable squadrons, so careless of death, but who had to be held on a light rein.

By the beginning of the XIXth century the Cossacks had become a caste of warriors – samurai, proud of their traditions. They were enlisted by the Russian army for a tiny wage, required to furnish their own horses and weapons, but with the understanding that they might pillage freely at every opportunity. There was an exclusive Cossack nobility. Every soldier attaining the rank of sublieutenant in the Russian army was, by law, ennobled; if he attained the rank of colonel, that nobility passed to his descendants.

Tolstoy has evoked with his customary genius the life in the Cossack villages on the Caucasian frontier, facing rebel populations which Russia was gradually reducing – with the help of the Cossacks. Their chalk-whitened houses were sparkling clean (in contrast to the filth in those of the moujiks), the farms, run by their strong and comely women, while their men served on the 'cordon', a line of fortified posts from which were launched raids into enemy territory, or into the mountains. The old and the very young hunted and fished, leading a fine 'ecological' life, despite some heroic drinking (but no tobacco – forbidden to the 'old faithful' by their religion). All Cossacks observed a strict moral code as regards the honour of women and of courage, but theft, rape and pillage from the enemy were held to be worthy. Many illiterates, as was common throughout Russia (and elsewhere in Europe) but, mark this, the Don Cossacks had public schools as early as 1765. The Don Cossack always carried a little bag of his native soil around his neck, and would not be separated from it.

In 1812 Platov, the commander of the units engaged at Inkowo, was 61 years old, had fought Tartars, Turks and Persians. General of brigade at 39, then lieutenant-general, promoted *ataman* (grand chief) of the Don province, he proved himself a world-class administrator. His cavalry had fought the French at Austerlitz, Jena and Eylau. In October 1812, when Napoleon abandoned Moscow, Platov was ordered to pursue the Grande Armée. We shall see the Cossacks collecting one of the most fabulous hauls of booty in history.

Platov himself would willingly have captured the Emperor, and had the following read to his riders: 'I wish you all to know the description of this man. He is short, corpulent, pale, with a short thick neck, large head, black hair. To be sure, arrest all short men and send them to me.' At the end of October 1812, at Gorodnia, a detachment of Cossacks nearly captured General Headquarters. These men were so intent on seizing the cannon that they paid no attention to a man in a fur coat and thus missed seizing Napoleon. Impressed by this incident, the Emperor asked his doctor to make up a phial of strong poison which he carried round his neck. Platov was to die three years before the Emperor, but before he did, he had bivouacked in the Champs Elysées.

The Cossacks did not stand in front of Smolensk; it was not their nature to do so in face of a major attack. Some accounts state that they were 'swept away' by Murat's light cavalry and Ney's infantry. No, they made off. The Napoleonic so-called light cavalry would advance at a slow trot, followed by the infantry. A thousand Cossacks had skilfully concealed themselves in a fold in the terrain covered by brush and had charged the French uttering a cry which sounded like 'Hurrah!' Some got so close to Marshal Ney that he had his collar ripped by a carbine bullet. Then, under steady pressure, the wild horsemen on their little ponies, split to right and left and made off like a cloud of insects.

Smolensk, on the left bank of the Dnieper, in a splendid location surrounded by mountains, is one of Russia's oldest cities: 12,000 inhabitants in 1812, 170,000 today. Sixteen of the thirty-two towers that graced the ramparts are still to be seen despite the desperate battle in 1941 between von Bock's forces and those of Timoshenko.

Ney's infantry found Smolensk a formidable-looking place. The walls seemed to surround the entire city and suburbs; from outside no house could be seen, only the five cupolas of the Cathedral of the Assumption. The walls were of brick, eight metres high and four metres thick. In 1812 it was ornamented by thirty-two towers, some already falling apart; others, transformed into redoubts, were bristling with cannon, which fired on the French army as it advanced. West of Smolensk was a large earthern fort called the Royal Bastion. On the far side of the bridge over the river was the junction of the roads leading to St Petersburg and Moscow. Ney summed-up: 'A city fully capable of resisting a surprise attack. But the suburbs will allow us to approach to the foot of the glacis without too much trouble.' His troops arrived there at 8 a.m. on 16 August and immediately started to mop up the sharpshooters who were endeavouring to prevent the advance on one of the suburbs. That evening fire was opened on the bridge which was being used by Russian troops, some leaving the city and some entering, why was not apparent. It transpired later that fresh regiments were relieving the garrison.

Napoleon seemed preoccupied; he asked Caulaincourt whether the Russians had at last decided to stand and fight or whether they were still retreating. 'I think, Sire, they are organising to retire.' 'If the Russian generals do that they will be abandoning one of Russia's holy cities and will dishonour themselves in the eyes of the population.' Then, after a silence, he explained what he intended to do if the enemy refused battle.

'I shall retire a little to be undisturbed and will fortify. We will rest and organise the countryside and we will see how Alexander reacts to that. I shall occupy myself with the Corps of the Dvina which is doing nothing, and my army will be more formidable, my position more threatening to Russia than if I had won two battles. I will call Poland to arms and I will choose later between Moscow and St Petersburg.'

This confidence was surprising given the oft-repeated statement that Moscow must be attacked at the earliest moment and that the Tsar would not negotiate until he saw his capital taken. Caulaincourt went to brief Berthier on these new dispositions. The Major-General shook his head. 'No. Once Smolensk is taken, he will want to go on.'

With the sharpshooters swept away, there was an infantry fire fight between troops on each river bank, but without much damage caused. The weather was very hot. Towards nightfall, there was a truce to allow the horses to be watered. A small tributary of the Dnieper separated the two armies and the cavalrymen led their mounts there. The Russian horses and the French horses drank deep, lifted their heads and looked at one another. So did the men who started to communicate by signs. Bottles and packets of tobacco were exchanged across the stream. The night was tranquil; tomorrow would be time enough to resume the war.

At 8 a.m. the guns on the ramparts fired and fighting raged in the suburbs. Some of the Russian troops held the heights on the right bank. All French manoeuvres that day were aimed at cutting off these troops from those inside Smolensk, but in this they were unsuccessful; the French cleared two suburbs at the point of the bayonet, one on the right of the city the other on the left.

The black powder smoke enveloped everything. The Russians, who now found themselves trapped, tried to sortie from the city, but were repulsed and their dead piled up in front of the Nikolskoie and Malakovskia gates. The French batteries fired continuously over the ramparts. As the day wore on, many districts of the city began to burn, gusts of red and yellow smoke piercing the black clouds of artillery smoke.

At nightfall, the scene became majestic, the salvos of cannon-fire punctuated by the rumble of collapsing buildings. A sharp cold had succeeded the day's heat. Napoleon surveyed the fire which lit the horizon and clapped Caulaincourt on the shoulder: 'It looks like an eruption of Vesuvius. Is not that a grand sight, Master of the Horse?' 'Horrible, Sire.' 'Bah! Remember the words of a Roman emperor: an enemy corpse always smells sweet.'

At 1 a.m. on 18 August, the last defenders of Smolensk retired, burning the bridges behind them; most succeeding in joining the bulk of the Russian army on the right bank. Two hours later, the French pillagers, always on the alert, started to slip through the old breaches in the ramparts. Napoleon was aware of it and gave orders to round them up; only formations of troops should enter the town. The bulk of the Russian army retired slowly in good order down the Moscow road.

Napoleon entered Smolensk at about 6 a.m.. This was not the first time that he had ridden into a conquered city through smoking ruins and dead piled high. The Russians had lost more than 9,000 men killed or wounded, the French about 6,000 – the figures are unconfirmed; I have also seen 15,000 dead and 4,000 wounded for the Russians, 1,200 dead and 6,000 wounded for the French. But who could keep an accurate account in this nightmare?

'In his progress across the city, the Emperor was constantly confronted by scenes of desolation.' Twenty-four hours would be needed before the streets could be cleared enough to allow the collection of the French and Russian wounded – those who seemed to have a chance of survival – and, once again, where should they be put? 'Fifteen large buildings were chosen as hospitals,' according to the official reports; in fact, only a few houses were still standing. As usual, the sick and wounded were piled into them. Lacking straw, they were laid out on paper and parchments taken from the archives. 'In the hospitals of

Smolensk,' wrote the Belgian surgeon Kerchove, 'or more accurately, in these cloaca of misery and infection, one could observe the impact of these putrid miasmas on the production of hospital gangrene.' For twenty-four hours, the wounded had practically nothing to eat or drink.

'In less than a month', said Napoleon to Caulaincourt, 'we shall be in Moscow and in ten weeks we shall have peace.'

No more talk of rest, or hesitation between Moscow and St Petersburg. He wrote to Marie-Louise: 'My love, I am at Smolensk as of this morning. We took this town from the Russians after having killed 3,000 and wounded more than triple. I am well. It is very hot. Things are going well.'

Some of the wounded were sent to the rear by various routes. Those travelling through regions spared from the war found food and drink, but not all were so fortunate. A Württemberg doctor looked in vain for the provision wagons said to be following the army. Where they were no one knew. The sick died from 'an acute form of diarrhoea'; the doctor had been unable to give them any food or fortifying drinks. He put an end to himself by cutting his throat with a scalpel.

On 19 August, while the army was continuing in pursuit of the Russians, Napoleon remained at Smolensk, issuing orders. 'I want this town divided into districts which will be constantly patrolled. Have the houses searched and arrest the so-called sick Russian soldiers that one sees everywhere. I do not wish to see a single corpse, detail more men for burial parties. Why have the entrances to the town not been sufficiently cleared?'

During the day, riding two leagues beyond the town, he met General Borelli of Murat's staff, who told him that the advance guard was engaged with a sizeable Russian corps. 'Sizeable? How many?' Strength not yet known. Napoleon ordered the advance guard to be reinforced and returned to Smolensk. Not until midnight was Gourgaud able to give him an account of the day's events. At Valoutina, the Russians had posted men on the heights overlooking the Moscow road and had opened fire on III Corps. Attacked by Ney's troops, they first retired and then reformed farther away, repeating the manoeuvre several times, their strength growing until they numbered 15,000. For two hours the fight had been indecisive, until finally there were 6–7,000 casualties without result since the Russians had been able to continue their retreat. Several generals cited Junot as being responsible for this check; his VIII Corps was nearby and yet did not intervene, despite an order from the Emperor and pleas from Ney: 'You are disappointed at not being a marshal. Here's a chance, take it and make sure of winning your baton.' Nothing would budge him and no reason ever emerged. 'Junot has given up,' said Napoleon to Berthier. 'I cannot leave him in command. Have Rapp replace him.' And a little later: 'Junot has let the Russians escape. He is making me lose the campaign.'

Then other issues seem to have seized his attention, for no other action was taken, and good news from the left wing raised his spirits. During an engagement with the Russians, Oudinot had been wounded and was immediately replaced by Gouvion Saint-Cyr. He counter-attacked brilliantly, driving in the Russian right and capturing some artillery. Napoleon, anxious for several days about his left wing, was so satisfied that he created Saint-Cyr Marshal of the Empire.

In the centre, the troops pursuing the Russians now had the feeling that their nightmare march would never end. They suffered from the heat and dust as they had in the first days of the invasion of Russia, always in front of them the same void, the same desert. Some soldiers had found wild honey in the forests through which they marched, word spread and the 'honey chase' became a game, a distraction – and then an obsession. Every village on the way was ransacked for food. At Dorogobuzhe it seemed as if the Russians intended to resist, but it came to nothing; the village was littered with broken carriages, dead horses, discarded harness and uniforms.

The bulk of the army was moving quite quickly, but the supply service, the wagons and vehicles of every kind were far behind with the stragglers. Among the latter were those who, after a spell of vagabondage, now showed a wish to rejoin their regiments. Some had acquired little Russian carts with one or two emaciated horses which hauled three or four of them with such food as they had managed to collect. Enormous cuirassiers rode little Polish horses, their heels scraping the ground. Others were on foot, often hobbling with staff or crude crutches. These groups of soldier-tramps shouted gross jokes at passing carriages full of women. Often repeated was: 'Roll on Moscow!' Not having struck a single blow, they saw the campaign as a rough but colourful adventure, at the end of which they would arrive in the land of plenty.

At Viazma, a rather pretty town of some 15,000 souls in normal times, but now half-burned, there remained some inhabitants: a sacristan, a beggar, a wig-maker from Strasburg, an apprentice-baker. The soldiers managed to save some houses from the fire and they found some grain, flour, brandy. The Emperor was billeted in a large, empty house, still intact. At the bottom of the garden in a small Greek temple the ADCs found a coffin containing the body of a very old priest dressed in rich sacerdotal robes. According to the sacristan, he had died of shock on learning of the approach of the French. Napoleon ordered that a funeral be conducted, the army furnishing the wherewithal, assisted by the sacristan. The weather had changed, a cold rain fell. It was only 29 August.

After Viazma it became really cold. 'Some cavalrymen started to wear their pelisses and to replace their shakos and caps with sheepskin bonnets. These accoutrements provoked constant jokes.' At 2 p.m. on 1 September, Napoleon arrived at Ghjatsk (150 kilometres from Moscow), that is, his horse walked down the single street of the village; all the houses were in flames. Rain helped the soldiers to put out the fires. The Emperor had known since the previous day that Field Marshal Kutusov had replaced Barclay de Tolly as commander-in-chief. He now learned that reinforcements were assembling in front of Moscow. 'The new general', he said, 'cannot continue the policy of retreat which public opinion has condemned. He has been appointed to head the army on condition . that he fight.'

On 4 September a reconnaissance in force, which had been roughly handled by the Russians, returned to report that the enemy were standing at the little River Kolocza. The rumour spread throughout the army that there would be a major battle. This aroused varying sentiments in the breasts of the troops, provoking lively arguments around the camp fires of the bivouacs. In the still, cold night could be heard German, French, Italian, Spanish, Portuguese, Polish, Flemish and other languages and dialects.

'On 5 September at 5 a.m.', wrote Bourgeois, 'our troops moved off and marched until 2 p.m.. We then observed the Russian army camped on the left bank of the Kalocza. His right extended towards the Moskowa, the defence running along the wooded heights backed by formidable redoubts.'

The French called the engagement of 7 September 1812 the battle of the Moskowa; for the Russians, it was the battle of Borodino, the name of a miserable village of twenty hovels. Both sides claimed victory. Napoleon called it a clash of giants, and 'my greatest battle'. It was certainly his most costly one: 60,000 dead, of whom about 45,000 were Russian. It was the least elegant – to use the expression of the expert tacticians – of Napoleon's battles. The partial success of the Grande Armée on that day was achieved by feeding battalions and squadrons into the furnace of what had become a slogging-match. This was largely because Napoleon was ill, but it is the more significant that he commanded everything without check or criticism, leaving a minimum of initiative to his subordinates.

'*Ma bonne amie,*' he wrote on 6 September to Marie-Louise, 'I am very tired. Bausset delivered to me the portrait of the King. It is a masterpiece. Thank you for your kind thought. It is as beautiful as you are. I will write in detail tomorrow. I am tired. *Adio mio bene.*' As we will see, this was about the portrait of the King of Rome; but to refer to his fatigue twice in four lines is striking. He had neglected a cold contracted four days earlier and which grew worse on the fifth while riding in bad weather, fog, wind, fine rain turning cold in the evening. But it was not only his cold. The Emperor was seen to dismount and to stoop with his head against the wheel of a cannon. He had send for Doctor Métivier: 'Well, doctor, you see, I am getting old. My legs are swollen; I can scarcely urinate. It must be the damp of the bivouacs since I only live in this skin.'

Métivier found his ankles and feet very swollen, pulse irregular, dry and hacking cough, breathing difficult and especially, 'much sand in the urine'. He prescribed calming potions and emollient poultices on the stomach. This therapy did not appear to have much effect in the short term, at least. During the battle, Napoleon had managed to ride, but less than usual and his behaviour proved that his respiratory and urinary troubles were affecting his mental capacity.

We have already seen in the previous days a most uncharacteristic wavering in his strategic decisions; if he had to be in Moscow within a month, to hibernate at Smolensk would be folly; then again, the hesitation in deciding between Moscow and St Petersburg: finally it would be Moscow. Arriving at the Moskowa, Napoleon had said, 'I need a big battle' and having before him the chance of one, he took no action, as we shall see. During the battle, we shall see him in turn hesitant, almost wandering, and, especially, despite the pleas of all his marshals and generals, obstinate, almost senile, in his refusal to commit the Guard.

Let us next look at the marshals and generals. They were none too enthusiastic at the start of this campaign. To have to say farewell to the gilded life which most of them had enjoyed for years was, they felt, a bit much. Bloody war! I place much weight in this nostalgia, despite another tolling bell heard here and there in some edited memoirs published long after the event. So what picture of the Moskowa should we get from the favourites who left for the war like a pack of whipped-on hounds; this one of the fabled valour, that one with his complete disregard for death? Let us name the generals who were killed in the battle:

Generals of division: Montbrun, Caulaincourt, Chastel: generals of brigade: Romeuf, Lambert, Marion, Compère, Huard, Plauzonne, Damas, Bessières (I Corps of cavalry reserve), Gérard (III Cavalry Corps). Generals wounded: thirty-seven; seriously: Morand, Friant, Compans, Rapp, Besnard, Nansouty, Grouchy, Saint-Germain, Bruyère, Pajol, Defrance, Bonamy, Teste, Thiry, Guilleminot. Try to find a butcher's bill of this size among the generals of the First World War or the Second. At the Moskowa, Marshal Davout was also wounded and if Murat was neither killed nor wounded it was purely by luck: he galloped everywhere with complete disregard for the enemy fire and there was no risk of his being overlooked with his huge gold-bedizened hat with its high white plume, green velvet pelisse embroidered with gold, sky-blue tunic with gold braid, gold-braided, crimson breeches in the Polish fashion, yellow boots.

We saw more than 400,000 men cross the Niemen and then Napoleon had split the Grande Armée into three great corps. How many took part in the battle of the Moskowa?: 120,000 according to Thiry, 127,000 according to Lachouque. What became of the others I do not know and I dare say that no one else does. Some regiments, having crossed the Niemen, had been sent north and south and we saw that fatigue, climate, hunger, alcohol and desertion (stragglers who never rejoined) had reduced by a third the army which marched on Moscow under Napoleon's command.

Those who arrived at the Moskowa were the survivors of a harrowing marathon; we have followed them closely enough to picture their state. The forced marches imposed a pitiless triage eliminating the feeblest, the least fitted for combat, but the survivors had empty bellies and soaking uniforms. In their huge cooking pots at the bivouacs of the Moskowa was nothing more than thin soup. While the Russians were fighting on their home ground, at the heart of their country and in defence of their capital and lacked for nothing, Napoleon's French soldiers were 800 leagues from France and the foreigners in the Grande Armée might well ask themselves for what country they were fighting. Now how would they behave, all these men thrown into this most brutal of battles? Like the generals listed above, like all the officers and NCOs, with a wild courage and complete contempt for death. Heroism, automatism – who can say?

From the very beginning, however, the mere sight of the Russian redoubts caused alarm. A redoubt is a fortified work, square in form, whose entry, known as the throat, is sited in the least exposed spot. It can contain numerous cannon; isolated, it can only resist for a limited time – such is its designated role. There were two redoubts near Borodino to defend the Moscow road: the Schwardino and the Grand Redoubt. Between these, on a knoll a little to the south, was another group of fortifications, triangular in shape, each smaller than a redoubt – the Three Flèches. The battlefield was about 12 by 10 kilometres on a plain cut by soft hills and deep gullies. The Moskowa is a winding river, here met by a tributary, the Kolocza, which runs through a sunken valley. The Russians faced Napoleon in an arc to the north-west in the angle formed by the rivers. Napoleon's army was in a slightly concave line on both sides of the Kolocza; south of the two armies was the forest of Outitza.

On his arrival on 5 September, Napoleon had wished to take the Schwardino redoubt, the farthest west and the first encountered on the Smolensk road. His order was carried out, not without difficulty. It took three assaults. Next day ambulance crews passing by saw a ditch filled with limbs and bodies. Apparently, Larrey and his colleagues had been operating there the previous day.

On 6 September at first light, Napoleon visited the lines. Overcoming his fatigue, he presented a 'confident demeanour'. Those near him could hear him humming snatches of 'Sing for Victory'. At the same time, the priests in the Russian army were parading an icon of the Holy Virgin brought from Smolensk and reputedly miraculous. The Russian soldiers knelt and sang; they could be heard from the French outposts.

According to Marbot, the Russian strength was about 130,000; Napoleon estimated them at 170,000. We saw these soldiers at fairly close range when they fraternised at Tilsit. Mostly illiterate brutes, their courage knew no bounds. Their gunners were better educated and fired very well: they had 600 cannon on this occasion. Kutusov, already appointed commander-in-chief on the Moskowa, supervised Bagration and Barclay de Tolly. A field marshal, related through his wife to the noblest families in Moscow, his success in Turkey had expunged the memory of his defeat at Austerlitz. Sixty-two years old, corpulent, very polite and apparently good-natured. For most of the battle, he sat on a small wooden bench, refusing any other, on a hillock a few metres high near the hamlet of Gorki, two kilometres east of Borodino, roughly in the centre of his army. As for Napoleon, he had his tent pitched just to the side of the Schwardino redoubt.

As I have said, the French were about 130,000 strong. Prince Eugène de Beauharnais, Viceroy of Italy (Napoleon was king) commanded the left wing, Marshal Davout the right and Ney the centre; Murat the cavalry; the Guard was in the rear in reserve. According to Caulaincourt (General de Caulaincourt, Duke of Vincenza; his brother, General Auguste de Caulaincourt, was killed at the Moskowa) Napoleon hesitated between two tactics. First idea: a grand movement on the right, which would allow him to turn the enemy position and avoid the redoubts. But would the Russians, threatened with being turned, once again retreat? Second idea: and adopted by Napoleon, was a mix: attack the centre 'frontally and from the rear, starting from the right'. Of course, it would be necessary to take the Grand Redoubt and the Three Flèches.

The Russians stood firm; obviously, they had but one idea, to stay put and parry each blow as it came. The scorched earth strategy hardly encourages tactical genius and, additionally, Napoleon intimidated every adversary. Seeing the immobile Russians, Napoleon decided (still at 6 a.m.) to give his army a day of rest and allow the circus time to catch up (especially the artillery reserve).

The weather: from the various accounts which do not wholly agree, one may deduce that it was damp and then cold and rainy on the 5th and 6th; on the 7th it was clear at first (Napoleon had spoken of an Austerlitz sun) and then grey, rainy and cold.

During the 6th two couriers reached the camp. One (Colonel Fabvier) brought news from Spain – bad news. Wellington, advancing from Ciudad

Rodrigo, had taken Salamanca. The armies in Portugal, concentrated by Marmont, 42,000 men in all, had clashed with the British at Arapiles, a series of small hills not far from Salamanca. After a bloody engagement – three French generals wounded, three on the British side, plus Field Marshal Beresford – the French had been forced to retreat in good order: 5–6,000 casualties on each side. Napoleon's reaction: 'The English are tied down in Spain. They cannot leave the country and come and scuffle in France and Germany. That is the essential.'

The other courier was the comte de Bausset, the palace prefect, coming from Saint-Cloud. He brought the portrait by Gérard of the King of Rome (aged 20 months). Napoleon declared it a masterpiece and displayed it to the officers of his household and to the generals awaiting his orders: 'Believe me, gentlemen, if my son was fifteen, he would not be here only in a painting.' He even summoned officers and soldiers of his Guard. Then suddenly: 'Take it away. He'll see the battlefield soon enough.'

On 7 September 1812 the working day had started well before dawn. Napoleon had called the duty ADC at 3 a.m. He had slept badly, suffering from a 'horrible migraine' and had called Bessières three times to ask him if the Guard lacked for anything: 'I want them to have three days' rations of biscuits and rice.' Waking a little later, he asked the grenadiers on guard at his tent if they had in fact received the food. Reassured, he went to bed again and finally fell asleep.

For the troops reveille had sounded at 2 a.m. The soldiers of the Guard, as was the tradition, had donned their full dress. The troops of the other corps had 'refreshed, that is, had combed their beards, dusted off their uniforms, blacked their boots, polished their buttons and cleaned their weapons. All this by torch light, which lent an air of solemnity to their work.

The company commanders mustered the men and read them the imperial proclamation which the colonels had just distributed, translating when necessary: 'Soldiers, here is the battle which you have desired so much. From now on, victory depends on you. We need it: it will give us abundance, good winter quarters and a prompt return home. Conduct yourselves as at Austerlitz, Friedland, Wagram, Smolensk, and let the most distant of your posterity mention with pride your conduct today under the walls of Moscow.' One senses a certain breathlessness on the author's part, with recourse to clichés, and it does not seem as if the proclamation aroused any great enthusiasm. Few or no cries of 'Vive l'Empereur!' – the historians speak of' 'a profound silence and a lot of serious thinking'. That said, all these men were convinced that the campaign must be ended and that they must do whatever was necessary.

They were hungry, especially the stragglers who had arrived during the night and had had no time to scrounge a meal. It was cold. The ritual distribution of schnapps (some called it schnick) would warm them, help them forget their hunger and generate some Dutch courage.

The sky lightened in the east, that is, behind the Russians. When the sun rose it blinded for a while but was soon behind the clouds. An unpleasant wind got up, but it masked the enemy's view by blowing clouds of dust into his face – the dust would be succeeded by cannon smoke.

At 6 a.m., at a signal from the Emperor, the massed batteries on the right opened fire and the Russians immediately replied. Some 120,000 rounds would be fired during this battle, the noise was continuous and masked the crackle of musketry almost completely despite its volume – three million cartridges would be fired. At this point we begin to read references in many accounts not only to cannon-balls but also to shells, though these were not the pointed projectiles with which we are familiar, but describe hollow projectiles. The shell filled with bullets would be used for the first time by Wellington's troops in Spain.

On the Moskowa, the troops of Eugène de Beauharnais opened the ball by descending and then climbing under enemy fire the ravine of the Kolocza and occupying Borodino which was already in flames, its inhabitants fled. At the same time Ney, Junot (centre) and Davout (right) attacked the Great Redoubt on the further right. Poniatowski charged to turn the Three Flèches and the extreme left of the enemy (Napoleon seems to have decided to order this move-ment at the same time as the frontal attack). But the Russian reserves counter-attacked and foiled a decision on that wing.

The general action quickly became murderous because, as a contemporary engraving shows, the regiments advanced in close order. No more of the deploy-ments inherited from the first fighters in the Revolution; this was more like the battles of Frederick II, but with increased fire-power. And with more ardour on both sides. The French – we use this word for the sake of convenience – wished to make an end and the alcohol they had taken was working on their nerves since they were practically fasting. The prayers and hymns of the priests had not prevented the Russians from drinking deep and they too fought fanatically. The compact masses of the French centre and right assaulted the Three Flèches eight times: the forts were bristling with cannon whose fire not only mowed down the French but also the counter-attacking Russians. The black smoke not only hin-dered but engendered courage, since it masked the extent of the slaughter. The generals fought in the front ranks with their troops. It was in making these repeated assaults against the Three Flèches , that Compans was seriously wound-ed and Davout, his horse shot from under him, lost consciousness. Murat arrived in his gaudy uniform at the head of his cavalry. The Three Flèches was eventually taken and their cannon silenced. It must have been close to midday. It was necessary to wait until the artillery on the left could advance in order to fire over the Three Flèches . Murat's cavalry was now pursuing the Russians who were retreating on the plateau: a demoralising rumour ran through their ranks – General Bagration had been mortally wounded.

There was an immense cheer from the French side – 'as if from all the voices of Europe in every language' when the Three Flèches strong-point fell. It was heard by the surgeons and doctors who had established their ambulance in a coppice fifty metres behind the lines. Later they were ordered to bring it forward. 'We started to receive wounded Saxons, Westphalians, Württembergers and even Russians. They were mainly cavalrymen with deep wounds or crushed limbs. An unusually tall Saxon cuirassier had been wounded in the thigh by an explosion. The shattered muscles had exposed the femur bone from the knee to the great trochanter. The wound did not bleed. Wounds from tissue torn away paralyses the vessels, while wounds from cutting instruments bleed copiously. The Saxon was alert and said "My wound is serious, but I shall heal quickly as I am healthy and my blood is pure." The French were quiet and patient. Many died before their turn came to be bandaged. In contrast, a Westphalian who had lost an arm cursed Napoleon and swore to take vengeance.'

The wounded were increasing in numbers, and were being evacuated to nearby villages or to a convent which was said to be capable of harbouring them. And all in disorder and uncertainty, for no one had instructed the surgeons beforehand as to the possibilities of evacuation. Many of the waiting wounded were laid out on the ground crying and groaning. It was cold. Instruments and dressings were scarce. At one point temporary dressings were improvised from strips of linen, clothing taken from corpses or from the patient himself.

Von Roos: 'We went to wash our instruments and our hands in the near-by stream. Enemy cannon–balls crashed frequently into the sides of the ravine or ricocheted to the bottom. During a lull, I went to see what was happening higher up. The fusillade, the artillery firing unceasingly, the cries were unend-ing, the aides-de camp galloped in every direction. Not more than thirty paces away, I saw General Montbrun turn pale and fall from his horse. I ran up, but two French doctors arrived before I did. The General was mortally wounded in the stomach from a bursting ball. The wound bled little. He was pale and yel-lowish. His alert gaze was extinguished.' Montbrun died shortly thereafter.

The Grand Redoubt had been built at the north-west end of the plateau and was held by the left wing of the Russian army. The redoubt was swathed in the smoke of its own cannon. The regiments of Morand's division, having climbed the slope of the Kolocza ravine, advanced step by step across the plateau under a hail of cannon-balls. Having reached the assault position, these soldiers – the 30th Line, charged with the bayonet and disappeared into the smoke. After a pause, the redoubt was taken under fire by the French artillery. Napoleon would soon be informed, doubtless a little after midday, that the work had been taken, but with heavy losses.

At this time, the 30th Line, now the only occupant of the Great Redoubt, saw swirling towards them a mass of Russian cavalry, followed by a mass of infantry. The regiment had lost two-thirds of its strength, including its colonel. General Bonamy was laid low 'with twenty-one bayonet wounds' and would be made prisoner. The survivors of the 30th had to retire, leaving the Grand Redoubt in the hands of the Russians.

Conspicuous among the mass of cavalry which threw themselves on Eugène de Beauharnais' infantry were the Cossack squadrons. The Russian heavy artillery fired on the Three Flèches , which were in French hands, and upon the Russian regiments.

A 'fresh' French division (General Friant), sent to counter-attack, advanced in good, even parade-ground order. In a moment, that good order was destroyed by the fury of the Russians. General Friant was wounded and fell from his horse. Colonel Galichet took command and ordered a retirement. A small group of cavalry rode up: Murat's staff, surrounding the Marshal, whose fabulous uniform was by now spattered with mud. 'What are you doing?' he shouted to the Colonel. 'You can see very well that I can't hold on here.' 'Well, I'm staying.' 'Fair enough,' replied Galichet, 'Soldiers, about turn. Let's go and get ourselves killed! Soldiers of Friant, you are heroes!' Many historians have reproduced this historic dialogue. Thiry provides a variant: Murat arrives after Friant had been wounded and a ball passes between him and Colonel Galichet. 'It's unhealthy here,' says Murat. 'But we're staying none the less.' One cannot fail to find some differences in the many accounts, all written long after the events (Coignet's, after the Restoration) of this furious and continuous hand-to-hand battle where the participants were out of their minds with noise, danger, fatigue, excitement. I myself attach more importance to details that recreate the atmosphere.

Napoleon surveyed the scene through his telescope, his view constantly obscured by clouds of smoke. From time to time he gave an order and an ADC left at a gallop. He was in turn, tight-lipped, 'strangely passive'. Surely, not a well man.

Messengers came bearing accounts of the brutal struggle that was developing in front of the Grand Redoubt, which the French were attempting to retake. All this, in a smoky world illuminated only by the yellow flashes of the cannon in the demented chaos. Nearly all the divisions of the army and many of its regiments lost their leaders, killed or wounded. 'Sire, the moment is approaching to use the Guard.' Many of the marshals and generals surrounding the Emperor must have uttered these words together, or perhaps one of them dared to speak for them all; in either case, the words were uttered. No reply.

Then Napoleon, learning that Rapp had been four times wounded in the space of an hour, and had just been carried to the first-aid post nearby, went to see him: 'So, it's your turn this time,' he said. How's it going?' 'Sire, I think that you will be obliged to use the Guard.' 'I disagree. I do not wish to see it destroyed. I am sure of winning the battle without using them.' Sure of winning the battle! But the Russians still held the Grand Redoubt. In front of the strong point the confused fight now involved five squadrons. 'All it is, in this hell on earth, is a confused mass of furious fighters clashing hand to hand,' Daru had come in turn to implore Napoleon to use the Guard – still in reserve behind the redoubt of Schwardino, in full dress, arms ordered. 'And if there is a battle tomorrow, what could I use?' A reply which gave rise to some mutterings even some shouts: 'The Guard to the battle!' Napoleon silenced the opposition: 'Eight hundred leagues from France, one does not gamble with one's last reserves.'

The Russian dead piled up in front of the Grand Redoubt to the extent that they were impeding the cavalry charges. The paroxysm of violence was such and persisted so long that all the accounts, using the same words to describe it, give rise to a strange feeling of monotony.

Meanwhile the French, having taken the Three Flèches , succeeded in turning these strong points' serviceable cannon on the Grand Redoubt. Russian troops could be seen staggering from the forts. Then the French cuirassiers charged, followed by Beauharnais' infantry and at about 4 p.m. the Grand Redoubt was retaken. A lull ensued; the artillery fire diminished. 'What are the Russians doing?' asked the Emperor. They had retired to the far end of the battlefield and were massing there. This defiance irritated Napoleon, who turned to General Sorbier, the artillery commander: 'Since they want more, give it to them!'

Four hundred guns fired into the mass. The two wings of the French army had now overrun the Russian centre. Many aides-de -camp arriving at the redoubt reported that everywhere the unit commanders were asking for the Guard to be committed 'to finish the business'. The senior officers around Napoleon were saying that this was the moment to release the Guard, cut the Russians in pieces and obtain the decisive victory which the Emperor had so coveted. Marshal Lefebvre even dared to shout: 'Forward, the entire Guard!' The pressure on Napoleon was such that he turned to the Guard and said, 'Go on then, you goddamned idiots!' But immediately after having allowing his hand to be forced, he rescinded the order. After the battle, he repeated that he had not committed his reserves because he would need them to strike the decisive blow in the battle which the Russians would certainly offer under the walls of Moscow.

Nightfall brought an end to the battle which in any case could not have continued because the surviving troops, French and Russians alike, were too reduced by fatigue. According to the official casualty lists, 6,547 French officers,

NCOs and soldiers had been killed and 21,453 wounded. These exact figures are meaningless, because they do not include men who had been blown to pieces, mangled, crushed or burned. In fact, 60,000 corpses, 45,000 of them Russian, lay on the battlefield, from which the groaning of 35,000 wounded men could be heard, few of whom would survive. Delirious cries in every language could be heard: 'To Arms!' 'The Cossacks!' and, eternally, the supplication 'Water!' Men wrenched themselves upright, staggered a few paces and fell again, others hobbled, groaning, Yet others went furtively from one body to the next – plunderers. Napoleon wrote to Marie-Louise that he had won the battle and Kutusov wrote in similar vein to his Tsar.

As usual, one reads in the Bulletin of the Grande Armée that the Emperor on the day after the battle visited the field and had the wounded of both armies removed. The clear and cold morning revealed a disgusting scene. The horse artillery was regrouping: 'I scarcely dare say', wrote Lieutenant Hubert Lyautey, 'that in some places, despite our precautions, we were compelled to drive our guns and caissons over the dead and wounded.'

Eugène de Beauharnais had spent the night on the battlefield, surrounded by some of his staff, all wrapped in their cloaks around a fire that had been built from bits of Russian gun-carriages. The sappers were digging trenches in the Grand Redoubt to bury the corpses around it. 'Suddenly', wrote von Roos: 'we saw a young Russian sit up amid the dead, rub his eyes in astonishment and get slowly to his feet as if the first rays of the sun had awoken him. Then he walked away in a direction where there were few of us and no one thought to stop him.'

At the place to which they had retired, the Russians had laid their dead neatly in rows. The plunderers searched the corpses openly – they were enemy; those who found only a few copper coins in the pockets swore, and their companions mocked them. Von Roos, collecting the wounded with his stretcher-bearers, witnessed another resurrection: 'In a wood, there was a body which we took for a cadaver, but he started to move his hands and to open his eyes. He was a wounded French officer, made prisoner by the Russians and then abandoned there.' The man had not been given first aid and was half-naked, only his trousers had escaped the thieves. Having fainted, he had spent the night on the bare earth, all his wounds open. 'He was a man growing grey, slightly bald. He had been long at war, since when showing us his most recent wounds, he also showed the old scars of wounds received in Italy, Germany and Spain.' Murat, who was passing, ordered him to be carried with the other wounded to a nearby village. On that day the surgeons and their aides ate the biscuits and nuts which they had found in the dead Russians' haversacks.

XI

MOSCOW
The Horizon Aflame

M adame de Staël has left an excellent description in a few lines of the
Moscow of that summer of 1812: 'Someone said rightly that it was
more a province than a city. In truth, one saw huts, mansions, palaces,
an oriental bazaar, churches, public buildings, lakes, woods and parks. In
Moscow, some of the palaces were of wood. Many had been burned for a celebration. Many houses were painted green, yellow or rose, elaborately carved like
the priest's dinner service.'

Before dawn on 14 September, Murat had already entered the city on the
heels of the Russian army, which was leaving. As the sun rose, the leading regiments breasted a rise from which they could see the city. It was called the Mount
of the Salute because any Russian reaching it would salute the holy city. The
cupolas sparkled like jewels in the morning mist. Napoleon's men had seen
nothing like it and stood, open-mouthed, overawed. Some pointed to a cupola
that sparkled more than the others – Ivan's Tower. Around the city which spread
far and wide could be seen wooded villages, pretty as toys.

Here follows as exact an account as possible of the events that occurred at
Moscow and nearby between 14 September and 19 October 1812, the date on
which the Grande Armée began to retrace its steps – say rather what remained
of the army, perhaps about 100,000 men of the 400,000 who had crossed the
Niemen.

The first units to enter the city on 14 September were the cavalry of the
advance-guard commanded by Murat: 10th Regiment of Polish hussars; the
Prussian Uhlans; then Württemberg chasseurs, leading four French regiments of
hussars and chasseurs and mounted artillery. 'We were so proud to have lived for
such a beautiful day that we forgot all our fatigue and privation.'

Many of these men had previously entered European cities as conquerors
and recalled having marched between hedges of men and women, often silent,
guarded, hostile, often merely curious, often applauding – it had happened.
Here, nothing! The music of the bands echoed off the walls. Despite the fine
weather (soon to change) the streets were empty.

They became less so as the troops advanced into the central districts,
where they swept up stragglers from the Russian army. Some staggered, visibly
drunk, and some were lying dead-drunk in the road, still clutching a wicker-cov-

ered bottle by its strap. From the saddle the cavalrymen could smell the alcohol; the Russians reeked of it. But for the troops of the Grande Armée entering Moscow, the penalties for pillage were extreme – death if one dismounted. So the men used the sabre to cut the strap and with a twist of the point, to slide a bottle within their reach.

The advance-guard noticed here and there a few liveried servants lurking in the shadows. To cross Moscow in pursuit of the Russians took at least three hours.

Napoleon arrived at the Mount of the Salute and received a note from Murat telling him that the enemy units had nearly all left the city and that a Russian army staff officer was asking for a suspension of fighting – approved on the express condition that the Russians continue their retreat.

On the same day at about 11 a.m. Napoleon learned that there had been a skirmish between the regiments of the advance-guard, who were arriving at the Kremlin in the city centre, and some hundreds of convicts with muskets endeavouring to prevent them from entering. A few rounds of artillery dispersed them.

French regiments were entering Moscow in a continuous stream, advancing cautiously through a deserted city. Patrols were sent out. Napoleon learned that there had been incipient fraternisation between the advance-guard and the Russian rear-guard. Some soldiers and officers had shaken hands, offering them drinks. A senior Russian officer arrived and put an end to these civilities, whipping the soldiers.

Murat's advance-guard and some other regiments, an entire division, were to follow the Russians for some distance northwards, the remainder were billeted in the city and in bivouacs outside.

At noon Napoleon with his ADCs and entire staff arrived at the Dorogomilov gate beyond the bridge over the Moskowa, west of the city. He was astonished not to find a delegation of notables to welcome him. 'Sire,' said General Durosnel, 'the population of Moscow has fled. But the houses still shelter some suspect persons. Your Majesty will not be able to sleep in the city until a service of patrols has been established in each district.' The Emperor, visibly disappointed, walked up and down for a while, then remounted his horse and rode across the district. Abandoning the idea of entering Moscow that day, he would spend the night at an inn in the Dorogomilov. The wooden building was reeking, noisome. An attempt was made to improve matters by burning vinegar in the room in which the Emperor was to sleep. In Moscow itself there were often houses like this rubbing shoulders with dream palaces – a very Russian contrast.

In fact, on 14 September 1812 Moscow, which normally harboured 300,000 inhabitants, was not completely deserted. It is true that practically every person of Russian origin had left the city; compulsorily. The order to evacuate the city had not been given after the battle of Borodino because the government had announced that Borodino had been a victory: salvos, music, balls. But after the battle at Mojaisk (70 kilometres west of Moscow), which the Russians lost, the Tsar left for St Petersburg and all Muscovites were ordered to leave; those who refused were regarded as traitors.

The order did not affect foreigners living in Moscow. Not only could they remain, they were obliged to do so. A number of them had applied for passports (no one could travel without one in Russia) in order to move, for example, to St Petersburg. Refused. So there were an unknown number of French and German nationals in Moscow; the foreign colony was reputed to be large and brilliant. For many years the sovereigns and nobility had welcomed to St Petersburg and Moscow French painters, artisans, actors (Moscow boasted a French theatre), hairdressers, cooks, cabinet-makers. Catherine II had welcomed many French *émigrés* including princes and gentlemen, some promptly favoured with pensions and dowries through imperial generosity, clergy, schoolmasters and professors (almost all of them retrained), soldiers – many served in the Russian army – the less affluent had to manage as best they could.

The sudden exodus began amid scenes of disorder and panic. The rich Russian landowners had wished to remain at Moscow with the foreigners. They had houses full of priceless marbles, chandeliers and mirrors from Italy, pictures which they were reluctant to abandon. They remained under cover while their compatriots complied with the evacuation order.,

A French actress, Louise Fusil, who had emigrated, first to St Petersburg and then to Moscow, 38 years old in 1812, found herself caught up in all this: 'I heard a sad song far off, then, a few moments later, a most touching sight came into view. A huge crowd, preceded by priests in their robes and carrying candles, men, women, children, all weeping and chanting holy hymns. This picture of a population abandoning its city and taking their penates with them was heart-rending.'

The first concern of those who stayed was to amass a stock of provisions, which were piled everywhere, especially in the cellars. Then it was rumoured that the city was to be destroyed and those remaining would be 'buried in the ruins'. This provoked another exodus, inside Moscow, to those quarters deemed the least exposed and most distant from those occupied by the invaders. Leaving furniture and pictures, taking only their jewels and food, the foreigners and those Muscovites anxious for their possessions moved to apartments, often in the palaces of friends who had fled. 'We climbed to the top storey with a telescope several times daily. We saw the fires of the bivouacs of the French. The terrified servants came to report that the police had been knocking on doors telling the occupants to flee as the city was to be burned and that the fire pumps had been removed.' To leave and go where? Anywhere! Without passports, with nothing? Just who was going to burn the city was not known. Panicky moves from one quarter to another were still occurring. Then, on 14 September came the invading army.

On that day some French men and even more French women, who had shut themselves up for some hours, dared to sortie. Once they had been identified they were not molested and did not lack for officers offering protection, often with a chivalrous disinterestedness.

Napoleon received from Murat, who was continuing to pursue the enemy army with the best part of a division, numerous reports in which the King of Naples stated that the Russian troops appeared very discouraged and that the Cossacks were discontented and wished to quit the army. These reports cheered the Emperor: 'We will soon receive peace proposals.' However, on 14 September at 11 p.m. an ADC arrived out of breath at General HQ (in the Dorogomilov quarter): 'The Moscow bazaar is on fire!' This was a development of brick-built shops north-west of the Kremlin. 'The Duke of Treviso and General Durosnel are on the spot. We have been unable to master the fire for lack of pumps. In defiance of their orders, the soldiers started to pillage.'

From many bivouacs around the city an explosion was heard – or, at least, so many soldiers believed: 'We thought that an ammunition magazine had exploded, or possibly an infernal machine.' Then came the flames. The officers and men billeted in the city as well as the headquarters staff thought that it was an accident, an imprudence. But soon more buildings were afire; eighteen according to many accounts. 'Numerous patrols were sent, and, by the light of the fire, they glimpsed figures in rags running from house to house, torches in hand.' These were the incendiaries; criminals, prisoners, and their appearance indicated that a Russian prison was no nursery. These men were hirsute, emaciated, indescribably filthy, naked under their rags which were held together by a leather belt or cord; terrifying and drunk, the odour they spread spoke volumes. Their gaolers, before fleeing, had distributed alcohol as well as sulphur matches. 'Set fire to everything and take anything you want.' This order had been given by General Count Vassilievitch Rostopchine, at that time governor of Moscow. His daughter, the Countess of Ségur, was to write many children's books including 'The Perfect little Girls'.

Three days earlier, this gentleman had had a proclamation posted up everywhere: 'General Kutusov will defend Moscow to the last drop of his blood and is prepared to fight in the streets of the city itself.'

'In 1823, Rostopchine would accuse the French of having caused the fires by placing candle ends, torches and firebrands in the houses. This assertion created sufficient stir that at St. Helena Napoleon, who had seen the incendiaries with his own eyes and had had some of them shot or hanged, began to wonder whether it was true. Even today, some people share his doubts. André Castelot put an end to the controversy by producing the deposition of Commisar Voronenko, held in the scientific and military archives at Moscow, reference 4346: 'On 14 September at 5 a.m. Count Rostopchine sent me to the wine market, to the Minty market and to the commissariat and ordered me if the enemy suddenly entered the city to try to destroy everything by fire, which I did, etc.' *Scripta manent.*

On the night of 14/15 September, Napoleon ordered the occupation of certain quarters of the city; twenty patrols of dragoons were to round up any Russians found and take them to Davout at a village outside the city; ten patrols of mounted grenadiers would perform the same duty at the Kremlin. The patrols deployed, but the Emperor can have had no idea of the wild fury of the incendiaries. Many soldiers, including Sergeant Bourgogne, have left good accounts of that mad night.

There was an army of torch-bearers and nothing could stop them, for they fuelled their fury until they dropped with gulps of alcohol found in the houses into which they had broken. Many were armed with weapons taken from the Kremlin armoury. There were bloody fights by the light of the flames, within the houses, courtyards, gardens, in magnificent greenhouses containing exotic plants and whose glass panes were burst by the heat. The incendiaries were pursued from floor to floor in these palaces; cornered, they did not hesitate to throw themselves from the windows. They killed themselves, wounded themselves, limped away torch in hand. A dragoon sabred the hand of one of them; without hesitation, the man picked up the torch with his other hand.

Those who staggered and fell dead-drunk had to be killed where they fell. Otherwise, the brutes awoke an hour later and resumed their task which proved as intoxicating as the alcohol. The soldiers themselves were also wild with fury as a result of the ferocity of their adversaries and because many comrades had been killed or wounded in booby-trapped houses: a bomb left to explode when the house was fired.

'Despite orders, the soldiers have started to pillage,' thus the ADC from Headquarters. The bazaar shops were crammed with goods of every kind, including food and drink; what trooper would hesitate for a minute? Dismount, and off we go!

Not only in the bazaar but throughout Moscow, despite the flames. Imagine these rough soldiers, some of whom had never been in anything but hovels, and who had been deprived of everything for weeks. A shot to break the padlocks, boots and musket butts to hammer in the doors; and there they were in houses such as they had never dreamed of. Bourgogne: 'I had never seen a house so richly and sumptuously furnished as those which we now saw. Among all these riches, the thing which attracted most attention was a case filled with arms of the utmost beauty. I took a pair of horse pistols whose sides were garnished with pearl and precious stones.' This was only the start. Other explorers, having plundered the rosewood wardrobes of silk shawls and satin robes, used these to wrap hams found in the kitchens or in the cellars, now awash with alcohol.

The civilians and others fleeing the fires, took to the street; both men and women were pursued. Those who could claim to be French were fairly well treated, but woe betide any Russians who had clung to their possessions, the soldiers arrested them, roughed them up, and stole their jewels and money. Naturally, the accounts from the French side are fairly discreet *apropos* these depredations, but Doctor René Bourgeois spoke of it freely, as he did of the rapes of the women. How could it have been otherwise in this madness which had exploded with the starting of the fires?

The dawn of Tuesday 15 September broke in flames. During the morning Napoleon, who had quit his reeking lodging, rode through the Dorogomilov gate towards the Kremlin, along the Arbate, normally the busiest street in Moscow, but now deserted. The Kremlin, built on a hill, dominated Moscow and was a city within a city. The surrounding walls and towers were of brick set within a deep ditch and contained the imperial palace, that of the ancient Greek patriarchs, the arsenal, the municipal building, many churches, the largest being that of the Annunciation, which had nine cupolas, of which the highest was Ivan's Tower, topped by a very elegant gilded cupola.

Napoleon rode around the walls then entered and installed himself in the quarters occupied by the Tsar when in Moscow. However he did not sleep in the imperial bed, but in his own little iron bed. The officers slept in the different buildings of the Kremlin.

At St. Helena, Napoleon spoke to Las Cases of that day. He thought then that the Russians might refuse to parley, in which case, the army would take up winter quarters in Moscow and nothing would have been lost. 'I would then have offered the odd sight of an army peaceably hibernating in the middle of an enemy nation which exerted pressure from every side, like a vessel held in the ice. Everyone would have spent the winter in Russia in a general state of torpor. Spring would also have come to everyone. With the first signs of the fine weather, I would have marched on my enemies and, having beaten them, would be master of their empire. But Alexander, you can be sure, would not have let matters go that far; he would have disappeared when faced by all the conditions that I would have imposed.'

Did Napoleon really harbour these ideas on 15 September 1812? In any case, he had not appreciated the situation entirely correctly. His army would not be a vessel held in the ice, but one on fire. At 8 p.m. a new fire broke out. 'Another imprudence by the soldiers,' said the imperial staff. The Emperor retired early, as did the staff. At 10.30 p.m. a servant woke Caulaincourt: 'Milord Duke, the whole city is on fire.' Caulaincourt awoke Duroc, grand marshal of the palace. From other reports, the whole city was not on fire, but new fires had broken out in the northern sector and the north wind was driving it towards the centre of the city. Duroc: 'Put the Guard under arms but don't wake the Emperor.' At 12.30 a.m. a new fire. At 4 a.m. two more; this time the Emperor was awakened. 'Send out officers in every direction to ascertain what is happening.'

First reports were ominous: the fire was spreading rapidly and not a single pump could be found. Near the Marshals' bridge, the grenadiers formed a chain of buckets and poured water on the roofs of threatened houses – it was useless. Napoleon paced the Kremlin terrace. Clouds of smoke wafted sinister odours of sulphur and bitumen; Moscow seemed to be engulfed by a sea of fire. The Emperor's previous optimism had evaporated. 'This', he said to General Mouton, 'presages the worst disasters.'

Later that morning he wrote a reassuring letter to Marie-Louise: 'Moscow is a city as big as Paris. There are 600 towers and more than a thousand beautiful palaces. The city is endowed with everything. The nobles have fled, the people remain. My health is good. My cold is gone. The enemy is retreating, apparently on Kazan. This fine conquest is the fruit of the battle of the Moskowa.' Not a word about the fires!

At 9 a.m. on 16 September, as the Emperor was walking in the Kremlin court, two incendiaries taken red-handed were brought before him. Not criminals, these, but 'military police' wearing the uniform of that corps. Questioned in the presence of the Emperor, they said that they had been ordered by their superiors to set fire to everything, and gave details of how it was organised, district by district. The plan was not entirely adhered to, witness the activities of the criminal incendiaries, running hither and thither like madmen, but the results were undeniable. Napoleon seemed very depressed by the confessions: 'See how the Russians make war! The civilisation of Petersburg has deceived us; they are still Scythians!' The military policemen were shot that morning. On the next and subsequent days, squads of incendiaries and others suspected of complicity would be escorted to various places of execution; having been shot, their bodies were hanged on gibbets as an example.

On 16 September houses surrounding the Kremlin started to burn. Some burning fragments were carried on the wind and fell on the tiled roof of the arsenal, full of powder and ammunition. Men threw buckets of water and swept the burning fragments off the roofs. The heat was suffocating. The grenadiers' bearskins were singed. The fire passed north of the Kremlin, whose windows burst. Bessières and Prince Eugène besought the Emperor to move away, but he said No. A moment later, Gourgaud: 'Sire, the Kremlin is now surrounded by the flames.' And Berthier: 'Sire, if the enemy attacks the army corps which is away from Moscow, Your Majesty has no means of communicating with it.' 'All right, I will go. I want to join IV Corps.'

Interest in the Napoleonic era has always been such that a thousand details have been scrutinised, studied and debated. For example: an acute argument arose between General Gourgaud and Philippe de Ségur (soldier, politician, diplomatist, officer and writer, a member of the French Academy) concerning which route the Emperor had taken when he left the Kremlin on 16 September 1812, and after the fall of the Empire the two historians fought a duel (Ségur was wounded) over the question. Whichever route he took, Napoleon left the Kremlin on the arm of Caulaincourt, necessarily on foot, a handkerchief over his face, crossing a burned-out district. Finally one of the grooms brought up a horse and the Emperor left for the ancient residence of Catherine II.

To start with, a folly of costume. On the squares where the army regiments bivouacked at will, one could see through the smoke soldiers dressed as Kalmuks, Chinese, Cossacks, Tartars, Persians, Turks – Moscow was nothing if not cosmopolitan. Everything came from pillage, pillage of barracks, homes, palaces, private theatres. Some troopers were wearing French court dress, swords at their side. 'Add to that a square covered with everything one could desire in the way of sweetmeats, wines and liqueurs in quantity, little fresh meat, many hams and large smoked fish, a little flour but no bread.' Amid this gluttony and Bacchanalian excess, the lack of bread was the most keenly felt. Whole houses burned and collapsed, but their cellars could still be got at. Here were jumbled together troops of every nation, criminal incendiaries, and women – the results can be imagined.

The serious pillagers wished to retain their sobriety. The soldiers and NCOs of the 1st Regiment of Chasseurs were well organised, celebrated modestly, happy to have appropriated 'many silver ingots from the Mint as big and heavy as a brick'.

The incendiaries were still pursued; it was sport, though the instinct of self-preservation was still to the fore. General Pernety arrived at one bivouac on horseback, pushing a young Russian in a sheepskin coat, hands tied. The General summoned Sergeant Bourgogne: 'Are you in charge of this post?' 'Yes, General.' 'You will execute this man with the bayonet. I just surprised him, torch in hand, setting fire to the palace where I am lodging.' Killing a captive in cold blood by bayoneting, what soldier wants to do that? 'We would, doubtless, have spared his life on account of his youth.' But the General was still there to see his order carried out. So, a musket shot. That was how it was there.

Nightfall lent an even more fantastic aspect to this apocalyptic scene. Groups of pillagers wandered blindly, eyes burning from hot ash, through districts where the topography changed almost hourly, thanks to collapsing houses and streets full of debris. Some groups were engulfed by the flames and were not seen again.

Others came to districts untouched by the fires, where a strange silence reigned. A patrol entered a grocery shop: no one there! On a table was some cooked meat, 'several sacks of small change and sugar'. They helped themselves. Enter a corporal from a nearby house: 'It is a carriage-maker's workshop. There are some beautiful carriages and also some wounded Russians.' Everyone went to see. The Russian wounded fell on their knees, nobody troubled them – the carriages were more interesting, pretty, light, surely ordered by boyars. 'Let's take them to carry the groceries from the shop.' They loaded the carriages, but lacking horses, manhandled them. A gang of criminals wearing animal skins rushed them, brandishing knives, but the soldiers had muskets and pistols and the gang was beaten off. Those who survived unhurt, more or less, were harnessed to the carriages. Forward! To return to barracks, it was necessary to cross a district still afire, using rifle butt and the flat of the sword to compel the terrified criminals. They passed through two walls of flame, where beams from the collapsing houses wrecked some of the carriages with their human crews. No matter, press on! It was now raining heavily, but the fire persisted. The procession was blocked for a time until a group of buildings had completely burned down. 'While we were waiting for a favourable moment, we noticed that in one corner house was the shop of an Italian confectioner.' The Napoleonic pillagers, hungry for bread and fresh meat, made themselves sick gorging confectionery and jam, and often the liqueurs found in the shops were of better quality than those found in the cellars. This patrol found here some 'pots of mustard from No. 13 rue Saint-André-des-Arts in Paris'.

At dawn on 17 September, this jumble of soldiers, prostitutes and criminals could scarcely distinguish night from day, thanks to the smoke under the rainy sky and the consequences of their orgies. By now, the officers had ceased trying to give orders to which the soldiers paid no attention. Besides, the officers were lodged in the palaces or in rich mansions and were none too badly off. Few talked of their condition at that time, but Stendhal, not an officer but a functionary in Daru's army administration, felt no such constraint when writing to his friends. I prefer to quote, rather than paraphrase him:

'I spent an hour or two at Joinville's [Baron Joinville, the army's Quartermaster-General]. I admired the voluptuous style of decoration of the house. We, with Billet and Busche, drank three bottles of wine which restored us to life. I read a few lines of an English translation of *Virginie* [*Paul et Virginie*, by Bernardin de Saint-Pierre, 1787] which, amidst the general grossness, restored to me a little of the moral life. We left at about 3.30, Billet and I, to visit the home of Count Pierre Soltykoff, which looks as if it would suit S. E.[Daru]. We went to the Kremlin to tell him so.

'The Quartermaster-General came to see it but did not agree. We promised to go and see other houses near the club. We found the club decorated in the French style, magisterial and smoky. There is nothing similar in Paris. After the club, we saw the nearby house, huge and superb; finally, a pretty house, square and white that we decided to occupy. We were given the good news that we could have the wine in the cellar of the club. We hurried our servants there. They sent a lot of poor white wine, damask tablecloths, some napkins idem but very worn. We pilfered those to make curtains. My servant was dead drunk; he loaded into the carriage the wine, a violin which he had stolen for himself and a thousand other things. We indulged in a small meal with wine with two or three colleagues. I went with Louis to see the fires. We saw one Savoye of the horse artillery, drunk, striking an officer of the Guard with the flat of his sword and shouting nonsense at him. He was wrong and ended up by having to apologise.' Note that Stendhal took precautions in his letters and did not tell the whole story. For example, in a letter to a friend at Grenoble: 'Pray pardon me and burn my letter, since it is advisable to allow only the Bulletin to speak of the army.'

Outside Moscow, in the palace of Peterskoïé, Napoleon studied his maps and dictated the outline of a new project. He now wished to march on St Petersburg. Eugène's divisions would lead, the other corps, based on the Duna, one wing anchored on the fortress of Riga and the other on Smolensk, would threaten the capital, etc. Hardly had the project been explained to the senior chiefs of the army than all of them except Eugène disapproved. 'Marching away! Even farther away! Burying ourselves in the north! Go in search of winter as if it would not be here soon enough!' No! And the Emperor dropped the idea.

On 18 September at 9 a.m. Napoleon, riding his horse Moscow, started back for the Kremlin. A large part of the city had been reduced to cinders, but the northern district near the Kremlin had finally been saved when the wind changed to the west. Some districts had not suffered; about one-third of the city was still standing. Napoleon looked serious when crossing the ruined city.

Scarcely had he entered the Kremlin than he was brought a poster miraculously preserved from the fire, which had reduced to cinders the secondary residence of governor Rostopchine. It had been posted on the façade and was addressed to the French invaders: 'For eight years I have beautified this region and lived here happily in the midst of my family. The inhabitants of my estate numbering 1,720 left at your approach, and I have set fire to my home so that it might not be sullied by your presence.'

Napoleon dictated more orders : take the Russian guns from the Kremlin arsenal; distribute provisions and help to the victims of the fires; go and ascertain the fate of the children in the Moscow Orphanage (abandoned to their fate by Rostopchine), and a letter to Alexander I in which he stated his wish to end the war as soon as possible. He finally decided to mention the fires to Marie-Louise: 'It was the governor and the Russians who, raging at their defeat, set fire to this beautiful city: 200,000 worthy inhabitants are in despair, in poverty in the streets.' Two hundred thousand, two-thirds of the populace? What of the exodus? But he must not paint too sombre a picture in a letter to Paris. 'There is enough left for the army,' he added, 'and the army has found lots of riches of every kind, for in this disorder all can be pillaged.' Yes! True, the imperial orders reduced the anarchy; there were remnants of discipline, and the troops bivouacking just outside Moscow received provisions from the city, but the pillaging continued, not excluding that by the officers who, less frank than Stendhal, would write that they had 'procured' some beautiful furs or had 'acquired' some object of value.

On 19 September the weather was fine and the Emperor held his first parade on the Kremlin square; at his side, was one of his ADCs, General Narbonne. To be an ADC at fifty-seven was unusual, but Louis de Narbonne-Lara was an exceptional figure in the Grande Armée; reputedly the natural son of Louis XV, in 1791 he had been Minister of War. It was perhaps his royal ancestry that endowed him with an air of distinction much appreciated by Napoleon and which contrasted with the manners of some of the marshals and generals whom success had scarcely refined. Throughout the Russian campaign, Narbonne was noted for his calm, his courage, his devotion to good deportment. Despite the biting cold and until it became absolutely impossible, he had his hair powdered and dressed in the 'royal bird' style. In the Bulletin, Napoleon lauded those who knew how to preserve 'their daily manners and their gaiety. It is of Narbonne that I am thinking.' 'Ah!' said Narbonne on reading that. 'The Emperor can say what he likes, but Gaiety is a bit much.' He died in 1813.

On 19 September Napoleon spoke to him in the Kremlin courtyard: 'Well, my dear Narbonne, how does such an army manoeuvring on such a fine day impress you?' 'I think, Sire, that the army is now rested and can be marched to barracks in Lithuania or in Greater Poland, leaving for the Russians their capital in the state to which they have brought it.' To leave before the cold and the snow, was that not good sense? The Emperor made no reply. It was fine that day, but it rained on the next; the great equinoctial change had begun, despite some misleadingly fine spells.

Rain or shine, the pillage continued; the officers took no action to stop it and Napoleon did not set a good example in having the enormous cross lowered from Ivan's Tower, reputed to be of gold. The cable broke and the cross fell to earth and was seen to be of gilded brass. Nevertheless the Emperor had it removed as a trophy. It disappeared in the icy hell that was to come.

On that same day, 19 September, Sergeant Bourgogne was one of a party of 200 men, including a squadron of Polish lancers, sent to the summer palace of the Empress on the city boundary. This was a wooden palace with stucco made to look like marble, superbly decorated and furnished. Napoleon wished to preserve it from any attack by the incendiaries. Shortly after the detachment arrived at 9 p.m. and the guard post and patrols had been organised, the first flames sprang up, 'in front, behind, to left and to right, with no sign of who had set the fires. At length, more than twelve parts of the building were seen to be ablaze.' The general commanding the detachment (perhaps Kellermann) ordered the sappers to try to contain the flames. They tried, but could do nothing; there were no pumps, and other measures proved useless. A group of incendiaries were surprised leaving one of the cellars, some still holding burning torches; their fate was sealed. A strong wind had got up, and the soldiers narrowly escaped being burned to death in the palace with the captured incendiaries.

On 20 September it poured with rain while patrols escorted to the places of execution incendiaries captured in various places, and others including policemen 'conspicuous in their uniforms' and 'an individual muffled in a well-kept green cloak weeping like a child'. This man had lost his wife and son in the fire. He claimed to be a Swiss from the Zurich canton and was a professor of German and French, seventeen years in Moscow. While crossing towards the Kremlin, he recognised the remains of his house and there found the burned remains of his family. The patrol leader took pity on him and released him. 'At midday, while looking out of the window of our lodgings, I saw a convict shot. He would not kneel and met his death with courage and, striking his chest, seemed to defy the firing- squad. Some hours later, those whom we had escorted met the same fate.'

Many NCOs were under house arrest for having allowed a group of prisoners to escape. No doubt, poorly guarded, for two of them, exploring a neighbouring house, found two women and a convict. At his side were weapons and a torch as thick as an arm. Beaten up, he tried to defend himself, but being drunk, without success. Thrown down the stairs, a patrol seized him. The two NCOs turned their attention to the two women who, to atone for having harboured an incendiary, offered cucumbers, onions and a large piece of salted fish with some beer. 'But no bread'. The women also produced some Danzig gin. All drank deep. There is no record of what followed, but the two NCOs decided to keep the women 'as laundresses'.

At this time, the troops who had been posted around Moscow were encountering very different problems. Bourgeois: 'They could hardly maintain life on the provisions sent to them from the city, little enough, since the fruits of pillage belonged to the pillagers and the military authorities were unable to claim them for general distribution.'

The outpost troops began eating horsemeat – cavalry horses. The officers tried to stop them from killing the beasts, but – we're hungry and anyway there is no forage for the mounts. Foraging parties were organised; it was necessary to travel 6 to 8 leagues from the bivouacs and these expeditions were in danger of ambush by the Cossacks and armed peasants.

Convoys from Smolensk arrived daily, but too often they brought nothing, having been harassed and pillaged by the Cossacks *en route*. The escorts brought horrific tales of the makeshift hospitals set up between Smolensk and Moscow, sepulchres they called them. Their presence could be discerned from afar by the putrid smell and the piles of rotting corpses, excrement and mud, forming a frightful cloaca around the buildings. Was this known in Moscow? No one seems to have given it a thought.

Napoleon wrote a long letter to the Tsar. He deplored and criticised the order given by Rostopchine to burn Moscow. He felt it impossible that the Tsar with 'his principles, his kindness, the justice of his ideas, had authorised such an excess, unworthy of a great nation'. In brief: 'I am making war on Your Majesty without malice: a note from you before or after the last battle would have stopped my advance. If Your Majesty retains some remnant of his previous sentiments, he will take this letter in good part. None the less, he can only thank me for have sent an account of the situation in Moscow.' The letter was confided to a Russian still living in Moscow, M. de Jakowleff, whose brother had been Russian minister at Stuttgart, and who claimed to be able to deliver the letter. Napoleon received no reply.

At every level in the occupying army, right up to Napoleon's household, a sole topic was argued endlessly: the Emperor would not spend the winter here. If he could not obtain a peace, he would retreat to Poland and go into winter quarters there. 'Don't believe any of it. Look at the orders which he has issued concerning the security of the city. We shall spend the winter here.'

The outcome – everyone agreed that this last eventuality could not be dismissed and that it would be prudent to provide against it. Provision became a key word: provision of warm clothing, food, drink, wood for heating. In short, here were new and valid reasons for pillage. The resources of the houses and palaces not consumed by the flames seemed unlimited. One count listed seven large cases of sparkling champagne, quantities of Spanish wine, of port, 500 bottles of Jamaica rum, 100 large sugar loaves, hams, salted fish in quantity, some sacks of flour, two large tubs of tallow and some beer.

The hunt for provisions had replaced the hunt for incendiaries; patrols constantly left and returned loaded. Between these fatigues, the men rested, lying on rich 'furs of mink, lion, fox and bear'. The patrols did not only bring back eatables. Bourgogne mentions 'many plaques of silver with designs in relief, ingots of that metal. The rest consisted of furs, Indian shawls, lengths of silk cloth embroidered with gold and silver. It is good to know that on everything that has escaped the fire we other NCOs always levy a tax of at least 20 per cent.'

On 24 September another parade in the Kremlin courtyard. 'On that day there were many promotions and decorations awarded. Those who received awards at this review richly deserved them for having shed their blood on the field of honour.'

At M. de Posnekoff's private theatre Napoleon attended a play given by French and Italian actors who had remained in Moscow. During the play ('Open Warfare') Louise Fusil sang a ballad by Fischer:

'A knight rushing off to the wars
By his farewells consoled his love:
"On the field of honour, love guides my feet,
Strengthens my arm, has no fear for my life.
I'll return with double laurels."'

'There was no applause because the Emperor was in the theatre,' according to Louise Fusil, 'but this ballad which no one knew, made quite a sensation. Napoleon did not hear it because he was talking. He asked about it and M. de Bausset, the palace prefect, came to tell me to give an encore.'

The NCOs who were amassing provisions organised a fancy-dress ball, the patrols having found all that was needed in the abandoned palaces and private theatres. 'We started by dressing our Russian women as Frenchwomen, that is, in the style of the *ancien régime*, as Chinese, as boyars. For an orchestra, we had a flute and a drum, but that sufficed for dancing because at the same time we were drinking large glasses of punch. The ball lasted all night.'

All this time, the advance-guard was marching painfully across an immense plain at the heels of the Russian army. The tracks of the enemy disappeared, the nights were cold and damp. The peasants came out of their hovels to watch the riders and foot soldiers who looked so tired, who seemed to be marching into a void. Von Roos: 'Our commander made signs to the inhabitants of a farm that he wanted a drink. One of them brought a large wooden bowl filled with a light brown liquid. The commander shared it with his men. This liquid tasted good and was so clear that one could see the flowers painted on the bottom of the bowl. He returned the empty bowl with a silver coin and the peasant made such a deep bow that his locks touched the ground. No one had ever thanked us before in that fashion. The drink was *kwas* [fermented barley].'

The retreating Russian army remained invisible, but each day the French were harassed by Cossacks. Daily the advance-guard gained ground but lost men. Orders were to evacuate the sick and wounded to Moscow – but how? The orders did not specify and the advance-guard had no transport. Of the seven senior surgeons at the crossing of the Niemen, only von Roos remained; the others had stayed behind or were sick or wounded or in charge of one of the putrid hospitals on the road to Moscow. The sick and wounded straggled as best they could, begging their comrades not to abandon them. They slowed down the march.

On 4 October on the road from Moscow to Tarutino, the Cossacks burst out of the woods, more numerous than usual, and attacked repeatedly, only retiring when Polish reinforcements arrived. Numerous casualties.

'On 5 October, with Poniatowski's corps and the cuirassiers we were established on the banks of the Tchernichnia near the village of Teterinka [where the infamous camp of the same name was to become so well-known]. For fourteen days, the assailants of the camp would not be the Russians – who kept their distance – but hunger and the night cold – pitiless. Murat lodged in a house nearby behind a wood. The soldiers, in order to feed their fires, demolished all the village buildings, only sparing a few hovels reserved for the sick and for senior officers. They slept outside on straw – which replaced blankets – and each morning this straw was stiff with white frost. For food: gruel of barley or buckwheat – and not nearly enough of it. One part of the grain was reserved for bread making – the yearned-for bread: 'We had to mould the grain, a painful task for our thin and feeble arms. In spite of all our efforts, we did not produce flour, but crushed grain and the bread was heavy and compact. Officers and soldiers took turns at turning the millstone; those refusing to help continued to fast. Lacking salt, we seasoned the stews with gunpowder. Recipe: when boiling, the charcoal floated to the surface; this was removed, leaving the salt. But the soup tasted bad and caused diarrhoea.'

At the camp one morning, a fantastic caravan emerged from the mist: men and animals, and when the men explained their presence they were not believed. They were driving a part of the herd of cattle that had crossed the Niemen in the wake of the Grande Armée, three months earlier. A part, rather say a vestige – a few steers, cows and emaciated sheep. Why these drovers had not scattered like thousands of other stragglers and deserters, even they could not explain. They had 'continued', surviving by eating some of the cattle and had arrived at Teterinka mostly by a miracle. The emaciated animals provided three days' of feasting.

'Occasionally, we receive from Moscow some tea, coffee, or sugar.' The coffee was kept for the nights; those nights when the cold made it impossible to sleep. Around a fire of debris, they talked. The officers were relying on the Emperor's genius: 'So long as he is at the helm, we should not despair.' But the women who prepared the coffee were bitter: 'He lives a soft life at Moscow with his Guard and sends us here to die of hunger.' The drovers also sat around the fires. They told some horrendous stories. They said they had seen mutilated soldiers on the devastated battlefield of Borodino, alive but incapable of moving, who survived inside the cadavers of horses from which they tore strips of festering meat. They were black and resembled animals. The arms and ammunition had been collected, but no one had bothered about these unfortunates. Others have confirmed these facts. Ségur reported that these abandoned wounded exhibited signs of cannibalism. Gourgaud denied this. Who should one believe?

At Moscow, at the end of September, it rained and sleeted. Caulaincourt asked for an audience with the Emperor. He spoke of the approach of winter, of the danger of the army being blocked in Moscow, of the danger of waiting too long, of 'a march in the cold'.

'What march?' Napoleon still hoped that Alexander would agree to peace negotiations. Then the good weather returned. On 4 October he wrote to Marie-Louise: 'The weather here is beautiful; as warm as Paris.' Morale improved; there was a wild rumour among the ADCs: 'We are leaving Moscow, not to retreat to the rear, but to go to the Indies!' 'So confident were we', wrote Castellane in his journal, 'that we did not take account the chances of such an enterprise being successful, but calculated the number of marches needed and the time needed for letters to reach us from France. We were accustomed to the infallibility of the Emperor and to the success of his projects.'

Speculation on this subject ceased abruptly when it was learned that Napoleon had given orders to arm and fortify the Kremlin, and for the evacuation of the wounded to Smolensk. There were some 15,000 sick and wounded in the hospitals in Moscow.

On 6 October the French theatre reopened. A poster announced that the first performance would be Marivaux's '*Le Jeu de l'Amour et du Hasard*', followed by '*L'Amant Auteur et Valet*' a one-act prose comedy by Céron. Louise Fusil was again in the cast. General verdict: a poor play. There were eleven performances, but Napoleon did not attend any of them.

During that week, despite the discretion demanded of the secretaries to whom Napoleon dictated for part of each night, another rumour circulated among the staffs: the Emperor had wanted to send Caulaincourt to St Petersburg, carrying another letter proposing peace. Caulaincourt had refused, saying that such a *démarche* would be useless. Napoleon had then sent for Lauriston whom he ordered to go to Kutusov's camp and offer a temporary armistice allowing for discussions of peace conditions. It was said that the Russian field marshal had refused to communicate anything to his sovereign. In the ranks, it was thought only that there had been diplomatic moves, exchanges of envoys, nothing more. Bourgeois: 'We awaited the conclusion of a peace which would put an end to the ills which we bore with courage and in the hope that they might end.'

Ills was a relative term when applied to the troops stationed in Moscow. One could see in many city squares large 'exchange markets'. The soldiers bartered with one another on behalf of the Jews and the traffickers who followed the army but did not dare enter the city.

On 14 October Napoleon wrote to Marie-Louise: 'We have had the first snows, but it is not cold.' Not cold, but the snow came as a warning. The Emperor suddenly made known his decision: 'Let us hurry. We must be in winter quarters within twenty days.' To find winter quarters meant first marching to Smolensk. By what route? Napoleon called a council of war. Present: Prince Eugène, Major General Berthier, Daru, Marshals Davout, Mortier and Ney. Murat and Bessières, still tracking the Russian rearguard, were absent. First let us count the troops of what was still called the Grande Armée. Davout had 72,000 combatants, Ney 11,000, Poniatowski 5,000; the Westphalians 2,000; the Guard 22,000 – a total of just over 100,000 men. Let us recall the strength when the Niemen was crossed: 400, 000.

Napoleon put two questions to the council: Should we leave? If so, by what route? Here are the opinions: Davout, leave, by the Kaluga road. Mortier, Yes, by the Vitebsk road. Ney, leave, by the Kaluga road. Berthier, leave by the Vitebsk road. Prince Eugène, Yes, the Vitebsk road. Daru, we must not leave but enter winter quarters here in Moscow. There are enough provisions in the city and we can get forage. Napoleon: Thank you, Messieurs. It seems that the Emperor had already taken his decision, for that very morning he had written to Murat to hold the position at Winkowo on the road to Kaluga. From Kaluga (150 kilometres south-south-west of Moscow) it would be possible to take a more southerly route to Smolensk than by the Vitebsk road, a route moreover that had not been used on the outward journey so the region would not be devastated.

On the 15th every one felt that events would now move quickly. Convoys of wounded left for Smolensk. These men were not in good heart, having learned that the Cossacks constantly harassed the convoys between Smolensk and Moscow. Also leaving westwards were carriage-loads of what were called 'trophies': colours, arms and armour (some collectors' pieces), in fact, the fruits of what was more or less official pillaging – the great cross from Ivan's Tower, taken down on the Emperor's orders. Also among the 'trophies' could be seen gold and silver ornaments from the churches.

That same day Napoleon, wishing to show that in any circumstances he had his finger on the pulse of the Empire's affairs down to the last detail, put the final touches to and signed a document that would engender much discussion: 'the Moscow Decree', which gave a charter to the Comédie-Française in Paris. Then, pacing up and down in front of his silent generals, occasionally stopping in front of the fireplace of gilded marble in the room which he occupied in the Kremlin, he expounded once again his ideas concerning Theatre. He addressed one of his aides-de-camp:

'I should, my dear Narbonne, have consulted you before sending my decree on the very subject of which we are speaking. I am sure that in your youth you were a lover of the theatre, you were a great connoisseur of it. I believe it would have been the comic theatre, the affectations of society, Célimène, Mademoiselle Contat. As for me, I prefer tragedy, high, sublime, as that which flowed from the pen of Corneille. There the great men are more true to life than in history: one sees them only faced by developing crises, in moments of supreme decision, etc.'

Then, regretting that no tragedy had been written concerning Peter the Great, Napoleon said that he would not mention the error of Charles XII, beaten at Poltava.

'After our army is rested and refitted here, and while the weather remains bearable, there will be time to march to Smolensk, to link up with our reinforcements along the way and to put the army into winter quarters in Lithuania and Poland.'

Sunday 18 October. Napoleon had decided that so far as the remaining populace was concerned, the departure should not seem to be an evacuation – an operation towards Kaluga, nothing more. The military parade took place as usual in the Kremlin courtyard, Ney's III Corps being reviewed by the Emperor. He descended the stairway, surrounded as usual by his numerous and bedizened staff. The band played.

Hardly had the review begun than a horseman in brilliant uniform arrived; he reined in his horse at a respectful distance and an ADC approached and spoke to him. The ADC returned to the staff: quite a ceremony. The horseman was invited to approach the Emperor, which he did, removing his hat. It was Béranger, ADC to Murat, and his news was not good.

'On 18 October before dawn,' recorded von Roos, 'we were awoken by two cannon-shots. As the horses were always saddled up at midnight, we were soon moving. We could already see the enemy lines both in front and behind us and Cossacks galloping everywhere. The Russian artillery opened fire before we could put ours into battery, having few horses left.' He was referring to the wretched camp at Teterinka mentioned earlier.

'Murat and Sébastiani let themselves be surprised,' exclaimed Napoleon after hearing the report. 'The French troops have fallen into the habit of slack security; reconnaissance was negligently executed. I have to see to everything myself!'

If he had seen with his own eyes the exhausted ghosts of soldiers in the Teterinka camp, no huts or barracks, no straw, men sleeping on the bare earth, packed against one another and rolled in their cloaks, he would perhaps better have understood what a tempting target they presented to the Russians and how it was that they could have been surprised.

The survivors of this action said that they had been saved by the skill of Murat and by his resolution which stopped the panic. A disaster was avoided, thanks to several energetic charges by Poniatowski's cavalry. The French had retreated towards Moscow in good order. Cost: 3–4,000 men out of action, including one of Murat's ADCs, General Dery, as well as the Pole Fiszer, chief of staff in Poniatowski's V corps. The Russians captured six cannon, caissons and wagons. It took an hour for Napoleon to calm down and finally announce his decision: 'It must not be said in France that a defeat had made us retire. We must cushion the impact of this surprise. Starting tomorrow, we shall march on Kaluga and God help those who get in my way!'

The waiting, the uncertainty on the part of a great mass of men, has the effect of creating, even though those concerned are mostly unaware of it, an electric tension favourable to the virtually instantaneous propagation of any kind of news. One has the impression that the news of the Russian strike at Murat's troops had become generally known within the hour. According to Caulaincourt, it produced on the army at Moscow and even farther afield, a 'strong impression'. It was, in fact, the first occasion that the Russian army had attacked since the Grande Armée had crossed the Niemen. The troops had scarcely time to discuss the affair for on the heels of the news, came an order: 'We are leaving! Leaving tomorrow morning. Prepare everything!'

The scramble that now took place, and which was to last all day and the following night, was indescribable. All over Moscow and beyond NCOs ran about madly trying to round up their men who, when off-duty, were dispersed to houses chosen by them, to tents, huts and bivouacs in the squares and in the near countryside, to cellars which the occupants never left unattended in order the safeguard their booty and their provisions. To muster these dispersed troops in their units seemed a task beyond human capacity, since although they wanted at all costs to leave, with their arms and their regular haversack, they wanted also their provisions and, above all, their booty.

Few of these men believed that it was merely a matter of marching to Kaluga to give the Russians a lesson. They were leaving to go into winter quarters, variously thought to be in the Ukraine, in Poland, in Lithuania; in any event, they would not return to Moscow. So take your treasure and provisions for the journey.

They would take the maximum with them, the rest would go in the carriages which had always followed the army: the *cantinières'* carts, service corps wagons, prostitutes' carts, carts bought or seized from Russian peasants, officers' carriages, those of their wives and mistresses. All the NCOs had the same concern as the troops, to carry off the maximum amount of booty. Its loading would take the rest of the day (18th) and the night following in an atmosphere of feverish haste. Some Germans and more Frenchmen who had remained (compulsorily) at Moscow and who had enjoyed good relations with the invaders, asked themselves whether they should depart with the army, plunge into an adventure where they would be involved in the fighting, or whether they should await the return of the Russian authorities, and who knew how they would be treated then? They consulted together, agonising, changing opinions hourly – and nearly all decided to leave.

On 19 October at 7 a.m. Napoleon wrote to Marie-Louise that he was leaving to visit the outposts, that the weather was warm with a sun like that at Paris in October. 'I intend to move into winter quarters and I hope to be able to bring you to Poland.'

The traffickers, mostly Jews, had arrived and were all over the city. Knowing what riches had been garnered by the soldiers, they had been emboldened during the last few days and were now clustered like flies around the departing soldiery. The Jews following the army had never resorted to pillage; they purchased. They showed the soldiers gold pieces. In a few hours a market was created on an unprecedented scale. The Jews trailed after the soldiers, now marching towards the Kaluga gate, reminding them that they could not carry such loads far. I think that I must here copy word for word, a historic document which is the list compiled by Sergeant Bourgogne of the contents of his haversack. Here was a man with no motive to lie or to show himself more of a pillager than he was: 'I had several pounds of sugar, rice, a few biscuits, a half-bottle of liqueur, a woman's Chinese costume made of silk embroidered with silver and gold, many luxuries in gold and silver. I also had my full dress uniform, a large cloak for a woman when riding, plus two pictures in silver one foot long by eight inches high with figures in relief, all finely executed. Beyond that, I had several medallions and the star of a Russian prince mounted with brilliants. I was wearing over my shirt a waistcoat of yellow silk which I had made myself from a woman's skirt, and on top of all a large collar of ermine plus a game-bag slung at my side containing many objects, including a gold and silver Christ and a small porcelain vase. And finally, my equipment, my weapons and sixty cartridges in the box.'

The lead regiments led off in the early hours, but it was evening before the last had gone. The Emperor rode in the middle of the Guard, but it would not be correct to imagine a military march such as we have often seen. The soldiers were more or less mustered into units, but each company was grouped in front of, beside and behind several carriages. These carried provisions and booty – even sizeable pieces of furniture – officers and civilians, men and women, with their belongings. One general of brigade left Moscow with twenty-five horses and six loaded carriages. The *vivandières* were crowded in with their husbands and their children on mountains of bundles, Jews held the bridles of emaciated horses harnessed to their carts loaded with booty which they had purchased; one could even see Russian peasants dragging carts and carriages full of objects which the soldiers had jettisoned. One could hear Russian, French, German, Spanish, Italian, Portuguese, Yiddish, and yet other languages; the children cried and screamed. The carriages moved in files of three, four or five, the cortège stretching back over five kilometres.

Before leaving, Napoleon had issued his orders. Mortier was to blow up the Kremlin next day after the last of the garrison had left. Murat was to rejoin the army on the march and form the advance-guard. Napoleon had understood that 'the vehicles following the Grande Armée were a considerable number'. He ordered that each owner carry two wounded men on demand: 'Every vehicle having been ordered to take one or two wounded and which is found travelling without them will be burned. The vehicles must be numbered or will be liable to confiscation.'

Numbered! This order to Berthier was dated that very morning, 19 October 1812. At this point the Emperor was out of touch with reality. According to one estimate, seemingly a conservative one (Denniée, *Itinéraire de Napoléon*) there were forty thousand vehicles on the road. Increase or reduce it as you wish. The retreat from Russia, which was about to go down in history, began with the greatest furniture removal in history.

XII

1812
Retreat in a Cold Hell

The heterogeneous mass trailed interminably towards Kaluga, stretched out over a distance of about twenty kilometres. Military formations were jumbled up with civilians, wagons, guns, carriages full of women and officers, peasant carts. On the day following the departure, the weather changed to rain which slowed everything down; by that evening, only 40 kilometres had been covered in three days of marching from sunrise to sunset. On 20 October, Napoleon had sent detailed orders to Mortier, who had remained behind: blow up the Kremlin and burn Moscow, set fire to the barracks and all public buildings, except for the Orphanage.

The 3rd Württemberg Regiment of chasseurs à cheval from the division that, under Murat, had long been dogging the footsteps of the retreating Russians was now a part of the rearguard of the Grande Armée with other troops from around Moscow who had joined the main body after the departure from the city. The men of these regiments found their comrades who had been billeted in Moscow, fat and sleek. These fortunates had loaves dangling from their haversacks, a brandy bottle slung from the sabre guard or cartridge box; not to mention the provisions in the carts and officers' carriages; to a man they showed little disposition to share their bounty. The deprived ones tended to console themselves with the rumour which ran the length of this disparate crowd: Napoleon was going to drive into the southern provinces, Russia's bread-basket, beat the Russians *en route*, destroy the large armament factory at Toula and put the army into good winter quarters. After which, they would all go home.

On the morning of 24 October, the 3rd Württemberg Regiment *en route* to Kaluga, had passed Borowski, 100 kilometres from Moscow. There had been a halt at the end of the morning and at that moment, gun-fire was heard from afar. The troopers said: 'Hey there's a fight!' but they weren't particularly concerned; they had heard gun-fire before. Their attention was directed to a scene which they found unusual: a long line of carriages had stopped and soldiers were unloading goods from them and laying them out on the ground in the style of travelling hawkers, except that no hawker had ever offered such merchandise. These treasures were examined, evaluated, bartered, sold – in order to lighten their packs. 'There were there,' wrote von Roos, 'the most beautiful carpets I had ever seen, tapestries, gold and silver-embroidered textiles, silk of every colour, men and women's clothing, embroidered and glittering as seen in princely courts. One heard: "So-and-So has so many precious stones, another has a strong-box full of brilliants, another a roll of ducats." I listened wondering.'

Far ahead, the cannon were still rumbling, but few paid attention because no orders had been passed down. The bartering continued until nightfall, when the treasures were hidden from view and the bivouac fires lit. Next day the cannon were heard again but intermittently. The treasure market resumed in front of the wagons. It ceased in the afternoon on receipt of shattering news: the Russians had attacked and wiped out the vanguard, the Emperor was a prisoner. Consternation: who would lead the army and whither? The Russians would certainly make a mass attack. One hour later other messengers arrived: the Emperor was not prisoner, although he had narrowly escaped capture. Thanks to the intervention of the troops of Eugène de Beauharnais, the advance-guard had been saved from disaster, but there had been a battle at the town of Malo-Jaroslavets which finally had remained in French hands, but devastated and burned. The Russians had once again retreated.

The mishap to Napoleon on the morning of 25 October has been recounted with variations by those who participated and by others who had heard of it – the latter often exaggerated and dramatised, showing the Emperor fighting against 5,000 Cossacks. The acceptable facts are that Napoleon had taken a risk in advancing too recklessly and with a small escort. He wished to see for himself whether the Russians were retreating or not. Dawn had scarcely broken. The Cossacks had at first been mistaken for French cavalry. Recognised, they were immediately engaged by the duty squadron, then by the Guard cavalry; finally, the troops of Eugène de Beauharnais had arrived. Napoleon had drawn his sword as had Berthier and Caulaincourt. Rapp was covered in blood, his horse having been struck by a lance.

Napoleon had laughed at the adventure and continued his reconnaissance. The Russians had retired in good order and Napoleon was vexed at not having been able to turn them. Should he continue the pursuit? Having discussed the matter, he had endorsed the opinion of most of the marshals, who recommended a retreat by the shortest route. On the morning of 26 October each corps was ordered to return northwards. They would rejoin the Moscow–Smolensk road at Mojaisk, which they had taken on their eastward march. Rumours continued to circulate – the Kremlin had been blown up; all the Russians there had been buried under the ruins; the rest of Moscow had been burned. 'A good job, too!'

In fact, the rain had severely limited the damage by soaking the fuzes which the French had lit. At the Kremlin, the arsenal and a part of the ramparts had been destroyed; the remainder was intact. But the idea that Moscow had been wiped out pleased the soldiers and the story circulated that the order had been to burn everything, as had the Russians when retreating on Moscow. All the villages between Malo-Jaroslavets and Mojaisk were burned. 'The pretty and romantic little town of Bronsk was put to the torch with a sort of frenzy by the first arrivals.' This was necessary, said the incendiaries, to prevent the Russians from pursuing the army.

Because of the length of the column those at one extremity knew nothing of what was passing at the other, or even in the centre. The leaders were surprised to have to move Russian corpses off the road because since Malo-Jaroslavets they had heard nothing of any battle, nor a single round of cannon-fire. These Russians, obviously killed recently by a bullet to the head, were prisoners being escorted by a Portuguese battalion. At departure they had numbered 1,200, nearly all in a pitiable state, and despite the slow rate of march many could not keep up; the Portuguese alleged that they had been ordered to do this. Castellane wrote in his diary that such barbarous conduct, if it became known, would certainly not improve the treatment of any Frenchman taken prisoner by the enemy.

Mojaisk was reached on the night of 28 October in a full-blooded snow-storm and a temperature of -4° C. The town was a miserable collection of wooden houses, in varying states of dilapidation. They emitted a frightful stench and torch light revealed piles of decomposing corpses; these were the wounded from the Moskowa who had been left in intact houses and public buildings where they had died. In the abbey of Kolotskoi there were still 2,000 wounded; the doctors who had been left with them had no medicaments and could do nothing against typhus and gangrene.

On the morning of 29 October, the following order was circulated: 'Each regiment is to identify their wounded and to put those who can be moved into the carriages; each vehicle to take one or two. The Emperor and his marshals have set an example by clearing one of their carriages for these unfortunates.' The wounded were rapidly sorted out and those who were dying were abandoned; this was to become routine during the retreat. Even before Mojaisk, soldiers and civilians had been able to see on the sides of the road the distorted bodies of French soldiers that looked as if they had been thrown there. And, in truth, they had been; dead, near-dead or even patients in reasonable shape were thrown out.

It was all very well to give orders that the wounded be put in carriages, but to get any carriage owner to comply was another matter. To take one wounded man meant ceding space occupied by sixty kilograms of provisions or treasure. And the wounded stank, and needed help to discharge their natural functions, far from convenient in those freezing temperatures! And this wounded man, for how long could he hold out in the conditions confronting the retreating army? One way or another, would he not be dead in a few days? So, heave him overboard! How many compassionate comrades looked after their wounded until they died? The reign of pitiless egotism had already started.

Sick or wounded soldiers, classified as convalescents, marched abreast or behind their regiments. They marched in the freezing wind alongside carriages and coaches carrying officers, women, French nationals from Moscow, carriages loaded with provisions jealously guarded by their owners. If they as much as laid a hand on one of them they were abused and chased away.

There were wagons reserved for wounded; in these the men huddled together against the ever-increasing cold. When one of them died, his comrades threw the body overboard: what else could they do? These wagons were drawn by the most wretched of the horses, the leanest and lankiest of those requisitioned, and the poor brutes were not adequately shod for icy conditions. After Mokaisk, they were seen to slip and fall by the dozen. The wagon immobilised, the driver fled, the wounded beseeching passers-by not to abandon them. Not a head turned. The wagon remained on the frozen plain like a sinking ship.

After leaving Mojaisk, Napoleon passed through a part of the battlefield of the Moskowa. This gave off an insufferable stench and clouds of crows circled around as the imperial procession approached. The sovereign saw with horror a wounded man who had survived amid the corpses. Incapable of walking, he had dragged the putrid corpse of a horse aside to feed himself. Recognising the Emperor, he summoned enough strength to curse him.

Most of the officers were well dressed in furs. Some soldiers had bearskins, others only their cloaks. The booty in their knapsacks included fur caftans, short fur-lined dresses worn by working women, elegant creations. They had no gloves; a musket could not be held for long in eight or ten degrees of frost. Between Mojaisk and Viazma many soldiers threw away their weapons, and many jettisoned everything except food and light booty. The road was strewn with precious objects – pictures, candelabra and books, as Sergeant Bourgogne noted: 'I spent more than an hour picking up volumes which I would glance at and then throw away, perhaps to be picked up by others who in their turn abandoned them. There were editions of Voltaire, J-J. Rousseau and Buffon's *Natural History*, bound in morocco leather and gilt-edged.' The hooves of the little Cossack ponies would soon crush these flowers of French culture.

Even before Mojaisk, the Cossacks had been a menace on the horizon. Their attacks began before the army reached Viazma. Surging from a wood at the gallop and spread out, they would approach from one side or the other, then form a phalanx and charge. In the time it took a squadron to deploy, or for a regiment to form a firing line, they had struck with their lances or opened fire at the gallop and dispersed across the plains, leaving a gash in the endless procession. The soldiers of the rearguard climbed over the corpses of the Cossacks' victims and, more and more, of the wounded who could no longer keep up.

The Moscow–Smolensk road ran approximately north-east/south-west, curving at times to avoid small hills or woods. The officers kept a lookout to the southward, knowing that Kutusov was marching parallel with the Grande Armée. Kutusov was following the southern route which Napoleon would have taken, had he not resigned himself to changing his itinerary after the battle of Malo-Jaroslavets.

On 14 November, the advance-guard reached Viazma, a little over 200 kilometres from Moscow. A few souls were still living in the unburned part of the town. A small garrison had been left there under General Teste with some members of the military administration, responsible for collecting and safe-guarding the provisions and forage. These men protested that they had had no warning of the army's arrival; there was only enough forage for the horses of the staff. No bread, only a small amount of rice and flour in the army depot. A first and inadequate distribution was made, and what remained was pillaged – by the Guard: 'In a few moments', wrote General Teste, 'the provisions acquired so painfully were dissipated, dispersed and expended by men who, issued with five days' rations, acted like starving madmen. The honour of our arms, above all by an élite corps confirmed on so many battlefields, forbids me to dwell on the details of such a fatal incident. It is, and will remain, the cruellest happening of my career.'

On 2 November, when the main body of the army left Viazma, the rumour spread that the Russians, coming along the Kaluga road, had cut the line of retreat and that sharp clashes were being fought in front. Then it was rumoured that the rear-guard had been attacked. Both rumours were true. Kutusov, still following the parallel route, harassed the army with his Cossacks and light cavalry, often with infantry and artillery, but without risking a serious engagement. He well knew that in the weather he had an invincible ally.

On 2 and 3 November, there were no more than 3 or 4 degrees of frost, and it was often sunny. This relative mildness reassured the troops, who were still attacking and counter-attacking brilliantly. The veterans of the Guard seemed to have lost none of their valour. Napoleon ordered an exchange of positions between the vanguard and the rear-guard and vice versa, and also directed them to one or other flank to attack the harassing Russians. Despite all the soldiers' impedimenta, these manoeuvres succeeded quite well. The army marched towards Smolensk as if it were a slow and heavy squadron at sea, firing first one broadside and then the other. The cold and the suffering would put an end to this.

They left Viazma late in the morning of 5 November. The Emperor urged haste and everyone congratulated themselves, persuaded that at Smolensk they would find the rations and shelter that would be their salvation. The next morning and in the days following, there were many dead around the bivouacs. They were left lying there after their comrades had stripped the corpses of everything of value. Clothing became less and less uniform, the soldiers donning any garments they could find, layered one upon another. 'Nothing would have been more pleasant if the occasion had not been so sad,' wrote the actress Louise Fusil, 'than to see an old grenadier with his moustache and his shako, covered with a rose-coloured cloak. The less fortunate protected themselves against the cold as best they could.' The cold would prove even more deadly to who had run out of food.

It started to snow on the night of 5/6 November, but the temperature stayed at minus 20° C. The wife of a company barber of the Guard, one Madame Dubois, gave birth to a boy in a shelter of branches hastily construct-ed on the border of a wood. The company surgeon was present and the colonel donated his cloak to cover the shelter. He also gave the mother his horse which she rode, carrying her new-born in her arms wrapped in a sheepskin; she herself wore two cloaks taken from soldiers who had died from cold during the night. The baby died from cold some days later; the sappers dug a grave with their axes.

On 6 November the Russian plain presented the picture which six gener-ations would retain of the retreat: white to the horizon with the pine woods white also. Minus 22° C and foggy. During the day, the weather cleared a little and the cold abated. For the first time, Napoleon was seen marching in front of his carriage, surrounded by marshals and ADCs, also on foot. The Emperor was concerned about the weather changes, for the thaw now much hindered the advance of the artillery and the transports. Towards night the temperature fell again, with, as a bonus, icy snow. The horses began to drop in their hundreds.

In every war before armies were motorised, the horses had been the martyrs. The supreme crown of martyrdom should be awarded to the horses of the Grande Armée in Russia. Massacred (like the men) on the battlefields, wounded and abandoned (often, like the men) legs broken, bellies ripped open, dying by inch-es, pecked by crows while still alive, then on the frozen snow, eaten alive by the men.

Fallen horses were attacked even before they were dead; the frost would harden them too quickly. They were seen whinnying and shaking their heads as the butchers went to work. In a few days, the repellent spectacle would cease to arouse pity and even become interesting. When a horse fell, and was being cut into, the gourmands went in quest of the liver, reputed to be the most succulent morsel, others cut the throat in order to collect the blood in their big cooking pots. This was taken scarcely cooked, smearing their bearded and blackened faces hideously. More deviant, men would cut steaks from a horse's thigh while the beast was still walking, harnessed to a cart. In the cold, the animal scarcely bled, continuing to walk, apparently without being aware of what was happening – a kind of local anaesthetic – at least temporarily, thanks to the cold.

A saying made the rounds: 'It is better to eat them alive.' When they left Moscow, the soldiers had some well-loved dogs. No dogs now – all eaten. And were men eaten by men? Here and there, some evidence; here and there hints. Usually denied, but the desperate instinct for survival overrides every taboo. Among the other survivors of the retreat from Russia, Sergeant Bourgogne has this to say: 'We fell in with some soldiers of the Line. They maintained that they had seen some foreign soldiers (Croats) enlisted in our army, withdraw from a fire in a barn a roasted cadaver, which they cut up and consumed. I suspect that this happened many times in the course of that fatal campaign, though I am no witness. What interest would these men facing death have had in saying so, were it not true?'

They had not yet reached Smolensk and each day a thousand men or more fell by the wayside, killed by the cold. In the bivouacs, those who awoke each morning were greeted by the bizarre spectacle of comrades transformed into statues: rigid, whitened, ranged in a circle, petrified in various attitudes, often seated as if thinking. Death while sleeping is gentle and tempting. A soldier would suddenly cease marching, throw away his burdens and crouch on the snow. Officers and comrades would shake him: 'You're mad! You will die!' 'That is what I want.' 'Come on, get up. We will soon be at Smolensk.' The prostrate man might refuse; some even smiled, as if relieved.

Before Smolensk, the 12th Cuirassier Regiment passed through the town of Dologobouch where there had been a fight earlier (I Corps had been attacked by Platov's Cossacks) and which was now in flames. It was 4 a.m. Hearing cries of distress from one of the burning houses, an officer went to investigate. On the stairway, in the smoke, a man both of whose legs had been amputated, was dragging himself from step to step. 'I am battalion sergeant-major of 30th Light Infantry. I have been sheltered in this abandoned house for six weeks. I wish to await the Russians but I do not wish to be burned alive. For God's sake, move me somewhere safe from the flames.' Carrying a double amputee is not easy and this man was corpulent. The officers ran for help and returned with men who carried the sergeant-major behind the house and left him at the foot of a tree. They could do no more for him. The wounded in other houses perished in the flames.

Still *en route* to Smolensk, at the start of the day's march, a carriage was seen to emerge from a coppice and head for the road, escorted by a senior officer and two sappers. The officer opened the carriage door and showed the sappers the corpse of a young girl. Sergeant Bourgogne: 'She was dressed in a grey silk dress, covered with a pelisse of the same material and trimmed with ermine.

This girl, though dead, was still beautiful, though thin. In spite of being hardened to such scenes, we were moved at this sight; for myself, I was moved to tears, the more so on seeing the weeping officer. As the sappers were moving this young person whom they placed on a cushion, curiosity impelled me to look in the carriage: I saw the mother and another girl lying one against the other. They appeared unconscious and finally expired the evening of that day.'

That was the evening when, shortly before reaching Smolensk, the surgeon Larrey saw a young woman push into a crowd of soldiers who had just disembowelled a horse. She plunged her hands in the animal's belly in order to tear away the liver. This was confirmed by other witnesses. Some have it that she was a *cantinière*, others, a colonel's wife.

We saw Smolensk when the Grande Armée fought there on the way to Moscow. Surrounded by mountains, in the Dnieper valley, circled by ramparts, one does not see the houses from a distance but only the cupola of the Cathedral of the Assumption. Now, all is white and snow-covered. By the time they reached Smolensk, the army had lost 30,000 men since quitting Moscow. The survivors were a huge mob clothed in rags and crawling with vermin. At the beginning of the retreat, the soldiers might have ventured to undress to de-louse themselves, but this was now impossible because of the cold. Faces were wrinkled, bearded, almost black.. The Guard were the only ones that did not exhibit these signs of misery.

As at Viazma, the victuallers said: 'We were not given any warning of your arrival.' The truth of the matter was that the head of the service responsible for supplying meat on the hoof was cooking the books: he had sold provisions and in particular cattle to the local traffickers who had immediately sold them on to the victuallers of the Russian army! Immediately brought before a court-martial and condemned to death, the unfortunate prostrated himself tearfully before the Emperor who, disgusted, eventually turned his head away and pardoned him.

The mob swirled into Smolensk, seeking shops to pillage, but such provisions as remained were well guarded, and an order was circulated: 'Only troop formations will be provisioned. Individuals will receive nothing,' but 'loners', who did not know that provisions were being distributed, spread out across the city, relying on their own efforts. Some units were still able to parade in good order, for example, the Guard who, with the Emperor's blessing, lacked for nothing.

Smolensk, its houses burned and churches become makeshift hospitals, presented a frightful spectacle. The so-called hospitals were virtually morgues; on entering one had to walk across rigid cadavers. But life continued. In houses that had remained intact, the traffickers sold food or bartered it for jewels looted by the troops. They were joined in their business by the *vivandières* of every nationality, both blessed and cursed by the troops; a warrant officer showed the remains of a cabbage-stalk: 'This is all I have had to eat in the last four days.' Lacking the wherewithal to buy anything, he wandered off through the city and disappeared. At nightfall the traffickers hid in the cellars together with the dregs of the army and their women. The pillagers often entered a town ahead of the vanguard; anyone seeking shelter in their lairs was likely to be held for ransom or killed.

Not all the troops were able to get into Smolensk; outside the walls could be seen thousands of bivouac campfires on the snow. Around one of these were a German officer of light infantry and his staff. His carriage was full of sacks of tea. At the halts, having little to eat, he would brew up, and would allow his staff to do the same only using the tea-leaves he had already boiled. Another officer criticised this 'cruel parsimony': 'My dear fellow, if I can manage to get this tea to Germany I shall make a fortune.' 'We left early next morning. The German lingered to have his tea. The Cossacks arrived and we have seen no more of him.'

The cold and the misery had all but wiped out social distinctions. 'M. Clément de Tintigny, ADC to the Emperor and nephew of M. de Caulaincourt, placed his men and his carriage at my disposition,' wrote Louise de Fusil, which is how she left Moscow. She noted that during the first few days of the retreat everyone was stealing: 'All day long one heard – "Ah Heavens! They have stolen my trunk; they have stolen my sack, my bread, my horse." It was so from general to private.' One day Napoleon, seeing one of his officers wearing a very fine fur coat, said to him laughingly, 'Where did you steal that?' 'Sire, I bought it.' 'Bought it from someone who was asleep?'

The disorderly horde of vehicles was still moving slowly: at each bridge, each narrow stretch of road, coaches and carriages collided and overturned. Orders were to burn any that obstructed the route, and Louise Fusil saw herself threatened. But she was a woman and an actress; she knew how to excite pity, soften adversaries and profit from her connections. 'General Lariboisière spoke to a gendarme and told him to include my carriage in the group of carriages of the Prince of Eckmühl [Davout],' Louise observed, with a very feminine observation of the turn-out of her companions in this exodus. 'The ladies do not wear cloaks except to protect from the cold, and they choose black. But the domestics, the shopkeepers, all classes of the people in short make it an affair of luxury and choose reds, blues, lilac or white.' Often finishing by scrabbling in a horse's belly for the liver. Without going as far as that, and managing pretty well, Louise would face hunger after Smolensk. Shivering in her carriage near a bivouac, the alarm was suddenly given – the Cossacks! The carriage must be abandoned. 'So here I was on horseback at midnight, possessing nothing but what I had on me, not knowing which road to follow and dying of cold.' She would survive.

The Cossacks tended to attack the bivouacs around Smolensk without any great conviction; the Guard would sortie and drive them off. The army left by echelons between 13 and 15 November, Ney remaining as rearguard with I Corps. Lacking vehicles, all wounded who could not march were left at Smolensk to the grace of God and the charity of the Russians. The cold was such as to harden hearts as well as cadavers. Now, when a soldier fell, his companions threw themselves on him and robbed him of his possessions even before he was dead, leaving him practically naked; from a certain point on the march, most of the corpses found on the road had been stripped.

On 15 November, the vanguard moved off very early for Krasnoë (30 kilometres from Smolensk). Before they could get there they found the road barred by a mass of Russian troops; these were visible against the snow from afar, in front and on the surrounding hills. The scouts who spotted them retired immediately, but the Guard was right behind and advanced deliberately towards the Russians, who made way for them, taking up positions on the hills to the left of the road.

The troops following the Guard went into bivouac behind the town. Shortly afterwards it was reported to the Emperor that substantial Russian forces had surrounded Krasnoë: 'I will attack them,' he said. I will deter them and disengage our corps which are still following.' To launch an attack using this mob that had been the Grande Armée might seem to be insane, but there was the Guard whom he kept under his eye, and besides, he thought that the Russians were probably in not much better condition than the French. To Caulaincourt he said: 'Kutusov will weaken himself as I do by these marches and will distance himself from his reserve. He is occupying a region which we have stripped. The Russians will die of hunger.'

The Guard received the order to attack on the night of the 15th. The soldiers started checking over their weapons. The idea of a battle was welcome to many. Some thought that a defeat would take heart out of the Russians and make the retreat more secure; others, that nothing could be worse than their present situation and that to die in battle was not such a bad solution. At 2 a.m. they moved off in three columns: fusilier-grenadiers in the centre, tirailleurs and voltigeurs on each flank.

The battle of Krasnoë started that evening and lasted for two days. Those accounts that have tried to depict the battle in terms applicable to Austerlitz, Wagram or Jena, with details of troop movements, timings of attacks and counter-attacks, etc., are, in my opinion, completely fictitious. The soldiers of the Guard, and those of Viceroy Eugène who arrived afterwards, fought in snow up to their knees in an unfamiliar theatre, often asking in which direction they should march. The first night was particularly costly for the Guard. In the moonlight and by the light of the flames – the Russians had set fire to their own camp – the veterans could see the Russian heavy cavalry, cuirassiers in white with black breastplates, bearing down on them, their artillery firing canister all the while. The fighting was hand to hand; the Russians employing one of their ruses: playing dead, then rising to fire at the backs of the enemy.

The NCOs urged their men 'Forward! Forward!'. A notorious sergeant-major of fusilier-grenadiers named Delaitre was detested by his men, who called him 'Peter the Cruel'. During the day, one of them said to a comrade, 'He'll soon be gone'. It is not unknown for brutal non-coms to be liquidated during the confusion of battle. In this case, however, a round removed both his legs. 'My friends,' he cried, 'for God's sake, blow out my brains!' Nobody obliged him.

On that day, the Emperor at their head, baton in hand, surrounded by his senior staff, the Guard prevented the Russians from encircling the army. I and IV Corps were engaged; Ney's rearguard was anxiously awaited but didn't arrive. The battle raged around Krasnoë while the Emperor led the way beyond towards Orcha. He was to sleep at Dubrovna on the 18th in the château of Princess Lubomviska. The survivors of the army left Krasnoë on the 19th. The Russians did not pursue them, but deployed to cut off Ney's rearguard.

The long march was resumed in a temperature of -28° C. Paul-Emile Victor assures me that marching in the snow in that temperature is practicable for any-one, provided they are in good health, properly clothed and nourished. The survivors of the Grande Armée now heading for Orcha (about 120 kilometres south-west of Smolensk) – not to mention the wounded – were under-nourished, verminous beneath their rags, and, psychologically in a deplorable state; each morning the frozen corpses of their comrades were left behind on the snow. Larrey has described the appearance of these cadavers: 'The skin and the muscles exfoliate as in wax statues, the bone remaining exposed, the nose removes itself like a false nose and the hands putrefy and fall off.'

Except for the Guard, officers and men marched in the same disorder, units of all arms intermixed. Some carried over their shoulder a beggar's wallet and at their belt a pot on a cord, others led by the bridle the ghosts of horses, each carrying a cauldron of pitiful provisions. However, in this long river of suffering humanity were still to be seen carriages carrying officers and civilians, both men and women.

It was impossible to bivouac in twenty-eight degrees of frost, so halts were made at villages, no matter how miserable; at least the hovels furnished firewood or shelter, being built from the trunks of pine trees erected in the form of a square, held in place by notches at the ends, the gaps filled with moss. They were easily demolished. Those who tried to keep one of these hovels intact had difficulties because other groups would try to demolish it for the timber, and if opposed would set it ablaze. I say 'groups' because after Krasnoë there were no more unit formations but only small bands which the soldiers called *coteries*, an old word derived from the trade guilds. The solidarity of the *coterie* could be seen, especially on arrival at the bivouac: acquisition of firewood, pooling of provisions. Any member who had nothing to contribute to the pot was rejected; so much the worse for him, let him steal, kill if need be – it had come to that. Anyone from another *coterie*, sick or wounded or who sought to beg, was driven off with curses, beaten, often killed. The French having invented these little groups, saw them immediately imitated by the foreigners, grouped by nationality.

Napoleon, still leading the army, now on horseback, now on foot, watched the disintegration of his army with dismay. The soldiers saw a man with a sad and anxious face, seeming to march hesitantly with numerous halts. Nothing had been heard of Ney and the rearguard – which gave cause for sombre anxiety.

At Korytnia, (25 kilometres west of Smolensk) he learned that the Cossacks had attacked and pillaged the military convoy carrying the 'trophies' removed from Moscow, including Ivan's Cross, intended for the dome of the Invalides at Paris. The Cossacks had also taken the effects of many general staff officers, and, more seriously, the caisson containing the supply of maps for the campaign. Napoleon was depressed also because at Dubrovna, while resting for a few hours, the Cossacks had surprised the Guard's outposts and entered the town: 'What would happen if I fell into Russian hands?' He had sent for doctor Yvan and had him make up a massive dose of poison which he carried in a small bag round his neck.

Finally, on 6 or 7 November he learned that General Claude-François Malet had escaped. He had been detained in an asylum at the Trône Gate, not on account of insanity, but for having earlier organised two revolutionary plots. Dressed in his uniform and accompanied by two accomplices, one disguised as an ADC, the other as a police inspector, he had presented himself at the Popincourt barracks at 3 a.m. on 23 October: 'The Emperor is dead. He was hit by a cannon-ball in front of Moscow. Here is the decree establishing a new government.' This document – forged, naturally – carried the names of the past minister Carnot, General Augereau, many senators and his own signature. He also produced a letter from the commander of the 2nd battalion of the Paris guard. This document gave him full power to release immediately from La Force prison General Fanneau de Lahorie, convicted of complicity in Moreau's conspiracy, and General Guidal, accused of having wished to sell Toulon to the British. The coup had proceeded. On 23 October at 10 a.m., Malet had acquired authority over three-quarters of the troops stationed in Paris, and Count Frochot, prefect of the capital, had opened the Hôtel de Ville to him. He then went to the place Vendôme which housed the headquarters of the division and where he was arrested, General Hulin having recognised the decree as being a forgery. Order was very quickly re-established. It was not the first conspiracy against the regime or the life of the Emperor, but the latter, despite the farcical nature of the ending, was deeply depressed because, believing him to be dead, no-one had seemed to remember that he had an heir and successor – the King of Rome.

On the route they had chosen, the town of Orcha on the Dnieper (today 65,000 inhabitants, textiles and construction industry; in 1812, wooden houses and one-sixth of the present population) was some 600 kilometres from Moscow. The army arrived there on 20 November, led by the Guard. The weather was a trifle warmer, the sun shone, the Guard marched behind its band. Once 35,000 strong, only 5,000 were left – and this corps was by far the least depleted.

The army stayed at Orcha only long enough for a bridge of boats to be quickly assembled by the Guard's bridging company. Many of the troops would remember this town with affection because it had not been destroyed and they could buy provisions. The merchants accepted bank notes acquired at Moscow ('collected' according to one mealy-mouthed officer) but at a very inferior rate of exchange. The buyers cared little, they had lost all notion of cost and were hungry.

The population welcomed the soldiers of the Guard with sympathy, but when the rest of the army arrived it created a panic and many doors were closed and barred. There were painful scenes as many soldiers and civilians, convinced that they would not survive if they continued to follow the retreat, decided to remain at Orcha. 'Prisoners of the Russians? tough luck!' For cash or jewels they obtained shelter. The wounded who wished to remain prayed for lodging, as the hospitals at Orcha were already full. But they either had nothing to offer in return, or not enough: 'They were chased away, often falling and being trampled underfoot.'

Borissov is on the Beresina, 120 kilometres away. Forward! The sick and wounded stumbled, they were pushed to one side, their pleas unheeded, often they were cursed. This ferocity was not, however, universal, because there are mentions of soldiers guiding blinded wounded. These men who had marched for weeks in a white waste were now suffering from acute ophthalmia, aggravated by the smoke from bivouac fires and by the irritation caused from rubbing their eyes with filthy hands, or with snow – in the hope of alleviating the pain. A priori, blindness excites pity – but few of the blind reached the Beresina.

Ney's reputation as the 'bravest of the brave' was known throughout the army. The soldiers knew that he had been the last to leave Smolensk, knew too that his rearguard had encountered the Russians at Krasnoïe the day before the

Guard were engaged. Not a word since then. And in this army, monstrously ego-
tist, the same question was uttered a thousand times: 'What news of Ney?'

Napoleon had left Orcha on the afternoon of 20 November and arrived
that evening at the château of Baranoi, 15 kilometres from Orcha. It was there
that he received a message from Eugène de Beauharnais that Ney had crossed the
Dnieper on the ice at Variski on the night of 18/19 November and that he was
bringing with his rearguard 4–5,000 individual stragglers as well as some French
civilians who had been late in leaving Moscow.

Nothing had been easy. Despite having attacked several times, the rear-
guard had not been able to break the front of the Russians barring the road at
Krasnoë. A Russian colonel had then appeared under a flag of truce, offering
terms for an 'honourable capitulation'. Ney had exploded: 'Never, Sir! You will
stay here and guide me to the nearest bridge, or I will cross the Dnieper on the
ice.' Denniée reported this incident in his *Itinéraires de Napoléon*. According to
other versions, Ney had sent back the Russian, saying 'I will find a place,' and
had ordered several competent officers to search for a practicable crossing. But
the ice was thin and dangerous and, though the river was not deep, there was a
swift current. Soldiers and civilians, men, women and children drowned. 'Cries
of anguish were heard, the confusion was indescribable. In the dark, it was
impossible to rescue those who were drowning or even to issue orders. Dark
shadows waved their arms, howling. Then the tumult subsided; those saved lay
panting, death had closed the mouths of the drowned.' Some 200 troops and
civilians crossed at the ford, in similar circumstances; neither the horses nor the
artillery could get across.

The days were shortening; it was not light before 8 o'clock, and it began to get
dark soon after 4 o'clock. The troops marched by day and by moonlight and,
occasionally, by the eerie light of the aurora borealis. Now all the corps were
intermingled. On arrival at the bivouacs, it was no longer a question of shouting for such and such a regiment or company, but 'first corps, fourth corps,
Imperial guard', for some of the corps that had mustered thirty regiments now
had no more than two.

On the road between Orcha and Bobr, a Westphalian soldier was sitting
on the ground, holding in his hands a silver ingot, which appeared to weigh
15–20 pounds. He had carried it all this way and was now offering it in
exchange for a loaf of bread. There were no takers and he was chaffed to 'eat his
ingot'. On that day, the dismounted cavalry were attacked by a party of Cossacks
armed with bows and arrows who took some prisoners. The officers were led
away without too much ill-treatment, but the soldiers were stripped practically
naked and were last seen staggering through the snow. They did not get far.

On the same day, a Major Castellane was marching level with a young and pretty dress saleswoman who had had a boutique in Moscow. The protection of Caulaincourt, Master of the Horse, had ensured that she could sleep each night in one of the Emperor's wagons. Castellane was sharing some chocolate which he had been given: 'There was no gallantry in this act. We were all so dog-tired that we all said that we would prefer a bottle of bad Bordeaux to the prettiest woman in the world.'

Since leaving Orcha, Napoleon had realised that the enemy would reach the Berezina before he did and had ordered the mustering of every man who could hold a musket. He kept the Guard under his eye, ensuring that it marched as a body in close order, and when passing through a village or town, all available resources were requisitioned for this unit.

On 23 November, before reaching Bobr (35 kilometres from the Berezina) he ordered that all the cavalry's eagles be burned to deny them to the enemy. Then wishing to have a personal phalanx even more devoted than the Guard, if that were possible, he amalgamated all the cavalry officers still possessing a horse and formed them into four companies of 'guards of honour'. In this formation, under Murat's command, generals of division became captains or lieutenants and generals of brigade sub-lieutenants. The soldiers called them the 'Sacred Squadron'. Some used the words ironically, others with religious fervour.

Despite the frightful privations they had endured, the prestige of the supreme commander still affected a part of the army. Cries of Vive l'Empereur! could still be heard, but these were becoming rare. Not surprisingly, for the wounded making their agonising way along the road, the acclamation no longer held any magic. Close to Borissov, an administration employee was lying with both his legs broken. As Napoleon passed at the head of the Sacred Squadron, he raised himself on his arms: 'Look at him, this miserable puppet, who has led us for ten years like sleepwalkers. Comrades, he is mad; beware of him. He is a cannibal and will devour us all!'

The Emperor rode by as if neither seeing nor hearing him, as did the escort and the Guard behind them and those again behind the Guard. What could one now do, other than to obey and follow the Emperor? The Berezina was reached.

Every event has its own legend that usually records an isolated incident, usually the most obvious, at the expense of everything else; but as a rule it is the 'everything else' that makes everything clear. Most people imagine that the crossing of the Berezina by the debris of the Grande Armée consisted solely of a blind rush across a bridge that was breaking up, of men killing one another and falling into icy water, all under a hail of Russian bullets. But there was rather more to it than that, and the horrors might have diminished somewhat had certain of the protagonists behaved less stupidly. A careful study of the accounts of eye-witnesses affords one a fairly clear view of the Berezina drama from beginning to end.

On 24 November at 5 a.m. Napoleon, still at Bobr, ordered the Guard and General Sorbier's artillery to make for Borissov, held by the Russians he thought, but where there was a bridge over the Berezina. To accelerate the march he ordered all vehicles to be burned except those of the artillery, but this order was not obeyed; we shall see carriages and coaches at the Berezina crossing.

On the night of 24/25 November, a reconnaissance by General Edouard de Colbert, commanding the 2nd light cavalry of the Guard, reported that a party of Oudinot's troops and of the Moscow garrison had retaken Borissov from detachments of the Russian advance-guard. Oudinot was commanding II Corps (8–9,000 men), Victor, IX Corps (11,000 men), these figures are all very approximate. Let me emphasise here that from this point until the end of the campaign in Russia, unit strengths quoted become more and more questionable. What we shall now see will fully explain why this is so.

The troops of II and IX Corps had remained in the sectors of Czergia and Bobr to cover the main force that had marched on Moscow. The bulk of the Russian troops were still fairly distant from the Berezina. Wittgenstein (30,000 men) was about 20 kilometres further north. Kutusov (90,000 men) was yet more distant and farther south on the banks of the Dnieper, 150 kilometres from the Berezina. Admiral Tchitchagov (45, ex-minister of marine, ex-governor of the Danubian provinces, recalled to bar the passage of the Berezina to the French) had 60,000 men, level with Borissov, about 10 kilometres from the right bank, and was not moving. Napoleon had to have time to organise the crossing as best he could – given the weather and the troops at his disposal.

On the 25th Oudinot and Victor's troops, who had suffered little and still maintained a military appearance, saw arriving in the Borissov sector the ghostly vestiges of the Grande Armée – pity, consternation and anxiety. What would happen if the Russians attacked *en masse?*

That evening Napoleon was installed in a property belonging to the Radziwills' agent Baron Korsach, nicknamed 'Old Borissov'. He went with Caulaincourt to examine the Borissov bridge which had been destroyed in three places. Beneath its remains flowed the Berezina, said to be shallow at this point, black, encumbered with enormous ice-floes, dividing here into several branches, and 700 metres wide. To rebuild the bridge would take too long; time was pressing, since it seemed certain that the Russians would soon attack. A ford must be found.

In fact, they didn't have to search. On the 23rd General Corbineau, commanding the 6th cavalry brigade of II Corps, had reported to Napoleon that, returning from the north to rejoin the Grande Armée, he had surprised a Lithuanian peasant whose horse was soaked up to its chest: 'You! – you have just crossed by a ford. Where is it?'. To have refused to reply would have meant death. The man showed Corbineau. The ford was 20 kilometres upstream at the village of Studianka. The river there was 100 metres wide, maximum depth 2–2.30 metres, the bottom muddy and irregular. The right bank was higher than the left and was marshy, but now frozen hard. Corbineau's troopers crossed but not without difficulty; many were drowned. Having entered the water, the infantry would have to swim some thirty metres before finding a foothold again.

At first Napoleon was not in favour of using this ford; he believed the bridge to be less damaged than was the case. Having seen it, he changed his mind, but there could be no question of marching the army into the ford, men and cannon. A bridge must be built at Studianka – no, two bridges, one for the infantry and another for the artillery, just upstream. On the night of 25/26 November, the bridge-builders of the corps of engineers of General Eblé and those of General Dode de la Brûlerie (IX Corps) went to work.

I have described how, at the battle of Wagram, these specialists built bridges, some on piles and others on trestles. On the Berezina, they built two bridges on trestles, twenty-three to each bridge, using timber from the demolished hovels of Studianka. They had only six caissons of tools and nails, two portable forges and two wagon-loads of coal. But these were minor difficulties; the main problem was having to work in the water up to their shoulders. Let us describe this as accurately as possible. The bridgers were not naked, as has often been reported. Why should they have been? One can survive longer in cold water if clothed than if naked. Contemporary engravings show them clothed. Not all of them had to enter the water, nor were they continually immersed; they had built rafts. Their professional skill was faultless. Which does not mean that a number of them (already much weakened and under-nourished) were not carried away by the current and drowned – farewell, comrades! Others who had survived this inhuman ordeal subsequently succumbed to tuberculosis; one of them was General Eblé.

On 26 November at 3 p.m. (1 p.m. in some accounts) the first bridge was ready, and 8–9,000 of Oudinot's troops and two cannon crossed from the left bank. They kept formation, though rather apprehensive at the undulations of the roadbed, in places almost awash, elsewhere 50–60 centimetres above the surface. As they crossed, the men shouted 'Vive l'Empereur!' Castellane: 'It was truly a pleasure to us to see the troops well ordered, real soldiers.'

Having gained the right bank, these troops attacked the vanguard of Admiral Tchitchagov's forces and put them to flight. One gets the impression that the Russians were not over-keen on joining battle. In fact, the Admiral's intelligence had proved faulty; he thought that the French had crossed at Borissov and had deployed most of his troops in that direction. At 4.30 p.m. the second bridge was ready, but, the trestles having been driven into the muddy bottom unevenly, it broke in three places. The bridgers repaired it.

At nightfall the greater part of the retreating army began to arrive on the left bank, plus the stragglers and many civilians in carriages, on horseback and on foot. Forty thousand in all, according to some witnesses. Bivouac fires were lighted and the scene was one of great disorder.

On the night of the 26th/27th a surprising thing happened. Officers had been sent by Napoleon to tell the people crowding on the left bank: 'Cross now while the bridge is free [the other one was being repaired]. It will be more difficult tomorrow because the Guard will be crossing and the Russians may arrive. So, be quick!' How many took this advice? Not more than twenty. The rest for the most part remained crouching over their miserable fires or curled up in their carriages – 'Yes! No! Tomorrow!' They were worn out, overcome by fatigue, hunger, misfortune. There were some who did not hear the officers, nor even knew that the bridge was open.

On the 27th the Guard spent the day crossing to the right bank, and now, as if signalled, the mob rushed the bridges. 'They all tried to cross at the same moment, men and horses bowled over those on foot and the carriage drivers claimed a place by running over anything in front of them.' No pity for the weak. Women and children were pushed into the icy water and disappeared. And who do we see quite calm, bless her, in the midst of this madhouse? The actress Louise Fusil.

We last saw her solitary on a horse in the freezing night between Smolensk and Krasnoë. She had retrieved a carriage and then lost it again; wandered throughout the night in burning Krasnoë after which she had collapsed in the snow: 'I experienced the sweet surrender of one who welcomes a peaceful sleep.' A gentle death from the cold. No, she did not die; by a miracle, Marshal Lefebvre found her, took her to his coach and fed her. So that was how she came to be at the Berezina on that morning, still in Lefebvre's coach, crossing the bridge with the Guard. 'The Emperor was at the bridgehead, hastening the march. I was able to observe him closely attentively because we were going very slowly: he seemed as calm as if at a review at the Tuileries. The bridge was so narrow that our carriage nearly touched him: "Don't be afraid," he said. "Go, go, go! Don't be afraid." These words, which seemed to be addressed to me personally, since there were no other women there, seemed to me to imply that there was an element of danger.' And here, also crossing, was Murat, leading the Sacred Squadron. 'The King of Naples reined in his horse and put his other hand on the door of my carriage. He made a gallant observation while looking at me. His costume seemed to me to be among the most unusual for such a moment and in a frost of twenty degrees: his collar open, his velvet cloak negligently thrown over one shoulder, his ringlets, his black velvet cap with its white plume gave him the appearance of a stage hero. I had never seen him before at close quarters and I could not refrain from staring at him. When he dropped back a little behind my carriage, I turned round to stare at him. He saw this and made a polite gesture. He was very flirtatious and liked women to be on their guard with him.' The crossings continued throughout the short day.

On the night of 27/28 November the temperature fell to -30°. A sort of paralysis covered everything; not a sound was heard. The bivouac fires were rekindled on the left bank. Among the troops still there could be seen men of the Guard, including Sergeant Bourgogne. He had fallen asleep near a fire, had had a nightmare and been woken by a cannon-shot. 'It could have been 7 a.m. I got up, took my weapons and without saying a word to anyone, made a run for the bridge and crossed, absolutely alone. I saw no one but the bridging crews on the two banks. When I got to the other side I saw on my right a large boat made of planks. It was there that the Emperor had slept and he was still there. As I was still cold from fever, I approached a fire where there were some officers looking at a map, but I was so poorly received that I had to retire. *The bridge had been free all night.*'

So far the Russians had not attacked despite their enormous numerical superiority. It would have been logical for Kutusov (south-east of Borissov), Wittgenstein (north) and Tchitchagov (west) to have made a concerted move to oppose the construction of the bridges, and throw themselves on this encircled mass of Frenchmen with their backs to the river. No. Tchitchagov apparently understood nothing of what was happening. (Later, perhaps aware of his less than brilliant role in this campaign, he resigned, left Russia and became a naturalised British subject.) And Kutusov had gone to the back of beyond, having managed to get 10,000 of his men across to the left bank of the Dnieper. To the north, Wittgenstein was making no great effort to attack Victor's force which was containing him.

There were two reasons for this torpor on the part of the Russians: they continued to believe (not without reason) that the climate alone would defeat Napoleon and his army, and they were afraid of him. The man's reputation was such that any European commander hesitated to confront him directly, even if his forces were small and partly disbanded. Let him turn on them, directing the remnants of his battalions, and they would fear the worst.   However, from dawn on the 28th, this fear lessened. The cannon-shot that had woken Sergeant Bourgogne was the first fired by Tchitchagov's artillery, whose troops would soon be engaged with those of Oudinot and Ney. The former would be wounded in the ensuing combats. On the left bank, Victor's troops (who had also to cross the bridges) conducted a slow and orderly retreat, continuing to hold Wittgenstein's force and making them retreat from time to time.

By now it was snowing heavily. The noise of battle and the soldiers' movements had at last alerted the crowd of stragglers and civilians that the left bank was no place for them, and the quicker they could cross the better. They surged forward, in a mass some 1,400 by 400 metres, and packed the approaches to the bridges which had been deserted for two nights running. It was 4 p.m., dusk was falling, and Wiittgenstein's artillery arrived within range and opened fire on the crowd. Chaos!

Some of Victor's troops were engaging the Russians, the rest were competing with the mob to get across the river. The fighting at the bridges' approaches was merciless under the snow, the cannon-balls, canister and musketry. This hail of fire could not drown the screams of terror from the women and children.

Such vehicles as succeeded in gaining the bridges became entangled, turned over, their passengers were thrown under the hooves of the horses, and women and children fell into the water and were swept away. Others voluntarily took to the water, using both the ford and swimming; many of these drowned, also. Yet others reached the right bank completely exhausted, only to be swallowed up in the marshes.

Castellane, who was trying to get back from the right bank, and was having to thrust his way through against the flow, saw a sutler in the water up to her waist, trying to climb on to the bridge. Soldiers were pushing her back, and she held out her child to Castellane. Before he could take it 'a wave of soldiers caught him up and carried him backwards for twenty paces without setting foot to ground'.

And here is the most tragic report, from a German doctor in the Grande Armée who returned home after the peace. No commentary could achieve the dramatic impact of this document, a letter addressed to von Roos: 'I must tell you of a scene encountered when I was crossing the Berezina. A pretty young woman of twenty-five, who had lost her husband in combat some days earlier, was riding nearby. Disregarding the scenes about her, she concentrated her attention on her little girl of four who was on the horse with her. She had tried in vain to breast the river and seemed to be in a mood of sombre disappointment. She did not weep and her look was directed first to heaven and then to her little girl. I heard her murmur "O God, why should I bear this misery. I cannot even pray!" At that moment, a bullet hit her in the leg and her horse collapsed. Then with the calmness of despair, she embraced her little girl who was crying, removed her bloodstained garter and strangled the infant. Then, clasping the body in her arms, she lay down beside her horse and waited for death. Shortly afterwards, she was trampled by the horses of those fighting to gain the bridge. Signed: Huber, Lauterbourg en Alsace, 30 October 1817.'

The damaged bridges were repeatedly repaired. That night, Victor was ordered to disengage. Some of his troops gained the right bank, others were killed or taken prisoner. The killing continued. On the left bank, Partouneaux's division would capitulate. 'To capitulate without fighting is shameful,' said Napoleon on learning of this. 'D'Assas, facing certain death, had cried: "Here, Auvergne!" If the generals lack the courage to fight, they should at least leave it to their grenadiers. A drummer-boy had saved his comrades from dishonour by beating the charge.'

Brave but unjust remarks. The 4,000 men of Partouneaux's division, trapped on the heights near Borissov, had held off 20–30,000 Russians for many hours, under a hail of fire and cavalry charges. Partouneaux was taken prisoner while trying to break-out. The 400 survivors of his division, out of ammunition, spent the night standing in the snow. It was not until then that they had laid down their arms.

On the evening of 28 November about 12,000 soldiers, stragglers and civilians were still on the left bank. The troops who had gained the right bank fought all day against the Admiral's forces. The fighting ceased at sundown, the Russians retreating and the French establishing their bivouacs near the village where they had their headquarters. Some of the wounded had managed to drag themselves there; the rest were left in the open without help or food. Those who had taken refuge in the huts were soon without shelter; complete demolition to provide firewood had by now become a routine. 'We left Napoleon the attic of the cottage he was using, taking only the roof-ridge.'

The extreme cold was even more painful in this marshy region. There was no food. The soldiers clustered around the fires. Here and there cries were heard that seemed to be coming from the earth, as indeed they were. In a number of hovels that had been demolished, there were wells, and as every morsel of wood had been taken, the well rims and covers were gone. In the dark men had fallen into the wells and were crying for help, perhaps a mere ten paces from a bivouac. 'Their cries were heard clearly. Nobody took any notice and they were left to die without anyone bothering to help them out, which would have been easy.'

Doctor von Roos, senior physician of the 3rd Regiment of Chasseurs, found himself among the troops who had remained on the left bank. His experience illustrates a lesser known aspect of the drama of the Berezina. Let us retrace our steps for a moment.

With many other officers he had spent the night of the 26th/27th in a barn at the end of the village of Studianka where the imperial HQ was established. Some infantry were bivouacked in a snow-covered copse nearby. The officers were chatting and von Roos and two others went to the next room to sleep. When they awoke at dawn they were alone. A soldier told them: 'The other officers left at 2 a.m. to cross the bridge. The Emperor is still at Studianka.' This explained matters, but von Roos and his two companions decided that they too had better cross. But they could neither see the bridge nor approach the river because of the dense crowd of soldiers and civilians. 'The Guard is now crossing,' they heard.

Indeed, they could see grenadiers and gunners waiting their turn. Von Roos left the other two and returned to the barn as it was still extremely cold. He tried again at midday. Impossible – 'The Guard is still crossing.' During the afternoon and evening, von Roos made three fruitless attempts to gain the bridge. Nobody seemed able to cross, or rather, some did but the doctor could not bring himself to employ the requisite aggressiveness. 'Pushed aside from every approach, not only had I been unable to cross by the bridge during the course of the day, but I could not even see it. I am astonished to have escaped the dangers of this atrocious scrum.' At nightfall (the bridge was deserted) von Roos, hoping for better luck next day, sought shelter, and spent the night in a barouche belonging to General von Hügel which had been left in the charge of a virtually blind cavalryman who was also waiting his turn to cross.

To claim one's turn involved a struggle for which Von Roos had little stomach. Cannon-fire could now be heard all around them and he entered a barn where he found two French staff officers with their attendants, and a woman. They invited him to have some coffee. A soldier came to tell them that the Russians had arrived and that nobody should move. 'The woman was from Hamburg and demanded imperiously that the staff furnish her with bread, and swore like a drover at the black bread which they produced, demanding white.' The staff did itself well enough!

The noise of artillery increased and cries were heard: 'The Cossacks!' And suddenly they came under fire. The cannon-balls whistled over the barn. The Russians had started to fire into the crowd which provoked a panic-stricken rush for the bridge. Leaving the barn, von Roos saw the tail-end on which the shells were raining down. Trying to approach the bridge, the soldiers used the flat of their weapons, the coachmen – there were still some folk who aspired to cross in their carriages – used their whips 'and swore in every known language. Add to this the cries of distress of the women and children.'

By now von Roos had given up trying to reach the bridges – those bridges that he had never seen; he still believed there was only one. Around him, people said 'There are some bridges upstream, let's try them.' Others who had already tried in that direction said No, there are no bridges, but they were not believed. The psychology of crowds in distress is aberrant. The group seeking these mythical bridges followed the river, entered the woods and encountered groups of soldiers: 'The Cossacks are here! Save yourselves!'

Too late, von Roos' was seized by a Cossack. 'Very frightened, I was relieved not to feel a lance transfixing my body.' With signs, and babbling a few words of German, the Cossack asked if he were an officer. On being told Yes, he seemed content. This cavalier of the steppes was young, raw, disfigured by small-pox, but neither ugly nor disagreeable. Dismounting, he led his prisoner to one side, made him empty his pockets, dividing the contents into two piles and taking only one of them. However, he made signs that he wished for something else – his watch. Von Roos had tried to hide it but had to surrender it as well as the decoration with which he had been honoured during the campaign. 'Seeing these things, he appeared delighted and assumed a benevolent air, then seized my bag of surgical instruments. In vain, I besought him to let me keep it. He would only leave me my pipe, some scissors and a few dressings. Then he added my decoration to the Legion of Honour which he was already wearing on his chest. He led me to the rear without harming me in any way. I soon understood that I was a prisoner behind the Russian lines.' We shall see more of von Roos and other French prisoners.

General Eblé had been ordered to set fire to the bridges at 7 a.m. on 29 November, but he decided to wait until 9 o'clock in order to save as many stragglers as possible. There was a large crowd of them as well as civilians. Squadrons of Cossacks now appeared, lances pointed, shouting their Hurrahs. The victims rushed for the burning bridges which were on the point of collapsing, others jumped into the water staggered a few paces and collapsed, frozen and drowned. But the Cossacks, jumping from their horses, rushed to the piles of booty that had been carried off from Moscow and were now lying on the snow.

The troops said: 'Once we cross the Niemen, we shall be almost home. To get to Vilna, that will be a good start.' Vilna was in Lithuania; one will find barracks there, food and rest for some days. From the Berezina to Vilna was 250 kilometres, and from there it only about 60 to Kovno on the Niemen. These soldiers did not reckon in kilometres, of course, but in leagues.

The army first had to crossed a marshy region. The temperature had moderated. They took a narrow road between the marshes, in places built on wooden overpasses. The infantry were intermingled with artillery caissons – some had survived – and carriages of officers and civilians. Some of these sank in the marshes.

Then the cold returned. Between the Berezina and Vilna the temperature varied between -20° and -30°, but on some days and nights it went down to -31°. Clouds of crows circled above the exodus; occasionally one would fall like a stone, dead of cold. The soldiers would watch to see whether a comrade were collapsing; scarcely did he hit the snow before he was being pillaged by his comrades, cursing, scrabbling and jostling. Some had no energy for such behaviour, but kept moving – like ghosts.

Their faces muffled in kerchiefs, shreds of clothing or anything that would serve, there was no talking because their breath froze on the face. The only noises were the croaking of the crows, the squeaking of the wheels of the carts and wagons and, here and there, a noise like wooden shoes on the hard snow. This was from men who had no shoes and had wrapped their feet in rags which hardened into blocks. Some, without feeling in their feet, were walking barefooted and made the same sort of noise. In the bivouacs, the men sat with their feet to the fire. Many could go no farther.

The Cossacks appeared intermittently, black dots on the snow which rapidly got larger. Only the Guard – what was left of them – were capable of withstanding their assaults. As for the others: 'Those who still had arms threw them away in order to be able to march the better, or to indicate that they would offer no resistance if taken prisoner. Men who had exhibited superhuman courage in past battles were now deadbeat, dazed, staring. Many would retain this frozen-faced aspect on their return to France; the soldiers called it 'the Muscovy'.

The Sacred Squadron was disbanded. Napoleon was sometimes on foot, sometimes on horseback at the head of the Guard, accompanied by marshals and generals. He did not use his carriage which was occupied by General d'Ornano, wounded at Krasnoë. He still had many vehicles but wished to show everyone that he still controlled the Guard and the staff. Caulaincourt wrote that the Guard was 'in an astonishing state'. As for the Emperor, he remained fearless, stone-faced, not at all emaciated. Thanks to the devoted ingenuity of the officers and servants of his household, he never wanted for anything throughout the retreat. White bread every day, beef or mutton, rice or lentils and his Chambertin wine.

During a retreat when so many men had deserted, the surgeons and physicians retained their honour. At Malo-Jaroslavets, Krasnoïe, and Borissov they had operated and ministered in the same lamentable conditions that the Grande Armée had encountered on other battlefields, with additionally, deadly cold which paralysed their fingers and killed the wounded under their hands, but which also became their ally on many occasions by limiting haemorrhages. In charnel houses with the abandoned wounded, with nothing but bare hands and charity to serve the desperate dying, they kept faith until death or captivity

The example of Larrey, the Guard's surgeon, set a high standard. At the Berezina we see him operating on his friend, the Polish General Zayonscheck, who commanded one of the cavalry regiments in that privileged corps. He amputated his leg while kneeling in the snow under a hail of Russian fire; to provide some shelter, four soldiers stood, holding with arms outstretched their cavalry cloaks. The operation, conducted with sensational dexterity, was a success and, later that day, Larrey operated on others under the same conditions of bombardment and snow.

During the savage rush for the bridges – the instruments and medicines being still on the left bank – he recrossed against the crowd. On his return from a second trip, he narrowly escaped being crushed and thrown into the river. 'I was about to perish when, fortunately, I was recognised. My name was shouted and I was passed by the soldiers from hand to hand until I reached the end of the bridge.' In a letter to his wife he wrote: 'I owe my life to these soldiers: those who ran to my aid when, surrounded by Cossacks, I was about to be killed or taken prisoner; those who hastened to my help when, at the end of my strength, I fell on the snow. Others again, seeing I was tormented by hunger, gave me what food they had; I had only to appear at a bivouac but what a place was made for me at the fire, I was surrounded by straw and their blankets. How many generals and officers were rejected and driven away pitilessly by their own soldiers!' A ray of light in the darkness of the retreat.

Between the Berezina and Vilna, on this road of horror where it seemed as if no one could help anyone any more, we see Larrey getting down from his carriage twenty times a day to walk the length of the column, distributing the few remaining medicines, adjusting a dressing with his own hands; acts by now nearly derisory, but no charity is such and Larrey persisted in going from one desperate man to the next. More and more of them by now wanted only to lie down and die. 'No! No! You must march. If you march, you will live!' Some of them, who knew him, listened. Zayonscheck, his amputee friend, could neither march nor ride. Larrey took him in his own carriage as far as Vilna where, the patient being in a poor way, he ceded the carriage to him to proceed to Warsaw and hospital, while Larrey himself continued on foot to Kovno and then to Königsberg, still on foot across the frozen plain. There he came down with typhus; but he was only forty-six and his time was not yet.

The inhabitants of every city, town and village in France felt as though they had been hit on the head with a hammer when reading or listening to the text of the white poster displayed at every town hall – the 29th Bulletin of the Grande Armée. On 2 December, Napoleon had decided to send a messenger to Paris with this official communiqué: 'I will tell them all. Better they learn it from me than from private letters.' The bulletin, comprising some 2,000 words, began: 'Up to 6 November, the weather had been excellent and the army movements had been attended with great success. The cold started on the 7th, at night; from that time, we lost many hundreds of horses which perished at the bivouacs. Arriving at Smolensk, we had already lost many cavalry and artillery horses.' The Emperor went on to tell of Volhynie's Russian army, the French right, of the pivot of the operations, with other remarks on tactical subjects. In the villages

the men listened without understanding a word of it. 'The cold which had started on the 7th became worse and from the 14th to the 15th and the 16th the
thermometer showed 16 or 18 degrees of frost. The roads were covered with ice:
the horses of the cavalry, artillery, the supply train, died each night, not by hundreds, but by thousands. More than 30,000 perished in a few days.' 'Hell, he
just talks about the horses. What about our lads?' The women, who had had no
news of their boys for weeks or months, started to cry. 'It was necessary to march
in order to avoid being drawn into a battle which lack of ammunition forced us
to avoid; it was necessary to occupy a certain amount of ground in order not to
have our flanks turned, and we had to do without cavalry to scout for us and
keep the columns in touch. This difficulty, with the excessive cold which arrived
without warning, put us in a difficult situation. Men whom nature had not sufficiently endowed to rise above the lottery of fortune, appeared overcome, lost
their gaiety and good humour and thought of nothing but misfortune and catastrophe. Those whose nature allowed them to rise above everything, kept their
gaiety and their ordinary demeanour and lived gloriously in the face of difficult
circumstances.' At this point, there were murmurs; the crowds groaned – this
high-falutin' style, even though the army was retreating. And one didn't have to
be too clever to realise that not only the horses had died of cold – and not only
the cold. 'The enemy, who could see along the roads the frightful calamity that
had struck the French army, strove to profit by it. He surrounded the columns
with Cossacks, who carried off, like the Arabs in the deserts, the isolated convoys and vehicles.' 'Frightful calamity'. Those were the words read out, so the
Emperor must have dictated them. And Cossacks? To abandon young French
lads to those savages! Well might the bulletin stress the success of the rear-guard,
the crossing of the Berezina which, on the whole, was successful; behind the
Duke of Reggio 'the whole army crossed to the right bank'; of the 6,000 Russian prisoners and the six guns captured – all that was very fine and one could
believe it or not, but it was the expressions such as 'frightful calamity' and others that stuck. 'The army, without cavalry, short of ammunition, tired to death
from fifty days' marching, carrying with them the sick and wounded of so many
fights.' In short – a rout.

After so many bulletins reporting victory – nothing but victories, so to
speak. How long had the Bulletins been lying? And, given that Napoleon had
decided to speak as he had, did that not mean that the situation was even worse
than he admitted? 'The generals, the officers and the soldiers had suffered
severely from fatigue and scarcity. Many had lost their gear when their horses
perished, others had lost theirs to Cossack ambushes.' As if the Cossacks confined themselves to baggage! And where were the wounded and who was caring
for them? And how many were dead? Would Napoleon ever tell them – oh,
calamity! Men and women wept – people hid their feelings less than today;

Louis XIV wept at the theatre. Doubtless, the Emperor never wept. The last sentence of the 29th Bulletin aroused astonishment, and then indignation: 'His Majesty's health has never been better.' In dictating that, the Emperor, it was said, was addressing anyone who might be thinking of imitating Malet, who had tried to seize power after announcing the Emperor's death: 'No, no, I am still here, still solid!' Solicitude for distressed populations, for families without news or who were sure their boy was dead, such is not of great account to those who would write great History.

While the French were learning of the disaster, Napoleon had left the army in the field and was travelling to Paris at maximum speed, by carriage, sleigh, and carriage again. On 29 November, he had written to Maret who was then at Vilna: 'The army is numerous but horribly disunited. It will take two weeks to recall it to the colours. Perhaps this army can only reorganise on the Niemen. In this state of affairs, I believe that my presence in Paris may be necessary for France, for the Empire, for the army itself. Tell me what you think.' His decision had already been taken. It had been ripening in his mind since the day on 6 November when he had been informed of the Malet conspiracy. The plot had revealed an unsuspected weakness in the régime, like a fissure. It must be taken in hand.

Napoleon had put together the 29th Bulletin on 5 December when he was still at the village of Smorgonie, less than 100 kilometres from Vilna. He had then sent for Major-General Berthier: 'I am leaving the army this evening for Paris. You will continue to discharge your duties with the King of Naples, who will command the army in my absence.' Berthier had been overcome, almost in despair. He tearfully besought the Emperor to allow him to accompany him. 'That is impossible. It is necessary for you to stay with the King of Naples. I am well aware personally that you are good for nothing, but others do not know this and your name has some weight in the army. If you persist in your disobedience, you can return to your estates, but you will never again be able to show your face in Paris, nor to appear before me.'

Berthier resigned himself. Then the Emperor sent for several marshals: Murat, Ney, Mortier, Bessières, Lefebvre, Davout: 'I am leaving you but it is to seek 300,000 soldiers. We must prepare to undertake a second campaign, since, for the first time, the first campaign has not finished the war.' Three hundred thousand soldiers. France's reservoir of manpower must be bottomless. The Emperor then launched into a lengthy discussion on the causes of the failure of the campaign, the first being that, at the start of the march on Moscow, Jérôme Bonaparte, King of Westphalia, had let 40,000 men of Bagration's army escape. 'As for us, our only defeat has been at the hands of the cold, whose premature onset deceived even the inhabitants themselves. The Russian campaign has, none the less, been the most glorious, the most difficult and the most honourable which modern history can record.' Then Napoleon spoke again of his departure for Paris as if the marshals present were being asked for their opinion on that point. Who would have dared to say: 'Sire, you are wrong. You are abandoning us'? A captain is the last to leave his sinking ship, but Napoleon might argue that his army was not in danger of sinking – was it not marching, once across the Niemen, into winter quarters? He could also argue that he was only leaving in order to save it. Moreover, the ship which he commanded was not the army, but France, the Empire, Europe; the army was merely an instrument.

Napoleon left Smorgonie at 10 p.m. in the lightest of the vehicles available, a barouche nick-named the '*chaise longue*'. The six least fatigued horses in the imperial stables were harnessed. Napoleon climbed aboard with Caulaincourt. Roustan and the captain interpreter, Count Wonsowicz, were on the box with the coachman, a footman rode behind on the valets' running board. In dead silence the barouche left accompanied by a squadron of mounted chasseurs of the Guard in front, another squadron, of Polish light cavalry, behind. They would be relieved at the next stage by 600 troopers of the Neapolitan royal guard coming from Vilna. Napoleon's party was followed some hours later by two carriages carrying the minister of state, Daru, Grand Marshal Duroc, the ADC General Mouton, Secretaries Fain and Moutier, the cartographer Bacler d'Albe and the surgeon Yvan.

The various accounts tell us that the army quickly learned of the Emperor's departure, but give differing reports as to the troops' reaction. Some 'unquestioning' historians have spawned the pious tradition that only the foreign troops disapproved. The worthy Sergeant Bourgogne has seen fit to adhere strictly to this view and even to add to it: 'Many foreigners profited from this event to heap opprobrium on the Emperor for taking a step which was only natural for, after the Malet conspiracy, his presence was necessary in France, not only to the administrative sector, but also to organise a new army.' This statement is so different in style from his usual manner of writing – plain and easy going – that one has the impression that he is writing to dictation. He even finishes by saying that those who blamed him were 'agents of England who frequented the army in order to spread disaffection'.

There were other versions: 'The greatest number,' wrote Lieutenant Hubert Lyautey, 'perhaps overcome by the weight of their misery, brutishly occupied in the search for food and in avoiding dying of cold, learned the news with indifference and did not foresee the consequences.' Brutishly is severe, but this reaction seems more probable. One cannot easily imagine these unfortunates whom we have seen on the road to chaos reflecting on the Emperor's departure, weighing the pros and cons and, finally, saying to their comrades: 'Yes, it is indeed necessary that he should leave to rally new forces.' Obviously the very idea of prolonging the war was repugnant to them. One should also remember that even those who did not cherish Napoleon and held him responsible for all their sufferings, regarded him as their indispensable guide and, less logically, their father. With his departure, what would happen? It was natural that this deprivation engendered anger in many of them.

Let us listen once more to René Bourgeois, MD of the Faculty of Paris, senior surgeon of the 12th Cuirassiers, whom I have already quoted, and who gives no sign of being a systematic detractor of Napoleon!

'His precipitous flight destroyed his prestige entirely and he was seen as a deserter who shamelessly abandoned the brave men who had so many times risked their lives for him. There exist no expressions sufficiently severe to characterise a departure considered to be base cowardice and treason.' Here Bourgeois lets himself be carried away. The exceptional vehemence of his language bears witness to his anger born of despair and implies that this surgeon was not alone in his feelings. Moreover, he said: 'Having approached a bivouac of the Guard where there were some senior officers, a major of the grenadiers arrived and openly said to one of them: "Well, so the brigand has now gone" – "Yes, he left in short order, just as he did in Egypt." Astonished to hear the word "brigand", I was later surprised to learn that it was applied here to Napoleon. Shortly afterwards, the army was officially informed of his departure.'

How could the Guard have failed to feel the most wounded of the units by this abandonment by their cherished protector? After his departure, they broke up; no more marching in formation, but mingling with the other troops, vagrant, worn-out. The new commander-in-chief, Murat, let things go, made no reference to it – in any event, what could he have done? 'It was really illusory to confide to a marshal the responsibility for managing the miserable debris which remained. Neither a plan nor the simplest tactical organisation could be executed. *Every man for himself* was the only order which we wished to hear.' Only one idea – to end it all. Even thoughts of Kovno and the Niemen had vanished; they were too far, one word only on everyone's lips – Vilna. The soldiers said: 'At Vilna, I shall sleep in a house and die content.' It had come to that.

Now, at Oszmiana, some 80 kilometres from Vilna, came another unforeseen happening. There arrived at a rendezvous, not an enemy force to bar the way, but reinforcements, an entire division, 12,000 men under General Loison. Young and healthy soldiers, a sight hardly credible. They stared with bewilderment at the spectres who questioned them. 'Yes, we have come from Vilna.' Actually, although they had spent some time there, they had come from all over Germany – most of them were Germans; but some had come from France. From France! But no one asked for news of France; the spectres were too concerned, brutishly, according to Lieutenant Lyautey, in something else – food. Loison's division had arrived with wagons loaded chiefly with biscuit – the soldiers' hard-tack – but there, on the snow, around the poor wooden houses of Oszmiana, the soldiers ate it and wept for joy. Loison's men had already moved off to provide the rear-guard of the retreat.

An event, not the most spectacular but certainly the most dramatic of the retreat from Russia – often barely mentioned in detail – was about to occur during the 48 hours between Oszmiana and Vilna: two-thirds of Loison's division were about to perish. Not from the fire of artillery or Cossacks – who were little in evidence between Oszmiana and Vilna – No. Some 8,000 of these ' fresh' reinforcements, died quite simply from the cold.

They were young and well-nourished, not worn-out by over-long marches, clothed normally for campaigning (though this was probably inadequate; better perhaps, after all, the layers of ragged clothing on top of the vermin and the grease). Confronted by this inhuman cold, most of them had no resistance. 'One saw them first stagger for a few moments and march uncertainly, as if drunk. Their faces were red and swollen and soon they became completely paralysed, their muskets fell from their lifeless hands, their legs buckled and they finally fell.' Another doctor's observation: 'Their eyes were very red and often blood exuded in drops from the conjunctiva. Thus one can rightly say that they shed tears of blood. This is no exaggeration; many have seen it.' In short, of 12,000 of these conscripts, 8,000 died of cold. The remainder survived to perform their duties in the rear-guard.

We saw Vilna when outward bound for Moscow. It was now the headquarters of the senior French military authorities in eastern Europe, still in thrall to Napoleon. One could see the steeples from afar, and when they came into view, the survivors of the approaching Grande Armée quickened their pace. This was on the morning of 9 December; the temperature was between -25° and -28°.

None of these survivors could imagine or know that three days earlier, Maret, Duke of Bassano, minister of foreign affairs resident at Vilna, had given a ball for the local populace, 'not suspecting the suffering and disasters suffered by the army. All that had been heard of our misfortunes had been some vague rumours which were not believed and were dismissed as coming from ill-disposed persons.' Despite the cold, Vilna was as lively as in peacetime, with busy cafes and well-stocked shops.

The troops entered the city in groups of various sizes on the 9th, taking several hours. The Vilna garrison was manned by troops of every kind who had taken no part in the march on Moscow. They were well uniformed, clean and well-nourished. They looked on these ragged survivors with suspicion, almost with censure. They had orders to send them to the monasteries, but the troops would have none of it. Those with money headed for the cafes and the shops; others, if they had the money, found billets with the locals – in barns, attics – they were not welcomed elsewhere, being so filthy, but they continued to arrive, in funds or penniless, demanding shelter. They hammered on doors, establishing themselves at random, causing immense disorder.

Disorder also reigned at Grande Armée HQ which had arrived the previous day. Maret sent Murat the Emperor's order to remain at Vilna. The King of Naples was outraged: 'No! No! I am not going to be trapped in this chamberpot!' Berthier asked for his orders for the army and he replied: 'Give them yourself. You know better than I do what must be done.' He left Vilna that same night, while at least ten thousand men wandered despairingly about the city. The inhabitants had at first regarded these unfortunates with pity, but as they saw more of them, fear became the dominant sentiment. Army supply dumps were besieged; they contained great quantities of flour, wine, brandy, dried vegetables, forage, clothing. Officers arrived, demanding supplies for their men: 'Have you a statement of ration strength for your unit? Otherwise, you will receive nothing.' Officers and soldiers became enraged, well knowing – as the Emperor himself admitted – that the staff corps enriched itself by selling army provisions. There was a groundswell of mutiny. A general of the retreating army – General Maison – ultimately gave the order himself to break into several depots; a furious pillage. The inhabitants, more and more terrified, barricaded themselves in, except for a few merchants in whom the taste for profit overcame their fears.

As night fell, the rioting increased, since the soldiers wished at all costs to find shelter from the pitiless cold; doors were stove-in. Men were seen to fall and die in front of barricaded houses. Suddenly, just before nightfall, the sounds of gun-fire. 'The Cossacks!' came the cry. In fact, the survivors of Loison's division found themselves in action against these wild horsemen for the first time. They fought bravely and their dead were scattered over the snow.

No polulation welcomes the idea of its city becoming a battlefield. The name 'Cossacks' produced an immediate effect; even those who had shown themselves sympathetic now furiously ejected the soldiers. The wounded were thrown out of windows. A mass of desperate men roamed the streets in the glacial cold of the night while the cannonade continued. No orders were issued to them, no directions on where billets were to be found, nothing. The temperature was down to -30°; the men tripped over the frozen corpses of their comrades of yesterday. Little by little, still in the darkness from which a lugubrious murmuring arose, a procession flowed through the Kovno gate. The locals, rushing from their houses, attacked the fugitives with clubs.

According to Larrey, 20–25,000 sick and wounded had been left at Vilna. According to others, this figure included many officers of all grades who preferred to be taken prisoner rather than continue on this calvary of a retreat. According to Louise Fusil, it included a very large number of civilians, men, women and children, who had left Moscow. Some of the latter, worn out and penniless, died at Vilna. Louise remained at Vilna to care for the wounded son of Marshal Lefebvre. She saw the Cossacks arrive, then other Russian troops, then Kutusov himself, whose wife had known the actress at St Petersburg. Thanks to her protection, Louise was able to remain there until she was able to return to France – a journey that took a year and was not without incidents, all recorded with spirit and humour: 'I can boast of having seen two unusual sights – the French in Moscow and the Russians in Paris.'

To allow oneself to be taken prisoner was a temptation; 'I have risked my life enough; I am exhausted; come what may.' A small number of officers and soldiers who had succumbed to this temptation had not regretted it too much and had finished by returning home. Others were dead and forgotten in the Urals or Siberia – fearing a lightning return by Napoleon, the Russians had forced-marched them well out of reach.

The Russian commander wanted officers who were taken prisoner to receive better treatment than that accorded to the common soldiers, but frequently before so much as laying eyes on a Russian officer, they were herded along with the rest by the Cossacks, who were champions at wielding the knout, and had scant regard for rating or rank.

Von Roos, whom we last saw under Cossack guard in a wood bordering the Berezina on the Studianka side, had had a stroke of luck. Taken to Borissov, he was interrogated by an officer of the administration: 'Ah, you are a doctor? Come with me." He was taken before General Wittgenstein. Other officer prisoners were there, so distressed that Wittgenstein had given orders for bread to be brought to them. He made himself agreeable to von Roos, having discovered that this German gentleman and he had friends in common at Stuttgart. Very sensibly, von Roos asked to be allowed to serve in a Russian army hospital during his captivity. Granted immediately. The hospital was not far away, in a village near Borissov. Von Roos was received cordially by his Russian confreres and immediately noted that the Tsar's medical services were no better than those of the Grande Armée. No medicine, derisory equipment; not a light in the wards, a candle in the operating-theatre, no lint, no bandages. 'We were brought dirty linen, black, gross, taken from the shirts of Polish peasants, no ointment, no splints – improvised from wooden slats.' Typhus, imported by the French according to the Russians, was raging in the hospital at Borissov and in the villages nearby.

Von Roos often returned to Borissov to look for instruments. In the woods he would come across peasants who had been put to collecting frozen corpses before the thaw, when they would putrefy. They could be seen removing the bodies of soldiers, frozen in natural attitudes, perhaps in a circle beneath a tree. They would carefully remove epaulettes, decorations and money which they had to turn over to an officer. All over Borissov were guns, wagons and baggage abandoned by the French.

Most of the wooden houses had been burned, but in the market-place a large stone house was almost intact. The Russians had used it as a prison for more than 300 women and children who had not managed to cross the Berezina. Roos' Russian colleagues asked how it was that there were so many women. He explained that the regulations allowed two or three women, canteen workers or laundresses, per company or squadron of the German regiments in the Grande Armée, more in some other units. He added that many of the French living at Moscow had followed the army with or without their children. On the night of the Russian Christmas this building caught fire – cause unknown. Some prisoners perished, 'others managed to escape this horrible death. They were taken in by compassionate people until peace was negotiated; the orphans were adopted by good-hearted folk.'

Weeks and months passed, and von Roos worked – any doctor would want to exercise his art. In the spring he accompanied some Russian engineer officers who had ordered to clear the river bed and build new bridges. The current had carried away the bodies of the drowned. Soldiers and peasants hauled from the river boxes, trunks, portmanteaux, chests, kitchen utensils, guns and arms of every kind, carriages, strong-boxes containing silver ingots, rolls of gold pieces, bracelets, watches, jewels. The peasants were supposed to deliver what they found to their masters, but they held on to as much as they could. The soldiers came out of it even better, the officers taking their share of the booty. All the arms were to be delivered to a representative of the crown.

At Borissov and Studianka, other teams had orders to search the ruins of the houses methodically. In the chests which the fires had spared they found quantities of papers – letters, maps, officers' commissions – which were collected and examined by a senior officer of the garrison. Of the French papers, for example, the most interesting were the correspondence and notes of the marshals; there was even a box containing letters from Napoleon, some addressed to his wife, others to his ministers, written or dictated, but never sent, lying forgotten at the time of the dramatic crossing. 'Napoleon's letters showed that he knew how to be affectionate; and that, despite the difficulties of this unhappy retreat, he was paying close attention to all that was happening in France.'

At the beginning of January 1813, von Roos had contracted typhus from his patients. Although without medicaments, he survived thanks to his robust constitution, and returned home to Germany after the spring of 1813.

What the commanders in their orders continued to call the army left Vilna on 10 December between 3 and 4 a.m. in 31° of frost. The men marched slowly and fell by the dozen. The horses, harnessed, but led by the bridle, moved at the speed of a hearse. And when the gentle light of day returned the men were afraid; the road which they faced was a ribbon of ice. This skating rink went straight up a steep slope between the mountains surrounding Vilna – the Polnari pass.

The caissons and carriages came to a halt in great disorder at the foot of this slope. None of them could make any progress on the ice. Some of the caissons contained the army treasury and all the precious belongings usually carried by the 'transports of the Emperor's household'. Napoleon had left all this behind when hastening back to France. And now there took place one of the strangest incidents in the history of the Grande Armée – less than two leagues from Vilna at the entrance to the Polnari pass. The official and unofficial accounts include some contradictory phrases: 'the idea was launched of having the troops carry the money of the imperial treasury' and 'the army's treasury was sacrificed'. Nowhere is the authority for such an order identified. The army treasure (or the imperial treasure, both expressions appear) exceeded five million francs, most of it in crowns. When it became evident that no vehicles could get up the icy slope, an explosion of pillaging erupted. The men threw themselves on the caissons and gutted them; not for the gold, for there was very little of it, but for the crowns (*écus*). These were bagged in sturdy canvas sacks. Gunfire from the rearguard against a Cossack attack could be heard, but the pillagers took little notice, being too busy shouldering as many sacks as they could manage. Many sacks fell to the ground, fighting broke out; others wanted their share: 'Give me some, you can see that you can't carry all that away.' 'Give me some or I will kill you,' or the man was simply thrown to the ground and the sack wrenched from him. On the edges of this scrum, men holding sacks of crowns between their thighs, kept up a fire against the swirling Cossacks who were performing their usual circus.

Even a small sack of crowns weighs heavily. The men knew that they could not carry such a burden far. As a gold *louis* weighs much less than four crowns, there developed an odd bartering: crowns against gold. Many of those present still had some, more than one would suspect and not only the officers. Sergeant Bourgogne admitted that on that day he had twenty crowns and twenty gold pieces. He did not wish to burden himself further and refused to trade his gold for crowns. But others, tempted by offers at very advantageous rates, accepted. Seeing which, those with crowns were increasingly tempted to dump them, the rate for gold climbed, the sellers, frightened at seeing the rates for their crowns falling, also exchanged them for gold, against anything of value – one saw a sale of a glass of brandy for ten crowns. Nevertheless, one officer, speculating on a fall, bought a barrel of crowns for five *louis*!

While the rear-guard's cannon boomed, the head of the column began to clamber up the icy slope while men squabbled over the contents of the imperial treasure wagons. 'Court dress, splendid furs were taken by soldiers in rags.'

But the rear-guard retreated; they must tear themselves away from this intoxicating pillage although the caissons had not yet been emptied. In the end it was the Cossacks who profited from the remains. For a long while, the inhabitants of Vilna would remember a Cossack who came into town wearing a purple mantle embroidered with bees, sceptre in hand and wearing a crown. Surely an exaggeration, but perhaps not without a basis of truth.

By 10 December the army was bivouacking on the heights. Next day they resumed the march and on the 13th reached Kovno, on the Niemen. The army? 'II and III Corps', wrote Ney to Berthier, 'are no more than a memory. The latter numbers only 60 men.' The town's shops were pillaged, casks were brought up and dumped in the streets; there was general drunkenness.

At the top of the hierarchy, there was another disorder. Murat called a council of war during which he criticised Napoleon vehemently. He would soon write to him that he no longer wished to continue in command, that he was having Eugène de Beauharnais succeed him. He was to leave for his estates without awaiting the sovereign's reply. It was Ney, once again, who, with the survivors of Loison's division, would defend Kovno to allow the frantic crowds time to cross the Niemen. Of the 400,000 men who crossed from the west between 24 and 30 June 1812, how many would get back over the bridges or the ice? The precise calculations made later in offices 400 kilometres away are fantasy. Let us say that of these 400,000, some 10–20,000 returned. The Russians took 100,000 prisoners. All the rest died. The Grande Armée no longer existed. But Napoleon had returned to France seeking 300,000 soldiers.

XIII

THE CONSCRIPTS
OF 1813

The notices appeared on the walls of the town halls during the first days of January 1813. These said that there would be a new conscription authorised by a senatorial decree. In ancient times a senatus consultus was a text embodying the opinion of the Roman senate. Now, it was a proposal from Napoleon to which the French senate could only say Amen. The posters announced that 150,000 young men who were over the age of 18 in 1813 were to be called up, plus those who had not been called between 1809 and 1812 either because they had drawn a 'good' number, or for health reasons.

The conditions appertaining to the drawing of lots had been laid down in the laws of 26 April 1803 and 26 August 1805. When the lists were drawn up in each commune, in the presence of the officers of gendarmerie and recruitment and of the conscripts, the mayor placed in an urn a ballot for each youth named on the list. 'Each ballot bearing a different number, starting with number one.' On the appointed day each conscript drew a ballot from the urn; or if absent, the mayor drew one for him. The number was announced by the sub-prefect. The higher the number the better the conscript's chance of not being called-up, because each commune had to furnish a fixed number of conscripts and no more.

That had been the case at one time. Today, these young men knew that the ballot was only a formality, that there were no more good numbers; the bottom of the manpower barrel was being scraped – the lame and the halt were being called. The first meeting of the board of examiners was held immediately after the ballot. 'Take your shoes off!' and the conscript passed under the measuring stick. If he were over 1.54 metres he was fit to serve. 'But I am ill, I have such and such a disease.' In which case he would appear before the recruitment board, composed of the prefect as president, the general commanding the department and a major. The examination was quick and public – 'subject to public decency'. A conscript declared fit for service could only escape by paying a substitute. This cost from 1,500 to 4,000 francs, varying by year and by region and subject to notarised private contract. As the required sum for exemption was a large one at that time, many paid annually. If the substitute were killed, the conscript had fourteen days in which to find another. Death while serving with the colours did not expunge the debt, which devolved to his heirs. Only rich families could assume these financial burdens. Moreover, in 1813, the system of replacements was as illusory as the balloting, because the replacement had to be from the same canton and the same class. Which meant that there were none available.

Final solution – desert or cheat. I have mentioned these gangs of deserters who hid in the woods and the mountains. In 1813, they were still more numerous than before, because they knew that having joined the army, there were at least two chances in three of leaving one's hide there. In his famous 29th Bulletin, the Emperor himself had hidden almost nothing concerning the disasters. There were no longer enough gendarmes to round-up deserters. In May 1813, there were approximately 160,000 absentees.

Cheating consisted, for example, of voluntary mutilation, breaking front teeth (or decaying them by eating herbs) so as to be unable to tear open a cartridge; amputating the thumb, so that the victim would be unable to hold a musket; inducing sores on the arms and legs by blistering agents, maintained by applications of diluted arsenic; breaking an ankle; some went as far as to put out an eye. But mutilations were arousing suspicion. Or false certificates of grave illnesses could be procured – some doctors cooperated in this traffic; secretaries at the mayor's office might provide identity documents falsifying age; often even false certificates of death – the deserter disappeared and the family faked a funeral. But this was risky, especially in the country, where people gossiped.

So, most of those called found no escape. Military bands played in front of the town halls during the lottery. With their families, the conscripts came out one after another, some looking gloomy, others swaggering and smiling. These latter went straight away to the stalls of the sellers of tri-coloured ribbons bearing the inscription 'Fit for service' which they proudly fixed to their hats. They either laughed at the others or commiserated with them, perhaps finally persuading them to buy a ribbon and urging them to a bar to drink and sing; it was necessary to create something of a hero's aura, since there was no more choice in the matter. Many found this difficult; some could be seen both singing and weeping.

In a few days, the accursed marching orders arrived. The betrothed wept, as did the mothers as they prepared warm clothing and provisions. Thus, throughout France and even well beyond her frontiers into Belgium and Italy, some 500,000 men, perhaps rather more, were being called-up: 250,000 would be assembled in Germany by 1 May 1813 and 300,000 by 1 June. Napoleon knew that these successive bleedings had not exhausted the human resources of France, at that time the most populous country in Europe.

Initially the Emperor would have at his disposal 200,000 combatants, not counting the cavalry. Seventeen divisions forming I, II, III, IV and IX Corps occupying Elbing, Marienburg and Thorn in Germany. Two other Corps covered Warsaw, the Bavarians concentrated at Plock, the Westphalians and the

Württembergers at Posen. A first and second 'Corps of Observation of the Rhine', each of 70 battalions, were forming at Erfurt, Wesel and Mainz. Ney commanded the first of these corps. To see these soldiers of the new Grande Armée a little more closely, let us follow the conscripts of Souham's division in Ney's I Corps. Many of them were from Alsace. Their marching orders had laid down that they were to join the army corps at Mainz by 29 January. They left their towns and villages, marching in snow or mud to the barracks at the assembly point. Their first surprise was to find there Piemontese and Genoese conscripts, three weeks on the road, unable to speak a word of French.

The conscripts left there in formations stiffened by a few veterans, survivors from Poland or Germany. Heading the unit was a captain on horseback, followed by drummers who sounded the beat when entering a village. Alsace was a fertile and populated region. Each night these young fellows presented a billeting voucher and were supped and lodged by the inhabitants who were well disposed, nearly all having a son in the service and often without news of him for months. 'Nearly always we had clotted cream and potatoes, sometimes fresh bacon, shimmering on a bed of sauerkraut. The children came to see us, the old ones asked us from which region we came and what we had been doing before being called-up, the young girls looked at us with sad expressions, dreaming of their lovers who had gone away, five, six, seven months earlier. Then they showed us to the son's room.'

After five days' marching the draft arrived at Mainz at 10 o'clock of a freezing night. All the shops and inns were open, the place was bustling and there were soldiers everywhere. At the barracks they received their billet vouchers and were dismissed. But how to find the houses and the streets in this unknown city? A *cantinière* was sitting at a small table under a large tricoloured umbrella lit by two lanterns, ready to provide directions. But first, 'what are you drinking?' They were all ready to be duped. Next day, muster at the barracks and receive their weapons: musket, bayonet or sabre, cartridge box, fit the equipment over their civilian clothes, get entangled in the straps and cross-belts; old sweats there to help for the price of a glass.

After arms, ammunition – fifty cartridges per man, and immediately the drums beat; prepare to march! As far as could be seen the Rhine was ice-bound, 'a magnificent and dazzling sight.' The ice was not slippery but was covered with frost so it was possible to walk on it, and there were even some carriages. They crossed and took the Frankfurt road. Fifty kilometres covered that day, actually a day and a night because the days were short.

It was at Frankfurt that the real military life began. Exercise and arms drill every day, eyes right!, eyes left!, three paces forward! one knee on the ground, grasp the musket at the second band to reload, and so forth, the day long in a snow-covered courtyard. These conscripts had to be trained in record time.

Next, the supply service. The battalion's uniforms had just arrived from France so, everyone to the stores to get them. The Jewish clothes-dealers were already there to buy their civilian clothes. It was necessary to slip the storekeepers some small change to persuade them to give one the right sizes, and to the corporals and sergeants to ensure fair play. The *cantinières* flattered the young lads, telling the spenders that it was easy to see that they came of good families – they were coining it.

Drafts of conscripts arrived daily from France, which pleased everyone, but morale dropped sharply on the day when they saw for the first time cart-loads of wounded arrive from Poland, bound for the Hospital of the Holy Spirit. Bundles of rags and misery the like of which they had never seen. For the most part, the wounded were stone-faced, but some had a sort of animal contentment at being out of it.

After a spell in hospital the walking wounded were allowed into the town. In the cafes they told of the horrors of the retreat. The conscripts listened in appalled silence, but some vowed vengeance – Russian bastards, we'll show them! With every step away from the family background the young men felt themselves more and more virile. The uniform, the drill – mustn't be a wet hen!

The battalion arrived at Frankfurt on 7 February and departed on the 18th for Selingenstadt where they stayed until 9 March. Thence to Schweinheim and then Aschaffenburg-on-Main where Souham's division was assembled. Next day they were inspected by Marshal Ney. Snow had given way to non-stop rain. The conscripts were impressed by the Marshal's bearing – Duke of Elchingen, Prince of the Moskowa – ('he was a handsome man with red-blond hair, who appeared extremely tough'), in his large hat, blue uniform and high boots streaming with rain.

The division moved off via Lauternbach and Neukirchen to Erfurt. In those towns there were barracks, the troops slept sometimes in a dormitory, two to a bed, sometimes billeted on the locals, always received correctly, but those who could speak German heard bitter remarks. They did not resent these youngsters who had been snatched from their families, but they had had enough of war and they cursed Napoleon. Some of them did not conceal their wish that the Saxons, Bavarians, Badeners and Württembergers enrolled in the French army would rise against the Emperor: 'Why should they fight against their own country, against their own brothers?'

The young men found this disconcerting. They had left France with the simple idea that they should march against the Russians in order to push them back to their own country, to discourage them from thinking that they could invade Europe. Why should the German people turn against France? The lads of the new Grande Armée knew nothing of the diplomatic and military manoeuvring that had been taking place since they left home. They were quite unaware that everything had started on 30 December 1812 when General Yorck, commanding the Prussian contingent in the Grande Armée, had signed the Convention of Tauroggen with Russia under the terms of which his unit would be 'neutral', and this led to the entry of Prussia into the 'war of liberation' on the Allies' side. The French forces occupying Königsberg had to retire towards the Vistula.

Marshal Schwarzenberg, commanding the Grande Armée's Austrian division, had abandoned the Volhynia (Wolyn) region which he was occupying, and instead of obeying Napoleon's order to rejoin Eugène de Beauharnais, who was holding Berlin, marched on Vienna. Count Metternich-Winneburg, the Austrian Minister of Foreign Affairs, master of the double-cross, secretly orchestrated the revolt of all the sovereigns who up to then had submitted to Napoleon. Among these was the Austrian Emperor Francis I who had but one idea: to get out of the alliance and declare war on his son-in-law, Napoleon. On 28 February 1813, the King of Prussia, Frederick-William, had signed a secret treaty with the Tsar, and on 17 March, dropping the mask, he declared war on France. Two weeks earlier, Bernadotte, ex-marshal of France and Prince of Ponte-Corvo, who had become Crown Prince of Sweden, signed a treaty with Britain in which he undertook to deploy a corps of 30,000 troops against Napoleon. On 25 March, Kutusov had directed a proclamation to the German people: 'Honour and Fatherland! Let every German worthy of his name promptly and vigorously join with us! Let each one, prince, noble or placed in the ranks of the men of the people, support with his goods, and according to his rank, his person and his life, heart and soul, the projects of liberating of Prussia and Russia.'

In short, practically the whole of Europe was arrayed against the Emperor of the French, including the Pope, Pius VII, virtually a prisoner at Fontainebleau and who, after having had a concordat extorted from him on 25 January 1813, had disavowed it two months later. Murat, so fearless under fire, had returned to his kingdom of Naples after the retreat from Russia, and took the first steps to an ignominious treachery. For Napoleon news from Spain was no better. The British were advancing in Leon and Castile and the bulk of the French forces were retreating northwards. The Emperor was resigning himself to holding the northern half of the peninsula only, and doubtless knew that this war was lost for him. He had taken steps to defend the Pyrenean frontier, and had recalled every general and staff officer not positively needed in Spain.

The young soldiers of Souham's division marched at maximum speed towards Erfurt, where Ney's corps was situated. Now they were marching past regiments, teams of artillery, ammunition wagons. The citadel of Erfurt was very strong and the town was rich. When the battalions were dismissed in the square opposite the barracks, the regimental postmen distributed the first letters from home. Parents, fiancées and friends gave only family news. In the days following, always drill. From the ramparts the sentries could see the bivouacs of the assembled regiments.

Suddenly, there was a rumour that the Emperor had arrived. Whence was not known, but he would take command of the new Grande Armée. The moustachioed sergeants told the young soldiers: 'Now you'll see! Things will hum!' On the dot of 5 p.m. they were ordered to parade under arms. 'Damn me if it isn't him!' But it was Marshal Ney with his gilded staff and General Souham with them. The latter addressed his division: 'Soldiers! You are going to form part of the advance-guard of III Corps. Don't forget that you are French. Vive l'Empereur!'

Vive l'Empereur! through the ranks. Napoleon had left the palace of Saint-Cloud on 15 April 1813 at 4 a.m. Driving day and night, he arrived at Mainz on 16 April at midnight. Eugène de Beauharnais sent officers to him bearing bad news. Eugène, having been forced to abandon Berlin, had collected the debris of the Grande Armée behind the Elbe. These comprised the small number of survivors of the retreat from Moscow, and the garrisons left in Germany which had not marched on Moscow.

Encamped between Magdeburg and Wittenburg, these troops had been unable to prevent the Russians from mopping-up between Torgau and the mountains of Bohemia. The King of Saxony (allied to Napoleon), seeing his capital, Dresden, invaded by the Russians and Prussians, had taken refuge with his family at Plauen. The Dresdeners had hailed the Tsar and the King of Prussia, throwing flowers under their horses' hooves. The Cossacks galloped across the plain between the Rivers Elbe and Weser. 'Sire, they are now threatening Erfurt.' 'I shall quickly strike them a major blow before Erfurt.'

Napoleon stayed some days at Mainz, issuing orders. He knew that the army could not be concentrated before the last days of the month and had no illusions as to its military capacity. There were too many young soldiers, hastily trained, and hardly a tenth of the officers were classed as capable. To replace the dead and missing from the retreat from Russia, retired officers had been recalled, old NCOs, many of whom were illiterate, had been promoted sub-lieutenants. The cavalry situation was worse: nearly 80 per cent of the recruits had never ridden a horse: 'They'll learn!' But at Hamburg, the captain of cuirassiers, Gonneville, having been ordered to leave on reconnaissance with his squadron, saw all his 'troopers' dismounted in ten minutes, the horses running free in the streets. The people of Hamburg laughed openly.

In order to be able to confine himself completely to military operations, Napoleon had vouchsafed the government of France to Marie-Louise, assisted by a council of regency directed by Cambacérès. On 28 April, he arrived at the army's concentration zone. Leaving his coach, he took to his horse and continued his journey surrounded by his military household and followed by the duty squadrons. On that day he had his first contact with his young troops.

'Vive l'Empereur!' When he appeared, the conscripts broke ranks, rushed towards him, cheering, their shakos on the ends of their bayonets. The old magnetism was still working. The mere sight of the legendary captain in person transformed them, transported them. They believed the veterans when they told them that now *Le Tondu* was with them, all would be well.

Napoleon spent the night at Eckartsberg where HQ had seen set up at the town hall in the main square. The 'palace' – do not forget that this was any house occupied by the Emperor – included the ground floor, two rooms on the first floor, bedroom and office. The tumultuous activity at Eckartsberg was unbounded. The bivouac fires in the streets were so close together that the whole town could have been in flames. Troops were marching everywhere, messengers galloped past, there were peasants with requisitioned carts, droves of cattle for the slaughter-houses, ammunition wagons, cannon and caissons; carriages raced each other and became entangled amid curses; one could also hear the shrieks of the inhabitants despoiled or ejected from their homes.

This noise and clamour reached the 'palace' whose front door remained open for the messengers and staff officers. Napoleon's retinue – officers, functionaries, messengers, servants – camped along the stairway, on the stairs and on the landing. But on the other side of the door, all was calm, order, silence. Twenty candles illuminated three sides of the room and a large map of the region lay on a table: Napoleon and Bacler d'Albe, pencil and compass in hand, leaned over the map. In a recess at a smaller table was Berthier, pen in hand, and at yet another, Baron Fain, secretary of the cabinet, replacing Méneval who had not yet recovered from the Moscow ordeal. Napoleon, turning from the map for a moment, dictated an order: 'Write to the Prince of the Moskowa to send Ricard's division to occupy Weissenfels by the left bank of the Saale. General Souham will be able to march by the right bank to Weissenfels.'

The young soldiers of Souham's division, having left Erfurt on the night of the 18th/19th, had arrived before Weimar where they remained for five days. There they heard for the first time the uncertain noises of war: pistol shots exchanged between French hussars and Uhlans. 'After two hours, the hussars returned: they had lost two men. This was the start of the campaign.'

Next day they spotted some Cossacks, but they kept out of range. 'The more these fellows retreated, the more our courage.' At sunset on the 29th, the division arrived on the banks of the Saale. Across the river, a plain extended as far as the eye could see, and one could clearly see under the red sky a large party of horsemen with shakos bent forward; behind them a forest of lances. The sergeants said: 'Those are Russian mounted chasseurs and Cossacks.' As soon as the French opened fire, these forces vanished. The division bivouacked on the banks of the river.

The moon rose in a sky full of stars. The bridge companies arrived with a long train of wagons containing their equipment and went to work. The bridges were completed by daybreak and the division marched across. In the morning dew, a mist rose from the river. By 5 a.m. the entire division had crossed the Saale. As each regiment reached the far bank, it formed square with arms ordered. As the sun dispersed the mist, visibility increased to three-quarters of a league. Somewhat to the right was an old town with houses with very steep roofs and, farther off, the château of Weissenfels.

Facing Souham's division was a deep fold in the ground. It might hide an enemy force, but the order was given to march towards Weissenfels. The squares of young soldiers, with a sprinkling of veterans, advanced in good formation at the quick march, colours leading, drums beating, sharpshooters and scouts extended. The sun sparkled on metal in the fold in the ground: there was a flash and a report – the Russian artillery had opened fire. For the first time, the young soldiers were marching in the face of the enemy. Those who looked to right or left, saw gaps in their ranks and heard their officers cry: 'Close ranks!' They obeyed, and to be elbow to elbow with their comrades reassured them. Fifty paces further, another flash and a whistle overhead and more gaps in the ranks. 'Close ranks!' All they could do was march. Suddenly, a general who had joined the first square, shouted 'Halt!' in a very loud voice. In front was a mass of Russian cavalry: 'Front rank, kneel, fix bayonets, present arms!' The young soldiers had performed this drill a hundred times in the barrack courtyards. But now the Russians were approaching, crouched over the necks of their horses, sabres drawn. 'Attention to the firing order: Aim! Fire!'

The four ranks of the front of the square fired together. The young soldiers, whose hearts were beating hard, saw with astonishment the Russian cavalry swerve and retire at the gallop. At the same time, they heard the guns fire behind them and saw the cannon-balls plough into the midst of the Russian horsemen. Again came the voice of the general: 'Charge!'

The soldiers began to trot, there were cries of 'Vive l'Empereur'. Those in the front ranks thought that the battle was won, but at two hundred paces from the fold in the ground, came the general's voice: 'Halt! Kneel! Fix bayonets.' More Russians arrived. The guns boomed. Orders could no longer be heard but the soldiers understood that they should fire into the mass. They saw horses rear, then smoke obscured them. When the smoke cleared, they saw the Russian cavalry retreating. 'Cease fire!'

The squares deployed; the drums beat the charge. They had to descend the ravine and climb the opposite slope, but the soldiers, excited by the flight of the Russians, ran, trampling the dead and wounded Russian cavalrymen and horses. 'Forward! Vive l'Empereur!' The front ranks arrived at the gardens of the houses surrounding Weissenfels whence Russian guns were still firing. Some instinct told them that the quicker they ran towards the guns, the less time their crews would have to fire. They arrived in the town, crossing hedges, gardens, hop fields, jumping over walls. The surviving Russians were in flight. The division was fallen in on the main square where Marshal Ney inspected them: 'Well done! Well done! I am pleased with you. The Emperor shall know of your good behaviour. He could not refrain from laughing at the way we had run at the guns.'

The battle of Weissenfels, a secondary engagement, had been an easy victory, even though Ney had only infantry at his disposal. The unexpected courage of the young soldiers of the new army had made up for the lack of cavalry. Without wishing to detract from their achievement, one could not say that they had had a very testing baptism of fire. I have described this battle in some detail since many of those that would follow would be much the same. The close order, reassuring for recruits, was in the end the most costly. But their leaders had to use it in view of the inexperience of these young troops.

Napoleon arrived at Weissenfels on 1 May 1813. He retired at 2 a.m. and next day wrote to Eugène de Beauharnais that he would proceed towards Lützen. 'If you hear cannon-fire near this city, march on the enemy right.' He had a plan of battle in mind.

A messenger arrived at 9 a.m. to say that fairly large enemy forces were established on the heights near the village of Poselna: 'Have Souham's division take this position!' And the Emperor rode off, followed by his staff. Marshal Bessières was already on the spot, as a spectator one might say, since he had no cavalry. His staff surrounded him and this colourful party was spotted by the gunners of an enemy battery. The first round decapitated a sergeant of the Polish light cavalry of the escort. Bessières, saddened, galloped toward the enemy to inspect their position more closely, then returned: 'I want this young man buried.' Hardly had he spoken, when a round from the same battery struck him full in the body. Napoleon, learning shortly afterwards of his death, appeared distressed. He esteemed and liked Bessières, one of the few whom he allowed to speak frankly. He remained for a moment, motionless, quiet, staring. 'So,' he said, 'he died Turenne's death. We should envy his fate.' When walking away, he murmured: 'Death is coming near to us.'

He had intended to take the initiative on 3 May, but the enemy general, Wittgenstein, had forestalled him: 70,000 troops threw themselves on Ney who had occupied a group of villages south of Lützen: Starseidel, Kaja, Rahna, Kleingörschen and Grossgörschen. The other corps commanders were slow to march to the sound of the guns. The enemy army debouched towards Kaja in several columns 'in a black depth' as Napoleon wrote in the Bulletin of 2 May

1813. The horizon was thick with them. Souham's conscripts division were to undergo a second baptism more arduous than the first. As at Weissenfels, close order: 'Form Square!' which was obeyed, but already enemy cavalry were swirling around the squares. The cannon-balls passed with a sharp roar; often they ricocheted, grazing the ground, breaking legs. Howitzers fired hollow shells which exploded, scattering canister which caused horrible injuries. Closing ranks, the conscripts heard this sinister command repeated and repeated. The French artillery was also firing; black smoke spread. The soldiers who were being bombarded had not yet fired a round. Finally, they saw the Prussian columns advancing with a 'strange confused noise like a rising tide'. These Prussians shouted 'Fatherland! Fatherland!' and now fought hand to hand, using the bayonet and musket butt, the French giving ground as the Prussians were so numerous and appeared invincible.

The battle was confused and endless. The village of Grossgörschen was lost, the most costly encounter being between Kleingörschen and Rahna. Ney's troops were thrown back on Kaja.

Napoleon had exposed himself more than usual. In front of Kaja, half a cannon-shot from the enemy, he was under fire for several hours. Around him, generals and ADCs fell wounded, General Gouré, Ney's chief of staff, was killed. The day was ending and the Prussians, despite having also suffered heavy losses, drove on Kaja. 'Close ranks! Close ranks!' – but in many of the conscripts' battalions the young men broke and scattered. Napoleon, on learning of this, approached them: 'Conscripts, for shame! It was on you that I was basing my hopes. I expected much from your young courage and you are running away!' Or, according to other versions, at perhaps another moment: 'Where do you think you are going? Can't you see that the battle is won? Come on, stand firm!' He pointing to a tree some two hundred paces in front of them: 'Seized with remorse, they ran to it and their officers succeeded in re-forming their ranks.' The conscripts, momentarily bewildered, rallied and advanced and took the village.

Now General Bertrand, commanding IV Corps, came to Ney's support. A tactical move by Napoleon settled the matter: a change of direction, the army pivoting on Kaja. The entire right (Marmont) changed front, the right leading. The battle was won, the enemy retreating. The cannonade did not stop until the light failed. In the evening, the Emperor wrote to Marie-Louise: 'Ma bonne amie, It is 11 p.m. I am very tired. I have achieved a complete victory over the Russian and Prussian army commanded by the Emperor Alexander and the King of Prussia. I lost 10,000 men killed and wounded. My troops covered themselves with glory and have given me proofs of their love which have touched my heart. Kiss my son. I am very well. Adieu, my good Louise.'

Next day he addressed an exceptionally long proclamation to the army: here I give only the essentials: 'You have rewarded my patience! You have made up for everything by your goodwill and your bravery. You have added new lustre to the glory of my eagles. The battle of Lützen will rank above the battles of Austerlitz, Jena, Friedland and the Moskowa.' An exaggeration, but a calculated one. It was necessary to inflate the pride of these young soldiers and galvanise them to face the future which was unlikely to prove easy. Napoleon had written to Marie-Louise of 10,000 men out of action, but the figure in the Grande Armée was to reach some 18,000 killed and wounded – 22,000 on the Russian and Prussian side. 'Sire,' said Ney to Napoleon: 'Give me a lot of these young fellows. I will lead them wherever I wish. The old sweats know as much as we do, they reason, they have too much sangfroid. These lads, on the other hand, are fearless and do not know the difficulties; they look straight ahead, not to right or to left.'

This was a trifle optimistic. And these innocents needed to be led by officers who were young, ambitious, ardent and with their fortune yet to make. Which was not the case. However, the victory at Lützen had left Napoleon master of the left bank of the Elbe as far as its mouth into the Baltic. Lauriston had taken Leipzig. The Emperor allowed Ney's corps, which had borne nearly the whole weight of the battle, one rest day in their present position. then, 'I will have them march on Berlin. The rest of the army will march towards Dresden in pursuit of the beaten armies' A pursuit too slow for lack of cavalry.

The Tsar and the King of Prussia were still at Dresden, capital of Saxony, where they had arrived on 4 May. The King of Saxony, Frederick-Augustus, had finally taken refuge at Prague. Bear in mind that three Fredericks appear on our present stage: Frederick-Augustus, King of Saxony, 63 years old, ex-Elector of that state, created king (1806) by Napoleon; Frederick I, King of Württemberg, 59 years old, ex-duke of that state, created king (1806) by Napoleon: his daughter, Catherine, was married to Jérôme Bonaparte, King of Westphalia; Frederick-William III, 43 years old, King of Prussia.

On their arrival at Dresden, the King of Prussia and the Tsar had published the news that there had been a bloody battle at Lützen and that Napoleon's army had been crushed. The delighted inhabitants had offered a serenade. But the arrival during the night of a great number of vehicles loaded with wounded gave food for thought. On 8 May, the anxious populace saw the Tsar and the King of Prussia leave the city in great haste and at midday, XI Corps of the Grande Armée entered the city. At that time, Dresden was a superb city, one of the great artistic centres of Europe, known as the Florence of the Elbe. On this 8 May 1813, the spring weather embellished it still further, but columns of smoke rose from the river banks, where the retreating enemy had fired the bridges: cannon-fire could be heard. At the same time, the bells in the steeples were ringing to welcome the arriving conqueror. The population dug-in: what reprisals would the Corsican Ogre exact? The municipal counsellors who brought him the city keys were in a tight spot. Napoleon received them with a face of marble and kept them waiting for a little while.

'You deserve to be treated as a conquered country. I know all that you have done since the Allies occupied your city. I have the list of volunteers whom you have clothed, equipped and armed against me. I am also aware of the celebrations which you organised when the Emperor Alexander and the King of Prussia entered your city. Your houses still bear traces of your garlands and we can see on the streets the remains of the flowers that your young girls strewed before the monarchs' feet. However, I wish to pardon it all. Bless your king, for he is your saviour; send a deputation to him praying he will join us here. I am only pardoning because of the love I bear him. I will ensure that this war causes you as little mischief as possible. Go!'

This high-speed homily and the pardon gave witness to a degree of civilisation not always within the reach of those conquerors and liberators whom we have followed, and also, Napoleon intended to influence the hesitant Frederick-Augustus I. If he defected to the enemy, it would mean the immediate rupture of all the alliances with the other states of the Confederation of the Rhine. It would, however, be necessary to send him an ultimatum of sorts, in order to impel him to return and place his troops at Napoleon's disposition. Impressed by the victory at Lützen, Frederick-William gave in. This reassured Napoleon to the degree that he made Dresden the linchpin of his operations in Germany. But the victory of Lützen had not been enough to reassure the marshals. On the night when Napoleon was installed in the royal palace of Dresden, the prefect, Bausset, had congratulated Duroc on the brilliant start to the campaign. Duroc had shrugged his shoulders, and with a gloomy expression said: 'It has gone on too long. It will be the death of us all.'

Eight thousand wounded at Lützen. As usual, they had had their wounds dressed in those ambulances that happened to be close to the battlefield. They were then sent to Leipzig. While passing Kaja they had seen the teams of peasants, escorted by soldiers, digging huge graves, long ditches in the fields; one of these was two kilometres in length. Wagons carried the corpses, which were thrown into the graves – one took the head, another the feet and plop! French, Russians and Prussians all mixed together – these soldiers in colourful uniforms who two days earlier, had been killing one another, were now fraternally bundled together and soon the clods of earth would cover them all.

The wounded arrived at Leipzig on a starry night. The hospital was in a suburb on the road to Halle. Lanterns illuminated the courtyard, orderlies carried the wounded on stretchers, which they had to carry up a spiral staircase. The main ward was upstairs, a huge room with hundreds of beds aligned in three ranks. There was a lantern hung at each open window, nurses, orderlies, doctors came and went. Beds – a real hospital – the veterans told the younger wounded that it was a paradise. A surgeon passed, surrounded by assistants, who directed him to one or other of the wounded. 'Undress him – why was he not already undressed? Gently, you will hurt him.' The humane surgeon examined the wounded carefully. His assistants called him 'Baron'. Many of the wounded would remember Baron Larrey for a long time.

Despite his care and the good order of the Leipzig hospital, some ten corpses were removed by the orderlies each morning. Immediately afterwards, the orderlies distributed the bouillon; this was one of the day's high spots. In the evenings, a little beef with a half-glass of wine. 'The mere sight of it heartened us and made the outlook brighter.' After some days, the walking wounded were allowed to go down to the large garden behind the hospital. This enjoyed a fine view of the Partha; poplar-lined, this river flowed into the Elster. They could see several white roads cutting through the fields of wheat, barley, oats, hop-gardens, a rich agricultural region already warmed by the suns of May. There were benches in the garden for those who needed to rest and other wounded walked together under the elms, chatting. 'We were like the proprietors.' The war seemed far away. However, shortly after 20 May, there was a rumour that there had been another battle at Bautzen, 12 leagues east of Dresden.

Napoleon, installed at Dresden, inspected the young troops who were constantly reinforcing the army. Daily he sent precise orders to the two groups into which the army was divided, one to the north towards Berlin, commanded by Ney; the other, to the south, commanded by Macdonald, was following the retreating enemy. The Emperor had expected the Prussians to retire on Berlin to protect their capital, while the Russians marched towards Silesia, where, according to reports, they were being reinforced. But no: the Prussians and the Russians remained together. 'Sire, they are marching on Breslau by way of Bautzen and Görlitz, skirting the Bohemian frontier.' Napoleon immediately understood why they were taking that route: in order to exert pressure on Austria to persuade the Emperor Francis to march against his son-in-law. Alexander and Frederick-William of Prussia dreamed of nothing else and this was also the goal of Metternich, Chancellor of Austria; this intriguing genius was also playing for time.

As he told the Prussian minister Hardenberg: 'We must not allow Bonaparte to attack Austria first. In a month, the army of Bohemia will be ready. Until then, I must dissemble.' He sent General Bubna to Napoleon with peace proposals. These were such that Napoleon could not accept them, but Metternich had at the same time suggested a procedure of negotiation to which the Emperor agreed. Nevertheless, not wishing to leave the field to Metternich, he sent Caulaincourt to the Tsar, with whom he still wished to arrive at an understanding. At the same time, he left Dresden to place himself at the head of his troops. 'All these will be more accommodating after I have gained a new victory.'

The enemy army was still concentrated east of Bautzen (50 kilometres east-north-east of Dresden) on the borders of the River Spree. The corps of Macdonald, Bertrand and Marmont were converging on the town. Ney had already been ordered to rejoin, marching to the sound of the guns and turning the Prussian right.

Napoleon launched the battle when he learned that the Tsar had refused to receive Caulaincourt. Most of the adversaries retained a confused memory of the happenings of the first day, 20 May, marching and counter-marching in a downpour. 'We could not see five paces before us. We could hear the guns. It continued to rain after nightfall, our uniforms were drenched and stuck to our bodies. To light a fire was impossible, impossible to lie down or even to sit.' The saturated ground would no longer absorb the rain which continued to fall in torrents. However, despite the rain, operations continued to conform to Napoleon's plan, which was to hold the enemy until Ney arrived.

At 8 p.m. the Emperor entered Bautzen, whose inhabitants showed gratitude for deliverance from the Cossacks and pillaging occupiers and rapists. Hoping to retake the ground lost the day before, the Russians attacked at daylight. The rain had stopped, except for a few showers. The attack failed and a war of attrition succeeded it, The French formed square behind the artillery which was under bombardment; the Russians did likewise. Worn-out after a sleepless night, the troops slept on the ground until a shower awakened them.

At about 1 p.m. Napoleon asked for his leather mattress, lay down on it and went to sleep, despite the noise of the gunfire. 'All his staff officers dismounted, lay down on the ground and went to sleep.' An odd sight. Awoken by Duroc, the gilded sleepers saw the Emperor already standing, observing the enemy through his telescope. He took out his watch and said in a satisfied tone: 'Ney has made his movement. The battle is won.' True, Ney had carried out his orders, but not fast enough to turn the enemy right. Blücher, who was in command of the latter, could be rescued and was free to retire if in danger of annihilation. Here is Jomini's opinion of this second day of the battle of Bautzen:

'If Ney had completely executed the order which Napoleon had given at 8 a.m. it would have been all up with the greater part of the enemy army. The fate of the Empire thus depended upon a moment of weakness on the part of the most valiant of his generals.' Henri de Jomini, Swiss, 34 years old in 1813, was deeply interested in everything to do with the art of war, despite his being a clerk in a bank. His treatise on the major operations of Frederick II, published in 1803, had made his reputation, and Ney had taken him on to his staff as a consultant. Major in the French army in 1804, colonel in 1806, he had managed the historical section of the Grande Armée, then fought at Eylau, and in Russia as brigadier general. Meanwhile, Ney, who was jealous of him, had withdrawn his protection. At Bautzen Jomini, placed under arrest for a questionable dereliction of duty, defected to the Russians and became ADC to the Tsar. Renowned military critic, many historians swear only by him.

It is true that after Bautzen the enemy, while retreating, was in no way in disorder. At every river or stream, or irregularity in the terrain, the Russian rearguard turned about and fought; men fell on both sides. When Napoleon rejoined the vanguard he learned that General Bruyère had been killed, his leg torn off by a cannon-ball and, at that moment, a chasseur of the escort was killed at his side. 'Ah,' said the Emperor to Duroc, 'fortune is smiling on us today.' All the officers in the group looked gloomy. 'My friend,' murmured Duroc to Marmont, 'the Emperor is an insatiable fighter. We shall never survive. It is our fate.'

The Russians, having retreated briefly, reformed behind a deep ravine. To observe them, Napoleon climbed a hillock overlooking the ground. Just behind him rode Mortier, the engineer General Kirgener, Duroc, Caulaincourt. At that moment a Russian cannon-ball struck a tree close by. Napoleon turned round and saw no one but Caulaincourt behind him. The latter rode up, his expression tense: 'Sire, the grand marshal of the palace has just been killed.' 'Duroc! It's not possible. He was here beside me a moment ago.' The round had struck the tree and ricocheted, killing General Kirgener immediately, and hitting Duroc in the stomach; his entrails were protruding. He was being carried to one of the nearby villages. General Gourgaud arrived. 'Sire, the enemy is retreating.'

Gérard-Christophe de Michel du Roc, 42 years old, born at Pont-à-Mousson, of the junior but authentic nobility, dropped the particle voluntarily in 1792. From the siege of Toulon until his death he had been one of the men most consulted by Napoleon. With Lannes, he was one of the few who could use the familiar 'tu' when speaking to the Emperor, but only when they were alone. On the Napoleonic canvas he is generally seen as an officer of the second rank, his fighting career having ended after Marengo, although at Austerlitz he had replaced General Oudinot on the spot in command of a division of grenadiers. Grand-marshal of the palace, but not marshal, his job was to organise the Emperor's life, plan his journeys, ensure that he enjoyed the maximum comfort possible on campaign, relieve him of material problems, and supervise his security. Having responsibility for the 'black cabinet', he was accustomed to opening private correspondence – he knew everything that was going on. The Emperor's shadow, silent and efficient, he was entrusted with many missions requiring discretion and secrecy. Had he lived long enough to write his memoirs, many obscure points of the great reign would have been cleared up and many judgements revised. Napoleon was shattered by his death. He ordered the Guard to halt and spent the rest of the day at a small table, staring at the ground in mournful silence. 'The marshals and the senior officers of the army kept a distance away. General Drouot came to ask for orders for the artillery. 'Everything tomorrow!' was the reply.

The surgeon Yvan and Doctor Ribes watched over Duroc in the hovel to which he had been carried. Larrey came to see him and at first glance, knew that he was lost. His face was pale, the pulse minimal. 'You can render me a friend's last service,' said the dying man. 'Your art cannot save me. But at least put an end to my sufferings.' All that Larrey could do was to soak a dressing in laudanum. Napoleon came to see Duroc, who shook the Emperor's hand and then put it to his lips. 'Sire, my whole life has been devoted to your service and I regret that I can be of no further use to you.' 'Duroc, there is another life and it is there that you will wait for me and where we shall meet again one day.' 'Yes sire, but that will be in thirty years' time when you will have triumphed over your enemies and realised all the nation's hopes. I have lived as an honest man and have nothing to reproach myself with. I leave a daughter. Your Majesty will be a father to her.' According to the Bulletin, these were the last exchanges. Napoleon remained for another quarter of an hour, 'his head resting on his left hand, in the deepest silence,' then Duroc said to him: 'Ah, Sire, leave me. This scene is painful to you.' 'Then farewell, my friend.' Napoleon re-entered his tent and received no one during the night. Duroc died at dawn.

According to the Bulletin of the Grande Armée of 24 May 1813: 'A flag of truce bearing many letters gave reason to think that it was a matter of negotiating an armistice.' Let us climb a little higher above these muddy roads where the new Guard was pursuing the enemy – too slowly for the Emperor's taste. The Allies were not in good shape. In the space of six months Napoleon had forced them to retire 350 kilometres. The Russian staff was desperate, the King of Prussia trembled, as did Metternich: 'Napoleon's march must be stopped.' Even though his country was not at war – not yet – it was at his instigation that on 29 May, the Russian Stadlov proposed an armistice to Napoleon which would lead to the opening of peace negotiations. Why did the Emperor, who was in an advantageous position, say Yes after no more than a momentary hesitation?

There seem to have been two reasons: first, pressure from the marshals and high functionaries in favour of peace. 'Bessières is dead and Duroc also, soon it will be my turn, then adieu my château and my fortune!' The second reason is a conclusion of Napoleon's: The two victories so far have been costly and indecisive, mainly due to lack of cavalry. A delay would allow us to acquire more cavalrymen. This was why, on 29 May 1813, Napoleon sent Caulaincourt to negotiate an armistice with the Russian general Schuvalov and the Prussian General von Kleist. Armand-Augustin, Marquis of Caulaincourt and Duke of Vicenza, more diplomatist than general, had been under the spell of the Tsar since his embassy to Russia (1807 to 1811) and was adamantly in favour of peace.

The armistice of Pleischwitz was signed between France and the Russo-Prussians on 2 June, and called for a peace conference to be held at Prague on 29 July. Concerning the fantastic game of diplomacy played at this time in Europe, I only wish to record those facts which show why the campaign in Saxony was resumed after a brief interval. It seems appropriate to recall two incidents, then unknown to Napoleon, which occurred between the armistice of Pleischwitz and the official opening of the congress of Prague.

On 14 June the Treaty of Reichenbach was signed between Britain and Prussia; Russia signed next day. Britain was to pay Prussia £1,333,334 and Russia £663,666 (or the equivalent cost in manpower of the two beneficiary countries). The Allies agreed not to sign a peace in any circumstances without the consent of Britain, who reserved the right to add other peace conditions to those conveyed to Napoleon.

On 27 June a new treaty of Reichenbach was signed, this time between Russia, Prussia and Austria. If Napoleon did not accept the initial conditions, Austria would execute the maximum programme of the others. In plain language: Britain was the boss, the Congress of Prague would be no more than a farce.

A conscript wrote to his parents: 'We have learned that meetings were being held at Prague in Bohemia to arrange a peace. That we find very good.' The soldiers could not imagine the international intrigues that were being launched so high above them, and besides, another subject which concerned them directly was being debated in every bivouac and in every officers' mess: the question of self-inflicted wounds. This affair had burst upon the army after Bautzen when reports circulated in high circles that the number of wounded among the young recruits was abnormal. These reports came from the senior surgeons and Doctors Lapiomont, Baulan, Eve, Yvan, and Desgenettes. Soult's reaction was immediate: 'They are doing it on purpose. We saw this in Spain. We must be severe.' Napoleon was told and listened with half an ear, having more pressing problems than the minor wounds of 2,000 soldiers. 'If they cannot hold a musket, they can at least hold a stretcher. Make them stretcher-bearers!'

After the armistice of Pleischwitz he found the time to read the reports. Some days later, the rumour reached Larrey that the Emperor had decided to condemn to death all those wounded in the right hand. The Chief Surgeon of the Guard was horrified and sought an audience which was granted on 12 June. 'Sire, these lads are innocent. You have been misled.' 'You presume a great deal in the defence of such wretches.' Larrey insisted eloquently that one could not at first sight tell whether a wound was self-inflicted or not. One must ascertain the circumstances, find out where the soldier was at the time of the wounding, etc. 'Sire, there should be an inquiry into each case. You need a jury of surgeons.'

The Emperor did not say No, but his farewell words were not encouraging: 'Go, sir, and fulfil your duty. Send me your findings officially.' Any dramatic news circulates like wildfire. The story ran through the ranks that all those wounded in the right hand were headed for the gallows – 'Two from each army corps will be shot. Chosen by lot.' The surgeons' investigation concerned 2,632 men and took four days. An official report was made concerning each wounded man, indicating the character and circumstances of the wounding and taking into account the testimony of the NCOs present at the time. Larrey's report, summarising the conclusions of the board, included the following sentences: 'There are no certain signs that will indicate which of two wounds received at point-blank range was voluntary or involuntary.' 'It is physically impossible to submit the smallest proof that any of the soldiers seen by the board had voluntarily mutilated themselves.'

Larrey had made no secret of his opposition to those favouring immediate and brutal punishment. Not only did these partisans include Soult and General Pradel, Provost in Chief of the army, in some degree *ex officio* (a tight rein sustains military justice), but also a number of other senior officers. The latter, having *a priori* pronounced against those wounded, now tried to fuel Napoleon's indignation. Such was their fear that he might change his mind that they even tried to steal Larrey's report when he submitted it.' We will present it ourselves. The Emperor is very busy.' 'I will wait just as long as is necessary.' Finally, at the audience: 'Well, Mr Larrey, do you persist in your opinion?' 'More than that, Sire, I have come to reveal the truth to Your Majesty.' He held out the reports. At first, Napoleon merely wished to glance at them, opened one of Larrey's pages at random and found some facts on military technique which interested him.

The musket in use at the time, the 1777 model, modified in 1802, had no sight. The user had to make a guess at the angle of presentation. He was advised to aim low as firing jerked the barrel upwards. The result, clearly demonstrated in Larrey's conclusions, was that when, for example, in a formed square there were three ranks of soldiers firing, 'the second and third ranks involuntarily pointed their musket barrels at the hands of those in the front rank'. Furthermore, even by merely manipulating the musket, those firing it could accidentally wound themselves.' Both NCOs and officers reported having seen this many times.

Napoleon, motionless, continued reading. He put down the file and paced up and down in his office without saying a word. Then he stopped in front of the surgeon: 'M. Larrey, it is a fortunate sovereign who has to deal with a man such as you. You will receive my orders.' An hour later, an ADC delivered to the surgeon a miniature of the Emperor, set in diamonds, six million francs in gold, and the deed to a state pension of 3,000 livres. For once, honesty and humanity had gained the day. In every regiment, faces brightened when the news spread that those with wounds to the hands, under suspicion and arrested, would be liberated. One person, however, would retain an unquenchable hatred for Larrey: twenty years later Soult, the collector of Spanish masterpieces, would still be trying to damage his son, Hippolyte.

The armistice ended at midnight on 10 August. On the 11th, Metternich declared the Congress of Prague closed, a charade on which the curtain had barely risen. On the 12th, the first return for his efforts: Austria declared war on France. The coalition troops numbered 500,000 – including 20,000 Swedes and 150,000 Austrians, being thus deployed: the Army of the North under Bernadotte, an army in Silesia under Blücher, an army of Bohemia under Schwarzenberg. Napoleon had about 400,000 men, including 40,000 cavalry under the command of Murat, who had returned from his kingdom of Naples.

Napoleon was well aware of the coalition's numerical superiority, but he didn't allow this to influence him; he felt that he was facing mediocre strategists. He had nothing but scorn for Bernadotte; Blücher was a German *Reiter* who knew nothing more than how to drive straight ahead; Schwarzenberg, whom he had under his orders in 1812, was pusillanimous. Napoleon's strategic intuition was still as sharp as it had been at the time of his great victories. Established at Dresden, at the centre of his dispositions, he could espy the movements of his enemies and take advantage of their errors, driving in person on the more reckless while his lieutenants dealt with the next two threats, and then mopping-up the remainder. This did not appeal to the lieutenants – the marshals. They felt that dividing the Grande Armée was too risky, that Germany should be evacuated and the defence line established on the Rhine and there a peace should be negotiated. But for the moment, they could scarcely make themselves heard.

The sole element that the inspired imagination of Napoleon had not reckoned with was treachery: three traitors, Bernadotte, Moreau (the general implicated in the Cadoudal conspiracy and who eventually became adviser to the Tsar) and Jomini had provided his enemies with a priceless crew of advisers. All three, when asked by the Tsar, had returned the same answer: 'You will never be able to beat this man in person. On the other hand, his lieutenants are vulnerable. So, whenever the Emperor is in command, avoid fighting him, even if you have to retreat twenty-five leagues. Anywhere where there are one of more of his marshals, drive on them. You will prevail, if only by force of numbers. In this way you will little by little ruin his effectives. In the end, Napoleon will not have enough troops. Then, concentrate all your forces and drive on him.'

The coalition adopted this policy and results were quickly forthcoming. On 19 August, as he had planned, Napoleon thrust into Bohemia to entice Schwarzenberg. But then he learned that five days earlier Blücher, opening the campaign, had fallen on Ney who was peacefully bivouacking on the Katzbach.

Ney's force had been driven back as far as the Bohne. Napoleon left Schwarzenberg in peace and on 20 August went to Ney's assistance, that is, to confront Blücher, who retreated without serious fighting. Napoleon would have preferred to pursue him but learned that Schwarzenberg, left to his own devices, had started to march on Dresden. On 23 August he decided to march against him. On that same day Oudinot was beaten by Bernadotte at Gross-Beeren, and reported that 10,000 Bavarians and Saxons had gone over to the enemy. Davout had to cancel his convergent movement. The northern operation was in ruins. On 25 August Gouvion Saint-Cyr, having let himself be driven back by Schwarzenberg to the outskirts of Dresden, called on Napoleon for help. Napoleon told Vandamme: 'I must march on Dresden. Keep Schwarzenberg busy.' No need to write more. As you can see, the strategy suggested by the turncoats succeeded, especially since the marshals had lost any trace of the sacred fire – and Napoleon found himself obliged to rush about all over the place. How much of this strategy was appreciated by the rank and file?

And now, rain! In mid-summer, an endless torrential downpour. The soldiers marched in the mud and through puddles on the ruined roads, bivouacking in the flooded plains, rarely able to light a fire, generally hungry, the rapid marching and counter-marching having left the supply services far behind. At the end of a march of 45–60 kilometres, could one ask an 18-year-old, chilled and starving, to clean and polish his weapons, groom his horse? More often than not the lad had lost his shoes in the mud. Thus were born the bacilli of dysentery and pulmonary diseases. On 17 August, of 4,856 soldiers billeted at Würzburg, 1,317 were recorded as sick, more than a quarter of the strength.

'I must march on Dresden' – Napoleon led at a gallop the reserve cavalry, Marmont's corps and the Guard, entering the Saxon capital with no more than a picket of mounted chasseurs. The enemy guns boomed from the heights, the inhabitants were terrified, the streets were full of wounded painfully dragging themselves to safety. Spies reported that the Austrians were enthusiastically crying – 'To Paris! To Paris!' The enemy columns slowly moved towards Dresden, each preceded by 50 guns. Gouvion Saint-Cyr's artillery barely slowed their advance. The Austrians closed on one of the gates, the Russians and the Prussians approached the suburb of Pirna on the banks of the Elbe. In fact Schwarzenberg could have taken the city, had he not, once again, showed his pusillanimity: 'I prefer to await reinforcements'. Yes, but it was Napoleon who was coming.   Napoleon was being briefed by Saint-Cyr on the situation – no recriminations; time was pressing. 'All I ask is that your troops stand firm for an hour or two on the city outskirts. Our reinforcements are on the way. I am returning to the palace.' The Saxon royal family was there, trembling. Napoleon reassured them, set up his HQ in a wing of the château and immediately left again. He knew the first requirement– to be seen. Looking as if he were holding a review, he left the city with no more than Caulaincourt and a page for escort, riding slowly towards the bombarded sector. Passing through a crowd of soldiers, a spent bullet struck the page three steps away from him. He kept on and even corrected the dressing of a battalion. Gouvion Saint-Cyr's troops, who had already visualised themselves dead or prisoner, took heart. 'Vive l'Empereur!' from every unit. An officer arrived: 'Sire, Marmont's corps is entering the city.' Turn back and gallop. Napoleon dismounted at a large bridge over the Elbe. As each colonel passed, he ordered them: 'Concentrate your regiment near such and such a gate. He had already planned the dispositions of the battle.

'Napoleon! Napoleon!' the name ran through the ranks of the enemy. The news of the arrival of the Emperor of the French had a more potent effect than repeated cavalry charges. In two hours, the troops descending from the heights began to retire. To say that the mere name of Napoleon produced all these movements would be ridiculous. The Guard had been engaged, the gunners had fired salvos, the conscripts had formed square and stood firm, Latour-Maubourg's cavalry had charged. But who had masterfully co-ordinated all these actions if not Napoleon? And, once more, it is undeniable that his presence inspired courage. In the course of this day, the coalition forces suffered 3–4,000 killed or wounded; the French 2,000.

During the night, freezing rain and violent wind. The end of this summer was undeniably detestable. Bivouacs were flooded, clothing drenched. The soldiers stood in the dark, backs to tree trunks, water up to their ankles, heads bowed against the squalls. With daybreak, the rain continued. Schwarzenberg had received his reinforcements; he was also joined by the Tsar and the King of Prussia. In total, 250,000 coalition troops were facing 100,000 French. In order to conform to the strategy prescribed by the turncoats to avoid combat so long as Napoleon commanded in person, they would not counter-attack, but manoeuvre to retire beyond the Bohemian mountains. But Napoleon sought a more decisive result.

Murat's cavalrymen had by now learned to mount their horses. Fortunately their charges, often represented as onslaughts, were in reality slow trots, as I have already said. These tyro horsemen, launched against the Allied left wing, opened the way for Victor's infantry. On the right, Ney pushed against the Prussians. In the centre, 1,200 French guns fired continuously. Every movement of this second day has been exhaustively described, but I think that a few lines from the memoirs of General Grabowski give a fairly accurate picture of the shape of the battle from about 10 or 11 a.m. when the Allied troops started to retreat faster than they would have wished. 'The King of Naples at the head of the cavalry, charged the batteries and the enemy columns. The artillery could escape, but the infantry formed square to receive us. The rain had so thoroughly damped the priming that muskets misfired and our cavalry broke the squares one after another.' Murat was wearing a blue, Polish-style tunic, with a gilded belt from which was slung a light sabre with a straight blade, violet breeches with a gold stripe, yellow leather boots, a hat with ostrich feathers and a white plume. His horse was wearing a huge sky-blue shabraque embroidered with gold – and all of it streaming with rain.

The French took more than 15,000 prisoners, including many generals and officers. Napoleon's 100,000 men had prevailed over 250,000 coalition troops. One of the three turncoats, General Moreau, was fatally wounded by a musket-ball.

Napoleon re-entered Dresden and made for the château. The streets were jammed with wounded and with columns of prisoners that no one knew where to lodge. The King of Saxony hastened to greet Napoleon. The grey coat streamed water, the corners of the small hat drooped. Napoleon left a trail of water on the flagstones of the hall. The king embraced him. The French victory stupefied the court and the city.

When Napoleon retired to his quarters he felt faint. Constant hastily stripped off his clothes which stuck to his body. A warm bath was ready. 'No, not a bath, my bed.' The sheets were warmed and the Emperor got between them. 'Send for Fain.' He wished to hear read the despatches that had accumulated in the office during the past three days. After two hours' work, he again felt ill. 'I want a hot bath. Boiling.' On leaving it, he began to vomit as a result of a fever. He returned to bed, forbidding them to send for a doctor. 'Do not call me except for events of the highest importance.' At 5 a.m. he sent for his valet and got up.

'The battle of Dresden, where I beat the large Allied army,' wrote Napoleon, 'was surely the best action of the campaign.' He was right. And the battlefield on the next day had its usual sinister aspect. Everywhere on the muddy, rain-soaked soil were corpses, naked or semi-naked, many mutilated or crushed by the wheels of the artillery, dead horses already swollen, wrecked caissons, scattered gear, bales of straw, puddles of blood. Shadowy figures moved slowly through the mist. The pillagers of the dead moved openly; some were seen loaded with weapons and breastplates, others made off hastily, their pockets bulging with money, watches and gems. The Dresdeners were trying to recover some of the losses they had suffered at the hands of pillagers.

Napoleon, meanwhile, was sitting in a folding chair in the suburb of Pirna, watching troops marching in pursuit of the army of Bohemia. He would have liked to have taken part personally in this pursuit, but he still felt tired. As the weather was now good, he wished to dine where he was and the 'food service' was laid up and served to him out of doors. Just as he was finishing his meal, destiny knocked. Although not a knock-out blow, it was sufficiently strong to give notice that from now on, despite some exceptions, matters would go badly for the rest of the campaign.

The messenger of destiny arrived mud-spattered on a foundering horse; he was an ADC to Macdonald, and brought news of a disaster. Two days earlier, the Marshal with 70,000 men had encountered Blücher's army and had been beaten with the loss of 3,000 dead, 20,000 prisoners, 100 guns, two eagles. Napoleon got to his feet, staggered and had to be supported. Suddenly, trembling with fever, he vomited as before. This relapse gave rise to the thought that 'His Majesty has been poisoned', a rumour that was to run for several days. For the moment, the Emperor, incapable of mounting a horse, had to return to Dresden in a carriage.

Hardly had he arrived, when the second piece of bad news reached him: Oudinot and his three army corps had been beaten by Bernadotte near Gross-Beeren, losing fifteen guns. The Saxon corps was virtually shattered. 'Have Ney take over command of the Army of the North and Oudinot resume command of his own corps. Macdonald must resist to the last man from every favourable position. I will come to his support as soon as the army of Bohemia is reduced. It would not be reduced, thanks to the slowness and the muddling of the generals. General Vandamme, full of ardour, ambitious for his marshal's baton, drove forward with the vanguard. Behind him trailed Saint-Cyr; one league and a half during the entire day of 29 August. Marmont also dawdled and Mortier was resting at Pirna. Murat with his cavalry was marching at the pace of Victor's infantry. In consequence Vandamme was taken in rear by two enemy corps. After a confused and heroic action, he was forced to surrender and was made prisoner with 7,000 of his men.

More disasters followed. On 5 September Ney, having relieved Oudinot, was beaten at Dennewitz. He had an excuse: of the 15,000 men lost during the battle, more than 8,000 were Saxons and Bavarians who had switched sides in the midst of the fight. Napoleon told himself that had he been there in command, it would have been entirely different. But how could he be everywhere on a front of one hundred leagues? During the entire month of September, he was to keep his HQ at Dresden, moving several times to threaten Blücher or Schwarzenberg. But whenever he appeared, these two adversaries retired, after having fired a few rounds of artillery.

Should anyone wish to know what state the conscripts of 1813 were in, morally and physically, at this time – here it is: they understood nothing and they were exhausted. The veterans had told them a thousand times over: '*Le Tondu* knows what he is doing.' And now? 'Yes, we are retiring, but he will come and then you will see.' The Emperor arrived, they advanced, 'Vive l'Empereur!', but a few days later the advance stopped and they bivouacked interminably under the rain – why? One novelty was that drafts from the army in Spain had joined several of the corps. These were hardened troops who had seen it all: tough, cynical, laughing at the conscripts who meekly accepted their miserable state. 'At the next town, you will see!' And they did. The conscripts learned the techniques of pillage and extortion.

At Dresden, Napoleon read the dispatches from the marshals and from his spies. Schwarzenberg, who was commander-in-chief of the Austrian forces (the army of Bohemia and the army of Wittgenstein), rather than retreating, invaded Saxony west of Dresden and drove towards Leipzig. Blücher crossed the Elbe, marching to rejoin Bernadotte; those two might very well turn south to link up with the Austrians. It was no longer possible to remain at Dresden.

Napoleon departed on the morning of the 7th, leaving behind Saint-Cyr with 30,000 men, his destination – Leipzig. After two halts he arrived at Düben, three leagues from Leipzig. While on the road he had received word of the armies' movements and had issued orders. From a ciphered message to Marmont on the 9th, we can deduce what his intentions were at that time: go northwards, beat Blücher and Bernadotte, push on to Berlin, free the towns on the Oder, reinforcing the garrisons from the Grande Armée, and then turn to crush Schwarzenberg. This plan seemed insane to the marshals, who had but one thought – to retreat to the Rhine.

'The Emperor stayed several days at Duben in a state of painful indecision. He remained almost entirely in his room, where they had installed his iron bed.' On 14 October, he abandoned his idea of marching north and decided to concentrate all the corps of the Grande Armée at Leipzig. What happened? To give a hard-and-fast reply would be dangerously misleading. Apparently, Berthier had at that time received news that Bavaria, leaving the Confederation of the Rhine, would join its forces with those of the coalition and the marshals had drawn conclusions in order to apply pressure to the Emperor. But few of them were at Düben. We could conclude that Napoleon had mainly based his decision on 'military factors arising from the position of these armies' which were cited by Colonel Drugne: assume a central position to prevent the coalition from concentrating: or alternatively, to fight them simultaneously, risking all on one throw. His letter to Ney dated 13 October 1813 ends: 'There will certainly be a major battle at Leipzig.'

At the outset of the XIXth century Leipzig was a compact and rich city, rich in history, in commerce (the Leipzig Fair) and even in industry, thanks to a nearby deposit of lignite. Its streets were straight and wide; three rivers, the Elster, Pleiss and Partha, with many tributaries, crossed the city; it was surrounded by a wall in which were four gates.

On 14 October it was raining. Napoleon arrived at midday at the village of Reudnitz, a half-league from Leipzig and established his HQ there. Cannon-fire could be heard to the south from Murat's troops who were trying to contain a thrust by Schwarzenberg. The boulevards and suburbs were full of soldiers and civilians. At HQ, there was an interesting conversation between the Emperor, Berthier, Marmont and Murat. He told them that he had ordered the formation of squares in two files. The enemy, accustomed to seeing the French formed into three files, over-estimated their strength. Napoleon had also considered the drawbacks to the three-file formation, for example, the matter of those wounded in the hand. Then he complained of his brothers, especially Joseph, who had managed to lose Spain. And turning to Murat: 'And you, have you never been ready to abandon me?' 'Sire, my enemies have poisoned Your Majesty's mind against me.' 'Yes, yes you have been as ready to do it as was Austria, but I forgive you. You are a good man, you have a fund of goodwill for me and you are a valiant man. Only, I was wrong to make you a king. Had I made you a viceroy, like Eugène, you would have behaved as he has. But, as king, you think more about your crown than of mine.'

Before the big battle starts, we have a moment to consider the most brilliant and picturesque person in the Grande Armée. Towards the end of the retreat from Russia, Napoleon had left the army, leaving the command on 5 December 1812 to Murat. He, on 13 December, having evacuated Königsberg, had returned to his kingdom of Naples, leaving Eugène de Beauharnais in his place. Murat had asked the British government if, in return for his joining the Allies, they would guarantee his retention of his kingdom after victory. Reply negative. So Murat turned again to Napoleon.

To continue. On 23 July 1813, Castlereagh, the British Foreign Secretary, authorised the British diplomatist Bentinck to tell Murat that his throne would be guaranteed him if he would make a complete break 'with Bonaparte'. On 16 August 1813, Murat took command of the cavalry of the Grande Armée. He fought bravely and effectively at Dresden on 26 September. Napoleon appointed him commander of all the forces facing Schwarzenberg while he himself was thinking of disposing of Bernadotte and Blücher.

So, at Leipzig on 15 October 1813, Murat had reported to Napoleon the position which he had assumed to defend the city against the Austrian army. Throughout the day, Napoleon visited the army corps then returning to his HQ. That night the sky was clear. The enemy's bivouac fires formed a huge arc. almost a complete circle. To the south was Schwarzenberg's army, to the west the Austrian army of Giulay, who would try to cut the road to France, to the east the Russian, Bennigsen.

At 7 a.m. on 16 October it was misty. The huge plain was crowded with troops moving in all directions without haste. The battle would start an hour later. During this day, there would be engaged about 140,000 coalition troops against about 96,000 of Napoleon's.

At 8 a.m. the Austrian guns opened fire, answered by 300 French pieces. The army of Bohemia, in three columns, marched determinedly across Murat's front. Black smoke rose everywhere. At a distance of five kilometres, French troops marching to concentrate were obliged to communicate by shouting. They said: 'It is louder than Eylau'. Napoleon was on a hill called the Thornberg, near the village of Liebertwolkwitz, six kilometres south-south-east of Leipzig. Shells burst near him, killing officers and horses. Undisturbed, he dismounted behind a tile-oven and continued to watch the progress of battle. The enemy tried to seize several villages south and south-east of Leipzig. From his point of vantage, the Emperor could see the brisk fire of the defenders, the fallen horses. He could even see, each time the enemy retired, the bodies of the fallen soldiers. At midday, three villages each assaulted six or seven times, remained in French hands. The French had taken 2,000 prisoners. Some 18,000 men were already casualties, more Austrians than French.

Shortly afterwards, distant cannon-fire to the north: this was Blücher approaching. Marmont's artillery replied. Then, another cannonade to the west, where Giulay was attacking Bertrand's corps which was defending the road to France. And the cannon boomed around the horizon, where to the east, Macdonald was attacking Bennigsen. The hard fighting spread. Napoleon gave orders, the ADCs galloped towards the unshakeable French squares, some of which were moving forward. The conscripts now obeyed orders like automata: 'Close ranks! Forward march! Kneel!' repeated endlessly. They knew nothing of the battle as a whole. Some strange situations arose: a battalion found itself isolated in the woods to the north of Leipzig between the Elster and the Parthe. Mission: shoot up Blücher's scouts. These men were relatively tranquil. They heard the artillery firing continuously, but in their sector there were only individual duels; a soldier seen suddenly between two trees who must be shot down before he saw you. Then came the order to leave the wood and climb a hillock covered with brush, when suddenly they were charged by Prussian hussars. 'These made so much noise that it gave you goose-pimples, the officers shouted commands in German, horses snorted, the sabre scabbards slapped against boots, the earth shook.' Soon afterwards, the battalion re-entered the forest.

On the plain, it was the French cavalry which charged. The battle was going quite well for the French. Told of this good turn of fortune, the King of Saxony had the bells of Leipzig rung to salute victory. But the army of Bohemia was held but not broken. According to some military critics, this relative lack of success was due both to the numerical inferiority of Napoleon's forces and to some slackness on the part of the marshals: Macdonald had attacked too late, Ney had kept Marmont too close to him, etc. One element is often overlooked in these judgements. During the campaign, as the ardour of Napoleon's marshals lessened, that of his enemies grew. Their troops were fighting to liberate their homelands and their officers were becoming more effective, their tactics less hasty.

Looking again at the French commanders; as regards Murat, one may question whether he had enough flexibility of mind to coordinate the movements of his troops to best advantage. In the middle of the battle, he ventured upon the most extraordinary communication with the enemy. He had earlier received at his HQ a dispatch from Cariati, the Neapolitan minister at Munich: Britain undertook to obtain from the Bourbon Ferdinand IV, King of the Two Sicilies, his renunciation of the throne of Naples and would guarantee it to Murat provided that he left the French army and did not send troops to help the viceroy, Eugène. The messenger had said: 'The Emperor of Austria wishes for a very early reply.' Now, on 15 October1813, a little before 3 p.m., Murat had sent his secretary to Austrian HQ. In substance, his message was simply: 'Agreed!'

Some minutes later, at exactly 3 o'clock, he received an order from Napoleon to send in all the cavalry. Certainly, replied Murat, and he unleashed his 12,000 sabres. The squadrons moved at the trot under a hail of enemy bullets. Cavalry charging against infantry nearly always prevailed and the squares disintegrated. But the enemy also had cavalry. The Cossacks of the Russian Guard had been trained not only in harassing tactics: they were an élite corps. The hussars of the Russian Guard were also present, as were the Austrian cavalry reserve under command of a field marshal. The movements of such an enormous mass of cavalry cannot be described.

The infantry saw themselves threatened from two directions, assaulted and crushed by a torrent of centaurs, first from one side, then another. At one moment, the dragoons of the French imperial guard and Poniatowski's Polish cavalry corps literally cut their way through several enemy squadrons. General Latour-Maubourg had his leg shot off by a round shot. The Austrian General Merveldt fell from his horse and was taken prisoner: he was immediately conveyed to imperial HQ. 'The victorious French troops were disordered by a difficult success.' In fact, neither the French squadrons nor the French squares were at that time gaining ground.

At 5 p.m. dusk was approaching. Napoleon wished to retake the village of Gossa which had fallen to the enemy. Impossible, the troops were too exhausted. Maison's division had lost five-sixths of its strength in front of Gossa. The artillery continue firing until 6 p.m. when it fell silent. The sky was dark and a light rain was falling. On the plain, the bivouac fires were lit at the same spots where they had burned out early that morning. Here and there, villages burned. This bloody battle had cost the Grande Armée at least 26,000 men, Generals

Vial, Aubry, Delmas, Friederichs and Ferrière were dead or dying and a dozen were wounded, including Latour-Maubourg.

On the battlefield that day, 16 October, Napoleon had redressed an injustice of a sort by promoting to Marshal of the Empire a man who had richly merited it earlier: Poniatowski. The soldiers admired him as he rode by, surrounded by his Polish lancers. 'He was a fairly tall man of some fifty years, thin, with a sad look.' Joseph Poniatowski, as brave as Murat, had never adopted the latter's theatrical costume and his character was quite the opposite. He was called 'The Polish Bayard'.

Born at Vienna in 1762, his father had been a field marshal in the Austrian army and brother to the King of Poland, Stanislas-Augustus. Ancestry which, in the context of the times, was to result in a lively career. At 25, Prince Joseph Poniatowski, Polish by nationality but serving in the Austrian army, distinguished himself against the Turks. At 30, recalled to his country by the Constituent Assembly, he fought successfully against the Russians. But, King Stanislas having joined in 1792 the Confederation of Targowitz, which incorporated the partition of Poland, Poniatowski resigned and went into exile. In 1794 came the Polish revolution. Poniatowski returned and enrolled as a simple volunteer under Kosciuszko. The revolt collapsed and he retired to Vienna, refusing tempting offers from Catherine II. In 1806, after Jena, and while the French armies were invading Poland, the King of Prussia made him governor of Warsaw. But nothing could withstand the French invasion and, like all Polish patriots, Poniatowski believed that it was a campaign of liberation and that Napoleon would restore Poland's independence and glory. He therefore embraced the cause of France and remained faithful for life. Appointed minister of war in the provisional Polish government, then after Tilsit, of the Grand-Duchy of Warsaw, he built an army consisting of twelve infantry regiments and sixteen of cavalry, the famous lancers.

In 1809, during the Franco-Austrian war, he repulsed with glory the Austrians attacking Warsaw. At the start of the Russian campaign, he offered his army to Napoleon. The Emperor – not from mistrust but because he knew of their courage – divided the various Polish corps throughout the French armies. They would take part in every major battle. In 1813 Poniatowski joined Napoleon in Saxony; we have seen his lancers at Leipzig. We shall meet him, his officers and men, again.

On the eve of the first day, Napoleon had a fairly good idea of the reinforcements the enemy could expect on the morrow; at least 100,000 men, while he could only count on the addition of some 15,000 men of General Reynier's from the area Lützen-Bautzen, of which two-thirds were Saxons of doubtful loyalty. At best, the odds against the Grande Armée were two to one.

On Sunday 17 October, the sky was dark, it was cold and raining. That morning, no gun, no musket fired, nothing moved. After inspecting the lines, Napoleon said to Murat: 'We must not deceive ourselves. It is time to think about retreat. Let us return to headquarters.'

Some provision wagons arrived and there was a distribution of meat, wine and brandy. The alcohol warmed them a bit, but around the bivouac fires could be seen plenty of feverish, exhausted men. 'And the distribution of alcohol made us think that we should soon be in battle again.' The soldiers could see the burned villages, the overturned guns and caissons, the ravaged earth. Farther away could be seen masses of enemy troops on the march who would soon be taking position. Troops were also moving on the French side, including reinforcements for Bertrand's units who were responsible for keeping open the line of communication with France. The soldiers also saw the requisitioned carts loaded with wounded and the walking wounded, arms in slings and heads bandaged, painfully hobbling, pale, with beaten looks.

Suddenly, some twenty hussars, brandishing pistols, galloped up shouting loudly 'The Emperor! The Emperor!' The battalions hastily fell in; the officers ordered arms presented. Seconds later, came the mounted grenadiers of the Guard – enormous men in huge boots and bearskins down to their shoulders, leaving nothing visible but noses, eyes and moustaches, sabre guards held close to the hip. Some horse-lengths behind, came the legendary person with his little hat and grey coat. Millions of conscripts had never seen him. 'Vive l'Empereur!', but he seemed to hear nothing: 'Frowning, he paid no more attention to us than to the fine rain which was falling.'

Napoleon was followed by the general staff. 'Imagine fifty to one hundred marshals, general officers, aides-de-camp, staff officers.' They were not as numerous as that, but such was their impact on the dazzled conscripts. 'So covered with embroidery and gold lace that it was hard to see the colour of their uniforms, some tall, thin with haughty looks, others, short, red-faced, stocky, others younger, sitting their horses like statues.' So moved the conquerors, now so threatened. Napoleon's subsequent conversation at his HQ with the Austrian General de Merveldt is enlightening. Sixteen years earlier, at Léoben, Merveldt had come to ask for an armistice of General Bonaparte. It was also he who, after Austerlitz, brought Napoleon the Emperor of Austria's peace proposals. Here is the substance of their conversation of 17 October:

> *Napoleon*: Let me compliment you on your courage yesterday during the fight for the bridge at Dolts. In token of our past good relations, I am going to send you under parole to the Austrian GHQ. Was it known on your side before the attack that I was here?
> *Merveldt*: Yes, Sire, we knew it.
> *Napoleon*: And you wished this time to give battle?

Merveldt: Yes, Sire, we wished to end the long struggle against you by a bloody and decisive encounter.

Napoleon: But you were wrong about my forces. How many soldiers do you think that I have?

Merveldt: At the most, one hundred and twenty thousand.

Napoleon: You are wrong. I have more than two hundred thousand. And how many do you have?

Merveldt: Three hundred and fifty thousand.

Napoleon; Ah, I had not thought you had so many (with good humour). And will you attack me tomorrow?

Merveldt: Surely, Sire. We intend to assure our independence, even at the price of our blood.

This conversation has been recorded by many witnesses, including Fain, the Emperor's secretary. It went on for a long while, the crux being a long, eloquent and adroit speech by Napoleon in favour of a peace founded firstly on reconciliation with Austria. 'Our political alliance is broken, but between your master and myself there is another alliance which is indissoluble. It is that one which I invoke, for I will always have confidence in my father-in-law's goodwill. Go and find him and repeat to him what I have just said to you.'

Here are the sentences which seem to have the most significance for us: 'For Austria to win at the expense of France is to lose. Think about that, General Merveldt. It is not too much for Austria, France and even Prussia to stem at the Vistula the flood of a semi-nomadic people, instinctively aggressive, whose immense empire stretches from our doors to China.'

Merveldt was escorted immediately to the outposts, whence he returned to the Allied camp and was received by the sovereigns. The attempt at negotiation was doomed. Merveldt was not allowed access to his Emperor. The march of events will show that he would have had some difficulty in doing so.

While Napoleon and Merveldt were talking, matters were at a standstill. The only encounter was farther to the north where there was a short engagement between the cavalry forces of Blücher and Victor. Early that night, other French troops neared the city – orders had been given to shorten the front. Then all was quiet. General Reynier advanced with his reinforcements: one Saxon and two French divisions. He did not know that at 5 o'clock on the previous afternoon, some officers from the Saxon division had appeared at Bernadotte's HQ and agreed that their units would desert to the enemy next day. Some soldiers of the Grande Armée, seeing the bivouac fires surrounding Leipzig for more than six leagues, said: 'Now, the whole universe is against us.'

Leipzig has been called 'the Battle of the Nations'. At 8 a.m. on the 18th, more than 1,500 guns boomed. As they had two days before, the enemy advanced in three columns. Drouot's artillery ploughed terrible lanes through their serried ranks, but the Austro-Russians were wreaking similar havoc on the French. Napoleon was watching every move from his vantage point on the Thornberg. Augereau's troops gave way, then the French cavalry charged, breaking the enemy squares, but behind these others were advancing. The battle hung in the balance until midday. The chroniclers, memorialists and historians do not agree as to how many combatants were engaged at this moment, but the following seems to me to be probably near the truth: 160,000 French against 320,000.

The enemy arc extended from north to east, to the south and south-west, and Bertrand's artillery could also be heard firing to the west. The bloodiest infantry battle was joined in the village of Probstheyda (five kilometres south-east of Leipzig) or rather in its ashes, between the Russo-Prussians and Murat's troops. Drouot had sited many batteries there, against which successive waves of infantry threw themselves with appalling losses. There was no longer any possibility of the coalition forces retiring, even though they were facing Napoleon in person as commander-in-chief. But the butchery at Probstheyda was so awful (more than 12,000 men in three hours) that Schwarzenberg gave orders to withdraw some hundreds of yards, and bombarded the French who advanced to fill the void. Men suddenly became aware that the noise of the second cannonade was increasing alarmingly. Blücher had crossed the Partha; his troops were securely joined with Bernadotte's and were driving on those of Ney and Marmont.

At 3 p.m. General Reynier ordered the cavalry of the Saxon division to support those regiments hard-pressed. The Saxon squadrons charged through the French lines, the enemy ranks opening to receive them. 'I have burned half my stock of munitions for the French, I will now shoot off the rest against them!' cried the chief of the Saxon artillery. And he turned his guns round. In the same sector, two Württemberger regiments turned on Durutte's division who were in line beside them and opened fire. 'In a few minutes', wrote some of the soldiers, 'these betrayals became known. Rather than destroying us, they increased our fury.' True, but this defection compelled Marmont's entire corps to retire. In the sector of the village of Schönfeld, north and north-west of Leipzig, some 28,000 French would now have to withstand the pressure of at least 90,000 Swedes and Prussians. The Swedes had 150 guns with ample ammunition. Marmont had only a third of that number and had to order his gunners to be economical with their fire.

The French infantry took the main shock. There is no exact account of the fighting. 'Officers and soldiers', wrote Barrès, 'fell like ears of corn before the scythe of the harvester.' Entire files were swept away by the artillery. Close Up! and the dead and wounded would be crushed under the feet of the enemy as the French retired. Every so often, the Swedish and Russian cavalry would throw themselves at the French squares. The ruins of Schönfeld were taken and lost seven times. To kill one another for a heap of ruins might seem ridiculous, but any old soldier will tell you that the most miserable ruin, a piece of wall, is a shelter for at least a while, a hope of prolonging his poor life for a moment, whereas in open country ...

Marmont found himself in the middle of a massacre. His chief of staff lay dying, four ADCs were dead, plus seven staff officers; their bodies lay on the ground side-by-side with those of senior officers, NCOs and soldiers.

During this time, Bernadotte advanced in the midst of his troops, riding a white horse, wearing a pelisse of purple velvet embroidered with gold braid, topped with a plumed hat and holding a baton covered in purple velvet. Napoleon, himself, looking solemn, headed a division of the Guard and marched towards HQ at Reudnitz, which was threatened by the enemy advance. The Swedes' drive was stopped there.

At nightfall, Schönfeld received its seventh assault from the Russians and Prussians. Every house was defended like a strong point, officers firing muskets with their men. It was necessary to retire to the houses, the gardens and then the cemetery 'where there were more corpses above than below ground'. Reinforcements arrived and the Russians were thrown back temporarily, but they rallied and returned and, being far too numerous, the French bugles sounded Retreat!. The defenders of Schönfeld pulled back as far as the suburbs of Leipzig without being pursued. Burning buildings illuminated their retreat. They marched over corpses, stumbled over dismounted cannon and overturned caissons. Stragglers wandered about the streets, looking for food and drink. The *cantinières* made fortunes selling wine and brandy.

At 7 p.m. Napoleon sent for Generals Sorbier and Dulauloy, commanding respectively the artillery of the army and the Guard. 'How much ammunition have we left?' 'Sire, 95,000 rounds have been expended today. We have 16,000 rounds left, about two hours' firing. We can only replenish from the depots at Magdeburg and Erfurt. 'We will go to Erfurt.' The Emperor immediately ordered the baggage, munitions, and artillery to cross the bridge over the Elster and take the road to France. The cavalry and the corps of Victor, Augereau and Ney would follow closely behind. Napoleon also sent messengers to the commanders of the fortresses in Germany. Their troops should return to France, brushing aside any opposition encountered on the road. The Emperor moved into 'The Prussian Arms' in Leipzig, and spent the best part of the night dictating orders. By first light on the 21st, two-thirds of the army had already crossed. Poniatowski came for orders: 'Prince, you will defend the central suburbs.' 'Sire, I have very few troops.' 'Well, defend them with what you have.' Napoleon went to bid farewell to the King of Saxony. Frederick-Augustus had wished to follow the Emperor; he still wished to do so and was inconsolable concerning the defection of his troops. Napoleon told him that he must remain at Leipzig and for his own safety must renounce his alliance with France. Too late: that same night the King of Saxony was made a prisoner of war. He would regain his kingdom in 1815, but reduced by a third. After this conversation, Napoleon left to cross the Elster and then wished to stop for a moment at a nearby mill. He was so exhausted that he fell asleep in a chair, despite the noise of the marching troops and the bombardment in the suburbs. It was there that the fighting continued. Many enemy regiments had encircled the city, pressing the troops who were securing access to the bridgehead. In the confusion and congestion, Poniatowski's lancers charged, turned round and charged again, their bravery impressing the other defenders who were in a tight corner. They too would have liked to have crossed the bridge, but were unable to do so until ordered. On the bridge there were collisions and fights. Survivors said that the Elster crossing was the Berezina minus the cold and so it remained until the end. A corporal and four sappers had been ordered to blow up the bridge as soon as the enemy appeared. At about midday, the corporal sighted Prussian troops and blew his mine. He was, of course, accused of having acted prematurely; those on the bridge were hurled into the river while those waiting to cross, cried 'Treason!', throwing themselves into the river, some without even shedding their haversacks. Among them was Prince Poniatowski, the newly created marshal. Bleeding from several wounds, he walked his black horse slowly into the water. The horse could not climb the opposite bank, which was very steep; the horse fell back on her rider and both were carried away on the swift current. Macdonald had been able to swim across. He himself recounted how those left on the river bank had cried: 'Marshal, save your soldiers, save your chaps!' He rode on in tears.

The vast battle of the nations, fought at close quarters had lived up to its promise. The coalition had lost more than 80,000 effectives: 35,000 dead, including eight generals, 45,000 wounded and (only) 1,500 prisoners, including General de Merveldt, later released. In the Grande Armée, 20,000 killed, including Marshal Poniatowski and three generals, 7,000 wounded, including Marshals Marmont and Ney and five generals, 23,000 taken prisoner, including a dozen generals. Total 50,000 men.

Recall the start of the retreat from Russia minus the snow. Also, with fewer vehicles. The sky was grey and it was raining. A cold wind blew. The soldiers moved with their heads lowered; how many it is difficult to say, perhaps 60,000 or a few more. Of this total, some half were troops marching in formation under officers' orders; the youngsters listened to the veterans who warned them to stay together and who encouraged them. 'If you leave the column, the Cossacks will have your skin; or the peasants, who have become hostile.' These survivors of the legendary retreat were not numerous, but other old sweats had fought the campaign in Saxony and had survived.

From Leipzig to Mainz, the retreat would extend to some 300 kilometres and last from 21 October to 2 November. About half the army moved in formed units, the rest in disorder. And this half in disorder did not follow, as is often the case; it went ahead, ahead even of the advance guard under General Bertrand. It went well ahead, dispersing during the march and thinning out. Most of them were youngsters who had escaped from the control of the veterans.

It often happens that units of young troops become dispersed when retreating. The striking psychological phenomenon is that these conscripts had earlier, even before their training was completed, shown surprising courage, as witness Ney's words after Lützen – 'The old sweats think too much, while the young ones press forward, etc.' Even later, even at Dresden and Leipzig, the conscripts as a whole did not dishonour themselves. Then, suddenly, without warning, at least half of them 'cracked'. Thanks to a long applied corset of discipline, the veterans held under defeat, the others did not. They broke up sometimes with a kind of frenzy, groups leaving to sack the villages, wrecking everything and, where they found nothing, setting the place on fire. Often they were attacked by groups of peasants who clubbed them; at other times, the Cossacks encircled them and killed them with their lances.

At the beginning of the retreat, Bertrand, defender of the road to France during the battle of Leipzig, had welcomed the Emperor to Weissenfels. 'Sire, do not stay here, leave this hell and return to France as fast as your horse will carry you.' Bertrand, being in command of the army of observation of the Rhine, had not lived through the horrors of the great retreat from Russia. He had blundered in speaking thus to Napoleon in the presence of hundreds of soldiers and was brusquely put in his place in consequence. This was the advance-guard, which would clear the way for the march of the army as far as Erfurt, where the troops would be re-mustered, rested and encouraged.

They reached Erfurt on 23 October. The army depots supplied munitions to the artillery, uniforms and shoes: 'Our new uniforms and our shoes fitted us like sentry-boxes, but that did not stop us from savouring their warmth. We revived.' Napoleon occupied the same palace at Erfurt which he had used in 1808, when amid excessive ceremony, the sovereigns and princes of Europe had come to pay court. Now alone, he worked through his mail which contained nothing but bad news. Bavaria's defection had obliged Eugène de Beauharnais, Viceroy of Italy, to retreat to the Adige. In Spain, after Joseph's defeat at Vitoria, Wellington had advanced to the Bidassoa. And in Germany the coalition forces would surely manoeuvre to cut the army's retreat. Fortunately, exhausted by the slogging-match of Leipzig, they had halted in order to reconstitute their forces. They were unwilling to attack without numerical superiority an adversary who still intimidated them. Napoleon was aware of this and still planned to field a force capable of opposing them – a mass of new conscripts. From Erfurt he sent a series of dispatches to the Council of Regency, ordering them to prepare an exceptional call-up of 300,000 men of the classes 1803 to 1814. This was the fifth resort to conscription since the beginning of 1813. On the staff, the senior officers shrugged their shoulders: 'More and more men are deserting. The product of this conscription will be derisory.'

In their own fashion, a number of the senior officers 'cracked'. Ney was the main malcontent and was heard to say, speaking of the Emperor: 'It is time to make an end, it is time to stop him, after having lost the army, from losing France.' And the 'bravest of the brave', on the pretext of recovering from a minor wound received at Leipzig, left the army and hurried to Paris. And in the confusion he was not even missed.

Murat left also – once again, leaving the sinking ship. But without concealment. He sought an audience of the Emperor. 'Sire, letters from Naples make it necessary for me to return to my estates. But I am only returning in order to serve Your Majesty better. I shall join up with the Viceroy Eugène with 30,000 men.' A little later, he gave an account of the interview to Mier, the Austrian Ambassador at Naples. 'I displayed such firmness that I wrenched consent from the Emperor and left immediately for fear he might renege.' Napoleon would never see him again.

After two days at Erfurt the army resumed its march. The rest had been insufficient and there were many typhoid victims, especially among the young soldiers.' 'Three leagues from Fulda on the road to Salmunster during a halt, it was learned that 50,000 Bavarians were barring the line of retreat and occupying the large forts on the route,' In fact, there were 30,000 Bavarians and 20,000 Austrians. The Bavarian General de Wrede had served from 1805 in the Grande Armée.

On the evening of 29 October Napoleon slept at the château of Prince Isenburg in the village of Langensebold. The enemy army was then in position in front of the town of Hanau and the River Kinsig. On the 30th he left his lodging and unhurriedly rode to a point where the woods overlooked the river.

The battle of Hanau was straightforward. To confront the 50,000 Austro-Bavarians Napoleon had only 17,000 men, but these included 10,000 of the Guard, light and heavy cavalry, grenadiers and chasseurs, not to mention the artillery. It was this élite force that he launched on that day. The artillery 'led the advance unsupported, but the thick smoke prevented the enemy from seeing that Drouot's guns had no accompanying troops.' Two battalions of chasseurs of the Old Guard followed, then the mounted chasseurs of the Old Guard, then the remainder of the available troops. The battle lasted from midday until 6 p.m. – the Austro-Bavarians were not swept aside without cost – 'The worst slaughter that I ever saw in my life,' wrote Coignet, exaggerating a trifle, but the French prevailed. The enemy never wholly recovered from the first blow. 'The sight of the Old Guard had struck terror into the Austrians and Bavarians.' The old sweats had had the best of it. The Austro-Bavarian army had beaten a retreat, having lost 10, 000 men, killed, wounded or prisoners.

It appears that Napoleon on this day felt that the issue was never in doubt. During the entire action, he had gone back and forth along the road through the forest. At one point, while he was talking to Caulaincourt, a shell fell into a nearby ditch. Caulaincourt ran to place himself between the Emperor and the shell, but it did not explode.

That night the enemy troops abandoned Hanau, and next day a deputation came to Napoleon, who had had his tent pitched in the forest. They asked for the Emperor's goodwill.

The victors of Hanau encountered the worst conditions while marching the 20 kilometres from Hanau to Frankfurt – torrential rain and mud. The soldiers jostled the stragglers and walking wounded. Carriages and cannon ran over the bodies of the fallen. At Frankfurt they had to bivouac outside the city in the vineyards, knee-deep in mud in the unceasing downpour. The fifty kilometres to Mainz were little better.

Napoleon arrived at Mainz on 2 November. Nothing had been prepared for the reprovisioning of the troops, the depots were empty. 'We did not think', said the culprits in the supply service, 'that the campaign would end in this retreat.' Inertia and muddle paralysed every corps and service of the army. The soldiers, who had been ordered to disperse throughout the villages and get the inhabitants to feed them, did the best they could in the circumstances. Many wandered in the town, exhausted, famished, dirty, flea-bitten. In the hospitals and churches, transformed into seed-beds of putrefaction, the sick suffered besides the corpses on the soiled straw. Typhus raged unchecked; the despairing doctors and surgeons had nothing with which to care for them. The epidemic did not spare the inhabitants. In one month there were 14,000 deaths among the military and as many again among the civilians. Convicts were conscripted to take the dead away for burial.

The enemy was approaching, the Rhine must be crossed and the crossings guarded. The campaign in France was about to begin.

XIV

1814
The Campaign in France

On 25 January 1814, Napoleon climbed into his carriage at 3 a.m. in the courtyard of the Tuileries, to travel to the front in Lorraine. Over most of France, snow was falling. In their cottages, the peasants huddled over the fire. Looks were gloomy and words few and bitter. Virtually everywhere there were supporters of peace at any price. Too bad if the Allies prevailed and reached Paris. But others said: 'If they reach Paris, their kings will be masters of everything, re-establishing forced labour and tithes and privileges. It will be as it was before the Revolution!'

A knock on the door. Who is there? Two gendarmes wished to know if so-and-so had been seen – they had quite a list. No, they had not been seen. Conscription got them and afterwards – nothing. A grandfather groaned: 'You know very well that there is no one here but women, children and the old. There are not even any horses!' Requisitioning had made large inroads in certain cantons. Lacking horses, it was necessary to work the fields by hand. The old had done so – causing distress. The gendarmes had not insisted and left.

More knocks on the door, this time by night. It surely could not be the gendarmes, and, besides, a name was spoken. 'Ah, it's you!' A deserter, cold and hungry. The deserters hid in shacks in the forests, in caves and ruins, in isolated houses whose inhabitants ran risks. Those they sheltered were always ready to disappear quickly while the peasants distracted the gendarmes. The deserters were quite a population, albeit an uncounted one.

Twenty years of war had been too much. Too many mourning families, too many feared to be. The authorities in the towns and villages knew that, under an apparent resignation, revolt simmered; unemployed workers where bread was not plentiful said that what was needed was a new revolution; at the same time, in the west, the royalists dared to come out of hiding and speak.

In northern and eastern France, it was snowing and colder than ever. Also, one could hear the guns. Blücher had crossed the Rhine on 1 January and since then Napoleon's marshals had done nothing but retreat before an enemy who, however, advanced only with prudence. The towns and villages of the invaded regions were full of uniforms, Prussian, German, Austrian and Russian and the occupiers were not tender. To the administrators who complained the officers retorted: 'Where we live, your soldiers did much worse.' On the roads, moving in front of the enemy were the pitiful tides of refugees, always the same down the ages. From time to time a shout: 'The Cossacks!' The women turned, open-mouthed, the children stood up to see. The Cossacks were now most wretched-looking – greasy, hairy, ragged – but they inspired terror; of all the invaders, they were they worst. Their extortions had provoked the bands of partisans who attacked the stragglers, the isolated, in the same way as the guerrillas in Spain had attacked the French. In the invaded districts, hatred of the invaders had eclipsed the desire for peace.

Between his return to France on 9 November after the German campaign and his departure for the front in Lorraine, Napoleon had resided now at the Tuileries, now at Saint-Cloud, governing a greatly reduced empire, attending to a thousand details, reviewing troops, giving receptions. The men around him murmured: 'He's mad!'

On 1 January, before a secret session of the Legislative Assembly, a deputy named Lainé had made a speech of unusual violence against conscription: 'For the last two years, men have been harvested three times a year. An endless and barbaric war swallows up our youth regularly.' There were open demonstrations. A vote to have this speech published was carried by 223 to 51. The Emperor came in haste and denounced the legislators, finishing by prophesy: 'In three months we shall have peace. Our enemies will have fled or I shall be dead.' Since then, the Allies had entered: Strasburg Saverne, Epinal, Toul, Chaumont, Lunéville, Nancy, Dijon, Saint-Dizier. Napoleonic power was crumbling away in great slabs. The Dutch had ejected the French occupying force – 2,000 men!; Spain had to be ceded to Ferdinand VII; Murat had bargained with the Austrians, bringing over 30,000 soldiers from his kingdom of Naples to the coalition; Eugène de Beauharnais, summoned to concentrate his troops with those of Augereau, had not budged; Pope Pius VII had regained possession of his States with the Emperor's blessing. Blücher, at the head of the army of Silesia, 80,000 men, was pushing ahead in Lorraine; Schwarzenberg and his army of Bohemia, 185,000 men, having violated the neutrality of Switzerland, was marching towards the plain of Langres. Other forces concentrated beyond the Rhine increased the total enemy strength to 400,000 men. In about mid-January, Napoleon had calculated that, to oppose the 220,000 enemy troops already in France, he could call on at least 120,000 disregarding the 170,000 of the national guards' 'active legions'. These figures were blindly optimistic; the intake from conscription was ridiculously low, thanks to the effect of desertion. In fact, against the rising tide of his enemies, Napoleon initially could muster 60,000 soldiers at most.

What soldiers? On induction, the conscripts of 1814 were no more than dispirited adolescents who had either not dared or been unable to follow the deserters, terrified at the idea of coming under fire. Their incorporation took place in worse conditions than those of the conscripts of 1813. Like the latter, assembled by an NCO at the principal town of the department, they were taken to a regimental depot, and from there by forced marches to the towns and villages near the front. They would still be dressed as they had left home, peasant blouses or the double-breasted suits of the bourgeois, the artisan's coat, round hat. They were pushed towards wagons loaded with uniforms, arms and equipment. The supply sergeants threw them selections as bones are thrown to dogs: 'Hurry up!' They had to undress, try on these military hand-me-downs in the rain, the snow, feet in the mud.

Often, the conscripts could not find clothes to fit them and had to recover their civvies. 'Hurry up, damn you!' Abuse rained down and sometimes blows. Finally, a forage cap and the belts, cartridge box and a sabre completed their outfit. 'Fall-in – don't you know anything?' Cartridges were distributed for the muskets which they did not yet know how to hold. 'This way, Forward!' The bewildered youngsters set out on the frosty road towards the front.

These conscripts were known as the *Marie-Louises* because the decree calling them to the colours had been signed by the Empress as President of the Council of Regency, Napoleon being with the armies. Their courage was legendary and we shall see that often it deserved to be so lauded. But they did not go into battle alone – they were backed up by old sweats.

It may seem surprising that the debris of the regiments recalled to the Rhine after the campaign in Saxony were still employable and that so many men were still valuable. They were, if one may put it so, the survivors of the survivors, the result of a form of brutal selection; now, they could endure anything, nothing could surprise or frighten them. They taught the conscripts how to shift for themselves – to loot, for example, but also they demonstrated the steadiness of seasoned troops, the automatism.

In 1814, these veterans were more numerous than during the campaign in Saxony, because, Napoleon having abandoned the war in Spain, more of them had been recalled. The dress of these last batches bewildered the conscripts and the population. Hats ranging from old, discoloured sombreros, turbans, skullcaps, priests' black hats, dressed in ragged capes, marching on home-made boots of untanned leather, faces tanned like leather.

We shall see, mixed with the *Marie-Louises* and the veterans, relatively older men, reservists or volunteers, foresters, gendarmes, who would serve as NCOs or in the ranks, and even some veterans, more or less mutilated, who controlled the drafting of the troops, one-armed pensioners from the Invalides, blind supporters of the Emperor (according to them, Napoleon retreated only after he had been betrayed) who had pulled strings to join up again. Bouvier-Destouches, ex-lieutenant of mounted grenadiers, ten fingers lost frozen in Russia, Legion of Honour, managed to hold a sabre and fell, covered in wounds, at Craonne.

Such was the heterogeneous mixture with which Napoleon would attempt to stop the invasion. He knew that, even more than in 1813, he would have to act with lightning speed. Three enemy armies were marching concentrically on Paris down the valleys of the tributaries of the Seine – natural invasion routes. Bülow was coming down the Oise valley with the Anglo-Prussians, Blücher was following the Marne with the army of Silesia which included Russian and Prussian troops, Schwarzenberg was on the Aube with the army of Bohemia, Austrians and Russians. As it happened, Napoleon would only have to concern himself with the armies of Blücher and Schwarzenberg. If these two could join he would be lost. If he could attack them separately he thought that he had a chance to beat them, despite each being superior in numbers. Many would regard the campaign in France as Napoleon's masterpiece: Brienne, Champaubert, Montmirail, Château-Thierry, Vauchamps, Montereau, Craonne, Reims – nine victories in fifty-five days. The record of the campaign in Italy was beaten. But that would not suffice.

On 23 January, in a moving ceremony, Napoleon, carrying the King of Rome in his arms, had confided him and the Empress to the 'courage of the National Guard'. He was never to see either of them again. He left Paris and that night he was at the prefecture of Châlons-sur-Marne.

'Where is Berthier? Where is the enemy? Where is the army?' Berthier arrived from Vitry. His news was not reassuring. The vanguard of the army of Bohemia had taken Bar-sur-Aube and Bar-sur-Seine. Blücher had just occupied Saint-Dizier where there was a Russian cavalry corps. There were many Cossacks between the Seine and the Marne. 'And the army?' Macdonald, coming from Belgium, should be at Mézières heading for Châlons. Mortier, with the Old Guard, was trying to slow the advance of the army of Bohemia; he was retiring towards Troyes. The country between the Rhine and Champagne had been abandoned almost without a fight. The marshals thought the cause was lost. Napoleon cast a glance at the map. 'It is evident that Blücher intends a junction with Schwarzenberg in the region of Bar-sur-Aube as the latter marches on Troyes. I will prevent this junction by first crushing Blücher.'

Orders were issued. At first light on the 26th Napoleon arrived at Vitry-le-François, finding there a large contingent of conscripts who had just arrived, all dropping with fatigue. The officers fell them in. 'Shout "Vive l'Empereur!" They bleated the greeting feebly.' Divide them between the units of Marmont's corps,' said the Emperor.

Instruction from the veterans. At dawn next day Duhesme's division, which was marching with Napoleon, ejected from Saint-Dizier a Russian division left there by Blücher to cover his rear. Napoleon entered the town at 8 a.m. Armed peasants proudly led before him some prisoners which they had taken. An interpreter repeated their information: 'Sire, Blücher passed through Saint-Dizier with about 30, 000 men, heading for Brienne. Napoleon hardly needed to consult a map: from Brienne, Blücher would aim for the road to Troyes which was being followed by Schwarzenberg.

'We march on Brienne!' Eleven leagues to cover. He knew from the prisoners that Blücher, to avoid the dirt road through the forest of Der, had taken the road via Vassy and Doulevant, twice as long, but with a macadam surface. 'There has been a month of frosts; the forest road should not be too difficult. We will take it. Leave in the morning the day after tomorrow.' Unfortunately there was a thaw during the night of the 27th/28th, and after they had started down the forest road, it rained in torrents. The infantry stumbled through mud to their knees, the artillery and the wagons got bogged down. It was not until nightfall that they reached a village (Montier-en-Der) where the conscripts dropped in their tracks without even looking for shelter.

At first light on the 29th – forward! Napoleon left with only 18,000 men. At 8 a.m., just before reaching a village hardly visible through the mist and the trees (Mézières), shots were heard: the advance-guards' cavalry had driven off a squadron of Prussian hussars. A moment later the priest appeared, threading his way through the horses to Napoleon. 'Bless you, Sire. Do you remember me?' Napoleon's memory never played him false: 'Father Henriot!' He had been in time past a master at the high school at Brienne and had known Bonaparte as a pupil. 'Father, you will serve me as guide.'

The heights of Brienne, immediately above the terraces of the château, were held by 30,000 Prussian and Russian troops. On the terraces and nearby, the young Bonaparte had fought sham fights. Thirty years on, Bonaparte-Napoleon had changed the face of Europe, and now, in the same surroundings, it was real guns that were firing and Napoleon was fighting in earnest, risking his life during day-long battles, a rough welcome for the *Marie-Louises*. Finally, the château was taken and held, despite a Prussian counter-attack.

Blücher retired at nightfall. At about 10 p.m. Napoleon, accompanied by Father Henriot and a small escort, was making his way to the presbytery of Mézières where he was to sleep. Suddenly the sinister shout 'Cossacks!' – one of these savages, lance in place, was already charging the leading rider in the grey coat; two generals were quicker than he and one of them, Gourgaud, shot the Cossack two paces from the Emperor. All this happened in a second.

They left on 31 January. Brienne had been a victory; Blücher had lost plenty of men but he was still moving. It was necessary to trap him before he joined all or part of the army of Bohemia. Napoleon, having concentrated with the corps of Marmont and Gérard, had now 45,000 men: 'With them, I will hold

Blücher.' Yes, but Napoleon was not to win this trick. The enemy junction was accomplished. On the 31st at Vendeuvre on the road Bar-sur-Aube–Troyes, Blücher was reinforced with three corps of the Army of Bohemia. On 1 February at La Rothière, 4 kilometres from Brienne, the 45,000 men under Napoleon collided with 180,000 coalition troops.

The front was one league long, along a line of villages, of which La Rothière was in the centre, in wooded, marshy country. The battle of La Rothière was remarkably confused, because most of it took place in a blizzard. Blücher had initiated the attack, but his blinded troops advanced very slowly and Marmont's gunners, even while firing blind, made good shooting. Victor was well dug-in in the village itself, which the *Marie-Louises* defended courageously, the more so since the whirling snow concealed the enemy masses from their view. From time to time the cavalry on both sides charged, disappearing into the mist. The old sweats said 'it's like Russia'. But this was a war of attrition and new units were arriving constantly. At nightfall, the defenders of La Rothière were facing the Russian Guard; it was necessary to evacuate the village; then scouts reported that yet another Austrian corps was arriving, the 40,000 Austrians of General Giulay. The Emperor ordered retreat, which was executed in good order by the Young Guard. The infantry retired to Brienne; the French lost 6,000 men, the enemy 8,000.

Napoleon, accompanied by the Guard cavalry, returned to the château of Brienne where he had already spent one night. But on this night (1/2 February) he did not sleep. He could see from his window the arcing fires of the enemy bivouacs, which seemed like a scythe menacing the small area where the fires of his army glowed. The French were now fewer than 40,000, whereas the enemy strength was some 250,000. Blücher – would he perhaps choose a dawn attack? Napoleon had already given his orders: at 1 a.m. the troops were to stoke-up their bivouac fires and decamp in silence, retreating towards Troyes. The army would have to cross two rivers, the Aube and the Voire, against which the army was backed; at each crossing there was but one bridge. At 4 a.m. the Emperor left the château. It was still snowing. He left on foot, a few soldiers with torches lighting the way, the staff following; they had covered some quarter of a league before the grooms and the escort caught up. Napoleon mounted his horse and arrived at the Lesmont bridge and crossed the Aube. Two hours later, the rearguard having crossed, the bridge was blown. At daybreak the enemy realised that he had been tricked and the pursuit started; but the French had a good lead.

The snow fell in squalls, the roads were swamped. The retreat had started in fairly good order, but after a few hours it changed into something like a rout. The command was slack – the generals: 'All that we can do is to make peace.' This was heard by officers and even by the rank-and-file. Nobody wishes to be killed a few days before peace is made. The retreat was to last two days and two nights. Some of the *Marie-Louises* in order to keep up were seen to throw away, first their haversacks, then their equipment and then their muskets. Some left the column and hid in the woods. Their naked bodies were found pierced by Cossack lances.

On 3 February 1814 Napoleon entered Troyes at 3 p.m. Doors and shutters closed, the city was frozen with terror. The news had spread that the Emperor had been beaten on the soil of France; this was the end. The exhausted troops marched through empty streets. Some soldiers stopped in front of the barricaded houses, knocked and asked for bread. Nothing. The inhabitants would keep their bread to satisfy the demands of the Russians, Austrians and Prussians, hoping thereby to avoid molestation. Some had the audacity to open a window and shout this harshly to the soldiers. This provoked anger, doors were stove-in, people beaten up, shops looted.

A period of calm ensued. The regiments were to remain for two days to regroup and recover their stragglers. During this time couriers bearing bad news reached Napoleon. Murat had concentrated his army to march on Eugène de Beauharnais who was engaged against the Austrians; the enemy had occupied Aix-la-Chapelle and Liège, General Maison's troops were being ejected from Belgium; Macdonald, who had been ordered to retire to Châlons-sur-Marne, had been expelled and had had to retreat to Château-Thierry; in the west, royalist bands were holding the region; in Paris, the Council of Regency had been struck with inertia. Napoleon muttered in Daru's hearing, 'All this will end with a Bourbon.'

At this same time, the Allied ministers met at Châtillon-sur-Seine in a form of congress to decide the terms of peace to be offered to Napoleon. We already know their first demand: the return of France to her old borders and the reconstruction of Europe to their orders. In reality, the coalition wished to see Napoleon humbled; this would require time. Napoleon had sent Caulaincourt to Châtillon with full powers 'to obtain an honourable peace'. In fact, he too wished to gain time, the more so since now the powerful army, pursuing the French army since its defeat at La Rothière, threatened Troyes. Time to go.

On 6 February the army resumed its retreat towards Nogent-sur-Seine. No snow, but icy rain and violent winds across a devastated land, the men suffering from hunger. Some conscripts wounded at La Rothière had not yet received even first aid. In one day, several hundred, incapable of marching further, fell down in the mud. The end for them.

On 7 February – Nogent. Napoleon received M. de Rumigny, bringing news of the congress of Châtillon. In a letter, Caulaincourt explained that, due to the harshness of the terms of the coalition, he had not felt able to use his plenipotentiary powers to conclude a peace. Napoleon read his letter, crumpled it and re-entered his room.

M. de Rumigny met Berthier, Lefebvre and General Belliard as he was descending the stairway. They appeared very excited. 'We no longer have an army. Tell the Duke of Vicenza to conclude a peace at any cost.' Lefebvre and Belliard asked Berthier to write in this sense to Caulaincourt. 'No. That should not go in writing. But I [will] formally instruct M. de Rumigny to say that he must make peace on the spot.' This was the attitude among the seniors. Napoleon was aware of it, but thought he could still keep them under his control. But, suddenly, a new turn.

On 8 February Napoleon received other news and, as he read, his face lightened. His enemies, who now thought that the campaign was ended and the road to Paris opened, had just committed a grave strategic error: they had in fact divided their armies. Blücher, with the army of Silesia, 60,000 men, was coming down the length of the Marne, while Schwarzenberg's army of Bohemia, 150,000 men, was following both banks of the Seine towards Paris. 'My maps!'

Napoleon had Bacler d'Albe get out the maps of the region between the Seine and the Marne. He had them spread on the table and bent over them, compasses in hand, measuring distances and inserting red-headed pins. Blücher hoped that by following the Marne he would enter Paris before Schwarzenberg. Having ejected Macdonald from Châlons, he sent his troops towards La Ferté-sous-Jouarre. His 60,000 men were disposed in four widely spaced groups. Having finished the examination of his maps, Napoleon straightened up: 'I am about to beat Blücher,' he told Fain.

Victor and Oudinot were to remain at Nogent with the task of holding Schwarzenberg's advance, giving Napoleon time to settle accounts with Blücher. On 9 February the army began to move towards Epernay. Napoleon took with him only Ney and Marmont's troops and the Old Guard, 6,000 sabres, 30,000 men in all. Speed was essential in order to 'upset the enemy by attacking him at those points where he expected it the least'. But speed is hard to achieve on flooded roads. But peasants, both requisitioned and volunteers, arrived with their horses to double the teams. The army pushed on through the mud and the rain. The first of the famous three victories in three days, Champaubert, would be the fruit of this effort, which had the advantage of surprise.

Very early on 10 February, the Russian regiments forming part of Blücher's army were unsuspectingly marching along the road from Châlons-sur-Marne to Meaux. They would be attacked in the flank by troops which had painfully travelled the flooded roads. As everyone knows, there is nothing worse than being taken in the flank. The Russian regiments were literally penetrated and rolled-up.

'*Ma bonne Louise*, victory!' Napoleon would write that same evening to the Empress. 'I have destroyed twelve Russian regiments, taken six thousand prisoners, 40 guns, two hundred caissons and the commanding general. I did not lose two hundred men.' As often, he exaggerated slightly, but the essentials were correct. Of course, the victory was not gained instantaneously. It took many charges of the cavalry and infantry, and General Alsufiev had had time to site his batteries on the heights of Champaubert, but the gunners had panicked when they saw the bearskins about to charge them; this was when victory started to smile on the French.

The Russians had been chased into the swamps of Saint-Gond. To avoid drowning or suffocation, they surrendered. Alsufiev himself had finally to flee but was taken by a young trooper of the 16th Chasseurs who held him at swordpoint and forced him to yield his sword. The young man (19 years) refused to allow his colonel to relieve him and, proud of his capture, wished to present him personally to the Emperor. The *Marie-Louises* who found retreating so painful, physically and morally, took heart from the fact that they were attacking. Marmont had picked out one who was steadfast under fire. 'But why did you not fire your musket?' 'I can fire as well as the next man, but I must have someone to reload it.' He did not know how to do this. Another, equally ignorant, approached his lieutenant: 'Sir, you have been at this for a long time. Take my musket and fire it and I will pass you the cartridges.' The officer agreed. Other memoirs mention young peasants, youths, who brought in 'their' prisoners. One of them, pushing two grenadiers before him, brandished a butcher's knife. 'These fellows wanted to make off, but I managed to make them march.'

Napoleon, again, was bent over his maps.' The army of Silesia is cut in two, but we must allow no respite to Sacken or Yorck, otherwise they will turn about and march towards Blücher.' Sacken, a Pomeranian, commanded the Russian troops of the army of Silesia, while Yorck, a Prussian, commanded a Prussian corps; together 35,000 men. On 11 February at 5 a.m., Napoleon swept off at top speed towards Montmirail with 5,000 veterans, 4,700 cavalry, 1,800 *Marie-Louises*. During the night of 10th/11th, the cavalry had been sent as vanguard and had cleared Montmirail of several squadrons of Cossacks whom the inhabitants would long remember.

The day before, these occupying troops had made as if to evacuate the town. 'A full hour later', according to a merchant, 'some 400 or 500 returned, charged the crowd with lances and sabres. They then dismounted and arrested some 30 persons, including 15 notables. These they stripped and gave 50 blows with a knout, both men and women were stripped. I was myself robbed by a leader who found that my clothes and boots fitted him. Most of the girls and women were raped, even in the streets. Some threw themselves from the windows in order to avoid such an outrage.'

Napoleon arrived at 10 a.m. at Montmirail as Sacken's riflemen were duelling with the French troops who were already in position. Fighting continued in the nearby villages, notably at Marchais, where the enemy had artillery and at l'Epine-au-Bois, where he occupied the Belle Epine farm defended by 3,000 infantry and 40 guns. The 1st Division of the Old Guard arrived, having been slowed down by the mud. It was they who turned the scales at l'Epine-au-Bois by taking the Belle Epine farm. Sacken's troops, deprived of this base and charged by the cavalry of the Old Guard, began to retire. Elsewhere, Sacken had only one idea – to work his way north in order to keep in touch with Yorck.

At 8 p.m. Napoleon wrote to Marie-Louise that he had beaten and routed the enemy army, taking more than 7,000 prisoners. He decided to distribute 1,750 crosses of the Legion of Honour, including 1,000 to the Guard. These must be awarded on the spot without delay, and was done by the light of the bivouac fires. Then Napoleon went and stretched out fully dressed in a room at Belle Epine farm. The footmen just had time to remove some corpses. The farmyard was packed with exhausted men, crouching on the dung-heaps which stank but gave off a little heat.

Next morning, up well before dawn, Napoleon placed the index finger of his right hand on the map: 'Yorck and Sacken are retreating in haste in order to cross the Marne at Château-Thierry. The town is on the bank opposite with only one bridge. We must catch the enemy before he gets to it.' At 9 a.m. the French army was on the march, formed in two columns, one led by the Emperor, the other by Mortier.

I have mentioned the behaviour of the Cossacks at Montmirail. Not far away, at Trezancy, French soldiers found the mayor tied by the neck to a bedpost, his wife on the floor, having fainted after having been raped in front of him. The baby was crying in its cradle. under which a fire had been lit. Elsewhere, the Cossacks had resorted to the traditional brigands' torture to elicit where money was hidden – burning the victims' feet.

Throughout Champagne, infuriated peasants, armed with hunting rifles or weapons taken from corpses, launched the same type of guerrilla warfare as had the partisans in Lorraine. And, like the Spaniards against the French, the peasant women helped in their fashion; at Essayes, a young widow had made sixty Cossacks drunk and then roasted them by setting her house afire. At a farm known as les Géraudots, some Cossacks, equally drunk, were massacred, a ploy repeated many times. At Presles, a servant eviscerated with a fork two Cossacks sleeping in a barn. Vengeance was equally wreaked upon the regular Russian troops and on the Prussians.

The French army was pursuing the troops of Yorck and Sacken. They eventually cornered them on the plateau of Nesles, near Château-Thierry and won a fairly easy victory, but then these enemies, hastily retreating again, had reached the bridge over the Marne and had destroyed it. Crossing the town to continue northwards was no picnic, especially for the last of them. The local inhabitants, roused to vengeance, massacred them with whatever weapons they had to hand.

The rebuilding of the bridge cost the French thirty-six hours. Billeted in a small farm on the left bank of the Marne, Napoleon dictated a stream of orders. Knowing that in Paris the recent victories had been greeted with some scepticism, he ordered Clarke, Minister of War, to parade the Russian prisoners along the boulevards, down the rue Napoleon (today the rue de la Paix). Some Russian generals, escorted by grenadiers of the National Guard led the march. The Parisians: 'Vive l'Empereur! Vive Marie-Louise! Down with the Cossacks!' After them came the prisoners, Russians and Prussians mixed together, filthy, mostly in rags, suffering. They carried their bivouac dixies on their back and made signs to the crowd that they were hungry: some showed their wounds. 'Poor devils,' said the Parisians, and gave them food, money and clothing.

To understand the events of the campaign in France, one can consult the map of operations or not, as one wishes. It is obvious that the soldiers of 1814 had never seen such a map. Most were illiterate and to the conscripts from Gascony, Limousin or Brittany, these place-names meant nothing. They marched to exhaustion in a countryside buried in snow or drowned in rain. No matter in which direction they marched, it was always the same thing, interminably. They fought and, overall, the battles became confused in their memories: the guns, the black smoke and the sinister order, incessantly repeated: 'Close Ranks!'

On reflection, only Napoleon had an overall, general view of the military events of this campaign. Even the marshals had no more than a partial view and the time would come when they would wish for nothing more. As for the enemy commanders, they of course consulted their maps, but almost until the end, they concentrated upon watching for and worrying over the initiatives of Napoleon. So it is only by placing ourselves in Napoleon's shoes that we can follow the course of events of this campaign.

Can one do this without presumption? Merely by scanning the orders which Napoleon issued almost continuously to his marshals – with details which indicate that he had less and less confidence in them – makes one giddy. I appreciate that the reader will tire of a recital of the orders issued, of these moves in every direction, but they do demonstrate the strategic genius of Napoleon. It seems to me that this succession of events will become clear at the price of an occasional glance at the map – we, who have the privilege of literacy, whereas the *Marie-Louises* marched like lost souls.

The people of Europe had seen the march of the Grande Armée as a torrent of devastation. Now, with the injustice of events, it was the French population that was to suffer and, even worse, these green *Marie-Louises* were the scape-goats, so to speak. I trust that the reader will have become aware of another change in the army – no more women. The retreat from Russia had swallowed up every kind of conveyance, the open carriages of the wives or mistresses of the officers, carts and wagons of mere prostitutes and even most of the *vivandières'* little carts.

Vivandières had followed the army during the campaign in Saxony and even that in France, but were less and less numerous as the army moved more quickly and painfully. As we shall hear no more of them, let us record that over-all they deserved well of the army. On the eve of Marengo, General Lasalle (killed in a charge at Wagram) had composed for a *vivandière* named Fanchon a song much sung by Napoleon's troops and even long after they were gone. 'Let us do something for them. Ah, how gentle is their care, how much merit they have and how much glory! She likes to laugh she likes to drink, she likes to sing like us.' The reader knows her successor – la Madelon.

With the Marne bridge repaired, Napoleon was acclaimed on arrival at Château-Thierry. While he was still there, he received from Marmont on the night of 13th/14th news that Blücher had taken the offensive and was advancing on Montmirail. Immediate reply: 'I hope to be able to be at Montmirail in person before 7 a.m. and to be able by midday to attack the enemy and teach him a sharp lesson. Choose a good position covering Montmirail. If possible, act so that the enemy neither suspects nor perceives anything.' By 8 a.m. he was there and summed up the situation in a flash: 'Grouchy, turn the right of the Pruss-ian army with your cavalry and take them from the rear.' And orders to Drouot for the guns.

At midday the Prussian cavalry, coming from Vauchamps, which would give its name to the battle, was received by a rain of shells. The French infantry seized the village and the French cuirassiers charged. 'Field Marshal,' said an ADC to Blücher, they are shouting 'Vive l'Empereur!" when they charge.' 'So – he is there.' And Blücher, who saw that he was already outflanked, ordered a retreat at 2 p.m. All had gone well for the French. Blücher's army, although not destroyed as Napoleon has claimed, had a good one-third of its effectives out of action until they could be reorganised to resume a part in the campaign.

'Now I have time to devote to Schwarzenberg's army.' We should remem-ber that on 9 February Victor and Oudinot had been left at Nogent to cover Schwarzenberg. By now, their troops had retired to Guignes (35 kilometres south-east of Paris). There, the two retreating marshals found an order from Napoleon: 'Hold your present positions. I will be there tomorrow.' From Vauchamps that evening, Napoleon had sent orders to Macdonald to march urgently from Château-Thierry towards Guignes. The Guard and Ney's corps, exhausted, were piled into peasants' carts and, with the 8,000 sabres at Napoleon's disposal, joined the concentration. Mortier and Marmont were ordered to take positions respectively on the Aisne and the Marne to prevent any offensive by Blücher: as always, to contain one of two adversaries while Napoleon disposed of the other.

On 17 February, the battle of Mormant, ten kilometres from Guignes. Napoleon mounted his horse at first light and the army moved in three columns. The centre column took the village, the enemy troops were turned by the cavalry, all went as well as at Vauchamps, the enemy losing 3,500 men and twelve guns. One might call it a banal victory, although there was not much of the banal about it as the cavalry pursued the retreating enemy.

At Valjouan, a squadron of hussars and mounted chasseurs commanded by General Bourdesoulle overtook a Russian division of the rear-guard, broke their square and did 'great execution'. The troopers pursued the enemy into the woods where they continued to sabre them. The surprising is fact is that this squadron consisted of recruits who had only been two weeks with the army. Here is what a Colonel Biot wrote of them before the battle. 'Not only were they incapable of directing their horses and handling their sabres, but even of holding the reins in one hand and their sabre in the other.' Then, how did they do it? Even if Bourdesoulle's action report of 17 February, which was submitted to Victor, exaggerated a trifle, the essentials are true.

The strategic and tactical machine which was Napoleon's brain never ceased to function. He now wished his army to rush south to seize and cross the Montereau bridges to capture an Austrian corps which had ventured there and was coming down the Seine towards the approaches to Fontainebleau. Then he would drive with his unified force on Troyes, where Schwarzenberg would surely not have had time to concentrate his units. Meanwhile, Napoleon himself, in order to remain in contact with all his corps, stopped at Nangis at the house of Justice of the Peace Salmon, where he set up his HQ.

It was Victor's corps that had been tasked with taking Montereau. But on the eve, Napoleon had reprimanded him for having retired too rapidly before Schwarzenberg. The Marshal was put out, dawdled and even, rather than driving straight on Montereau, stopped one league from the bridge and went no farther.

Now for a diplomatic note. The Tsar, the King of Prussia and Schwarzenberg met at Bray-sur-Seine (40 kilometres east of Fontainebleau) for a council of war. Napoleon's string of victories had unnerved them. Schwarzenberg, who had just seen a part of his army pushed towards Montereau and Provins, said that the situation with the army of Silesia was no better. 'Napoleon must be stopped at all costs.' 'Well, do it,' said the Tsar. But how? Schwarzenberg sent a letter to Berthier through the French outposts in which he stated that, believing that preliminaries of peace were to be signed at Châtillon, he had ordered his troops to refrain from any offensive movement. Napoleon shrugged his shoulders. He was on a winning streak. On 18 February, he ordered Victor to attack before daylight. Victor had not budged until 8 a.m. and, instead of making a coordinated attack, allowed his units to attack successively. The Württembergers opposite had profited from this and decimated three of his divisions. General Chataux was mortally wounded. On arrival, Napoleon had appraised the situation. To Victor: 'You may go home.'

He took command himself and was everywhere. As he was about to lay a gun himself, his ADCs besought him to expose himself less. This provoked the historic reply: 'The bullet that will kill me has not yet been cast.' The situation was essentially re-established, except that, at one moment, the French batteries fell silent. 'Why are they not firing.' 'Sire, they have no more ammunition.' 'Berthier, convene a court-martial tomorrow and arraign Digeon before it.' Digeon was the artillery commandant of II Corps. Fortunately the Prince of Württemberg, who was in command of the enemy forces opposite, had ordered a retreat as soon as he saw his flank threatened. In the streets of Montereau, the inhabitants hurled tables and chairs, sniped at the Württembergers from basement windows and from the rooftops.

The 15,000 men holding Montereau had lost 1,500 killed or wounded and 3,500 prisoners and had not had time to blow up the bridge. But Victor's inertia had had one consequence: the Austrian corps which had ventured on to the left bank of the Seine had been able to retreat and march on Troyes unscathed. On the evening of 18 February, Napoleon retired to the château of Surville, overlooking Montereau – tired but relaxed; this was the moment for the day's defaulters to try their luck. 'Sire,' asked Berthier, 'do I really have to send General Digeon before a court-martial?' 'No, tear up the papers.'

When Victor arrived he was met by an avalanche of reproaches: you serve with ill grace, you avoid headquarters, you secretly drag your feet. I know that even your wife avoids the Empress. Victor's wife was a lady of honour. 'Sire, I have served you since Italy. You cannot banish me from the battlefield without dishonouring me. If I have committed a military fault, I have paid dearly for it in the wounding of my son-in-law [General Chataux].' 'Is there any chance of saving him?' No, and Victor started to cry, and in turn, the Emperor was moved. 'I shall take up a musket,' said Victor through his tears; he would join the ranks of the Guard. Napoleon held out his hand. 'Well, Victor, you may stay. I cannot restore your corps, since I have given it to Gérard, but I will give you two divisions of the Guard. And you will stay and dine with me.'

On 20 February, while the French army was pursuing the army of Bohemia towards Troyes, Napoleon moved his HQ to Nogent-sur-Seine. It was freezing, the town looked sinister, gutted houses, smoke-blackened walls. There had been fighting there on 11 and 12 February. That morning, Ney and Oudinot asked for an audience. Napoleon received them leaning against the mantelpiece: 'Well, gentlemen?' The two had come as something of a delegation, representing, they said, all the marshals. They had to urge the Emperor to make peace. 'This time, we will speak firmly to him,' Ney had said. Yes, but facing that blue regard which transfixed the head, his arrogance evaporated. In a flat monotone he explained clumsily the reason for their visit: the Emperor seemed to ignore the redoubtable strength of the Allies; how could one hope to prevail with an army no more than a sixth of their size? To his surprise, Napoleon listened with unruffled composure.

'What are you saying? You misrepresent the situation. Ney, sit there and write!' From memory, he reeled off the effectives of each army corps. Incorrectly, he quoted the figures of the ration strengths of each unit. Since January, these had been reduced by at least one-third through losses due to combat, sickness and desertion.' You, Oudinot, you have 15,000 men. And you, Ney, 9,000.' 'Sire, I have only 10,000 present.' 'Sire, I have only 3,000.' 'It is not true.' Ney hedged. 'It is true, Sire, that I had forgotten 1,500 cavalry.' 'Ah, I was right when I said that you had 9,000 men.'

Mistrust, and then anger. When a flaming log fell from the fireplace, Oudinot bent down to replace it. Napoleon could not resist seizing the Marshal by the scruff of neck and holding him bent over. 'Now, sir, I have you there! Confess that you two agreed to come and deter me.' Oudinot got up, trembling a little. The two marshals maintained their devotion. 'Well, gentlemen, in spite of this, we shall dine together.' The meal was disposed of in a few minutes in a pregnant silence. The two marshals escaped, leaving the Emperor alone. 'My maps!'

These marshals are mad, thought the Emperor. The army of Silesia is nearly destroyed. The Bohemian one is retreating everywhere. 'I shall cross the Seine at Méry with part of my army and fall on Schwarzenberg's right flank. Have Boyer leave immediately with a part of the Guard to clear the Austrians from Méry, if they are still there and, above all, prevent them from destroying the bridge over the Seine.'

Pursue, reach the bridge before the enemy, or if he is there, prevent him from destroying it; this was an obsession. This time Boyer's division would stop nothing. Because what they would find at Méry was not a few Austrians, but the Prussians. Blücher's army had been reorganised and reinforced by a Russian corps, and now totalled 50,000 men. And the two enemy armies were close to each other: 200,000 men. With this concentration, Blücher and Schwarzenberg only had to throw themselves on the advancing 30,000 French.

No. The Allies' doctrine was unchanged from that of the campaign in Saxony; always avoid confronting Napoleon personally and play for time. When the Emperor was at Châtres, one league from Méry on the right bank of the Seine, the Prince of Liechtenstein came to ask him on behalf of the Allies – those allies who now had operational on the ground seven times more men than he – for a suspension of hostilities!

'No, no suspension of arms for the moment. I am thinking of sleeping tonight at Troyes. I will send a general to your outposts tomorrow to negotiate an armistice.' An ambiguous reply. Did Napoleon also hope to gain time? Or to make a quick dagger thrust at this enemy so overwhelmingly superior in numbers? Fighting and negotiating simultaneously is not unknown, though it is risky. The news of the arrival of a flag of truce from the enemy spread quickly through the ranks. 'Yes, peace quickly!' shouted the soldiers. But nothing happened – no armistice. 'Then, how much longer?' The troops by now were marching like automatons.

On the night of 22 February, the enemy abandoned Méry, set the village afire and destroyed the bridge. Remaining on the left bank of the Seine, the army marched on Troyes where the enemy was still standing. The French bombardment set fire to the suburbs and to several nearby villages. The enemy troops evacuated the town, destroying everything. And at the same time, negotiations continued. Napoleon had sent General Flahaut to Lusigny to conclude an armistice but 'negotiations must not hinder operations'. Further, the conditions on which the Emperor would sign an armistice were as unacceptable to the Allies as were those which they had repeatedly proposed. What would be the outcome?

Napoleon entered Troyes on 24 February, surrounded by a deliriously enthusiastic crowd. The locals kissed his boots and embraced the stupefied troops. 'But how many more towns must we liberate?' asked the soldiers.

On the night of 26/27 February, Napoleon learned that Blücher had fallen on Sézanne, ejecting Marmont's forces, and that he had passed down the valley of the Marne *nach Paris!* There was no more talk of an armistice (the talks would be finally broken off next day), the Prussians must be stopped at any cost – 'crushed,' was the word used by Napoleon. Once again, the same exhausting march between two adversaries constantly beaten and constantly resurrected, as in Saxony.

It really was as if the same orders were being re-issued from the campaign in Saxony. 'Macdonald and Oudinot are to remain in contact with the army of Bohemia and slow it down until Blücher is finished off. I plan to take him in the rear while Mortier and Marmont bar the road to Paris. Blücher will have to accept battle and will be exterminated. If he escapes northward, I will trap him on the Aisne: he must surrender or perish.' Such was the substance of the orders and briefings which Napoleon gave to his marshals.

It was 100 kilometres from Troyes, at the confluence of the Marne and the Ourcq, that Napoleon hoped to corner Blücher. The proportion of *Marie-Louises* remained about the same, because since the beginning of the campaign the depots had been sending a steady stream of recruits to fill the gaps. These youngsters had to tie their boots on with string in order not to lose them in the mud. For the past week they had been hungry. None the less, the 100 kilometres between Troyes and Jouarre were covered in three days. By means of a few words which Napoleon sent down the columns and which were repeated, he managed to persuade them that this time it was for good and all.

The troops of Mortier and Marmont had managed to halt the march on Paris of the army of Silesia and were occupying the line of the Ourcq. On 1 March at dusk, the army marching from Troyes gained the heights of Jouarre. Through a veil of rain could be seen the ribbon of the Marne. Forgetting their fatigue, the soldiers cried 'Forward!', wanting to make a finish. But some of the artillery was lagging behind, bogged down in the wooded, marshy country between Rebais and Jouarre. Ney in the vanguard, entered La Ferté-sous-Jouarre and, what did he see on the far side of the Marne? The army of Silesia, retiring after destroying the bridges. Blücher, knowing that Napoleon was on his traces, *renounced – for the time being – his march on Paris* and was heading north.

'All right,' said Napoleon, 'I will corner him on the Aisne!' It took at least 24 hours to restore the bridges over the Marne. The sappers went to work by night in the rain. Next day Napoleon went down to encourage them. Some peasants who had crossed the river in a boat reported that the retreat of the Russians and Prussians resembled a rout: 'They are abandoning guns and caissons.' Napoleon did not yet know what had caused this haste. Blücher wished to cross the Aisne and join up with the troops of Bülow coming from the north, which up to now had taken no part in operations. Now, at that time, there were not thirty-six bridges that could be used by an army to cross with its guns and wagons. Blücher's immediate objective was the bridge at Soissons.

'Soissons is in French hands,' said Napoleon. It was half-true. The Soissons garrison numbered 700 Poles of the Vistula regiment, 140 French gunners, 80 scouts from the Guard and 300 men from the urban guard. The town commandant was a General Moreau, namesake of the deserter killed at Dresden. The Poles were commanded by Colonel Kozynski.

On the night of 2 March, the Marne bridge was ready and the French army crossed with Napoleon. On 4 March, they reached Fismes between Soissons and Reims, in other words, they were in a position to cut Blücher off if, being unable to cross the Aisne at Soissons, he chose to retreat to the east. Ahead, he would collide with the troops of Marmont and Mortier, bent on denying him the road from Villers-Cotterets, while to his rear, the imperial army was preparing to fall on him. What better? For the first time in months, no more gloomy faces were seen at HQ and there were no more allusions to peace at any price. Fismes would be the high point of Napoleon's strategic brio during the campaign in France.

Late in the day, one of Marmont's ADCs galloped into HQ covered in mud: 'Soissons has capitulated.' One might ask how long the Soissons garrison of 1,220 men could have withstood the 43,000 of Bülow's army who reached the Aisne from the north. On the morning of 2 March, the vanguard of this army had deployed on the roads to Laon and Reims. The Poles manned the ramparts. The town was heavily bombarded and then the Russians and Prussians attacked. The defenders' musketry stopped them. Kozynski at the head of his 300 troopers, charged so effectively that the enemy retired to the plain.

Despite their overwhelming numerical advantage, the Allied command was anxious. Blücher had infected Bülow with his brand of panic: the Ogre was at his heels. 'And it would take at least twelve hours to open a breach, even thirty-six! Better try for a surrender.'

The weak point of the Soissons defence was at the top – Moreau. In his situation, agreeing to receive a flag of truce was tantamount to surrender. In succession, they flattered and threatened him: 'Your defence has been heroic, but is hopeless. Look at our numbers. The population of Soissons would be annihilated for nothing, etc.' Moreau had summoned a 'council of defence' to bargain with the enemy. He himself was inclined to surrender. The Polish colonel, although wounded during his charge, was adamant – better death than shame! An ADC was sent to call him away and the capitulation was signed in his absence of ten minutes. His horsemen, when they learned of it, chewed their carbines with rage; the populace insulted Moreau. Almost immediately gunfire could be heard from the direction of the Ourcq. 'It is the Emperor. We must tear up the capitulation!' Too late: enemy troops had already entered the town. Moreau took the arm of a Russian officer: 'I am a dead man. The Emperor will have me shot. He would never forgive me for having surrendered the town at such a time.'

Moreau was not shot. The board of inquiry before which he appeared first decided that he should stand trial before a court-martial. The court did not deliver its verdict until 24 March and Moreau was saved by the entry into Paris of the coalition troops. Joining the Bourbons, he was made a knight of Saint-Louis, brigadier-general and given command of the department of the Indre.

Napoleon received more bad news at Fismes. La Fère had surrendered after even less resistance than Soissons, the Allies gaining 100 guns from the arsenal. Oudinot allowed himself to be surprised and beaten by Schwarzenberg at

Daulaincourt and had retreated behind the Seine at Nogent and Montereau. The army of Bohemia, which was coming down the Seine, was within 50 kilometres of Paris. What to do? Napoleon still dreamed of crushing Blücher. The army was ordered to cross the Aisne at Berry-au-Bac and pursue.

Craonne lies 20 kilometres north-west of Berry-au-Bac on a plateau which forms a spur, ending in an impressive scarped promontory. It would become tragically famous in 1917 under the name 'Chemin des Dames'. On the morning of 17 March 1814 it was held by 28,000 Russians and Prussians and it was these whom Napoleon planned to attack on arrival, without delay – faster, ever faster, before the other corps, delayed at Soissons, could arrive.

The enemy artillery started bombarding and counter-battery fire was ordered. But to prepare to fire when under fire oneself is no picnic. And most of the artillerymen and service troops that had arrived so far were such novices that they took an interminable time. Some guns were demolished by the enemy's fire before being able to fire a shot, the least ill-served firing one round for every six from the enemy. General Drouot, seeing their disarray, took pity on them, leaving the staff and trotting over to the batteries to show the recruits how to load and lay a gun, wielding the sponge himself.

The *Marie-Louise* infantrymen were sent in to the assault. We know that, if deployed, they fell apart in minutes, less from cowardice than from lack of combat experience. It was essential to keep them in close order, guided by veteran NCOs. They clambered over the bodies of their comrades. A second brigade, held in reserve, was soon brought forward from its shelter in a wood. Fix bayonets! Their charge had some initial success, but the Russians quickly brought up more artillery, their infantry advanced, their cavalry assembled and they slowly began to counter-attack.

'Send in the Guard!' Neither the chasseurs, the lancers nor the gunners of the Guard were novices, and one must recall that the appearance on the battlefield of the bearskins had a magic effect on any troops. 'The artillery of the Guard silenced the Russian guns. The Emperor, noticing some hesitation in the enemy ranks, ordered the whole line to attack.' Blücher also noticed this hesitation and he could see the French rapidly advancing on both his flanks. After a few words with his chief of staff, the ADCs galloped away bearing an order: 'Retire on Laon and concentrate the army.'

Was this a French victory? Yes, because the army of Napoleon remained mistress of the huge, sterile plateau and even pursued the retreating army. Night ended the pursuit, but did not interrupt the killing. On the plateau of Craonne, the inhabitants of Paissy, Ailles and Oulches finished off the Russian wounded. Others, pursued by Cossacks, hid in the quarries of the 'mountain'. The Cossacks smoked them out; many children died of suffocation. 'This battle of Craonne was glorious,' wrote Napoleon to Marie-Louise. 'I had 7–800 men killed or wounded, the enemy losing 5–6,000 men.' In fact the enemy did lose 5,000 men, but the French lost 6,000. Victor and eight generals, including Grouchy, were wounded.

Laon, 9 March. It snowed all night and in the morning there was fog. Laon is built on a steep hill, surrounded by walls pierced by eleven gates. The slopes are steep with the suburbs at the bottom; the surrounding plain is cut by small streams. The enemy was solidly established on the slopes – 90,000 men in all. Napoleon arrived with 40,000 men. Naturally he wished to conquer, he always wished to conquer, he wished it now more than ever because one thought dominated his life – to crush Blücher. He still thought that, with Blücher crushed. he could change objectives and assault Schwarzenberg who was still marching towards Paris. The dismembering continued.

In the long view, it seems evident, given the situation and the position of the forces, that Blücher could not be crushed. This time, and for the first time, he would not have to order a retreat. The first day of the fight for Laon had been bloody and in vain; the Guard had suffered losses. That night the young soldiers slept around the fires, crushed against one another, the old sweats had scattered in search of rations. On the 10th, the Prussians advanced very stealthily before the French had time to rush to arms.

The best that one can say is that the retreat – on Soissons – was difficult. The French column was beset by a swarm of enemy cavalry. A bizarre note: the cavalry bands played selections, whereupon the cavalry halted and fired on the column for some minutes, then rode off again. A little later, another tune, a stop and a fusillade and so on. Night fell. Marmont on the French right had lost 3,000 men and nearly all his guns.

Here is one last glimpse of the French: 'The last smile of Fortune,' according to Marmont. Some 15,000 Russians commanded by a French *émigré*, the Count of St-Priest, occupied Reims. On 13 March, the French vanguard burst into the town and captured a complete Russian regiment marching to the cathedral for a Te Deum. Napoleon arrived at 4 p.m. and took charge. All was going well. Just before the battle, one of St-Priest's officers asked what would be the line of retreat if Napoleon attacked. 'Why, sir, are you thinking about retreat when you could get yourself killed?' However, as soon as St-Priest knew who it was that was attacking him, he immediately ordered a retreat. Fate did not favour this man, who was almost immediately struck by a shell. His leg had to be amputated and he died. Napoleon added one detail: St-Priest was struck by a round from the same gun-layer who had hit Moreau, the turncoat. The cavalry finally charged the enemy retreating through the streets. At nightfall, the inhabitants illumined their windows, decorated them and shouted 'Vive l'Empereur!'

In another French city, Bordeaux, at about this time, the inhabitants were shouting 'Long live the King!' Soult had been beaten by the British near Orthez. Bordeaux surrendered without a fight to the Duke of Angoulême who took possession in the name of Louis XVIII. At Toulouse, Caffarelli, commanding the military region, was no longer obeyed. 'The inhabitants will make no resistance to the enemy's progress, believing that they would be better off under his yoke.' They refused all requisitions. In the department of the Lot, the gendarmes rounding-up the conscripts were attacked by armed mobs. At Tours, in Mayenne, in the Sarthe and in Maine-et-Loire conscription was officially suspended. Bands of brigands were seen near La Flèche and Baugé. The Emperor could no longer count on receiving the smallest reinforcement.

Napoleon asked himself, must he continue to dream of 'crushing' Blücher, or was there something else more urgent? The news from Paris was as bad as that from the provinces. The council of regency thought of nothing else than compelling the Emperor to make peace. If the enemy appeared before the capital, it seemed certain that it would not be defended. Now, the army that most menaced Paris was not Blücher's, but Schwarzenberg's – so, leave Blücher.

Once again, leave one prey to run after another. On 20 March Ney arrived with his vanguard at Arcis-sur-Aube and learned there from peasants fleeing from the south that an immense army was approaching in order of battle. The explanation: Schwarzenberg, suddenly finding a fund of courage which he had never displayed hitherto, had turned his army that had been moving on Paris, and was now marching to meet Napoleon.

When Napoleon himself arrived at Arcis during the afternoon, he found himself in a battle and one which was going badly for the French. During this day they were to pit 14, 000 men against 40,000, then 22,000 against 90,000. The odds make it clear that at no time was there a hope of victory. Here is what one can deduce from the various accounts. First, in the town itself, the Guard cavalry defended itself clumsily against a Russian cavalry force four times greater. A French infantry division made a rush for the bridge at Arcis, shouting 'Every man for himself!' Napoleon was jostled, swept into the torrent of runaways and only managed to extricate himself by drawing his sword. Leaping into the bridgehead, he faced about: 'Which of you would pass before I do?' The fugitives paused and turned back to the fighting. To my knowledge, the propaganda machine did not seize on this replay of the bridge at Arcola because it did not end in a victory. Napoleon once more gave evidence of his physical courage. A shell fell in front of a group of conscripts, who recoiled. The Emperor walked his horse forward and pushed the missile aside. The shell burst and his wounded horse collapsed, the Emperor disappearing in the smoke. He was then seen to get up and, without a word, mount another horse which a groom walked up.

'Vive l'Empereur!' – the conscripts moved forward. At nightfall, the Guard still held Arcis-sur-Aube, now only a blazing ruin. The enemy held the heights bordering the river. Next day, the entire army of Bohemia, 100,000 men, was concentrated there. Napoleon had 18,000 infantry and 9,000 cavalry. Retreat was imperative.

Having crossed the Aube, heading north, most of the soldiers thought that they were to march on Paris. No! To the east. They didn't understand why. Napoleon was playing a strategic poker game. Since it seemed impossible to triumph by interminably running between Blücher and Schwarzenberg, he had thought of another solution: leave the field to the west to the enemy and attack their rear from Lorraine. Call in the sparse garrisons in the region, threaten the Allies' communications with Germany. This offered a chance that they would panic and call off the march on Paris.

The plan might succeed. Two incidents were to ruin it. The couriers riding between Paris and the army, mostly by night, had often been intercepted. This time, on 23 March, a patrol under Lieutenant Redlich of the Hanseatic Legion seized a pouch containing a letter from Napoleon to Marie-Louise. 'I have decided to move to the Marne in order to push the enemy armies further away from Paris and to bring me closer to my base.'

This was immediately reported and the Tsar called a council of war, attended by the King of Prussia, Schwarzenberg and many generals. Blücher, in bed, suffering from ophthalmia, was absent. Here is their decision: 'The armies of Silesia and Bohemia are to join together and move to attack Bonaparte's rear and flanks. Battle may be joined between Vitry and Metz.'

On 24 March a squadron of Cossacks captured another courier, carrying a large packet of dispatches. In these messages, many high functionaries professed themselves shocked by the lack of ammunition in the arsenals as well as by the anxiety and discontent of the population. The same (or maybe the following) day, Cossacks seized yet another courier, carrying this time, a letter from Savary (a member of the Council of Regency): 'The public treasury, the arsenals and the magazines are empty. We are completely at the end of our resources, the population is discouraged and dissatisfied, wishing for peace at any price. The enemies of the imperial government conspire and foment in the population an agitation still latent but which will be impossible to repress unless the Emperor succeeds in driving the Allies away from Paris and drawing them far away from the bridges of the capital.'

Another Allied council of war. After discussion, the opinion prevailed that the best way to overthrow Bonaparte was to drive on Paris. This decision marked the end of the campaign in France. No suspension of fighting, no armistice or peace preliminaries had held. The war was not ended; it was to last another two weeks. But this would be a war without fighting, without a battle, except for a day's fighting in Paris – a sop to honour. Napoleon would be the only one wishing still to try the impossible.

On the evening of the 27th, Napoleon arrived under the walls of Vitry, defended and all gates closed by a strong enemy garrison, barring the passage over the Marne. He was joined by Macdonald who brought a bulletin of Schwarzenberg's found on a prisoner. 'Translate!' '200,000 coalition troops are marching on Paris.' The whole staff turned to the Emperor, who appeared very calm. 'This changes everything. There is a decision to take.' A discussion followed, the counterpart of the enemy's deliberations. Macdonald maintained that the Allies' march on Paris need change nothing of the earlier plan. He was alone in this opinion. Napoleon thought for a moment and then ordered all troops to stand fast in their positions. 'For myself, I am returning to Saint-Dizier.'

It would later become known that the coalition troops were shaken when the French army marched on Lorraine. They had feared that Paris would not be seriously defended until Napoleon could come to the rescue with a reinforced army. They had been reassured by M. de Vitrolles, Talleyrand's secret emissary, by M. Hedelhofer, secretary to the Duke of Dalberg, by MM. de Polignac, Adrien de Montmorency, de Montagu and even – every one wanted peace, every one betrayed – by Thiriot, deputy director of the imperial police. The royalist party, which included some important members of the government, was ready to welcome the Allies as saviours.

Napoleon was reunited with his staff at Saint-Dizier. He had once again studied his maps. He had torn up the plan for marching into Lorraine. 'I shall fly to Paris, raise the people, arm the workmen in the suburbs and throw them, mixed in with the soldiers, to the defence of their capital.'

He was fifty leagues from Paris, the enemy less than fifteen. The capital was not fortified and the defence consisted of 10,000 garrison troops, 12,000 national guardsmen of no military value. Napoleon had ordered the transfer to Paris of the 50,000 men distributed between Vitry, Saint-Dizier and Doulevant. The weather was frightful, sleet succeeded by snowstorms and freezing rain. The countryside was ravaged, towns partly burned and roads transformed into bogs. Napoleon's coach left Saint-Dizier escorted by the duty squadrons, overtaking the columns of soldiers bent before the squalls. At his approach, the troops quit the roads for the flooded fields, regarding the imperial carriage dolefully. By now they understood nothing and had ceased to think for themselves – well, perhaps one thought: if they marched on Paris perhaps the war would end. At Doulevant (30 kilometres south of Saint-Dizier) Napoleon received a ciphered dispatch from a courier disguised as a peasant. 'I wish to see him.' In came the man, streaming rain, exhausted. 'Sire, all the roads within fifteen leagues of Paris are in enemy hands. The royalists are distributing proclamations in the capital. There is talk of forcing the Legislative Assembly to meet and ask for peace.

"Surely," they say, "the Russians will burn Paris to avenge the burning of Moscow."' During this interview Fain brought in a dispatch from La Valette, the Postmaster. 'The Emperor's presence is necessary. If he does not wish the capital delivered to the enemy, there is not a moment to lose.'

Not a moment to lose was a bit much. In the evening of this same 28 March, the council met to choose what course to follow. First, they decided to welcome the Allies, since the Empress would doubtless obtain acceptable peace terms from her father. But Joseph Bonaparte had read a letter from the Emperor, already two days' old, in which he formally instructed the high authorities to move towards Blois if matters took a bad turn.

At 9 a.m. on 29 March, under the rain, a convoy of vehicles escorted by chasseurs of the Guard climbed the Champs-Elysées heading for the Rambouillet road. These carriages bore the Empress, the King of Rome, Letizia Bonaparte, Cambacérès and the ministers among others.

Precisely at this time, Napoleon gave Berthier new orders intended to accelerate the army's march. No stop, day or night. If artillery teams were lacking, bury the cannon and the mortars which could not keep up.

The imperial berline rolled towards Troyes under a heavy sky and increasingly black clouds. A cutting wind swept the plain of Champagne. At nightfall, the escort and the generals drew their sabres and closed up on the berline; Cossacks were prowling. The army followed as best it could. A little before midnight on the 29th, Napoleon and escort were in the suburbs of Troyes. Before going to rest for some hours at the château de Pouilly, the Emperor sent for Berthier: 'I had thought to leave you leading the troops, but I shall need you in Paris. I will order Ney to march the army to Fontainebleau. Send for him.'

'I shall need you in Paris.' Napoleon was convinced that once he had reached Paris, everything would change. The royalists would go underground, the capital would defend itself and Napoleon, returning to head the army concentrated at Fontainebleau, would attack the coalition forces, now far from their bases, and who would be demoralised by the resistance in Paris. It was a beautiful dream.

Napoleon left Troyes before dawn on the 30th. At 3 p.m. on the 31st he was at Sens. As he was dining, he received a message from Clarke, Minister of War: there was fighting in Paris – the Allies had attacked. 'We are leaving!' The carriages followed the left bank of the Yonne. Every minute, Napoleon leaned out of the window 'Faster!' At 10.30 p.m. they reached the Fromenteau relay, near Juvisy, where the horses would be changed. In the foggy night, Napoleon looked through the lamplight to see the chief postillion talking with some one on horseback. 'Who is that?' 'Sire, it is General Belliard.' 'Belliard?' What was the general commanding the cavalry of Marmont's corps doing here if his squadrons were fighting in Paris? Belliard himself has left a record of the conversation: 'Well, Belliard, what is this? What are you doing here with your cavalry? Where is the enemy?' 'At the gates of Paris, Sire.' 'And the army? 'Following me.' 'And who is guarding Paris?' 'It is evacuated. The enemy should enter tomorrow at nine.' 'And what has happened to my wife and son? Where is Mortier, where is Marmont?' 'The Empress, your son and the whole court left for Rambouillet two days ago. Marshals Mortier and Marmont are surely at Paris to finish the arrangements.' The race had been lost.

For a moment, Napoleon could not grasp it. Having succumbed to a terrible fit of anger: 'What cowardice to capitulate, etc.,' he then wished to go on to Paris. 'I will put myself at the head of the national guard and my troops and we will put things right. General Belliard, give orders for the troops to turn about.' He sat at the verge of the road, despondent. 'Alexander in Paris!' He then went into the post-house where he asked for writing materials – for a note to Marie-Louise. 'My love, I returned to defend Paris, but I was too late. The city had been surrendered this evening. I am concentrating the army near Fontainebleau. I am in good health. I feel for what you must be suffering.'

The imperial dream was to continue: to manoeuvre on the Loire, linking up with the troops in the south, sending to Lyons for Augereau's army and taking some of Soult's forces, fighting around Toulouse. Then, another idea: negotiate – to gain time? Perhaps. Nothing is certain any more. The Emperor dictated a letter to Caulaincourt giving him full powers 'to negotiate and conclude peace'. What, in truth, did this man, overwhelmed by destiny, really hope for? This is what he said to Caulaincourt as the latter was about to leave: 'You will arrive too late. If you see that the only salvation lies in our courage, we will fight and die gloriously.' He then got in his coach bound for Fontainebleau, where he arrived at 6 a.m. on the 31st. Marmont told him, more or less, what had been happening.

Nothing could be more difficult than to throw light on the events leading up to a capitulation. Who can say afterwards that he never for a moment betrayed the truth, excused himself, added a bit more sparkle to a personally courageous deed, censured those who had not shown equal courage? During what has been called 'the battle of Paris' on 30 March 1814, the soldiers of the ghost of the Grande Armée fought and died courageously. But, rather than a true battle organised on one side or the other, it was a series of disconnected actions.

We recall that, after the French failure at Arcis-sur-Aube on 20 March, while Napoleon was marching on Saint-Dizier with part of his army, he had left the corps of Mortier and Marmont to guard the road to Paris. On the 25th, these two corps, attacked at la Fère-Champenoise by the entire army of Bohemia, had retreated. On the 28th, Clarke had ordered them to fall back on Paris itself, leaving at Bray and Nogent the troops of General Souham.

Before dawn on 30 June, the drums of Paris sounded the alarm to the national guard. Commotion in the suburbs, formed units started marching towards the place Vendôme where the city commandant, General Hulin, had his HQ. From the assembled crowd came shouts: 'Muskets! Muskets!' A delegation was received, but how could General Hulin give them muskets when he did not have enough for the national guard as well as his own troops? Besides, what general would willingly give arms to a crowd of excited civilians? But with daylight, the cannon boomed; the soldiers were fighting.

Schwarzenberg was to attack Pantin and Romainville; Blücher, Clichy and the heights of Montmartre, at that time outside the city proper. A total of 39,000 troops were to defend the capital against 100,000 coalition soldiers. All these troops would not be engaged at the same time. Marmont and Mortier's soldiers were tired after a week of retreating. In addition, many knew that the previous day, an enemy flag of truce had met General Compans, who was defending Bondy, to ask for an armistice of four hours; that another, a Colonel Blücher, namesake of the General, had appeared at the outposts at Clayes-sous-Bois with peace proposals. He had been sent away, after having produced a proclamation from Schwarzenberg inviting the Parisians to follow the example of the Bordelais; that is, to allow the coalition forces enter.

Despite their numerical inferiority and fatigue, despite the diminution of energy which affects troops who know that negotiations have begun, the coalition forces were repulsed everywhere. At many points, at Pantin, Romainville, on the right bank of the Ourcq Canal, the French even gained ground. But on the plain outside the city, the coalition forces were becoming ever more numerous.

The appearance of the city was astonishing. In the place Vendôme, the workmen continued to shout for arms, while at the Cafe Tortini the clients declared that it was useless and even stupid to fight. In his memoirs, the Duke of Broglie described how he took a walk along the boulevards between the Madeleine and the rue Montmartre. 'One could see a crowd of well set-up men, with elegantly dressed women, almost like a public occasion. The booths, which had been carefully shuttered, were now full of men and women hastily lunching. The noise of the fighting was very clearly heard. The rumours that were passed around were, as one might expect, of every sort and very contradictory, nobody believed anything, everybody believed some of it.'

At 2 p.m. the Prussian guard went on the offensive at Pantin and the French battalions fell back on Belleville. Major Evain held the Trône Gate with 28 guns served by the pupils of the Ecole Polytechnique. Charged by the Russian cavalry, fired on by the Prussian artillery, charged by the Uhlans, these young men, still inexperienced, showed a courage which would later become famous. On the point of being overwhelmed, they were rescued by a charge of the Polish lancers – these, once again! But the law of numbers was telling more and more. Late that morning, Joseph Bonaparte, before leaving Paris, authorised Marmont and Mortier to treat with the enemy 'if they could not hold out any longer'. At 3.30 p.m., Marmont, who had fought with exemplary courage, reckoned that the moment had arrived. Flags of truce were exchanged.

Despite a cease-fire order, fighting continued here and there. A few shells fell in the city, rue Montmartre, rue Saint-Antoine, rue Saint-Denis, rue Saint-Martin. Negotiations dragged on, in part because Mortier refused to capitulate. He gave in, but his opposition was useful, since the Allies, fearing a return of Napoleon, offered concessions. The text of the capitulation was signed at Marmont's home in the rue Paradis. His corps and that of Mortier were to evacuate the city by 7 a.m. on 31 March, with their arms and baggage. The national and urban guard was to be retained, disarmed or dismissed as the Allies chose. The city of Paris was 'commended to the generosity of the high Allied powers'.

'Far into the night, the suburbs rumbled and echoed with the cry of "Treason",' heard at the crisis of every defeat. The capitulation revolted those who feared the return of the kings; others rejoiced. At midnight on 30 March 1814, Prussian soldiers and even Cossacks danced with the girls in the cabarets on the ramparts.

Those Parisians who wished to see the entry of the Allies began to collect at 9 a.m. in the faubourgs Saint-Martin and Saint-Denis, and along the boulevards. Some royalists were told to assemble in the place de la Concorde to march in front of the Allied sovereigns. They appeared in excellent spirits. One of them had attached his cross of the Legion of Honour to his horse's tail. They moved down the boulevard of the Madeleine shouting 'Long live the King'. The crowd's reaction was one of indifference. They did not go beyond the rue de Richelieu.

At 11 o'clock a murmur ran through the faubourg Saint-Martin 'They are here!' The Allied troops were preceded by trumpeters, then came the Cossacks of the Guard, no rags there, but smart red uniforms, caps, lances in hand; hussars, dragoons. Then came the sovereigns: the Tsar, the King of Prussia, Schwarzenberg, representing the Emperor of Austria, 1,000 staff officers, as bedizened as those of Napoleon. These were followed by numerous battalions of the élite corps, Russian, Prussian, Austrian; forty-seven squadrons of Russian cavalry brought up the rear.

Along the faubourgs Saint-Martin and Saint-Denis, the crowds were solemn, sad; the atmosphere rather hostile. A larger crowd was ranged along the boulevard. The Allied troops marched in good order; they looked healthy, their hair shining. Over it all hung a strong smell of horse manure. Enthusiasm broke through around the rue Poissonnière, triggered by two or three shouts of 'Vive

Alexandre!, Vivent les Alliés'. The superb Russian monarch reined in his horse. 'We bring you Peace,' he cried loudly.

He added other remarks which were lost in the cheers of the crowd. Some ran towards his horse, others knelt! The enthusiasm became delirious when the bands started to play French airs. The pseudo-conquerors of Napoleon received more cheers than had ever greeted the Emperor of the French in his own capital. In fact, it was peace the people were acclaiming. This euphoria reached its peak on the Champs-Elysées, where men and women kissed the Tsar's boots and his horse. In order to see better, some women climbed on to the cruppers of the staff officers' horses. Alexander turned, laughing: 'So long as they do not abduct those Sabines!'

After the procession, tens of thousands of Parisians flocked to see the troops encamped on the Champs-Elysées, at Neuilly and on the avenue de la Motte-Piquet. Flags in the wind, trumpets sounding, field-kitchens, all added to the picturesque scene. On the Champs-Elysées, the bivouacs of the English, Irish and Scots were popular, with their red coats, tartan kilts, and pipers. But the greatest curiosity was the camp opposite, that of the Cossacks. Their huts were built of bales of straw over lances driven into the earth. Bearded, hairy, slant-eyed, genially delousing themselves, playing cards, cooking their rations. Good-natured when addressed by signs, ready to barter or swap: an enamelled Russian cup for French tobacco, a watch-chain of unknown provenance. Many of these sons of the steppes showed a want of tact in setting up at the Pont-Neuf a bazaar where they tried to sell various objects which they had pillaged in the environs of Paris. Some victims appeared and tried to retrieve their goods, resulting in some fights: no rose without a thorn. From all these events a business sprang up. Less than forty-eight hours after the Allies had entered Paris, shops were selling and hawkers offering broadsheets, songs denigrating Napoleon, comparing him to Robespierre, Attila, calling him an ogre, an assassin. Note that these hawkers were careful to stay in the city centre; the faubourgs were mostly faithful to the Emperor.

On 1 April, the Senate named a provisional government consisting of Talleyrand as president, and four of his faithful supporters. One of the first acts of this directory was to publish an address to the army: 'Soldiers: You cannot support one who has ravaged the capital, delivering it without weapons, defence, who had made your name odious to every nation, who would perhaps have sullied your glory if a man who is not even French could ever tarnish the honour of your arms and the generosity of our soldiers. You are no longer Napoleon's soldiers; the Senate, the whole of France free you from your oaths.' *A man who is not even French!*

Next day there was a sumptuous dinner, attended by the provisional government, the Tsar and his principal officers. The sovereign later appeared at the

Opera. The theatre was packed with royalists, men and women in full dress and white cockades. 'Vive le Roi! Vive le Tsar!' A famous tenor sang a popular song: 'Vive Henri IV!', adapting the words in flagrant flattery to laud the Tsar, the King of Prussia and their 'valiant warriors'. The audience spat on the eagle over Napoleon's box until a workman came and covered it.

Fifteen leagues away from the capital was Fontainebleau, which resembled a far-off planet with its bitterness, unreality and intrigues. The military genius with whom the sovereigns now being acclaimed in Paris had avoided a clash, not understanding that Fortune had abandoned him and that power was slipping through his fingers like water, wished to march on Paris.

'I shall concentrate the army between the Essonne and Fontainebleau. I will attack in a few days.' What army? The Guard, which the Emperor had left behind when he had rushed towards the capital, had not yet arrived at Fontainebleau by 1 April. Behind it trailed the corps of Macdonald, Gérard and Oudinot, now mainly composed of conscripts, the youngest of the latest call-up. Their forced marches took them through country already ravaged, drained of its last resources by the troops of Ney, of the Guard which preceded them. Worn-out by hunger and fatigue, verminous, racked by fever and dysentery, staggering under the weight of their weapons, they left dying men in every village.

Waiting for them on the heights dominating the Seine between Corbeil and Essonne, Napoleon inspected 'his advance guard', wretched regiments reduced to a few hundred men with ravaged faces. The drums beat when the Emperor arrived, shakos on the bayonets fixed to their muskets, 'Vive l'Empereur!' He walked slowly down the ranks, gesturing his thanks, smiling, visibly moved. He stopped, dismounted, pinned on decorations. 'You have fought like lions and only the numbers of the enemy have bested you. I thank my brave soldiers. Patience, the army is coming. In a few days, you will have your revenge.' The Guard arrived on 2 April. In his office, Napoleon re-read yet more news from Paris. Pasquier, the prefect of police, reported that the senate had proclaimed the fall of the Emperor.

On the morning of 3 April, Napoleon announced that he would review the Guard at 11 o'clock. Then, having again inspected his outposts, he received Lefebvre, Oudinot and Ney. He showed them his maps, on which he had worked part of the night. 'I shall attack south of Paris.'

A dismal silence. Then the marshals suggested that it would be better to fight on the Loire. Why not the Garonne, where the enemy is also present? The meeting was cut short and the Emperor dismissed his visitors without either a conclusion or an order. To Caulaincourt, who arrived later, he voiced his disappointment: 'But I shall change nothing in my project.' 'In that case, Sire, there is not an instant to lose. Contact with Paris is poison to the army, it ferments, it

erodes, especially the seniors. We must fight immediately or retire on the Loire.'
'I know all that, but the corps of Macdonald, Gérard and Oudinot will not be
here before tomorrow evening. I shall attack at first light on the 5th.' At midday
An ADC came to tell the Emperor that the Guard had been fallen in under arms
– and under the rain – for the last hour in the courtyard of the White Horse, so
named for its horseshoe shape.

A few minutes later, Napoleon appeared at the top of the staircase, surrounded by many marshals and generals: impassive, as at the reviews in Vienna
and Berlin. The drums beat the salute '*Au Champs!*', the troops presented arms
and the review started. Napoleon had the men open ranks, spoke to soldiers,
questioned them, awarded crosses. Then he took post in the middle of the
courtyard.

'Officers, under-officers and soldiers of the Old Guard.' His voice was
firm. In a few simple phrases, the Emperor explained that he had offered the
Tsar a peace 'bought by great sacrifices'. Not only had Alexander refused but,
outwitted by the *émigrés*, he had authorised the wearing of the white cockade
and soon would substitute it for the national cockade. 'In a few days, I shall
attack Paris. I am counting on you.' Silence. Many seconds, perhaps ten. An
eternity. 'Am I right?' resumed the Emperor. This time, his voice was raised.
Another few seconds of silence, then the old mechanism ticked over: 'Vive l'Empereur! To Paris! To Paris!' The magic still worked on the Old Guard, but on
them only.

Next morning, 4 April, Napoleon issued further orders for the troop concentration prior to the march on Paris. He would hold one more review, of the
troops who had just arrived. These were – at last! – the 'army corps' of Macdonald, Gérard and Oudinot. They looked like ghosts. The soldiers of the
Guards battalions, left in town for the security of headquarters, tried to cheer
them up. 'Nothing is lost! The Emperor will attack Paris.' The ghosts made no
reply. They fell-in for the review, but the few, thin cheers came from the officers
and the few long-service soldiers.

Napoleon could not but feel this lassitude. No proclamation this time, and
when he re-entered his office in the palace he started to 'pace up and down, ani-
matedly' saying nothing. With him were Maret, Caulaincourt, Ney, Berthier,
Lefebvre and some generals. All looked gloomy. 'Gentlemen, what news from
Paris?' The news was of nothing but problems. Ney, with the support of the others, said that the worst of it was that one could see no end to this situation. 'The
end will depend upon us!' The Emperor mentioned the soldiers' courage; they
had no rank or fortune at risk and only thought of marching and dying to
wrench France from the hands of the foreigner. The seniors bowed their heads.
Thiers recorded the sequel to the speech: 'The coalition forces are split between
the two banks of the Seine and we hold the main bridges, which are in an

immense city. Vigorously assaulted in this position, they are lost. The Parisians are agitated; they will not let them pass without pursuing them and the peasants will finish them off. They can doubtless return. But Eugène is on his way back from Italy with 36,000 men, Augereau has 30, Suchet 20, Soult 40. I will call in the greater part of these forces. I have 70,000 men here and with this mass I will push into the Rhine anyone who leaves Paris and tries to re-enter. We will save France, defend our honour and then I will accept a moderate peace. What do we need to achieve all that? One last effort which will allow you to enjoy a rest from twenty-five years of toil.'

None of the figures mentioned by Napoleon was exact. For many years, the strengths he had quoted had been eroded by a third or more, by losses in combat, and from sickness and exhaustion. Macdonald, who arrived shortly after this meeting, confirmed that the troops still under arms were tired and discouraged. The marshals said feebly that they were ready to give battle, but that they did not wish Paris to become another Moscow. There are variations in the accounts of this conversation. The crux is that the marshals were determined to make an end. Napoleon suddenly appeared overwhelmed. 'So, what do you wish to do, gentlemen?' It was then that the word abdication was uttered, probably by Ney and Oudinot. To the surprise of the marshals, the Emperor wasted little time before surrendering. 'Do you wish the King of Rome to be my successor, and the Empress as regent?' Yes, all present wished that. 'Good. We must first obtain a suspension of fighting and I will send commissioners to Paris. Gentlemen, you may now retire.'

Was that the whole story? Napoleon did not believe so – the march of the events that followed is well known. The Emperor threw himself on a sofa and beat his thigh with his fist. To the marshals: 'Bah, gentlemen, enough of that; let us march. We will fight tomorrow.' No, the marshals withdrew.

For several days the army had not fought. The soldiers knew nothing of the events that were unfolding in high places. They did not know that the Emperor had signed an act of abdication in favour of his son, and that three commissioners briefed by him were *en route* for Paris to meet the Tsar. Neither did they know that on this morning of 4 April, Marmont, commanding VI Corps, replying to a proposal sent him by Schwarzenberg the evening before, had said that he was ready to 'stop the effusion of French blood' and quit Napoleon's army with his troops. This on condition that they could retire on Normandy and that some agreement could be reached with the vanquished Emperor.

The path of treason is rarely simple and clear. The proceedings are tortuous, hesitant, beset with desertions, lies and half-truths, and those who venture on this course finish by lying to themselves. Thence lies psychodrama.

Having written to Schwarzenberg, Marmont had told all to his generals, swearing them to secrecy. He passed command of VI Corps to General Souham, then hurried to join Ney, Macdonald and Caulaincourt who were going to see the Tsar. To them he recounted a part of the truth: Schwarzenberg's proposal and that he had replied with a counter-proposal. Faced with their indignant protests, he assured them that nothing had been signed and even said that he would write to the Austrian to recant. He did neither and was received with the others by the Tsar who said that the conditional abdication was not wholly satisfactory, but that he would consult with his allies. The Tsar promised a reply the next day.

Essonnes, at 7 p.m. By the light of torches, the officers read to the assembled troops a proclamation by Marmont announcing (contrary to the secret orders) the Emperor's abdication, without revealing that it was conditional. On being dismissed, the shaken soldiers returned to their bivouacs, some saying: after all, we shall have peace, others spoke of treason.

At this point, enter General Gourgaud, principal ADC to the Emperor, with an order summoning all the marshals to Fontainebleau at 10 p.m. Napoleon intended to ask the commanders of all the army corps to draft a statement that they were opposed to the return of the Bourbons. Now, neither Marmont, nor General Souham, his successor in command of VI Corps, was present. Gourgaud saw first Fabvier, chief of staff to Souham. 'Where is the Marshal?' 'At Paris with these gentlemen.' 'What, without orders? He has left his army corps? The others have a task, but not he.' 'What do you expect? You can see that everything is breaking down, the machine is failing. The Emperor is abdicating. Many men are leaving, each thinking of himself. For the rest, don't worry. The Marshal has gone, but General Souham is in command. If you have orders for the corps you may give them to him. He is twenty minutes' upstream from here on a bluff.'

Gourgaud rode off. He did not see Souham, sending a message by his ADC to report to Fontainebleau. Once Souham knew of this, he called in the seven corps commanders: 'The Emperor knows everything! If he sends for us it will be to have us shot.' The only solution, that foreseen by Marmont in his letter to Schwarzenberg – go over to the enemy. The generals sent an officer to Schwarzenberg to negotiate the passage of their regiments. They should start to march towards the enemy outposts at Versailles. The troops began to move off. The generals had put it about that they were to occupy new positions: 'We have been recalled to Fontainebleau.' The night was dark; once again they were making a night march. But after a while, the officers started to ask themselves: why were they marching north when Fontainebleau was to the south?

A new rumour spread: 'We are going into battle.' Yes? Well, obey orders. The soldiers marched on, resigned. A little later the officers asked themselves other questions: why was there no advance-guard? What was the enemy thinking of to allow 10,000 men to advance without opening fire? They had been marching for an hour without a single musket-shot. They were now at Juvisy. 'What is that noise?' In the darkness, on either side of the road, they could sense that there were squadrons moving, swords clicked, horses snorted. Whose cavalry was there? The soldiers passed the word between the files, speaking in low tones. Dawn was about to break. At the rear of the column, the commander of a squadron of Polish lancers, suddenly mistrustful, detached several flankers who discovered that VI Corps was being escorted by two long columns of Bavarian cavalry: 'Treachery!' About turn! Sabres drawn, the Polish squadron charged, intending to break through to Fontainebleau.

It was too late for the rest. With the dawn, the sun burned away the mist. In the meadows, an immense army, both Russian and Prussian, drawn up on both sides of the road, presented arms. There was first a stupefied silence, then a mutter, then shouts, contradictory orders. Bordesoulle turned to Colonel Ordener, namesake of the General, commanding the 30th Dragoons: 'Draw swords and render the honours.' 'If my dragoons draw swords it will be to charge!' But the generals rode the length of the columns in order to calm everyone. 'There is no treason. The Emperor has abdicated. The whole army is under the orders of the new government. VI corps is marching to Normandy for a rest period.'

Other generals told the soldiers that the Austrians were allied to the French to keep the Emperor on the throne! What did the soldiers believe? There were still shouts of Treason, but finally the men marched, more or less resignedly, on Versailles. The disorder was in their hearts.

On 5 April, Marmont dined at Ney's home with Caulaincourt and Macdonald. He had just told them that he had warned his generals that all contact with Schwarzenberg had been broken and that VI corps was not to move from its positions under any pretext. 'I am really happy to have listened to you and to have joined my fate to yours.' A servant came in: 'Monsieur le Maréchal, an officer is asking for you.' It was Fabvier. 'Your corps has gone over to the enemy under the guidance of General Souham.' Marmont turned to the others, 'his face astonished, scarcely able to speak.' 'I am dishonoured! I am lost! I shall never get over it. Souham has disobeyed me; he has betrayed his duty!' A good piece of theatre; we would say today 'of cinema'. The marshals and Caulaincourt were overcome.

'I would have given an arm', said Marmont, 'for this not to have happened.' Ney, in a hard voice: 'An arm? Say, rather, a head and that would not be too much.' Marmont said that he was going to place himself at the head of his corps to make it return. He took his sword and left. Napoleon's three negotiators learned within the next hour the irreparable political result of this betrayal; the Tsar, who knew it all, now demanded an unconditional abdication. Marmont trotted towards Versailles with four ADCs. At the gate to Versailles, he found all the generals together. 'Where is the bulk of the army?' 'On the Rambouillet road.'

The generals explained that the inhabitants of Versailles had sent a delegation to them. 'There are 30,000 Russians here, in the barracks or bivouacking around the Swiss lake.' The streets were empty. A revolt had then blazed up. The soldiers said they would not be disarmed and made prisoners of war. They broke their muskets; officers tore off their epaulettes. Souham had them fall in on the parade ground and had harangued them. Shots rang out and the generals were forced to retire. An officer came to say that, after they left, the colonels had decided that VI Corps must return to Fontainebleau at all costs. The enemy was holding the road by which they had come; they would have to march by Rambouillet. 'I am going to rejoin my soldiers!' cried Marmont. 'Don't do that,' said General Compans, 'they will fire on you.' 'I have made up my mind. In an hour I shall either be dead or they will have accepted my authority.'

He caught up with the column and followed at a distance, sending an ADC to see how the soldiers were behaving. They were marching in silence. Marmont sent word to the officers that he was coming and that the corps should halt and wait for him. The soldiers did not receive him badly. They were now less mutinous than tired from their long march. And, above all, as Marmont had not been present at the moment of their defection, they nearly all thought that he did not know of it. He addressed the troops in moving terms, showing them his arm in a sling. 'I have shared your battles and your perils, your privations. Since when could you defy me? They had planned to break and disarm you! But your honour and your preservation, are they not as dear to me as my own honour and my life? Are not all of you my family and my cherished family?'

The Marshal spoke with conviction, with evident sincerity. His emotion touched them, bringing tears to their eyes. The officers themselves were convinced and re-assured those men who were still unconvinced. 'You can well see that we are neither prisoners nor disarmed. We are going to rest.' 'Rest' was a magic word to men so tired. and VI Corps marched towards Normandy.

Marmont hastened to Paris where Talleyrand and the members of the provisional government congratulated him. Jean Thiry, to whom we owe the clearest account of this conspiracy, concluded by quoting a passage from the memoirs of Bourienne (diplomatist, counsellor of state): 'After the passage of fifteen years, I can see again the Marshal arriving at M. de Talleyrand's just as everyone had finished dining. I saw him dining alone at a small table in the middle of the room. He was the hero of the day. Each of us came to talk with him and to compliment him.' 'Marmont was to atone for the rest of his life for this one-day triumph,' concluded Jean Thiry. Yes, but later he would find his defenders. These would say: this marshal played the game of the provisional government because he thought that, with Napoleon in the position he was now in, to confound him was to preserve France from civil war. It is true that the other marshals wanted peace as much as Marmont and hence the fall of Napoleon. He took upon himself its secret fulfilment.

On the evening of 5 April, Ney wrote to Talleyrand: 'The Emperor appears to be resigned and consents to unconditional abdication. I hope that tomorrow morning he will deliver to me the formal and official instrument.' On the 6th, Napoleon received Ney, Macdonald and Caulaincourt and, once more, spoke of assembling troops and trying his luck one last time. There was no reply. 'You want a rest, then take it! You do not know what sorrows and dangers await you in your feather beds!' He edited a first text of an act of abdication which the marshals made him modify. This is what he finally signed:

'The Allied Powers having proclaimed that the Emperor Napoleon is the only obstacle to the re-establishment of peace in Europe, the Emperor Napoleon, faithful to his oath, declares that he renounces, for himself and his heirs, the thrones of France and Italy and that there is no personal sacrifice, including his life, that he is not ready to make in the interests of France.'

'Vive l'Empereur! To Paris! Death to Traitors!' Who is shouting this when, twenty-four hours ago, the Emperor had abdicated unconditionally? The grenadiers and chasseurs of the Guard and a handful of Poles in the streets of Fontainebleau in the middle of the night. These men had left their barracks and were running through the dark, carrying torches.

'Everyone to the château!' But, at the château, the alarm had been given. Grand-Marshal Bertrand with his ADCs and the grenadiers of the security guard closed the gates in the faces of a flood of protesters. 'Vive l'Empereur! To Paris! Death to Traitors!' The traitors were the marshals, the generals, all who had compelled the Emperor to abdicate when he was about to crush the 'Kaiserlicks', the Russians, the Prussians, and to save France. Forgotten was the exhausting campaign that these men had just survived; they had forgotten their sufferings and their privations of years past, their bitterness towards Napoleon, the curses they had hurled at him in Spain. The Emperor's dream was their dream.

It would be the last. Through the gate, Bertrand parlayed with the officers of the Guard, who were mixed with their men, recalling them to their duty in the name of the Emperor. He managed to persuade them to re-establish order. The old sweats calmed down and consented to return to barracks. These men saw the Emperor once more before he left for exile, one more time. The soldiers of other units would not. And none of them knew what had happened at the château of Fontainebleau and at Paris during the following days: the negotiations of Caulaincourt and Macdonald in Paris to obtain for the Emperor a new and derisory sovereignty; the race between the marshals and generals for new powers: the arrival at Paris of Count d'Artois, received by Talleyrand, Ney, Marmont and Moncey: the attempted suicide of the Emperor, who swallowed the poison which doctor Yvan had given him during the retreat from Moscow when he feared capture by the Cossacks. He had vomited and survived. How would the Guard have reacted if they had known of this despair, if the Emperor had died? But nothing happened.

On 20 April at midday, all was ready for the departure. Carriages were waiting. The Guard was fallen-in in the courtyard of the White Horse which was to become the Court of Farewells. At 1 p.m., Napoleon appeared at the top of the stairway, surrounded by senior officers and generals, but not a single marshal. He shook hands rapidly, descended the stairs and addressed the Guard 'in the midst of a deep religious silence'. His words should be quoted, since they form a part of the folklore of the Grande Armée. Here we have a man, emerged from his stubbornly held dreams, reasonable, desirous above all to spare France civil war. What he would have said and done had the marshals, instead of compelling him to abdicate, had said 'Yes, Sire, fight to the death.' That we shall never know.

'Soldiers of my Old Guard, I bid you good-bye. For twenty years, I have seen you constantly on the road of honour and glory. Recently, as in those times of our prosperity, you have never ceased to be models of bravery and fidelity. With men such as you, our cause was not lost, but the war was endless: it would have meant civil war and France could only become more miserable. I have therefore sacrificed all our interests to those of our country. I am leaving. But you, my friends, continue to serve France. Her welfare has been my only thought and will be the object of my prayers. Do not bewail my fate.'

And now the situation overwhelmed the Emperor. 'If I have chosen to survive, it is to witness your glory. I wish to write the great things that we have achieved together. Farewell, my lads! I would like to press you all to my heart; let me at least embrace your colours!'

The Epinal pictures have shown three generations of Frenchmen the Emperor seizing the eagle and kissing the colours. The 'grumblers' were racked with sobs. The foreign commissioners responsible for escorting Napoleon to the embarkation point were 'transported' by the sight. The Austrian General Koller put his hat on the point of his sword. The Englishman Campbell said loudly: 'Here is a very affecting scene which is worthy of this great man.' The Emperor, repressing his emotion, said again in a loud voice: 'Once again, farewell my dear comrades. Keep this last kiss in your hearts.' And he walked to his carriage.

The Grande Armée had ceased to exist. I could have said that after the retreat from Russia, for what then remained? But Napoleon had extracted from the entrails of France a new army, then yet another after the campaign in Saxony. And you well know that that was not the end. We must march until the last battle.

XV

1815
The Flight of the Eagle, Elba to Paris

'You, my friends, continue to save France.' The marshals read this as, 'I release you from your oath of fidelity.' That was one of the last remarks of Napoleon in the Court of Farewells. The marshals asked nothing more. On 29 April 1814, it was Berthier who headed their delegation to salute Louis XVIII on his arrival at Compiègne: 'Sire, after twenty-five years of uncertainty and upheavals, the French people have once again offered the responsibility for its happiness to the oldest existing dynasty that so many centuries of glory have consecrated in the history of the world. As warriors and citizens, the marshals of France have been impelled by every impulse of their hearts to foster this manifestation of the national will.'

Such flattery caused several present to turn their heads away. With a physique disastrous in a monarch, gouty, enormous, quasi-impotent, Louis XVIII possessed a great fund of shrewdness – he understood very well the motive of this monarchist fervour. But he believed that the total submission of the military leaders would ease his task. He replied that the marshals would be some of the strongest pillars of the state, he thanked them, he congratulated them, he flattered them, he made them stay for dinner and cajoled them yet more. 'I wish to drink with you to the armies of France.'

He would be the only one to show himself adroit. At Compiègne, in front of the marshals, the Duchess of Angoulême was as cold as ice, the Prince of Condé and the Duke of Bourbon uttered nothing apart from various inaudible whispers. From this point on, the nobility set out on a trail of blunders that would in large measure bring about the collapse of the first Restoration. While the monarch was piling honours on his military chiefs – sixteen marshals created peers of France, a lavish distribution of Crosses of Saint-Louis, prestigious appointments – the nobles treated most of them with the utmost contempt. And, supreme stupidity, their wives competed in this wounding of their self-respect: 'Who is this person. I do not know her. She is the wife of a marshal.' That was the sort of talk heard at the Tuileries. It was in part why Ney vacillated when the Emperor returned: 'I do not want to be humiliated further. I do not want my wife to come home with her eyes full of tears due to the insults which she has received during the day. The king does not want us, that is evident.'

The king, perhaps yes; his entourage, no. On 3 May 1814, Louis XVIII entered Paris. From the Saint-Denis gate, the Guard formed a hedge on each side of the procession. It had been decided to bring from Fontainebleau the old sweats who two weeks earlier had been shouting 'Vive l'Empereur'. Here is an extract from Chateaubriand who witnessed the affair: 'I do not believe that human figures had ever expressed anything as menacing and as terrible. The grenadiers, covered in wounds, conquerors of Europe, who had seen so many thousands of bullets pass over their heads, who had smelt the fire and the powder, these same men, deprived of their chief, were forced to salute an old king, an invalid from age, not war, under the eyes of the armies of the Russians, Austrians and Prussians.' It is true that the Allies were still there, camped in Paris and the suburbs. They did not evacuate Paris and France until 3 June. The Guard, brought to Paris, were right to feel themselves prisoners. Let us listen again to Chateaubriand, speaking of the grenadiers: 'Some, wrinkling the skin of their foreheads, worked their large bearskins down over their eyes as if not wishing to see, others turned down the corners of their mouths in scorn and rage, others again, below their moustaches, bared their teeth like tigers. When they presented arms, there was a crash of fury and the noise made one tremble.'

The officers, sabres drawn, deliberately wiped their eyes. The marshals, escorting the royal coach, were as gay as undertakers' mutes. The crowd cried, 'Berthier to Elba!' and 'Vive la vieille Garde'. Laughter greeted the progress of the Duchess of Angoulême, dressed English-fashion, and of the Prince of Condé, frizzed pigeon-wing fashion, and few and far between were the cheers for the King. A few days before, the same crowd had gone mad at the sight of a foreign prince, the Tsar. That was from joy at the thought of peace and because he was very handsome and a superb horseman. Presented with an impotent monarch, surrounded by persons who, like him, had appeared from a past that was thought to have been jettisoned, what disillusion!

The remnant of the Old Guard had also been fallen-in in the courtyard of the Tuileries. While they certainly did not like the King, they were prepared to be inspected, as was customary. Fatigued, Louis XVIII, adroit with the marshals, passed the soldiers by without seeing them. A king has no right to be tired. The officers asked if the Guard would find the detail for the Tuileries, as in the past. They were told, No. Another affront. Neither quarters nor rations had been provided for this detail, called to Paris. These soldiers were kept waiting and then given individual lodging vouchers. Too late, every door was closed. They scattered through the city, furious, provoking the first of what were to be many incidents.

Peace meant the return of prisoners. They came from Spain, Italy, Germany, Belgium, the Netherlands, England. They had suffered in camps and prisons, in the hulks in England and Spain and on the island-hell of Cabrera. A total of perhaps 200,000 men, a Grande Armée in itself. Nothing had been provided for their return. 'Here is your release. You are free to go home.' They formed long processions of misery and rags along the roads. Villagers shut their doors at their approach.

Many of these men, having been isolated from any news, did not even know on reaching France that Napoleon was no longer on the throne. They had believed they would rejoin their chief, their idol, their father. With him gone, they were nothing and nobody paid attention to their plight. Often anger seized them, blinded them. At Morlaix, they fought with royalist volunteers and killed thirty of them. Count de Ferrière, commissioner for the departments of the west: 'Far from being grateful to the sovereign who has restored their liberty, the prisoners declare themselves for those who threw them behind bars!' At Strasbourg, the prisoners snatched the cockades of the royalists and fought with the soldiers – 'You have sold your flag for a flagon of brandy!'

The military chiefs received reports of very many desertions: 'I do not wish to serve under the white flag.' The white flag was a pretext for many young men recently torn from their homes. Another reason was that, during the upheaval created by the change in regime, pay arrived late or not at all. Moreover, at the first meeting at the Tuileries, the new government found that the army was much too large. Why did they need all these soldiers? 'We must completely dissolve the old army and replace it with young men free of the revolutionary taint.'

Who had been chosen as Minister of War? General Dupont, defeated at Baylen. He espoused the wishes of the princes who were deeply distrustful of the officers. From 12 May, some 30,000 officers were placed on half-pay. Captains drew 75 francs monthly, lieutenants 44 francs. They were forbidden to absent themselves without a passport, nor to marry without the Minister's permission. They were forbidden to follow another profession on the pretext that they were liable to recall without notice. Thus, a new type of outcast was created: the legendary half-pay officer.

At the same time, the new government reconstituted the royal military establishment, which would have to be as large as that of Louis XIV in order to distribute commissions to all the importunate *émigrés*. Among the resurrections were the 'Guards of the Gate', the 'Cent-Suisses', the ancient companies of musketeers: these bodies were commanded by princes and dukes. Also created were the 'bodyguards': an élite corps of six-footers, commanded by the prince de Poix, the Duke of Gramont, the young Duke of Luxembourg, the Duke of Havré. They created two extra companies of these guards which were given to marshals Berthier and Marmont 'to cement the fusion of the two armies'. They were known to the half-pay officers as the Companies of Saint Peter and Judas. The total strength of the royalist military: 6,000 men costing 20 millions, or a tenth of the total army budget. The cost aroused less indignation than the irregular promotions: officers were promoted general on the basis of seniority which included time spent at home. 'If Louis XVIII had been on the throne,' they said, 'we would have served.' While the Guard was at Fontainebleau, the Duke of Berry (Charles Ferdinand de Bourbon, second son of the comte d'Artois – who would become Charles X – assassinated on 13 February 1820 by Louvel) came to review them. Squat, choleric, he assumed an air of casual and paternal good-fellowship. He joked with the old sweats, tapped them on the shoulder, even going so far as to pinch their ears. The soldiers said, 'He is mad and cares nothing for us!' Later, on his orders, Dupont organised a mock war for the princes on the Neuilly plain which was grotesque and exasperating to the soldiers. Hoping to conciliate the Guard, Dupont reaffirmed their status as an élite corps: they would be known as the 'grenadiers of France'. But, to reassure the princes, he scattered the Guard among many garrisons in the provinces. These were the first fruits: at Clermont, some chasseurs arriving from Fontainebleau found the town dressed in white and a Te Deum in progress to celebrate the re-establishment of the monarchy. The white and fleur-de-lys flags in the streets were torn down and thrown into the stream.

On 28 June 1814, the general commanding the sub-division of Seine et Marne reported to the minister the departure from Nemours of 150 grenadiers of France, marching on Paris with their arms and equipment in order to claim their back pay from the king. Passing through Fontainebleau, they were joined by the grenadiers of the 1st Regiment. General Maison, having been alerted, took two battalions and a troop of police and managed to bar the road to the capital. In July, at Belle-Isle, 260 men of the 36th Light Regiment learned that they were destined to leave for the colonies: 'We won't go!' They killed an officer, stole a boat and sailed for the mainland. Intercepted at Vannes, they were put in prison. In their place was sent a battalion of the 75th Line – which repeated the exploit of the 36th Light: a boat from Belle-Isle, the continent and a march on Paris. General Maison had to intervene once again, in the same conditions, in order to suppress these mutineers.

Another of Dupont's initiatives was to replace the profile of Napoleon on the cross of the Legion of Honour with that of Henry IV. In five months of peace, they would distribute 2,593 crosses, 1,633 by the hands of the Dukes of Angoulême and Artois, mainly to functionaries and right-thinking merchants. Lynch, mayor of Bordeaux, who had opened the city gates to the British, was given high rank.

Officers of noble origin who had taken part in the campaigns of the Empire naturally served in the royal army and were not placed on half-pay. Often, their morale was no better. Sylvain Larréguy de Civrieux, enlisted at sixteen, had campaigned in Spain and at the age of 18 was a sergeant-major in a company of grenadiers of the 77th. Dupont had sent this regiment to Besançon. In June 1814, General Lecourbe came to hold a review. A direct order was given to all officers, NCOs and soldiers: 'You will shout "Long live the King!"' 'We resolved', wrote Civrieux, 'to supplement this by a cry of "Vive Arbois!" where we had drunk such good wine. But the commanding officer, Villetard, from habit, absent-mindedness, deliberate error, cried "Vive l'Empereur!" and this cry was repeated enthusiastically by the company of grenadiers.' The commandant was placed on half-pay, the major went to prison.

15 August 1814. For the past fifteen years, the whole army had celebrated the feast of Saint Napoleon. Even on the island-hell of Cabrera, the starving prisoners had celebrated the day. Louis XVIII could not say officially: 'Bravo, continue.' To break the tradition, he ordered that there should be processions everywhere on that day to celebrate the vow of Louis XIII to place France under the protection of the Virgin. In principle, detachments from each regiment were supposed to participate; the order was rarely obeyed. In most of the barracks, the soldiers shouted 'Vive l'Empereur!', drank his health and sang the songs of the Empire in their rooms lit by candles.

Officers were required to attend Mass. Like many of their men, absent from the country for long periods of war, they had retained the anti-clerical and anti-religious sentiments of the time of the Revolution. The half-pays, meeting in their cafes, sniggered: 'No Mass, no promotion,' and many other remarks. A police report of 20 July 1814, reported the following observation, publicly expressed by a half-pay officer: '*Le Tondu* got men killed, but he also knew how to reward them. This idiot is only at home with the God-botherers.' and 'The King and the priests are like knife and fork.'

When Soult replaced Dupont, in December 1814, one of his first actions was to expel from Paris all the half-pay officers who were 'not habitually resident there'. Those who had campaigned had had no permanent residence anywhere for years. They were expelled to the provinces and dispersed. Soult drew up a list of generals authorised to reside in Paris, a total of eighteen. The police were instructed to take the names of all visitors received by Davout at Savigny-sur-Orge. The general commanding the military division of Tours was invited to investigate the personal sentiments of General Ornano, who appeared to have a 'bad influence' on the views of the dragoons of France (previously the dragoons of the Imperial Guard). Soult denounced General Vandamme in high places as 'undesirable'; when he presented himself at the Tuileries, he was publicly expelled. To General Travot, who came to solicit a command, the pillager of the Spanish museums replied: 'I will not employ you until you surrender the goods of the *émigrés*'.

Soult would exhibit the full extent of his magnanimity in the Exelmans affair. Rémi Isadore Exelmans joined as a volunteer in 1791, became a cavalry officer, colonel at Austerlitz, general at Eylau, master of horse to Murat and a personal friend. In November 1814, he imprudently sent the King of Naples a letter reiterating his fidelity. The letter was intercepted and the writer was reprimanded by Dupont. Pursued by the royal police, he managed to escape. The worthy Louis said: 'Drop it, file the dossier.' But Soult was now minister: 'Exelmans must be punished.' He relieved the General of his command, placed him on the inactive list and ordered him to retire to Bar-le-Duc, considered to be his domicile. 'My wife cannot travel at this time,' wrote Exelmans, 'she is about to give birth.' Soult was not concerned about that. 'Arrest him. Take him to Soissons where he will be under supervised residence.'

On the arrival of the general commanding the city of Paris, Exelmans kicked up a fuss and aroused the district. Without success, though he succeeded in escaping and appeared voluntarily before the local authorities at Soissons.' Send him before a court-martial.' In the end, it was at Lille that he was tried. The president of the court was Lieutenant-General Drouet d'Erlon, a past comrade in arms. He was declared not guilty. He left the court to cheers and was carried off in triumph.

This was on 23 January 1815; in exactly thirty-six days, Napoleon, having escaped from the isle of Elba, would disembark at Golfe-Juan. This is a study of the Grande Armée. I do not wish to describe in detail the local events which, despite the widespread desire of the French people for peace, had disenchanted them with the first Restoration. I believe that I have shown that the administration, including some marshals who had been won over, had been guilty of so many blunders and persecutions that the army would quickly move at the critical moment in support of the exile who would not admit defeat.

On the mainland, it began with the reports of the gendarmes. On the night of 1/2 March 1815, the sergeant of gendarmerie of Cannes dismounted at the gendarmerie post at Fréjus and awoke the mayor. 'Napoleon has landed at Golfe-Juan with some troops.' 'Tell the gendarmerie,' said the mayor. The duty gendarme had overheard his colleague. 'Good, I will send a message to the chief of the squadron at Draguignan.' He sent a horseman with a note: 'The Cannes gendarmerie report that 50 men of the ex-Emperor's guard have landed at Golfe-Juan.' The squadron chief at Draguignan, having hesitated to wake General Morangies, the city commandant, decided to do so: 'General, this message has just arrived.' 'All right, I shall send it to Toulon.' Toulon was the station of General Abbé. 'I will send it to Marseilles to General Masséna.' The message was sent with a reassuring cover-note: 'The naval prefect tells me that he is advised that the grenadiers on the isle of Elba have been granted leave to proceed to

France to visit their families.' Masséna received the message at 9 a.m. on the 3rd. 'I am none the less not going to alert the Marseilles garrison to keep watch on fifty men. I will, however, send it to the Minister of War at Paris.' He finished his dispatch: 'I personally agree with the opinion of the naval prefect that this is merely the landing of a few men bored with remaining on the isle of Elba.'

I have outlined this buck-passing burlesque because it illustrates a psychological fact: In a period of tension (during the Great Fear in the countryside during the beginning of the Revolution, for example) transmission inflates and deforms any fact in a threatening and frightening way. Here, the contrary was true because all concerned had but one idea: 'At last, we have peace; we are calm. Let sleeping dogs lie.' However, the prefect of the Var and General Morangies had dispatched other gendarmes from Cannes to reconnoitre. They returned in the evening and reported that it was certainly Napoleon who had disembarked. The prefect informed Masséna who, at 9 p.m. on the 3rd, sent another dispatch to Paris and sent for General Miollis: 'Take the 83rd Line and six companies of the 58th and take position on the Sisteron. If Napoleon chooses to march on Paris, he will go that way.'

The prefect Bouthillier had, at the same time as he alerted Masséna, sent a message to the prefect of the Basses-Alpes, who in turn called on General Loverdo, commanding the department: 'What is the strength of the Digne garrison?' 'One hundred and twenty-two men, Monsieur le prefet. Their fidelity is doubtful, only a week ago, my officers sent some of these soldiers to prison for having shouted "Vive l'Empereur!" I did not endorse this punishment for fear of a mutiny. All the rest said that they too should be put in prison as they were all prepared to shout "Vive l'Empereur!"'

'I will convoke all the brigades of gendarmerie, the national guard and will distribute arms to the population,' said the prefect. Hardly had these orders been given than the notables came running. 'For heaven's sake, Monsieur le prefet, do not attempt to oppose Bonaparte if he comes. You surely do not wish our town to be sacked?' 'All right, I shall put the public funds in a place of safety and disappear. This won't last long.' He retired to a neighbouring village, intending to resume his post after the Napoleonic column had passed. General Loverdo moved his troops beyond the Durance to the Aix road 'to avoid all contact'.

Napoleon remembered only too well his journey across Provence *en route* for Elba. Threatened, he had had to disguise himself as an Austrian officer. 'I shall go to Grenoble and Lyons by way of the road over the Alps.' Before disembarking from the brig *Inconstant,* he had written two long proclamations, one addressed to the French people, the other to the army, justifying his decision to reconquer his throne. The latter included a sentence which has become famous: 'The eagle with the national colours will fly from steeple to steeple to the towers of Notre-Dame.'

Progress was slow to begin with, at times no more than a crawl. After Grasse, which the little force (1,200 men and four cannon) had bypassed because the population was demonstrating and rather hostile, it was necessary to get to Digne where they could follow the road to Grenoble. But there was no road between Grasse and Digne, merely mountain tracks, covered in snow. The guns had to be abandoned. Napoleon went on foot, supported by his officers; in single file, this was by no means a triumphal march. Nor was there any triumph at Digne, where the population (remember, they had asked the prefect to offer no resistance) showed itself more curious than enthusiastic; there was sparse applause for Napoleon's speech. However, two half-pays and four youngsters decided to follow the Emperor.

At 1 a.m. on 4 March, Napoleon's advance guard entered Sisteron. Cambronne, who was in command, ordered the mayor to provide shelter and lodgings for 3,000 men – he exaggerated their numbers – and the vouchers were immediately signed by the municipal council, which was sitting continuously. Not a sign of any military opposition. The troops whom Masséna had dispatched from Marseilles were still far away and, as we have seen, General Loverdo had no wish to impede the Emperor's party, which he called a 'fabulous outfit' – he meant 'a bunch of maniacs'. Farther down the road, at Gap, the prefect of the Hautes-Alpes and General Rostollant tried to put the town into a state of defence, but had to desist in the face of popular protests: 'Above all, no resistance, no battle'.

Cambronne had a talent amounting almost to a vocation for commanding an advance-guard. During the campaign in Saxony, after the rebuff at Leipzig, when the French troops clashed with the Bavarians at Hanau who were barring the road to France, it was he with his chasseurs who began to cut a way through: 'The way he swept aside everything in his path', wrote Marmont, 'was the admiration of all who witnessed it.' This time Cambronne again had to cut a way through, but without violence. He had accompanied Napoleon into exile and had come with him from Elba.

'Cambronne', said the Emperor as they landed, 'I am confiding to you the advance guard of my finest campaign. You will not fire one shot. I wish to reclaim my crown without shedding one drop of blood.' In 1815 Cambronne, at 45, was merely a divisional general. He had no talent for intrigue, and was perhaps too human. Engaged as a volunteer in 1791, he served in the armies of the North and the Ardennes. NCO, then lieutenant in the armies of the West, charged both with coastal defence and the repression of the Chouans, he had exhibited a character both generous and energetic. He participated in the ejection of the Vendéens from Nantes (where he was born) but allowed his mother to shelter a refractory priest. He fought the *émigrés* at Quiberon, but let escape many who, having violated their paroles, were to be shot. His entire military career was unblemished. At the camp at Boulogne, he had received the Legion of Honour from the Emperor. He distinguished himself at Jena, fought bravely everywhere: in Spain, Germany, where he was promoted to the imperial Guard, in Spain again, in Russia, in Saxony. Suffering multiple wounds during the campaign in France, he was stretched out on a hospital bed when the Allies were attacking Paris. He got up and rejoined the fighting, was wounded twice more. Volunteering for Elba, he was appointed to command the 'Napoleon battalion'. A fervent and blind supporter of the Emperor. On 23 February 1815, Napoleon had warned him to be ready to leave. 'Cambronne, where shall we go?' 'I have never sought to know the secrets of my sovereign.'

Let us anticipate, because we shall have little time to follow Cambronne after Waterloo, where he did not merely distinguish himself by saying 'Merde!' to the British. Wounded in the head in one of the last squares, prisoner of the British but even so, condemned to death *in absentia* at the second Restoration, he returned to France in 1815 and was imprisoned, court-martialled, defended by the famous counsel Pierre Antoine Berryer (son of Pierre Nicolas Berryer who would defend Ney) he was acquitted and freed, but without pension. Retiring to Nantes, he married a rich English widow. The King then created him a viscount, recalled him to service as commander of the 16th Division at Lille. Did Cambronne accept these favours reluctantly? After Napoleon's death, he asked to be retired. He spent the last years of his life as a gentleman-farmer, and died aged 72.

The first link of Chappe's optical telegraph had been operating between Paris and Lille from 1794, but in 1815 it did not extend to the south beyond Lyons. The ciphered message which Masséna had sent on the evening of 3 March to Soult, Minister of War, had been carried by relays of couriers to Lyons, thence by optical telegraph, reaching Paris on 5 March at about noon, and delivered, after deciphering to Claude Chappe, manager and inventor of the telegraph. He was greatly moved and took it, sealed as was the custom, to secretary of state Vitrolles, who delivered it to the King, who opened it. 'Do you know what this is?' 'No, Sire.' It is Bonaparte who has landed on the shores of Provence,' said Louis XVIII calmly. 'You must carry this dispatch to the Minister of War. He will see what can be done.'

Vitrolles, as agitated as Chappe, departed in his carriage, but it was a fine Sunday with promenaders everywhere. They were delayed and Vitrolles was fretting, when, miraculously, he sighted Soult who was strolling, on his way to a meeting of ministers. He stopped his carriage, beckoned to the Marshal and read him the dispatch. 'We must wait for confirmation,' said Soult, 'then I will see the King.' The Marshal is mad, thought Vitrolles, still rather agitated. I will go to see Monsieur (the comte d'Artois, brother to the king and the future Charles X.) But Monsieur was at vespers. Vitrolles waited, still fidgety. When he returned, he gave him the news. 'There is not a moment to lose,' he concluded. Monsieur was calm. Finally, after a minute: 'I think you are right and we must "get our skates on".' 'No, Monsieur, we've got to be quicker than that.' Vitrolles went to see the King again. Soult also saw him in the evening of 5 March. He presented to the council of ministers a plan approved by the King and the princes. The comte d'Artois would leave for Lyons whither 30,000 men were marching. The Duke of Berry would manoeuvre on the left, supported by Marshal Ney, with HQ at Besançon. On the right, the Duke of Angoulême would march on Nîmes to take Bonaparte in flank 'and cut his retreat'. He would be supported by Marshal Macdonald (in fact, Macdonald would be co-opted by d'Artois, who had need of him at Lyons).

General Marchand was much upset on learning on the evening of 4 March, in a letter from the prefect of the Var, that Napoleon had landed and was marching on Grenoble, base of the 7th Division which Marchand commanded.

Born in Grenoble, a lawyer under Louis XVI, Marchand had left the city of his birth in 1791, elected captain (as was then the custom) by his comrades of the 4th Battalion of volunteers of the Isère. At the end of 1813, he returned as a divisional general, grand-eagle of the Legion of Honour, count of the Empire with an income of 80,000 livres. His immediate adherence to the Bourbons in April 1814 had allowed him to retain the command of the 7th District. But the soldiers said: 'He is a traitor.' Fourrier, prefect of the Isère, was no less troubled than Marchand. Having been appointed by Napoleon, he had only kept his place thanks to his immediate adherence to the Bourbons.

Aside from the nobles, the populace of Grenoble was mainly Bonapartist. The prefect and the general sought advice in one quarter and another. Then: 'So, what do we do?' They decided to defend their new-found royalist loyalty. 'I will draw up', said the prefect, 'a proclamation against the usurper.' 'I am ordering the 7th and 11th Line from Chambéry as well as the 4th Hussars at Vienne to report here as soon as possible,' said the General.

At 8 a.m. on 5 March, the generals, colonels and majors assembled at General Marchand's. All now knew the big news. 'The prefect and I remain faithful to the King,' said Marchand, 'and I hope that you approve?' The reply was Yes. 'Good. The question is whether we should march against Bonaparte or whether we await him behind these ramparts.'

After a short consultation, the first alternative was adopted. 'I shall review the troops and have them swear allegiance,' said Marchand. This provoked a problem. Some officers said that it would be better if it were the unit chiefs who spoke to the men. No one dared tell Marchand that he was too unpopular.

The news of Napoleon's march had reached the people of Grenoble during the morning of 5 March. The royalists were fearful or furious, the many half-pays in the city were very excited, others were indifferent or fairly favourable, but said, like the people of Digne, 'So long as it does not involve a battle.' At 5 p.m., when the prefect's official proclamation was posted up outside the city hall – the 'brigands of Bonaparte' had raised eyebrows – a cry of 'Vive l'Empereur!' was heard. A single cry, because the man was immediately arrested, which gives food for thought.

On the morning of 6 March, there was a new meeting of the chiefs at Marchand's. Now the officers were perplexed, especially those of the 4th Artillery: 'Our men persist in remembering that Bonaparte had served in their regiment as lieutenant before the Revolution. They venerate the Emperor because of that memory.'

All the colonels said that it would be imprudent to march against Napoleon with troops of such doubtful loyalty. 'We will shut ourselves up in Grenoble', said Marchand, 'and wait for Bonaparte to pass. If you exhort your men as you should, they will reflect, and at the right time they will do their duty. I will also address a proclamation to them.' Finally, he contented himself with having it posted up: 'Soldiers, Bonaparte has disembarked on our shores. Let us remember that he has freed us from our oaths and that we have taken others to the King. You will be faithful to your honour and your duty and this storm will soon pass. We shall see our beautiful country grow powerful and happy. If on the contrary, you let yourselves be led astray by perfidious advice, every sort of misfortune will fall on you.' Having read this or had it read to them, the soldiers said: 'We really would be idiots if we harmed a man who has brought us nothing but good. We should not be listening to this stupid clown, but to the other side.' Almost everywhere, the general's name was scratched out and replaced 'with a gross word'.

In order to slow down Napoleon's advance, Marchand sent to La Mure (35 kilometres south of Grenoble) an engineer company and a battalion of the 5th Line with orders to blow up a bridge over a torrent. The operation was commanded by a Major Lessard. At 9 p.m., the sergeant who had been sent ahead to prepare billets returned saying that his advance guard and that of the Bonapartist force had met at La Mure. 'I see that we are wearing different cockades,' said Napoleon's sergeant. 'Are we friends or enemies?' Old comrades in arms are always friends. 'So, let's sort out the billets together.' The two men shook hands, but Lessard's sergeant returned to warn his chief of the incident. Lessard recalled his entire force to the neighbouring town of Laffrey.

At Grenoble, the troops worked hard at organising the defence of the ramparts. During the course of the morning, the 4th Hussars arrived from Vienne and the 7th and 11th Line from Chambéry. The infantry colonels told Marchand that the sooner their men manned the ramparts the better. 'Otherwise the populace will disband them. That would not be difficult.'

During the morning Napoleon arrived at la Mure where he was acclaimed by the populace. He had dismounted before reaching the little town and stationed himself on a small hillock beside the road. A picket of foot-chasseurs kept the crowd in a circle around him, while he talked easily with the mayor and the municipal counsellors. A corporal brought a bucket of wine for the chasseurs, each filling the glass and drinking. Napoleon gestured to the corporal and, in turn, drank some wine. The crowd applauded.

The advance guard approached the narrow entrance to Laffrey which was guarded by Lessard's battalion. Towards midday, Napoleon sent one of his officers who asked to speak to their commander. Reply: 'I have orders not to communicate.' Napoleon was then in a coach: he got out and mounted his horse and rode into the defile. The 5th Line barred the road. Napoleon looked at them through his spy-glass and realised that his grey coat had been identified. Lessard's men looked at him from their position, then looked at one another. Napoleon sent another officer to Lessard, who replied that he would do his duty. He sent a third who said to the troops of the 5th Line: 'The Emperor is going to march towards you. If you fire, the first round will hit him. But remember that you will answer to France for all the misfortunes that will follow.' The Polish lancers and the grenadiers of the Old Guard moved forward. Lessard turned his men about in order to retreat, then turned them about again: 'Halt! Fire to the front. Target, the lancers!' Captain Randon, Lessard's second in command, shouted 'Fire!', but not a shot was heard. The lancers dismounted and walked forward, hands extended. Then the Emperor walked alone towards the 5th Line until he was within pistol-shot. 'If there is among you a soldier who wishes to kill his Emperor, here I am!'

Once again, a scene immortalised in the Epinal pictures; the soldiers, muskets aimed, crying 'Vive l'Empereur!' The game was won. This was really where the eagle began to fly. Some episodes are picturesque and revealing.

On the morning of 6 March, Louis XVIII had signed a decree declaring Bonaparte 'traitor and rebel' and enjoining every soldier, national guardsman and simple citizen 'to fall on him'.

Next day, Grenoble was in ferment. It was known that the battalion sent to la Mure had acclaimed Napoleon. 'He is coming with ten thousand men who have rallied to him. And he has the support of Austria, his father-in-law is for him.' The royalists were already taking off their white cockades; they put them on again when the prefect posted up a dispatch from Lyons announcing the arrival of the comte d'Artois with 40,000 men.   Marchand tried to be reassuring. 'I know that last year some troopers of the 4th Hussars shouted 'Vive l'Empereur!' at a review by the comte d' Artois, but I am counting on the 7th. I have no doubts about La Bedoyère; heir of excellent family and married to Mademoiselle de Chastellux, grand-daughter of the Marquis of Dufort-Civrac. Her connections allow no doubt as to her monarchist loyalty.'

Count Charles de la Bedoyère, 29 years old, ex-ADC to Lannes, then to Prince Eugène, colonel of the 12th Line in 1813, and twice proposed for the rank of general during the campaign in France, one of the most brilliant officers of the Grande Armée, had in all sincerity joined the Bourbons. Then, like some of his comrades, and despite his origins and marriage, he had been rejected by the nobles who had returned to France with the King. Retiring into himself, he had said nothing and had done his duty. But the news of the Emperor's landing, which came to him at Chambéry, had shaken him. That afternoon, Marchand had ordered his colonels to pass their regiments in review again and to harangue them against Napoleon. Hardly had his men fallen in than La Bedoyère drew his sword: 'Here, soldiers of the 7th, my brave comrades. I will show you the road to follow. Forward! Let those who love me follow!' Further words were unnecessary and the 7th left Grenoble by the Bonne Gate and marched south.

From our distance in time these reversals seem natural because of Napoleon's magnetism and because we know the outcome – Napoleon became a legendary hero. We should, however, consider what it cost a soldier to cross into disobedience and rebellion. Immediately, there is an internal drama. And the soldiers of the 7th in this town, torn by conflicting passions, could not forget that they risked severe punishment. That was to be for La Bedoyère the supreme penalty: shot at Louis XVIII's second restoration.

The comte d' Artois arrived at Lyons on 8 March: 'I trust that the guns of Grenoble will have stopped Bonaparte. In any case, I will prevent him from crossing the Rhìne.' That same day Napoleon reached Grenoble and made a good impression with his reasonable and reassuring sentiments. At this stage of his journey, he had 7–8,000 men, powder magazines and an arsenal of guns of every calibre. And Artois? The 30,000 men dispatched by Soult were still far away. The garrison of Lyons comprised two line regiments and the 13th Dragoons. Plus the national guard: 6,000 men and 1,500 muskets. Artillery: two guns – unserviceable, according to their crews. A thousand guns and a garrison ten times more numerous would not have sufficed to stop the Emperor: not one soldier wished to march against him. The comte d'Artois was reminded of this truth on the day following his arrival at Lyons. He unburdened himself to the Duke of Orléans who had just reached the city. 'All you can do is to try to make the troops march and to retreat,' said the Duke. 'I want first to consult Marshal Macdonald who should arrive soon.' When Macdonald arrived later in the evening, d'Artois had already reached a decision. 'You take over command here. I give you the widest powers. Here we have neither ammunition, nor guns. The troops demonstrate and say that they will oppose any resistance, and the greater part of the populace has declared against us. I have ordered the city evacuated early tomorrow morning.' Macdonald was bewildered. 'But where can you stand once you have left the barrier of the Rhìne? Let us at least try to persuade the troops to defend Lyons. Let us muster them tomorrow morning. We will put it to them as a point of honour, always so sensitive, so cherished by Frenchmen. We will show them the evils that would emerge from a civil war and the danger of having all Europe in arms fall upon France.'

At 10 a.m. on 10 March, a delegation of officers presented themselves to the Marshal. 'The troops refuse to be reviewed by the princes. But they will welcome you with respect.' When he arrived at the place Bellecour in driving rain, the troops cheered him. He formed them into squares and made a royalist speech. 'I only ask as guarantee of your loyalty and patriotism to respond to my cheer.' He shouted 'Long live the king!' twice over at the top of his lungs. Dead silence. An error of judgement then impelled him to seek out the comte d'Artois. This prince, approaching an old and much decorated sapper of the 14th Dragoons, 'spoke to him in friendly fashion, praising his courage'. The sequel was ridiculous and painful. In front of this soldier, who looked at him fixedly, his mouth open, the Prince cried 'Vive le Roi!' Macdonald did the same, as did several colonels who came to encourage the sapper to do likewise. No result. Red with fury, d'Artois hastily retired. He passed through a crowd who cried 'Vive l'Empereur!' to his face. An hour later, Macdonald saw him to his post-chaise in which, preceded by the Duke d'Orléans, he hurried back to Paris.

Macdonald himself had to escape on horseback a little after 2 p.m. when Napoleon's hussars broke in through the district called la Guillotière, accompanied by a crowd of peasants shouting 'Vive l'Empereur!, Vive la liberté.' At 8 p.m. the mayor, baron de Fargues, welcomed Napoleon at the same spot and offered him the keys to the city. Processions ran through the streets with blazing torches. Men and women sang the Marseillaise and shouted, not only 'Vive l'Empereur!', but also 'Down with the priests! Down with the nobles! Death to royalists, Bourbons to the scaffold!'

In order to erect a human rampart against Napoleon's advance, a royal decree of 9 March had authorised the recruitment of three million national guards. The prefects and the generals had raised their arms to heaven: how were they to organise such a mass of men in a few days, how to arm them? Some thousands of unemployed presented themselves but no one knew what to do with them. Soult had also recalled to the colours 120,000 soldiers who were on leave and some 'absent without leave'. Only ten thousand responded, including the half-pays who had but one idea: to rejoin the Napoleonic forces at the first opportunity.

In mid-March, during a meeting of the council of ministers, the Duke of Blacas had another idea: 'The King must present himself before Bonaparte in full array and in his open coach accompanied by members of the Chamber of Deputies, all on horseback, together with the princes of the royal family. His Majesty would then ask Bonaparte: 'Sir, what have you come to do in Paris?' Overcome by the grandeur of the spectacle, the Usurper could only withdraw.' His audience kept straight faces. Vitrolles was sarcastic: 'I believe that this project lacks one essential element. The procession must be led by the archbishop of Paris, carrying the Blessed Sacrament, like Saint Martin de Tours leading the Visigoths.'

Marmont recommended fortifying the Tuileries and retiring inside with 3,000 men and provisions for two months. 'We can put things in a state to withstand a siege.' Louis XVIII shrugged his shoulders .'We do not wish to play a ridiculous role.' How was France divided? North, west, south-west, Ile de France, or in other words, four-fifths of the land remained under royal rule, to which must be added Provence where the Duke of Angoulême and Masséna still flew the white flag, apart from the coastal regions. In the south-east, the key cities of Lyons and Grenoble were under the imperial regime. A corridor between the Saône and the Loire extended eastwards to the Jura and southwards to the Bourbonnais; here, two currents collided. This was the theatre of decision. We have already explained that, beyond the forces which rallied to him, Napoleon's principal asset was his own person. And he was driving on in Burgundy while the King sat in the Tuileries. On 14 March at Saint-Brieuc, fishermen and workmen tore down the royal ordinances to cries of 'Vive l'Empereur!' at Lille mobs of locals raised the same cry. At Nancy, students distributed tracts and songs:

Return, return is the cry of France
To end her shame and suffering.

White cockades were ripped off and trampled in the barracks at Sarrguemines, Mézières, Amiens, Le Havre, Brest, Auch. Five infantry regiments and the 31st Hussars stationed between Moulins and Bourg, rebelled and started marching on Maçon to join the Emperor. At Dijon a group of young people – one of them, François Rude, had already won the Prix de Rome for sculpture – stopped two squadrons of chasseurs who were riding, without visible enthusiasm, to oppose the Emperor. They persuaded them not to go further. The populace enthusiastically tore up cobblestones, the bourgeois national guards threw in their lot with the Bonapartist movement which prevailed at Beaune and the entire department of the Côte d'Or. The prefect fled, General Veaux, commanding the region, proclaimed the restoration of the Empire.

Now the most celebrated of the marshals of the Grande Armée that had gone over to the Bourbons makes his appearance on the scene. Summoned by

Soult to Paris on 7 March, Ney had talked to the King. He sincerely thought that the return of Napoleon to France would be a catastrophe, and told the sovereign: 'I will bring him back to Paris in an iron cage. I guarantee the support of the troops.' He became less certain of this when, on 12 March, he met the colonels of his regiments at Besançon. 'Monsieur le Maréchal, morale is bad. There are desertions. Napoleon's agents have brought two eagles.' 'The first soldier that goes over, I will run through with my sword. But soldiers always march to the guns.' He made battle dispositions, issued orders to his generals. He had only 6,000 men to oppose the 14,000 now available to Napoleon. This numerical inferiority did not disquiet him, nor did what he was told of the indecision of his soldiers. 'I will take a musket and fire the first shot and they will all march.'

However, Ney had read the famous proclamation 'The eagle, with the national colours, will fly from steeple to steeple to the towers of Notre-Dame.' He had exclaimed: 'That's no way to write. The King should write that.' But his resolution was now flawed. Having joined the Bourbons in all sincerity, he had since continually had to suffer a series of humiliations: 'The comte d'Artois has never deigned to invite a marshal of France to ride in his carriage.' And he brooded over the slights inflicted on his wife. This noble and courageous heart was divided.

Napoleon himself was convinced that Ney's soldiers, like all the others encountered up to then, would rally to him. But he knew the impulsiveness of the man who, to all intents, had forced him to abdicate in April 1814. 'He is quite capable, when excited, of winning over some battalions, even if it means firing the first shot.' Now, the Emperor did not wish blood spilt. He had sent Ney a hand-written letter: 'My cousin, my major–general is sending you our order of march. I do not doubt that as soon as you have learned of my arrival at Lyons you will have had your troops re-display the tricolour flag. Obey Bertrand's orders and rejoin me at Châlons. I will receive you as I did on the eve of the battle of the Moskowa.'

Later, during the trial which would end in his condemnation to death, Ney justified his decision to rejoin Napoleon with these words: 'Never, since the time when I made the fatal error for which I have so long atoned, have I had other thought than to shield my country from civil war and from all the ills which flow from it.'

On 15 May 1814, when he had reached Lons-le-Saulnier, he assembled his troops in the allées de la Chevalerie. The soldiers were surrounded by a crowd. There had been rumours of an important event. The officers' faces were 'deathly pale', as were those of the soldiers. Ney, with no cockade in his hat, took post inside the square and drew his sword. 'Officers, NCOs and soldiers, the Bourbon cause is irretrievably lost.' 'Vive l'Empereur!' The cheers were fervent. The

Marshal gestured for silence. 'Soldiers! The time has passed when we could be governed with ridiculous prejudices, when the rights of the people were distrusted and suppressed. The legitimate dynasty which the nation has adopted is about to re-assume the throne. It is for the emperor Napoleon alone to rule over our beautiful country. Soldiers, I have so often led you to victory. Now, I will lead you to the immortal phalanx which the Emperor is marching to Paris.' They broke ranks, delirious with enthusiasm. The *vivandières* dispensed free brandy, officers and men embraced. Ney, jostled, surrounded, also embraced his neighbours. Soldiers brought out the tricolour cockades which they had hidden in their haversacks and put them on. Only a few senior officers refused to join in the general enthusiasm. The colonel of the national guard of Lons-le-Saulnier, knight of Saint-Louis, publicly broke his sword.

Ney reached Auxerre on the night of 17/18 March and saw the Emperor next morning. He had drawn up a memorandum justifying his conduct at Fontainebleau. Napoleon would have none of it. 'You need no excuse. Your reason as mine lies in the events which have been stronger than mere men. But, no more talk of the past. Let us not remember it except to guide us better in the future.' He told Ney that he was in favour of peace and a degree of liberty. That he had written to Vienna and that he hoped to avoid a new clash with Europe. He appointed Ney to a division of four regiments of infantry and three of cavalry and told him to meet him in Paris.

In Paris, at the moment following the news of the rallying of Ney to the Emperor, someone fixed a placard to the railings of the Vendôme column: 'Napoleon to Louis XVIII. My good brother. It is unnecessary to send me any more soldiers. I have enough.' This jest was true. The end of the march on Paris was no more than a promenade. 'I see that it is over,' said Louis that evening of the 18th. 'Let us not engage in useless resistance. I have decided to leave.' His followers tearfully kissed his hand. He had signed a last proclamation which was posted throughout Paris. 'The King had not wished to fight in the capital for fear of unleashing civil war.'

Bands of workmen took to the streets from the districts of the Temple, Saint-Denis and Saint-Antoine, marching and singing as they headed for the boulevards to the south. They sang the Marseillaise and shouted 'Vive l'Empereur!' though, as at Lyons, the shout of 'Down with the priests!' was also heard. The palace of the Tuileries was full of counsellors of state, generals, old servants and ministers with their wives wearing court dress.

At Fontainebleau, the Emperor had transferred to a coach, escorted by many mounted officers. His carriage moved more and more slowly through the crowds. He reached the Tuileries at 9 p.m. and was carried shoulder-high to the first floor.

XVI

THE GUARD DIES

O n 14 June 1815, the Grande Armée marched on the enemy. It was now
called the Army of the North, but the Guard was by far the largest unit
and Napoleon was commanding it in person. There were practically no
foreigners in the ranks. The Saxons, Belgians, Hanoverians, Württembergers, all
the troops of the ex-Confederation of the Rhine, were now serving in the ranks
of the coalition of Europe against the Corsican Ogre, returned from the isle of
Elba.

The new army was fairly homogeneous. There were some conscripts, but
a good half were old soldiers who had rejoined during the first Restoration, from
the prisons in England, from Russia or from the garrisons in Germany and
Poland; among the officers were many half-pays, rejoined with enthusiasm.
Some had been fighting under Bonaparte since the days of the Boulogne Camp
and even earlier. We know nothing of how these men fared; a few have been
saved from oblivion because they wrote down their memories. Before the last
guns open fire, I should like to mention two, simply to show what adventures,
what dangers these men had been able to surmount.

The first, Captain Coignet, is well known, better known in fact than some
marshals of the period. Hundreds of historians, including myself, have quoted
him. Jean-Roch Coignet was born on 26 August 1776 at Druyes-les-Belles-
Fontaines in the Puisaye, department of the Yonne. An unhappy childhood,
escaping from his home, he had to find a job. Luckily, he found a good master,
a horse dealer. At 23, Jean-Roch enlisted in the army and fought in the campaign in Italy, managed to get in the Guard by fudging his height, as he said. All
the same, one can't conceal a difference of four inches, which leaves one to suppose that there were not only colossi in the Guard and that legend has been
exaggerated. Coignet fought at Austerlitz, Jena, Friedland. Corporal in 1807, a
brief period in Spain, sergeant in 1809, the second Austrian campaign. In 1812,
by the eve of the invasion of Russia, he had learned to read and write, which
enabled him to be promoted to lieutenant. He survived the march on Moscow,
the fire, the retreat. In 1813, during the campaign in Germany, we see him a
captain on the staff, handling convoys. Life became less harsh. After the first
abdication he retired to Auxerre where he heard the whistle of the wings of the

flying eagle. He ran to the colours; and the captain would fight at Waterloo. At the second Restoration, he was at home on half-pay.

After 48 battles, not one wound. 'Some soldiers fall in their first battle, others walk through every fire.' Yes, but let us remember the name which the other soldiers gave to the Guard: the Immortals. Except on rare occasions, the Guard were not engaged until things were going really badly. It is true that then they would allow themselves to be cut to pieces, though this happened rarely. Their death-rate was far lower than that of the Line.

At Auxerre, the half-pay Coignet, 73 francs monthly, had to sell his three horses and install himself in a modest pension. He amused himself by recounting his adventures at the host's table, glorifying *le Tondu*, castigating the *émigrés* and the ultras. The police kept an eye on him, as they did all half-pays; his name figures in many reports. In 1818, however, he married at the age of 42. In 1830, he enthusiastically supported the Revolution. No more police surveillance, elected colour-bearer of the National Guard, rosette of the Legion of Honour in 1847. His wife died in that year and to assuage his grief he began to write his memoirs, the first appearing in 1851. Reading them, one must admire the way in which Coignet could recall precisely, at forty years' distance, so many of the details which appear in his writings. Knowing so well the context, the intellectual climate used in his memoirs, what does it matter if occasionally he exaggerates a little? What author has not? Let us salute the agile pen of a man who, at 30, could neither read nor write. He died in his bed aged 89.

The career of Captain François, who also fought at Waterloo and survived reads like a novel. Born a year after Coignet, in 1777 at Guinchy on the Somme. Enlisted at 15 and two weeks later, wounded at Valmy. In October, he fought at Jemappes, saw the fall of Brussels, the sieges of Antwerp and Namur. Promoted corporal on 2 December 1793. A second wound at Neerwinden. After the campaign in the Netherlands, he left the Army of the North and, with the Army of Sambre et Meuse, crossed the Rhine. In 1796, Salzbach and a third wound and made prisoner. He escaped and in 1797 rejoined the 9th Demi-brigade then marching to Italy. Fought at Tagliamento and joined a mobile column under Lannes. On 19 May 1798 he sailed from Toulon for the expedition to Egypt. François, then promoted sergeant, was aboard the bombard *Hirondelle* and served as storekeeper during the voyage. Drafted to Reynier's division, he took part in the expedition to Syria and the siege of St-Jean-d'Acre. Here comes the romance; next he is a member of the Camel Corps, blue turban, sky-blue tunic with red facings. But the campaign in Egypt was not going well and one day a column of prisoners was marching through the desert. François was one of them and their destination was the prison at Damascus. In the east, prisoner means slave. François had the luck to be picked by an Emir who treated him well, took him into his service and even on to his military staff. Another sumptuous costume, this time entirely Turkish. The Arabised François saw Jaffa, Baghdad, Nablus, Jerusalem, Constantinople, where the Sultan gave him a rank in the mounted Janissaries.

The magic of the Orient can pall; the Janissary escaped, presenting himself at the French embassy. General Sébastiani provided him with him European clothes and 400 francs and passage in a ship sailing for Dalmatia. On 2 October 1803, François rejoined a French regiment – his old 9th Line – with the rank of sub-lieutenant.

At Jena he was wounded four times, not too seriously apparently, because he then fought in Spain where fortune did not favour him: made prisoner at Baylen, consigned to one of the hulks at Cadiz. We know how this old tub was cast up on the coast one stormy night when 700 prisoners escaped; one of them was none other than François. How could he have kept going? We next see Captain François in the mud and dust of Russia: Vilna, Smolensk, yet another wound on the Moskowa. Like Coignet, he entered Moscow, retreated and crossed the Beresina, surviving everything. He also fought at Waterloo and lived. In the evening of his life, he lived at Nantes and was married. Like Coignet, he wrote his memoirs which appeared in 1829. He would die, as did Captain Coignet, the death of many adventurers – in his bed.

Since 2 June, Napoleon had been outlawed by the Congress of Vienna. And yet here were soldiers, many of whom had had more than enough of war, marching willingly against the enemy monarchs who wished to reverse the victories of the French people dating back to the Revolution.

This sentiment was emphatically not shared by the aristocrats or the rich, nor by the bourgeoisie. Not every merchant or even peasant went along with it, but it was truly that of the soldiers and most of their officers, and was good for morale, except that this resurrection of the revolutionary ideal was accompanied by another, that of distrust.

On the ground the situation was simple; we have only to glance at the map to understand the preliminary battles – Ligny and Quatre Bras – then Waterloo. Wellington's army, 85,000 men had its HQ at Brussels, covering Antwerp, the port of escape in case of failure. Blücher's army, 117,000 men, which was to cover the Rhine, had its HQ at Namur. The two enemy commanders had their troops spread over distances as vast as two French departments, with merely some advanced elements for surveillance.

Napoleon had available 112,000 men; his strategic plan was simple: one might almost say it was the same as always: to attack his enemies with a lightning blow, beating first one and then the other. He must first cross the Sambre which formed a moat parallel to the frontier. In the greatest secrecy, the Emperor had assembled the bulk of his army behind the forest of Beaumont, facing

Charleroi. 'We shall attack at 3 a.m. on 15 June. None of our enemies expects that.'

At Avesnes, on the eve, Napoleon addressed his army in unusually solemn tones: 'Soldiers! Today is the anniversary of Marengo and Friedland, both of which decided the destiny of Europe. Then, as after Austerlitz, we were too generous. We believed the protestations and promises of the princes whom we left on their thrones. Today, associated together against us, they threaten the independence and the most sacred rights of France. They have committed the most unjust of aggressions. Let us march to meet them! Soldiers! we have forced-marches to make and battles to join, risks to run. But, with constancy, victory will be ours. Our rights, the honour and welfare of our country will be reclaimed. For every Frenchman of good heart, this is the time to conquer or die.'

Napoleon knew that these words, which echoed the times when the nation was in danger, would touch the hearts of the veterans; he had no fears on that score. But he had no grounds for such complacency as regards the senior officers who must carry out his orders.

When he returned to Paris he had counted on seeing his old lieutenants rallying to him. Aside from Ney, five had joined him during the eagle's flight: Suchet, Brune, Jourdan, Davout, Soult. Where were the rest?

Berthier, Marmont and Victor had left France with Louis. Others were voluntarily confined to their estates. Berthier was doubly absent, having left this world on 1 June. Detained at Bamberg, while trying to rejoin the Emperor, he had thrown himself in despair from a window.

Murat continued to pursue a fantasy. We saw how at Leipzig, when commanding the imperial cavalry, he secretly made overtures to the Austrians in the hope of keeping his throne of the Kingdom of Naples. He had obtained assurances, but of dubious reliability. On 30 March 1815, turning against the Austrians, he launched a manifesto summoning the Italians to unity and independence. Beaten, first at Occhiobello then at Tolentino, with his troops utterly routed, he had abandoned the struggle and on 21 May embarked for France, arriving on the 25th at Cannes. He had offered Napoleon his services and had met with refusal ('My soldiers would refuse to obey him'). Let us cut short this saga which is starting to turn black. After Waterloo and the second abdication, Murat, pursued by the royalist police, fled to Corsica, then crossed to Calabria, still dreaming of regaining his throne. Betrayed, sold, arrested and condemned to death – a death which could expunge in part his follies and betrayals. Facing the firing-squad, Murat refused the traditional eye-bandage and, last conceit of the lady-killer, ordered the firing squad: 'Soldiers, do your duty, fire at my heart, but spare my face.' He was buried in a common grave at Pizzo.

On how many marshals who had remained or returned to their allegiance could the Emperor rely? Davout had been appointed Minister of War. Suchet had been given command of the Army of the Alps. Brune that of the Army of the Var, yet to be formed, Jourdan the governorship of Besançon, Mortier, having secretly defected to the Bourbons, was posted sick. That left Soult and Ney.

The Emperor had called in Grouchy, promoted marshal, quite why no one knows. After his short campaign in the south against the Duke of Angoulême, Emmanuel de Grouchy, 49 years old, had displayed great gallantry as a cavalry officer at Hohenlinden in Germany and at Eylau in Austria, at Friedland, Wagram and on other fields of battle. In 1812, Napoleon had appointed him to command the 'Sacred Squadron' charged with watching over his personal safety, but, knowing his limitations, had never given him command of an army corps. So why, this time? Why Soult, whose attachment to the monarchy at the time of the first Restoration bordered on baseness? Lack of choice? In any case, Napoleon had committed a major error of judgement in appointing Soult as chief of staff in succession to Berthier.

Napoleon used to scold Berthier and often teased him cruelly, saying he was 'good for nothing'. But he knew that this marshal, who was not capable of exercising high command, was the perfect chief of staff. Scarcely had the supreme commander's thought been formed than Berthier had grasped it, both wholly and in its nuances. He never argued over it, never called it into question, and with an uncommon speed and efficiency, sent it to the various units in terms of absolute clarity.

Soult's brain was that of a good tactician, capable of rapid combinations on the battlefield, but totally deficient in the capacity for the order and organisation needed to direct a large, or for that matter, a small staff. We shall see Soult commit omissions and errors in his orders, forgetting to send them to one unit, not knowing that two or three copies of an important order should be sent by two or three messengers – at the least. So, even before starting the march towards the enemy, in his orders for the concentration of the army, Soult had forgotten to task the cavalry reserve. This omission had to be put right at the last moment before the attack. The twelve divisions and 15,000 horses which formed this reserve would have only 24 instead of 48 hours to make their rendezvous and some regiments would have 80 kilometres to travel. They arrived tired out.

Another unpardonable negligence: the order for the attack at dawn on 15 June was sent to each corps on the evening of the 14th by one messenger apiece. The messenger to Vandamme's III Corps, broke his leg and the order was never delivered. Now, it was precisely III Corps that was to lead the way. It was not until the corps scheduled to follow arrived that Vandamme became aware of the situation. Result: III Corps was unable to move until 6 a.m. The delay of three hours cost the army the element of surprise. The German General von Ziethen, commanding the corps nearest to the frontier, would have time to concentrate his units and make a defence which should not have been possible.

In the evening of the 14th, Napoleon occupied the château of Prince Cara-man-Chimay at Beaumont, a large village south of Charleroi. The troops bivouacked by army corps around the château: orders were given to conceal fires. Summer was but one week old; the weather was heavy and it was raining.

On 15 June, from 3 a.m. the army started to advance in three columns. On the left, the corps of Drouet d'Erlon (I Corps) and Reille (II Corps) moved towards Marchienne, the bulk of the army, the centre, towards Charleroi; Gérard's IV Corps on the right towards Châtelet. Vandamme's III Corps, which had not been ordered to move, as I explained, would not start until 6 a.m.

The march was no picnic. No roads, only dirt tracks, some rather narrow. The country was wooded and hilly. The soldiers were heavily laden: in addition to his equipment, each carried all his cartridges and four days' ration of bread, However, morale was good, partly thanks to the welcome of the Belgians.

From the first hours, the French light cavalry seized the Prussian advanced posts and were now at Charleroi. The sappers and marines of the Guard had reached the bridge over the Sambre before the enemy had been able to destroy it. The cavalry crossed the town and pursued the enemy, who retired hastily. But, thanks to Soult's negligence, General von Ziethen was alerted and started the movement of the large units of his army corps.

And on that morning, the enemy were about to receive another present, this time in the shape of treason.

General de Bourmont, commanding one of IV Corps' lead divisions, was an ex-Chouan to whom Bonaparte, as a gesture of amnesty, had offered a senior post in the French army. On 15 June at 5 a.m. he left Florennes with his staff (a colonel, a squadron chief, three captains, all but one of noble blood) and five chasseurs. Having passed through the advanced posts, Bourmont sent back the chasseurs with a letter to General Gérard and with his officers, galloped towards the enemy. Here is the text of the letter: 'I do not wish to contribute to the estab-lishment in France of a bloody despotism which will ruin my country. I would have resigned and gone home had I been able to believe that I would have been left alone. That seems to me unlikely and I have had to assure my liberty by other means. You will not see me in the ranks of the enemy, nor will they have from me any information capable of harming the French army, composed of men whom I love and to whom I will not cease to bear a continuing attach-ment.'

Fifteen minutes after gaining the German lines, Bourmont declared to Colonel Schutter: 'The French will attack this afternoon.' Then he met Colonel de Reiche who asked him what was the strength of the French army and Bourmont told him: 120,000 men and he produced the order of march of his division for the day. At about 3 p.m. near Sombreffe, he was presented to Blücher who only addressed a few words to him. A Prussian officer observed to the Field Marshal that Bourmont was wearing the white cockade: 'What does it matter what he is wearing! A scoundrel is still a scoundrel.' In spite of the information given to the enemy, this treason had no physical effect on operations, which proceeded normally, but which spread a temporary disquiet among the rank and file. 'Some officers are traitors, especially the nobles.' General Hulot, commanding one of the brigades in Bourmont's division, overheard these remarks. He made speeches, swearing to fight with them against the enemies of France to his last breath. Gérard, the corps commander, rode down the front of the troops, greeting them cordially. He was cheered.

From Charleroi, one road, on the left, led to Brussels – and the British; on the right one led to Namur – and the Prussians. Napoleon had decided send the bulk of his army against the Prussians who were closer. Had he first attacked the British, the alerted Prussians could have attacked his right flank. The Emperor therefore sent Grouchy (with the four corps constituting the cavalry reserve) and supported by Vandamme on the right-hand road.

On the left, it was a matter of preventing the British and Prussians from joining. Such interdiction was possible so long as they could hold the Namur road, on which was the only possible point for such a junction: a cross-roads named Quatre Bras. Napoleon, who had arrived at Charleroi at noon, sent for Ney: 'Marshal, do you know the position at Quatre Bras well?' 'Yes, Sire, how could I not? I have been campaigning in this territory for twenty years. That position is the key to everything.' 'Good, take your two corps there.' In other words, seize the position. 'Trust me, Sire. We shall be at Quatre Bras in two hours, so long as the enemy is not there already.' It was then 3.30 p.m. The light cavalry was already on the Brussels road and the army corps of Reille and Drouet d'Erlon were closing by way of the Marchienne bridge. To seize Quatre Bras, Ney therefore disposed of I and II corps and their attached cavalry, plus the light cavalry of the Guard, in all some 48,000 men, more than one-third of the army.

On the right, late that day, the Grouchy–Vandamme column pushed back von Ziethen's troops, who retired at maximum speed. Napoleon was now certain of being able to deploy on the 16th beyond the wooded zone, which would give him better freedom of movement. He returned to his HQ in the Hôtel Puissant at Charleroi and slept. It was 11 p.m.

At midnight, Napoleon rose, as Ney was announced. Ney recounted the day's events. Had the Prince of the Moskowa occupied Quatre Bras, as ordered? No. Had he been repulsed by superior force? No. Having himself arrived near the famous cross-roads, he observed that there were only 4,000 British troops with four guns. He had only 'made some charges' then had recalled his advance-guard to Frasnes, four kilometres south of the cross-roads. Why this hesitation, this inertia on the part of the Bravest of the Brave? It was incomprehensible. None of the suggested reasons – including 'Ney had gone mad' – is convincing. The Marshals's conduct could still hold some surprises.

It was nearly as surprising to learn that Napoleon, hearing this report, had not severely reprimanded Ney. No; he contented himself merely with 'again recommending to him the importance of the Quatre Bras position' that he must take the next day. Then the Emperor retired for a further two or three hours of sleep.

Napoleon slept, while Wellington danced. At Brussels, he opened the ball given by the Duchess of Richmond. At 6 p.m. he received a dispatch forwarded from Namur by Blücher: 'Major attack by the French.' No rush, for fear of frightening the Belgians. Besides, why deprive these young officers of their ball, for which they had donned full dress? The British commander-in-chief merely dictated some movement orders which only covered the roads between the frontier and Brussels. Supper was served at 11.30 p.m. It was magnificent weather and the dancers were supremely elegant. The pipes of the Gordon Highlanders played in the garden and kilted officers performed a sword dance – ah! how pretty is warfare! Then, the ball. Wellington had received another dispatch and had brought forward by two hours the departure time of the troops stationed at Brussels. But in the illuminated rooms, the couples still waltzed; the ball would last all night. Byron wrote: 'that night on which was to rise so bloody a dawn'.

It was already dawn when the officers left the ball. A painting by Hillingford depicts the romantic scene: young girls with bare shoulders and silk dresses making their tender adieux to handsome young men in red capes and helmets, many already on horseback. A square of pipers of the Gordon Highlanders marched into the distance, followed by the colours and a forest of muskets.

At 4 a.m. on the 16th, Napoleon awoke at his HQ at Charleroi and read the reports from his army corps. Grouchy stated that the Prussian army had taken up a position in front of Fleurus where there was now a force of French cavalry. Having reflected, the Emperor dictated orders for Ney and Grouchy. The message to Ney was long and very detailed, dealing with twenty eventualities, but the substance was the same as the order given at midnight: seize Quatre Bras as quickly as possible. The order to Grouchy stated that Napoleon wished to finish personally the action started the previous day against Blücher's troops. Having crushed the enemy on that side, he would rush up the road to Brussels, which by then would have been liberated by Ney, after having taken Quatre Bras that morning. The march on Brussels with all forces concentrated, could not fail to be victorious, all being ready for a triumphal entry

At 11 o'clock Napoleon reached the mill at Naveau, which was just in front of Fleurus (in these accounts, it will be called the mill at Fleurus) some ten kilometres north-east of Charleroi, where he wished to survey the battle-field. In an hour the sappers had built a circular platform around the tower. The Emperor, in a grey coat, high boots, small hat, looked at the map held before him by a page. Behind him was a group of his staff and, lower down, some chasseurs of the escort, in green, and busbies with plumes of red and green, some of them on horseback, others standing and holding their chargers. It was extremely hot. Napoleon surveyed the countryside through his spy-glass. An undulating plain, covered with crops, mainly rye – and the rye was motion-less, not a breath of wind. To the east, the plain was cut by deep ravines. To the north, a road ran east–west, bordered by trees; to the left, a bare road, stone-based, built by the Romans. Here and there, steeples and villages. Some long dark-green smears were moving north: the Prussian regiments taking up their positions. Napoleon snapped shut his telescope. No trace of emotion on his pale face. All would go well if Ney managed the business properly at Quatre Bras.

As I have said, Quatre Bras was the junction of the two roads Charleroi–Brus-sels and Namur–Nivelles. At that point, they were wide, and the terrain was flat, small woods, clear of the roads, but not far distant. At the cross-roads itself, a large farm and some houses. Some thousands of British troops were there, red-coats everywhere, riflemen in green, gunners in blue.

Ney had left early from Marchienne, west of Charleroi, and reached Frasnes, three kilometres from Quatre Bras. He could see the cross-roads from there, and all seemed unchanged from the previous evening. The Prince of the Moskowa had had it from Napoleon himself that he must take Quatre Bras and now, at 8 a.m. he had substantially the means to do so, even though not all his forces had yet arrived. To hand were the troops of Reille's corps, 23,000 men with the rest coming up. So, Forward! No – Ney did not move, doing nothing until the receipt of Napoleon's written order at 11 a.m. Then, and only then, did he send his generals orders which expressed the Emperor's hopes to be able to march on Brussels that evening

On the previous evening, the British had had 4,000 men at Quatre Bras. But since then Wellington, warned, had started to send reinforcements. By 11 a.m. next day, when Ney received Napoleon's order, the British were 7,000 strong; by 2 o'clock, when Ney eventually started his troops marching, they numbered 30,000 and soon after, even more.

477

On the battlefield on the right, Blücher had deployed his troops on the plain of Ligny, east and west of this village. Ligny is about nine kilometres east-south-east of Quatre Bras. Napoleon was still standing on the platform of the mill at Fleurus, looking through his telescope. It was 1 o'clock; nothing from Ney, what was he doing? Napoleon could see the enemy positions filling with troops. At 3 o'clock the Guards' guns fired three blank rounds from the battery below the mill. It was the signal.

The infantry of Lefol's division, III Corps, sitting in the corn, got to their feet: the band of the 23rd played the *Chant du Départ* (the Song of Farewell) ,the drums beat the charge. The charge would be slow, since the soldiers were overburdened and could not move quickly through the high crops. General Gérard sent his troops against two hamlets, St-Amand-la-Haye and le Hameau, on the enemy's right and it was quickly apparent that their right would be enveloped.

At 2 o'clock, Napoleon had Soult send Ney the following order: 'The Emperor orders me to warn you that the enemy has concentrated a corps between Sombreffe and Brye and that at 2.30 Marshal Grouchy with III and IV Corps will attack it. His Majesty's intention is that you should attack what faces you and that, having made a vigorous attack, you fall back on us to assist in the envelopment of the corps mentioned above.' It is clear that if Ney, having seized Quatre Bras, had struck towards Ligny, while Gérard was already threatening to envelop the Prussian right wing, Blücher's army would have been finished.

But – no Ney, and Blücher had seen the danger. He struck with a brigade of infantry to the front and to the flank with two cavalry regiments. From then on, the battle of Ligny became general and furious.

The troops shot at each other as they closed on the villages, where hand-to-hand fighting took place in the streets with musketry and bayonet thrusts delivered house-to-house. Human torrents collided in the black smoke, houses caught fire. Having fought in the houses until they were no longer tenable, the soldiers fought around the piles of corpses in the open, amid a foul odour of burning flesh, both of dead and helpless wounded. Ligny was burned from end to end, gutted as far as the cemetery. The adversaries, their cartridges spent, too closely engaged to use their bayonets, fought with musket butts. A fight of hatred, rarely seen.

Between the villages and hamlets, the cavalry clashed. Squares were formed to ward off charges. Troops of horses, their riders killed, swirled around the formations in terror and confusion. The weather continued torrid and the sky was thick with black clouds. At the foot of the Fleurus mill, Napoleon paced up and down, pale and nervous. Soult appeared: 'If d'Erlon carries out the order which Your Majesty has given, the Prussian army is lost.' We shall see who is this d'Erlon and what he was to do. Napoleon shrugged his shoulders. He was still thinking of Ney.

Was Ney mad? Among the thousands of critics of Waterloo, he has his defenders. He had complained that Napoleon's order received at 11 p.m. was unclear. According to d'Erlon's recollection, when first ordered to go to his support, he had then been ordered to envelop Blücher's right at the moment when he was fully engaged against the entire British army – and other complaints. While the debate will never end, the salient and established facts are these: Ney, having done nothing on the 15th, had wasted the morning of the 16th in having his infantry close the few kilometres which separated them from the British outposts. Again, at midday, a determined attack by Reille's infantry would have thrown the British off the cross-roads.

Ney had decided to attack when almost the entire British army was at the cross-roads. And then, an error almost as serious as his procrastination, he committed his units piecemeal, without manoeuvring or using any tactical imagination, in a manner which was at once the most costly and least effective. Ney had led his squadrons ten times in charges with blind courage, sword drawn, bareheaded, his red hair streaming like a flame. How many horses were killed under him? Two, five? One gains the impression that death would not have been unwelcome to him. And all without gaining a decision; against the British, courage alone was not enough. Against whom would it have sufficed?

At about 5 p.m., Ney ordered Kellermann to join him with one of the brigades that was still at Frasnes – still there! why? Ney galloped up to Kellermann as soon as he was in sight: 'My dear General, the future of France is at stake. We need an extraordinary effort. Take your cavalry and charge the British centre. Crush them: ride over them!

But, Monsieur le Maréchal, I have only one brigade of cavalry with me. As you ordered, the rest have remained at Frasnes. 'No matter! Charge with what you have. Ride them down! I will back you up with all the cavalry present. Go! Go now!' Kellermann rode in the lead of Guidon's brigade, formed from the 8th and 11th Cuirassiers, which in 1815 were scarcely different from those which as a child I saw in 1914 at the beginning of the war: breastplate, sheepskin breeches, iron helmet topped by a crest of yellow copper, black horse-tail. Kellermann turned to his men: 'Charge, at the gallop!'

In a valley, on something of a reverse slope, was a British brigade, red coats, grey trousers, shakos, formed in square awaiting the shock. The British bullets clanged against the breastplates and helmets of the cuirassiers. The brigade was shattered, its colours taken, and the French cavalry reached Quatre Bras. Victory!

It would perhaps have been victory, had Kellermann's other brigades been present or if his infantry could have occupied the terrain. But they were not there. The British, occupying the houses at the cross-roads, fired on the French cavalry. Horses fell and the squadron began to waver. Kellermann, his horse killed under him, fell, spraining a foot. To avoid being taken prisoner, he had to hold on to two cuirassiers who carried him back between them to the French lines.

At this moment, Major Baudus appeared with a message from Napoleon, telling Ney that the most serious fighting was now at Ligny, that he should send Drouet d'Erlon (I Corps) without delay and that Ney, if necessary, should deal with the British. The Marshal made as if to comply for a moment, then, 'seeing his infantry in disorder' ran to rally his men and lead them again towards the enemy. On the enemy side, new battalions were constantly appearing. Ney gave the order to begin retreating. Fortunately, Wellington did not have the boldness to follow. At 9 p.m. firing ceased. The British established their bivouacs more or less perpendicular to the Charleroi–Brussels road about two kilometres south of Quatre Bras. Ney led his troops to the north of Frasnes, his point of departure.

The most senseless manoeuvre of the 16th was, apparently, that of Drouet d'Erlon's army corps, consisting of four infantry divisions, a cavalry division, six batteries of artillery and train and five companies of engineers, in all 20,371 men according to the muster rolls. Shortly after 4 p.m., the fighting at Ligny was still very hard. Napoleon, still not seeing Ney arriving, thought of calling on Drouet d'Erlon who, marching behind Ney, could not have joined up with him. A messenger intercepted d'Erlon: 'By order of the Emperor, you are to change direction and march on Ligny.'

D'Erlon immediately started to comply. At the same time, as a disciplined soldier, he reported the order directly to his superior, Marshal Ney. Ney, receiving his message, raised his arms to heaven. 'I am being placed in a frightful position. Here I am engaged with the entire British army and I am suddenly deprived of a whole army corps. I shall be destroyed! Delcambre, go and ask d'Erlon to come here.' 'General, Marshal Ney wishes to have you with him. He is waiting for you with impatience.' But it is on the Emperor's order that I am marching in this direction.' Did Delcambre really tell d'Erlon that the Emperor was informed of the whole matter and that it was with his agreement that Ney was recalling him to Quatre Bras? Had Ney told him to say so? Another grey area in this day of disorder. Whatever the truth of the matter, d'Erlon, although very disturbed, again changed direction and marched towards Quatre Bras.

I say that d'Erlon did this and that, but we well understand that it was his army corps, not d'Erlon personally. One cannot get an entire army corps, cavalry, infantry, artillery and train plus 20,000 men suddenly to change direction like a section of cavalry. The result was that I Corps did not return to Quatre

Bras until night had fallen, having zigzagged for a whole day between Napoleon and Ney. Not only had it contributed nothing, but by evening the soldiers were exhausted and absolutely furious – there were even cries of 'Treason!'

Even though deprived of the support of I Corps, Napoleon still disposed of some 25,000 men in the Ligny sector. Fighting was still under way at 6.30 p.m. Now the rumble of thunder matched that of the guns, more and more black clouds gathered and large drops of rain began to fall. The Emperor decided to commit the Guard. Having failed to envelop the right of Blücher's army, he would strike the centre.

The Guard artillery opened with counter-battery fire on the Prussian guns. Then the grenadiers advanced towards Ligny, which was still burning and from which two Prussian divisions were still firing. The march forward of the Guard was one of those moments of which legends are made. Men in bearskins formed square and moved irresistibly, while on the flanks the cavalry clashed. Despite his age, Blücher plunged into the mêlée, leading a charge which failed and which resulted in a retreat pursued by the French cavalry. Suddenly the Field Marshal's horse was hit and collapsed, trapping its rider. The French cuirassiers passed Blücher without recognising him. Immediately afterwards, a Prussian charge rescued Blücher, though it was not without difficulty that he was disengaged from his mount. He rode back on an NCO's charger. The Prussian centre had been broken, but with darkness and a rainstorm, the battle of Ligny ended.

Before leaving Ligny in response to Ney's recall, Drouet d'Erlon had detached one of his four divisions, that of Durutte, to Wagnelie at the extremity of the French left. Durutte had received from d'Erlon no order other than a general caution to be prudent. He reached Wagnelie as Blücher's beaten army was streaming back northwards. As no order was given, one of his brigadiers, General Bruc, approached him: 'It is unheard of for us to stand with folded arms watching the retreat of a beaten army when there is every indication that we need only attack to destroy it.' 'It is a very good thing that you are not in command here,', replied d'Erlon. 'Would to God that I were. We would be engaged by now.' This conversation closed the day of this phantom army. In the Ligny sector, the French had lost about 8,000 men, the Prussians 15,000. At Quatre Bras, Ney had 4,200 men disabled. The losses in human lives did not stop Wellington from sleeping. 'Soldiers', he said, 'are brutes who only think of getting drunk.' Told of Blücher's defeat at Ligny, he exploded with laughter: 'The Prussians have had the devil of a beating.' Yes, they were certainly retreating, but Blücher's army was not destroyed as Napoleon had wished. Ligny was a tactical victory for Napoleon but he had failed in his strategic object – to separate Germans from British and, having beaten one, to throw himself at the other. Such failure stemmed from a series of blunders, from Soult's errors to the incomprehensible inertia of Ney. To pursue the retreating Prussians and crush them completely was the obvious objective offered to Napoleon on the evening of 16 June. Would a night pursuit have been possible? Napoleon thought not. He decided to sleep at Fleurus. He would later say that this was a mistake: 'The battle of Waterloo would have been fought 24 hours earlier. Wellington and Blücher would never have joined together!'

In a fine room in the Château de la Paix, not far from the mill at Fleurus, Napoleon slept, lying on his back. His face was pale, slightly greenish, absolutely motionless, like a death-mask, except that it was slightly less swollen. Even before the departure for Belgium, the whole household had been struck by the often recurrent expression of lassitude, of absence. The eyes, once so piercingly blue, were now dull.

Fifteen years of reign, of wars, conquests, political and dynastic upheavals, of victories, disasters, defections, betrayals – and separation from wife and son.

The Hundred Days ends in disillusionment. After all that his spies had told him on Elba, Napoleon, after landing at Golfe-Juan, had expected to be greeted by an outburst of enthusiasm. He had been sustained only by the faithfulness of the army and the hatred of the little people for the Bourbons. He had the impression that the rest of the population distrusted him. He felt alone. He found men to be faithless, cowardly, weak. Even unworthy of punishment or prosecution. Consider these examples: Augereau, whose negligence had ruined his most promising manoeuvres during the campaign in France; Marmont, whose defection delivered him to the Allies. Both had been left undisturbed during the Hundred Days. Fouché, who for years had worked openly for his downfall, had regained his ministry and resumed his intrigues with the European coalition. 'Monsieur Fouché, I should have you hanged.' 'I cannot at all agree with Your Majesty.' And matters rested there. Then there was this choice of marshals, this inaction in the face of their faults. Then lassitude; in the coach which took him north, Napoleon spent most of the time dozing. On 15 June in early afternoon, while the troops marched past cheering him, he sat in a chair in front of a small cafe, the Belle-Vue, drowsing, despite the noise of the cheering. On Sunday 11 June, after a family dinner, he turned to Fanny Bertrand with an expression of mixed melancholy and disquiet: 'Well, Madame Bertrand, let us hope that we do not regret the isle of Elba!' And, shortly afterwards, after dozing in an armchair, waking suddenly and believing he was alone: 'Fate will decide the outcome!' Fatalism leads to fatality. We shall still see some fine bounds, but never again from the man he had been.

On 17 June, Napoleon boarded his coach and left Fleurus for the battlefield of Ligny. It moved slowly over poor roads and across fields; the Emperor emerged and mounted his horse. He had himself shown over the whole field of yesterday's battle. The streets of the villages and hamlets were piled with dead, wounded and the debris of war. Napoleon spoke with the wounded, distributed money and brandy, including the Prussian casualties: 'I wish them to be cared for as our own.' During this visit, he received intelligence of the enemy's movements. Ney reported that the British were arrayed in front of Quatre Bras: eight infantry regiments and 2,000 cavalry. The Emperor sent three divisions and some cavalry, plus the Guard and Milhaud's cuirassiers. He dictated orders to Grouchy to pursue the retreating Prussians, while he, Napoleon, took care of the British. To do this, Grouchy had two army corps and a division of infantry, three corps of cavalry, some 33,000 men in all. He was to 'actively pursue the Prussians, roll up their rear-guard and push them while keeping them in view'. At the same time, he was to remain in constant touch with the army. And the Emperor. Grouchy was none too enthusiastic about his task.

'The Prussians started their retreat last night at 10 p.m. I must now round-up my scattered troops in the plain. The soldiers are eating and do not expect to be engaged today. I have no exact information of the route taken by the mass of the Prussians. The cavalry reports indicate that it may be Namur. If I move in that direction, I shall be isolated and cut-off from Your Majesty.'

Napoleon replied impatiently that it was up to him to discover where the Prussians were heading. 'I will keep in touch with you by the paved road from Namur to Quatre Bras.'

Grouchy left Napoleon at 11.30 a.m. A little later the Emperor sent him a written order, long, too detailed and none too clear overall, wherein he repeated that Grouchy was to remain in constant communication with the Emperor. At midday Napoleon dictated to Soult an order to Ney: attack the British at Quatre Bras and push them from their position. After which, the Emperor mounted his horse and rode towards Quatre Bras.

He arrived at about 2 p.m. and a heavy storm was threatening. Ney's troops had barely arrived. When the Prince of the Moskowa appeared Napoleon burst into a torrent of reproaches: 'What, such indecision, such foot-dragging! You have just wasted three precious hours.' Ney stammered pitifully that he had believed that Wellington was still at Quatre Bras with his whole army.

He was not. A *cantinière*, captured by scouts, was brought to the Emperor and she told him that Wellington, learning of Blücher's defeat at Ligny, had ordered a retreat on Brussels. This was true. Wellington had left at Quatre Bras only a rear-guard, a cavalry corps and some batteries of light artillery, commanded by General Lord Uxbridge.

'I shall establish myself at Mont Saint-Jean below Waterloo,' 'Wellington had told his generals. 'I shall await Napoleon there and force him to give battle so long as I have the hope of support of merely one Prussian corps. But if that support is lacking, I shall be compelled to sacrifice Brussels and take up positions behind the Escaut.'

He had even had a plan developed in secret for the re-embarkation of his army at Antwerp. Disembark, re-embark was the strategy of the islanders which had often disconcerted the continentals. Napoleon himself was counting on sleeping that night in Brussels.

The British rear-guard at Quatre Bras was in no position to resist Napoleon with 74,000 men and who was now pursuing in foul weather, fog and cloudbursts, soldiers foot-slogging up to their knees in mud. The British marched fast, 'as if on a fox-hunt' according to Mercer in his *Journal of the Waterloo Campaign*. Lord Uxbridge shouted to his cavalrymen, 'Faster, for God's sake, gallop faster or you will all be captured.' The French lancers pursuing them laughed and shouted insults. Napoleon took part in the race, marvellously restored and riding his white mare, Désirée. At Genappe, where they had to cross the Dyle, Uxbridge tried, in torrential rain, to organise a counter-attack, which failed.

At 7.30 p.m., the French advance-guard reached Plancenoit, about six kilometres south of Waterloo. The British were established a little further north in front of a small hill named Mont Saint-Jean on the edge of the forest of Soignies. Some fifteen of their guns opened fire, but in the fog and rain it was hard to make out their line. It was obvious that there could be no battle that day.

'What would I not give', said Napoleon, 'to have the power of Joshua to stop the sun for two hours!' He dismounted and, accompanied by three officers, walked the length of the British line, inspecting it through his spy-glass. The little party stumbled in the mud, Napoleon leaning on the arm of the page, Gudin. Shells were falling into the mud. 'My friend,' said Napoleon gaily to his page, 'you have never been invited to a party such as this. Your baptism is harsh, but you will learn fast.'

His inspection lasted until 9.30 p.m. when he remounted his horse and rode to the farm of Le Caillou at the side of the Brussels road. The servants had placed a camp-bed in a small room at street level where a big fire was burning. Napoleon got into bed, where his supper was served. He then dictated a letter to Grouchy which an officer was waiting to take immediately. It said in essence that there would be a major battle next day, that Grouchy should conform generally to the movements of Blücher's army, while keeping contact with the main French army's right wing. At the same time, Grouchy was writing to Napoleon that he had established his HQ at Gembloux. Some hours later he wrote again that, in following Blücher, he had set up two advance guards, one between Gembloux and Wavre (on the Brussels road) and the other towards Liège. Thus started an exchange of messages throughout the night and a part of next day, and which finally came to nothing because events overtook the messengers, because Soult continued to issue imprecise orders dictated at top speed by Napoleon as he concentrated on what was happening before him, and because Grouchy, as we have seen, preferred sticking to orders rather than marching to the guns.

At the Le Caillou, in the first-floor rooms, the seniors of the Emperor's household and headquarters slept on bales of straw. Every nearby inn was crowded with officers, but many had been unable to find a billet – and as for the rank-and-file! It was still raining. Along the walls, seated or crouched in the dark mud, the soldiers huddled together. Others tried to tend bivouac fires, yet others wandered like ghosts on the plateau. These men had marched 25–30 kilometres in pursuit of the British army in conditions which we have described.

And nothing to eat! The four days' bread rations carried by each man at the start of the campaign had long been eaten. Only possibility, pillage: a door stove-in, a sheepfold attacked. Carcasses smoked heavily on spits in the rain. Why was the supply service so inefficient? The soldiers said: 'it smells of treason!' At the same time, the general view was 'Let's get it over quickly!'

At 1 a.m. on 18 June, Napoleon awoke, mounted his horse and went to inspect the outposts. The rain, which had ceased temporarily, had resumed with even more gusto, the mud was deep. The Emperor feared that the British would take advantage of the weather to retire. But no, fatigued by their retreat, they slept around their fires. There was a profound silence. Napoleon returned to the Caillou still in the rain. At 3.30 the reconnoitring officers and scouts confirmed that the British had not budged.

The generals at HQ said: 'It is raining too much for us to fight. The artillery will be bogged down.' Napoleon paced up and down rather nervously. At 5 a.m. he dictated the following to Soult: 'The Emperor orders the army to be ready to attack at 9 a.m. The commanders of the army corps will muster their troops, put their arms in order and allow their troops to make a meal in order that at 9 a.m. exactly each corps will be ready to join battle immediately with its artillery and its ambulances in the positions which the Emperor indicated in his order of last night.'

On his return, and many times thereafter, the Emperor consulted his maps and memorised the position of each corps in different places on the field of battle, all of which were clearly fixed in his mind. It would be an illusion to claim to be able to follow too precisely the movements of each unit once battle had been joined, since such movements could only be recorded approximately after the event. I have already noted how in earlier battles, the black smoke always obscured parts of the field and that nervous excitement often prevented the combatants from knowing where they were. Only the Emperor, unrivalled observer, endowed with tactical genius as we know, could follow such movements as were not masked by smoke. As to the configuration of the battlefield, a map will give an idea, provided we remember that the 'dreary plain' was indeed just that: slightly undulating and the points labelled mount, valley, plateau, were very insignificant features.

Napoleon had not yet dictated to Soult the order of battle, although, over a stretch of three leagues in the morning gloom under driving rain, the drummers of the French army were sounded reveille. Few of the troops had really slept; they got up, stretched their aching joints in their soaked clothes, stirred up their miserable fires, cooked their 'soup', which was, more often than not, whatever edibles they had left, something plundered, some bread, which belatedly the supply wagons were distributing here and there. Men wandered about, searching for any form of shelter, a barn, a shack, in order, with a staggering professional conscience, to be able to clean and prepare their weapons. They well knew that their lives might depend upon them. As the hours passed they looked hopefully at the sky, which was now a little less sombre and the rain a little lighter.

The rain ceased just after 8 a.m. and the sun came out. Some gunners who had surveyed the ground came to tell the Emperor that the artillery could manoeuvre. The ground dried out as the sun rose higher. Napoleon conferred with his lieutenants. He asked Reille his opinion of the British army: 'I think the British army is impregnable, thanks to their tenacity and calm and the superiority of their musketry. Before being able to attack with the bayonet, one can expect to receive 50 per cent casualties. But the British army is less agile, less supple, less manoeuvrable than ours. Although they may not be overcome by direct attack, it may be possible to beat them by manoeuvring.' 'I know', said the Emperor, 'that the English are difficult to beat when in position. Therefore, I will manoeuvre.'

He went out and took horse towards la Haye-Sainte to examine the enemy lines once more. He told the engineer General Haxo to go closer to try to see whether the British had built redoubts or entrenchments. No, they had not done so. Napoleon said that he intended to pierce the centre of the enemy army, to push it up the trunk road to Brussels and, on reaching the edge of the forest of Soignies, to cut the enemy retreat from left and right. He then returned to the hummock at the Rossomme farm from which he wished to watch the battle. This farm was on the road from Charleroi to Brussels, some 600 metres north of the Caillou farm and about three kilometres south of Mont Saint-Jean where the British army was now in position, and about 1,600 metres south of La Belle-Alliance farm, mentioned in every account of Waterloo, not only because of its name, both striking and easily remembered, but also because Napoleon was to stop there a little later. At Rossomme the Emperor dictated to Soult a letter to Grouchy: 'His Majesty wishes you to move towards Wavre in order to close us.' He then dictated the order of battle, expressing the intention which I have just mentioned. Two generals sitting on the ground, copied the orders and passed them to the ADCs for delivery to the army corps. Since 5 a.m. the previous day, the Emperor had slept for only three hours and was now tired. He lay down on his camp-bed. 'It is now ten o'clock,' he said to Jérôme Bonaparte. 'I shall sleep until eleven.'

The army was moving to its allotted positions; the Emperor awoke while the units were still marching. They were formed into eleven columns – four leading, then seven. The drums rolled as they passed the Emperor, colours were dipped, bands played 'Let us watch over the safety of the Empire'. The infantry were uniformed in blue and white, the Guard in blue greatcoats and bearskins (with their full dress in their haversacks for the parade in Brussels), the cavalry, sparkling in uniforms of various colours, the sun glinting on helmets and breastplates, the gunners wearing dark uniforms, their guns polished. It was staggering that the army could put on this spanking turn-out after spending such a night as the previous one. Napoleon was to write: 'The earth seemed proud to support so many brave men.' The good weather allowed the men to see the dark-red line of the British troops At the start of the battle Wellington had in place some 84,000 men. His force was as heterogeneous as the Grand Armée had been at the start: 24 brigades, of which 9 were British, 10 German, 5 Dutch or Belgian: 11 cavalry divisions, composed of 16 British regiments, 9 German and 6 Dutch. The French, numbered about 74,000, were commanded by the man whom most of his adversaries believed to be the greatest captain in history. All the auguries were good.

Except that, at that very moment, Grouchy was writing to Napoleon: 'By this evening, I shall be concentrated at Wavre and will thus be between Wellington who is, I assume, retreating before Your Majesty, and the Prussian army. I need further instructions as to what Your Majesty wishes me to do. The country between Wavre and the plain of the Chyse is difficult, cut up and marshy. I can easily reach Brussels before those who will be held up by the Chyse. Deign, Sire, to send me your orders. I can receive them before starting my movement tomorrow.' Tomorrow?

'A battle', Napoleon wrote, 'is a dramatic action which has a beginning, a middle and an end. The order of battle assumed by the two armies, the first movements made in order to make contact comprise the introduction, the counter-movements of the army attacked form the knot which compels new dispositions and leads to the crisis which produces the outcome or *dénouement*.'

On 18 June 1815, at 11.30 a.m., the Guard battery situated a short distance in front of the Emperor's observation post, fired three rounds. 'A battle is a dramatic action.' This one was, in fact, the last act of an immense Wagnerian drama played by the Grande Armée on the theatre of Europe.

The first action of the day, directed at the enemy right, was intended by Napoleon to distract Wellington's attention from his centre, the target of the main blow. On this side (the British right) was the château of Hougoumont, a fairly strong position, comprising a massive house surrounded by farm buildings, in front of which was a wood, part copse, part forest. Classically, the first action is a bombardment. Three British batteries responded. Half an hour's cannonade, and then the infantry. It was Reille's II Corps which had been ordered to occupy the approaches to Hougoumont; he had delegated the task to Jérôme Bonaparte. Forward! II Corp's divisions – Foy's, Jérôme's and Bachelu's – came down the valley (it was an easy slope) and began to attack from each direction at once, an impetuous frontal attack of precisely the wrong sort. The object was, not to take Hougoumont by assault, but to 'occupy the approaches'. Also, the position was occupied by strong detachments (British, Hanoverian, Dutch) dug into the complex, which formed a redoubt. The garden walls, two metres high, had been crenellated and pierced with loopholes. The British had even erected in the garden a scaffold from which they could fire down on the attackers. One General (Bauduin) was killed and the French made only very slow progress. Wellington, who was watching the battle through his glass, sent reinforcements. Hundreds of French corpses were already strewn on the approaches. Reille, who was also watching the action, lamented: 'I told the Prince to remain in the bottom behind the wood while maintaining a strong forward line of sharpshooters.' Had he, in fact, clearly explained this to Jérôme who, in any event, was the last person to whom to confide a diversion, a feint?

Jérôme was impetuous, and the feint was turning out to be more and more costly to the attackers. Jérôme had rounded-up the remains of the brigade of Bauduin, the dead general. They took the orchard, but then found themselves in the open under an ever-increasing fire. They also advanced to the west wall of the château. The assault would assume a character reminiscent of the Middle Ages. Leading was a lieutenant of the 1st Light, a colossus named Legros, known to the men as 'the Smasher'. From their windows, the British poured a heavy fire into the soldiers who were vainly trying to break down the gates to the courtyard. Legros threw away his sword, seized an axe from a sapper and beat on the door like a madman. The door splintered and Legros rushed in, followed by some ten men who were immediately bayoneted in the courtyard. Legros defended himself with wild swings of his axe – he was the Iron Man! He advanced as far as the chapel in the middle of the courtyard, back to the wall, bleeding from twenty wounds, his bloody axe still in his hand. He was finally felled by a volley. Outside, the survivors of the French battalions took refuge in the woods. The feint had been costly. Fighting flared up again and continued, causing heavy losses to both attackers and defenders.

Ney had been tasked to lead the first serious attack: to drive in the enemy centre. As the fighting around Hougoumont continued, he had sent one of his

ADCs to tell the Emperor that all was ready and that he was awaiting the signal to take his troops forward. His artillery was already firing.

Shortly afterwards, Napoleon, who continued to survey the battle through his glass, spotted far away on the horizon to the north-east 'a cloud which seemed like troops'. To Soult, who was nearby: 'Marshal, what do you see beyond St-Lambert?' 'Sire, I believe I can see five or six thousand men. It is probably part of Grouchy's advance guard.'

Every spy-glass of the staff was pointed in that direction. The Emperor sent for General Domon who commanded a light cavalry division: 'I want to be sure of what we can see. Proceed in that direction with your division, contact promptly the troops who are arriving. Join up with them if they are those of Marshal Grouchy, or hold them if they are enemy.' Napoleon did not have to wait. A Prussian Black Hussar was brought before him. The man had been taken prisoner by a flying column of 300 chasseurs. He was carrying a letter from Blücher to Wellington: 'I am coming by St-Lambert with IV corps.' It was not Grouchy's advance guard, but Blücher's. Napoleon seemed unconcerned. He said that Grouchy was surely on the heels of the Prussians, who would shortly be caught between two fires. At 1 p.m. he sent an officer to find Grouchy, inform him of the situation and invite him to speed his march.

At 1.30 he gave the order which Ney was awaiting. The army corps tasked to drive in the enemy centre was Drouet d'Erlon's, the one which, two days earlier, had shuttled between Quatre Bras and Ligny: four divisions of two brigades each, totalling 21,000 men. Napoleon wished to begin by seizing the farm of la Haye-Sainte, situated approximately in the centre of the enemy position, on the Brussels road on the slope of the plateau.

Ney had had placed at his disposal the four divisions of d'Erlon's corps in four columns in echelon. The left column was to lead and to be the first to attack la Haye-Sainte. This column consisted of one brigade only, led by Ney.

Echelons, or divisions, were normally spaced out with 400 paces between each. But no one seems to have understood why Drouet d'Erlon had chosen that each division should form a bloc more compact than anything seen under the *ancien régime*. The battalions were spaced five paces behind the next, so that the mounted officers could scarcely take their posts there. Each division was formed in a rectangle 200 metres wide by 60 deep. One cannon-ball could kill a file of 24 men, and only the leading battalions could fire. Visually, the effect was terrifying. The four living masses advanced like coloured monsters, irresistibly, crushing the rye underfoot. The bayonets formed a steel carapace above them. The British gunners on the plateau fired at will. The brigade commanded by Ney advanced on la Haye-Sainte. Up and down the ranks were cries of 'Vive l'Empereur!' They crossed the shallow valley which separated the two armies.

The French guns then stopped firing for fear of hitting their own men who were now climbing the opposite slope.

The big farm of la Haye-Sainte formed a very extended rectangle. First, there was an orchard, 250 metres long, surrounded by hedges, then came buildings around a huge courtyard. The second light battalion of the King's German Legion, commanded by the British Major Baring, defended la Haye-Sainte. Baring had had the walls crenellated, and stationed three companies in the orchard, two in the buildings and one in the kitchen-garden behind.

Since this was no feint, as at Hougoumont, but an all-out assault, the first step should have been to demolish la Haye-Sainte by artillery fire, opening a breach in the south face of the farm. The two guns accompanying the infantry should have sufficed. This elementary idea never occurred to d'Erlon nor to Ney, seasoned warriors of more than twenty years' campaigning.

Naturally, as soon as they closed, the brave soldiers of the leading brigade were mowed down by volleys from the defenders. Those following, climbing over the dead and wounded, charged and were shot down in their turn and so on ten times. A battalion of the 55th which circled the farm to the west and tried to break in by the kitchen-garden, were likewise cut down.

During this time, on the right d'Erlon had crossed the gentle slope of the plateau with his three and a half divisions. It was now extremely hot. The soldiers marched slowly under enemy fire in the rich, soaking farmland and through the rye. They reached the edge of the plateau known as Mont Saint-Jean. Around the Emperor were looks of satisfaction. 'Our cavalry will enlarge the breaches which the infantry have made in the British defences.'

These seniors were not looking closely enough at the situation. In fact, d'Erlon's corps had lost a lot of men and those who were now on the plateau were exhausted by the climb and by breasting the hedges under enemy fire. This was the moment which the British General Picton chose to launch his counter-attack. His infantry were well hidden, crouching in the crops. They jumped up and delivered a volley. The leading French brigade received the blast full in the face and recoiled. The French soldiers heard orders shouted in English and saw the enemy infantry charging them with the bayonet. Hand-to-hand fighting followed. A French officer who attempted to seize the British colours was killed; Picton received a ball in the head.

A second mêlée followed when a Scottish brigade charged in turn, well deployed. The soldiers fired at 20 metres and the French replied, though feebly, hampered by their close order. Lord Uxbridge, who had commanded the rearguard on the retreat from Quatre Bras, was now in command of the British cavalry. The units which he ordered to charge were the flower of this arm: the Blues, the King's Dragoon Guards, the 1st and 2nd Life Guards; the Royal Dragoons, Scots Greys and 6th Inniskilling Dragoons. They were very tall men mounted on enormous horses from Ireland. Their charges passed through the French infantry and swept aside the French cuirassiers who came in support. Lord Somerset reported that the Life Guards beat on the cuirassiers 'like tinkers at work'.

Drouet d'Erlon's corps had already lost a third of its effectives when Wellington launched the Scots Greys into the battle. These were also colossal men on heavy horses. Their charges were not rapid but devastating. Normally, the French infantry would have been formed into squares, but here they could not do so, being hampered by their over-close order and also because the soldiers were exhausted. The Scots cut swathes through their ranks with their sabres. The French gunners did not dare fire for fear of killing their comrades and watched the massacre helplessly.

Lord Uxbridge, anxious that his cavalry should not venture too far, sounded the retreat, but carried away by their success, they held on until a charge by the cuirassiers of Milhaud's brigade persuaded them to turn about. Then followed a lull in the battle. The French drive had failed but Napoleon was not dissatisfied in view of 'the disorder which reigned in the British army'. On the left at Hougoumont, the French had managed to retake the orchard. The enemy were seen running towards the Brussels road.

Let us not forget: on the evening of 17 June, Napoleon had dictated to Soult an order telling Grouchy that a major battle would take place on the next day, that he should manoeuvre according to the movements of Blücher's army and that, at all costs, he must march to join with the French right. A little later, the Emperor had questioned his chief of staff: 'How many officers did you send with that order?' 'I sent one, Sire.' 'Ah, Sir, Berthier would have sent a hundred.' It seems evident that Grouchy never received the order. During the night of the 17th/18th, reports from the cavalry having led him to believe that the Prussians might have halted at Wavre, he had decided to march in that direction and we know that he had told the Emperor, adding that he wanted further orders.

On the morning of the 18th Grouchy was at Walhain, 20 kilometres from Wavre and 50 kilometres from Brussels and 20 kilometres from Mont Saint-Jean as the crow flies. At 10.30 a.m. he stopped at the house of a notary, dining in the summer-house as it was raining. He considered the table with satisfaction, then sat down with Generals, Gérard and Vandamme, and other officers. When dinner was nearly over and they were eating strawberries, the sound of gunfire was heard in the west. Some officers put their ears to the ground, Red Indian fashion. The rain stopped and the sound of gunfire became more distinct. A peasant guide was questioned and gave his opinion that the battle was at Mont Saint-Jean.

'I think', said Gérard, 'that we should march to the guns.' The notary was called and told them where Mont Saint-Jean was. Gérard repeated that they should march to the guns. Grouchy was irritated. 'The Emperor told me last night that he intended to attack the British army if Wellington accepted battle. I am therefore in no way surprised at the engagement which is now taking place. If the Emperor had wished me to take part, he would not have sent me away at the very moment he was moving on the British. Besides, in taking bad roads cross country, flooded by yesterday's rain, I would not arrive in time on the battlefield. My duty is to carry out the Emperor's orders which require me to pursue the Prussians. To follow your advice would be to disregard his orders.' Grouchy continued to pursue Blücher's army and engaged a part of it, with both merit and success and, after a skilful retreat, would lead back to France the greater part of the troops confided to him by Napoleon. If, rather than doing that, he had marched to the guns and joined the Emperor, would Waterloo have finished with a French victory? Only God knows. History has judged Grouchy harshly for his absence. As our purpose is to follow the Grande Armée, we can but bid him adieu.

The episode which follows has always been called 'Ney's charges'. Many painters of battles have depicted it. We see in a terrifying and grandiose movement, concentrated masses of horses, coloured uniforms, glittering breastplates and helmets, the brandishing of flashing sabres. Generally, the horses in these compositions, always at full gallop, seem to be flying; whereas they were usually trotting in the mud, but it is true that courage was not lacking. How much courage was wasted on that day!

Drouet d'Erlon's offensive having failed, Napoleon had profited from the lull to prepare another attack on the enemy centre. He had quartered the battlefield on horseback, indifferent to the bullets, and then returned to La Belle-Alliance. To his way of thinking, a major attack could be conducted only by using proven tactics: pin down the enemy by a strong bombardment, then launch an infantry assault and finally, use the heavy cavalry.

Now at 3.30 p.m. 'the Duke of Wellington suddenly saw through the smoke a great movement of cavalry'. He and his staff were astonished. Why was Napoleon launching cavalry against infantry which was not softened up and which, protected by the folds in the ground, had suffered little from bombardment?

It had all started, according to Louis Madelin, 'without precise orders, without plan, without direction'. Without precise orders? At some moment, Napoleon had told Ney, doubtless after the former's return to La Belle-Alliance, that he was placing Milhaud's 4th Cavalry Division, eight regiments of cuirassiers, under his command. When did he tell him to charge with it? Never. It was Ney who suddenly decided, placed himself at the head of this body of cavalry, and Forward! Passing close to general Lefebvre-Desnouettes, commander of the light cavalry of the Guard, he shouted: 'I am attacking! Support me!' Lefeb-vre-Desnouettes, thinking that the movement had been ordered by the Emper-or, followed him. Sabres were drawn, horses trotted, nearly 4,000 cavalrymen followed the huge hat with the white plumes beneath which rode the man whom the soldiers always called 'Ginger'. First, down the slope towards la Haye-Sainte. The cuirassiers leading, on their heavy horses, then the chasseurs, bus-bies with red bags, green jackets with yellow braiding, scarlet pelisses, curved sabres. Behind them, 1,000 Lancers of the Guard in tall chapskas decorated with brass, red-and-white pennons on their lances.

At the foot of the slope, a stop to regroup into attack formation. The British artillery was seen to be posted in front of the infantry. No matter, for-ward! The gunners waited until the leaders were within one hundred paces before firing. The guns were double loaded with ball and canister. The volley only checked the *furia francese* for an instant. 'Vive l'Empereur! Charge!' a fair-ly slow trot. The guns were taken and overrun, now for the squares!

There were fourteen squares, some three-quarters of which were manned by red-coats. Each square consisted of 1,000 men in four ranks, front rank kneeling, musket butts in the turf, the barrel sloping forward. The next two ranks fired volleys. Horses reared up before the lines of bayonets, hooves beat-ing the air, bellies exposed, falling on the implanted bayonets. The struggle was unequal, since the horses were already tired from marching and fighting and now had to climb the muddy, slippery slope. On reaching the summit, they were blown, and there was not enough space for them to regain momentum. After a moment, heaps of eviscerated horses piled up in front of the squares; addition-al protection for the defenders.

Wellington's talent was mmainly defensive, but talent he had. He also launched cavalry. Coming from his right, they passed through the intervals between the British squares and attacked the French cavalry in flank. The cuirassiers gave way, turned tail and abandoned the plateau, fired on by the British gunners who had regained their pieces.

Ney was everywhere, powder-blackened, two bullets through his hat, uni-form torn, shouting. Two horses had already been shot from under him. He sig-nalled to Lefebvre-Desnouettes to close, to throw his squadrons forward, Ney himself leading the new charge, a second and a third, until count was lost. A cuirassier officer of Milhaud's division has told how, in course of these repeated charges, the adversaries grew to know one another, recognised and hurled insults, man to man.

'The enemy centre is broken,' cried the jubilant officers surrounding Napoleon at La Belle-Alliance. He saw the situation differently: 'That was a pre-mature move which may have fatal consequences for the day.' Speaking of Ney, he said to Jérôme: 'The wretch! This is the second time in two days that he has compromised the fortunes of France!' Then, pensive for a moment, he added: 'It is an hour too early. However, we must support what has been done.' And he sent an ADC to Kellermann on the left, telling him to support the cavalry which was struggling for mastery of the plateau.

It was not an hour too early – it was 4.30 and too late. Blücher's advance guard was by now debouching less than three kilometres to the east of La Belle-Alliance. 'A battle is an act of drama.' Yes, and control of the action was slipping away from Napoleon. Soon, all he would be able to do would be to submit.

Blücher had used his artillery against Domon's cavalry, which was barring his advance, to let Wellington know that he was approaching with 30,000 troops. His men were tired from interminable marches, but who on this field was not tired from having fought since morning in the stormy heat? The heavy atmosphere seemed to be crushing everything. Leading his army, Blücher marched the heavy Silesian regiments in blue greatcoats, preceded by fifes and drums. Soon the music would stop and the guns and muskets would be heard and men would begin to fall. Napoleon had sent General Mouton with his VI Corps to stop the arriving army. Initially, his men managed to hold the Prussians, the Silesians losing cohesion. But behind them came an army and one corps cannot hold back an army whose soldiers have a superiority of three to one. Blücher's army continued to gain ground, inexorably. A deadly threat, they drove towards Plancenoit, just to the right and *behind* La Belle-Alliance.

Let us raise ourselves in imagination above the battlefield. Blücher's approach to Plancenoit was crab-like, with one claw pushing his prey, Napoleon's army, towards the crab's mouth, towards this impregnable British defence which finally devoured all that was thrown to it.

Napoleon had ordered Kellermann to support Ney's cavalry in their charges on the British squares and now dragoons and carabiniers charged with the cuirassiers, the former in green with scarlet revers, the latter in white with gilded breastplates. The cavalry shouted 'Vive l'Empereur!' as they plunged into the mêlée. Into this nightmare. Yes, one had the impression of one of those nightmares that repeats over and over. One saw happenings unimaginable earlier. Two thousand horses charging on so narrow a front, so crowded that some horses were lifted from the ground! Some British squares sustained thirteen successive charges without flinching.

Ney had lost his hat and had had a fourth mount killed. He had shouted to Drouet d'Erlon, 'Hold on, my friend, for you and I will not be killed by British bullets, but by those of the *émigrés*.' At least a third of the French cavalry had been felled. Behind and to the right, Blücher was still advancing; the crab claw reached the village of Plancenoit and squeezed it.

And suddenly, on the other wing, facing the plateau, that vital space where the cavalry was being worn down, there was heard from the direction of

Hougoumont the sound of military bands. They were playing 'Let us watch over the safety of the Empire' as they advanced, followed by a massed column of six infantry regiments. The charges having failed, Ney had looked for help – too late– from his infantry. The objective was, as before, the farm of la Haye-Sainte. Once more, trying to climb the gentle but fatal slope, men marching bent without cover or support. 'A hail of death,' was how General Foy described the volleys which greeted them. Bodies piled up on the ground, trampled a hundred times already, but still the adversaries clashed. And this time the door to the farm was breached and the position was taken. Ney – finally with a flash of common sense – brought up a battery which fired at point-blank range (less than 300 yards) at the British squares.

Did the fortunes of battle see-saw? For a moment, the British feared that they might. An ADC to General Alten wrote: 'The centre of our line was open. We were in danger. At no time was the issue of the battle more doubtful.' To officers who came for orders, Wellington replied: 'There is only one thing to do, to hold on to the last man.' The British were mistaken in their fears. They had played throughout on the defensive, like those rugby teams which refuse to play an open game and whose opponents are more worn down than they are, and whose measure they now have. Ney, still hoping to be able to strike a decisive blow, sent a colonel to the Emperor to ask for infantry. 'Infantry! Where can I find infantry? Do you wish me to make them? Look at what I have on my hands and what I have left.'

'The Guard, supreme concept, supreme hope.' There was the Old Guard and the Young Guard. The infantry of the Old Guard: 3,800 grenadiers and 4,600 chasseurs. Infantry of the Young Guard: 4,200 men. Cavalry 4,000 sabres: artillery 3,000 men. Total 19,600 men and 118 guns. An enormous reserve.

Throughout the years, the strength of the Guard had constantly grown. We saw the birth of the Young Guard in Spain. It seems that year by year it approached its elder unit in military valour and very often they were not differentiated when in action. Furthermore, the proportion of truly veteran soldiers in the Old Guard at this time is unknown. A detail: the 3rd and 4th Grenadier Chasseurs were often called the Middle Guard. The figures quoted here were taken from the situation reports of the Guard for 16 June.

At the moment when Napoleon decided to commit the Guard, the most pressing threat came from Blücher's army – the crab's claw – which was squeezing Plancenoit. The Emperor ordered the Young Guard to march on this village in the theatrical fashion proper to an élite corps. Twelve drummers beat the charge, the bearskins advanced without firing, muskets slung. Around Plancenoit, 2,000 Prussians awaited them, dug in behind banks and hedges, Firing broke out.

Plancenoit would be taken by the Young Guard and held for a deadly half-hour. Blücher's artillery plastered the village with shot at the risk of killing the Prussians who were still there, then six fresh enemy battalions were launched in assault. The fighting was as furious as any that we saw at Ligny. The Prussians finally prevailed. Napoleon thought the situation so critical that he sent for General Morand: 'You will advance on Plancenoit with four battalions of the Old Guard and sixteen guns. But first I wish to speak to these men.' 'He addressed the soldiers in their ranks: 'My friends. We are now at the supreme moment. It is not necessary to fire, you must attack the enemy hand-to-hand and, at the bayonet's point, throw them back into the ravine whence they came to threaten the army, the Empire and France.'

At 7.15 p.m. the Emperor learned that the Young Guard had retaken Plancenoit. But the 'supreme moment' was to come during the last act of this tragedy. Napoleon would lead the remnant of the Guard in person, six thousand soldiers. He had placed five battalions under Ney's command; d'Erlon and Reille had been ordered to act in support of the Guard with the survivors of their corps, and the commanders of the cavalry were ordered to charge at every favourable opportunity with their survivors.

'Bring forward the last reserve battery!' The artillery officers, looking at their almost empty caissons, said to one another: 'Let us hope they make a quick end of it.' To sustain morale, Napoleon had ordered La Bedoyère to gallop across the field, shouting that Grouchy had arrived. The drummers beat the charge, the Guard deployed in front of Napoleon, who pointed to the spot where they should attack. The soldiers, full of enthusiasm, cried 'Vive l'Empereur! one last time.

Once again, the climb up the slope of Mont Saint-Jean but this time, it is the Guard who lead. The British guns boomed, the shots cut swathes through the battalions, but the bearskins still moved forward. The first regiments reached the plateau. In front was a void. The centre of the British line was a concave arc. Forward!

And, suddenly, from out of the earth rose a line of red-coats followed by a wall of fire. Once more, two thousand guardsmen of Maitland and Adam's brigades, crouching in the crops, had stood up. Five minutes later, half the first wave of attackers had fallen.

Momentum was lost. The survivors, deploying to return the British fire, masked the guns which were to support them. For five, maybe ten, interminable minutes the chasseurs of the Guard were exposed to a hail of fire from the British artillery. Ney was brought down, his fifth horse having been killed beneath him. Wellington saw, wonderful sight, Napoleon's Guard in difficulty! No more a question of to the last man, but of throwing the last possible man into the pursuit: 'Forward, lads, this is the moment!' The red-coats surged forward. For a moment, the battalion of the 4th Chasseurs of the Guard succeeded in holding the flood of enemy troops, but the British were too many, too determined, feeling that the scales were tipping in their favour.

Reille had just started to move his troops of I Corps to open an attack on the British right. These men suddenly saw before them, coming down the valley which they were preparing to climb, a mass of bearskins. 'The Guard are retreating! The Guard are retreating!' Napoleon himself has left a dramatic account of the sequel. 'The broken troops passed the ravine, the nearby regiments who saw some units of the Guard break ranks, believed that they were from the Old Guard and joined the rout. Cries of "All is lost! The Guard is defeated!" were heard. The soldiers even claimed that in many places, ill-disposed agents shouted "Every man for himself!" However that may be, panic spread rapidly over the whole field of battle, men rushed in complete disorder on to the lines of communication, soldiers, gunners, caisson drivers scrambled to reach them; the Old Guard which was in reserve was swept up and itself carried away.' The sun was setting – the sun of Austerlitz.

Wellington arrived on horseback at the edge of the plateau. He stood in his stirrups, and waved his hat in the air. As one man, the British regiments, the squadrons, the battalions, the batteries bounded in pursuit of the routed French army.

I crave your indulgence here to say farewell to a man whose courage and humanity we have admired on so many occasions: the surgeon Larrey. During the campaign in Belgium, at Ligny, at Waterloo, he practised his art. At Waterloo, his ambulance was posted close to La Belle-Alliance, but he frequently left it in order to operate in the field, and he was even seen assisting the stretcher-bearers to move the wounded who were under fire. Wellington, who, like Napoleon, constantly used his spy-glass, had noticed the surgeon's comings and goings and had questioned his ADCs: 'Have you seen this audacious fellow? Who is he?' 'It is Larrey, your Grace.' Larrey's reputation had passed frontiers. 'Go and tell them not to fire in that direction,' ordered Wellington. And he raised his hat. 'Who are you saluting?' he was asked. 'I salute honour and loyalty which are passing by.'

On that day, Larrey continued to follow his profession, and it was Napoleon, when all was lost, who gave him the peremptory order to leave and to cross the frontier with his ambulance to avoid capture. But nothing lasts for ever. Run down by Prussian lancers, sustaining two sabre cuts which made him lose consciousness, Larrey was finally captured by other Prussians who, seeing his grey coat, took him for the Emperor. They brought him to their divisional general, an idiot who, not appreciating the enormity of his offence had the prisoner been Napoleon, had Larrey stood against a wall to be shot. Providentially, the surgeon-major who was detailed to bandage his eyes had been a pupil at Larrey's courses in surgery at Berlin. Recognised, taken first to Bülow then to Blücher, whose son had been cared for by Larrey when wounded and a prisoner, Larrey was treated on his merits and was set free at Louvain. Wellington's salute to Larrey and the rescue *in extremis* of this good-hearted man cast a ray of sunshine on this so sombre day.

Napoleon had ordered the remnant of the Old Guard to form square – three squares of 500 men apiece. On their retreat, the grumblers had repelled the charges of the British cavalry. Their intact squares were overtaken by the flood of enemy troops which flowed past them, sabring the fugitives. Many cried 'Where is the Emperor?' as if seeking a father, and others replied that he was dead. Night added to the disorder. Plancenoit, where generations of worthy villagers had laboriously raised their families, was burned out; under their collapsed roofs were a thousand charred bodies of French soldiers.

In the middle of the disaster, the square of the 2nd Battalion of the 1st Chasseurs, commanded by Cambronne, climbed the slope of La Belle-Alliance surrounded by the enemy. The British officers shouted to them to surrender and it was then that Cambronne had snapped his furious '*Merde*', bowdlerised as we know, for the sake of school-children and the drawing-room set. In truth, soldiers' language, even that of senior officers and often of the Emperor himself when he was with the army, could scarcely be described as polished. Likewise, the language exchanged in the field during the charge and hand-to-hand fighting consisted generally of insults of the grossest kind. Cambronne was struck by a bullet to the forehead, was left for dead and was stripped of his uniform by the plunderers of corpses. He managed to survive, as I have recounted, and married an English woman.

Napoleon reached a spot between Plancenoit and the Rossomme farm where he found the square of the 1st Battalion of the 1st Regiment of Grenadiers of the Guard, the supreme élite. The ranks opened for him and he mounted a horse in the square's centre, a living fortress. Behind him, also mounted, were three or four staff officers wearing large hats, and General Petit, wearing a bearskin like his grenadiers. The latter were standing, calm, their long muskets grounded or sloped, some being reloaded in the twelve steps prescribed by the manual. The square was like an immobile island in the flood of the rout. Night was falling. Shortly, Napoleon would order General Petit to retreat southwards towards Genappe. The last square had marched off into the night led by the band, yes, one hundred and fifty musicians – while the tide of fear and fury flowed past them.

The moon, sometimes obscured by heavy clouds, lit the battlefield where the British soldiers, 'dead tired' according to Wellington, had gone into bivouac, while the Prussians continued to pursue and cut down the routed French. The redcoats lit their fires in the midst of the dead and the groans of the wounded.

Wellington's army had lost in killed and wounded 13,000 men, including two generals killed. In the Grande Armée, three generals had been killed, another, taken prisoner, would die next day; sixteen generals had been wounded. The numbers of killed and wounded has varied: 23,600 men including 7,000 prisoners, according to Napoleon; 18,500 killed or wounded and 7,000 prisoners according to Gourgaud.

Genappe, on the high road to Charleroi, was a small town on the Dyle. Over this river was a bridge and, as at Dresden and the Beresina, the fugitives fought savagely to cross it. The mantle of night gave the chaos an extra touch of madness. Troopers' sabres flashed, blood flowed, infantrymen fired at hazard into the crowds. At midnight on 18 June 1815, Napoleon was still at Genappe and was about to board his coach, when suddenly, there were shouts: 'The Prussians! The Prussians!' A body of enemy cavalry clattered down the main road, sweeping all before them, sabring the men backed against the walls. Napoleon got down from his carriage, mounted a horse and left at a brisk trot into the night with a small cavalry escort. Within a week, he would have abdicated for the second time. In four months' time he would be at St. Helena.

XVII

THE LAST BIVOUACS
1840

S t. Helena, 16 October 1840, at dusk. At the base of a narrow fault which opened in the mountain, on a dark river was a large launch, immobile on calm water. On land, the procession escorting Napoleon's coffin was wending its way through the settlement of Jamestown. Leading was a platoon of British infantry in full dress with arms reversed. The band played 'The dead march in Saul' with muffled drums.

Standing on the quay was the Prince of Joinville, youngest son of Louis-Philippe, accompanied by Generals Bertrand and Gourgaud, Las Cases and Count Philippe de Rohan-Chabot. The British General Middlemore delivered officially to the Prince de Joinville the body of the Emperor who had died nineteen years ago after six years' captivity on this sterile rock.

The coffin was loaded into the launch, which made for the frigate *Belle Poule* anchored in the roadstead. 'The moment was beautiful,' wrote the Prince. 'A magnificent sunset was followed by a profound calm. The notables and the British troops stood motionless, ranked on the beach while the ship's guns fired a royal salute. The seamen, crepe bands on the arms of their white uniforms, rowed in silence with admirable precision, moving slowly and majestically, escorted by the boats of the staffs. It was very moving and the whole scene evoked a high national sentiment.' Napoleon's last wish was being met: 'I wish that my ashes may repose on the banks of the Seine in the midst of the French people whom I have loved so much.'

History's vagaries are surprising. It was following the Revolution of July 1830 – a violent reaction against the *ordonnances* decreed by an absolute monarch – that the press had launched the idea of repatriating the body of one of the most absolute rulers that France had known, but the consequences of the great Revolution and of Waterloo had not effaced the memory of the victories. During the next year, thousands of Parisians filed past a work of Daguerre representing the tomb of the Emperor on St. Helena, an iron grille, a stone slab without name. The death of the King of Rome in 1832 revived both the memory and the emotion. Victor Hugo prophesied:

'Sleep, we shall come for you. The day will come, perhaps,
For you were our god, but not our master.'

It would be necessary to wait for eight years before the event occurred in an unforeseen way. Lord Palmerston, British Foreign Secretary, informed the French Prime Minister, Thiers, secretly: 'The Irish member O'Connell is to ask the London government to restore to France the body of Napoleon.' Thiers consulted the Duke of Orléans, the King's eldest son, who approved. Louis-Philippe, having hesitated awhile, acted as a monarch genuinely anxious to foster national unity and approved the return of the body.

After Waterloo, as after the campaign in France, we had seen the survivors of the Grande Armée crossing France in small stages, staff in hand, going home. This time, they were less ragged and emaciated because the ordeal had been shorter.

But to find a job, or simply their daily bread, had not been easy. Many of those demobilised had been young and had no trade. They had been told that they would receive their arrears of pay, but it didn't arrive, any more than that owed to the officers placed on half-pay, who, this time, knew that it would be for a long, long while. In order to be recognised and to be able to recognise others, they had adopted a sort of uniform dress: a broad-brimmed hat, a blue frock-coat, long and pinched at the waist, broad trousers, tight at the ankles, a twisted cane with a big handle, moustache, red or violet carnation in the buttonhole and, of course, the red ribbon of the Legion d'Honneur which most had been awarded – the cross, so-called.

They had started to band together, telling of their campaigns in loud voices, in order to irritate the royalists. Should one of these contradict them, they would laugh at them or shrug their shoulders or, in the street, merely look at them impudently, which provoked insults and fights. The police kept a close eye on the half-pays, more so than during the first Restoration. They were classed as revolutionaries, Jacobins, plotters. The Count of Bourdonnais, deputy for Maine-et-Loire, had spoken thus to his fellow commissioners: 'To stop these criminal plots, we must use irons, hangmen, torture.'

Ney, La Bedoyère and four other officers of general's rank had been shot. Marshal Brune was murdered and his body thrown into the Rhine. At Marseilles, thirteen ex-Mamelukes of the Guard were also murdered. Offences classed as 'seditious demonstrations' were tried by summary courts from whose verdicts there was no appeal. History records that Louis XVIII ended what had been called the second White Terror by dissolving the 'invisible Chamber' on 5 September 1816.

Napoleonic fervour had grown irresistibly, fuelled at the start by the reminiscences of the survivors of the Grande Armée, and nothing remains to be said of Napoleon, inspired propagandist of his own glory. The *Memorial*, published in 1823, had already inflamed many minds when, on 7 July 1840, in the presence of the Prince of Joinville, the Bishop of Fréjus had blessed the *Belle Poule* which was about to sail for St. Helena.

The return voyage took 41 days; on their arrival, Cherbourg was bedecked with flags. The locals were allowed to file past the imperial coffin displayed on the frigate's deck. The crowds came during four days of glacial weather; the deck was piled with flowers and wreaths of *immortelles*.

On 4 December, the coffin was transferred to a steamer which, accompanied by a flotilla of river boats, was to carry it up the Seine. A catafalque had been constructed in such appallingly bad taste that the Prince had it destroyed. 'I ordered the boat painted black overall and demolished all in the bows to allow the coffin to be placed there alone, in full view, covered with a mortuary blanket of purple velvet.'

At Rouen, the coffin had to be transhipped to a smaller craft. The funeral flotilla slowly steamed through the river's bends. On the banks were delegations from towns and villages, headed by the mayor in his tricolour sash, the men waving their hats, the priests blessing. On the afternoon of 14 December, the flotilla anchored for the night below Courbevoie, near the Neuilly bridge. Soult, ex-Marshal of the Empire, ex-minister of Louis XVIII, ex-chief of staff at Waterloo, now President of Louis-Philippe's new ministry, came to greet the princes. Then he knelt in tears before the coffin. Why not? Despite a cold which grew increasingly bitter, a large crowd had gathered on the river's banks. In the dusk, a movement could be discerned, the crowd, which was beginning to drift away, made room for groups of shadows, no, they were groups of men and they were formed into units. They had arranged several rendezvous when still distant and they now marched silently. Some walked with the help of a cane. We can recognise them, despite the dusk. This is not fiction. These survivors had donned their old uniforms, there were grenadiers of the line, nearly all white haired, foot dragoons in their tall black gaiters, chasseurs in flared shakos, guards of honour from the campaign in France. Only officers of the rank of colonel were permitted to go aboard, but these veterans did not presume to ask for permission. To mount guard around his boat, as some had mounted guard around his tent, that was all that they wanted, and, on the frozen grass, they once again followed the same procedure. They had brought wood with them and the bivouac fires blazed; four hundred survivors would sleep around the fires, rolled in their old cloaks, in the December night with the thermometer at -8° C. Some of them would not wake up. Others would die of the cold in Paris and the surroundings, both that night and the next.

At 9 a.m. on 15 December, the carriage which was to carry the coffin to the Invalides was on the quay at Courbevoie. With the aid of papier-maché, plaster and painted canvas, the quay had been transformed into a sort of Greek temple. The carriage measured 17 metres by five, ten metres high, weighing five tons. It was covered in flags, eagles, fantasies, garlands and victory wreaths. The decorations along the route were no more tasteful, but no matter, the aura of the event eclipsed other considerations.

A twenty-one gun salute. As the procession was about to move off, the strains of the Marseillaise, a seditious song, were heard from three thousand students from the Latin Quarter. No space had been allotted them in the procession, nor for the grumblers who had kept vigil in the freezing night. But, at the last moment, they were both admitted and marched behind the carriage, immediately behind the notables, As they passed, the crowds applauded and even, carried away, cried 'Vive l'Empereur!' as in years past. So many years of war, so many sons taken and never again seen, or returned crippled; the misery, the suffering of invasion, Cossacks fouling the soil of France; all that was forgotten. What remains is the legend created by one man and cherished by his people. As legends are by all peoples.

The magic continues. Each time I walk from my nearby street, I pass down one side of the Invalides and see files of visitors walking towards his tomb, a line constantly renewed, like the thousands of regiments which we have seen over-running Europe. My thoughts go back to those old veterans which a man to whom I had spoken had seen with his own eyes. The Grande Armée was yesterday.

APPENDIXES

1. CHRONOLOGY

1803

16 May	Rupture of the Peace of Amiens.
23 June	The first Consul leaves Paris for an inspection trip in northern France and Belgium.
28 June	The First Consul at Boulogne
1 July	At Calais.
12 July	Draws up an overall plan for the invasion of England.
11 August	Returns to Saint-Cloud.
3–18 September	At Boulogne.
30 November	The First Consul at Etaples.
2 December	Formation of the Army of the Ocean Coasts.
October–December	Discovery of the Cadoudal–Pichegru conspiracy.

1804

1–6 January	The First Consul at the Boulogne camp.
15 February	Arrest of Moreau.
28 February	Arrest of Pichegru.
9 March	Arrest of Cadoudal.
15 March	Abduction of the Duke of Enghien from Ettenheim.
20–21 March	Execution of the Duke of Enghien.
21 March	Publication of the Civil Code.
18 May	Napoleon proclaimed Emperor.
19 May	Creation of eighteen Marshals of the Empire.
15 July	Oath-taking by members of the Order of the Legion of Honour at the Invalides.
16 August	Distribution of Eagles at Boulogne.
2 December	Coronation.

1805

17 March	Napoleon proclaimed King of Italy.
9 August	Formation of the Third Coalition.
27 August	Camp of Boulogne struck.
25 September	Grande Armée crosses the Rhine.
14 October	Victory of Elchingen.
19 October	Mack surrenders at Ulm.
21 October	Naval defeat at Trafalgar.
13 November	French enter Vienna.
2 December	Victory at Austerlitz.
26 December	Peace of Pressburg.

1806

12 July	Formation of the Confederation of the Rhine.
9 October	Creation of the Fourth Coalition.
14 October	Victories of Jena and Auerstadt.
27 October	Grande Armée enters Berlin.
21 November	Continental blockade established.
27 November	Napoleon arrives at Posen.
19 December	Enters Warsaw.

1807

1 January	Napoleon meets Marie Walewska at the inn at Bronie.
7–8 February	Battle of Eylau.
March	Napoleon stays at Osterode.
April–May	Napoleon stays at Finkenstein.
26 May	Danzig falls.
14 June	Victory of Friedland.
7 July	Treaty of Tilsit.
30 November	Junot enters Lisbon.
November	French enter Spain.

1808

20 February	Murat promoted Lieutenant-General in Spain.
18 March	Uprising at Aranjuez.
24 March	French army enters Madrid.
14 April	Napoleon reaches Bayonne.
20 April	Ferdinand VII arrives at Bayonne.
30 April	Meeting at Bayonne.
2 May	Uprising in Madrid.

5 May	Ferdinand VII abdicates.
10 May	Joseph named King of Spain.
14 July	Bessières' victory at Medina del Rio Seco.
22 July	Surrender at Baylen.
1 August	Wellesley (later Wellington) lands in Portugal.
2 August	Joseph flees from Madrid.
13 August	Spanish recapture Madrid.
30 August	Convention of Cintra.
September	Talks at Erfurt. Talleyrand's treason.
30 October	Napoleon enters Spain.
4–20 November	Napoleon at Burgos.
30 November	Battle of Somosierra.
4 December	Madrid surrenders.
22 December	Crossing of the Guadarrama.

1809

19 January	Battle of Corunna.
22 January	Saint Cyr's victory at Tarragona.
	Joseph returns to Madrid.
23 January	Napoleon returns to Paris.
21 February	Fall of Saragossa.
29 march	Soult takes Oporto.
April	Formation of the Fifth Coalition.
21 April	Victory of Landschut.
22 April	Victory of Eckmühl.
13 May	Vienna surrenders.
21 May	Battle of Essling.
31 May	Death of Marshal Lannes
5–6 July	Victory of Wagram.
26 October	Napoleon returns to Fontainebleau.
14 December	Napoleon divorces Josephine.

1810

1 February	Fall of Seville.
1 April	Civil marriage to Marie-Louise at Saint-Cloud.
2 April	Religious marriage in the Louvre.

1811

February	Tension between Napoleon and the Tsar.
11 March	Soult's victory at Badajoz.
20 March	Birth of the King of Rome.

16 May	Battle of Albuera.
28 June	Suchet's victory at Tarragona.
30 October	Suchet's victory at Sagunta.

1812

19 January	Wellington's victory at Ciudad Rodrigo.
6 April	Wellington takes Badajoz.
27 April	Audience with Prince Kourakine and the Tsar's ultimatum.
17–29 May	Interview at Dresden with the Austrian Emperor and the King of Prussia.
22 June	War declared on Russia.
24 June	Grande Armée crosses the Niemen.
26 June–16 July	Napoleon at Vilna.
11 August	British enter Madrid.
17 August	Battle of Smolensk.
7 September	Battle of the Moskowa.
14 September	Napoleon enters Moscow.
19 October	Grande Armée evacuates Moscow.
23 October	General Malet's conspiracy.
1 November	French re-enter Madrid.
28 November	Crossing of the Beresina.
5 December	Napoleon leaves Smorgonia.
19 December	Napoleon reaches Paris.

1813

17 January	Murat quits the army.
31 January	Russo–Austrian armistice.
2 February	Marie-Louise proclaimed regent.
28 February	Russo–Prussian alliance.
16 March	Prussia declares war.
15 April	Napoleon leaves for the campaign in Germany.
1 May	Death of Marshal Bessières.
2 May	Victory at Lützen.
20 May	Victory of Bautzen.
22 May	Death of Duroc.
4 May	Armistice of Pleiswitz.
5 July	Congress of Prague opens.
21 June	Wellington's victory at Vitoria.
10 August	Failure of the Congress of Prague.
15 August	Austria declares war.

26–27 August	Victory of Dresden.
8 October	Bavaria defects. Wellington invades southern France.
16–19 October	Defeat at Leipzig.
2–4 November	French retreat to the Rhine.
11 December	Treaty of Valençay. Napoleon abandons Spain to Ferdinand VII.
20–21 December	Austrians cross the Rhine at Schaffhausen.

1814

January	Murat's treason. Campaign in France opens.
27 January	Fight at Saint-Dizier.
29 January	Fight at Brienne.
1 February	Defeat at la Rothière.
10 February	Fight at Champaubert.
February–March	Congress of Châtillon.
11 February	Victory of Montmirail.
18–19 February	Skirmish at Montereau.
7 March	Battle of Craonne.
9 March	Battle of Laon.
13 March	Battle of Reims.
20–21 March	Battle of Arcis-sur-Aube.
30 March	Paris surrenders.
3 April	Senate dethrones Napoleon.
10 April	Soult defeated at Toulouse.
11 April	First abdication of Napoleon.
20 April	Farewells at Fontainebleau.
3 May	Louis XVIII enters Paris. Napoleon arrives at Elba.

1815

21 January	Remains of Louis XVI transferred to Saint-Denis.
26 February	Napoleon escapes from Elba.
1 March	Napoleon lands at Golfe-Juan.
4 March	Napoleon reaches Digne.
7 March	Triumphal entry into Grenoble.
10 March	Enthusiastic reception at Lyons.
17 March	Ney rejoins Napoleon at Auxerre.
19–20 March	Flight of Louis XVIII.
20 March	Napoleon reaches Paris.
25 March	Renewal of the Pact of Chaumont.
31 March	Seventh Coalition formed.

11 June	Napoleon leaves for the campaign in Belgium.
16 June	Battles of Ligny and Quatre Bras.
18 June	Defeat at Waterloo.
22 June	Second abdication of Napoleon.
8 July	Louis XVIII returns to Paris.
17 July	The White Terror. Massacres at Nîmes.
2 August	Assassination of Marshal Brune.
5 August	Arrest of Ney.
19 August	Execution of La Bedoyère.
13 October	Capture and execution of Murat at Pizzo.
15 October	Napoleon reaches St. Helena.
7 December	Execution of Marshal Ney.

1821

5 May	Napoleon dies at St. Helena.

1840

December	The return of Napoleon's remains to France.
15 December	Napoleon at the Invalides.

2. THE STRENGTHS OF THE NAPOLEONIC ARMIES

1805 The Boulogne Camp and the Austrian campaign The Grande Armée numbered 200,000 men.

1806–7 The campaign in Prussia and Poland November 1806, the army increased to 500,000 men by the early call-up of the 1807 class.

1808–9 The Peninsular campaign At the start of 1809, 300,000 men were in the peninsula and would continue to fight there until 1813.

1809 The Austrian campaign Formation of a new Grande Armée of 350,000 men, including 10,000 men of the Rhine Confederation. In Italy, an army of 100,000 men, including some 25,000 Italians.

1812 The Russian campaign The Grande Armée numbered 400,000 men (of whom 125,000 were French). Nearly 300,000 men were still in Spain, 130 battalions in the depots, and 120,000 men not yet enrolled. Total: 1 million men under arms.

1813 The German campaign 500,000 men, conscripts of 1813 and 1814. earlier classes recalled plus 100,000 in National Guard units incorporated in the army. 250,000 men still in Spain.

1814 The campaign in France 300,000 men dispersed about Europe, including 190,000 garrisoning forts. That left only 56,000 on the Rhine when the coalition forces broke in.
1815 The Belgian campaign 180,000 men under arms. From the end of March, about 300,000 men plus 200,000 national guards for fortress garrisons.
TOTAL from 1802 to 1815 1,600,000 Frenchmen served with the colours. Allied forces should be added to this total.

3. HOW MANY DIED?

So many soldiers of the Grande Armée disappeared without trace that the figures of those killed or mortally wounded on the battlefields of Europe must be accepted with fairly major reservations. It is generally agreed that the wars of the Revolution and the Empire cost France 850,000 dead and 550,000 missing. Below are the least inaccurate figures of the losses of the Grande Armée in the course of the principal battles.

Austerlitz, 2 December 1805. Forces engaged 71,000. Losses, killed and wounded, 7–8,000.
Eylau, 7–8 February 1807. Forces engaged, 54–75,000. Losses, 15,000 dead, 20,000 wounded.
Friedland, 14 June 1807. Forces engaged 80–120,000. Losses, 7,000. Russian losses, 25,000.
Essling, 21 May 1809. Forces engaged, 80,000 French. Losses, 18,000. Austrian losses, 27,000.
Wagram, 5–6 July 1809. Forces engaged, 150,000. French losses estimated, 17–50,000. Austrian losses about 23,000.
The Moskowa (The Beresina), 7 September 1812. Forces engaged, 120–130,000 French, 140–160,000 Russian. Losses, about 10,000 dead, 14,000 wounded. Russian losses, about 45,000.
Leipzig 16–19 October 1813. Forces engaged, about 185,000 French, 320,000 Coalition. French losses, 20,000 dead, 7,000 wounded, 23,000 prisoners. Coalition losses, 35,000 killed, 45,000 wounded, 1,500 prisoners.
Ligny 16 June 1815. Forces engaged, 124,000 engaged over two days.
Waterloo 18 June: 74,000 French (at the beginning of Waterloo), 84,000 under Wellington. 18 June losses, various estimates: 30–45,000 French killed or wounded, including Ligny. British and Prussian losses at Waterloo, about 22,000.

4. FOREIGNERS IN THE GRANDE ARMEE

At the Rhine crossing in September 1805, during the first campaign in Germany, the Grande Armée had some 30,000 foreigners in a total of 200,000 men. Later, the proportion grew considerably: in Spain, to about one-sixth, in Russia, more than a half, still more than a fifth by 1814. Few people know that the Grande Armée included 190 foreign general officers, whose numbers breakdown as follows: Germany, no details, 21, Palatinate 7; Prussia 2; Baden 1; Bavaria 1; Hesse-Cassel 1; Saxony 1; Württemberg 1; Switzerland 29; Poland 26; Holland 25; Belgium 19; Italy, no details 4; Genoa 1; Naples 1; Piedmont 11; Papal States 2; Ireland 13; Portugal 6; Austria 5; Britain 3; Courland 3; USA 2; Denmark 1; Spain 2; Greece 1; Venezuela 1. The Greek was named Loverdo, the Venezuelan, Miranda. Many other foreign officers served in the Grande Armée but did not attain general's rank. These figures illustrate its cosmopolitan composition, although at the end it was almost wholly composed of Frenchmen and, thus, became a national army once more.

5. RATES OF PAY

The table below shows the official pay scales of general officers of the Grande Armée. In practice, these senior officers received much more. The Emperor made enormous gifts of châteaux, estates and cash. More than 16 million francs were given to 824 generals. This does not take account of the 'spoils of war' at a time when the Grande Armée was everywhere victorious.

General Officers

	Basic monthly salary	Monthly war supplement	Ration Allowance
Marshal of France	3,333	–	–
Army C-in-C	3,000	–	12
Army Quartermaster General	3,000	–	10
Paymaster in Chief	1,833	–	8
General of Division	1,250	312.5	8
Chief Inspector	1,250	362.5	8
General of Brigade	833.33	208	6
Paymaster	833.33	–	3
Inspector	833.33	208	6

Senior Officers

	Basic monthly salary	Monthly war supplement	Ration Allowance
1st Colonel	} 562.5 – 486	} 168 – 123	3
Town Major			2
Commissioner of War	} 562.5 – 486		3
Sub-Inspector			
Major	} 408 – 300	} 104 – 83	2
Battalion or Squadron Chief			

Junior Officers

	Monthly Salary stage	Daily war or March allowance
Captains	233 – 200	3
Lieutenants	141.6 –104	2.50
Sub-Lieutenants	125–83	

NCOs and Men

	Ration allowance (daily)
Warrant Officers	1.75 to 1.90
Surgeons	0.95 to 1.69
Sergeants	0.87 to 1.23
Corporal, Brigadier	0.60 to 0.96
2nd Class	0.45 to 0.62

As the ranges show, there was a wide spread.

6. THE FATE OF THE MARSHALS

Augereau, Duke of Castiglione. In the Second Restoration, he regained the baton which Napoleon had withdrawn in consequence of his conduct in 1814. Detailed, with other marshals, to judge Ney, he declined and was quickly placed on half-pay. Died at La Housaye on 12 June 1816.

Bernadotte, Prince of Ponto-Corvo. On 5 February 1818 he became King of Sweden. Died on 8 March 1844 at 81 from an attack of paralysis.

Berthier, Prince of Neuchâtel, Prince of Wagram. During the Hundred Days he accompanied Louis XVIII to Ghent and then left to meet his family in Bamberg. Died on 1 June 1815 having fallen from a window.

Bessières, Duke of Istria. Died near Lützen from a bullet while leading the Imperial Guard.

Brune, Count of the Empire. Victim of the White Terror. Shot at point-blank range on 2 August 1815 at Avignon. His body was thrown into the Rhìne.

Davout, Duke of Auerstadt, Prince of Eckmühl. Defended Ney in 1815 and was exiled. In 1819, the king restored his title of Peer of France and awarded him the Cross of Saint-Louis. Mayor of Savigny-sur-Orge until he died on 1 June 1823.

Gouvion Saint-Cyr, Count of the Empire. Louis XVIII appointed him to the Chamber of Peers. Marquis in 1817. Minister of Marine, then Minister of War. He retired in 1819 to Hyères where he died in 1830.

Grouchy, Count of the Empire. Banished in July 1815 by Louis XVIII, he went to Philadelphia where he spent five years. Amnestied in 1821, he returned to France at the Restoration, but his rank of marshal was not recognised until restored by Louis-Philippe in 1831. Member of the Chamber of Peers in 1832. He died in Paris in 1847.

Jourdan. Ennobled in 1818 by Louis XVIII as Count. He sat in the Chamber of Peers from 1819. Minister of Foreign Affairs under Louis-Philippe. Governor of the Invalides until his death on 23 November 1833.

Kellermann, Duke of Valmy. Rallied to the Bourbons in 1814, Peer of France and liberal party member. Died 13 September 1820 at his estate in the valley of Montmorency aged 85 years.

Lannes, Duke of Montebello On the evening of 22 May 1809, was struck by a shot which mangled his legs. The left leg was amputated, gangrene followed. Died on 30 May. Buried in the Pantheon.

Lefebvre, Duke of Danzig. Declared for Louis XVIII in 1814, created a Peer of France. Dismissed in 1815 for having sat in the imperial Chamber during the Hundred Days. Pardoned in 1819; died in 1820.

Macdonald, Duke of Taranto. Grand chancellor of the Legion of Honour in 1815 with the task of running-down the army. In 1824, he remarried, for the fourth time, Mademoiselle de Bourgouin, who bore him a son and who died in 1825. Died 24 September 1840 at his estate at Courcelles.

Marmont, Duke of Ragusa. Peer of France under Louis XVIII whom he followed to Ghent during the Hundred Days. Promoted major-general of the royal guard at the Second Restoration. Left for exile voluntarily at the accession of Louis-Philippe, travelled widely, often in contact with the Duke of Reichstadt. Moved to Vienna and died alone and abandoned on 22 July 1852.

Masséna, Duke of Rivoli, Prince of Essling. Rallied to the Bourbons in 1814. Inactive during the Hundred Days, named governor of Paris after Waterloo. Died of a chest ailment in 1817

Moncey, Duke of Corvegliano. Retained as Inspector of Gendarmerie at the Restoration and created a Peer of France. At the trial of Marshal Ney, he refused to be president of the court-martial and was dismissed and imprisoned in the fortress of Ham. Titles and functions restored in 1816. Commanded IV Corps in the war in Spain and conquered Catalonia 1823. Governor of the Invalides in 1833. Died at Paris in 1842.

Mortier, Duke of Treviso. Deputy for the North department in 1816, awarded the orders of the Saint-Esprit, of Saint Louis and Saint Michael. Grand Chancellor of the Legion of Honour, Ambassador to Russia. Minister of War 1834-1835 and President of the Council. Killed by a bomb of Fieschi.

Murat, Grand Duke of Berg and Cleves, King of Naples. In 1815, Metternich negotiated his return to the throne of Naples with Ferdinand IV, King of Sicily. Murat drove through northern Italy, calling the populace to arms. After Waterloo, fled to Corsica. Tricked by emissaries of Ferdinand, he landed on 8 October 1815 at Pizzo, Calabria, Italy. Arrested, condemned to death and shot on 13 October.

Ney, Duke of Elchingen, Prince of the Moskowa. Convicted of treason after Waterloo. Court-martial declared itself incompetent; judged by the Chamber of Peers and condemned to death. Shot on 7 December 1815.

Oudinot, Duke of Reggio. Louis XVIII created him Peer of France and gave him command of the national guard. Remained neutral during the Hundred Days, his fortune was not compromised. 1839, Grand Chancellor of the Legion of Honour; 1842, governor of the Invalides. Died in 1847 aged 80.

Pérignon, Count of the Empire. Peer of France under Louis XVIII and extra Commissioner of the first military district. Organised the defence of Toulouse after Napoleon landed from Elba. Retired to his estates during the Hundred Days. Governor of Paris under the Second Restoration, marquis, grand cross of Saint Louis died 25 December 1818.

Poniatowski, Prince of the Holy Empire. On the third day of the battle of Leipzig, was charged with protecting the retreat, containing the attack by superior forces on the banks of the Elster. As the bridges had been destroyed, attempted to swim his horse across the river and drowned.

Sérurier, Count of the Empire. Nominated Peer of France by Louis XVIII. Held aloof during the Hundred Days. Lost governorship of the Invalides under the Second Restoration. Died 21 December 1819.

Soult, Duke of Dalmatia. Banished at the Second Restoration, retired to the Duchy of Berg where he married a German woman. Restored to favour 1819. He regained his marshal's baton and became a Peer of France. Minister of War in 1814, of Foreign Affairs in 1839, of War again in 1840. In 1847, promoted exceptionally to Marshal-General of France. Died in 1850.

Suchet, Duke of Albufera. In 1815, Peer of France and commander of the 2nd Military District. Compromised during the return from Elba and disgraced, losing his title of Peer. Restored in 1819. Died at the château of Montendon near Marseilles on 3 January 1826.

Victor, Duke of Belluno. 1815, Peer of France, commanding the 2nd Military district, major-general of the royal guard. Minister of War 1821–23. Forced to resign in a parliamentary scandal, became minister of state. Refused to support the July monarchy. Died at Paris in 1841.

MAPS
The Theatres of Operations

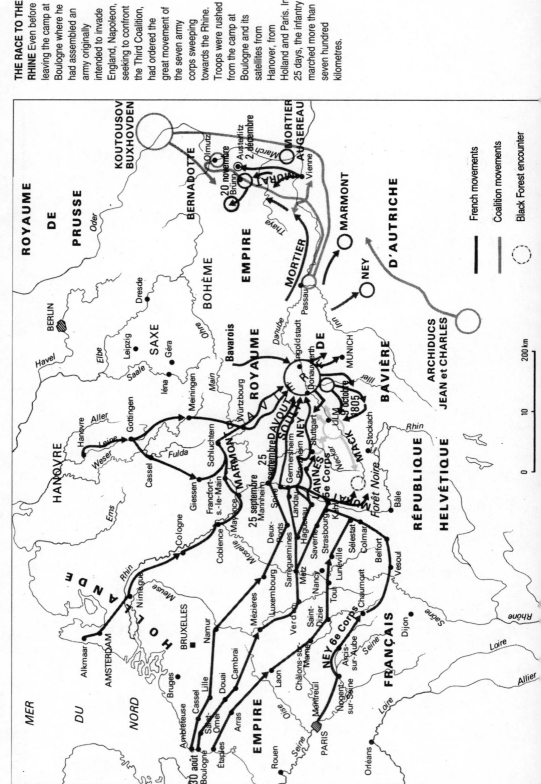

THE RACE TO THE RHINE Even before leaving the camp at Boulogne where he had assembled an army originally intended to invade England, Napoleon, seeking to confront the Third Coalition, had ordered the great movement of the seven army corps sweeping towards the Rhine. Troops were rushed from the camp at Boulogne and its satellites from Hanover, from Holland and Paris. In 25 days, the infantry marched more than seven hundred kilometres.

French movements
Coalition movements
Black Forest encounter

MER DU NORD

ROYAUME DE PRUSSE

HANOVRE

HOLLANDE

EMPIRE FRANÇAIS

SAXE

BOHÊME

EMPIRE

ROYAUME DE BAVIÈRE

RÉPUBLIQUE HELVÉTIQUE

D'AUTRICHE

ARCHIDUCS JEAN et CHARLES

KOUTOUSOV BUXHOVDEN

BERNADOTTE

MORTIER AUGEREAU

MARMONT

NEY

MURAT

MACK

LANNES 5e Corps

NEY 6e Corps

SOULT DAVOUT

MARMONT

BERLIN
Dresde
Leipzig
Iéna
Géra
Meiningen
Würtzbourg
Gottingen
Hanovre
Cassel
Fulda
Schluchtern
Giessen
Francfort s.-le-Main
Cologne
Coblence
Nimègue
Amsterdam
Alkmaar
Bruges
BRUXELLES
Namur
Mézières
Lille
Douai
Cambrai
Arras
Laon
Oise
Rouen
PARIS
Châlons-sur-Marne
Saint-Dizier
Verdun
Metz
Nancy
Toul
Lunéville
Nogent-sur-Seine
Arcis-sur-Aube
Chaumont
Dijon
Orléans
Luxembourg
Sarreguemines
Deux-Ponts
Landau
Haguenau
Saverne
Strasbourg
Sélestat
Colmar
Belfort
Vesoul
Bâle
Stockach
Germersheim
Spire
Mannheim
Mayence
Stuttgart
ULM
Neckar
Forêt Noire
MUNICH
Donauwerth
Ingolstadt
Passau
Vienne
Brünn
Olmutz
Austerlitz
30 août
Boulogne
Étaples
Ambleteuse
Saint-Omer
Montreuil

25 septembre
25 septembre

20 novembre
2 décembre

8 octobre 1805
20 octobre

Rhin
Meuse
Moselle
Main
Saale
Elbe
Havel
Oder
Ohre
Weser
Aller
Leine
Ems
Seine
Marne
Saône
Loire
Allier
Rhône
Danube
Inn
Iller
Thaya

Bavarois

0   10   200 km

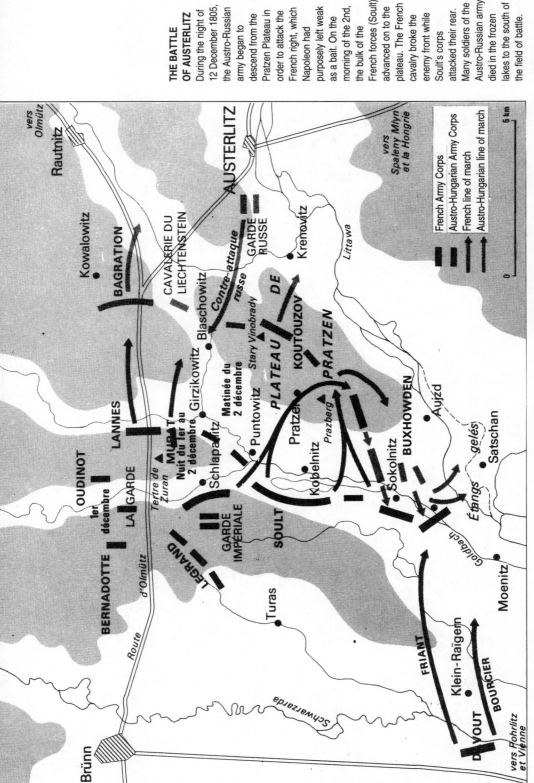

THE BATTLE OF AUSTERLITZ

During the night of 12 December 1805, the Austro-Russian army began to descend from the Pratzen Plateau in order to attack the French right, which Napoleon had purposely left weak as a bait. On the morning of the 2nd, the bulk of the French forces (Soult) advanced on to the plateau. The French cavalry broke the enemy front while Soult's corps attacked their rear. Many soldiers of the Austro-Russian army died in the frozen lakes to the south of the field of battle.

French Army Corps

Austro-Hungarian Army Corps

French line of march

Austro-Hungarian line of march

0   5 km

vers Olmütz

Rautnitz

Brünn

Route d'Olmütz

Turas

vers Pohrlitz et Vienne

Schwarzarda

Klein-Raïgern

Moenitz

Kowalowitz

BAGRATION

CAVALERIE DU LIECHTENSTEIN

LANNES

OUDINOT

1er décembre

BERNADOTTE

LA GARDE

MURAT

Nuit du 1er au 2 décembre

Tertre de Zuran

LEGRAND

GARDE IMPÉRIALE

SOULT

DAVOUT

BOURCIER

FRIANT

Schlapanitz

Girzikowitz

Blaschowitz

Contre-attaque russe

AUSTERLITZ

GARDE RUSSE

Krenowitz

vers Spaleny Mlyn et la Hongrie

Littawa

Puntowitz

Matinée du 2 décembre

Stary Vinobrady

PLATEAU DE PRATZEN

KOUTOUZOV

Pratzen

Prazberg

Kobelnitz

Sokolnitz

BUXHOWDEN

Aujzd

Étangs gelés

Satschan

Goldbach

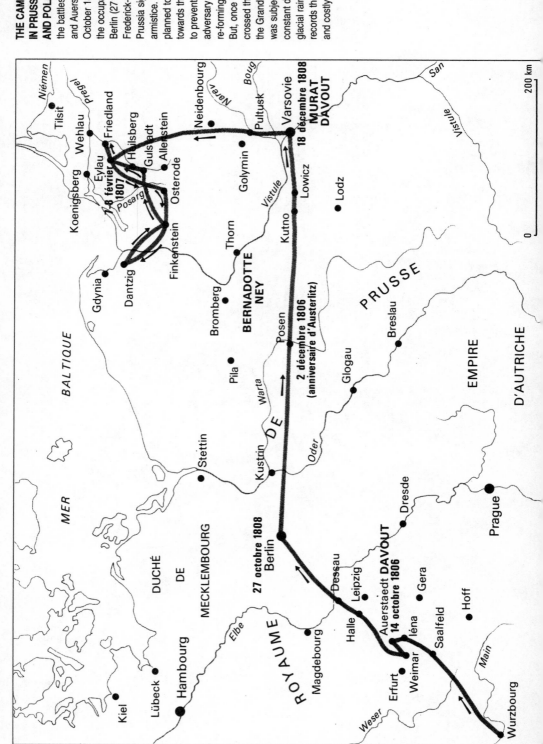

**THE CAMPAIGN
IN PRUSSIA
AND POLAND** After
the battles of Jena
and Auerstadt (14
October 1806) and
the occupation of
Berlin (27 October),
Frederick-William of
Prussia signed an
armistice. Napoleon
planned to drive
towards the Vistula
to prevent this
adversary from
re-forming his army.
But, once having
crossed the Oder,
the Grande Armée
was subjected to a
constant downpour of
glacial rain. This map
records their slow
and costly advance.

THE CAMPAIGN IN PRUSSIA AND POLAND

0   200 km

Niémen
Tilsit
Prégel
Koenigsberg
Wehlau
Friedland
BALTIQUE
Eylau
7-8 février
1807
Gutstadt
Heilsberg
Allenstein
Posarg
Osterode
Neidenbourg
Narev
Pultusk
Boug
Varsovie
18 décembre 1806
MURAT
DAVOUT
Gdynia
Dantzig
Finkenstein
Golymin
Vistule
Lowicz
Lodz
Bromberg
Thorn
Kutno
San
Vistule
MER
BALTIQUE
Stettin
Pila
Warta
Posen
2 décembre 1806
(anniversaire d'Austerlitz)
BERNADOTTE
NEY
PRUSSE
Breslau
Oder
Glogau
Kustrin
EMPIRE
D'AUTRICHE
LÜbeck
Kiel
Hambourg
DUCHÉ
DE
MECKLEMBOURG
Elbe
Magdebourg
27 octobre 1806
Berlin
Dessau
Halle
Leipzig
Dresde
DE
Prague
Auerstaedt DAVOUT
14 octobre 1806
Gera
Iéna
Erfurt
Weimar
Saalfeld
Hoff
ROYAUME
Weser
Main
Wurzbourg

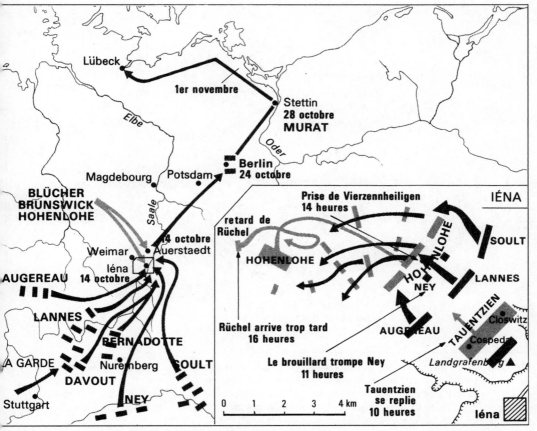

Iéna

1er novembre

Stettin
28 octobre
MURAT

Berlin
24 octobre

Magdebourg   Potsdam

**BLÜCHER
BRUNSWICK
HOHENLOHE**

retard de Rüchel

14 octobre
Weimar   Auerstaedt

Iéna
14 octobre

HOHENLOHE

AUGEREAU

LANNES

BERNADOTTE

A GARDE   Nuremberg

DAVOUT

Stuttgart   **NEY**

SOULT

Prise de Vierzennheiligen
14 heures

HOHENLOHE

SOULT

LANNES

NEY

AUGEREAU

TAUENTZIEN

Closwitz

Cospeda

Rüchel arrive trop tard
16 heures

Le brouillard trompe Ney
11 heures

Tauentzien
se replie
10 heures

Landgrafenberg

0 1 2 3 4 km

Iéna

THE BATTLES OF JENA and EYLAU The Battle of Jena (above, 14 October 1806) was one of Napoleon's lightning victories. On that same day, Davout beat the Brunswicker army at Auerstadt. Eylau (below, 7–8 January 1807) was by contrast a butchery in a snowstorm. Twenty French generals were killed or wounded.

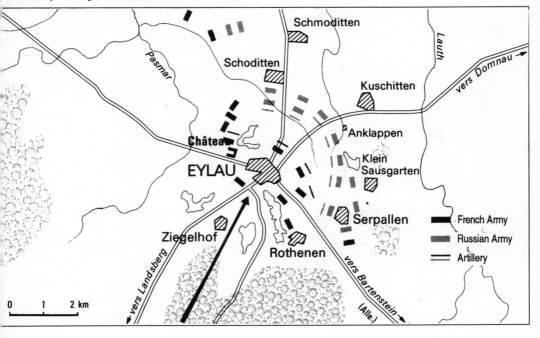

Schmoditten

Schoditten

Kuschitten

vers Domnau

Pasmar

Lauth

Château

Anklappen

EYLAU

Klein
Sausgarten

Ziegelhof

Serpallen

Rothenen

vers Landsberg

vers Bartenstein

(Alle.)

French Army

Russian Army

Artillery

0 1 2 km

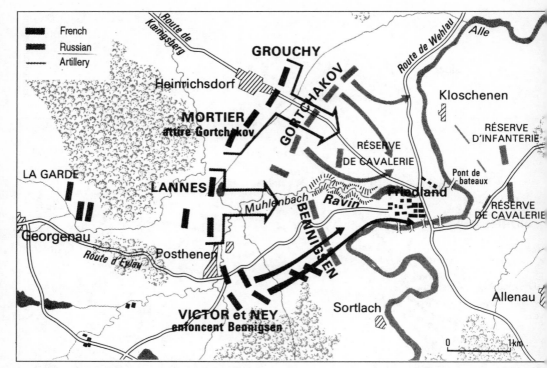

THE BATTLES OF FRIEDLAND AND WAGRAM At Friedland, (above, 14 June 1807) the Russian general, Bennigsen, rashly deployed his troops with their backs to the River Alle. Napoleon attacked, siting artillery in advance of his infantry. Success was complete. Friedland is considered the model of the victorious offensive. Before giving battle on the plain of Wagram on 5–6 July 1809 (below), the French had to rebuild the bridges over the Danube, destroyed by the Austrians. Napoleon broke the enemy front, using a mass of infantry and cavalry with artillery in support.

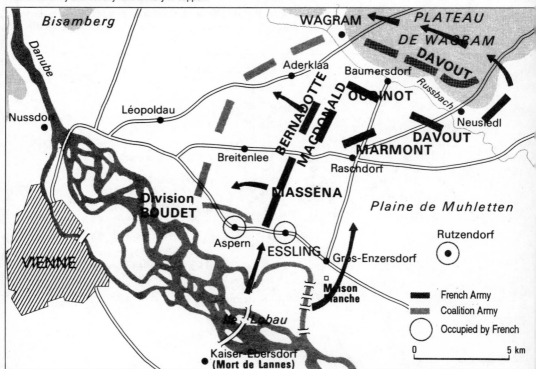

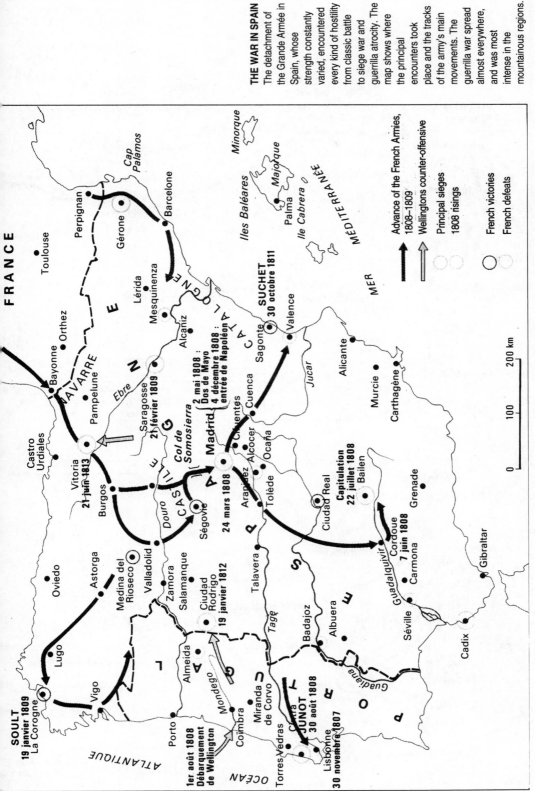

FRANCE

Toulouse

Perpignan

Cap Palamos

Gérone

Barcelone

Minorque

Iles Baléares

Majorque
Palma
Ile Cabrera

MÉDITERRANÉE

MER

Castro Urdiales

Bayonne

Orthez

NAVARRE

Pampelune

Ebre

Lérida

Mesquinenza

Alcaniz

CATALOGNE

Sagonte

SUCHET
30 octobre 1811

Valence

Vitoria
21 juin 1813

Saragosse
21 février 1809

Col de Somosierra

Burgos

Douro

CASTILLE

Ségovie
24 mars 1808

Madrid
2 mai 1808 : Dos de Mayo
4 décembre 1808 : entrée de Napoléon

Cuenca

Jucar

Alicante

Oviedo

Astorga

Medina del Rioseco

Valladolid

Zamora

Salamanque

Ciudad Rodrigo
19 janvier 1812

Aranjuez
Alcocer
Ocaña
Tolède

Cifuentes

Ciudad Real

Capitulation
22 juillet 1808
Bailen

Murcie

Carthagène

SOULT
19 janvier 1809
La Corogne

Lugo

Vigo

Almeida

Mondego

Miranda de Corvo

Coimbra

1er août 1808
Débarquement
de Wellington

Porto

ATLANTIQUE

Torres Vedras

Lisbonne
30 novembre 1807

JUNOT
30 août 1808

PORTUGAL

Tage

Talavera

Badajoz

Albuera

Guadiana

Séville

Cadix

SIERRA

Guadalquivir

Cordoue
7 juin 1808

Carmona

Grenade

Gibraltar

OCÉAN

0   100   200 km

Advance of the French Armies, 1808–1809

Wellingtons counter-offensive

Principal sieges

1808 risings

French victories

French defeats

THE WAR IN SPAIN
The detachment of the Grande Armée in Spain, whose strength constantly varied, encountered every kind of hostility from classic battle to siege war and guerrilla atrocity. The map shows where the principal encounters took place and the tracks of the army's main movements. The guerrilla war spread almost everywhere, and was most intense in the mountainous regions.

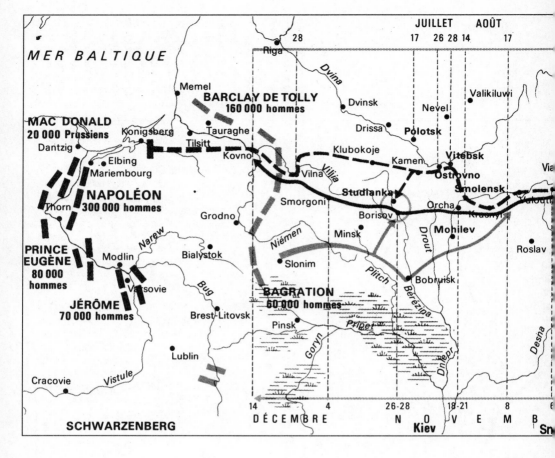

MER BALTIQUE

Riga

JUILLET   AOÛT
28   17   26 28 14   17

Dvina

MAC DONALD
20 000 Prussiens

BARCLAY DE TOLLY
160 000 hommes

Memel

Dvinsk

Valikiluwi

Königsberg   Tauraghe

Drissa

Nevel

Dantzig   Tilsitt

Klubokoje

Polotsk

Elbing   Kovno

Kamen

Vitebsk

Mariembourg

Vilna   Villia

Ostrovno

NAPOLÉON
300 000 hommes

Smolensk

Smorgoni

Orcha

Vi

Thorn

Grodno

Borisov

Studianka

Krasnyi

Yaloutt

PRINCE
EUGÈNE
80 000
hommes

Modlin

Niémen

Minsk

Drout

Mohilev

Roslav

Bialystok

Varsovie

Slonim

Bobruisk

JÉRÔME
70 000 hommes

Bug

Plitch

Bérézina

Brest-Litovsk

Pinsk

Pripet

Dnepr

Desna

Lublin

Goryn

Cracovie

Vistule

14   4   26-28   18-21   8
SCHWARZENBERG   DÉCEMBRE   N   O   V   Kiev   E   M   B   Sn

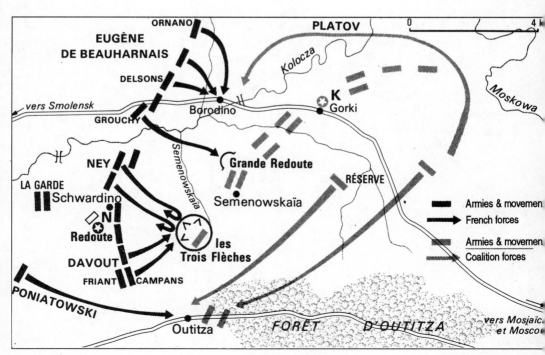

ORNANO   PLATOV   0   4 k

EUGÈNE
DE BEAUHARNAIS

Kolocza

Moskowa

DELSONS

K
Gorki

vers Smolensk   Borodino

GROUCHY

NEY   Semenowskaïa   Grande Redoute

LA GARDE
Schwardino   RÉSERVE

N
Redoute   Semenowskaïa

DAVOUT   les
Trois Flèches

FRIANT   CAMPANS

PONIATOWSKI

Outitza   FORÊT   D'OUTITZA   vers Mosjaïc
et Mosco

Armies & movemen
French forces

Armies & movemen
Coalition forces

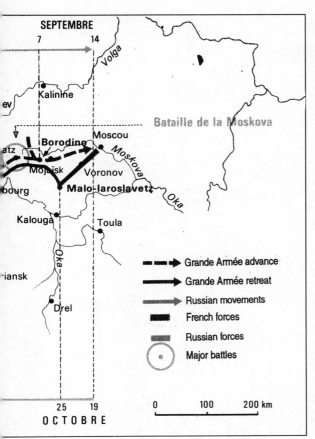

Volga

Kalinîne

ev

Bataille de la Moskova

Moscou

Borodino

atz

Mojaïsk   Voronov

bourg

Malo-Iaroslavetz

Kalouga   Toula

iansk

Orel

- - - ▶ Grande Armée advance
━━━▶ Grande Armée retreat
━━━▶ Russian movements
▬▬▬ French forces
▬▬▬ Russian forces
◎ Major battles

25   19
OCTOBRE

0   100   200 km

THE CAMPAIGN IN RUSSIA The map on the left shows chronologically the progress of the advance to and the retreat from Moscow. Barely one third of the Grande Armée was French. At first, they suffered from heat and dust, and the victualling service lagged behind them. The Russians retreated, destroying everything behind them. A major clash occured on the Moskowa (Borodino) 100 km west of Moscow. The army eventually retreated in a cold hell to the drama of the Berezina. Only 10,000 to 20,000 survived.

BATTLE OF THE MOSKOWA (below left)
The Russians called this the Battle of Borodino, a wretched village of twenty hovels. It was the least 'elegant' of Napoléon's battles. 65,000 died, 45,000 of them Russian. The partial, unexploited success of the Grande Armée was bought at the cost of squadrons and battallions thrown into the cauldron. The most furious fighting took place around two strongpoints: the Three Flèches and the Great Redoubt.

THE CROSSING OF THE BEREZINA (below)
The bulk of the Russian troops (Wittgenstein to the north, Kutusov to the south-east) were far off when the French reached the Berezina crossings. General Eblé's pontoon units built two bridges at Studienka. Victor and Oudinot fixed the enemy. Some of the troops crossed unhindered on 26 November 1812, but the rest encountered frustrating delays. Once the Russians arrived, they started to bombard, causing a fatal panic.

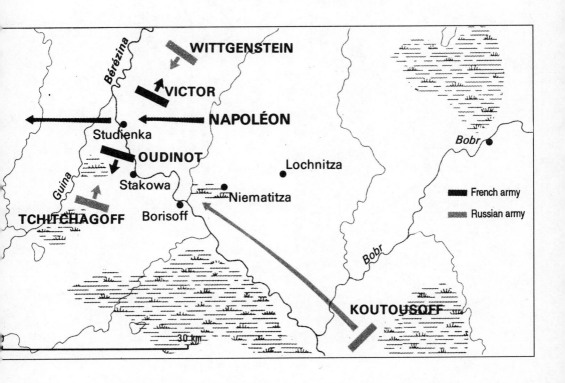

WITTGENSTEIN

VICTOR

NAPOLÉON

Bérézina

Studienka

OUDINOT

Lochnitza

Bobr

Stakowa

Niematitza

TCHITCHAGOFF   Borisoff

Bobr

KOUTOUSOFF

▬▬▬ French army
▬▬▬ Russian army

30 km

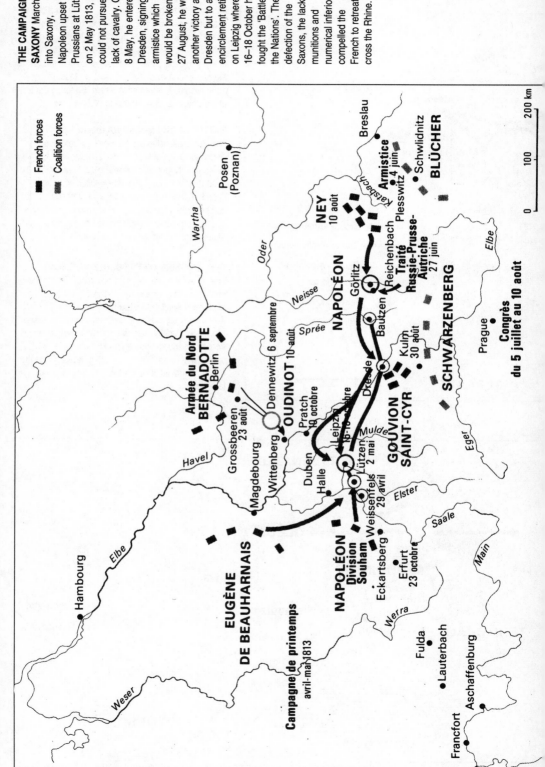

THE CAMPAIGN IN SAXONY Marching into Saxony, Napoleon upset the Prussians at Lützen on 2 May 1813, but could not pursue for lack of cavalry. On 8 May, he entered Dresden, signing an armistice which would be broken. On 27 August, he won another victory at Dresden but to avoid encirclement retired on Leipzig where on 16–18 October he fought the 'Battle of the Nations'. The defection of the Saxons, the lack of munitions and numerical inferiority compelled the French to retreat and cross the Rhine.

French forces

Coalition forces

0   100   200 km

Hambourg

Weser

Elbe

Havel

Magdebourg

Berlin

**Armée du Nord
BERNADOTTE**

Posen (Poznan)

Wartha

Oder

Neisse

Breslau

Schwidnitz

BLÜCHER

Plesswitz
Armistice
4 juin

Schwidnitz

Kätsbach

NEY
10 août

Reichenbach

Görlitz

Bautzen

NAPOLÉON

Sprée

OUDINOT 10 août

Dennewitz 6 septembre

Wittenberg

Grossbeeren
23 août

Duben

Halle

Leipzig
16–19 octobre

Pratch
19 octobre

Mulde

Lützen
2 mai

Weissenfels
29 avril

Eckartsberg

Erfurt
23 octobre

**NAPOLÉON
Division
Souham**

Elster

Saale

Werra

**GOUVION
SAINT-CYR**

Dresde

Kulm
30 août

**Traité
Russie-Prusse-
Autriche**
27 juin

SCHWARZENBERG

Eger

Prague

Elbe

**Congrès
du 5 juillet au 10 août**

**EUGÈNE
DE BEAUHARNAIS**

Campagne de printemps
avril–mai 1813

Fulda

Lauterbach

Main

Francfort

Aschaffenburg

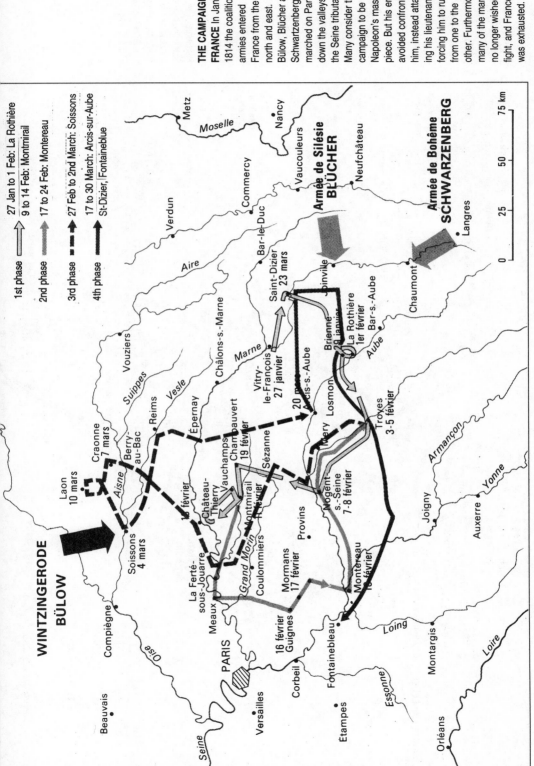

THE CAMPAIGN IN FRANCE In January 1814 the coalition armies entered France from the north and east. Bülow, Blücher and Schwarzenberg marched on Paris down the valleys of the Seine tributaries. Many consider this campaign to be Napoleon's masterpiece. But his enemy avoided confronting him, instead attacking his lieutenants, forcing him to rush from one to the other. Furthermore, many of the marshals no longer wished to fight, and France was exhausted.

1st phase — 27 Jan to 1 Feb: La Rothière
9 to 14 Feb: Montmirail

2nd phase — 17 to 24 Feb: Montereau

3rd phase — 27 Feb to 2nd March: Soissons

4th phase — 17 to 30 March: Arcis-sur-Aube
St-Dizier, Fontaineblue

Metz

Moselle

Nancy

WINTZINGERODE
BÜLOW

Verdun

Commercy

Vaucouleurs

Neufchâteau

Aire

Bar-le-Duc

Armée de Silésie
BLÜCHER

Saint-Dizier
23 mars

Joinville

Langres

Armée de Bohême
SCHWARZENBERG

0   25   50   75 km

Châlons-s.-Marne

Vouziers

Suippes

Vesle

Marne

Vitry-
le-François
27 janvier

Brienne
29 janvier

La Rothière
1er février

Bar-s.-Aube

Chaumont

Craonne
7 mars

Berry-
au-Bac

Reims

Épernay

Aisne

Laon
10 mars

Soissons
4 mars

Compiègne

Oise

Beauvais

La Ferté-
sous-Jouarre

Meaux

Château-
Thierry
1 février

Vauchamps

Montmirail
11 février

Chambauvert
19 février

Sézanne

Provins

Coulommiers

Grand Morin

Mormans
17 février

Guignes
16 février

PARIS

Versailles

Corbeil

Fontainebleau

Étampes

Essonne

Seine

Orléans

Montargis

Loing

Loire

Auxerre

Yonne

Joigny

Armançon

Montereau
18 février

Nogent
s.-Seine
7-8 février

Troyes
3-5 février

Méry

Losmont

Arcis-s.-Aube
20 janvier

Aube

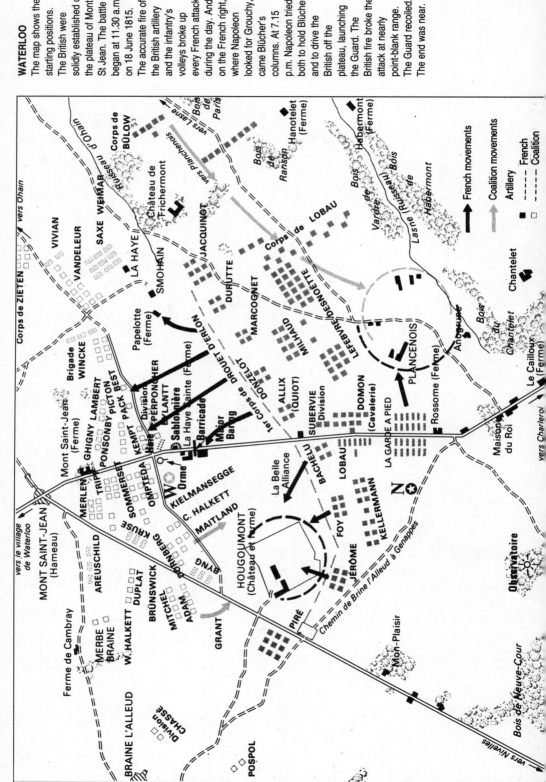

WATERLOO

The map shows the starting positions. The British were solidly established on the plateau of Mont St Jean. The battle began at 11.30 a.m. on 18 June 1815. The accurate fire of the British artillery and the infantry's volleys broke up every French attack during the day. And on the French right, where Napoleon looked for Grouchy, came Blücher's columns. At 7.15 p.m. Napoleon tried both to hold Blücher and to drive the British off the plateau, launching the Guard. The British fire broke the attack at nearly point-blank range. The Guard recoiled. The end was near.

Legend:

French movements
Coalition movements
Artillery

— French
---- Coalition

Map labels:

vers Ohain
Corps de ZIETEN
Ruisseau d'Ohain
SAXE WEIMAR
Corps de BÜLOW
vers Lasne
vers Plancenoit
vers le village de Waterloo
VIVIAN
VANDELEUR
LA HAYE
Château de Trichermont
Bois de Paris
Brigade WINCKE
SMOHAIN
Papelotte (Ferme)
JACQUINOT
DURUTTE
Bois de Ranson
Hanotelet (Ferme)
Mont Saint-Jean (Ferme)
GHIGNY LAMBERT
PONSONBY PICTON
PACK BEST
KEMPT
Division PERPONCHER
LANTT
DROUET D'ERLON
MARCOGNET
Corps de LOBAU
LEFEBVRE-DESNOETTE
MILHAUD
Vardre de
Bois de Habermont
Bais (Ruisseau)
Habermont (Ferme)
MERLEN
TRIP
SOMMERSET
OMPTEDA
Orme
KIELMANSEGGE
Sablonière
La Haye Sainte (Ferme)
Barricade
Major Baring
1er Corps de DONZELOT
ALLIX (QUIOT)
SUBERVIE Division
DOMON (Cavalerie)
PLANCENOIS (Ferme)
Angebure
Bois du Chantelet
Chantelet
MONT SAINT-JEAN (Hameau)
AREUSCHILD
KRUSE
DORNBERG
C. HALKETT
MAITLAND
BYNG
La Belle Alliance
BACHELU
LOBAU
LA GARDE A PIED
Rossome (Ferme)
Maison du Roi
Le Caillou (Ferme)
vers Charleroi
BRAINE L'ALLEUD
Division CHASSE
MERBE BRAINE
W. HALKETT
DUPLAT
BRUNSWICK
MITCHEL
ADAM
GRANT
HOUGOUMONT (Château et Ferme)
FOY
JÉRÔME
KELLERMANN
Chemin de Brine l'Alleud à Genappes
PIRÉ
Mon-Plaisir
Observatoire
Bois de Hieuve-Cour
vers Nivelles
Ferme de Cambray
POSPOL
vers le village de Waterloo
N

BIBLIOGRAPHY

An enormous number of books have been written about the Grande Armée. Listed here are the principal general works that I have consulted.

Abrantès, Duchess d', *Mémoires*. Paris, 1831.
Bainville, Jacques, *Napoléon*. Paris, 1931.
Baldet, Marcel, *La Vie quotidienne dans les armées de Napoléon*. Paris, 1964.
Barrès, General, *Mémoires*. Paris, 1883.
Blaze, Elzéar, *La Vie militaire sous le Premier Empire*. Paris, 1888.
Blond, Georges, *La Beauté et la Gloire*. Paris, 1976.
Boigne, Countess de, *Mémoires*. Paris, 1907.
Brice, Raoul, *Les Femmes aux armees sous la Révolution et l'Empire*. Paris, s.d.
Brunon, Jean et Raoul, *Les Mameluks d'Égypte et les Mameluks de la Garde Impériale*. Marseilles, 1963.
Cadet de Gassicourt, *Voyage en Autriche, en Moravie et en Bavière*. Paris, 1818.
Castelot, André, *Bonaparte*. Paris, 1967.
— *Napoléon*. Paris, 1968.
Castelot, André, and Decaux, Alain, *Histoire de la France et des Français au jour le jour (1764–1814)*. Paris, 1977.
Castelot, André, Decaux, Alain, and Koenig, General, *Le Livre de la famille impériale*. Paris, 1969.
Caulaincourt, General Armand de, *Mémoires*. Paris, 1933.
Chardigny, Louis, *Les Maréchaux de Napoléon*. Paris, 1977.
Chlapowski, General Désiré, *Mémoires sur les guerres de Napoléon*. Paris, 1908.
Choury, Maurice, *Les Grognards et Napoléon*. Paris, 1968.
Coignet, Jean-Roch, capitaine, *Les Cahiers*. Paris, 1883.
Constant, *Mémoires du premier valet de chambre de Napoléon*. Paris, 1969.
Desboeufs, Captain, *Souvenirs*, Paris, 1901.
Dupont, Marcel, *Napoléon en campagne*. Paris, 1952.
— *Murat*. Paris, 1934.
— *Napoléon et ses grognards*. Paris, 1945.
Fleischman, Théo, *L'épopée impériale; Souvenirs inédits du caporal Martial-Joseph Delroeux*. Paris, 1964.

Funcken, Liliane and Fred, *L'Uniforme et les Armes des soldats du Premier Empire*. Paris, 1973.

Harsany, Zoltan-Étienne, *La Vie à Strasbourg sous le Consulat et l'Empire*. Strasbourg, 1976.

Hautpoul, General, Marquis d', *Souvenirs sur la Révolution, l'Empire, la Restauration*. Paris, 1904.

La Barre de Nanteuil, Henri, *Le Comte Daru ou l'administration militaire sous l'Empire*. Paris, 1966.

Lachouque, Henri, Commandant, *Napoléon, 20 ans de campagnes*. Paris, 1969.

— *Napoléon et la Garde Impériale*. Paris, 1957; translated by Anne S. K. Brown as *The Anatomy of Glory: Napoleon and his Guard, A Study in Leadership*, Rhode Island and London, 1962; reprinted London, 1978.

Larrey, Dominique, baron, *Mémoires de chirurgie militaire et Campagnes*. Paris, 1812–1817.

Latreille, A, *L'Ère napoléonienne*. Paris, 1974.

Lefebvre, Georges, *Napoléon*. Paris, 1935; translated, London, 1969.

Lenôtre, Georges, *Croquis de l'Épopée*. Paris, 1932.

Levy, Arthur, *Napoléon intime*. Paris, 1892.

— *Napoléon et la Paix*. Paris, 1902.

Lucas-Dubreton, *Soldats de Napoléon*. Paris, 1977.

Ludwig, Émile, *Napoléon*. Paris, 1928.

Madelin, Louis, *Histoire du Consulat et de l'Empire*. Paris, 1937.

Marbot, General Baron de, *Mémoires*. Paris, 1891; translated, London 1913.

Marmont, Marshal, *Mémoires*. Paris, 1856.

Massin, Jean, *L'Almanach du Premier Empire*. Paris, 1964.

Masson, Frédéric, *Cavaliers de Napoléon*. Paris, 1893.

Maze-Sencier, *Les Fournisseurs de Napoléon*. Paris, 1893.

Miot-Putigny, *Putigny, grognard de l'Empire*. Paris, 1950.

Mistler, Jean, *Napoléon et l'Empire*. Paris, 1968.

Napoleon I, *Correspondance*. Paris, 1858–1870

— *Mémoires et Œuvres*. Paris, 1926. (Tancrède Martel).

— *Proclamations, Ordres du Jour, Bulletins de la Grande Armée*. Paris, 1964. (Jean Tulard).

Palluel, *Le Dictionnaire de l'Empereur*. Paris, 1969.

Palluel et Lovie, *L'Épisode napoléonien*. Paris, 1972.

Percy, Baron, *Journal de Campagne du baron Percy, Chirurgien en chef de la Grande Armée*. Paris, 1904.

Parquin, *Souvenirs et campagnes d'un vieux soldat de l'Empire*. Paris, 1843.

Quennevat, Jean-Claude, *Atlas de la Grande Armée*. Paris, 1966.

— *Les Vrais Soldats de Napoléon*. Paris, 1968.

Robiquet, Jean, *La Vie Quotidienne au temps de Napoléon*. Paris, 1944.

Ravignant, Patrick, *Napoléon pas à pas*. Paris, 1969.

Sauzey, *Les Allemands sous les aigles françaises*. Paris, 1902.

Schuerman, A, *Itinéraire général de Napoléon*. Paris, 1911.

Six, Georges, *Les Généraux de la Révolution et de l'Empire*. Paris, 1948.

Soubiran, Dr André, *Le Baron Larrey, chirurgien de Napoléon*. Paris, 1904.

Thiard, General, *Souvenirs diplomatiques et militaires*. Paris, nd.

Thiers, Adolphe, *Histoire du Consulat et de l'Empire*. Paris, 1874.

Thoumas, Charles, *Les Grands Cavaliers du Premier Empire*. Paris, 1909.

Tulard, Jean, *Napoléon*. Paris, 1977.

— *La Vie Quotidienne des Français sous Napoléon*. Paris, 1978.

Vachée, Colonel, *Napoléon en Campagne*. Paris, 1913; translated as *Napoleon at Work*, London, 1914.

Valynseele, Jean, *Les Maréchaux du Premier Empire*. Paris, 1957.

— *Les Princes et Ducs du Premier Empire*. Paris, 1959.

WORKS DEVOTED TO SPECIFIC CAMPAIGNS AND PERIODS

The Camp at Boulogne

Blond, Georges, *La Beauté et la Gloire*. Paris, 1976.

Chatelle, Albert, *Napoléon et la Légion d'honneur au camp de Boulogne*. Paris, 1956.

Maine, René, *Trafalgar*. Paris, 1955.

Revue de l'Institut Napoléon, *Napoléon a-t-il dicté à Daru le plan de la campagne de 1805?* Paris, 1971. *A propos de la dictée de Boulogne*. Paris, 1972.

Austerlitz

Alombert et Colin, *La Campagne de 1805 en Allemagne*. Paris, 1902.

— *Le Corps d'armée aux ordres du Maréchal Mortier*. Paris, 1897.

Bonnal, Henri, *De Rossbach à Ulm*. Paris, 1903.

Manceron, Claude, *Austerlitz*. Paris, 1960.

Thiry, Jean, *Ulm, Trafalgar, Austerlitz*. Paris, 1962.

Jena

Bonnal, Henri, *La Manoeuvre d'Iéna*. Paris, 1904.

Foucart, Pierre, *La Campagne de Prusse*. Paris, 1887.

Guye, Alfred, *Le Bataillon de Neuchâtel au service de Napoléon*. Neuchâtel, 1964.

Lachouque, Henri, *Iéna*. Paris, 1964.

Thiry, Jean, *Iéna*. Paris, 1964.

Eylau and Friedland

Bertaut, Jules, *Le Roi Jérôme*. Paris, 1954.

Fabre, *Jérôme Bonaparte, roi de Westphalie*. Paris, 1952.

Foucart, Pierre, *La Campagne de Pologne*. Paris, 1882.

Grenier, Pierre, *Les Manoeuvres d'Eylau et de Friedland*. Paris, 1901.

Martinet, A, *Jérôme Napoléon, roi de Westphalie*. Paris, 1902.

Melchior-Bonnet, Bernardine, *Jérôme Bonaparte*. Paris, 1979.

Thiry, Jean, *Eylau, Friedland, Tilsit*. Paris, 1965.

The War in Spain and Portugal

Bapst, *Souvenirs d'un canonnier de l'Armée d'Espagne*. Paris, 1892.

Boppe, *Les Espagnols á la Grande Armée*. Paris, 1899.

— *La Légion portugaise*. Paris, 1897.

Chastenet, Jacques, *Godoy*. Paris, 1961.

— *La Vie Quotidienne en Espagne au temps de Goya*. Paris, 1966.

Clerc, Lieutenant Colonel, *La Capitulation de Baylen*. Paris, 1903.

Fee, *Souvenirs de la guerre d'Espagne*. Paris, 1856.

François, Captain, *Journal*. Paris, 1903.

Fugier, A, *Napoléon et l'Espagne*. Paris, 1930.

— *Napoléon et le Portugal*. Paris, 1931.

Geisendorf des Gouttes, *Geôles et Pontons d'Espagne*. Genève, 1937.

Geoffroy de Grandmaison, *L'Espagne et Napoléon*. Paris, 1930.

Grasset, A, *La Guerre d'Espagne*. Paris, 1914.

Guillon, E, *Les Guerres d'Espagne sous Napoléon*. Paris, 1902.

Lucas-Dubreton, J, *Napoléon devant l'Espagne*. Paris, 1947.

Nabonne, Bernard, *Joseph Bonaparte*. Paris, 1949.

Roux, Georges, *Napoléon et le Guêpier espagnol*. Paris, 1970.

Spillmann, General Georges, 'Le Maréchal Suchet, stratège et pacificateur' in *Souvenir napoléonien*. Paris, March 1977.

Thiébault, General Baron, *Mémoires*. Paris, 1893.

Thirion, *Souvenirs militaires*. Paris, 1892.

Thiry, Jean, *La Guerre d'Espagne*. Paris, 1966.

Wagram

Augustin-Thierry, A, *Masséna*. Paris, 1947.

Bonnal, Henri, *La manoeuvre de Landshut*. Paris, 1905.

Buat, Edmond, *De Ratisbonne à Znaïm*. Paris, 1909.

Thiry, Jean, *Wagram*. Paris, 1966.

The Moscow Campaign

Bourgeois, René, Surgeon-Major, *Tableau de la Campagne de Moscou en 1812*. Paris, 1814.

Bourgogne, Sergeant, *Mémoires*. Paris, 1898; translated by Paul Cottin and Maurice Hénault as *The Memoirs of Sergeant Bourgogne, 1812–1813*, London, 1899; reprinted 1979.

Deniée, Baron, *Itinéraire de l'Empereur Napoléon pendant la campagne de 1812*. Paris, 1842.

Fusil, Louise, *J'étais à la Bérézina*. Paris, 1977.

Grundwald, Constantin de, *La Campagne de Russie*. Paris, 1963.

Longworth, Philippe, *Les Cosaques*. Paris, 1972.

Lucas-Dubreton, *Le Maréchal Ney*. Paris, 1941.

Olivier, Daria, *L'incendie de Moscou*. Paris, 1964.

Roos, Henrich von, *Souvenirs d'un médecin de la Grande Armée*. Paris, 1913.

Savant, Jean, *Les Cosaques*. Paris, 1944.

Ségur, Philippe de, *Histoire de Napoléon et de la Grande Armée pendant l'année 1812*. Paris, 1824.

Stendhal, *Journal*. Paris, 1908.

The Campaign in Saxony

Doher, Marcel, 'Napoléon en campagne' in *Souvenir napoléonien*. Paris, November 1974.

Erckman-Chatrian, *Un Conscrit de 1813*, being the notebooks of Captain Vidal. Paris, 1977.

Nabonne, Bernard, *Bernadotte*. Paris, 1940.

Thiry, Jean, *Lützen et Bautzen*. Paris, 1971.

— *Leipzig*. Paris, 1972.

The Campaign in France, Treason among the Marshals and the First Abdication

Chateaubriand, *Mémoires d'outre-tombe*. Paris, 1823.

Chuquet, Arthur, *L'année 1814*. Paris, 1914.

Dupont, Marcel, *Napoléon et la trahison des maréchaux*. Paris, 1939.

Fain, Baron, *souvenirs de la campagne de France*. Paris, 1823.

Ségur, General, Count de, *Du Rhin à Fontainebleau*. Paris, 1969.

Thiry, Jean, *La Campagne de France*. Paris, 1938.

— *La Première abdication*. Paris, 1939.

Zeller, André, *Soldats perdus*. Paris, 1977.

..

The Return from Elba

Berthier de Sauvigny, *La Restauration*. Paris, 1955.
Houssaye, Henri, *1815*. Paris, 1896.
Manceron, Claude, *Napoléon reprend Paris*. Paris, 1965.
Ravignant, Patrick, *Le Retour de l'île d'Elbe*. Paris, 1977.
Thiry, Jean, *Le Vol de l'Aigle*. Paris, 1942.

The Waterloo Campaign

Dupont, Marcel, *La Garde meurt*. Paris, 1931.
Lachouque, Commandant Henri, *Waterloo*. Paris, 1972; illustrated edition by
    Juan Carlos Carmignani, Paris, 1972; translated edition, London, 1975.
Thiry, Jean, *Waterloo*. Paris, 1943.

The Return from St Helena

Bourguignon, Jean, *Le Retour des Cendres*. Paris, 1941.
Joinville, Admiral Prince de, 'Vieux Souvenirs' in *Revue Neptunia*, 1977–1978.
Lucas-Dubreton, *Le Culte de Napoléon*. Paris, 1960.

INDEX

A Selective Index of the Principal Names mentioned